The Domain Of Reasons

IN MEMORY OF MY MOTHER

Thou thy worldly task hast don,
Home art gon, and tane thy wages.

The Domain of Reasons

JOHN SKORUPSKI

OXFORD
UNIVERSITY PRESS

OXFORD
UNIVERSITY PRESS

Great Clarendon Street, Oxford OX2 6DP

Oxford University Press is a department of the University of Oxford.
It furthers the University's objective of excellence in research, scholarship,
and education by publishing worldwide in

Oxford New York

Auckland Cape Town Dar es Salaam Hong Kong Karachi
Kuala Lumpur Madrid Melbourne Mexico City Nairobi
New Delhi Shanghai Taipei Toronto

With offices in

Argentina Austria Brazil Chile Czech Republic France Greece
Guatemala Hungary Italy Japan Poland Portugal Singapore
South Korea Switzerland Thailand Turkey Ukraine Vietnam

Oxford is a registered trade mark of Oxford University Press
in the UK and in certain other countries

Published in the United States
by Oxford University Press Inc., New York

© John Skorupski 2010

The moral rights of the author have been asserted
Database right Oxford University Press (maker)

First published 2010

All rights reserved. No part of this publication may be reproduced,
stored in a retrieval system, or transmitted, in any form or by any means,
without the prior permission in writing of Oxford University Press,
or as expressly permitted by law, or under terms agreed with the appropriate
reprographics rights organization. Enquiries concerning reproduction
outside the scope of the above should be sent to the Rights Department,
Oxford University Press, at the address above

You must not circulate this book in any other binding or cover
and you must impose the same condition on any acquirer

British Library Cataloguing in Publication Data

Data available

Library of Congress Cataloging in Publication Data

Data available

Typeset by SPI Publishing Services, Pondicherry, India
Printed in Great Britain
on acid-free paper by
MPG Books Group, Bodmin and King's Lynn

ISBN 978–0–19–958763–6

1 3 5 7 9 10 8 6 4 2

CONTENTS

Preface		xiii
Synopsis		xvii

1	**Introduction**	1
	1.1 What this book is about: a brief outline	1
	1.2 Global realism versus Critical philosophy	5
	1.3 Kant	9
	1.4 Vienna	13
	1.5 The Normative view	18
	1.6 Autonomy and the unity of reason	20
	1.7 Will and feeling: practical reasons and value	23
	1.8 Morality	28
	1.9 Is the world our world? Are we in it?	29

PART I THE STRUCTURE OF NORMATIVE CONCEPTS	33

2	**Reasons**	35
	2.1 Epistemic, practical, and evaluative reasons	35
	2.2 Specific, overall, and sufficient	37
	2.3 Epistemic fields: *prima facie* and 'all-things-considered reasons'	41
	2.4 Epistemic fields in space and time	45
	2.5 Reasons and indicators	47
	2.6 'Should', 'ought', and 'right'	48
	2.7 Can 'R' and 'R$_o$' be defined in terms of 'S'? Degrees of belief and feeling	50
	2.8 Interpretative explanations	52
	2.9 Epistemic, evaluative, and practical: an irreducible trichotomy	53
	2.10 Facts, reasons, and supervenience	55

3	**Indexicality, Universalizability, and the Range of Reasons**	57
	3.1 Reflexivity, acting from reasons, and self-determination	57

3.2	Indexicality: neutral and relative reasons	60
3.3	Reasons as nominal or substantial facts	61
3.4	Relativity to agent, patient, and thinker	63
3.5	Relativity to time and the general formula	67
3.6	The universality and the universalizability of reasons	68
3.7	The universalizability of evaluative reasons	70
3.8	What determines the range of a reason?	71
3.9	Cognitive internalism	73

4 Normativity — 77

4.1	Semantic reduction and concept possession	78
4.2	Normative sentences and normative predicates	80
4.3	Defining 'good'	82
4.4	Objections to the definition	87
4.5	Thick evaluative terms: (i) wholly normative	93
4.6	Thick evaluative terms: (ii) mixed	96
4.7	Functional goodness and cost-effectiveness	98
4.8	Reasons and conditionals	99
4.9	The Transmission principle	103
4.10	Categorical and hypothetical	104

5 Warrant — 107

5.1	Self-accessibility and warrant	107
5.2	Epistemic self-audit	109
5.3	Epistemic states	112
5.4	Having a reason	113
5.5	Acting from a warrant: (i) knowledge of one's epistemic state	114
5.6	Acting from a warrant: (ii) normative insight into complete reasons	115
5.7	Apperception and independent objects	119
5.8	Some theses about warrant	121
5.9	Warrant and justification	124
5.10	Reliability and knowledge	127
5.11	Rational commitment and rationality	130
5.12	Autonomy	133

PART II EPISTEMIC REASONS — 135

6 The A Priori — 137
- 6.1 Three models of apriority — 138
- 6.2 Intuitionism — 142
- 6.3 The Critical argument — 144
- 6.4 Against intuitionism — 146
- 6.5 A priori propositions — 148
- 6.6 A priori warrants — 150
- 6.7 The normativity of a priori propositions — 152
- 6.8 Offshoots of normative propositions — 155
- 6.9 Apriority and defeasibility — 156
- 6.10 A priori knowledge — 160

7 Analyticity — 164
- 7.1 Kant, Mill, Frege, and Vienna — 165
- 7.2 The empty-inference approach — 167
- 7.3 Sentence, proposition, and truth condition — 172
- 7.4 Are the basic principles of truth analytic? — 174
- 7.5 Analyticity and implicit definition — 176
- 7.6 Verificationism and its difficulties — 178
- 7.7 Fixing a reference and apriority — 181
- 7.8 Propositions and content — 184

8 Modality — 186
- 8.1 Logic — 187
- 8.2 Acts of inquiry and epistemic reasons — 189
- 8.3 The dynamics of supposition — 191
- 8.4 Modality as unconditional exclusion and inclusion — 192
- 8.5 Normative interpretation of modal logic — 195
- 8.6 Modal knowledge and fallibilism — 198
- 8.7 Modality and normativity: cart and horse — 200
- 8.8 Factualism versus the normativity of logic — 203
- 8.9 Empiricism and reasons — 204

9 Non-monotonic Norms — 207

- 9.1 Apperceptual and perceptual reasons — 207
- 9.2 Evidence and reasons to believe — 210
- 9.3 Inductive evidence — 213
- 9.4 Defeasibility and monotonicity — 214
- 9.5 Non-inductive, non-monotonic norms: norms of receptivity — 217
- 9.6 Probability, frequency, and propensity — 220
- 9.7 Do epistemic reasons satisfy the probability calculus? — 223
- 9.8 Bayesianism — 227
- 9.9 The dynamics of inquiry — 230

PART III EVALUATIVE AND PRACTICAL REASONS — 233

10 Rational Explanation: Belief, Feeling, and Will — 235

- 10.1 Explaining belief, feeling, and action — 236
- 10.2 Cognitive and non-cognitive models of motivation: psychological arguments — 239
- 10.3 Cognitive and non-cognitive models of motivation: philosophical arguments — 242
- 10.4 Instrumentalism — 245
- 10.5 Against instrumentalism — 247
- 10.6 Williams on internal reasons — 248
- 10.7 The requirement of effectiveness — 252
- 10.8 Cognitive internalism and the range of practical reasons — 254
- 10.9 Reason, feeling, and autonomy — 256
- 10.10 The will: *Wille* and *Willkür* — 259

11 Reasons and Feelings: (i) The Bridge Principle and the Concept of a Person's Good — 263

- 11.1 Sentimentalism: the Bridge principle — 264
- 11.2 The concept of a person's good — 267
- 11.3 Desire and reason to desire — 270
- 11.4 The irreducibility of reasons to desire — 272
- 11.5 Categorial and particular desires — 274
- 11.6 How a person's good can expand — 278
- 11.7 Personal good and rational care: acting for someone's sake — 282

	11.8	Egoism	285
	11.9	Ideals and practical necessity	287
12	**Reasons and Feelings: (ii) Moral Concepts**		**290**
	12.1	Wrongness and blameworthiness	291
	12.2	Blame as withdrawal of recognition	294
	12.3	Morality, blame, and practical reasons	295
	12.4	Morality, self-determination, and autonomy	301
	12.5	Cognitive internalism and autonomy	304
	12.6	Rights and duties of right	307
	12.7	Justice, desert, and fairness	313
	12.8	The epistemology of blame	317
	12.9	Moral wrongness: predicate, property, and concept	318
13	**Impartiality: (i) The Principle of Good**		**321**
	13.1	The limits of sentimentalism	322
	13.2	Impartiality and autonomy	324
	13.3	Impartial good and the disinterested will	327
	13.4	Practical reason and the will	330
	13.5	Good and rights	333
	13.6	Telic reasons	334
	13.7	Utilitarianism	336
	13.8	Utilitarianism and moral obligation	339
	13.9	Rule utilitarianism	340
	13.10	Other indirect options	344
14	**Impartiality: (ii) The Demand Principle**		**347**
	14.1	Sidgwick's three methods of ethics	348
	14.2	The Demand principle	351
	14.3	Demand and the disinterested will	353
	14.4	On the mutual relations of the sources of practical reasons	356
	14.5	Can it be wrong to pursue the Good?	359
	14.6	Hegel on conscience	361
	14.7	Esotericism and abstraction	364
	14.8	The principles of safety and conscience	366

x   Contents

15	**Moral Judgement and Feeling**	369
	15.1 British sentimentalism and German idealism	370
	15.2 Moral recognition	373
	15.3 Blame and avoidability	376
	15.4 Ethical punishment as atonement	378
	15.5 Recognition and respect	382
	15.6 Respect and honour	385
	15.7 The elementary forms of the moral life	387
	15.8 Liberal community: freedom and impartiality	390
	15.9 Criticism of morality	392

PART IV THE NORMATIVE VIEW   399

16	**The Epistemology of Reason Relations**	401
	16.1 Facts	403
	16.2 Spontaneity	405
	16.3 Normative harmony and reflective equilibrium	410
	16.4 Convergence	412
	16.5 Receptivity versus self-evidence: intuitionism again	413
	16.6 Receptivity and spontaneity in Kant	416
	16.7 Free thought	418

17	**The Ontology of Reason Relations**	420
	17.1 Semantics versus metaphysics	421
	17.2 Existence and actuality	424
	17.3 The causal condition	426
	17.4 Reason relations and abstraction	428
	17.5 Truth and correspondence	430
	17.6 Quietism is too quiet	434
	17.7 Non-cognitivism is not required	436
	17.8 What turns on 'realism'?	439

18	**Rules, Norms, and Concepts**	442
	18.1 Rules and norms	443
	18.2 The normativity of rule-following	444

18.3	Moore's open question	447
18.4	Wittgenstein's open question	451
18.5	Norms and concepts	452
18.6	Cart and horse: supervenience	454

19 Self and Self-Determination — 458

19.1	Apperception, consciousness, and 'inner sense'	458
19.2	What is it to grasp and act for a reason?	462
19.3	Self-determination and the unity of apperception	464
19.4	Self-determination, freedom, responsibility, and autonomy	465
19.5	Why treat reasons as nominal, not substantial, facts?	469
19.6	The ontology of persons	472
19.7	Empirical and intelligible	475

20 The Critique of Reasons — 477

20.1	Reasons and Reason	478
20.2	In defence of the trichotomy	480
20.3	Constructivism and cognitive irrealism in Kant	484
20.4	The Normative view as Critical philosophy	487
20.5	How do epistemic norms apply to reality?	489
20.6	Are epistemic norms defeasible?	492
20.7	Scepticism	494
20.8	Naturalism	499
20.9	Can Critical dualisms be overcome?	502

Appendix: Symbols, Terms, and Theses	505
References	511
Index	519

PREFACE

This book covers a lot of ground across fields that are nowadays not often studied together. Yet it is a monograph, inasmuch as it covers all these fields from a single point of view. It works out the consequences of an account of normativity according to which all normative properties are reducible to what I call *reason relations*, so that normative propositions in all fields are propositions about reasons.

Part I sets out the foundations of this analysis; Part II applies and extends it to epistemic reasons, hence aprioricity, modality, and probability; Part III to evaluative and practical reasons, hence value, practical reason, and morality. Finally Part IV moves to the meta-normative, showing how the epistemology and ontology of reason relations grounds a new Critical philosophy, one that does not fall to the difficulties of previous Critical ventures. Although the positions developed in this book cannot be said to be Kantian, and in some respects differ sharply from Kant's, his starting points, particularly his contrast between receptivity and spontaneity, and much of what he says about the will (though not the feelings), are also mine.

The widespread of topics covered means that not all readers will read all parts of this book. For example, readers with more interest in metaphysics and epistemology than in moral philosophy may want to omit Part III, while those with more interest in moral philosophy may want to omit Part II. Others may want to pick their way through the book in other ways, or to follow an order other than its order of presentation. To facilitate all these kinds of selective reading I have provided a synopsis, and an appendix of notes on symbols, terms, and some theses. I have also put rather a lot of cross-references into the text, which I hope will not be too distracting. Readers who want a brief survey of the overall view may find the Introduction helpful. Chapter 5 examines the notion of *warrant*, which is central to the book as a whole. A final pulling together is provided in the last chapter, Chapter 20. It remains my guiding conviction, however, that to show how a unified account of normativity can be provided across *all* areas is to strengthen the account in *each* of them.

One other point follows. Many of the areas of philosophy traversed in this book are much discussed and controversial. In all of them it would be possible to delve deeper into the issues, discuss an extensive literature on the subject and explain what criticisms I have of positions I disagree with. By and large I have not done this because it would make a long book even longer, and produce even greater challenges for both author and reader. The aim of this book is constructive, rather than polemical—furthermore, my criticisms of other views would often merely recapitulate criticisms already made by others. For example, I agree with the main criticisms that have been made of non-cognitivist theories of the normative. But I have confined myself to noting (17.7) that if the irrealist, yet cognitivist, account offered in this book is right—together with the natural account of rational motivation that goes with it—then the pressures favouring non-cognitivism dissipate. Non-cognitivists make sound criticisms of meta-normative realism; but on my account that does not force us to non-cognitivism. Some other important lines of thought I have had to leave out entirely: these include, in particular, constitutive accounts of normativity of the kind offered by Christine Korsgaard and David Velleman, and the non-descriptive or 'expressivist' cognitivism in meta-ethics advanced by Terence Horgan and Mark Timmons.[1] This is not at all because I find these approaches uninteresting—although I do disagree with them—but on the contrary, because there is no space for the detailed assessment that I would like to make.

This book results from thinking and discussion with others over rather more years than I care to remember. More recently I have benefited from several periods of study leave. I owe thanks to the School of Philosophy and Anthropology at St Andrews, which has been generous in granting me leave, especially for a year's leave of absence after I completed a three-year stint as Head of School. Special thanks are due here to Peter Clark, who took over as Head. I was able to spend that year as a visiting fellow at All Souls College in Oxford in 2002–3, where I crystallized rough ideas into Part I of this book, and became much clearer about the book's overall aims. I am grateful to the College for the generous facilities and hospitality it offered me as a visiting fellow. While at All Souls, and since, I gained much from discussion with John Broome, Jeremy Butterfield, Roger Crisp, Jonathan Dancy, Brad Hooker, Derek Parfit, Thomas Pogge, Philip Stratton-Lake, and Ralph Wedgwood.

Then I was lucky enough to receive a two-year major research fellowship from the Leverhulme Trust in 2006–8, together with another semester's leave from St Andrews after I realized that two years would not be, as I had optimistically thought, quite enough. In this period of two and a half years I completed a first draft of the book.

Finally, I owe thanks to the Philosophy division of the Research School of Social Sciences at the Australian National University. The time I spent in Canberra as a visiting fellow in June to September of 2009 was a happy and rewarding period during which I was able to revise my book and provide a synopsis for it.

Without the generous support of all these institutions it would have been, at the least, very much harder to complete this book.

I am also conscious how much I owe over the years to many discussions with friends in St Andrews and elsewhere. Heartfelt thanks especially to Sarah Broadie, Roger Crisp, Dudley Knowles, Graham Priest, Wlodek Rabinowicz, Jerry Schneewind, and Crispin Wright, for various kinds of criticism and support. From earlier times I owe much to discussion with Bernard Williams. I have received valuable comments on particular sections of this book, in earlier drafts as well as in response to various ideas in it, notably from David Copp, Stephen Darwall, Antony Duff, Allan Gibbard, Andy Hamilton, Brad Hooker, Tim Mulgan, Jonas Olson, Ingmar Persson, Peter Railton, Stephen Read, Simon Robertson, Toni Rønnow-Rasmussen, Tim Scanlon, and Elea Zardini. And I have profited from much discussion of its topics with a splendid group of graduate students in St

---

[1] See, for example Horgan and Timmons 2000, 2006; Korsgaard 2008, 2009; Velleman 2000.

Andrews (as they were then)—Andy Fisher, Iwao Hirose, Kent Hurtig, Brian McElwee, Paul Markwick, Andrew Reisner, Simon Robertson, Raffaele Rodogno, and Enzo Rossi.

As well as this personal level of discussion, the ideas or scholarship of a number of philosophers have greatly influenced me through my reading. Among them are Allan Gibbard, John MacDowell, Derek Parfit, Hilary Putnam, Joseph Raz, Tim Scanlon, and Allen Wood (my first guide to Hegel's ethics). The amount of time I have spent thinking about their ideas or benefiting from their scholarship is not captured by the specific references that follow.

Finally, to my mind traditions of thinking matter in philosophy. In a note on the development of his ideas, Henry Sidgwick revealingly cited Mill and Kant, followed by Butler, as his 'masters'. (The note was published posthumously by E. E. Constance-Jones as a preface to the 6th edition of *Methods of Ethics*.) They are my masters too; I would add, in the domain of ethics and morality, Hegel—and, of course, Sidgwick.

A number of ideas in this book have been canvassed in earlier articles. Some of these were collected and revised in Parts I ('Reasons') and III ('Morality') of my *Ethical Explorations* (1999). I have also drawn on some other articles, notably the following:

> 'Logical Grammar, Transcendentalism and Normativity', *Philosophical Topics* 25, 1997; 'Irrealist Cognitivism', in Jonathan Dancy (ed.), *Ratio*, 1999: 436–59; 'The Ontology of Reasons', in C. Bagnoli and G. Usberti (eds), *Meaning, Justification and Reasons*, *Topoi* 1, 2002: 113–24; 'Blame, Respect and Recognition, A reply to Theo van Willigenburg', *Utilitas* 17, 2005; 'Later Empiricism and Logical Positivism', in Stewart Shapiro (ed.), *The Oxford Handbook to the Philosophy of Mathematics*, Oxford University Press, 2005; 'Welfare and Self-Governance', *Ethical Theory and Moral Practice* 9, 2006; 'Propositions about Reasons', *European Journal of Philosophy* 14, 2006; 'Internal Reasons and the Scope of Blame', in Alan Thomas (ed.), *Bernard Williams*, Cambridge University Press, 2007.

Some other articles that have appeared more recently were based on earlier drafts of this book:

> 'What is Normativity?', *Disputatio* 2, 2007; 'Buckpassing about goodness', in T. Rønnow-Rasmussen, B. Petersson, J. Josefsson, and D. Egonsson (eds), *Hommage à Wlodek, Philosophical Papers Dedicated to Wlodek Rabinowicz*, 2007, www.fil.lu.se/hommageawlodek/site/papper/SkorupskiJohn.pdf; 'L'utilitarismo e l'obiezione dell'arroganza' (Utilitarianism and the Arrogance Objection), *Rivista di Filosofia* 9, 2008; 'Back to Kant?', *The Polish Journal of Philosophy* 3, 2009; The Unity and Diversity of Reasons', in Simon Robertson (ed.), *Spheres of Reason: New Essays in the Philosophy of Normativity*, Oxford University Press, 2009; 'Moral Obligation, Blame And Self-Governance', *Social Philosophy and Policy*, 2010, 27: 2.

SYNOPSIS

1 Introduction

An outline of the main themes of this book.

1.1 Brief summary of contents.
1.2 The characteristics of Critical philosophy. How it is opposed to global realism, and what global realism is.
1.3 Critical philosophy in *Kant*.
1.4 Critical philosophy in *Wittgenstein* and the *Vienna Circle*.
1.5 Critical philosophy as proposed in this book: the Normative view.
1.6 Autonomy and self-determination; reasons and warranted reasons. The meta-unity of reasons, epistemic, practical, and evaluative. The possibility of autonomy presupposes that reason relations are a priori.
1.7 The normative sources of practical reasons. Relation of the view advanced in this book to sentimentalism and to *Kant*.
1.8 Moral concepts are characterizable in terms of the sentiment of blame. Outline of implications of this thesis. The role of moral judgement.
1.9 Summary statement of the Normative view. Outline of its implications and limits.

Part I The Structure of Normative Concepts

2 Reasons

Chapter 2 gives an account of *reason relations*. It distinguishes between epistemic reasons (reasons to believe), evaluative reasons (reasons to feel), and practical reasons (reasons to act), and makes some main points about their logic.

2.1 Epistemic, practical, and evaluative reasons distinguished.
2.2 In all three cases there are three reason relations: specific (R); overall (R_o); and sufficient (S). 'S' is not definable in terms of 'R' and/or 'R_o'. Nor is 'R_o' definable in terms of 'R'.
2.3 Epistemic reasons have a special feature; they are relative to epistemic fields: sets of facts knowable to the actor. A *prima facie* reason is an apparent reason in an epistemic field, which may or may not really be a reason in that field when all facts in the field are considered.

2.4 Since inquiry takes place in space and time, we can if necessary think of the inquirer as having a tree of epistemic fields available at any given time.

2.5 Epistemic reasons should be distinguished from indicators. X *indicates* Y if and only if X tends to produce Y, or vice versa, or both X and Y tend to be produced by a common cause. Indicators that p may or may not be reasons to believe that p—it depends on the epistemic field.

2.6 'x should ψ', 'x ought to ψ,' and 'it is right for x to ψ' can all be used to say that there is sufficient reason for x to ψ (uniquely sufficient reason in the case of practical reasons). We call this the designated use, indicating it where convenient by an asterisk, e.g. 'should*'.

2.7 'R' and 'R_o' cannot be defined in terms of 'S'.

2.8 'Normative' and 'explanatory' reasons: a potentially misleading distinction. 'Normative reasons' are reasons *to* ψ: these are the reasons discussed in this book.

2.9 The distinction between epistemic, evaluative, and practical reasons is irreducible. See also 20.2.

2.10 To be a reason is to stand in a reason relation (just as to be a father is to stand in the father relation). Normative supervenience reduces to reason relations.

3 Indexicality, Universalizability, and the Range of Reasons

Chapter 3 examines a distinction between neutral and relative reasons. It also considers the universalizability and range of reasons. Reasons are universal: they apply to all actors. But over what entities does 'all actors' range?

3.1 We are readier to impute reasons than to impute the concept of a reason. However, self-determination—'acting *from* reasons'—requires the latter, because it requires the capacity to assess reasons as such.

3.2 A reason is relative if it essentially comprises indexical facts. Otherwise it is neutral.

3.3 A distinction is made between a nominal and a substantial sense of 'fact'. We take reasons to be facts in the nominal sense.

3.4 This leads to another way of stating the distinction between relative and neutral reasons, worked out for practical, evaluative, and epistemic reasons.

3.5 And for the case of temporal neutrality / relativity. A general formulation.

3.6 Reasons, when stated completely (see 5.6), are universal. More strongly, they are universalizable. Illustrated by *Sidgwick's* discussion of irrational as against rational egoism.

3.7 Evaluative reasons are universalizable, just as epistemic and practical reasons are.

3.8 Although reasons are universal that does not determine their range. What determines the range of entities, or actors, to which a given reason can be ascribed?

3.9 Cognitive internalism is the thesis that only an actor that can grasp a reason falls within the range of that reason. Initial account of its implications.

4 Normativity

In this book 'normative' is used broadly to contrast with 'descriptive', not narrowly to contrast with 'evaluative'. Chapter 4 presents, and begins discussion of, the Reasons thesis, which states that the concept of a reason is the fundamental normative concept.

4.1 Two versions of the Reason thesis: the definability thesis and the concept–possession thesis.

4.2 'Normative sentence' and 'normative predicate' defined.

4.3 Interlinked definitions of 'good' in terms of reasons.

4.4 Objections to these definitions; replies.

4.5 Some 'thick' evaluative terms may be wholly normative; even so they can convey factual information about the evaluated items.

4.6 In other cases there are inextricable factual and normative ingredients.

4.7 Why the notion of cost-effectiveness must be understood as a normative notion.

4.8 How S works in conditionals: 'ought' and 'rational requirement'.

4.9 The Transmission principle, governing objective-and-means reasoning, stated, argued to be analytic, and contrasted to the Instrumental principle.

4.10 A factor which lends spurious plausibility to the Instrumental principle. How our discussion relates to Kant's distinction between hypothetical and Categorical Imperatives.

5 Warrant

Self-determining actors must be able to know what reasons they have. They must be able to audit those reasons, to assess whether they have *warrant* for a particular response. Chapter 5 defines warrant and discusses its structure, distinguishing it from justification and knowledge. It argues that if self-determination is possible reason relations must be a priori.

5.1 Warranted reasons must be self-accessible. Autonomy is a special case of self-determination: to respond autonomously is to respond *from* warrant.

5.2 Self-determiners must be able to tell, just by self-examination and reflection, whether they have sufficient reason for a belief. Argument for this view.

5.3 A fact belongs to your *epistemic state* just if constitutes in itself a sufficient reason for you to believe that it obtains.

5.4 There is warrant for x to ψ if and only if x's epistemic state gives x sufficient reason to believe that there is sufficient reason for x to ψ.

5.5 Only facts about yourself that you can know solely by attending to them satisfy the requirement of Section 3.

5.6 If warrants are self-accessible, knowledge of reason relations must be a priori. A priori knowledge of reason relations is formally universal.

5.7 We say that actors *apperceive* the facts in their epistemic state. One cannot apperceive facts about objects that are independent of one's mind.

5.8 Some theses about warrant. We can relativize warrants to a particular actor's normative powers or to his epistemic state. The theses assume the latter reading.

5.9 We may often be justified in our response—not criticizable in respect of rationality—whether or not the response is warranted. This is because the normative is complex and time is scarce. Nonetheless we aim at warrant.

5.10 The WK principle: if x is warranted in believing that p then, were x to recognize that warrant and on that basis believe that p, x would be warranted in believing that x knows that p.

5.11 Some principles of rationality proposed. Rationality is responsiveness to warranted reasons; how it connects to justification and to warrant.

5.12 Seeking to respond from warrant—autonomously—whenever possible can be a practical project. Whether it is warranted depends on the substantive theory of practical reasons.

Part II Epistemic Reasons

6 The A Priori

Chapter 6 gives a normative account of what it means to say of a proposition, of a warrant, and of knowledge that it is a priori; it then argues that all synthetic a priori propositions are either normative propositions or non-normative offshoots of normative propositions.

6.1 Three models of apriolicity described: intuitionism; the no-content view; and the Normative view that is propounded in this book. The Normative view of the a priori compared to *Kant's* view.

6.2 Intuitionism (as the term is used in this book) holds that a priori propositions state substantial facts knowable by intuition. It models its account of a priori warrant and knowledge on perceptual warrant and knowledge.

6.3 The Critical thesis: no factual proposition is a priori. An argument for it is set out. The basic premise: no real relation holds between distinct existents a priori. *Kant's* transcendental idealism considered in this light. It entails the unknowability of cognition-independent facts.

6.4 Intuitionism leads to a vicious regress.

6.5 A proposition is a priori in e if there is outright sufficient reason to believe it in e. It has some degree of a priori support in e if there is that degree of outright reason to believe it.

6.6 A person, x, has a priori warrant for the belief that p when in x's epistemic state the fact that x is spontaneously disposed to judge outright that p gives x sufficient reason to believe that there is outright reason to believe that p.

6.7 Discussion of 'Nothing is simultaneously wholly red and wholly green'. Simple identities and non-identities are non-factual.

6.8 Certain non-normative propositions 'derive' from epistemic norms, but not deductively and *a fortiori* not definitionally. These 'offshoots' are a priori, but non-factual as well as non-normative.

6.9 If there is a priori support for a proposition in e, then it is a priori in e, and in all strict improvements on e, that there is this support in e. But is there a priori support for the proposition in all strict improvements on e? The question left to 20.6.

6.10 x has a priori knowledge that p if and only if (i) p; (ii) x believes that p on the basis of normative dispositions to believe that p; and (iii) which are reliable. The reliability of a normative disposition is measured by the degree to which it can be trusted to provide an epistemic basis for an a priori warrant.

7 Analyticity

Chapter 7 explains what notions of analyticity, proposition and truth are adopted in this book. It also reviews the version of Critical philosophy developed by *Wittgenstein* and the *Vienna Circle* in the 1920s (the 'Vienna School'), and the reasons why their attempt at a Critical perspective fails.

7.1 If the notion of analyticity is to serve a Critical epistemological purpose an analytic sentence must be *empty of informative content*. Notions of analyticity in *Kant*, *Mill*, *Frege* and the *Vienna School*.

7.2 *Mill's* 'empty-inference' criterion of analyticity satisfies this requirement. In doing so it makes logic synthetic.

7.3 Explanation of our use of the terms 'proposition' and 'truth condition'. Truth conditions distinguished from 'truth makers'.

7.4 Three principles of truth are proposed. It is argued that the first of these—*it is true that* $p \leftrightarrow p$—is analytic by the empty-inference criterion.

7.5 The Vienna School's notion of analyticity by implicit definition. An objection to it considered: implicit definition does not guarantee reference.

7.6 The Viennese reply: existence and truth are internal to the framework of conventions. Objections.

7.7 A sentence can express an a priori proposition in virtue of fixing the reference of a term. But where the reference is to an existent this does not make such propositions necessarily true (whether or not they are).

7.8 Discussion of the sense in which aprioricity based on reference fixing can be said to be 'linguistic' or 'analytic'.

8 Modality

Chapter 8 argues that (i) though some modal necessities that govern thinking are a priori and some are not, the nature of the necessity involved is the same; and (ii) the modal concept of necessity is analysable in term of epistemic reasons: reasons to exclude and include suppositions in the course of eliminative inquiry.

8.1 Logic as such is not demarcated in any philosophically significant way from the general domain of a priori necessity. Our question is about the nature of modality in general, and about how it is that some modalities are known a priori while others are only known a posteriori.

8.2 *Eliminative inquiry* proceeds by eliminating branches from a tree of suppositions. Although the reasons for engaging in any given inquiry are practical reasons, the reasons for cognitive acts within the inquiry are epistemic.

8.3 *Inclusion* and *exclusion* as acts within eliminative inquiry. Conditional and unconditional inclusion/exclusion.

8.4 The *maximal field*, μ, is the epistemic field consisting of all the facts. Definition: it is *impossible* that p if and only if there is sufficient epistemic reason in μ to exclude unconditionally the proposition that p. Definitions of possibility and necessity.

8.5 The system of modal logic that holds on this interpretation is S5. Necessities of identity and origin also hold.

8.6 How can a limited epistemic field give us sufficient reason for modal beliefs, if these beliefs are about what suppositions should* be unconditionally included/excluded in μ? Discussion of two relevant principles in the logic of reasons. Fallibilist versus sceptical reading of these principles.

8.7 Objection: our normative analysis of modality puts the cart before the horse. It's *because* it is impossible that p that there is sufficient reason in μ to exclude the supposition that p. This objection can be raised for all our analyses in terms of reasons; it is considered in general terms in 18.6.

8.8 Factualist views of logic contrasted with the Normative view.

8.9 The fundamental objection to empiricism: if self-determination is possible there must be a priori norms. This does not rule out empiricism about logic and mathematics; however, on the Normative view there is no philosophical reason to deny that these are a priori.

9 Non-monotonic Norms

In Chapter 9 normative definitions of *evidence* and *probability* are proposed, and the norms that govern a posteriori warrants and non-deductive reasoning are surveyed.

9.1 When I apperceive that p the fact that p itself gives me reason to believe that p—whereas when I perceive that p it is not the fact that p itself that gives me reason to believe that p. It is, rather, the fact that I perceive that p.

9.2 *Inductive* and *indicative* evidence distinguished. The fact that q is inductive evidence that $p =$ the fact that q constitutes a non-deductive, inference-based reason to believe that p. The appropriateness of the term 'evidence' in the case of indicators traces back to a looser connection with reasons.

9.3 Inductive norms: the straight norm of induction and the norm of inference to the best explanation.

9.4 Monotonicity defined for practical and evaluative norms, and for epistemic norms. The former are all monotonic; but not all epistemic norms are monotonic. Inductive norms are non-monotonic. We can also ask whether a norm—monotonic or not—is *defeasible*.

9.5 Some proposed norms of receptivity (perception, memory, empathy, testimony) considered. Norms of receptivity, like inductive norms, are non-monotonic.

9.6 Probability is degree of (specific or overall) reason to believe. Frequency and propensity are not themselves probability concepts but provide epistemic grounds for probability judgements via inductive and propensity norms.

9.7 Overall epistemic reasons satisfy the probability calculus. The underlying norm is the norm of indifference.

9.8 The Normative interpretation of probability is closer to Bayesianism than to frequency and propensity views, but differs in two respects. It does not postulate degrees of belief, as against degrees of reason to believe, and it holds that claims about the latter are true or false assertions.

9.9 Inquiry is a dynamic process taking place in time. Non-monotonic norms yield warrants for judgement that are 'innocent until proved guilty'. This is an inevitable feature of inquiry: without it inquiry could neither get started nor produce revisions of belief.

Part III Evaluative and Practical Reasons

10 Rational Explanation: Belief, Feeling, and Will

The aim of Chapter 10 is to describe the form of 'rational explanations', i.e. explanations in terms of recognized warrant, and to show that exactly the same form of rational explanation applies to beliefs, actions, and feelings. In all three cases a cognitive account applies: the *explanans* in a rational explanation consists of the actor's factual and normative beliefs.

10.1 'Rational explanation' explains an act as caused by recognition of warrant; it is a special case of interpretative or 'personal-level' explanation. All interpretative explanation appeals to intelligible reasons. 'Humean' or non-cognitive accounts of such explanations.

10.2 We should distinguish an aim-eliciting and a substantive sense of desire. It then becomes clear that the Humean model of motivation cannot be defended empirically, either directly or by appeal to implicit definition.

10.3 As for philosophical arguments for it, these require special premises: either empiricism, or a combination of factualism with a strong open-question argument. If these are sound, they refute a purely cognitive account of rational explanation in all cases—for beliefs and feelings as well as for actions.

10.4 We should also consider instrumentalism as an account specifically of practical reasons. There can be a constitutive and a Normative version of this account. The constitutive version is a species of reductive realism, and as such falls under the objections to all reductive realisms advanced in Chapter 18.

10.5 Some objections specifically to instrumentalism, normative as well as constitutive, considered, and upheld.

10.6 *Williams'* theory of internal reasons is not a version of instrumentalism, but does entail a peculiarly individualistic relativism about practical norms.

10.7 However, even though *Williams'* motivational internalism should be rejected, cognitive internalism (3.8) may still hold. If it does, it has many of the implications for the scope of blame which *Williams* believes his internalism to have.

10.8 Cognitive internalism considered as a constraint on practical reasons. Moral obligations, unlike ideals, entail reasons that do not depend on 'subjective conditions', nonetheless cognitive internalism could apply to both moral obligations and ideals.

10.9 Interpretative explanation can apply to involuntary behaviour as well as to intentional acts. Normative reasons come into play in these cases: reasons for feelings. And since there are reasons for feelings, one can feel, as well as act and believe, autonomously.

10.10 To have a will is simply to have the power of acting from what one takes to be reasons for the action. There is also 'willpower'. This distinguishes action from belief and feeling: we can act, but not believe or feel, at will; we can make ourselves *do* something, but not believe or feel something. *Kant's* distinction between *Wille* and *Willkür* reflects this.

11 Reasons and Feelings: (i) The Bridge Principle and the Concept of a Person's Good

Chapters 11 and 13–14 describe the normative sources of evaluative–practical reasoning, and analyse its distinctive concepts. One such source is a principle we call the 'Bridge' principle, since it is the bridge by which thought crosses from evaluative reasons to practical reasons. The concept of a person's good and the concept of personal ideals both belong within this sentimentalist territory. They, together with the Bridge principle, are the topics of Chapter 11.

11.1 How the term 'sentimentalism' is used in this book. Basic principle of sentimentalism—the *Bridge* principle: whatever facts give x reason to feel ϕ give x reason to do the ϕ-prompted action, in virtue of being a reason to feel ϕ.

11.2 A person's good comprises whatever there is reason for that person to desire, in the substantive sense of desire (see 10.2).

11.3 But how does one tell what there is reason for a person to desire? Desire is the sole criterion of desirability, as *Mill* in effect said. Difficulties in applying this criterion.

11.4 What a person desires, and would desire under various conditions, is the epistemic criterion of what there is reason for them to desire; it does not *constitute* what there is reason for them to desire. An epistemic circle noted—further discussion left to Chapter 16.

11.5 We can distinguish between categorial desires and desires for a particular object under a category. It does not follow that an 'objective list' of categorial desirables can be drawn up.

11.6 What there is substantive reason for a person to desire is a part of that person's good, whether or not its object is a state of the person.

11.7 *Darwall's* characterization of a person's good, in terms of what there is reason to want (or do) for him for his sake, considered. Although it may be a priori correct, our account makes a better definition.

11.8 The truth in egoism is that there is a specific reason to pursue one's own good, irrespective of other practical reasons; this follows from the definition of a person's good together with the Bridge principle. But it is not true that egoistic reasons are the only practical reasons.

11.9 The truth in perfectionism is that the admirable is a source of value distinct from the desirable. But to give a person reason to pursue it, as against supporting it, the admirable object has to become desirable to that person.

12 Reasons and Feelings: (ii) Moral Concepts

We develop our account of morality in two stages. Chapter 12 is concerned with the conceptual connections between moral concepts, the sentiment of blame, and practical reasons. A fuller account of moral judgement and feeling, and its place in communal life is given in Chapter 15, after we have completed, in Chapters 13 and 14, our account of the normative sources of evaluative–practical reasoning.

12.1 The connection between moral wrongness and blameworthiness stated, and the meaning of 'blameworthiness' discussed. The sentiment and the act of blame distinguished.

12.2 Preliminary account of the sentiment (continued in Chapter 15): blame disposes to 'withdrawal of recognition'.

12.3 If I blame someone for doing something I must think he had a belief-relative reason not to do it (or was relevantly negligent in forming his beliefs). The categoricity of moral obligation follows from this hermeneutic principle of blame.

12.4 The concept of moral agency requires that a moral agent is self-determining; it does not require that a moral agent is autonomous (cp. 5.1). However, 'modern morality' holds that moral agents are autonomous: the Insight principle.

12.5 *Williams'* critique of modern morality is unconvincing so far as based on motivational internalism (10.6). But a similar critique arises from cognitive internalism (3.9), and cognitive internalism about moral obligation is inherent in modern morality's commitment to equal autonomy. This further discussed in Chapter 15.

12.6 *Mill's* definition of rights rejected, on the basis of *Hart's* objection that it 'puts the cart before the horse'. An alternative definition is proposed in terms of what it is morally permissible to *demand*.

12.7 *Desert* always reduces to reasons for certain person-evaluating feelings. It engages with *justice* where permissible demands are involved. Likewise fairness engages with justice where it generates permissible demands.

12.8 The criterion of blameworthiness, and hence moral wrongness, is the blame feeling. But spontaneous judgements of blameworthiness could be defeated by a substantive theory of practical reasons.

12.9 Our account of moral wrongness is a 'buck-passing account', like our account of goodness in 4.3 and 4.4.

13 Impartiality: (i) The Principle of Good

Chapters 13 and 14 argue that sentimentalism can give no account of how *impartiality* enters into the sources of practical reasons. Impartial principles underlie our notions of Good and of Rights; their epistemic basis cannot be the affective dispositions, it can only be the disinterested dispositions of the will. Chapter 13 discusses the principle of Good.

13.1 Sentimentalism cannot account for the impartial elements in morality and practical reasons. Some sentimentalist options considered and dismissed.

13.2 *Kant* takes it that impartiality can be derived from autonomy. But this cannot be done by appeal to the universalizability of an autonomous will's maxims. (Cp. *Sidgwick's* discussion, noted in 3.6). Nor can it be done by appeal to the 'open-question' point.

13.3 But can we postulate the existence of *disinterestedness* in an autonomous will? If so, that disinterested moment can be the epistemic basis for a requirement of impartiality. A thought experiment suggests that there is this moment of disinterestedness, and exhibits it as the epistemic basis of a principle of impartial good.

13.4 This is not a form of intuitionism: it does not postulate a receptive faculty whereby we know normative facts, but bases normative principles of impartiality on dispositions of the will. Similarities and differences between *Kant's* view and our view described.

13.5 An impartial principle of Good contrasted with an impartial principle of rights. *Mill* sought to base the latter on the former; but the next chapter will argue that both are separately founded on the disinterested dispositions of the will.

13.6 If the fact that an action will promote a state of affairs is a complete reason to do it, that state of affairs is a *final end*. Where an action promotes a final end the fact that it does so is a *telic* reason to do it. Utilitarianism holds that all practical reasons are telic reasons.

13.7 Characteristics of *pure* and *dominance* utilitarianism.

13.8 What account can a utilitarian give of moral obligation? Warranted act utilitarianism; objections.

13.9 Rule utilitarianism: definition, substantive moral thesis, or theoretical reduction? Objections to these.

13.10 Strategic adoption of moral common sense, combined with philosophical rejection of the concept of the moral; objections. What of the Dominance view: is it more genuinely friendly to moral common sense?

14 Impartiality: (ii) The Demand Principle

Whether there can be a disinterested will is a major turning point for ethics. In Chapter 13 we accepted that there can be and is, and made its dispositions the epistemic basis of a principle of Good. Chapter 14 introduces a third and final principle of practical reason—the Demand principle—basing it in the same way. It then asks how *moral judgement* plays on these three principles of practical reason.

14.1 *Sidgwick's* dualism of practical reason can be seen as structurally similar to our position in that (i) it is pluralist about practical reason; and (ii) it passes the buck with respect to moral obligation.

14.2 But dualism is not enough, because it cannot explain the connection between rights and reasons. The *Demand* principle: if it is morally permissible for x to demand that *y αs*, the fact that it is is a complete specific reason for *y* not to fail to *α* without *x*'s permission.

14.3 The epistemic basis of the Demand principle, and thus of rights, is the demands of the disinterested will.

14.4 How do Bridge, Good, and Demand combine to generate sufficient reasons? How do they combine with reasons for blame to generate moral obligations? The latter combination is the task of *moral judgement*, to be considered in the remainder of this chapter and the next.

14.5 A *prima facie* conflict between Good and Demand considered: the case of Galahad. Is Galahad arrogant?

14.6 *Hegel's* criticism of *Kant's* conception of autonomy. His own conception: conscience in modern *Sittlichkeit*. His 'private morality argument' compared to *Wittgenstein's* 'private language argument'. The exoteric principle.

14.7 In moral judgement discussion with others is epistemically indispensable, but how much and with whom? When do abstract normative theories outweigh the judgements of moral common sense?

14.8 The principle of safety. The principle of conscience and the temptation to esotericism. On avoiding esotericism, whether by the individual or the group.

15 Moral Judgement and Feeling

The question considered in Chapter 15 is why do we engage in moral judgement, as well as practical judgements about what to do? Understanding the role of moral judgement requires a deeper understanding of the moral feelings than has been undertaken so far, so Chapter 15 examines the moral feelings and their relation to moral judgement.

15.1 Our account of moral judgement and feeling has some similarities to *Adam Smith's*. But differences are noted; in particular, we do not take the moral feelings to be based on 'resentment'. We can draw on *Fichte* and *Hegel* to achieve a better account, in terms of 'recognition'.

15.2 Forms of recognition distinguished: *summons*, *demand*, and *moral recognition* proper.

15.3 Blame presupposes avoidability, the capacity for moral agency, and the possibility of moral resolve; thus the capacity for self-blame. In these respects it differs from both horror and disgust, and contempt and disdain, which make no such assumptions.

15.4 Blame and guilt are the first stages in what (if completed) is a three-stage process: withdrawal of recognition; liminality and repentence; atonement, reconciliation with oneself and others. 'Ethical punishment' is the travail involved in the second two stages. How ethical punishment impinges on legal or institutional punishment.

15.5 *Kant's* notion of *respect* and its connection with the moral examined, and compared with our account of the moral in terms of recognition.

15.6 The modern ideal of human dignity, as *Kant* appeals to it, compared and contrasted to the bedrock of the moral sentiments.

15.7 The roles of moral judgement: verdictive; disciplinary; and emancipatory. The verdictive role.

15.8 How the disciplinary and emancipatory roles of moral judgement are connected. What kind of autonomy the freedom of moral integrity requires; and how it depends on well-functioning moral community.

15.9 Withdrawal of recognition gives morality a potentially dangerous charge. Are we, through our wish to recruit everyone into morality, led into unrealistic assumptions about people (*Williams*)? Cognitive internalism again.

Part IV The Normative View

16 The Epistemology of Reason Relations

Part IV moves to the epistemology and metaphysics of reason relations. Chapter 16 describes the epistemic circumstances in which a person is said to have warrant for a normative belief, or to have normative knowledge. It argues that an accurate description of our epistemic practice is inconsistent with taking purely normative propositions to be substantially factual.

16.1 The distinction made in 3.3 between nominal and substantial facts is reviewed. Further characterization of substantial facts.

16.2 Spontaneity is characterized, and some relations to *Kant*'s distinction between spontaneity and receptivity noted. The notion of normative harmony is explained. A *norm of spontaneity* is stated.

16.3 How normative harmony expands into reflective equilibrium.

16.4 The epistemology of reason relations is inherently dialogical. This arises because any judgement incurs a rational commitment stateable as the *convergence thesis*. The argument for the convergence thesis. Upshot: warrant for normative claims requires the twin pillars of individual spontaneity and discussion with others, and nothing more.

16.5 If spontaneity and convergence provide a sound basis for normative knowledge, normative knowledge is not factual.

16.6 How our account of the epistemology of reason relations compares with *Kant*'s account of understanding and practical reason. (To be continued in Chapter 20.)

16.7 This epistemology is the foundation for liberty of thought and discussion.

17 The Ontology of Reason Relations

Chapter 17 shows how reason relations differ from other relations in ways that can be summarized by saying that, unlike these other relations, reason relations are *irreal*. It also endorses a 'minimalist' account of truth. It then argues that there is no reason to hold a non-cognitivist view of the normative.

17.1 The semantic and the causal condition of existence. We reject the semantic condition. Our use of the terms 'exist' and 'real'.

17.2 Existence is opposed to non-existence; actuality to possibility. Fictional objects, and 'putatively real' objects that do not exist, are contingently actual but necessarily non-existent or irreal. The semantic condition is a condition on actuality, not existence.

17.3 The causal condition should be understood broadly, in terms of any philosophically defensible notion of productive power. It is proposed that existence is causal standing; this is a synthetic not an analytic identity.

17.4 Reason relations, unlike fictional objects and putative reals, are *objective* (mind independent) actual irreals. All abstracta are reducible to reason relations.

17.5 'Minimalism' about truth characterized and endorsed. The correspondence theory rejected.

17.6 Quietism—the claim that there are only nominal facts—rejected.

17.7 Three arguments for non-cognitivism considered and rejected.

17.8 Why call our position 'irrealism'? In what way does it differ from non-naturalistic realism?

18 Rules, Norms, and Concepts

Chapter 18 discusses the normative dimension of language use and concept possession. It is shown how *Wittgenstein*'s discussion of rule-following develops the 'open-question' challenge in such a way as to lead to the Normative view. Concept possession, it is argued, consists in grasp of epistemic norms.

18.1 Rules and conventions distinguished from norms.

18.2 On the sense in which a judgement about how to apply a rule is normative.

18.3 *Moore*'s 'open-question' defended as an argument against reductive realism about the normative.

18.4 *Wittgenstein*'s 'open-question' defended as an argument against realism about the normative as such.

18.5 To possess a concept is to have spontaneous recognition of a pattern of epistemic norms for introduction and elimination of the concept in thought. Putative concepts may be specious; genuine concepts may be uninstantiated. The notion 'conceptual truth' does not *explain* apriority or necessity.

18.6 The normative definitions we have given of *good, a priori, necessary, probable, morally wrong,* and *a right* considered together. A 'cart before the horse' objection can be made to each of them. The objection diagnosed as involving a certain reification. In contrast, our account eliminates the middleman and sweeps away normative 'supervenience'.

19 Self and Self-Determination

A certain group of concepts hang together as ingredients in our understanding of ourselves and others as persons: apperception, grasp of reasons, self-determination, will and freedom. They are surveyed in this chapter.

19.1 Our notion of apperception compared with various notions of consciousness. *Kant* on apperception and inner sense: his notion of inner sense rejected.

19.2 Levels of imputation: explanation in terms of states with intentional content; attribution of reasons; and attribution of self-determining power. Acting from self-determination calls for possession of the concept of a reason; but not all acting for reasons does.

19.3 Self-determination requires certain apperceptual, perceptual, and conceptual unities; distinctively, the ability to place oneself and one's epistemic field within a spatio-temporal and causal framework that gives rise to reasons.

19.4 We distinguish freedom as responsibility and freedom as autonomy. The latter can be understood more or less strongly, in a *Kantian* or a *Hegelian* way. Either way it is stronger than self-determination, which is all that is required for responsibility.

19.5 Reasons should be regarded as nominal facts, or truths, because they can include indexical and normative truths; more generally because what a self-determiner recognizes as a reason is *that* something is the case.

19.6 Difficulties in accepting either the reality or the irreality of the self. But these lie beyond the scope of this study.

19.7 Contrary to *Kant*, the contrast between 'empirical' and 'intelligible' is not a contrast between things as they appear and things as they really are. Yet it remains fundamental to this study, in that the basic category of the intelligible domain is the concept of a reason.

20 The Critique of Reasons

This chapter reviews the account of normativity developed in this book, and its foundation in the analysis of reasons. It explains how this account—the Normative view—constitutes a version of Critical philosophy; it assesses the similarities and differences between its metaphysics and *Kant*'s metaphysics of experience.

20.1 We should not reify 'Reason', nor assume that there must be a unitary faculty underlying all normative competence. While reason *relations* all have the same meta-status, *reasons* themselves are indefinitely diverse. So might be the capacities to recognize them.

20.2 Epistemicism (there are only epistemic reasons) and pragmatism (there are only practical reasons) considered. Our trichotomy of reasons preferred to epistemicism on grounds of economy, power, and naturalness. And to pragmatism, on the ground that pragmatism cannot account for warrant and self-determination. Dualism (there are only epistemic and practical reasons) also dismissed.

20.3 *Kant* is a constructivist about nature, but not about morality or reason. His view is that we 'give ourselves the moral law' as *law*—but that no one is or could be the 'author' of its content and validity. His view of requirements of reason in general is cognitivist and irrealist.

20.4 The Critical standing of the Normative view rests on its claim that not all content is factual: factual and normative content are distinct. We have shown that this claim does not require non-cognitivism about the normative.

20.5 Epistemic norms do not hold in virtue of any facts. Logic and mathematics can be stated as universal non-normative truths because their underlying norms are monotonic. Non-monotonic norms have no such offshoots.

20.6 Evaluative and practical norms are indefeasible. So are epistemic norms, both monotonic and non-monotonic. However, this is consistent with a weak empiricism about the universal propositions of logic and mathematics.

20.7 The Normative view refutes forms of scepticism that are based on global realism. But it does not, and is not meant to, deal with sceptical doubts that might arise from other, internal, sources.

20.8 Unlike *Kant's* transcendental idealism and *Viennese* verificationism, the Normative view is consistent with naturalism.

20.9 All Critical philosophy involves a fundamental dualism. For us, as for *Kant*, it is that of spontaneity and receptivity. Does this lead to a kind of transcendental idealism after all, or to the conclusion that truth is internal to our best overall conclusions about the world?

1

INTRODUCTION

1.1 What this book is about: a brief outline

This book is about normativity and reasons. By the end, however, our subject becomes the relation between self, thought, and world. As I hope to show, getting the metaphysics of normativity right is the high road to understanding this relation. But the high road is also a long road. We reach our final destination only in Part IV. On the way lie topics in the domain of reasons, which are important in their own right.

The elusiveness of the interplay between self, thought, and world is both striking and strange. It has proved remarkably difficult to resolve all the issues into a single philosophically clear picture. By now in the history of philosophy it may be unrealistic to expect that any attempt can satisfy everyone. Still it seems defeatist not to aim for a comprehensive resolution to which at least some people can give serious and settled assent.

What then is normativity? I use the word 'normative' in the broad way that draws a distinction between normative and descriptive. The normative includes *ought* and *should*, *good* and *bad*, as well as the various 'thick' normative concepts discussed in Chapter 4. It extends to epistemology as well as ethics and aesthetics. We assess arguments and evidence as good and bad: we talk about what one should believe on the evidence.

Specifically, this book focuses on the normative concept of a reason. That this concept should have increasingly attracted the attention of philosophers is unsurprising; the only surprise is that it has taken so long. It is a concept fundamental to all thought. It is pervasive—actions, beliefs, and sentiments all fall within its range; primitive—all other normative concepts are reducible to it; and constitutive of the idea of thought itself. Thinking is sensitivity to reasons. Thought in the full sense of autonomous cognition is possible only for a being sensitive to reasons and capable of deliberating about them. That is why reflection on the logical structure, epistemology, and ontology of reasons must finally lead us to an account of the interplay of self, thought, and world.

To be sure, each of the points just made can be questioned. First, as regards pervasiveness: philosophers have had a historic tendency to dismiss the idea that sentiments properly fall under the concept of a reason—at least, that they fall under it as squarely and surely as actions and beliefs do. This tendency is so marked as to generate a kind of rationalistic distortion of reasons: philosopher's syndrome, blindness to the fact that feelings have their own reasons. 'The heart has its reasons of which reason knows nothing'. That remark of Pascal's is perceptive, but still takes a contestable view of 'reason'. What sort of 'reason' knows nothing of these reasons? One main aim of this book is to get beyond over simple notions of reason, by providing a unified account of all three kinds of reason—reasons for belief, reasons for action, and reasons for feelings, such as admiration, gratitude, fear, and desire. Treating all three of them entirely on a level allows us to look carefully at the role reasons for feelings play in the structure of reasoning, particularly in giving an account of value.

Second, as regards primitiveness: there is vigorous debate about whether the concept of a reason is the primitive normative concept.[1] I shall try to make it plausible that it is, by showing how all normative content can be seen as consisting in propositions about reasons—call this the 'Reasons thesis'. What is it that has to be shown, however? The hard-edged version of the Reasons thesis is explicitly semantic: any normative predicate is definitionally reducible to a reason predicate (as well as descriptive predicates if it is not itself wholly normative), using the existing resources of our language alone. I shall examine how far this version of the thesis can be taken, but I shall conclude that it cannot do all the work. Overall, the thesis should be put instead at the level of concepts: the sole normative ingredient in any normative concept is the concept of a reason. To grasp its distinctively normative content it is necessary and sufficient that one grasps the concept of a reason. This claim is weaker, in that the semantic thesis entails it but the converse need not hold. Furthermore, given the indefinitely large number of 'thick' normative concepts, it has to be put forward as a conjecture. The conjecture can, however, be made increasingly plausible, to a point at which it becomes reasonable simply to stipulate it as a definition of 'normative'.

Third, as to the idea that responsiveness to reasons is the constitutive feature of thought: that is not so much controversial as unclear. A central thesis here is that self-determining thought involves what I call the capacity for *epistemic self-audit*—the capacity to assess reflectively what one has reason to believe and in particular whether one has reason to inquire further. A further thesis, for which I argue in Chapter 18, is that a being cannot exercise concepts at all without the capacity for such epistemic self-audit.

The groundwork for the Reasons thesis is laid down mostly in Part I. Chapters 2 and 3 deal with the logical structure of propositions about reasons; Chapter 4 defines normativity and discusses the analysis of normative concepts in terms of the concept of a reason. Chapter 5 sets out the concepts of self-determination and warrant. Self-determination, and

---

[1] Allan Gibbard (1990) approaches normativity in terms of the notion of 'what is rational'—not the same concept as that of a reason, as will emerge in 5.11. Nonetheless, it is the concept of a reason that effectively emerges as primitive in his 'norm-expressivist' position. T. M. Scanlon explicitly takes 'the idea of a reason as primitive' (1998: 18). Joseph Raz, another pioneer in this field, agrees: 'The normativity of all that is normative consists in the way it is, or provides, or is otherwise related to reasons' (Raz 2000: 67). All three have been influential in focusing attention on reasons and rationality. As to the word 'primitive': note that even if the concept of a reason is the primitive normative *concept*, it is a further question whether reason *relations* are primitive in the sense of not being identical with any non-normative relations. The latter question belongs to the metaphysics, as against the conceptual analysis, of normativity; it will be argued in Part IV that reason relations are indeed primitive in the latter sense.

the concept of warrant that a self-determiner must operate with, are the pivots connecting analysis of reasons to the epistemological and metaphysical arguments of Part IV.

But before we come to these final, meta-normative, arguments in Part IV, Parts II and III respectively consider in more detail reasons for belief and Reasons for action and feeling. A main aim is further development of the Reasons thesis. Thus in Part II, I argue that aprioricity, necessity, evidence, and probability, which may not seem to be normative at all, are in fact normative concepts analysable in terms of the concept of a reason. In Part III, I argue the same for the concept of a person's good, and for moral concepts including the concept of a right.

I am not mainly concerned in this book with substantive normative theses in epistemology, aesthetics, and ethics. Yet some substantive discussion is indispensable. Epistemic norms are discussed in Chapters 8 and 9. My interest is more in their structure as pure propositions about epistemic reasons than in their substantive content; nonetheless, some questions about their substantive content are unavoidable, since the way epistemic reasons work turns crucially on that content. This particularly applies to norms of perception and self-consciousness (apperception, as I call it, with a reference to Kant). Still, Part II does not go into the controversies of first-order epistemology to the extent that Part III goes into the controversies of first-order ethics. In Part III, I put forward substantive claims about the normative sources of practical reasons, as well as giving analyses of practical–normative concepts. I argue that there are three such sources: the Bridge principle (Chapter 11); The principle of Good (Chapter 13); and the Demand principle (Chapter 14).

There are a number of reasons for this greater first-order involvement in Part III. They can only emerge gradually but I indicate them here. First and foremost, the basic structure of practical reason is far less understood than that of epistemic (theoretical) reason. There is very little agreement about it. Indeed it is not surprising that interest in the notion of a reason has emerged more from ethics than from epistemology, for the kinds of reasons that enter into practical reasoning are so obviously diverse. Behind this diversity of practical reasons, on my account, lies an *ultimate* diversity of practical–normative sources. That being so, another important issue arises, and further entails that Part III must be more substantive than Part II. It is the question of what role morality, and in particular the moral concepts, plays within the structure of practical reason. How does moral judgement relate to the basic practical–normative sources? I give a fuller outline of Part III in Sections 1.6 to 1.8 below.

Part IV moves to the epistemology and metaphysics of reasons. In recent decades questions of normativity have been much discussed in epistemology and in the philosophy of language as well as in the philosophy of value. But these separate discussions have only rarely been approached in a unified way. In meta-ethics the main lines of dispute have been between non-cognitivists, on the one hand, and realists of various kinds, on the other. Non-cognitivists hold that an ethical claim is not, strictly speaking, the assertion of any proposition, while realists hold that it is the assertion that an 'ethical fact' obtains. In the heyday of conventionalism about the a priori there was a somewhat analogous discussion in epistemology, insofar as conventionalism was a form of non-cognitivism. Nowadays non-cognitivist views are less prominent in epistemology than in ethics.

Moreover, whereas the view that there are practical norms—a priori truths about reasons for action—is at least fairly uncontroversial (what they are is, of course, controversial) it is by no means uncontroversial that there *are* epistemic norms: a priori truths about reasons to believe. Not everyone thinks it obvious that epistemology is a normative subject. Meanwhile in philosophy of language there has been extensive discussion of normativity and 'rule-following'. Here too, similar lines of approach can be discerned: denial that normativity is involved, or if its presence is acknowledged, non-cognitivism about it, on the one hand, and various forms of realism about 'semantic facts', on the other.

This book argues quite generally—against non-cognitivist views—that whether we make claims about reasons to believe, reasons to feel, or reasons to act we are asserting genuine propositions: judgeable, truth-apt contents. At the same time it also argues quite generally, against realist views, that these normative propositions must be distinguished from factual propositions. It takes a uniform view of all normative propositions in all domains: holding that they do not represent states of affairs and that their epistemology differs correspondingly from that of factual propositions.

I call this standpoint about the normative *cognitivist* and *irrealist*. (I know the dangers of labels, but they can be helpful in aiding memory and saving space.) It restates an old distinction: the distinction between descriptive and normative, which becomes a distinction between propositions about the world and propositions about reasons. The distinction has been out of fashion, but I believe that its foundations in the Critical tradition (which we shall come to below) remain as strong as ever. Putting the contrast in terms of propositions about the world and propositions about reasons, as against 'is' and 'ought', or 'fact' and 'value', is, I hope to show, illuminating.

Still, it should be noted that the meta-normative standpoint, I argue for in Part IV, is logically independent of many of the analyses of normative concepts in terms of the concept of a reason proposed in Part I. In most cases neither entails the other: one can accept the analysis without accepting irrealist cognitivism, and vice versa. Nonetheless, I believe they hang together, as Parts II and III will help to make clear. In particular, and crucially, whether or not one analyses aprioricity as a normative concept depends on whether or not one is a realist about the a priori. And in general, irrealist cognitivism can be put more elegantly, and explained more perspicuously and persuasively, once we focus on the nature of reasons. To see normativity as a matter of reasons is to be prompted, though not compelled, to the meta-normative account I propose.

Note also that we cannot assume there is only one way of inter-defining the circle of normative concepts. It could turn out that reductive analysis of normative concepts can be done in more than one way. If so, the case for making the idea of a reason the basic normative idea would have to turn on philosophical considerations. We can urge, for example, that its affinity to irrealist cognitivism counts in its favour, if we can make a plausible case for that meta-normative view. We can favour it on more specific grounds; for example, that it clears up the obscure relation of normative supervenience, which simply reduces to the reason relation (2.10), or that it opens up a plausible sentimentalist account of value in terms of reasons for feelings. I shall be putting all these arguments. Beyond these, there is an underlying, stage-setting thought that I myself find very persuasive: 'normativity' can be nothing more than a way of talking about that by which self-determining—reason-sensitive—agents steer. It must come down to their reasons for belief, feeling, and action, to the normative relation between facts, on the one hand, and those reason-responsive actions or states, on the other. The elaborations of normative discourse must issue in propositions about reasons or they are idle wheels. However, I do not try to prove the negative: that no other way of inter-defining normative concepts is possible. It is for others to show alternative ways, if they exist.

In the rest of this Introduction I offer a fuller outline of some guiding ideas in this book. Even in outline it will become clear that a major point of reference and contrast throughout is Kant. The meta-normative view I argue for (the 'Normative view', for short) is a new version of Critical philosophy: Sections 1.2 to 1.5 and 1.9 sketch out how. Sections 1.6 to 1.8 outline the picture of practical reason that emerges in Part III. In both cases there is continuity with Kant as well as fundamental difference, though in Part III the discussion also moves in some fundamental (and well-trodden) ways towards Hegel.

Readers who prefer to jump straight in to the argument may want to omit some or all of these sections; they may, however, want to come back to them at the end, or in the course of their reading, treating them as a recapitulation rather than an introduction.

1.2 Global realism versus Critical philosophy

Irrealist cognitivism about reasons has very wide-ranging implications. I consider its relation to the idea of autonomy in Sections 1.6 and 1.7. However, I want to begin by placing it, over the next four sections, within what can be called the *Critical* tradition in philosophy, indicating how it differs from two historically influential standpoints within this tradition: that of Kant[2] and that of Wittgenstein and the Vienna Circle in the early twentieth century. Each of these begins with admirable aims, from promising starting points, yet founders by committing itself to theses which most of us find impossible to accept. Thus the question arises whether any other Critical perspective can do better.

The Critical project seeks to find a satisfactory and stable way of avoiding two views which it takes to be equally untenable, that of the sceptic and that of the dogmatist. Its characteristic method is to do so by examining the nature and limits of human cognition. This sounds attractive; it turns out to be far from uncontroversial or easy. Being non-Critical is not the same as being uncritical: on the contrary, sceptics and dogmatists have powerful criticisms to make of any attempt to find a path that avoids the choice between their two positions. Their criticisms have a certain distinctive source. Seeing how they work against the Kantian and the 'Viennese' versions of Critical philosophy will help us to see what it is.

Scepticism puts in question all our alleged warrants for belief and finds no satisfying answer. Dogmatism holds that some answers must be simply accepted. Warrants can be

---

[2] The word itself, in its philosophical application, comes from Kant, referring originally to the philosophy developed in his three Critiques—see *Critique of Pure Reason*, Axii ff. (References to Kant will follow the convention of citing A/B editions for the *Critique of Pure Reason*, and the volume/page number of the *Academie* edition for other works.)

provided only in a context where some claims are accepted without warrant.[3] In fact the two standpoints have a disconcerting way of flipping into each other, whereas the Critical standpoint stands in contrast to both of them. It holds that we should not believe without warrant and that we do indeed have warrant for some of our beliefs—sufficient reason to hold them. It then seeks to show how this can be so: how it is that what we regard, in ordinary reflective practice, as sufficient reasons can legitimately (in most cases) be regarded as such.

This non-revisionary attitude towards 'common cognition', to use a phrase of Kant, marks out the Critical stance. A notion of common cognition—roughly, the way we think when we think methodically, with care, but in a certain sense not at the level of *philosophical* reflection—is highly important to it. On the one hand, it holds that what common cognition regards as sufficient reasons must in general, and contrary to the sceptic, be accepted as such, on the other hand, contrary to the dogmatist, it holds that common cognition both requires and can be given a philosophical vindication. It is not enough to stop at simply accepting its resilient attitudes; we have to show (at the meta-level of 'critique') why it is justified, and not merely evasive, to stop there.[4] Like dogmatism, the Critical attitude starts from acceptance that common cognition does achieve some knowledge. It doesn't engage with scepticism as a *live* option; but unlike dogmatism it wants to achieve a clear meta-understanding of *why* it is not a live option. What it criticizes is not common cognition and the methodized application of common cognition that is science, but sceptics who reject it and metaphysicians who think they can go beyond it.

It is essential, of course, that this vindication should not itself put forward philosophical dogmas, or it will itself amount to a dogmatic response to scepticism. Hence the characteristically deflationary, 'anti-metaphysical' character of the Critical stance. It targets assumptions that, it claims, are (a) uncritically assumed by the sceptic and/or the dogmatist and yet (b) form no part of common cognition. It seeks merely to remove extraneous philosophical material. Hence also the aim of its critics: to show that the Critical attitude itself rests on contestable philosophical dogma after all, dogma that does not just go beyond common cognition but is positively at odds with it.[5]

If the dialectic between the Critical stance and its sceptical or dogmatic opponents has this broad shape then it is likely to be highly elusive. Each side tries to show that unargued, unnatural assumptions are being made by the other. Can the Critical ambition, that of finally seeing its opponents and thereby itself definitively off the scene, be fulfilled? Or is there something ineradicable about what Kant called 'transcendental illusion'?

---

[3] This formulation is reminiscent of the later Wittgenstein; as we shall see however, there is a question about where, on the territory between a dogmatic and a Critical stance, to place his later thought. Chapter 18 argues that his account of rule-following is best read as cognitivist and irrealist; that places it in the Critical camp.

[4] That is, to stop there philosophically—to accept the resilient attitudes of common cognition as a starting point. I do not mean that the Critical stance necessarily holds them to be unrevisable; in itself it holds no brief against revisions of common sense at the scientific or ethical as against the philosophical level, and so can be compatible with radical forms of fallibilism.

[5] This is the force of Barry Stroud's treatment of Kant and Carnap, in Stroud 1984.

We can characterize the position that the Critical tradition rejects in a philosophically more specific way. It rejects, in one way or another, an outlook that I shall call 'global realism'. This consists of two tenets:

(1) factualism: to assert any proposition is to say that some fact obtains,

(2) cognition independence: facts are cognition independent.[6]

The Critical standpoint says that if we accept both (1) and (2) then no knowledge at all is possible. It further argues that global realism is no part of common cognition.

Yet it can easily appear that global realism is the natural stance and its rejection is what runs counter to common sense. Thus any version of the Critical stance must try to show how and why that appearance is to be expected, while also showing it to be illusory—as Kant tried with his just-mentioned notion of transcendental illusion. It is also to be expected that this will be no straightforward task: the illusion, if that is what it is, is unlikely to be easy to dispel, or we would long ceased to have suffer from it. It may even be, as Kant thought, impossible to dispel it. This is a tantalizing question that we shall come to in the final chapter. At any rate, inasmuch as irrealist cognitivism is a version of the Critical stance it is committed to the task, and the whole of this book is an attempt at carrying it through.

A distinction we should note before going further is between what I shall call a purely *nominal* notion of factuality, and various ontologically *substantial* notions. This distinction will be important in our discussion (see in particular 2.3, 16.1, and 19.5). The nominal notion identifies facts with true propositions. I shall take 'proposition' in pretty much the way Frege takes his notion of a 'thought' (*Gedanke*)—as the sense or meaning of an assertoric sentence on an occasion. So the nominal notion of fact is pretty much the Fregean notion: 'a fact is a thought that is true'.[7]

On this view, if 'Hesperus' and 'Phosphorus' have different senses then 'Hesperus is a planet' and 'Phosphorus is a planet' express different propositions and state different facts. Plainly if 'fact' is taken in this sense, (1) is trivially true. To assert that p is to assert the truth of the proposition that p, and thus to assert it to be a fact—in the nominal sense—that p. Here no substantial notion of fact is being deployed. In contrast, a *substantial* notion of fact takes facts to be perfectly distinct from propositions. A global realist understands (1) in the substantial way: any assertion says that some facts obtain, and is true just if those facts do obtain. Understood in this way, (1) is not trivial. I shall call (1), understood in this way, 'factualism'.

---

[6] Local realism is the assertion of (1) and (2) about the propositions in some particular area of discourse. In rejecting global realism, Critical philosophy may or may not reject local realism, as we shall see. Note also that 'realism' as I understand it does not include the claim that the cognition-independent facts that are asserted to exist in some realist discourse *do* exist. Thus, for example, 'error theory' about moral assertions is by my classification a form of realism, not a form of cognitivist irrealism. In what follows, when there is possible doubt about what kind of fact is being referred to I shall disambiguate by referring to nominal or to substantial facts, as appropriate.

[7] Frege 1977: 25. It would be better to identify the nominal fact that p with the truth of the proposition that p (rather than the proposition itself). More on 'proposition' in 7.3, and on nominal versus substantial facts in 3.3, 16.1, and 19.5.

A correspondence theory of truth also understands the notion of fact in this substantial way, for it holds that truth consists in a binary relation of correspondence between a proposition and a substantial fact. It is very important to note, however, that one does not have to be a correspondence theorist to accept that there are substantial facts. The correspondence theory is often rejected on the grounds that it cannot provide a defensible notion of fact that will do the job that it requires. I suspect that criticism is correct. However, even if we grant that we have no notion of substantial fact that would do the job *required by the correspondence theory*, it does not follow that we have no notion of substantial fact at all. On the contrary, the ordinary notion of fact is a substantial notion. Facts in this ordinary sense can be picked out by differing modes of presentation, can play causal roles, etc. None of this fits the nominal notion of fact.

In this ordinary sense of fact, it is a truism that a factual proposition is true only insofar as the fact that it says obtains *does* obtain. But this truism is not the correspondence theory of truth. Acknowledging this ordinary sense of fact is consistent with any theory of truth whatever.[8] Furthermore, unlike the correspondence theory, this truism does not imply that all propositional content is factual content. To argue, as I shall argue, that there are factual propositions and also wholly normative propositions that are not factual is to endorse a substantial notion of fact, but to reject factualism, the thesis that all propositions are substantially factual, and thus *a fortiori* the correspondence theory of truth.

Let us turn to (2), which says that the nature and existence of a fact in no way depends on anyone's way of knowing that it does.

The facts are as they are—independently of whether and how we know them. They are thus and so, this way rather than that, 'already there', 'there anyway',[9] irrespective of what we think. This undoubtedly calls for further clarification; we shall be concerned with various ways of understanding it. Take facts about one's own cognition, for example. In one way they are obviously not cognition independent. The fact that I am thinking is hardly independent of my thinking. But are they cognition independent in the *relevant* way? Can we say that whether such a fact obtains is not dependent in any way on my or anyone's knowing that it does? What is the implication of realism here? That is a question about the objects of our self-knowledge. What then about the rest of our knowledge? How does the basic notion of cognition-independence stand there? Does it lead us to scientific realism, or to the sophisticated position that used to be called 'naïve realism'? Or are these philosophical options undetermined by the common sense notion of cognition-independence?

However, although the thesis that facts are cognition independent may not be clear, the question for the Critical theorist cannot be whether it is true in any significant sense at all, but only in what significant sense it is true. To deny that facts are cognition independent in any significant sense at all would certainly infringe the Critical attitude to

---

[8] Not with the 'identity theory of truth' (the theory that facts are truths), but then this is more a theory of factuality than a theory of truth. It says that the only available notion of fact is the nominal notion. Frege, who believed this, also held truth to be indefinable. But one can agree that truth is not explicitly definable without accepting that the only available notion of fact is the nominal notion (see 17.5 and 17.6). Note also that it is the correspondence theory, not the ordinary notion of a substantial fact, that imposes such questions as whether there are negative, disjunctive, existential, etc., facts.

[9] Bernard Williams' phrases: 1985: 138, ff on the 'absolute conception'.

common cognition, which is supposed to be non-revisionary. That there are substantial facts, and that they are in some significant sense independent of our knowledge of them, is too much a part of common sense to be baldly rejected. The common sense picture of our place as knowers in the world holds that facts are at once cognition-independent (always) and cognition-accessible (often). That it's getting dark, for example, is a fact that in no way depends on my or your awareness of it. Nonetheless, one can often just see that it's getting dark, as against inferring it or being told. Many facts are accessible to our cognition, whether by simple perceptual awareness or by scientific inference, but many facts are not accessible at all. These deeply entrenched platitudes form part of our idea of *fact* (and thus of *object* and *property*); they have the structuring 'givenness' of common sense. The facts are *there*—we receive information through our senses about them. A philosophy which simply rejected this rudimentary notion of cognition-independence would be at a fatal disadvantage.

How strongly should we understand it though? Take the example I've used. Common sense takes no stand on whether the fact that it's getting dark really is an 'absolute', scientifically pukka, etc., fact. When it says that whether it's getting dark doesn't depend on our knowing that it is, it is not saying something that either entails or is incompatible with a scientific theory of secondary qualities. Bernard Williams' 'absolute conception' seems to take a further step towards scientific realism than is present in the rudimentary view, which simply says that the fact that it's getting dark is there anyway, irrespective of what we think or know.

Here then is the *shape* of a debate: whereas global realism holds that asserting any proposition at all is asserting that a substantial, cognition-independent fact obtains, the Critical standpoint says that knowledge is possible only if this global realism is false. It denies some element of global realism: that all propositions are factual, or that all or any facts are cognition-independent. In doing so it must find a way of refuting global realism that doesn't get it into a losing battle with the common sense notion of cognition-independence. So what is and is not a part of that common sense notion is likely to be important. It is not enough, moreover, simply to show that global realism leads to scepticism: scepticism might be the correct conclusion. One needs to find some element in global realism, be it (1) or (2) or both, which independently looks like a philosophical error. What is needed is a diagnosis, and a diagnosis compatible with common cognition.

1.3 Kant

The original Critical philosopher is Kant. If we characterize that tradition as a critique of global realism, how does he fit in? Does he reject (1) or (2), or both? Consider Kant's celebrated statement of his 'Copernican Revolution':

> Up to now it has been assumed that all our cognition must conform to the objects; but all attempts to find out something about them *a priori* through concepts that would extend our cognition have, on this presupposition, come to nothing. Hence

> let us try whether we do not get farther with the problems of metaphysics by assuming that the objects must conform to our cognition...

The daring thesis Kant wants to try is that the very constitution of objects is structured by our receptive capacities:

> If intuition [i.e. cognition of objects] has to conform to the constitution of objects, then I do not see how we can know anything of them *a priori*; but if the object (as an object of the senses) conforms to the constitution of our faculty of intuition, then I can very well represent this possibility to myself.[10]

His claim is that a strictly cognition-independent conception of objects renders a priori knowledge (and thus in his view knowledge) impossible. He is not saying that our cognizing faculties are receptive to some properties of things and not others—only to the ones that can pass our cognition-gate, so to speak. On this view, we would know that things in themselves, things as they really, 'already', are, had *some* properties, the ones that pass through the gate, even though we could not know anything of other properties which do not pass the gate. In contrast, Kant thinks we cannot know *any* properties things have in themselves. His view is that we can know the properties of 'the object (as an object of our senses)' only because the object as an object of our senses is a product of the way our sensibility structures the input from objects as they are in themselves. The object of our senses is a joint product of the forms of our sensibility and of things in themselves. Furthermore, Kant thinks that the contribution our sensibility makes to the constitution of these objects can be traced to forms that structure *all* knowable objects. It is this structuring contribution that gives rise to the synthetic a priori character of arithmetic and geometry, and makes empirical knowledge in general possible.

The sense in which Kant rejects thesis (2) in global realism—cognition-independence—is thus clear. The objects of the senses, the temporal and spatio-temporal facts that we can know, are cognition dependent. They are cognition-dependent in a strong sense: knowable facts about them are in part cognition constituted. Cognition by us of facts not so constituted is impossible. In another sense, however, Kant can also be thought of as rejecting (1)—factualism. He accepts the intelligibility of the cognition independent conception of fact, and holds that there are such facts—facts about things as they are in themselves, independently of our cognition. These facts, however, we cannot know. The upshot is that our empirical assertions say nothing about these facts, the facts as they really are. Thus when factuality is understood in this way, i.e. in conformity with (2), then Kant's rejection of (1) is radical: *none* of our empirical assertions are factual. Kant saves the synthetic a priori by removing cognition-independent factuality from all our phenomenal claims, while at the same time he retains the cognition-independent notion of fact and accepts that there are such facts. This is his transcendental idealism.

It is a deeply perplexing position. It polarizes the common sense picture, according to which the world consists of often knowable cognition-independent facts, into two

---

[10] *Critique of Pure Reason*, Bxvi–xvii.

separate elements—*phenomena*, knowable cognition-dependent facts, and *noumena*, unknowable cognition independent facts. The need for the latter arises because transcendental idealism is a 'joint-product theory': the phenomenal facts are joint products of the forms of our sensibility and things as they really are, with the former structuring the input received from the latter. One can obviously ask whether that is itself a knowable fact, and if so, how it is knowable. Not that I am suggesting that this theory contains no insights. Far from it. By the end of Part IV we shall be in a position to appreciate how difficult it is to escape something like it altogether (20.9). Nevertheless, we should try to capture Kant's insights without this joint-product theory and thus without the contrast between noumena and phenomena. That is a very reasonable constraint to place on any new version of the Critical stance.

At this point another side of Kant's philosophy is helpful: his view of reason as against his view of sensibility.

Kant's account of principles of pure reason seems to require definite rejection of (1). Take practical reason first. Kant holds that there are objective imperatives or laws of practical reason. In other words, there are true propositions to the effect that such-and-such an action or aim is required by practical reason. Does he then think these propositions are factual claims about some sector of reality, phenomenal, or noumenal? He cannot think they are phenomenal claims. He makes no distinction between reason as it knowably appears to us and as it unknowably is; he thinks we have unmediated insight into the laws of reason. Does he then think these propositions are factual claims about the noumena? This doesn't fit either. True, Kant thinks that we are subject to the requirements of reason just insofar as we are free, and further, that freedom is our noumenal essence. We cannot know that it is, any more than we can know any noumenal fact, but Kant claims that we necessarily postulate our own freedom whenever we deliberate, and that he can show, by appeal to his transcendental idealism, that our postulate is coherent. Yet it is not the fact that we are free, if it is a fact, that makes it true that there *are* requirements of reason. It only makes it true that those requirements apply to *us*. That there *are* requirements of reason is not made true by any fact.

That is the position in the Groundwork; in the *Critique of Practical Reason* Kant seems to take it as a fact that we are *aware* of pure practical reason's requirements as requirements on *us*.[11] But again it is not the fact of our awareness that they apply *to us*, if it is a fact, that makes it true that there *are* requirements of reason. Kant does not hold that *any* fact, phenomenal or noumenal, makes principles of pure reason true. These principles are not factual propositions at all. He is not a constructivist about practical reason, if constructivism is understood as a view that maintains that principles of reason are somehow products or constructions of our own thinking, and thus accepts (1) but rejects (2). That account fits his view of nature, not reason. In the sense in which we can be said to

---

[11] This is Kant's notorious appeal to 'the fact of reason'. All the relevant passages are cited in Allison, 1990: 231. As Allison points out, 'in his more careful moments' Kant talks only about 'the fact as it were'. I have followed Allison in my understanding of what that 'fact as it were' is.

part construct the phenomenal world of nature, we cannot be said to construct the requirements of practical reason, as against making them a law to ourselves.

It therefore seems that Kant is a cognitivist about practical reason but not a realist, and that directly implies that he must reject (1). The point extends to his view of reason in general, as one might expect, given his emphasis on the unity of reason. We can see this by considering the contrast he draws between receptivity and spontaneity—a Kantian contrast that will be of fundamental significance in this book.

Our senses are receptive faculties in that they give us access to (phenomenal) facts by receiving information from them. In contrast, pure judgements of the understanding involve no receptivity. They are acts of pure spontaneity. Let us consider an example of how receptivity and spontaneity interact. I receive an aural representation as of a higher note followed by a lower note. Such a representation, Kant thinks, has already received considerable formation in *sensibility*, notably by acquiring there the form of temporality. But consider the step in which I proceed to judge, on the basis of this representation, that I have heard a certain objective sequence of sounds. This step involves the *understanding*, whose distinctive power is that of applying concepts to the materials provided by sensibility. The understanding has the capacity to identify particular epistemic states of the self as giving the self reason to form judgements that deploy particular empirical concepts—such as that of x being a higher note than y, or of y being later than x. To have empirical concepts is among other things to grasp, of various possible states of sensibility, that they constitute reasons to make judgements deploying those concepts. This capacity of concept-application or reason-recognition is spontaneous, in that it is an active power involving no further form of receptivity. 'Concepts are grounded on the spontaneity of thinking, sensible intuitions on the receptivity of impressions', and hence '*receptivity* can make cognitions possible only when combined with *spontaneity*'.[12] A given epistemic state is the outcome of various forms of receptivity, such as hearing; but recognizing that it provides reason to make this or that judgement does not involve *another* form of receptivity, to some *further* domain of substantial facts.

So what is Kant's view of this kind of reason-recognizing judgement of the understanding—say, the judgement 'My aural representation gives me sufficient reason to believe that I am hearing a lower note followed by a higher one'? He clearly rejects an intuitionist account, according to which reason-recognition is a form of receptivity that is *sui generis* to the understanding. That is the point of talking about these cognitive acts as acts of spontaneity. Furthermore, he thinks that where the epistemology of a judgement involves spontaneity only, and no receptivity, one cannot regard its content as factual in the phenomenal sense. At this point his transcendental idealism might seem to leave open the possibility that its content is factual in the noumenal sense. But according to Kant no substantive proposition about the noumena can be known to us. To take another example, consider the judgement, 'My visual representation gives me sufficient reason to believe that I am being presented with an object that falls under the concept *blue*'. This is a judgement of pure spontaneity, so it is not factual in the phenomenal sense.

---

[12] *Critique of Pure Reason*, A68/B93, A97.

Its content is intelligible and knowable, so on Kant's own account it cannot be factual in the noumenal sense. The only possible conclusion is that these spontaneous reason-recognizing judgements of the understanding are not factual judgements at all. In this respect they differ from synthetic a priori judgements arising from the form of sensibility, which Kant holds to be factual in the phenomenal, though not in the noumenal sense. So his position about these reason-recognizing, or normative, judgements is simultaneously cognitivist and irrealist. These judgements, like pure judgements about practical reasons, are counter-examples to thesis (1).

This is an attractive and important position: I shall be arguing for it in this book. I shall also argue that Kant's contrast of spontaneity and receptivity, or at least a demystified version of it that sees spontaneity as a matter of spontaneous normative dispositions, can help us to see how it works. However, I shall not be defending Kant's transcendental idealist version of the Critical stance. As noted above, I take it as a reasonable constraint on any defensible version of the Critical stance that it should not endorse Kant's 'joint-product' view of the objects of our receptive sensibility. But I shall also argue that since Kant had the essential idea of irrealist cognitivism about normative claims, he never needed transcendental idealism for his Critical project anyway (20.3). Irrealist cognitivism about normative claims was enough.

1.4 Vienna

As it turned out, Kant's transcendental idealism only produced a new stalemate in nineteenth century thought, between 'naturalist' or 'positivist' forms of global realism, on the one hand, and, on the other, post-Kantian forms of idealism which strove to overcome unsatisfactory dichotomies in the philosophy of Kant—not least that between 'phenomena' and 'noumena'—but did so in what seemed to many to be highly implausible ways.[13] This debate between positivism and post-Kantian idealism gave rise to a strongly realist reaction. Then came a second great formulation of the Critical standpoint—that of the Vienna School. I have in mind both Wittgenstein's philosophy and the ideas associated with the Vienna Circle, notably with Carnap.[14]

In what sense do they belong to the Critical tradition? Interpretation of Wittgenstein's philosophy is notoriously controversial. This particularly applies to the *Tractatus*. At first appearance it is a paradigmatic exposition of global realism. Against that, there are the 'transcendental' elements, and the hard to interpret remarks about sense and nonsense. Then there is the evolution of his thought in the 'Viennese' period of his conversations with members of the Vienna Circle, and finally, the ideas that develop in the *Philosophical Investigations*, in which the status of rule-following emerges as a central theme. In my

---

[13] In what follows I draw on the historical accounts offered in Skorupski 1993 and 2005.
[14] Calling them the Vienna School might be thought a misnomer, in that what is really *Viennese*, or *Austrian*, it might be said, is realist opposition to all forms of the Critical tradition. I take the point. My 'Vienna School' is about as Viennese as the 'Second Vienna School' in music was.

view Wittgenstein is engaged with the Critical standpoint throughout, and in Chapter 18 I shall offer an interpretation of what he says about rule-following that fits into that; however, our focus at the moment is his Viennese period.

What about the Vienna Circle? Its members thought of themselves as empiricists, in the specifically anti-Kantian sense of denying that there are any synthetic a priori propositions. They also held that all content is factual content (for analytic propositions have no content). Now one way to get to empiricism is from global realism. Given a cognition-independent conception of fact, the principle that no factual proposition is true a priori seems to follow very plausibly. How can mere thinking tell one that any fact other than the thinking itself obtains? Thinking is a process which is about processes and states other than itself. The existence of the thinking is one fact, the existence of its objects is another fact. If they are genuinely independent, there must be some way in which information about the objects is transmitted from the objects to the thinking, and a capacity to receive that information on the part of the thinker. But that there *is* such transmission and receptivity cannot be a priori truth. So if all content is about cognition-independent facts then no content is a priori. In effect Kant himself accepts this inference from global realism to empiricism. He argues that empiricism makes knowledge impossible and contraposes to the rejection of global realism. In contrast, one interpretation of logical positivism is that it argues in the opposite direction: from global realism to empiricism.

However, leading philosophers in the Vienna School were not as distant from the Critical tradition as this interpretation would suggest.[15] They were not transcendental idealists, but they agreed with the Kantian idea that knowledge is possible only within a framework to which knowable objects must conform. For them, however, the necessary framework was provided not by forms of intuition or categories of the understanding but by a system of conventions. Knowledge, they agreed, requires a prior framework; though against Kant they emphasized that there is no unique framework that it requires. The conventions that provide the framework can vary. Nor is there any meaningful distinction to be made between objects as they can be known and objects as they really are. There is no intelligible standpoint outside the empirical standpoint—only free choices of framework.[16] Things are as they could, in principle, be known to be within a framework stipulated a priori. And this conception opens up, as they thought, a new account of the apriority of logic and mathematics. Kant took mathematics to be synthetic a priori. The Vienna Circle held that logic and mathematics owe their apriority, their exactness, and their certainty to the fact that they belong to the framework of conventions. By the same token they are empty of content. Content can exist, be conveyed, only within a framework.

It is natural to think that particular languages are merely contingent vehicles for the expression of contents of thought. The thought contents themselves are a language-independent domain about which there are language-independent truths. The Vienna

---

[15] Affinities between Kant's views and those of the logical positivists and Wittgenstein have been discussed by a number of interpreters: among them Coffa 1991; Friedman 1991; Garver 1996; and Stroud 1984. Of course individual philosophers differed in this respect—Schlick had much less affinity to the Critical stance then Reichenbach or Carnap, or arguably Wittgenstein.

[16] See, for example, Carnap on 'internal' and 'external' questions, in Carnap 1956.

School denied this. There is no such domain of thought contents. There are no language-independent facts or norms constituting it. There are only rules of particular languages and empirical, natural facts expressible by true sentences in a particular language. That a particular set of linguistic rules exists is itself an empirical fact; yet without some set of rules there can be no expression of empirical facts. All discourse and thought is language relative. One can sum up this 'linguistic turn' as follows:

- Thought requires a determinate language: a framework of rules which renders it possible and at the same time fixes its 'limits' (by fixing what sentences have sense).
- These rules confer content on a given sentence by determining when it is assertible within the framework.
- The rules themselves are free conventions.
- Sentences in the language that simply express or record these rules are empty of content.

This was a radically new Critical standpoint. It was expounded by Wittgenstein in his conversations with the Vienna Circle and developed in independent, divergent ways by him and by Carnap among others. Its characteristically Critical ambitions were in a way even grander than Kant's. It envisaged the end of philosophy, which should be replaced by the systematic activity of describing or laying down rules of 'logical syntax' (Carnap) or alternatively, kept at bay by administering reminders of 'logical grammar' (Wittgenstein).

The meaning of an assertoric sentence, on this new view, is determined by the conditions in which it is assertible. Whether or not an assertion is licensed is determined by data of experience plus the conventions constituting the framework; these conventions are its 'syntax'. Epistemology reduces to syntax—the set of conventions that license moves within the language. There is nothing 'beyond' or 'outside' these conventions. Fact and existence are internal to the conventions, as are meaning and truth.[17]

Thus, for example, once geometrical axioms have been set down and co-ordinated with experience by ostensive and metric conventions, there is no further question about whether there exists a unique set of appropriate geometrical objects to satisfy those axioms. In the case of logic itself the same point applies. The only meaningful question concerns the pragmatic convenience of this or that language. What objects, properties, and facts there are is a matter of the ontological commitments of the best scientific theory within a pragmatically determined set of conventions.

So the Vienna School belongs to the Critical tradition because it rejects (2), the cognition-independence of facts. It is factualist, in the sense that it accepts (1). However, what facts there are is determinate only in the context of rules of discourse that we choose. Furthermore, the scheme/content distinction made by the logical positivists requires rejection of the correspondence conception of truth and adoption of an epistemic

---

[17] This was interestingly consonant with a governing idea of 1930s modernism: the idea that what fixes our form of life, our cultural framework, is nothing but a social system of conventions for acting and thinking in. There is no deeper structure, in either the individual or the world, of trans-linguistic essences, things as they absolutely are, or normative requirements. In contrast the argument of this book is that there is a normative structure which is neither 'in' the individual nor 'in' the world.

conception of meaning. The logical positivists were factualists, but not correspondence-theory factualists. It was in this sense that Wittgenstein and Carnap 'offered in the early 1930s' as Alberto Coffa put it, 'the first genuine alternative to Kant's conception of the a priori'.[18] He aptly described this new conception as another Copernican revolution:

> One could, in fact, mimic Kant's famous 'Copernican' pronouncement to state [Carnap's and Wittgenstein's] point. If our a priori knowledge must conform to the constitution of meanings, I do not see how we could know anything of them a priori; but if meanings must conform to the a priori, I have no difficulty in conceiving such a possibility.[19]

There is a question about how best to formulate this position. The strict formulation would be that there are only factual propositions and rules. On this strict account, an analytic sentence expresses no proposition. It must be interpreted not as the assertion of something true or false but as the laying down or expression of a rule. Construed in this way, the Viennese view can both agree with (1) and deny that there are *any* a priori propositions.

However, it is convenient to be able to speak of analytic propositions. Indeed more than convenient: analytic sentences can be embedded in complex sentences, and feature in the expression of arguments, and this dictates treating them as expressing propositions with truth-value. The core notion of analyticity is absence of informative content (7.1); that is not the same as absence of meaning. We can distinguish between linguistic meaning and informative content. 'Eggs are eggs' and 'eggs are not eggs' both have linguistic meaning in English; it is natural to say that the former is true while the latter is false, even if neither conveys information to someone who understands English. Since they have meaning it fits with the broadly Fregean notion of a proposition to say that they express propositions, even though they have no informative content. I shall follow this way of putting it, even in stating the Viennese view, according to which, or at least some versions of which, it may be convenient but is not strictly correct. In this way of putting it (1) is strictly false; we should say instead that any proposition *that has content* is factual. And the Viennese view is that all a priori propositions are analytic propositions rather than that there are no a priori propositions.

We can make a further point. The drive to align truth-value with factual content is actually a mark of the presence of non-Critical elements in the Viennese view. There is a motive for it if one adheres to the correspondence conception of assertoric content—of what a proposition is, and what it is for a proposition to be true. In this perspective, arguably that of the *Tractatus*, possession of truth-value and representation of a state of affairs go together. However, if one abandons a correspondence conception, as the verificationist side of the Viennese view requires, then the realist motive disappears. Without global realism, there is no clear rationale for the view that all non-analytic sentences in the language express factual propositions—unless one simply stipulates that 'fact' is to be understood intra-linguistically in terms of 'truth-stating informative sentence'.

---

[18] Coffa 1991: 263.
[19] Ibid.

However, the logical positivists had a stronger notion of fact. They held that any assertoric sentence that has cognitive meaning either belongs to the logico-mathematical framework of a scientific theory or is a sentence within the framework of that theory. Non-scientific sentences, such as those of ethics or aesthetics, lack cognitive meaning. So why this view of ethics and aesthetics? Two elements are separable here: the convention/content distinction, on the one hand, and what can fairly be called a form of scientism, on the other. The first says that a discourse that has content requires a framework of rules. This can be presented (whether successfully or otherwise) as resulting not from any philosophical dogma, but from reflection on the presuppositions of content. The second says that knowledge must consist in scientific inference from sense experience. This second claim certainly looks like a philosophical dogma. *Why* should we hold that all knowledge is based in this way on sense experience? The underlying line of thought seems to be: (a) knowledge is of facts; (b) the only facts we can know are those given directly or indirectly by our receptive faculties; and (c) the only receptive faculties we have are the familiar faculties of sense experience. Note that (c) is also held by Kant, and that (b) is held by him when 'fact' is understood in a substantial way. Note also that the Viennese School could say that their argument for (c) is empirical rather than metaphysical: there is no empirical evidence for the kind of non-sensible receptivity that intuitionists claim to exist, nor do they set out any scientifically intelligible model of how it is supposed to work.

(b) can be understood as a thesis about the very notion of a substantial fact, one emphasized in any Critical standpoint (see 16.1). However, to understand it in this way is to put (a) in question. The convention/content argument says nothing about whether content must be factual in this substantial sense, connected with receptivity. It only says that content is language relative (in the sense of the bullet points above). A metaphysical claim, of the kind the Critical position tries to disclaim, is required to reach the conclusion that all knowledge is factual in a substantial sense. The most obvious metaphysical suspect is the correspondence theory of truth, which the logical positivists rejected. Thus it should have been possible to develop a non-scientistic version of the Viennese view that accepted the convention/content distinction but accepted neither non-cognitivism about normative claims nor realism about them.

Nowadays the Viennese view is thought to face insurmountable problems. The outstanding one is that its verificationist account of meaning denies (2), the cognition-independence of facts, far too strongly. This is a weakness it shares with transcendental idealism, though it arises in a different way. Our best scientific conception of the world itself implies that there are verification-transcendent facts. Science itself gives us good reason to believe that some instances of 'p but we can never have good reason to believe that p' are true. But for a verificationist, there is a problem about the meaningfulness of such instances. There may be ways of responding to this problem, but I shall not pursue them. Just as we must seek a version of the Critical stance that does not subscribe to Kant's 'joint-product' view, so I shall take it that we must seek a version that does not subscribe to Viennese verificationism.

Two other problems, however, both about the convention/content dichotomy, are more instructive for the purposes of this book. There is Quine's problem: how do we tell whether a sentence expresses a linguistic rule or conveys an empirical assertion—i.e. whether it is analytic or synthetic? That is a good objection to the Viennese notion of analyticity. This notion is far too promiscuous: it seems that sentences can be labelled analytic at will, without a well-grounded and motivated account of what it is for a sentence to lack informative content. True—as others have argued—Quine overstated his point.[20] There is a perfectly defensible account of analyticity in terms of lack of informative content. To be defensible, however, this notion must be very narrow indeed. And this very narrow notion of analyticity, the strict notion of truth by definition, is epistemologically toothless. It doesn't even sustain the idea that logic is analytic. Thus the thrust of Quine's argument, that one can work no epistemological magic with the wand of analyticity, is sound. These issues are discussed in Chapters 6 and 7.

The other problem is the most telling one for our purposes. Is it even coherent to hold that 'There are only empirical facts and linguistic decisions'? Whereas Quine's question was whether we can draw a clear line between the two, the question raised here is whether the dichotomy could even in principle be exhaustive. The claim that it could not be is a central theme in the later Wittgenstein's account of rule-following. I believe that this account developed from a critique of the convention/content distinction itself—to which Wittgenstein, in his 'Viennese' period, himself adhered. Wittgenstein began to ask, when one judges that the application of a word to an object is in accordance with the rule that has been laid down for its use, what sort of judgement is that? Is it simply a further stipulation rather than a genuine judgement, or is it a judgement of empirical fact? If it is neither, that undermines the Viennese, linguistic version of the Critical standpoint. There remains of course the possibility that it is a judgement of non-empirical fact based on intuition. Wittgenstein does not give this option very serious attention but it is plainly a way for the global realist to go. If, however, it too turns out to be indefensible, then we are led to the conclusion that there are normative propositions that are not factual. That important argument will be discussed in 18.4.

1.5 The Normative view

Just as a swing to global realism followed the post-Kantian debate, so a swing to global realism followed the failure of the new version of Critical philosophy formulated in Vienna. With hindsight it appears that both these Critical standpoints undertook a hopeless task. The task was hopeless not because of this or that particular difficulty but because, in the end, neither standpoint concedes enough to the common sense cognition-independent notion of fact. Despite their ambition to leave common cognition 'as it is', they end up clipping its wings.

What then about global realism? Is this attitude naturally rooted in pre-philosophical common conceptions? Is it merely a tidied-up statement of the outlook of common

---

[20] See, for example, Putnam, 'The Analytic and the Synthetic', in Putnam 1975, vol. 2 (cp. ' "Two Dogmas" Revisited' and 'There is at least one *a priori* truth' in Putnam 1983).

cognition, or is it, as the Critical tradition takes it to be, the product of some uncritically accepted philosophical prejudices?

(2) certainly seems rooted in the natural, pre-philosophical attitude. There is wiggle room available here, in that the notion of cognition-independence remains to be clarified, but certainly the natural attitude takes it to be true in some pretty robust sense. What about (1)—is there a pre-philosophical case for it, rooted in our natural attitudes? That is not so obvious. It is a mere truism, as I noted above, that when one asserts a factual proposition one asserts that a fact obtains. And obviously we make plenty of factual assertions. Yet nothing in our ordinary thinking commits us to the idea that *all* our assertions are factual assertions. On the contrary, common sense positively favours the idea that there is a fundamental difference of kind between stating the facts, on the one hand, and discussing what to think, how to react, what to do, on the other. In many cases such discussion reaches normative conclusions, but these conclusions are not about some further set of facts.

This contrast between factual and normative propositions is not a scientistic imposition, as some normative realists like to urge. On the contrary. To deny it is to adopt a philosophical posture which stands provocatively at odds with common sense, and is typically felt that way. Support for realism about the normative (I shall argue) comes not from common cognition but from a distinctly philosophical imposition, the correspondence conception of truth. Then there is also the fear that rejecting realism about normative propositions somehow relegates them to a second-class status. It is that fear, not the rejection of normative realism, that is revealingly scientistic: what it calls for is Critical therapy. Or so I shall argue.

These points lead to a version of Critical philosophy which seeks to maintain (2) while rejecting (1). Its guiding thought is that normative and factual propositions should be distinguished; I will simply call it the *Normative view*. I give a fuller account of it below, in Section 9, but for the moment the point to note is that it agrees with Kant that there are synthetic a priori propositions. Knowledge, it holds, is possible because some wholly normative propositions about epistemic reasons are a priori. However, it denies that these propositions are (substantially) factual. It agrees with the Viennese version of the Critical tradition inasmuch as it rejects the correspondence conception of content. But it requires no verificationist theory of meaning.

This looks attractively commonsensical in outline. But can the Normative view really leave (2), the cognition-independence thesis, wholly in place? As we shall see, things are not so simple. It can accept that any factual claim is revisable in the light of experience, thereby affirming an important empiricist insight. But it must also accept that some non-normative 'offshoots' (6.8) of normative propositions are a priori. This forces further reflection about how our notions of apriority, normativity, and factuality are related. Just how much and what kind of cognition independence our thinking is pre-philosophically committed to, and whether the Normative standpoint has to disturb that, remains a crucial issue. There is, one might say, a tension between cognition-independence and apriority to which the Critical stance is sensitive. Thought through global realism is at one end of the polarity, leaving (according to the Critical theorist) no room for aprioricity at all. Transcendental idealism and verificationism seem to go too far in the other direction, making the domain of fact cognition-dependent in a very implausible way. But where is common sense, and where is the Normative view?

Is it true that thought through global realism leaves no room for aprioricity? The Normative view says two things: that knowledge is possible because some wholly normative propositions are a priori, and that no wholly normative proposition is factual. Obviously one might accept the first thesis but reject the second. *Intuitionistic* realism says that wholly normative propositions are about a special realm of *sui generis* facts known to us by special receptive faculties of intuition. More recently, however, realism about the normative has tended to be reductive. It tries to show that normative propositions have as truth-makers facts which can also be characterized in non-normative ways. An obvious difference between these two forms of realism is that the first is anti-naturalistic while the second is predominantly naturalistic.[21]

It is notable that neither the Kantian nor the Viennese standpoint considered realism about the normative, of either of these forms, at all seriously.[22] We do not have that option. I shall keep track of the differences between the Normative version of the Critical stance, on the one hand, and these two currently influential forms of global realism, on the other. My argument will be, in a nutshell, that intuitionistic realism involves a vicious regress in its account of a priori knowledge (6.2 and 6.3), while reductive realism can give no account of a priori knowledge at all. Since the choice between these two forms of global realism is exhaustive, it follows that thought through global realism leaves no room for aprioricity. However, I shall not develop extended criticisms either of realist or of non-cognitivist views of the normative. All these positions have been well criticized by others (realism by non-cognitivists and non-cognitivism by realists)—my aim is the positive one of developing my own view, showing how the difficulties that seem to force an unappetizing choice between non-cognitivism and realism can be removed. In the last part of the book we shall find ourselves returning instead to some comparisons with the two other versions of the Critical tradition, first to Vienna, via Wittgenstein's discussion of rule following, and then finally to Kant. In 20.5 to 20.8 we come back to a final assessment of how well the Normative view preserves the cognition-independence of facts.

1.6 Autonomy and the unity of reason

In outlining the Critical tradition I have so far focused on epistemic reasons. But, as indicated in Section 1.1, it is a rule of this book to keep thinking of all the kinds of reason together—epistemic reasons for belief; practical reasons for action; *evaluative* reasons for feeling (as I shall call them)—and to search for a uniform account. Here two further

---

[21] Predominantly, but not always. Logically speaking, the reduction could be to supernatural just as well as to natural facts (Adams 1999). This new, reductive, realism was facilitated by a clarification in the 1960s of the differences between analyticity, aprioricity, and necessity that highlighted the existence of synthetic identities which are necessary but not a priori. See especially Kripke 1971.

[22] For further discussion see 20.3.

Kantian themes provide us with a starting point. They concern autonomy and the unity of reason.

Autonomy, as understood in this book, is personal insight into and self-determination by reasons. Some other influential ethical or political ideals of autonomy are related to this basic notion but I will not be concerned to trace such connections. As the term is understood here, a person who acts autonomously grasps reasons by first-person insight and believes, feels or acts 'from' or 'out of' the reasons he grasps. Thus autonomy requires the power of assessing for oneself, by one's own reflection, what one has sufficient reason to believe or to feel, or to do. In particular autonomous actors must be able to assess whether they have sufficient reason to believe something, or whether they need to do some further investigating. You realize that you do not have sufficient reason to believe this rather than that about something that matters to you: 'if I need to have a view about this', you reflect, 'I shall have to inquire further'. Call this process of assessing what reasons one has in one's epistemic state *epistemic self-audit*.

Self-determination by reasons (acting 'from' them) presupposes the possibility of epistemic self-audit, because what one has reason to feel or do depends on what one has reason to believe. Furthermore, self-audit must be completable by self-examination and reflection alone. The question whether further empirical investigation is required cannot always require further empirical investigation (5.2). Nor is it a question that can only be answered non-rationally. The very idea of self-determination requires that this question can be rationally appraised in a first-person way: if autonomy is possible it must be possible to audit one's reasons by reflective self-examination and thereby give a warranted answer to the question, 'Do I have sufficient reason for this belief, sentiment, or action?'

I have been speaking here about the reasons one *has*. I do not mean that what there *is* reason for one to feel or do depends on one's reasons to believe. On the contrary, what there *is* reason to feel or do turns on the relevant facts, which include facts about what one believes only in very special cases. Whether there's reason for you to slow down depends on whether there's danger ahead, not on whether you believe there is; whether there's reason for you to admire Jane's bravery depends on whether she was brave, not on whether you think she was, and so on. The distinction can be made for epistemic reasons themselves: what there *is* reason for us to believe depends on the facts available to us, the facts we could discover, whether or not we *have* discovered them. This will be an important distinction throughout the book; unfortunately no good labels for it are readily available. I shall distinguish between the *reasons there are* for x to ψ and the *warranted reasons x has* to ψ, referring to the former simply as x's reasons and to the latter as x's warranted reasons, or (where possible) simply as the reasons x has. The basic concept is that of a reason: warranted reasons are defined in terms of reasons in 5.4.

The notion of self-determination, and thus the notion of self-audit, shapes the notion of a warranted reason. What one has reason to believe, feel, or do is determined by one's epistemic state—the set of facts one can be aware of by self-examination alone, or in the somewhat Kantian terminology I shall use, the set of facts one apperceives.[23] Furthermore,

---

[23] The differences between my and Kant's notion of apperception are set out in 19.1.

as well as having the capacity to be self-aware of these facts, one must be able to tell a priori what reasons are warranted by them. If knowledge of reasons, and thus autonomy, is possible at all, knowledge of norms—a priori truths about reason relations—must be possible. An explanation of the concept of autonomy thus requires a conception of warranted reasons that is doubly 'internalist'. First, the facts that determine warranted reasons are facts about the actor who has the warranted reasons, facts of which the actor can be self-aware. Second, *that* they determine warranted reasons is something the actor can tell a priori. This point about *warranted* reasons is quite compatible with recognizing that the basic notion of a reason, as against a warranted reason, is 'externalist' in the sense that there can be reasons for a person to ψ that that person cannot know.

So far, so—more or less—Kantian.[24] What about the other Kantian theme, that of the unity of reason?

I have said that it is a main objective of this book to keep in mind all three kinds of reason and search for a uniform account of them; it is also a main thesis of this book that the three kinds of reason, epistemic, evaluative, and practical, are irreducible. In particular, it will be important that evaluative reasons, reasons to feel, are not analysable in terms of reasons to believe and to act, and that practical reasons are not reducible to epistemic and evaluative ones either. The three kinds of reason are not just conceptually but substantively diverse.

Talk of Reason can easily mislead. If 'Reason' is just a non-committal label for all a priori knowledge of reasons, there is no problem. It becomes misleading, however, if it leads us to suppose that there is some interestingly unitary faculty called Reason—even more so if it leads us to think that this unitary faculty can detect some substantive common principle underlying all propositions about reasons.[25] That should not be assumed. On the contrary, we should be prepared to find that diversity reigns. For all that has been said so far, pluralism may obtain within each category of reasons as well as across categories. There may be a plurality of norms governing belief, another plurality of norms governing action, and not least, a plurality of norms governing feeling. And so (I shall argue) it turns out to be. We human beings have a whole range of normative competences, and we differ quite a lot in our profile of competence across this range.

Granted, however, that reasons are substantially multiple and diverse, reason relations nevertheless have an epistemological and ontological unity which necessarily arises from the nature of self-determination. About all reasons there must be propositions that are true a priori. Intuitionistic realists would agree with that. But if they cannot give a satisfactory account of a priori knowledge then they cannot give an account of our

---

[24] To act from one's own, first-personal, recognition of a sufficient reason is in a certain sense to act fully freely (autonomously). Furthermore, acting from first-personally recognized moral obligation is acting fully freely in that sense. These are Kantian doctrines with which I agree. But Kant identifies autonomous action with acting from moral obligation, whereas I take autonomy more broadly to refer to any fully free response. Not all fully free acting is acting from moral obligation; furthermore, since belief and feeling as well as action can stem from first-personal recognition of a sufficient reason there can be autonomy of belief and feeling as well as of action. It is not Kant's basic analysis of freedom, it is other doctrines of his (about feeling, giving oneself the law, moral obligation) that would force him to disagree. Note also that autonomy is a stronger notion than self-determination. On this see 5.1, 12.4, and 19.4.

[25] As Kant may have supposed. See 20.1.

knowledge of any truths about reasons, thus of any normative knowledge, and thus of knowledge as such. There is, it will turn out, an indissoluble Critical tie between *autonomy*, *knowledge*, and cognitivist irrealism about reasons: if autonomy and knowledge are possible there must be norms knowable a priori; if there are such norms, knowledge of them must be a product not of receptivity but of pure spontaneity; if that is possible norms cannot be factual propositions. 'Unity of reason' in this sense—the common source in spontaneity of all propositions about reasons—is a precondition of autonomy.

1.7 Will and feeling: practical reasons and value

We have been considering autonomy in its recognitional aspect: the ability to recognize and assess reasons. Autonomy is also executive: your recognition of what there is sufficient reason for you to believe, feel, or do can itself give rise to the appropriate belief, feeling, or action. We have autonomy, fully insightful self-determination, only when it does.[26]

The recognition of reasons to believe can give rise to belief; the recognition of reasons to feel can give rise to feeling; the recognition of reasons to act can give rise to action. *Will* is nothing but the moving power of our beliefs about our practical reasons; furthermore, one way in which we acquire these beliefs is the autonomous way—simply by recognizing that they are warranted. So one could say, with Kant, that in autonomous action practical reason itself motivates. I defend this account of motivation by reasons in Chapter 10.

Not that it exhausts Kant's view of will and practical reason. There is a good deal more to it, and it will be important to distinguish various stronger things that he thought.

Kant thinks that we can acquire the concept of a *pure will* through our awareness of pure practical laws:

> We can become aware of pure practical laws just as we are aware of pure theoretical principles, by attending to the necessity with which reason prescribes them to us and to the setting aside of all empirical conditions to which reason directs us. The concept of a pure will arises from the first [awareness of pure practical laws], as consciousness of a pure understanding arises from the latter [awareness of pure theoretical principles].[27]

One point Kant has in mind in making this analogy has already been noted: there must be a priori awareness of epistemic and practical norms if there is knowledge of epistemic and practical reasons at all. In each case, the theoretical and the practical, we become aware of a priori, universal truths about reasons by setting aside all 'empirical conditions', that is, truths about what the facts happen to be. In the practical case, this includes facts about our actual inclinations.

The point in itself is abstractly epistemological, telling us nothing about the *content* of norms. A priori norms will not state that any empirical condition actually obtains, but they

---

[26] It is another issue whether autonomy is always the thing to aim at—see 5.12.
[27] *Critique of Practical Reason*, 5: 30.

will generally *refer* to possible empirical conditions that would, if they obtained, constitute reasons for a particular belief, feeling, or action. It could still be, in the practical case, that what they refer to is our inclinations. Consider, for example, the following putative norm: 'If x desires y then that fact is a reason for x to try to get y'. As a matter of fact I shall argue that this is false, but for the moment that does not matter. The point is that this norm abstracts from empirical conditions in one sense—that is, from the actual facts about what any particular x wants—but still refers to wants. This norm can give warranted reasons for action only when combined with warranted beliefs about one's desires.

Kant means more than this. Pure will, he thinks, can dispose to warranted action even when it sets aside all facts about one's own inclinations, desires, feelings, or sentiments. Hence pure practical reason must contain norms which give rise to reasons for action irrespective of all such facts.[28]

This may seem very strong. However at this point we can still distinguish two theses:

(a) Practical norms determine what there is reason for you to do irrespective of what you actually feel.
(b) Practical norms determine what there is reason for you to do irrespective of what there is actually reason for you to feel.

Kant's claim is (a); he doesn't even consider (b), because he does not admit the existence of evaluative reasons. Yet even if (a) is true (as I believe it is) (b) could be false. One might agree with (a) just because one holds that what there is reason for a person to do always depends on what there is reason for that person to feel, rather than what he or she actually does feel. To make this distinction is by no means to deny that claims about what there's reason for someone to feel are often *epistemically* supported by consideration of the kinds of thing that person does feel, or that people in general feel, or would feel with relevant information. It just implies that such supporting inferences are never deductive—a point that will be important when we consider the epistemology of value—see 16.2.

If what there is reason for you to do can depend on what there is reason for you to feel then (b) is not true for all practical norms: at least some of them determine practical reasons on the basis of evaluative ones. How does this dependence work? I shall argue that it works through a principle I call the *Bridge principle*. Bridge says that there is reason for x to do what the affective responses that there is reason for x to feel would characteristically dispose x to do (11.1). For example, desiring something characteristically disposes one to try to get it, so Bridge says that there is reason for one to try to get what there is reason for one to desire. There are plenty of other instances of the Bridge principle. It still agrees with (a), but it introduces nothing like the gulf between 'reason' and sentiment that Kant's actual position envisages.

It would be a distinctly stronger view to hold that this is the *only* principle of practical reason: that *all* reasons for action must come over this bridge. I call this stronger view

---

[28] He sometimes seems to think it contains *only* such norms. I leave open the question of what he did think, since it raises vexed (perhaps unanswerable) questions about how he understands hypothetical imperatives, and whether he thinks there are non-moral truths about what there is reason to do.

sentimentalism about practical reasons. Distinguish then between sentimentalism about practical reasons and *sentimentalism about value*. The latter holds that all value can be analysed in terms of reasons for feeling—desire, admiration, respect, pride, gratitude, resentment, sorrow, pity... and so indefinitely on. On this analysis value generates reasons for action via Bridge. However, sentimentalism about value does not say that the Bridge principle is the *only* principle of practical reason. There could be others. There could, for example, be practical reasons that are not *value*-based—as Kant thinks there are.

I shall argue that the stronger doctrine, sentimentalism about practical reasons, cannot be sustained. The most significant counter-examples consist in variously formulated principles of impartiality. Take a formulation that says that there is reason to pursue anyone's good impartially. It generates reasons to act that do not depend on what there is reason for the actor to feel. One can try to deny this by basing this formulation of impartiality on a sentiment of universal love. By the Bridge principle, if there's reason for me to love you, then there's reason for me to pursue your good (that being the characteristic disposition of love); so if there's equal reason to love everyone, then there's equal reason to pursue everyone's good. But—at least for most ordinary human beings—there simply isn't equal reason to love everyone.[29] For example, although there's almost certainly reason for you to love your children (assuming they're not despicable ingrates like Goneril and Regan), there isn't necessarily any reason for you to love mine. Whether there's any reason depends on many empirical conditions, about you, them, and your relationship to them. Quite likely there is no reason for you to feel anything about them at all. Nonetheless, whenever the circumstances of justice apply, you should certainly be strictly impartial as between your children and mine. Moreover, most ethical views agree that there is always reason for you to take the interests of anyone at all into *some* account. Neither of these truths can be derived from a sentimentalist appeal to benevolence (understood as a sentiment, not literally as 'goodwill'). Theories which appeal to what someone with universal love for all human beings *would* do, clearly give up on sentimentalism about practical reasons as defined above. They are not inferring what there's reason for you to do from what there is actually reason for you to feel; instead they infer to what there's reason for you to do from the practical dispositions of a certain kind of hypothetical agent. They are implausible anyway: whereas the first inference has the force of the Bridge principle behind it, it is unclear why the second should have any force.

Impartiality must be grounded in a spontaneous disposition of the will that still exists in the absence of any spontaneous sentiment. It is in this sense a disposition of the *pure will*. Furthermore, the grounds which dispose the will to take the interests of any being into account, or to regard any being as an end itself (in Kant's preferred formulation), must be characteristics of the being that do not essentially involve a non-trivial relation to the actor—they must be agent-neutral grounds. In the utilitarian tradition, the relevant characteristic is that the being is capable of enjoyment and suffering, while in the Kantian tradition, it is that it is rational. However the general point, about the

---

[29] A saint's equal love for all human beings, or all created things, may be reasonable, or it may be self-deluding or dotty. Whatever one thinks about that, few of us are saints.

grounding of impartiality in pure will, is one of Kant's firmest insights, as I try to show in 13.3 and 14.3.

Yet Kant's view is more ambitious still, in two notable ways. In the *Groundwork* at least he was not satisfied with a bare appeal to the spontaneity of the will. There he famously tried to get to impartiality by analysis of the very idea of acting from a reason, that is, from the concept of autonomy itself. Furthermore, Kant thought that *morality* could be derived from a notion of impartiality alone, and moreover a formulation of impartiality— the Categorical Imperative—that makes no appeal to the notion of a person's good, but only to the fact of autonomy. I shall not be defending either of these doctrines. Impartiality does not follow analytically from the concept of autonomy as such. Morality is not exclusively impartial. Justice requires impartiality, and justice is an important part of morality, but many moral principles quite properly invoke partial or agent-relative considerations. Nor can morality be characterized either formally or substantively without appeal to evaluative reasons.

Formally, the morally wrong is definable only by reference to what there is sufficient reason for anyone to blame. I refer to the sentiment of blame, not the action of blaming, so that is a sentimentalist account of morality: a characterization of moral wrongness in terms of what there is reason to feel. I defend it in Chapters 12 and 15. Tellingly, Kant himself may be thought to give a sentimentalist account of morality in this respect, that is, of what makes a principle (for us) a *moral* principle. He does this in terms of a key evaluative reason—what there is reason to respect; he then has a special story to tell about the supposedly a priori basis of respect. I discuss this in 15.5 and 15.6.

So we have sentimentalism about *practical reasons*, sentimentalism about *value* and sentimentalism about *morality*. Of these I defend the last. 'Sentimentalism about value' is not an exactly accurate description, for although (I shall argue) all value concepts are characterizable in terms of the concept of a reason, it is not true that they are all characterizable solely in terms of *evaluative* reasons. Good evidence and good corkscrews are not evidence, and corkscrews we have reason to feel anything in particular about. Still, often when we talk about value we have in mind value concepts that are indeed definable in terms of evaluative reasons, and these will generate reasons for action by the Bridge principle. Many moral principles trace back in this way to evaluative reasons—obligations of gratitude are an example. We can certainly still ask why these principles should have the status of *moral* principles; but the attempt to explain even that status in terms of some underlying appeal to impartiality, whether Kantian or utilitarian, is contrived. Note also that one of the principles of impartiality we should accept—impartial concern for everyone's good (the principle of Good mentioned above)—cannot be formulated without appeal to evaluative reasons. For the notion of a person's good is, I shall argue, one of the value notions to which a sentimentalist account applies: it is definable as what there is reason for that person to desire. This does not apply to the other impartial principle we should accept—the Demand principle—which underlies impartial respect for everyone's rights. Nonetheless, what substantive rights human beings have is surely grounded on what values and ideals matter to them.

The deep distortions in Kantian ethics seem to me, as they have seemed to many others, to stem from a profoundly false contrast between 'Reason' and feeling. The root problem is his failure to recognize that there are *sui generis* reasons for feeling. Insofar as rationality enters the appraisal of feelings at all, Kant thinks it does only in the form of *practical* rationality. When it serves the ends of practical reason that one should feel more of this or less of that, then we should try, with what success we can, to cultivate these feelings and not those. He does not recognize that the feelings have their own immanent rationality: that there is right and wrong feeling in the sense of what the facts as such give one reason to feel, irrespective of what the moral project, or any other practical project, might make it sensible to try to feel. The stilted rhetoric of Kant's dealings with emotions reflects this. He humours them because he has ulterior plans for using them.[30]

Failure to recognize evaluative reasons is the greatest, most damaging error in Kant's philosophy of freedom. He fails to recognize them even when he implicitly appeals to them, as in the case of respect, where the sublimity of the moral law gives rise to respect via the 'causality of freedom'—presumably not unreasonably but because its sublimity is recognized as a *reason* for respect.

Kant's positive hostility to any trace of sentimentalism in moral philosophy does not arise from anything that is required by his overall Critical stance, his epistemology of reasons, or his transcendental idealism. If the epistemological basis of reasons for action and reasons for belief is spontaneity of the will and spontaneity of belief, why shouldn't the epistemological basis of reasons for feeling be spontaneity of feeling?

It might be said, on his behalf, that feelings are not spontaneous in the *relevant* sense, as against currently common senses—we do not originate them, they just happen to us. Perhaps this, to some extent, explains why Kant so disastrously sends feelings to the phenomenal as against the noumenal side: to the self as it appears, as against the self as it is. But do the emotions 'just happen' to us any more than beliefs 'just happen to us'? Is there anything more to this than the simple point that feelings, like beliefs, are not subject to our will? That point does not undermine their spontaneity in the relevant philosophical sense, any more than it undermines the spontaneity of cognition. Recognition of reasons for feeling is based on the spontaneity of feelings, in exactly the way that recognition of reasons for belief or action is based on the spontaneity of dispositions to believe or act. In no case does it involve receptivity to a special domain. Feeling has the potential for self-determination just as belief and action do. Failure to recognize this forces Kant into an unpalatable choice— either to adopt a non-Critically intuitionistic view of value, or (as he does) to dispense with value as a *basic* category in his theory of practical reason altogether. He thus distorts the content of morality, ignores reasons other than moral requirements, enters into contortions about the rationality of respect, and—joining a strange alliance with Hume—destroys the possibility of a non-instrumentalist account of hypothetical imperatives.

We need a better critique of morality to fill out our Critical story. It will have to give space to the Bridge principle, to the impartial principles of Good and Demand, and to the distinctively moral judgements of conscience and moral common sense.

---

[30] One might say that his sentimentality arises from his failure to see the truth in sentimentalism. What to learn from this? Quite a lot, it seems to me, about certain main distortions in the modern ethical tradition of the West—which Kant did much to shape, and which remain influential in current moral philosophy.

1.8 Morality

As will become apparent in Chapter 12, the connection between moral obligation and reasons for the sentiment of blame is decidedly tricky. Nonetheless, I argue there that the moral can be defined by reference to that sentiment. This, if correct, is an important illustration of the Reasons thesis. However, if we define the moral in that way, we obviously cannot identify the sentiment we have in mind as that sentiment which there is reason to feel towards moral wrongdoing. We must individuate the sentiment in a non-circular way, by its objects and the actions to which it disposes. That in turn leads on to further important issues.

In the first place, an examination of the proper object of blame can help us to understand the categoricity of morality. By the thesis that morality is categorical I mean that it is a priori that if someone has a moral obligation to a he has reason to a. This has been contested. But the basic point, according to my account of blame, is that it makes no sense to blame someone for doing something he had no reason not to do. This is inherent to the sentiment of blame, in the way that it is inherent to gratitude that its object is a good turn that has been done to you by another, or to the sentiment of resentment that its object is a brazen insult or unapologetic injury. It makes no sense to blame someone if you think they had no reason not to do what they did, just as it makes no sense to be grateful to someone unless you think they have done you good, or at least tried. Hence if there is reason to blame a person for doing something, there must have been reason for him not to do it. Not any reason of course—a reason which it was blameworthy on his part to ignore. What are these reasons? It is our considered blame responses that tell us what they are. I develop these ideas in 12.3.

Examining blame's dispositions takes us further. Different sentiments dispose to different actions. These differences can be subtle; pinning down the distinctive actions to which the sentiment of blame disposes illustrates that very clearly. And yet these subtle differences are of utmost significance in understanding morality and the role it plays in all societies. The disposition of blame, as against contempt, anger, resentment, and the like, is *withdrawal of recognition*. So given the connection between moral wrongdoing and reason to blame, and combining it with the Bridge principle, we see that moral wrongdoing without extenuation gives reason to withdraw recognition.

To withdraw or withhold recognition is to cut off relations or refuse to enter into them, to exclude, in however partial and temporary a way. It is essential to this response, however, at least in its healthy state, that it should not be final and irreversible. The whole point is that recognition can be restored. The wrongdoer remains a moral agent; atonement, in the old sense of restoration of at oneness, always remains possible. Hence the internal connections between blame, remorse, forgiveness, or reconciliation. This is the emotional dialectic in terms of which to understand the ethical notion of punishment. (The rationale for legal punishment is a more complex matter compounding a number of strands, of which ethical punishment is only one—though it should always be one.) None of these connections can be understood if we do not keep clearly in mind that emotions have their reasons: evaluative reasons which cannot by reduced to practical reasons but must be immanently understood.

Finally, to fill out the relations between practical reasons and morality we must give an account of the role and the epistemology of moral judgement. The basic principles of practical reason, I argue in Part III, are Bridge, Good, and Demand. Contrary to sentimentalists, rational utilitarians, and pure rights theorists, these are not further reducible. We seek to set-up, more or less, adequate *axiomata media* to help us balance them, or to balance them by direct judgement in particular cases when such middle principles are of no avail. This balancing is not always a case of *moral* judgement, but it is important that it sometimes is.

In such cases moral judgement plays a verdictive role. It is *moral* judgement because it also has disciplinary and emancipatory roles. Normative judgement in general is founded purely on spontaneity and discussion; that applies to all norms, epistemic, evaluative, and practical. Spontaneous normative dispositions, evolved and educated through discussion with others, are basic to the epistemology of all norms. With moral judgement, however, the two pillars of spontaneity and discussion acquire a special role, because moral judgement, in its disciplinary function, is the justifier for withdrawal of recognition. In moral judgement the dialectic of spontaneity and discussion become the dialectic between individual conscience and the moral common sense of a community—what Hegel called *Sittlichkeit*. But in social contexts in which conscience and moral common sense can be at one, moral judgement also plays its most important emancipatory role. There 'the individual' can be at home—can find 'his *liberation* in duty'.[31] Hegel gives the best reply to critics who find morality oppressive, or want to go beyond it—even granted that a social order in which common morality can play its emancipatory role is not always easy to attain. The functions of moral judgement are discussed in Chapter 15.

1.9 Is the world our world? Are we in it?

Let me now state the Normative view in the form of four theses. (i) Normative propositions are propositions about reason relations; (ii) there is a fundamental epistemological and ontological distinction between factual propositions and a priori propositions about reason relations—call these *purely* normative propositions; (iii) all (synthetic) a priori propositions are in the first place normative;[32] (iv) reason relations are irreal objects of true and false thoughts. These theses, when applied to epistemic norms, make the Normative view a new form of Critical philosophy.

All Critical philosophies start from an epistemological dualism between self-determining thought and its data. This dualism arises from the very nature of self-determining thought. Viennese Critical philosophy interprets it as a dualism of convention and experience. Like Kant, I see it as a dualism of spontaneity and receptivity: the dualism between self-determining thought's own epistemic materials—its spontaneous epistemic–

---

[31] Hegel, *Philosophy of Right*, 1942: 149.
[32] 'In the first place' because certain (monotonic) epistemic norms generate non-normative offshoots. See 6.6, 9.4, and 20.5. Since the norms are a priori these are too.

normative dispositions—and the epistemic materials it receives from something other than itself, the facts as they are. In the Viennese critique, thought determines itself by laying down rules. It does not do so on the Normative view. It determines itself by responding to norms—synthetic a priori normative truths. Yet its judgements about these are products of pure spontaneity, involving no receptivity to anything real.

How a purely *spontaneous response* can found a genuine—true or false—normative *judgement* is the subject of Part IV. In Chapters 16 and 17, I argue that neither epistemology nor semantics commits us to realism about reason relations. Indeed an accurate epistemology of reasons positively precludes it. Any knowledge of real objects independent of oneself requires receptivity—but when we consult our practice, we find that normative knowledge rests on just two pillars, individual spontaneity and free dialogue with other inquirers. No special receptivity to a putative domain of normative fact is involved.

Normative knowledge is adequately supported by these two pillars because its objects—reason relations—are actual, objective, and *irreal*. I explain what I mean by this in Chapter 17, which deals with semantics, existence, and truth. As philosophers have found over the centuries, the notion or notions of existence, reality, are extraordinarily elusive. Two criteria have long been used to pin them down. There is what I call the semantic condition, according to which whatever we can talk (or think) about exists, is real; and there is the causal condition, according to which the real is whatever has causal standing.

In recent decades, the first of these has had extraordinary influence. However, there are many things that do not exist; we talk about non-existent entities all the time. The previous sentence can be regarded as self-contradictory only if we attach ontological significance to the 'existential' quantifier. Yet the semantic condition is no part of semantics. Semantics has done its job when it has assigned semantic values to terms and truth conditions to sentences. To make the further claim that semantic values must be real is to step out of semantics into metaphysics. The only condition semantics *as such* places on a semantic value is that we should know what we are talking about when we talk about it. The same applies to the idea that truths must have 'truth makers', substantial facts that make them true: this too goes beyond semantics into metaphysics. We know what it is for a proposition to be true when we grasp the proposition.

We should reject both the semantic criterion of existence and the correspondence theory of truth. But we should accept the causal condition. The real is that which has causal standing. How widely the notion of cause should be understood is a further philosophical question; but *however* widely we understand it, I argue, this criterion makes reason relations irreal. It does not follow that propositions about them cannot be true, and it does not follow that reason relations are fictions or constructs. They are what they are, independently of what we think they are. Their objectivity is the unconditioned condition on which the Normative view explains the possibility of knowledge and freedom.

The Normative view can explain how these are possible without introducing any form of transcendental idealism. It is compatible with naturalism, the thesis that the natural facts are all the substantial facts there are. (Take natural facts to be facts wholly constituted by attributes falling under relations of causality—causality of a kind that can be studied by whatever we should seriously regard as science.) Furthermore since, as I shall argue, Kant was a cognitive irrealist about 'Reason' it follows that *Kant* didn't need transcendental idealism to carry out his Critical project. Still, transcendental idealism retains strengths that become manifest when we ask ourselves whether scientific inquiry can be guaranteed to converge on a unique or 'absolute' conception of reality. And even without transcendental idealism there still remains, on the Normative view, a sense in which the world is our world.

We can approach this in a number of ways. One is to consider how the Normative view responds to scepticism. Another is to consider how the a priori sciences of logic and mathematics function as pivots between the normative and the factual. Another, that follows on from that, is to note that our 'world theory' is not an inert picture or 'mirror' of nature but a way of thinking about nature and acting in it. It is both product and basis of our self-determining activity; it has normative as well as factual dimensions which cannot be neatly separated. These issues are explored in 20.3 to 20.8.

The world is 'our' world rather than 'my' world. The Cartesian reply to scepticism makes it 'my' world in the sense that Descartes' approach requires me to recover it, complete with a population of other people, from egocentric premises. Now the Normative view is by no means a nostrum against every kind of sceptical challenge. However the form of scepticism to which Descartes attempts to reply loses its menace on the Normative view, for it poses a challenge only on globally realist assumptions (20.6). Moreover, the epistemology of norms cannot function in a purely egocentric manner. It indispensably requires discussion with others as well as individual spontaneity. True, if I am to reflect autonomously on my reasons, I have to determine their soundness *for myself*; but that is something for which I need a dialogical context. I cannot do it entirely *by* myself. For this reason the factors mentioned in the previous paragraph make the world in a sense 'our' world, rather than 'my world'.

So are we in the world? The reasons for questioning whether we are, are not epistemological. They have to do with whether persons are identical with any objects in the best account of natural reality. This question is not settled one way or the other by the epistemology of the Normative view.

Given a naturalistic account of reality how do persons fit in? Are persons natural objects? I do not try to answer this question, for it falls beyond the scope of Normative critique. However, I do point out that its importance is reduced given the ontology of reasons proposed in Chapter 17. If reason relations are actual, objective and irreal, might not persons—self-determiners—be so too? That might be the case even if all facts about persons supervene on natural facts. On this view, even if persons are no more natural objects than reason relations are, it would not follow that naturalism is false. Persons, like reason relations, would not be 'in' the natural world, but they would not be 'out' of it either—that is, in a domain of substantial non-natural facts. These questions are broached, though not answered, in Chapter 19.

Sections 1.2 to 1.9 have outlined in broad terms the main ideas of this book. We now turn to their detailed development. In Part I we consider the logic of reasons and the structure of normative concepts. This analysis will provide the foundation for Parts II to IV.

PART I

The Structure of Normative Concepts

2

REASONS

Let us begin by introducing what I shall call *reason relations*. They are the fundamental topic of this book. We set out, in this chapter, what reason relations there are and make some main points about their logic.

We should start with some examples of the way we use the concept of a reason.

2.1 Epistemic, practical, and evaluative reasons

We talk about reasons to believe—think, judge, conclude, and so on:

> The fact that the freezer door is open is a reason to think the ice cream will melt.
> The fact that the governing party is alienating so many interest groups gives one reason to believe that it will not be re-elected.
> All the components we've had so far from that supplier have had this particular flaw, so there's some reason to conclude that all of them have it.
> Data gathered from underwater sea currents give us some reason to believe that global warming is taking place.

Call reasons of this kind, reasons to believe something, *epistemic* reasons.[1] We also talk about reasons to do things:

> Is there any reason to go to this lecture? Yes, you'll enjoy it.
> Since there's likely to be a traffic jam down this road there's some reason to try the other route.
> She had good reason to leave. The bus was going in 5 minutes.
> The fact that Nice will be pleasantly hot and sunny is a reason to have our weekend break there; the fact that it will be expensive is a reason not to.

---

[1] Reasons to make a purely cognitive step *within* a train of reasoning to a conclusion (introduce a supposition, make an inference, exclude a supposition, etc.) are also epistemic reasons. They should not be confused with practical reasons for engaging in such reasoning in the first place. More on this in 8.2.

These we shall call *practical* reasons. And third, we talk about reasons to feel. (By a feeling I mean a sentiment, emotion, affective response to an object or circumstance.) This third class of reasons will play a prominent part in this book. We can call them *evaluative* reasons:[2]

> He has reason to feel proud of himself: despite all the pressure he won the match.
> That electrician has failed to turn up again! Yes, you have every reason to be annoyed with him.
> There's good reason for my gratitude—she helped me out of a very tight corner.
> There is no reason for you to feel ashamed of yourself—the mistake you made in reading the navigation chart was perfectly understandable.

The difference between the three kinds of reason is as clear as the difference between action, belief, and feeling: a clear enough difference, though puzzles can as ever be raised.[3] I assume that they constitute a trichotomy that is both irreducible and exhaustive: we can take this as a postulate, to be vindicated by our discussion overall.

In all three cases, the epistemic, practical, and evaluative, *being a reason* is a relation—between facts, persons, and beliefs, actions, or feelings. The fact that Nice is expensive is a reason to go somewhere else. The fact that currents are changing in such-and-such a way is a reason to think the oceans are warming. The fact that the electrician has failed to turn up again is a reason to be annoyed with him (unless, for example, he has an excuse). I take the notion of fact in play to be the nominal one mentioned in the Introduction—a nominal fact is the truth of a proposition. This is, of course, a significant assumption—we shall come back to it (3.3 and 16.1).

In all three cases, reasons can be stronger or weaker, that is, they can vary in degrees of strength.[4] Also in all three cases they can vary with time. There may be reason to believe, feel, or do something at a given time for which there wasn't reason before and may not be reason after. So far, then, reason relations can be thought of as having five places, as follows:

(1) The epistemic reason relation:

the fact that p is at time t a reason of degree d for x to believe...

(2) The evaluative reason relation:

the fact that p is at time t a reason of degree d for x to feel...

---

[2] This is an unfamiliar and somewhat awkward term, unlike 'epistemic' and 'practical', but on the whole I find it better than some possible alternatives. The idea behind it will come to the fore in Chapter 3, where we shall argue that judgements of aesthetic and ethical value (evaluations) are judgements about reasons to feel.

[3] There is, for example, the case of adopting a hypothesis (say about where the enemy will attack) for purposes of action. This can be guided by epistemic reasons but finally justified for practical reasons. Deciding whether to consider a particular supposition in the course of an inquiry has similar features. We shall come back to these cases in 5.9. Consider also reasons to hope: these encompass both reasons to believe that something may turn out to be the case and reason to desire or wish that it will. Questions have been raised about reasons to intend; I take it that reasons to intend to α are either (properly speaking) reasons to α or (improperly speaking) reasons to *make yourself* intend to α—see 2.9 and 4.4. Either way they are practical reasons.

[4] This does not assume that degrees of strengths are always comparable, or indeed that they can be mathematically represented at all. However, Eric Carlson (2006) shows how incomparable values may be mathematically represented in an ordering of values. The same can apply to incomparable strengths of reasons, if there are any.

(3) The practical reason relation:

the fact that p is at time t a reason of degree d for x to do . . .

In order to talk more generally about these relations it is useful to have a term that covers all three cases. I shall refer to beliefs, feelings, and actions as *responses*. The being or entity to which a response can be imputed I shall call the *actor*. By 'responses' I do not mean responses to stimuli, but responses to what the actor takes to be reasons. Responses are 'intentional acts', in the broad sense that they all have an intentional content that is linked essentially to their answerability to reasons. The notion of an 'intentional act' is useful inasmuch as it suggests that beliefs and feelings, while not themselves action, can be an *active* response—as in 'he responded with gratitude', 'he came to a conclusion'. An actor can be said to respond to, or be sensitive to reasons, and to have a reason for a response. Almost all human beings are actors in this sense, and so perhaps, are some animals. There could be other actors who are not human beings, perhaps including machines. What the conditions of reason-sensitivity are, when it can be attributed, and to what extent, are questions we shall have to consider. But we can set them aside for the moment, while we consider the logical structure of propositions about reasons.

Think then of epistemic, evaluative, and practical reason relations as particular cases of a general relation, R, which holds between the following items: facts; times; degrees of strength of reason; actors; and acts:

$R(\pi_i, t, d, x, \psi)$—π_i is/are at time t a reason of degree of strength d for x to ψ.[5]

Reasons can consist not just in one fact but in a number of facts (the facts at your disposal, the facts that constitute the evidence, etc.) So we can think of 'π_i' as ranging over pluralities and replaceable by plural terms. Or we can think of it as ranging over sets comprising the facts which constitute the reason. It won't be necessary to decide about this. Either way, this plurality, or set, can consist of one or more facts. In dealing with the notion of the a priori it will be convenient to allow it also to refer to the empty plurality or empty set.

Finally, note that instead of saying that the fact that p *is* a reason to ψ, we can also say that it *gives* x a reason to ψ; provides x with a reason to ψ; constitutes a reason for x to ψ. These phrases will be used in this book completely interchangeably, to mean exactly the same thing. They all say that being a reason to y is a property of the fact that p.

2.2 Specific, overall, and sufficient

'R' is not the only reason predicate. There are two others. In the first place, we often take stock of how strong is the reason to feel, believe, or do something *overall*—when all specific reasons are taken into account. We consider how strong a reason there is for ψ-ing overall, in the light of all relevant specific reasons, or as we say, in the light of all the relevant

---

[5] Epistemic reasons, as we shall see, are also relative to epistemic fields, and practical reasons to choice sets. (For notes on symbols in this book, see the Appendix.)

considerations, or all the relevant facts. And second, having considered how strong a reason for ψ-ing there is overall, we sometimes conclude that there is *sufficient* reason to ψ is a property of the fact that p.

Suppose, for example, that an industrial tribunal is considering a case of unfair dismissal. The employer cites various incidents as grounds, that is, specific reasons, for dismissing the person. Without holding that any of them were in themselves a sufficient reason for dismissal, he claims that taken together they did constitute sufficient reason. The dismissed employee does not question that each of these incidents is a reason for dismissal but argues that they did not, taken overall, constitute a sufficient reason. What the tribunal has to determine is how strong the *overall* reason for dismissal was and whether it amounted to sufficient reason. It could quite intelligibly conclude that while there was some reason for dismissal overall, it was not sufficient.

The tribunal could also conclude that there was more than one sufficient reason for dismissal. It would then trivially follow that the facts overall constitute sufficient reason for dismissal. We do not distinguish 'specific' and 'overall' in the case of *sufficient* reasons, since wherever some facts constitute a specific sufficient reason they remain a sufficient reason when all reasons are taken into account. *Vice versa*, wherever there is sufficient reason, there is at least one set of facts that constitute a sufficient reason.

So we have specific and overall reasons of degree,[6] and sufficient reasons, yielding the following three reason predicates:

> Specific reasons—R(π_i, t, d, x, ψ): π_i are at time t a specific reason of degree of strength d for x to ψ.
> Overall reasons—R$_o$(π_i, t, d, x, ψ): π_i are at time t overall reason of degree of strength d for x to ψ.
> Sufficient reasons—S(π_i, t, x, ψ): π_i are at time t a sufficient reason for x to ψ.

Can any of these three predicates be defined in terms of the others?

Take 'S'—can it be defined in terms of 'R' or 'R$_o$'?[7] In the case of practical reasons, it may seem plausible that it can. We shall take it that there is *sufficient* reason to do an action if and only if there is more reason overall to do it than any other action. When we think of sufficient reasons for doing something in this way, we assume some exhaustive partitioning of actions, within which one and only one action must be done. Call an exhaustive partitioning of actions a choice set; 'inaction' and likewise the action of further deliberation are members of the set. When there is more than one action that there is most reason to do there is sufficient reason to do one of them but not sufficient reason to do either of them; we have S(α_1 v α_2) but not Sα_1 v Sα_2. The same applies to the putative case of incomparable optimal actions, where there is at least as much reason to do each one of the optimal ones as any others with which they can be compared, but comparisons within the optimal set are in some cases indeterminate.

---

[6] I take the term *'pro tanto reason'* to refer to specific reasons of degree. Susan Hurley contrasts *pro tanto* and *prima facie* reasons in Hurley 1989, 7:3. My use of *'pro tanto'* coincides, I believe, with hers, but my use of *prima facie* (in the next section) seems to be different. As I use them, these terms mark cross-cutting distinctions.

[7] I argue that it is impossible to define 'R' and 'R$_o$' in terms of 'S' in Section 2.7 below.

Often, it is true, we assess proposed actions on an individual basis without seeking to partition in any way the whole range of available options; we consider directly, with each possible action that comes up for consideration, whether there is *sufficient* reason to do it. In this way of deliberating about sufficient reasons it does not seem to follow from the fact that there's *sufficient* reason to act in a particular way that there's no action there's more reason to do. We say that there is *sufficient* reason to spend the afternoon at the cinema, without taking that action to be optimal. Maybe someone could come up with something better, but this will do. Here we seem to take the notion of a sufficient reason as a reason that's 'good enough' for action.[8]

It is relevant that decisions about what to do are often collective. In such cases, e.g. if we're deciding together what to do this afternoon, the need for compromise can defeat what is *ex ante* optimal from any individual's point of view. Sufficient reason for the collective may have to be construed by reference to decision-making conventions, issues of courtesy, etc. which lead us to seize on something which we can all agree is a good enough decision. That still leaves it open to anyone to hold that although that is what there is collectively speaking sufficient reason to do, it's not what there is in fact most reason for the collective to do. So it is at least not obvious, even in the case of practical reasons, that 'sufficient reason', as used in ordinary talk entails 'optimal reason'. However, from now on I shall take it that a sufficient practical reason is a uniquely optimal practical reason. If we considered practical reasons alone, therefore, we might think that 'S' is definable in terms of 'R_o'.

When we turn to the case of epistemic reasons, however, it is clear that 'S' cannot be defined in terms of 'R' or 'R_o'. For example, say that there is at present more reason to believe that a federal European state will emerge than that it will not emerge. If that is right, the proposition that there will be such a state is what there is currently most reason to believe as regards that question. But it's not true that there is currently *sufficient* reason to believe it. At this stage it would be a very unsafe conclusion.[9]

In the epistemic case we can be confronted with something partially analogous to a partitioning of actions. We may be able to specify that the answer to some particular question must lie within a set of possibilities. Thus, for example, we may know that Mary has gone to some capital city but not know which one she has gone to. There may be more reason to think that she's gone to Paris or Rome, but no more reason to think it's Paris than to think it's Rome. However, in a case like this, unlike the superficially analogous case in practical reasoning, it *still* does not follow that we should believe that she's gone to Paris or Rome. It's not true that one should believe the disjunction of things there's most reason to believe. For we can conclude that there's *insufficient* reason to

---

[8] The cost of deliberation and inquiry is obviously an important factor, and raises issues about strategy which will be discussed later. See 5.9.

[9] What about defining 'there's sufficient reason to believe that *p*' as 'there's more reason to believe that *p* than not to believe that *p*'? It is unclear what 'there's reason *not* to believe that *p*' means (if it is distinct from both 'there's no reason to believe that *p*' and 'there's reason to believe that it's not the case that *p*'). Perhaps it's definable as 'there is reason to believe that given the facts available there isn't sufficient reason to believe that *p*'. In that case, 'there's more reason to believe that *p* than not to believe that *p*' means something like 'there is more reason to believe that the reasons to believe that *p* are sufficient than to believe they are not'. That does not give us a definition of S in terms of R_o.

believe anything within the set of possibilities—including any disjunction formed from a proper subset of possibilities in it—even while we conclude that some such disjunction is what there's *most* reason to believe. In contrast, we can't conclude that there's insufficient reason to do anything within the choice set, including disjunctions within it, while also holding that some disjunction is what there's most reason to do.

The same point holds for feelings. There may be some reason to feel grateful to Pierre for his would-be good turn, and some reason to feel irritated. Perhaps irritation, as against gratitude, is what there's most reason to feel—but still, taking all the facts into account, maybe the reasons for feeling irritated aren't sufficient. Sometimes we can specify a feeling set, similar to a belief set, or an action set: for example, I may be unclear whether I should feel annoyed, flattered, or embarrassed about the fact that p, even though I'm clear that no other reaction is appropriate. The case here is like that of belief. That is, it may be that this is the disjunction of feelings that I have most reason to have, but it does not follow that I should have one or all of them. For example, it may be that, there's about equal reason to feel annoyed, flattered, and embarrassed by your offer, and less or no reason to feel anything else, but it may still be true that there's insufficient reason to feel any of these things.

In short, the analogy between optimal disjunctions of action and optimal disjunctions of belief or feeling is only partial. The difference, obviously, is that inaction counts as a form of action, whereas non-belief and non-feeling are not beliefs or feelings. This generates a gap between reasons of degree and sufficient reasons in the epistemic, and the evaluative case that does not exist in the practical case.

What about defining R_o in terms of R? Note first that the degree of strength of an overall reason can differ from the degree of strength of any of the specific reasons. Nor can we treat the overall reason as the specific reason that is constituted by all the relevant facts. Such a specific reason would be *in competition* with the other specific reasons: it would be one specific reason to take into account along with any others. In the case of the industrial tribunal, for example, some of the relevant facts may be reasons *not* to dismiss, so that the overall reason for dismissal may be weak, even though some specific reasons for dismissal are strong. We cannot argue that this weak overall reason is outweighed by one of the strong specific reasons, for they have already been taken into account. We can say that the set of facts constituting all specific reasons to ψ, including where appropriate specific reasons not to ψ, determines the strength of the overall reason to ψ. This truth is not a definition, however, since if we tried to write it out as a definition we would find the concept occurring in its own characterization. ('How much overall reason there is to ψ' 'is defined as' 'how much *reason* there is when all relevant specific reasons have been taken into overall account.' Here the italicized occurrence of 'reason' refers to overall reason.) Thus R_o is not definable in terms of R.[10]

---

[10] I may seem to be disagreeing with Jonathan Dancy, who denies that 'there are such things as overall reasons in addition to the contributory ones' (Dancy 2004: 16). However, his point, I believe, is that overall reasons do not constitute *additional* reasons in the sense that they cannot change, so to speak, the reason-giving situation determined by the totality of specific reasons. Exactly: that is why one must distinguish the concept of an overall reason from that of a specific reason.

It is certainly plausible that truths about R_o depend on truths about R, and truths about S depend on truths about R and about R_o. I believe it to be true. A difference in sufficient reasons must rest on some underlying difference in degrees of reason. However normative insight, not grasp of definitions, is required to infer from one level to another. We might try to find substantive principles linking the levels in all cases, or in some. Moving from judgements about specific reasons to ψ to a judgement about the overall degree of reason to ψ may be a matter of weighing reasons, or it may involve, for example, lexical discontinuities. Likewise with moving from a judgement about the overall degree of reason to ψ to a judgement about whether there is sufficient reason to ψ. We should not assume that an overall reason that is sufficiently strong always becomes a sufficient reason. Other, qualitative, factors about the nature of the reason may be involved.[11] Perhaps in moving from one level to another we often rely on overall judgements that are highly case specific. For example, that might apply to a lot of hypothetical inferences in science. All these questions will arise in substantive theories of reasons. All I want to claim here is that the three predicates are not inter-definable, and are all the reason predicates there are, so that all talk about reasons can be formally characterized in terms of them. More strongly, it will be a main argument of this book that the three reason predicates also suffice to characterize the whole field of normative concepts, and are not themselves reducible (either analytically or by a synthetic identity) to non-normative predicates. So R, R_o, and S are the three primitive *normative* predicates.

2.3 Epistemic fields: *prima facie* and 'all-things-considered reasons'

Epistemic reasons have a special feature: they must be *knowable* facts.

Your practical and evaluative reasons do not in general, depend on what you do know or even could know. For example, the fact that a friend of yours has done you a great favour is a reason for you to feel grateful, whether or not you could come to know it. I might truly say: 'There's reason for you to feel very grateful to one of your friends, but I can't reveal what it is, or who it is.' Likewise, the fact that the garage is cheating you is a reason for you to be annoyed with it, whether or not you know that it's cheating you. And the fact that this stuff is poison, not water, is a reason for you not to drink it, whether or not you do or could know that fact. An observer could know that there's reason for you not to drink this stuff. Again, if a truck has broken down round the bend and you'll avoid hitting it only by braking right now, then there's reason for you to brake right now, even though you haven't seen the truck and don't know that there is reason to slow down. In all these cases, others can know that there are reasons for you that you cannot know—unless they tell you (for example, by putting up a warning triangle by the side of the road).

---

[11] Consider the case of the stadium. There are n people in it; m people ($n>m>0$) went through the turnstile. Is there an m low enough to give sufficient reason to believe that an arbitrary individual did not go through the turnstile, or are qualitative considerations about the type of evidence we have relevant?

Unsurprisingly, however, this lack of dependence on the actor's actual and possible knowledge does not apply to epistemic reasons, reasons for belief. There must be some epistemic restriction on the facts that can give me reason to believe that a fact obtains. Otherwise what gives me reason to believe that p obtains could be just that fact, the fact that p—unrestrictedly for any fact at all. Now we shall be arguing that for each actor there must always be some facts with respect to which that is so (Chapter 5). In such a case, the fact that p is indeed the very reason for x to believe that p. For example, the fact that I'm thinking is a reason for me to believe that I'm thinking. That is a non-inferential reason. But in many cases our reason for believing some fact to obtain can only be inferential. In these cases the fact itself is not a reason for believing that it obtains. Furthermore, we take it for granted that there can be propositions that are true even though there is no reason to believe that they are true. So in the case of any such true proposition that p, which there is no reason for us to believe, the fact that p cannot itself be a reason to believe that p.

Suppose exactly three gulls died on the West Beach at St Andrews on 26 June 56 BCE. Is that fact itself a reason for me now to believe that three gulls died on that beach then? No. Why not? Because I cannot know it. I wasn't there to see it, there are no records which, or observers who, could tell me of it. The facts that are knowable by an actor x, and can thus be epistemic reasons for x at a time t are limited by what x could at t know of by reflection or by further (physically possible, spatio-temporal) inquiry, or just by 'stumbling across' them. These are the facts that are *epistemically accessible* to x at t: x could come to know them by skill or by luck. Call them x's *epistemic field* at t.

There will be epistemic dependencies within this field. Take the fact that physical space is not uniformly Euclidean. It cannot itself be the reason, or part of the reason, to believe that it itself obtains. We could have reason to believe the proposition that space is not uniformly Euclidean only by theoretical inference from other facts. It is those facts that are our reasons for believing the proposition. Still, given that we can know it, it can give us reason to believe other things.[12]

Facts in an actor's epistemic field can constitute epistemic reasons for that actor whether or not he has become aware of them. Suppose the fact that there are small and distinctive scratches on the window sill, together with other facts which a careful inspection of the scene of the crime would reveal, is a reason to think that the criminal escaped through the window. Sherlock Holmes says to Watson 'Well, I think there's some reason for us to conclude that the criminal escaped through the window, don't you?' But Watson is baffled, because he hasn't noticed those highly significant scratches. Nevertheless, Holmes is quite right to speak in the first-person plural. Those scratches *are* a reason for Watson to think the criminal went that way; Watson *could* have noticed them if he'd been more careful or lucky—the fact that he hasn't noticed them just is the fact that he's missed a reason for concluding something about the criminal's escape route.

---

[12] When I remember that p, the fact that p can give me reason to believe that q. Suppose I remember that you spent the whole day in Edinburgh yesterday. Then the fact that you did so is a reason for me to believe that you weren't in St Andrews at the time of the seminar that took place there yesterday. But, in that case, cannot a fact I remember, such as that space is non-Euclidean, be a reason for me to believe that it itself obtains (putting 'p' for 'q')? No: in this case it is the fact that I seem to remember that p that gives me now a reason to believe that p. See Chapter 9.

Crucially, however, the existence of the scratches constitutes a reason for thinking that the criminal escaped through the window only relative to all the other facts accessible to Holmes and Watson. Suppose the housekeeper, who could easily be interviewed, would tell them that the scratches were there before the crime. If that's so, then the scratches on the window are *not* a reason for them to believe the criminal went that way.

Suppose, though, that the housekeeper is mistaken: the scratches were not there before the crime—they were indeed left by the criminal. It may nevertheless still not be the case, given the facts accessible to Holmes and Watson, including the housekeeper's testimony, that the presence of the scratches is a reason, all things considered, for Holmes and Watson to believe that the criminal went that way. That will be the case if they have no reason to doubt the housekeeper's honesty or memory and if there is no other way in which they could discover that the scratches were not there before the crime, contrary to the housekeeper's mistaken evidence. They would have to have access to some independent facts that would give them reason to dismiss the housekeeper's testimony as mistaken. Only if they do have access to such facts do the scratches on the window still give them reason to think the criminal went that way.

Epistemic reasons are relative to their field: whether a subset of facts in an epistemic field constitutes a reason—and how good a reason for belief it constitutes—depends on the other facts in the field. (This is a version of Carnap's much-cited requirement of total evidence.[13]) They are also defeasible. An actor's epistemic field can be enlarged over time as more facts become available, and a fact which was a reason to believe in the earlier epistemic field may cease to be so in the enlarged epistemic field. In both respects epistemic reasons differ from evaluative and practical reasons. The latter are neither field-relative nor defeasible—although of course reasons for *believing* that a practical or an evaluative reason exists are indeed both field-relative and defeasible.[14]

This is a good place to put the notion of a '*prima facie* reason'. The presence of the scratches is a *prima facie* reason to believe the criminal went that way—an apparent reason—but it turns out, when the whole epistemic field is taken into consideration, not to be a reason. Suppose Holmes's brother Mycroft is also on the case and has questioned the housekeeper. Mycroft says to Sherlock 'Yes, I agree these scratches look like a reason to think he went this way, but as it turns out they aren't: I've questioned the housekeeper, and she is confident that the marks were here before'.

An epistemic reason is an all-things-considered epistemic reason. (Distinguish 'all-things-considered reason', which contrasts with *prima facie* reason, from 'overall reason', which contrasts with *specific* reason.) To say that a fact is, *prima facie*, a reason is to say that it seems to be a reason when not all facts in the epistemic field are known. Thus a *prima facie* epistemic reason may be defeated *within* its epistemic field, whereas an all-things-considered epistemic reason (a reason proper) can only be defeated in an *enlarged* epistemic field. Put another way: a *prima facie* reason may or may not be a reason (all things

---

[13] Carnap 1950: 211–13.
[14] *Warranted* evaluative and practical reasons, which we shall define in Chapter 5, are both field-relative and defeasible, because they inherit these features from the epistemic reasons that support them.

considered) in the actual epistemic field—but would indeed have been a reason in a more restricted epistemic field. If the marks had in fact been on the window sill before the crime, but no one noticed them, or the only person who noticed them is away and unavailable for questioning, then the fact that those marks were there before the crime would be inaccessible to Mycroft and Sherlock: it would not be in their epistemic field. Hence the presence of marks would be a specific reason, all things considered, for them to think the criminal left through the window.

Further, since the distinction is in this way relative to an epistemic field, it applies only to epistemic reasons. As I am using the terms 'prima facie' and 'all-things-considered', then, no distinction exists between *prima facie* and all-things-considered *practical* or *evaluative* reasons.[15]

The upshot is that in the case of epistemic reasons the epistemic field itself can be regarded as one of the terms in the epistemic reason relation.[16] It remains, however, as indicated by the Holmes/Watson example, that we typically talk of *specific* subsets of facts within an epistemic field constituting an epistemic reason, rather than talking of the epistemic field as a whole constituting a reason. For example, we may want to distinguish, within an epistemic field, between a specific set of facts that give reason to believe that p and another specific set of facts that give reason to believe that not-p, or between different sets of facts which give distinct reasons to believe that p; and to consider the relative strengths of these various specific epistemic reasons. In the epistemic case, then, R becomes a six-place relation as follows:

$R(e, \pi_i, t, d, x, \beta(p))$.
In x's epistemic field at t, facts π_i are a reason of degree of strength d for x to believe that p.

Of course we don't usually make all the terms in this relation explicit. Context and interest determine which ones to make explicit in a particular case. What is there reason to believe? What is there reason to believe given the available evidence, e? What is there reason for this particular person, x, to believe? What do these particular facts, π_i, give anyone reason to believe? What was there then, at t, reason to believe?[17] One reason why reference to the epistemic field is often redundant is that in the actual world (though not across possible words) fixing the actor and time fixes the epistemic field. However, the field may be what we want to talk about: in an inquiry into whether the police should have caught the criminal, for example, we are interested in what they could have known, that is, discovered. So though in a particular context it may be otiose to make some of the

---

[15] There can, however, be *prima facie warranted* evaluative and practical reasons; that is, there can be *prima facie* reason to believe that one has certain evaluative or practical reasons. Hence also, given the analysis of moral obligation in Chapter 12, there can be *prima facie* moral obligations. (This is not, I think, quite the same as Ross's notion of a *prima facie* moral obligation (Ross 2002 (1930): 19–20): our notion, seemingly unlike his, is strictly epistemic.)

[16] To maintain formal unity across epistemic, evaluative, and practical reasons we could treat the requirement that epistemic reasons are knowable facts as a *constraint* on what facts can be epistemic reasons, rather than treating the set of knowable facts as one of the *relata* of the epistemic reason relation. The latter approach will, however, be very convenient (though not at all indispensable) for the rest of our discussion.

[17] Correspondingly, we can write '$R(t, p)$', '$R(e, p)$', and so on.

terms of the epistemic reason relation explicit, any one of them may come into focus, in this or that context, depending on our interest.

2.4 Epistemic fields in space and time

Human inquiry is a dynamic process that takes place in space and time. The inquirer is spatio-temporally situated, and the activity of searching out some facts precludes him from discovering others. These facts and those will not belong to the same set of jointly discoverable facts. In reality, then, he always has before him more than one realizable epistemic field.

A way to capture this would be to think in terms of a tree structure of possible inquiries. Epistemic fields then consist of maximal sets of facts which the actor could discover jointly if he pursued a programme of inquiry 'down a branch of the tree' over some period. On this account, x's plural epistemic fields at t would consist of the various sets of facts that x could jointly discover, come to know, at t. What facts are in these fields is determined by the inquirer's epistemic powers, the actual technology of inquiry available to him, and the time available.

Take the fact that the lawn is wet. This fact may, in one of my current epistemic fields, be a reason for me to believe that it has rained recently. I'm not aware of it, because I haven't looked out of the window; but I could easily become aware of it by looking out, even though I'm busy checking what books are on my shelf. However, the same fact may also be in another of my current epistemic fields *without* being a reason for me to believe that it's been raining. For suppose that another fact in that epistemic field is that the water hose is on and leaking onto the lawn. Although I can't see that this is so just by looking out of the window, if I gave up my inquiries at the bookshelf I could discover it by going out and checking in the garden. In that case I have another epistemic field available to me right now that contains all those facts about the hose and the lawn, but fewer facts about the books on my shelf—and in this field the fact that the lawn is wet is *not* a reason for me to believe that it has rained recently.

So in the case of epistemic reasons, we could represent R like this:

$R(e_j, \pi_i, t, d, x, \beta(p))$
In x's j-th epistemic field at t facts π_i are a reason of degree of strength d for x to believe that p.

Similarly for S:

$S(e_j, x, t, \pi_i, x, \beta(p), t)$
In x's j-th epistemic field at t facts π_i give x sufficient reason to believe that p.

On this approach what reason there is for x to believe something at a time depends on which of his epistemic fields at that time we consider. It may not be clear, for example, whether there's sufficient reason for x to believe a given proposition at t. That's because a range of epistemic fields may be open to x at t, some of which provide sufficient reason to believe and some of which do not.

And yet we often want to ask, *tout court*, whether there is or was sufficient reason for *x* to believe some proposition at *t*. In particular, we can ask what evidence was available to a person at a time. We ask 'for example' whether there was enough evidence available for the police to have made a case against a suspect. It's unclear what we mean: do we mean what evidence was available in one or other of their epistemic fields at that time, or what evidence was available in *all* those fields taken together? Or something more complicated and/or vaguer—what evidence they could have been *expected* to discover? What they would have discovered if they had conducted a disciplined inquiry?[18]

In the example we've just considered, is there some reason for me to believe that it has rained? To answer we must fix my field. Suppose we fix it as the specific branch of the tree down which I in fact go. I don't go out into the garden but remain at the bookshelf checking the books. On that branch of the tree I could still look round and see that the lawn is wet. So relative to that branch there is reason for me to believe that it has rained. To see that the hose is leaking I would have to have got on to a different branch, by going out to the garden and seeing the water hose. In that branch the fact that the lawn is wet would be defeated as a reason for thinking it has rained. But I am not on that branch. These points also apply to Watson: if he devotes his inquiries to something incompatible with looking at the window sill, he is in a branching epistemic field which does not contain the fact that the scratches are there. If he does something compatible with noticing the scratches, then he is in a branching field in which there is reason for him to believe the criminal went through the window.

The dynamic picture of an inquiry tree of epistemic fields is more realistic than just talking about the actor's epistemic field as though it was a static, unitary thing (as though, so to speak, the actor could stop time while he explored his field). However, it is also more complex. The important point for our purposes is the relativity of epistemic reasons to epistemic fields. And note that it remains true, despite this relativity, that there can be reasons for a person to believe something, *whether or not he knows that there are, or could come to realize that there are by reflection alone*, just as there can be reasons for him to feel or do something whether or not he knows that, or could come to realize it by reflection.

These unknown but not unknowable epistemic reasons will be facts in his epistemic field that he hasn't accessed. They include facts that he couldn't access without undertaking an inquiry that involves action in space and time. However, as will be discussed in Chapter 5, we are also very often interested in a sense of 'reason' according to which a person could come to see that he has a reason *just through sufficient reflection*, without further inquiry of this kind. I shall call reasons in this sense *warranted* reasons, and I shall call a warranted sufficient reason a *warrant*. In the Holmes/Watson example, there's so much that Watson has failed to notice about the scene that he is not warranted in believing that the criminal escaped through the window. In fact he *has* no warranted reason

---

[18] Then there is the question of how much time was available to them. Perhaps in concrete cases this is fixed contextually: for example, if what we're interested in is how much of *the evidence discoverable before the attack* the police discovered. (These indeterminacies also generate corresponding indeterminacies in the distinction between *prima facie* and all-things-considered reasons.)

to think that at all, even though there *is* reason for him to think that, as Holmes truly says to him. The facts accessible to both Holmes and Watson provide a reason for Watson as well as Holmes to think that the criminal escaped through the window. It's just that Watson has not been observant enough to put himself in possession of that reason. Similarly, Holmes may say to himself: 'I have no reason at the moment to think Smith is the criminal, but there may well be a reason to think so that I haven't yet discovered—I'd better look into it.' What Holmes has done here is what I shall in Chapter 5 call an 'epistemic self-audit': he has asked himself what warranted reasons for belief he has, and decided that further inquiry is needed.

This concept of warrant is crucial for the whole theory of normativity in virtue of its connection with the possibility of self-audit, and thereby with justification, self-determination, and autonomy. As we shall see, however, warrant is not a new primitive concept; warranted reasons are definable in terms of the three reason predicates we have already introduced. So until we get to Chapter 5 we can concentrate on these.

2.5 Reasons and indicators

Do *all* epistemic reasons relativize to an epistemic field? One important aspect of this question turns on what we should say about a priori epistemic reasons. That there are such reasons will be important for the overall argument of this book. We shall treat them as reasons to believe in which the set of facts, π_i, is the empty set; they are, I shall say, *outright* reasons to believe. It does not follow, however, that such reasons lose their relativity to an epistemic field. It remains an open possibility that there might be outright reason to believe that p in e_1 but not in e_2. In that case we have:

$R(e_1, \varnothing, \beta p)$

but not

$R(e_2, \varnothing, \beta p)$

(where '$\varnothing$' denotes the empty set, or empty plurality). The proposition that p would be a priori in e_1 but not in e_2: aprioricity would be relative to epistemic fields.

These questions will be discussed in Chapter 6. For the moment we can focus on a posteriori epistemic reasons (reasons consisting of a non-empty set of facts).

Suppose that in the crime scene we have just been considering, the scratches on the window sill were, in fact, caused by the criminal's boots. In that case we can say that they *indicate* that the criminal went that way. Indication in this sense involves nothing more than a productive connection, deterministic, or propensity-based, between objects: X indicates Y if and only if X produces or tends to produce Y, or vice versa, or both X and Y are produced, or tend to be produced by a common cause.

The scratches indicate the criminal's path because they were produced by it. Medical symptoms, traces of a quarry, behavioural signs of a feeling, are indicators. The fact that bubbles are forming at the edges of the pan indicates that the water in it is about to boil.

Here the indicator and the fact indicated are effects of a common cause: the application of heat.

Indication gives us one of our concepts of evidence: indicative evidence that p consists of facts that indicate that p (see 9.2). However, though the scratches on the window are indicative evidence that the criminal went that way, they may or may not be a reason for Holmes and Watson to think that. In the first place, to be a reason for Holmes and Watson to believe that, they must be in Holmes's and Watson's epistemic field. Indicative evidence that's not in your e cannot be a reason for you to believe anything. But second, these scratches will be a reason for Holmes and Watson to think that the criminal went that way only if there's reason for Homes and Watson to *regard* them as indicative evidence of that. Holmes and Watson may spot them but remain unsure whether they really are indicative evidence or not. Similarly, if the discolorations on the bark of a tree indicate that the tree has some disease D, they are indicative evidence that the tree has the disease—whether or not anyone could ever observe them, and even if no one could ever establish that they indicate the presence of D. Seeing them on a tree will, however, give a person reason to believe that the tree has D only if there is also reason in his epistemic field to believe that they indicate D. Indicative evidence is not a subclass of reasons to believe.

We could, it is true, introduce the notion of an 'indicative reason'. On this account the fact that p would be an indicative reason to believe that q if and only if it indicates that q. There would then be an indicative reason for Holmes and Watson to believe that the criminal escaped through the window, even though, in the sense of 'reason' that I find more natural, there might not be reason for them to believe that—because their epistemic field included misleading testimony from the housekeeper, for example. *Indicative* reasons would not be relative to an epistemic field.

This, however, would be confusing terminology. I prefer to distinguish *indicative evidence* that p from *reason to believe that p*. That a fact qualifies as one of these does not entail that it qualifies as the other. True, taking something as an epistemic reason often involves taking it to be an indicator or hypothesizing that it is, as in the example of the scratches on the window. But that is not always so, and as will emerge in Chapter 9, could not always be so. The fundamental concept of an epistemic reason is that of a reason relation on an epistemic field. It can be convenient to talk of indicators as reasons, but that is only against a background assumption that the epistemic field in which we find ourselves *contains* the fact that facts of this kind are indicators.

2.6 'Should', 'ought', and 'right'

As well as judging whether there's reason for someone to ψ we also make judgements about whether they should or ought to ψ, or whether it's right for them to ψ.

'x should ψ', 'x ought to ψ' and 'It is right for x to ψ' can all be used to say that there is sufficient reason for x to ψ. In the practical case, as we noticed above, there may be more than one thing there is most reason to do—in which case there is no one thing that one should do. When more than one action is optimal it is false of any one of them that there is sufficient reason to do it. It remains true, however, that there is sufficient reason to do one or other of them—hence that one should do one or other of them—with the disjunction occurring within the scope of the 'should'.

I will call this use of 'should', 'ought', and 'right' the designated use, and where convenient I shall indicate it by an asterisk, e.g. 'should*'. When we wonder, for example, whether we ought to take the car; whether we should be feeling quite as annoyed as we are at the way we've been treated; whether it is right to conclude from the evidence that this substance is dangerous; we are using these terms in the designated way.

They are also regularly used in other ways, both normative and non-normative.[19] I illustrate for the case of 'should'. (Similar points could be made about 'ought' and 'right'.) Suppose A says 'It should be getting colder soon', B says 'You shouldn't park here—it's a double yellow line', and C says 'You should show some consideration for other people's feelings.' Is the word 'should' in these three statements being used in the designated way? Take the case of A. If A could have said exactly the same thing by saying 'There's sufficient reason to expect it to get colder soon' then he's using 'should' in the designated way. But without further context it's not clear that that is what he's saying. What about B's statement? Suppose B could have said the same thing by saying 'It's illegal to park on yellow lines'—is what he did say normative? On a positivist view of law, if that is all he meant then his use of 'should' is not normative at all. For according to legal positivism the fact that a law exists in a population is a fact about certain attitudes, dispositions, and actions in that population, and their causal antecedents. That this fact obtains may well be a reason to do something, such as driving on; nonetheless saying that it obtains is not in itself saying anything about reasons; and I shall argue in Chapter 4 that *normative* claims should always be understood as claims about reasons. Legal positivism is of course a contested position, so consider also the case of statements that can be agreed to be purely conventional. Consider 'You should move the king one square at a time.' If this sentence is used just to state the rules of chess then again 'should' is not being used in the designated way. Of course it may often be simply indeterminate what a person meant. It may be simply indeterminate, for example, whether B is just saying that it's illegal to park on double yellow lines, or saying that there's sufficient reason for you not to do so, because it's illegal. In that case it's indeterminate whether B's use of 'should' is the designated use.

As for C, in a given context he may be saying that you have a moral obligation to consider other people's feelings. I shall argue (12.3) that if you have a moral obligation to do something you have sufficient reason to do it. However, I don't think this is true by definition. So if C is using 'should' to express a moral obligation he is not using it in the designated way. This does not imply that the concept of moral obligation is not a normative concept at all—that question will be discussed in 12.2.

In the designated sense of these terms, it can be the case that a person should or ought to ψ—that it is right for that person to ψ—even though that person does not realize that

---

[19] Whether these various uses correspond to distinct *senses* is a question for semantic theory. For example, is the use of 'should' as an auxiliary verb—'If I should die, think only this of me'—a distinct sense of 'should'? Is the use of 'ought' to express moral obligation a distinct sense of 'ought'? I shall talk about the designated *sense* of 'should', 'ought', and 'right' when convenient, as well as the designated *use*, but in doing so I do not mean to answer the semantic question.

that is so. While this may be because he hasn't put two and two together, it may also be that he is simply unaware of some of the facts in virtue of which he should* ψ. Indeed it could be impossible for him to know what he should* do.

As I have said, however, we shall also consider the notion of *warrant*. A basic principle governing this notion will be that when actors are warranted in ψ-ing they can (in principle) *tell* that they are, solely by reflecting on what there is sufficient reason for them to believe that they know. The fact that one can come to a conclusion about one's warrants by reflection alone is highly important. Such reflection may lead to the conclusion that one doesn't yet know what one should* ψ—further inquiry would be necessary to answer the question, though sometimes it may remain unanswerable. In the Holmes/Watson example, Watson is not *warranted* in believing that the criminal escaped through the window. Given how little he's noticed, there would have to be some faulty reasoning on his part for him to come to that conclusion. Yet Holmes could intelligibly say that Watson should* have concluded that the criminal escaped through the window: the facts accessible to both of them provide sufficient reason for Watson as well as Holmes to reach that conclusion. There was sufficient reason for a conclusion on Watson's part there, in his epistemic field—it's just that he wasn't observant enough to put himself in possession of that reason.

2.7 Can 'R' and 'R$_o$' be defined in terms of 'S'? Degrees of belief and feeling

'S', we have argued, cannot be defined in terms of 'R' or 'R$_o$'—but what of the possibility of defining 'R' or 'R$_o$' in terms of 'S'?

I can see no way of doing it for the case of specific reasons. Could we say that a specific reason to ψ is one which in the absence of other reasons pro or con constitutes a sufficient reason to ψ? That is clearly false for epistemic and evaluative reasons. But in any case it cannot be a definition of 'specific reason', since 'in the absence of other reasons' refers to specific reasons. Even in the practical case, orderings of actions by R$_o$ do not 'reach back' to the underlying specific reasons—they 'lose' that information. So it is unsurprising that neither 'S' nor 'R$_o$' can define 'R'.[20]

However, the case of overall reasons is not quite so unpromising. The approach is most plausible in the case of actions. For here it can be argued that in any choice set there will always be some action or disjunction of actions that there is sufficient reason to do. A choice set is an exhaustive set of alternate actions open to an individual at a time. We can consider restricted choice sets that result from ruling out some of these actions.

---

[20] John Broome proposes that 'a reason why x ought to ψ' can be defined as 'an explanation of why x ought to ψ'. (Broome, forthcoming, Chapter 3). If this worked for 'ought' it would work for 'S'. But explanation in the *relevant* sense is explanation in terms of reasons, and thus presupposes the notion of a reason. A fact explains, or contributes to explaining, why you ought to ψ just if it is a reason to ψ. If you don't understand why the fact is a reason to ψ you don't understand the explanation.

We then define 'there is more (overall) reason to α_1 than to α_2' as 'in the restricted choice set α_1, α_2 there is sufficient reason to α_1'. And we can define 'there is reason to α_1' as 'there is some α_2 in the choice set such that there is more reason to α_1 than to α_2. (So in the case where all actions in the choice set are equally choice-worthy it is false of any one of them that there is some degree of reason to do it and false of any one of them that there is sufficient reason to do it.)

What about the case of beliefs and feelings? Here we might try appealing to the notion of *degrees* of feeling and belief. The idea is to define degree of reason in terms of the degree of belief or feeling for which there is sufficient reason. In the case of feelings we could say that π_i give you some degree of reason to ϕ, just in case π_i give you sufficient reason to ϕ *to that same degree*. And likewise in the case of beliefs we could say that π_i give you some degree of reason to $\beta(p)$, just in case π_i give you sufficient reason to $\beta(p)$ *to that same degree*. Instead of saying, for any e, that it gives such-and-such degrees of reason to believe various things, we say on this approach that it gives sufficient reason to believe various things to various degrees.

But this line of thought will not work, in either case. If there is some small degree of reason to feel annoyed, does it follow that there is sufficient reason to feel annoyed to the same small degree? I think not. There may be insufficient reason to feel annoyed at all, even though there is some degree of reason. The degree to which some fact gives one reason to feel something, and the strength of feeling for which it gives one reason, are separate issues. There is, for example, strong reason to fear midges slightly, and weak reason to fear a normally placid but very occasionally dangerous elephant strongly.

In the case of belief this approach is even less plausible. For despite the appeal made to this notion by Bayesians, belief does not (literally) come in degrees. The contrast with feelings is telling. One can literally have a feeling more or less strongly. But one cannot literally believe more or less strongly, as against being more or less strongly *inclined* to believe. To give sense to the notion of a degree of belief one must interpret it: either (i) in terms of a degree of inclination to believe that p; or (ii) in terms of a belief about what degree of reason there is to believe that p; or (iii) in terms of how much reason there is to make a practical conjecture, or 'working hypothesis', for the purpose of action even in the absence of belief—e.g. that the stock market will go down, when one doesn't have much evidence either way, or that the enemy will attack on the right rather than the left, when one has no specific reason to believe either.[21] If degree of belief is thought of purely as a psychological concept, the only plausible interpretation is (i). But we shall argue in 9.6 to 9.8 that everything a rational choice theorist needs can be provided in terms of (ii) and (iii), without any psychological notion of 'degrees of belief'.

---

[21] Apart from the options mentioned here there is the usage 'I strongly believe that.' Two points about it. (i) Saying 'I believe that p' in many contexts disclaims knowledge or certainty ('I believe you'll get to the station if you take this road here.') In such contexts it's odd to say 'I strongly believe.' (ii) 'I strongly believe that' typically occurs in ethical or policy discussions—'I strongly believe that this will have the most awful consequences for our party.' Here, while not claiming knowledge or certainty, one is nevertheless intending to issue a strong warning, make it clear that one disassociates oneself from a particular policy decision, etc.

However, even if there are no literal degrees of belief, can we not always convert the proposition that there is reason of such-and-such degree to believe that p into the proposition that there is sufficient reason to believe that it's probable to such-and-such degree that p? Does this give us a reduction of R to S in the epistemic case?

There is this equivalence; the question is, whether it can be exploited to provide an illuminating reduction of R to S in terms of an *independently* explicable notion of probability. Or is 'probable' itself definable in terms of epistemic reasons? Does 'It's probable to some degree that p' simply mean 'There's reason of some degree to believe that p'— with the latter phrase being the *analysans* rather than the *analysandum*? We shall argue in Chapter 9 that that is what 'probable' means, and that *overall degree of reason to believe* (R_o) satisfies the probability calculus.

Finally we come to a fundamental objection to these attempted definitions. It is that they overlook the difference between specific and overall reasons. In the case of beliefs, a variety of different facts within an epistemic field may give stronger or weaker specific reasons to believe that p, while other facts within the field may give specific reasons to believe that not-p. To get the overall degree of reason to believe—which may or may not be a sufficient reason—we need to take them all into account. Analogous points apply to evaluative and practical reasons.

It is worth noting here the difference between rational choice theory and the general philosophy of reasons. The former is a theoretical construct whose usefulness should be measured in terms of its own projects. From the point of view of the philosophy of reasons, however, it has the potential to be seriously misleading. For what *is* the project of rational choice theory? An immediate question is whether it is descriptive or normative. If it is the former, then the rational-choice-theoretical notions 'x should α', or 'there is more reason for x to α_1 than α_2', are not normative, and not to be identified with the concepts studied in this book. If, on the other hand, we think of the theory as a set of axioms specifying a complete theory of practical reasons, there is much to criticize, even if a Normative version of rational choice theory is restricted in its remit, for example, to being a theory of cost-effectiveness. Some of these criticisms could be derived from the positive views that will be defended in this book. I shall note this at some points. However, our overall aim is a philosophical account of normativity in all its aspects; a Critical study from this standpoint of expected utility theory (for example) would be a special first-order normative topic in its own right.

2.8 Interpretative explanations

In explaining people's beliefs, feelings, and actions we assume that they take themselves to have, and in one or another way respond to, reasons. How such interpretative explanations work will be discussed in Chapter 10. Clearly, however, the directly relevant question in an explanation of this kind is what a person *takes* to be reasons to ψ. He may be wrong in thinking that these were sufficient reasons, or even reasons at all. Yet it's still important that we should be able to understand why the reason the actor took himself to have could have *been* a reason, and why he took it to be so. Otherwise something remains that is unaccountable from the intelligible or interpretative point of view. And while it sometimes has to be left like that—something unaccountable, in the sense of normatively unintelligible, remains in the act—the preferred outcome of explanation in terms of reasons is that such unintelligibility should be dispelled.

Explanations in terms of reasons are causal explanations. When you act from reasons what directly causes your act is your factual and normative beliefs. Your factual beliefs are themselves caused—in favourable circumstances—by the facts that make them true. However, neither your factual nor your normative beliefs are explicable exclusively in terms of causation by the facts. The capacity to form factual beliefs requires the capacity to form normative beliefs, and that capacity in turn requires reason-sensitivity. *This* sensitivity—to truths about reason relations—is not a causal form of sensitivity, as the various forms of sensory receptivity are. There are no 'normative facts' that *could* cause normative beliefs.

These claims will of course be discussed and defended. We shall see that they require no departure from a sensible naturalism (20.7). Nonetheless, their implication is that while interpretative explanation certainly has to be 'causally adequate' (in Max Weber's phrase), it also goes beyond the category of purely causal relations among worldly states, requiring also 'adequacy at the level of meaning'. For we attribute to an actor whose action, belief or feeling is interpretatively explained *the capacity to acknowledge reasons* of the relevant kind: intelligible actors are reason-sensitive actors, to some greater or lesser degree. They may be more sensitive to some kinds of reasons than to others, or not sensitive to some kinds of reasons at all. In all cases, however, what they are sensitive to are the reason relations that have been discussed in this chapter. And this is not a causal form of sensitivity.

It is somewhat misleading to call these 'normative reasons', for there *are* no 'non-normative reasons'. If we say that the reason why the bridge fell is that its cables had rusted, we are referring to the cause of its fall. The fact that the cables had rusted was not a reason *for the bridge to* fall. The bridge does not have reasons. Likewise if the reason the ice melted was that the door of the freezer was left open: here again the word 'reason' signifies nothing more than cause; we are not giving an interpretative explanation of the ice's reasons for melting.[22] It is similarly misleading to distinguish an explanatory and a normative concept of a reason. There are just reason relations, and these reason relations can feature both in the context of interpretative explanation (in or out of the actor's attitude contents) or in the context of deliberation about what there is reason to think, feel, or do.

2.9 Epistemic, evaluative, and practical: an irreducible trichotomy

The trichotomy of reasons—epistemic, evaluative, and practical—is irreducible. We cannot yet set out the case for this view fully, since it is best vindicated in the context of a complete theory of normativity, one that also covers the epistemology and

---

[22] Perhaps the use of 'reason' to refer to cause has some connection with epistemic reasons. The fact that the cables are rusty is 'a reason for it to fall' in the sense that in a sufficiently rich epistemic field it is a reason to expect the bridge to fall; the fact that the door of the freezer was left open is likewise a reason to believe the ice has melted.

metaphysics of the normative. We shall return to it in 20.2. But we can take a preliminary look.

On a purely semantic test it is trivially true that there are epistemic, evaluative, and practical reasons. There are truth-expressing sentences which contain the corresponding predicates—'reason to β'; 'reason to ϕ'; 'reason to α'. To reject the trichotomist view is presumably not to deny that. It is to hold that sentences in one or more of these classes are definable in some way that shows we can always eliminate one or more of these predicates; or more weakly, that in some sense, despite the surface data, one or more of these types of reason is not 'really' a fundamental category.

Clearly this possibility cannot be ruled out in advance. One alternative to trichotomism that seems to me to be fairly influential may be called *epistemicism about reasons*. Its guiding idea is that all talk of evaluative and practical reasons can be analysed in terms of other normative concepts. Thus one might postulate a valoric scale of goodness and badness, and/or a deontic concept we can refer to as *Ought*. One or both of these would be taken as primitive. Propositions about evaluative and practical reasons would be analysable in valoric and/or deontic terms. Value and obligation, not evaluative and practical 'reasons', would be taken as basic. What one Ought to do would be determined by what action has the most valuable outcome, or by some set of principles determining what Ought to be done, or some combination of these.

Perhaps we could push this further and analyse epistemic reasons out as well. One line of thought would treat them as a priori epistemic probabilities. We would also have an irreducible epistemic Ought which could govern beliefs, including beliefs about these probabilities. Thus talk of reasons would completely disappear.

The contrary view, which we shall argue for, is that the three types of reasons should be taken as basic. Propositions about value all reduce to propositions about reasons, epistemic, evaluative, and practical. As for propositions about moral obligation, these reduce to propositions about evaluative reasons, in this case about what there is reason to blame.

To be sure, even if this is a viable direction of analysis we cannot assume it to be the only possible one. The epistemicist's direction of analysis may be another. Normative concepts may be inter-definable in the way that the truth-functional operators are inter-definable. In the case of the operators it's not obvious, though it's not ruled out, that philosophical reasons can be given for taking some pair of operators, say negation and implication, as primitive, even though alternatives are formally available. Likewise in the normative case. If reductive analysis can be done in more than one way, then the case for making the trichotomy of reasons basic will have to be philosophical. We shall consider some philosophical reasons in 20.2.

Another somewhat influential view may be called *pragmatism about reasons*. This says that the only irreducible propositions about reasons are propositions about practical reasons. What to believe or feel is in reality a *practical* question. You have reason to believe or feel what it will be useful, practically valuable, for you to believe or feel.

To this it is natural to respond by distinguishing between reason to believe or feel something, and reason to bring it about that you believe or feel it. Bringing it about that you believe something, or feel something (causing yourself to be believe or feel it) is an action, so the reasons for doing so are indeed practical reasons. And there can be such practical reasons. I may be on an extremely dangerous mission which there is no reason to believe I will survive. But it will greatly aid my peace of mind if I *believe* that I am fated to survive it. So if swallowing this drug or saying this prayer will in fact cause me to believe that I am fated to survive then I have a practical reason to swallow the drug or say the prayer. It does not follow that I have any epistemic reason to believe that I will survive. In this situation there is reason for me to bring it about that I believe something that there *is* no reason for me to believe.

The same point holds for the distinction between evaluative and practical reasons.[23] There is, for example, no reason for me to admire my boss's taste in wine, but it's important for my promotion prospects that I manifest admiration. The best way for me to do this is actually to feel admiration, so there is practical reason to bring it about that I do feel it, if there is some means available of causing myself to feel it. In this case there is practical reason for me to bring it about that I admire something which there is no reason for me to admire.

Once a pair of reason relations has been clearly distinguished—an epistemic and a practical reason, or an evaluative and a practical reason—we can say without contradiction that one holds when the other does not. There can be reason for me to bring it about that I believe or feel something that there is no reason for me to believe or feel, and *vice versa*. Cases of this kind, the trichotomist will say, give us no reason at all to deny the distinction between epistemic and practical, or evaluative and practical, reasons.

This point seems to refute pragmatism on its own. But pragmatists have some possible replies. We shall examine these and reject them in 20.2, on grounds to do with the essential connection between reasons and self-determination. Meanwhile I shall assume that the trichotomy of epistemic, evaluative, and practical reasons is fundamental.

2.10 Facts, reasons, and supervenience

Finally a note about reasons and supervenience. Reasons do not supervene on facts. They *are* facts. Consider the following:

(1) The reason for Jim to have a drink is that he will enjoy it.

We can treat this as an identity statement:

(1*) The reason for Jim to have a drink = the fact that Jim will enjoy having a drink.

The singular term on the left picks out the fact by means of one of its properties, namely, being a reason for Jim to have a drink. Thus we have:

---

[23] Many philosophers have thought that there are no evaluative reasons; far fewer have thought there are no epistemic reasons. Not surprisingly, then, it is much more common to find all reasons for feeling treated as though they were practical reasons to bring it about that one felt something than it is to find the same treatment given to epistemic reasons.

(1**) ɩx: R(x, Jim, have a drink) = the fact that Jim will enjoy having a drink.

Compare:

(2) The father of Jane is Jim.
(2*) The father of Jane = Jim.
(2**) ɩx: father(x, Jane) = Jim.

The structure is exactly the same in each case: each proposition is true if the item referred to on the left by means of a relation it has to some other items is identical with the item referred to on the right.

It is easy to be misled about this. One can say, for example, there's reason for Jim to have a drink *in virtue of the fact* that he will enjoy it. But this says nothing more than (1); it says a little less, in that it leaves open the possibility that there are other reasons for him to have a drink. All it says is:

(3) The fact that Jim will enjoy having a drink is a reason for him to have one.

The observation that reasons are facts is important, in that it highlights one of the ways in which a demonstration that all normative properties are reducible to the reason relations would be illuminating. It would show that the rather puzzling relation of supervenience that holds between the normative and the factual simply reduces to those reason relations. Since reasons are facts, if you fix the facts you fix the reasons,[24] and thus if normative properties are all reducible to reason relations, you fix them too.

However, these points do not show that propositions about reason relations are themselves factual. Granted that supervenience reduces to the reason relations, we can still ask about the epistemology and ontology of these relations, and thus of a proposition such as (3). That meta-normative question will be the topic of Part IV. Realism—the view that propositions about reasons relations are about one or another distinctive kind of fact—is one answer to it, an answer that will be rejected in this book. Irrespective of that meta-normative issue, however, it would still be worthwhile to replace the notion of supervenience, which has caused so much puzzlement, with the notion of a reason. At least we would then have one puzzle to deal with instead of two.

---

[24] This assumes that propositions purely about outright reasons are necessarily true or false, a claim to be defended in Chapter 8.

3

INDEXICALITY, UNIVERSALIZABILITY, AND THE RANGE OF REASONS

In this chapter we examine a distinction that will serve us as a tool throughout this book, especially in Part III: the distinction between neutral and relative reasons. Both kinds of reasons are 'universalizable'—this is an intrinsic property of reasons as such. We should, however, also examine the *range* of reasons. Reasons are universal: they apply to all actors—but over what entities does 'all actors' range?

A thesis that looks plausible is that only an actor that can grasp a reason as a reason falls within the range of that reason. If you can't grasp it as a reason it's not a reason for you. I shall call this thesis 'cognitive internalism'; it will be discussed in Sections 3.8 and 3.9.

But then what is it to grasp something as a reason? Does it require the concept of a reason? We act for reasons, but we mostly do so unreflectively. In what circumstances do explicit thoughts about reasons come to the fore? If an actor can be said to be acting for reasons must we also impute the capacity to formulate questions about those reasons in explicit terms? On the whole, the answer seems to be 'no'. Nonetheless this capacity, the capacity of *self-determination* as I shall call it, will be of great significance in this book. We shall see in later chapters that the very notion of a reason is shaped by it.

3.1 Reflexivity, acting from reasons, and self-determination

In thinking about what to believe, to feel, or do, I don't normally formulate reflexive questions to myself of the form 'Is there reason for me to ψ now?', or 'Should I ψ now?'. Quite often I have no explicit thoughts about the present moment (except in the sense that that my thinking is tensed), more often I have no explicit thoughts about myself, and even more often, I have no explicit thoughts about reason relations.

Seeing a delivery man taking the path to the side of the house I think to myself 'He must be coming round the back...where's the key to the back door...in the kitchen probably'—and I head for the kitchen. Seeing a lorry blocking the middle of the road

I steer for the pavement hoping to get past that way. Or, hearing that our flight has been cancelled yet again, I say to you 'This is getting quite intolerable—they really must start paying out some substantial compensation'. And perhaps I go home and write a letter.

Ordinary action and reaction takes place under conditions of everyday unreflectiveness: within accepted frameworks of belief, projects, intentions, taken for granted environments. Yet it's also true that we can be asked why we thought there was reason to do, believe, or feel what we did, that we can be asked for advice about what to do, and that we can consciously reflect in our own case on our reasons, in particular, on whether there is or was sufficient reason to do this or that. This last case will be our topic in 5.1 and 5.2. It requires a capacity for what I there call *epistemic self-audit*, that is, reflection as to whether some particular belief, action, or feeling is warranted, or whether further inquiry is needed.

In all these contexts, of self-explanation, advice to others, and reflective self-audit, we move beyond everyday unreflectiveness to varying degrees. Reasons, considerations about the actor and the moment may be cited in fragmentary and allusive ways or they may become more explicit. At the limit of normative ascent[1] they are fully formulated as considerations about what *reasons* there are (or were, or were thought to be) for the actor to ψ now (or then), and about the strength of those reasons.

Normative ascent normally takes place when a decision is difficult, or its nature, subsequently, controversial. Should I have gone on to the pavement? Did I slow down enough? Couldn't I see that someone might run out of the garden gate? How pressing was my business? Is there really much reason to be annoyed at this flight cancellation? Has it got to the point where there's enough reason to complain?

In retrospective self-scrutiny and assessment I can often recover to a very considerable extent what my reasons for acting actually were and formulate them as reasons. Obviously I may not have perfect recall, I may be prone to self-delusion, and the line between recall and retrospective hypothesis can be difficult to draw. Nevertheless, I can often give a reflective account of my reasons, even though I did not consciously formulate them to myself at the time. And I can ask myself whether they were sufficient reasons.

How much of this capacity for reflective self-scrutiny and audit is required for an actor to be describable as responsive to reasons? *Reflection* about reasons requires possession of the concepts of self, time, and reason. Must an actor possess these concepts to be *acting* for reasons? I headed for the kitchen because I thought the delivery man would come to the back door, because I thought I'd need to open it, and because I thought the key was in the kitchen. Though I didn't think about it at the time, those were my reasons,[2] and

---

[1] I borrow this phrase from John Broome.

[2] That is: that the delivery man would come to the back door, that I'd need to open it, that the key was in the kitchen. Often when we refer to a person's reasons in this way we are referring to what he *took* to be the facts; our reference is then not to facts but to the putative facts which he thought obtained. (The status of such 'putatively real' irreals is discussed in Chapter 17.) But if we know that the facts were as he took them to be, we may refer to those facts as his reasons: 'He went to the kitchen because the key was there'. Either way, however, the immediate *explanans* of the act is what the actor *took* to be the facts.

I could tell you that. The dog headed for the back of the shed because it wanted to catch the cat, saw that it had run into the shed and expected it to come out through an opening at the back when it thought the coast was clear. Here too one might say that those were its reasons—even though the dog could *not* tell you that. It does not have the capacities of reflective self-scrutiny and reflective deliberation, does not engage in normative ascent, and it is debatable how far one can attribute to it a conception of itself, of present and future, let alone of a reason.

We seem readier to impute reasons than to impute the concept of a reason. At the same time, however, explanation by reasons is narrower than teleological explanation. We can explain plant behaviour teleologically—for example, when we say that a plant's leaves move in order to track a light source—but we are not attributing reasons to the plant or its leaves. In explaining the dog's behaviour, in contrast, we are attributing reasons even though we don't attribute to it possession of the concept of a reason. Are we imputing *reason-responsiveness*—not just recognition of the facts, but also recognition that they stand in a certain reason relation to the action? Does the dog recognize reasons and act from them? If it can see where the cat is likely to come out *soon*, and where *it* needs to be *itself* to ambush the cat—without having concepts of time and self—why can't it also see these facts as *reasons* to head for the back of the shed, without having thoughts which require possession of the concept of a reason? Can't we say that it is heading for the back of the shed because it thinks that that's where it's got to be to catch the cat? That means that it is locating itself within a map of its environment. To explain its behaviour in this way we must place it within its own plan, based on its own self-locating map, and take the plan as its reason for what it does.

Acts directed by responsiveness to reasons involve awareness, at some level, of what there is *reason* for *self* to do *now*. How much reflective ability, and what degree of concept possession, must be attributed in order to attribute such awareness and thus reason-responsiveness? There seems to be no very clear-cut answer: just a spectrum of intuitions ranging from the restrictive to the liberal. We shall pursue the issue a little further in 19.2. Meanwhile for clarity I stipulate that a being can be said to act *from* (and not just *for*) reasons only if it has the capacity for full-blooded reason-responsiveness— the capacity reflectively to identify and audit reasons, at a level that does require possession of the concept of a reason, of itself, and of the present. It must have the capacity; it need not actually be exercising it when it acts from reasons. When I go to the kitchen to get the key to the back door I am acting from reasons, even though I do not reflect on these reasons.

This capacity to identify and audit reasons is the capacity of self-determination; a response from reasons is a self-determined response. We can and do impute reasons to the dog, but I suggest that we are not thereby compelled to regard it as self-determining, an actor capable of recognizing and acting from reasons. This notion of self-determination will be important throughout the rest of this book.

3.2 Indexicality: neutral and relative reasons

To act from a reason I must recognize it as a reason for me to act now. However, it does not follow that the reason *itself* must consist in an indexical fact about me now.[3] Plenty of reason-giving facts are not indexical.

The fact that hot air rises is a reason for me to believe that if a balloon were heated it would rise. The fact that a liquid turns a litmus paper red is a reason for me to believe it's an acid. The fact that paper is permeable is a reason not to transport liquids in a paper bag. The fact that someone behaves with heroism and self-sacrifice is a reason to admire them. These are all reasons, reasons for you and for me, even though they are not *about* you or me. They are expressed in tensed sentences, but the tense is inessential. One doesn't need to know *when* the liquid turned the litmus paper red to know that it's an acid; likewise, if you hear about someone's heroism and self-sacrifice your admiration is reason-supported[4] even if you don't know when it happened. In all these cases you have reason to ψ now, even though the fact which gives you reason is not about some relation to the present moment.

In stating reason-giving facts I may use demonstratives to pick out objects implicated in those facts: *this* paper bag; *this* liquid; *that* heroic act. I might establish the reference of the demonstrative by a description that uses indexicals (though I can also do so just by selective attention)—'the paper bag I'm holding'; 'the liquid in my test tube'; 'the heroism I'm reading about in the paper'. However, that does not mean that these reason-giving facts are indexical. We should distinguish (i) whether indexicals feature in securing demonstrative identification of some object; and (ii) whether they are essential to the reason-giving force of a fact about that object (i.e. to that fact having that reason relation). The liquid in my test tube turned the paper red. That gives me reason to believe, of it, that it's an acid. But that it's in *my* test tube *now* is no part of what gives me reason to believe it's an acid.

Often, however, the reason is *itself* an indexical fact. The fact that *I* have promised to come to see you gives me a reason to come to see you. The fact that *I* am being called to the information desk is a reason for me to go there.

My mother is moved by an old photograph of a house. She has reason to be: it's a photo of the house *she* was born in. You look at the list of people to be sacked and you realize that there's reason to think you'll be sacked—why? Because you see that *your* name is on the list.

The fact that the train is meant to leave in 5 minutes from *now*, and that it's *now* 12.15, is a good reason to believe that the train will leave at 12.20. The fact that you're *now* an hour late gives me reason to be annoyed with you, and to remonstrate with you when you arrive.

We can say that a reason-giving fact is *essentially* indexical when the actor, in order to grasp it as a reason for *him*, or a reason for him to ψ at some *time* identified by its relation to the present, must grasp it indexically as a fact about himself or about the present; that

---

[3] We can assume that indexicals of place are analysable in terms of indexicals of person and time.
[4] We shall say that a response for which there is some reason is *reason-supported*. This is distinct from 'reasonable' and 'rational', which have different meanings.

is, when its indexicality is essential to its reason-giving force. In this case we shall say that the reason is actor-relative, or temporally relative, or just 'relative' for short. A reason is relative if and only if it is essentially indexical. When that is not the case, when the reason-giving force of the fact, for the actor, does not rest on its indexicality we shall say the reason is *neutral*. Both kinds of reason exist, even though in all cases, as we noted, to respond to a reason now I must in some sense recognize it as a reason for me now. Indexicals of person and time appear in my thought whenever I take myself to have reason, but that does not mean that they appear in my representation of the fact, as I take it to be, that *gives* me the reason. The reason in question is relative only if indexicals must appear in my representation of that fact for me to recognize the fact as a reason for me, or as a reason for me at some time characterized by reference to the present.

The distinction between relative and neutral reasons will be of some importance in this book. In Section 3.4 I set out another (equivalent) approach to it, which makes it easier to observe how it interacts with the universality and the universalizability of reasons. This discussion will in turn give rise to a further question that can usefully be broached in this chapter: granted that reasons are universal, over what domain of actors do they range? Reason are reasons for everyone—but who or what is covered by 'everyone'?

3.3 Reasons as nominal or substantial facts

First, however, we should consider an important question about what it means to say that reasons are facts. I have just been referring, in the previous section, to indexical facts—but can a *fact* be indexical?

It depends on what notion of a fact we choose to use. As noted in 1.2, two concepts of fact feature in this study: the nominal and the substantial concept. The nominal concept maps facts onto true propositions. In the nominal sense of 'fact' the fact that p is identical with the fact that q if and only if the statement that p is true and has the same sense as, expresses the same proposition as, the statement that q.[5] One might say that the nominal fact that p is identical with *its being true that p*, or *the truth of the proposition that p*: one could say 'Its being true that p is a reason to ψ', or 'the truth of the proposition that p is a reason to ψ'. We can regard nominal facts as a *sui generis* type of abstract item standing in a one–one relation to true propositions, or we can simply, though somewhat artificially, identify them with true propositions.

In contrast, on the substantial concept of a fact, facts involve substantial properties, *attributes*, as I shall also call them. The substantial fact that p is identical with the substantial fact that q if and only if the fact that p is isomorphically constituted of the same attributes and (where relevant) objects as the fact that q. Attributes of things are to be understood neither as senses nor as (Fregean) semantic values of predicates. They can

---

[5] Sentences containing indexicals of time and person express distinct propositions when uttered by different persons, or at different times, even though they can be held to preserve the same 'meaning'. 'Sense' and 'proposition' go with mode of presentation of truth conditions, rather than with 'meaning' in this conventional sense. (Points made in this and the next paragraph are further discussed in 7.3 and 16.1.)

be described or picked out in different ways, by predicates that differ in sense. We may not be aware that these different predicates pick out one and the same attribute (for example, that being live, as an attribute of electrical circuits, is having electrons flowing through).[6]

Global realists hold that *all* true assertions state that a substantial fact obtains. They may also hold, naturalistically, that all substantial facts have causal powers, or they may deny that. For example, they may hold that normative facts are substantial facts but deny that they have causal powers. Either way they need a special substantial notion of fact, one that will fit their correspondence conception of truth, for global realism postulates that truth is a relation between a proposition and something non-propositional that makes the proposition true. However, as I emphasized in the Introduction, to reject global realism's conception of fact is not to reject the notion of a substantial fact as such. It is quite consistent to reject the correspondence theory but still maintain that factual assertions state, while purely normative assertions do not state, that a substantial fact obtains.

So should we take reasons to be nominal or substantial facts? The answer is not obvious; either or both options might be viable. However, taking reasons to be nominal facts has at least the advantage that some things can be said more easily.

In the nominal sense of 'fact' it makes perfectly good sense to talk of indexical facts. An indexical fact is simply a true proposition expressible by a declarative sentence containing indexicals. We can refer to it by means of a nominalized sentential clause, 'the fact that . . .', where the gap is filled by the sentence in question. By this definition the fact that my name is on the list is an indexical fact. And by the identity conditions for nominal facts this is not the same fact as the fact that John Skorupski's name is on the list, since the sentences 'My name is on the list' and 'John Skorupski's name is on the list' differ in sense. In contrast, in the substantial sense of 'fact' it makes no sense to talk of indexical facts. The fact that my name is on the list consists in the possession of the very same attribute, by the very same particular object, as the fact that John Skorupski's name is on the list. Indexicality is a feature of the *mode of presentation* of a substantial fact.

Suppose we take reasons to be substantial facts. The fact that my name is on the list is a reason for me to feel desperately worried, and a reason for me to take evading action. So is the fact that JS's name is on the list a reason for me to respond and to act in those ways? Well, it's the very same substantial fact. So if reasons are substantial facts we can conclude that the fact that JS's name is on the list is a reason for *me* to respond and act in those ways. It's a reason for *me*—but I don't know that it is unless I know that I am JS.

Do we then want to say that the fact that I am John Skorupski is part of my reason for being anxious, and for taking evading action? That can sound right in appropriate contexts, and is unexceptionable if we are taking reasons to be nominal facts. But if we take reasons to be substantial facts, then it can be objected that there *is* no such substantive fact as the fact that I am John Skorupski, since identity is not an attribute (a substantial

---

[6] Clarity would be served if instead of talking about substantial and nominal facts we talked instead about facts and truths. But I have found that this becomes too circumlocutory and distracting.

property). I believe this objection is sound.[7] On the view that reasons are substantial facts we should hold that some facts can be known by you to be a reason *now* for *you* only under the appropriate indexical mode of presentation (or we could say that reasons are not just facts *simpliciter* but pairs consisting of a fact and a mode of presentation).

Taking that line, we can say that a reason is *relative* when, if I am to recognize it as a reason for me to ψ, or as a reason for me to ψ at some time characterized by reference to the present, the fact which constitutes the reason must be *presented* to me in the corresponding indexical way (the 'me/now' way). Thus suppose the fact that a car is heading for me out of control is the fact that that car is heading for JS at 2.15 on a particular date. That substantial fact is both an agent-relative and a temporally-relative reason for me to act, because for me to recognize it as a reason for me to jump now, it needs to be presented to me in the 'me/now' way. In contrast the fact that any contribution to some particular charity at any time will be used effectively by that charity for famine relief is a reason for me to act which is neither agent-relative nor temporally relative. I can recognize it a reason for me to contribute to the charity now, without it being presented to me in the me/now way.

I shall take reasons to be nominal, not substantial, facts. It is at least easier to talk about the logic of reasons in that way. In 19.5 we shall consider whether there are decisive arguments that favour one view or the other. But for the moment we turn to another (though equivalent) way of making the distinction between relative and neutral reasons. This way will allow us to make a crisp connection with the universality and universalizability of reasons, so it is worth analysing it in some detail, although it involves some complication.

3.4 Relativity to agent, patient, and thinker

It is familiar, for the particular case of agents and practical reasons, from Thomas Nagel's *The Possibility of Altruism*[8]—in this case it's the distinction between what are now often called 'agent-neutral' and 'agent-relative' reasons.[9] Consider the schema:

(It's being the case) that Pα gives x reason to α

where 'x' is replaceable by terms denoting agents and 'α' by terms denoting actions open to x.[10] (That is, for any given x, 'α' ranges over the action-types open to x.) If all instances of the schema are true then 'P' is a *reason-giving predicate on agents and actions open to the agent*. Now we define agent-neutral and agent-relative reasons as follows:

---

[7] See 7.2.
[8] Nagel 1970, Chapters 7 and 10.
[9] Nagel 1970. I am using the terms 'agent-neutral' and 'agent-relative' to coincide respectively with the terms 'objective' and 'subjective' as Nagel uses in them in this book. More recently The terms 'agent-neutral' and 'agent-relative' have come to be used in other, rather confusing, ways (including by Nagel). However, I believe Nagel's original distinction, as he made it in his 1970, is the useful one for a general study of the logic of reasons.
[10] Uniformly replaceable—though we can allow, for example, pronominal reference back, as in 'It's being the case that John has promised gives *him* (namely, John) a reason to...' Note that since we have taken reasons to be nominal facts, quantification into a statement of a *nominal* fact is quantification into an intensional context and should be understood substitutionally. (I have benefitted from discussion of this point with Elya Zardini.)

(i) If 'P' contains a free occurrence of 'x' then it is an agent-relative predicate. If it does not, it is an agent-neutral predicate.
(ii) A reason for action which is expressible by an agent-neutral predicate is agent-neutral. A reason for action which is not so expressible is agent-relative.

Suppose I have promised to send Mira a book. We could say that the predicate which expresses, in universal terms, my consequent reason for sending her a book is given by the schema:

(It's being the case) that x has promised to α gives x reason to α.

This reason cannot be expressed by an agent-neutral reason-giving predicate: that is, one that contains no free occurrence of the relevant agent-denoting term.

The question is whether the *reason*, not the action, can be specified without use of a term denoting the agent. Suppose the actions open to you are confessing or shooting yourself. 'Shooting yourself' refers indexically to the agent. But the reason to shoot yourself may be agent-neutral. For example, if your reason for shooting yourself is to save humanity, then the action α, is shooting yourself, and the reason-predicate is 'α will save humanity', which contains no agent-denoting term. On the definition this reason for shooting yourself comes out, as it should do, as agent-neutral.

Can an analogous distinction be made for evaluative and epistemic reasons? Consider first the case of reasons to feel. The fact that Sylvia has done me a good turn gives me reason to feel grateful, but it doesn't give you any reason to feel grateful. So with my mother: the fact that this is a photograph of the house she was born in, now long destroyed, is a reason for her to feel moved but not a reason for you to feel moved (or at least not the same reason). By the definition of relative reasons in terms of essential indexicality that I gave in Section 2, these are relative reasons. We can call them 'patient-relative reasons'—'patient' standing to 'passion' (feeling, sentiment, affective response) as 'agent' stands to action. Patient-relative reasons to feel can give rise to agent-relative reasons to act, as in the example of gratitude.

There are also patient-neutral reasons to feel: important cases are aesthetic and moral evaluations, which concern what there is reason to admire or to blame. If the fact that Tom cheated his opponent is a reason to blame him, then it's a reason for anyone to blame him, irrespective of facts about *them*, the blamers. (I'm referring here to the affective attitude, not the action, of blaming.) If the novel features of this building's design are a reason to admire it, they're a reason for anyone to admire it.[11]

However, in defining patient-relativity and patient-neutrality we cannot work with a 'reason-giving predicate on feelings' analogous to the reason-giving predicate on actions used in the definition above. For whereas the facts which give one reason to do something can be represented as facts about that action, the facts which give one reason to feel something must be represented as facts about the *objects* of that feeling. The relativity of my

---

[11] This I think amounts to the Kantian claim that such evaluations are 'universally legislative' (Kant, *Critique of Judgement*, 5: 239–40). Kant's claim is stronger than saying that they are universalizable in the sense discussed below. A patient-*relative* reason, like my reason for being irritated with the garage, is also universalizable in that sense.

mother's evaluative reason and your epistemic reason arise because the reasons in question comprise facts about the relation between her and the *object* of her feeling, and you and the *object* of your belief. We should take account of this point in building a definition of neutral and relative reasons for the evaluative and epistemic cases. Thus consider the schema:

(It's being the case) that $Py_1,\ldots,y_n$ gives x reason to feel ϕ with respect to $y_1,\ldots,y_n$

where 'ϕ' is a name for some particular type of feeling, and '$y_1,\ldots,y_n$' range over objects with respect to which x may have that feeling. If all instances of the schema are true we can call 'P' a *reason-giving predicate on objects with respect to* ϕ. Our definition of patient-neutrality and patient-relativity with respect to evaluative reasons is then as follows:

(i) If 'P' contains a free occurrence of 'x' it is a patient-relative predicate. If it does not, it is a patient-neutral predicate.
(ii) A reason for feeling which is expressible by a patient-neutral predicate is patient-neutral. A reason for feeling which is not so expressible is patient-relative.

Example: if some garage, y, were to charge x surreptitiously for a repair which y had not carried out, that would give x a specific reason to be angry with y. That is true for all x and y. Here 'Py' = 'a garage y charged x surreptitiously for a repair which y did not carry out'. Thus 'P' contains a free occurrence of x; nor is the reason it expresses expressible by a patient-neutral predicate; so the reason in question is patient-relative.

Is this equivalent to the definition in terms of essential indexicality? It is. To know that there's reason for me to be annoyed with the garage I must know that it has cheated *me*. Note, however, that I can have reasons to feel something, for example, proud or ashamed, about *myself*. I myself am the object of my feelings. This complicates things. We have, say:

The fact that x has made a silly mistake is a reason for x to feel ashamed of x.

Here the reason-giving *sentence* ('x has made a silly mistake') contains a free occurrence of x, but the reason-giving *predicate* does not. An obvious response is to redefine in terms of sentences rather than predicates. But if we did that for the case of practical reasons, we would get the wrong result, as we see if we think again about agent-neutral reasons for shooting oneself:

The fact that shooting x would save the world is a reason for x to shoot x.

The point is that we want to *distinguish* between x as the person for whom there is a reason to ψ and x as an object of ψ. Let us do this by requiring that any identity of actor and object is made explicit in the reason-giving predicate:

The fact that y has made a silly mistake and $y = x$ is a reason for x to feel ashamed of x.

Now our predicate on y is patient-relative.

What about feelings about non-existent objects such as the characters in a play? And can there be reasons for feelings that are not object directed at all?

In 17.2 we shall be led to distinguish between the existent, or real, as against the irreal, and the actual as against the possible. We shall take it that actual objects can be referred to and quantified over, whether or not they exist. There are general arguments for this account, but it has relevance here. Specifically, there can be reasons to have feelings about actual non-existent objects. King Lear is a case in point. Is there reason to be impatient with King Lear's foolishness and self-conceit? Is there reason to think he would have been wiser not to part with his kingdom? Surely yes. If you and I have these attitudes to King Lear then there is one thing to which both of us have them. If King Lear is one of Shakespeare's characters, then we have them towards one of Shakespeare's characters. Beliefs about fictional characters are beliefs *de re*, and fictional objects fall within the range of '$y_1,\ldots,y_n$' in the definition of patient-relativity and neutrality given above.

Further, suppose I had reason to believe there would be a view here, and have walked some distance to get to it. That's a reason to be disappointed that there isn't one. We can say that I am disappointed with this spot, which turns out not have a view. But we can equally well say that I am disappointed that the view you told me about, turns out not to exist. Intentional identities of this kind, about what we shall call 'putative reals', are easily handled on the account proposed in Chapter 17.

Finally, can there be reasons for feelings which are not object directed? Consider an objectless feeling of elation. That's precisely the kind of feeling which there can't be reason to have—or reason not to have—though there can be an *explanation* of why one has it. If I'm elated because my team has won the cup, my elation has an object and a reason. If I'm elated this morning because the sun is shining, then that's my reason for elation. (If you're feeling grumpy you can question whether it's a good enough reason for elation.) In contrast, if I'm just elated this morning, and my elation apparently has no object, then we might just as well say that I'm elated for no reason. Reasons for feelings must always be facts about objects to which those feelings are directed. Objectless moods do not fall within their scope.

Let us now turn to the case of reasons to believe. Here too, by the definition in terms of essential indexicality, some reasons to believe are 'thinker-relative', whereas others are 'thinker-neutral'. The fact that you are walking away from St Andrews gives you reason to believe that the person walking in the opposite direction to *you* is walking towards it. The fact that Mary is walking quickly gives you reason to believe that she is in a hurry. The first reason is thinker-relative, the second is thinker-neutral.

As in the case of feelings, to give a definition in terms of neutral and relative predicates we must represent the facts which give a person reason to believe something as facts about the *objects* of that belief. So consider the schema:

(it's being the case) that $P(y_1,\ldots,y_n)$ would give x reason to believe F of $y_1,\ldots,y_n$

where '$y_1,\ldots,y_n$' ranges over n-tuples of objects of which x may believe F. If all instances of the schema are true, we call '$P(y_1,\ldots,y_n)$' an *epistemic reason-giving predicate on objects with respect to* F. Here again we want to distinguish between x as the person for whom there is a reason to ψ and X as an object of ψ. Again we require that any identity of actor and object is made explicit in the reason-giving predicate:

The fact that y's name has been called and $y = x$ is a reason for x to believe x is wanted.[12]

This predicate on x is thinker-relative. The definition of thinker-neutral and thinker-relative reasons to believe proceeds as before—turning, that is, on whether 'P' contains a free occurrence of 'x'. Thus:

(i) If 'P' contains a free occurrence of 'x' it is a thinker-relative predicate. If it does not, it is a thinker-neutral predicate.

(ii) A reason for believing which is expressible by a thinker-neutral reason-predicate is thinker-neutral. A reason for believing which is not so expressible is thinker-relative.

Suppose, for example, that Smith hears his name being called by someone else. Does that give him reason to believe that that other person wants *him*? On this account it does—a thinker-relative reason.

True, Smith may not *realize* that it gives him a reason for that belief. He may hear his name being called without realizing that it is *his* name that is being called—that is, without realizing of himself, *de se*, that *he* is being called.[13] In that case he does not have, what in Chapter 5 I shall call a *warranted* reason, to believe that he is being called. There *is* reason for him to believe that he is being called, but he *has* no reason to believe that there is (unless, for example, we tell him that there is, because *we* know that his name is being called).

We shall come back to this in our account of warrant in Chapter 5, in which knowledge *de se* will play a crucial role.

3.5 Relativity to time and a general formula

So far we have been ignoring time; but reasons are relations between a fact, an actor, a response, and a *time*. This can be important, because there can be temporally relative reasons—epistemic, evaluative, and practical. The fact that I have a meeting in the conference room at noon, and that it's now noon, gives me reason to go now. The fact that there is still a chance that my horse will win gives me a reason to hope that it will. What makes a reason temporally relative is that the fact in which it consists is temporally indexical. So a definition along the same lines as those above will turn on the presence or otherwise of a free variable ranging over time in the reason predicate. But since epistemic, evaluative, and practical reasons can all be temporally relative or neutral, we need a general formula covering all these cases.

To achieve that we must bring the account of agent-relativity and agent-neutrality into line with the account of relativity and neutrality in the other cases. In the case of practical reasons we made no distinction between an action and its objects, as we did in the case of beliefs and feelings, and their objects—we simply treated 'P' a reason-giving-predicate on

---

[12] Both facts, not just the fact that y's name is being called but also the fact that $y = x$, must be in x's epistemic field.
[13] On *de se* reference, see Lewis 1979.

actions. To get uniformity, think of '$\alpha(y)$' as consisting of a verb, 'α', referring to an act of 'actioning' (cp deciding to, willing to), and a variable, 'y', ranging over types of action which can be actioned. So now α is one value of the variable ranging over responses, 'ψ', all of which can take objects $y_1,\ldots,y_n$. The other values are particular types of feeling, and particular beliefs. The *general schema* is then:

it's being the case that $P(y_{1\ldots n})$ would give x reason to $\psi(y_{1\ldots n})$ at t.

Relativity involves the free occurrence of 'x' or 't' in 'P':

(i) If 'P' contains a free occurrence of 't' or 'x' it is a relative reason-predicate. If it does not, it is a neutral reason-predicate.

(ii) A reason which is expressible by a neutral reason-predicate is neutral. A reason which is not so expressible is relative to x or t.

3.6 The universality and universalizability of reasons

It is implicit in what has been said so far that reasons in general (epistemic, evaluative, and practical) are universal. Consider again the general schema of the last section. Instances of this schema for a specific predicate 'P' may or may not be true a priori. Where they are true a priori, they state what in 5.6 we will call a *complete reason*: i.e. one whose reason-giving force is knowable by normative insight alone, without a posteriori knowledge of further facts.

Reasons are universal in the sense that *complete* reasons are universal: when it's a priori that:

it's being the case that $P(y_{1\ldots n})$ would give x reason to $\psi(y_{1\ldots n})$ at t

then

(x) it's being the case that $P(y_{1\ldots n})$ would give x reason to $\psi(y_{1\ldots n})$ at t.

Incomplete reasons may not be universal. To anticipate an example from Chapter 5: the fact that the building is on fire may be a reason for me to leave, but for you to enter. Both assertions are true; but that's because you are a fireman and I am not. (I should add that whether universal reasons are *general* enough to be worth calling 'principles' is a separate matter; I am not here raising an objection to any form of particularism that accepts that the content of normative insight is inherently universal.)

As well as being universal, reasons are also *universalizable*. Universalizability involves something more than universality: namely, the elimination of objectual rigid designators from a full statement of the reason.

We can approach this by considering a famous context in which the distinction between agent-neutral and agent-relative reasons plays an essential role. I have in mind the contrast drawn by Sidgwick between the position of a 'rational' egoist, who, Sidgwick thinks, cannot be accused of incoherence, and the position of an egoist who, he thinks, cannot resist utilitarianism without incoherence. (This contrast is part of the build-up to Sidgwick's conception of a dualism of practical reason, according to which both rational egoism and utilitarianism are dictates of practical reason.)

The rational egoist and the utilitarian respectively believe that the following—enriched by an account of what determines the strength of their respective kinds of reason—are the sole foundations of ethics:

> Rational egoist: if it were the case that α-ing had a propensity to benefit x that would give x reason to α.
> Utilitarian: if it were the case that α-ing had a propensity to benefit y that would give x reason to α.

But there is also an egoist who 'puts forward, implicitly or explicitly, the proposition that his pleasure or happiness is Good, not only *for him* but from the point of view of the Universe'. To this egoist it can be pointed out that '*his* happiness cannot be a more important part of Good, taken universally, then the equal happiness of any other person'.[14] Denying that, Sidgwick thinks, would be irrational. Why?

The irrational egoist's sole principle is:

> If it were the case that α had a propensity to benefit me that would give x reason to α.

His view is that benefits to him are, as such, agent-neutral reasons for action. He does not derive his principle by substituting the indexical term 'me' for 'y' in the utilitarian's principle. He takes his principle as primitive. But, Sidgwick thinks, what makes my benefit an agent-neutral reason for action cannot be the fact that it is MY benefit. If it is to be an *agent-neutral* reason for action that must be because it is a benefit—not because it is *my* benefit.

Sidgwick's train of thought allows that reasons for action can be agent-relative but insists that they must be universalizable. The rational egoist's principle is agent-relative and universalizable, whereas the irrational egoist's principle is agent-neutral but not *universalizable*. It is not that this latter principle, stated in its universal form as above, is false. The utilitarian, for one, would agree that it's true, since it's a straightforward corollary of *his* principle. The relevant point is that the reason-predicate, 'α has a propensity to benefit me' has a term functioning as an objectual rigid designator in it—'me'—which as far as the irrational egoist is concerned is essential. This rigid designator (or one with the same referent) cannot be eliminated without losing his fundamental thought. If you ask the rational egoist why the fact that your α-ing would have a propensity to benefit him gives *you* reason to α, he will insist that there is nothing more to say: the reason for you to α is just that your α-ing probabilizes a benefit to *him*. In contrast, the utilitarian's fundamental thought is: this is a being capable of enjoying benefits, and there is reason to promote the benefit of any being capable of enjoying benefits.

---

[14] Sidgwick 1981 (1907): 420–1.

If we ask the irrational egoist what it is about him that gives us reason to benefit him, his answer attaches reason-giving force to the fact that he is who he is: that he is he. Sidgwick thinks that is irrational:

> The mere fact (if I may so put it) that *he* is *he* can have nothing to do with [the] objective desirability or goodness [of his happiness].[15]

The point is that this merely nominal fact is a tautology: an analytic truth that expresses no substantial fact.[16] Given that such nominal facts, of the form '*x* is *x*' cannot have reason-giving force, the universalizability of reasons follows directly.

3.7 The universalizability of evaluative reasons

But does universalizability apply to evaluative reasons?

Suppose someone says 'I love Freda and only Freda will do! It's not anything about her, it's just that she's Freda!' He is unlikely to be claiming that Freda's being the very person she is, viz. Freda, is a *reason* to love her. More likely he is saying that there is no *reason* for him to love Freda—he just does. Assuredly, however, there can be reasons to love or hate someone. People can be loveable or hateful. The fact that someone is notably kind, warm, free of resentments, and open to others is reason to love them. That they are malicious, spiteful, resentful, sadistic, etc., that they do not make efforts to control these feelings but positively glory in them, that is reason to dislike or even hate them. Even in this case, however, we wouldn't necessarily say that loving someone like that is *irrational*. It happens all the time.[17]

Still, while a love for which there is no reason is not necessarily *irrational*, it sets up some tension, epistemic and explanatory. There is some impetus towards explaining why you love. In some of these cases you simply don't know *why* you love X, nor can anyone else see why. This is a pure case of loving without reason; questions about its pathology can soon begin to arise. In other much more frequent cases you can point to something about X that explains *why* you love X, though you don't think it's a very good reason *to* love X. Nonetheless, for this sort of interpretative explanation to work (in contrast to a purely non-interpretative explanation that simply says that you've been injected with a drug, or swallowed a love potion) the feature you point to must be at least intelligible as a reason to love X. One can find a much wider variety of reasons intelligible than one thinks to be good to any serious degree, but one must still grasp them as *reasons*. Suppose that what you love about Joe is his curly blond hair. I can understand that as a reason— curly blond hair is quite nice, whereas say the fact that he weighs exactly 12 stone is hardly intelligible as a reason to love him. Still, I reserve the right to think his curly blond

---

[15] Sidgwick 2000 ('Utilitarianism'): 9.

[16] Note Sidgwick's apologetic tone in referring to this 'mere fact' as a *fact*. More on the analyticity of instances of '*x* is *x*' in 7.2.

[17] Hating someone for no particular reason also happens, but we don't think that is acceptable, whereas in the case of love we do. However, this is a matter of morality, not rationality. If there's no reason to hate someone you should try not to hate them; just because there's no reason to love someone, it doesn't follow that you should try not to love them.

hair is not a very good reason for the degree of passionate devotion that you evidently feel. The point applies to actions and beliefs as well as feelings. To *understand* why someone believes something or does something, you need to understand their reasons as reasons. But you don't have to agree about their strength.

Feeling something without reason is not necessarily irrational, because to say that a feeling is irrational is to say something much stronger than simply saying there is no reason to feel that way. Nor is failing to feel something there is reason to feel necessarily irrational. Suppose my mother is moved by the newly discovered photo of the house she was born in, whereas my aunt, who was also born there, is not. My mother loved the place. Perhaps my aunt did not; in that case there may be no reason for her to be moved. Or she loved it, but now all these memories have gone dead. She can see why my mother is moved, why she is moved with reason, but the photograph does nothing for her. That can happen. Likewise you might see that there is reason to admire a performance but in fact feel no admiration. You are too tired, have heard it too often before, etc. None of this undermines the universalizability of evaluative reasons.

There is a different case, however, in which my aunt simply cannot *see any reason* to be moved: she is completely baffled as to what could be moving about a photo. What is moving about a photo? It's just a piece of glossy paper. That (if genuine as against a refusal to feel) is a pure deficit of normative insight, and it leads us to the topic of the next two sections.

3.8 What determines the range of a reason?

Reasons are universal and universalizable. But what determines the *range* of a reason? That is, what determines the actors over which it ranges? In the general schema of Section 3.5, over what objects does 'x' range? Do all reasons have the same range? Or do ranges vary depending on the type of reason in question?

T. M. Scanlon notes that some reasons may include 'subjective conditions'.[18] For example, the fact that I like playing chess and that there's a chess club in the neighbourhood is a reason for me to join it, but not a reason for you to join it since you're not interested in chess. A fact about personal likes and dislikes is part of the reason. So far that is just an instance of the general point that practical and evaluative reasons are often relative. The fact that I'm interested in chess is a reason for me to join the chess club; the reason for you would be that *you're* interested in chess. This agent-relative reason can still be stated universally:

> (x)(its being the case that x likes playing chess and that there's a chess club near by would be a reason for x to join that club).

You fall within the range of this reason just as much as I do. It's just that you don't like playing chess. So there's no reason for you to join the chess club, because the subjective condition included in the reason doesn't apply to you.

[18] Scanlon 1998: 367.

But what, in contrast, of my pet snake? Does *it* fall within the range of *x*? Should we say that there's no reason for it to join the chess club, because it doesn't like playing chess—or should we say that snakes just *don't fall* within the range of this kind of reason? In general terms: what condition must be satisfied by any entity *x* for reasons of a given kind to be ascribable to it?

At first sight the answer seems obvious—it must be reason-sensitive. So trees, rocks, and planets, at least, don't instantiate reason relations. Since the variable that ranges over actors simply doesn't include them in its range, they're no counter-example to the universality of reasons. However, all we've said about actors so far is that they can be said to respond to or be sensitive to *some* reasons. As noted in Section 3.1, we are assuming for the purposes of this book a full-blooded model of reason-responsiveness, involving concept possession and the capacity for reflection on reasons. But it was also noted that we often attribute reason-responsiveness less full-bloodedly, say to dogs, dolphins, and primates as well as people. They may be reason-sensitive 'to some degree', in different areas and to different levels. So we need to think more carefully about the conditions that suffice to bring a thing within the range of a particular type of reason—suffice, that is, to make it an actor in relation to *that* type of reason.

Suppose that $(x)R(\pi, x, \psi)$. There are three *prima facie* plausible suggestions as to what conditions some particular entity x would have to satisfy to fall within the range of '*x*'—conditions that must be met for it to be true that $R(\pi, x, \psi)$:

(a) x can entertain the thought that π obtains

(b) x can entertain the content of the act ψ

(c) x can recognize *de se* that $R(\pi, x, \psi)$.[19]

I want to suggest that (c) must be satisfied. If (c) must be satisfied then (a) and (b) must be. But clearly one might argue for a weaker view—for example, that only (a) and (b) must be satisfied, or a different view involving, for example, the community to which x belongs. And obviously a lot hangs on how we understand 'can' in (c).

Suppose the paper boy has come to collect our weekly payments for newspapers delivered. I've trained my dog to carry the envelope with the money over to him. We could say that the dog is giving the weekly payment to the paper boy, in an extensional sense which carries no implication as to its intentions. But in the richer sense of action that's relevant for us, that isn't really true: the dog isn't performing an act whose intentional content is *giving the money to the paper boy*. It can't perform *that* act because it can't grasp that content. But maybe it is performing some other intentional act, such as *doing the routine its leader wants it to do*. If it's performing the latter act it may also be able to grasp that by doing this it will conform to its role as follower. If so, then perhaps it's also true that the fact that doing the routine will conform to its role may be its reason for doing the

---

[19] Can't the conditions for x to fall within the range of a reason be included in the subjective conditions—so that every object, including every electron in the universe, falls under all reasons? Distinguish (i) what counts as a reason to ψ; and (ii) what conditions must be satisfied for *x* to fall within the range of the reason. Having a recognitional capacity is not a *reason*—it's a condition on falling within the range of a reason.

routine—in which case (c) is satisfied: that is, the dog can recognize *conforming to it's role as follower* as a reason for *doing the routine its leader wants it to do*. But just as the dog can't grasp the content *giving the money to the paper boy*, so it can't entertain the thought that *giving the money to the paper boy is paying our weekly bill*. Hence both condition (a) and condition (b) would rule out the more ambitious reason ascription: *viz.*, that there is a reason for the dog to give the money to the paper boy, and that that reason is the fact that giving the money to the paper boy pays off our weekly bill.

This is plainly right: the dog simply doesn't fall within the range of that particular reason, though it falls within the range of other reasons. Moreover, though in this case either one of (a) and (b) removes the dog from the range of that reason, both are in general necessary. For example, while *going to the porch* may be an act content the dog can grasp, condition (a) certainly rules out, as a reason for the dog to do so, the fact that an interesting political debate is about to take place in the street just next to the porch.

Now what of the case where x can entertain the thought that π obtains and can ψ, but simply can't see that $R(\pi, x, \psi)$? That is, x can't see that π, if it obtained, would give him *reason* to ψ?

Suppose that y has done x a good turn out of sheer goodwill. x knows that, and knows what it is to do a good turn out of goodwill—to confer a benefit just because it is a benefit, and for no ulterior reason. What he can't see at all is that the fact that y has done him a good turn is a reason for him to do a good turn to y. He simply has no sense of reasons of reciprocity. The maxim that one good turn deserves another means nothing to him. *Is there then reason for x to reciprocate? Is the fact that y has done x a good turn a reason for x to do y a good turn?*

3.9 Cognitive internalism

Our response to this kind of case strikes me as uncertain. If we say that there is no reason for x to reciprocate, the thought that moves us is that a fact cannot be a reason for an actor to ψ if its reason-giving force cannot be recognized as such by the actor. This follows from what in 10.7 I call the 'the requirement of effectiveness' on reasons—if something is a reason for x, it must be possible for x to act for that reason. What we are concerned with is not the actor's knowledge of the reason-giving facts but his ability to recognize them as reason-giving. It is not a question of whether the actor has the information which enables him to know that the reason-giving fact obtains; the point is that the actor must have the ability to recognize the *reason-giving force* of that fact were it to obtain. He must be able to appreciate in his own right, or see for himself, that that fact *as such*, were it to obtain, would indeed be a reason for him to ψ. Only then can *this reason* prompt him to act. This is condition (c). Let's call the thesis that it must be satisfied *cognitive internalism*:

> Cognitive internalism: π_i are a reason for x to ψ only if x has the ability to recognize that π_i are a reason for x to ψ.

Cognitive internalism says that only considerations which an actor has the ability to recognize *as* reasons can *be* reasons for that actor. But how should we understand 'can'?

We are talking about x's normative ability to recognize reason relations, not his calculative competence or ability to recognize what facts obtain. The weakest understanding, which has attraction just because it is the weakest, requires only that it be within the actor's nature, or determinate potential, to come to recognize the reason as such, i.e. to recognize the reason relation that it satisfies. He need not have the *realized* ability to recognize the reason. The difference between realizing one's potential to grasp a reason and being merely indoctrinated into counting it as one is crucial here. It will be central to our discussion of the epistemology of the normative in 16.2; in Kantian terminology to be explained and discussed there, the reason-giving force of the facts must be *spontaneously* accessible to the actor.

Spontaneity in this sense may be achieved only with difficulty, and can be damaged or temporarily disturbed. Much preliminary clarification may be needed before spontaneous insight occurs. The degree and extent to which it is actually working in a person can vary greatly depending on the circumstances. People can suffer a temporary blockage on their spontaneous ability to see a reason, or they can have an ability that has not yet developed. On the condition suggested, we can still put them within the range of reasons they're currently unable to see, or are not yet able see—so long as they have a determinate potential to see them.

Does cognitive internalism also hold for evaluative and epistemic reasons? Let's consider evaluative reasons first. Where y has done x a good turn, is there reason for x to feel grateful to y? In this example one could argue that it's (b) that does the work. If x can't see that the fact that y has done him a good turn is a reason to feel grateful, that is because x doesn't know what gratitude is, and so can't grasp the content of ψ, which is, being grateful to y. But if grasp of concepts is grasp of reasons (as will be argued in 18.5), often (b) and (c) will be hard to disentangle, in that the concepts that feature in ψ may be concepts one can grasp only by grasping truths about reasons to ψ.

What about the case of epistemic reasons? Does cognitive internalism apply in the same way here?

We should set aside issues that arise simply from the fact that epistemic reasons are relative to an epistemic field. If one knows that dark clouds on the horizon often indicate rain then in that epistemic field the fact that there are dark clouds on the horizon is a reason to believe that it will rain. But on its own it is not a reason for everyone to believe that it will rain, because the fact that dark clouds on the horizon are often followed by rain may not be in everyone's epistemic field. In universalizing we must consider complete reasons, and complete epistemic reasons must include a reference to the actor's epistemic field. This holds independently of the truth or otherwise of cognitive internalism. To get at the specific issue of cognitive internalism we have to consider complete reasons (see 5.6). For example, *the fact that there are dark clouds on the horizon together with the fact that dark clouds on the horizon often indicate rain* jointly constitute a complete reason to believe that it will rain. To call it a complete reason is to say that the following is an a priori truth:

(1) R(e_x, the fact that there are dark clouds on the horizon, the fact that dark clouds on the horizon often indicate rain, x, β(it will rain)).

We can now ask: what conditions must be satisfied by x if x is to fall within the range of *x* in (1)? Cognitive internalism says that x must be capable of normative insight into the truth of (1). (Some complete epistemic reasons may be too complicated for *direct* insight. But let's leave this complication aside for now.)

Imagine a community of actors whose default epistemic position is Brouwerian intuitionism in logic and non-Euclideanism in geometry. That is, they don't accept that the principle of excluded middle or the parallels postulate (understood as a claim about physical space) have *a priori* status. Nor could they be brought by philosophical discussion into a state in which they were spontaneously disposed to accept them as such. They do recognize them as pretty safe a posteriori conjectures. So they will agree that in general, it's pretty safe to reason on the basis that either it's the case that *p* or it's not the case that *p*, and likewise, pretty safe to infer, for most lengths one encounters, that if two lines of that length are shown to enclose a space, then they're not both straight. Or perhaps they take these principles as very well-established principles of their science, on a par with the principle that light travels in straight lines, say. It is not that they *do* experience these principles as *a priori* but take a sophisticated intuitionistic or empiricist view about logic or geometry—and thus suppress such experiences of apriority as misleading. They simply don't have those experiences.

Suppose we think the law of excluded middle is a priori—that is, that there is outright sufficient reason to accept the law of excluded middle. We have a powerful, spontaneous disposition to accept outright that $pv\neg p$. It seems to us quite evident that it must be true. We may think, not just that there's outright sufficient reason to believe excluded middle in our *e*, but that there's outright sufficient reason to believe it in all *e*s. On our view, in that case:

(2) $(x)(e_x)S(e_x, x, \beta pv\neg p)$.

But do the thinkers of this other community fall within the range of *x*?

If we come to the conclusion that the intuitionistic community is simply unable to achieve a priori insight into (2), we have two options. The first is to abandon our own view. Maybe they're right—what seems to us a priori isn't really. But we may be more confident in our stance. (We might not be so confident, of course, if it was the parallels postulate that was being considered.) We may conclude that they are unable to grasp, even potentially, that there is outright sufficient reason to believe (2), even though there is. What do we say then? Do we say that there is outright sufficient reason for *them* to believe that $pv\neg p$? Or do we exclude them from the range of *x*?

If we accept cognitive internalism we will exclude them. The attraction of cognitive internalism is that it enables us to claim that if something has reason-giving force for you then you can at least potentially tell that it has. What, in contrast, would count in favour of a practice of ascribing reasons to actors who are quite impervious to such reasons? As we have now seen, the principle that reasons are universal does not do so.[20] The question is not whether reasons are universal but over what domain they are.

Cognitive internalism will be a recurrent topic in this book. It is a significant issue in the theory of reasons. In the case of ethics, as we shall see (12.4), a factor pulling in its favour is our idea that moral agents are autonomous and are able to grasp morally salient reasons for themselves. A factor pulling against it is the wish to bring everyone within the range of morality, and in particular to hold them to moral obligations even if they are unable to grasp them. In general, cognitive internalism is an aspect of the idea of autonomy, and thereby is in turn connected to cognitive irrealism. So we shall have to come back to the relations between irrealism, internalism, and the implication for a relativism of reasons in Chapter 20—but not until some specific issues in ethics and epistemology have been tackled.

[20] *Pace* Scanlon 1998: 367, 372.

4

NORMATIVITY

A main thesis of this book—the 'Reasons thesis'—is that the concept of a reason is the fundamental normative concept. As we can now put it, the Reasons thesis states that the three concepts, we identified in Chapter 2, R, R_o, and S, can be treated as the fundamental normative concepts. A corollary is that all normative propositions can be regarded as propositions about reasons—propositions about R, R_o, and S. We should begin to clarify and makes progress with these claims. Not all the concepts that I claim to be normative will be considered fully in this chapter, however. Some of them require chapters to themselves: aprioricity; necessity; evidence; probability—the concept of a person's good, the moral concepts. The aim of this chapter is to provide and illustrate a general framework of analysis.

'Normative' is a technical term of philosophy, used in various ways. I use it broadly, to contrast with 'descriptive', not narrowly, as some writers use it, to contrast with 'evaluative'. The circle of terms that are normative in this broad sense comprises a vocabulary that is diverse and wide. It is surrounded by a thick margin of terms as to whose normativity or otherwise there is dispute, often because their meaning is in dispute. We cannot in practice consider all putative normative terms, or even all classes of such terms. The Reasons thesis is best seen as a conjecture which we aim to make plausible by exploring a variety of cases. If this exploration can be carried far enough successfully, it will become reasonable to stipulate, as a definition of 'normative', that a normative term is a term that satisfies the thesis.

Even if we achieve this goal it does not follow that there is no other way of inter-defining the circle of normative concepts. It is possible, in principle, that reductive analysis of normative concepts can be done in more than one way; for example, by taking value, obligation, or rationality as fundamental normative concepts. I don't find these possibilities plausible; however, I am not going to try to prove that all such possibilities fail. My aim is to explore and vindicate the Reasons thesis in detail. Should it turn out to be possible to define the normative concepts in another way, the case for thinking the Reasons thesis is particularly illuminating would have to turn on more general philosophical considerations. I think such considerations can be given; they will gradually emerge in Part IV.[1]

---

[1] I also leave to Part IV the question whether reason predicates are *irreducible*. They are irreducible if the relations they express cannot be expressed in non-normative terms; Part IV will argue that they are indeed irreducible in this sense.

4.1 Semantic reduction and concept possession

The simplest and sharpest version of the Reasons thesis is explicitly semantic: any normative predicate is definitionally reducible to a reason predicate (as well as non-normative predicates if it is not itself wholly normative). Call this the *definability thesis*.

An alternative is to put the Reasons thesis at the level of concepts: the sole normative ingredient in any normative concept is the concept of a reason. Call this the *concept-possession* thesis. This claim is weaker, in that the definability thesis entails it but the converse need not hold.

To illustrate the difference, consider the moral concepts, which are obviously a major case in any general discussion of normativity. Let's allow that the basic concept here is that of moral wrongness: a moral obligation, for example, is by definition something with which non-compliance is morally wrong. And let's allow for the sake of argument that the morally wrong is that which (absent extenuating circumstances) there is reason to blame.[2] So that promises a reduction of moral sentences to sentences about reasons. But it may plausibly be objected that it cannot yield a *definition* of 'morally wrong', since 'blame' in the relevant sense should be defined as that sentiment which is appropriate—which there is reason to feel—towards the *morally wrong*. A good objection, but not the end of the story. Suppose that there is a distinctive sentiment of blame whose object is the morally wrong; suppose also that we can be given an independent characterization of this sentiment that enables us to grasp what it is—say by a characterization of the distinctive actions which it prompts, or by having it explained as the sentiment we feel when we consider some specific representative cases. Suppose, finally, that when we have been made familiar, in the first-person way, with the sentiment, we find ourselves able to go on spontaneously, and reasonably convergently, making confident new judgements about when there is reason to feel that specific sentiment towards an action. In that case we have everything we need to grasp the concept of moral wrongness. The concept can in this sense be exhaustively captured in terms of the concept of a reason and the concept of a certain sentiment, even though 'morally wrong' cannot be defined in terms of 'reason'. Furthermore if we can individuate the sentiment by these methods we can also use them to introduce a term to refer to the sentiment, say 'б'. The morally wrong is that which, in the absence of an excuse, is б-worthy—towards which there is sufficient reason to feel that sentiment.

Colour concepts provide a partial analogy. To grasp the concept of yellow you have to be familiar in the first-person way with the sensation of yellow, and take the presence of the sensation as reason to think it indicates a particular objective feature, while also being able to recognize cases in which that reason is defeated. If you have all that, you have what's needed to possess the concept. Nonetheless, 'yellow' is not definable in terms of 'sensation of yellow'. 'Yellow' is simple, 'sensation of yellow' is complex: you need to know what the former means to know what the latter means. G. E. Moore was right about the indefinability of 'yellow' (if not, as I shall argue later, about the indefinability of 'good').

---

[2] This is by some way too simple, as will emerge in 12.1 and 12.2. However, it will do to make the present point.

The partial analogy with moral wrongness is that a being which has the blame response, and an ability to distinguish between having it and having reason to have it, has what's needed to possess the concept of moral wrongness, even though 'morally wrong' is not definable in terms of 'what there is reason to blame'.

This is an approach that captures a concept by saying what is required for possession of the concept, rather than by the semantic route of explicit definition. Nonetheless, if the story is right we have shown that the normative concept of moral wrongness can be fully captured in terms of the normative concept of a reason, and in this sense made progress in defending the Reasons thesis. Attributing full possession of either concept, that of wrongness or that of yellowness, involves attributing reason-sensitivity to its user, in that it is a condition for grasping a concept that one is sensitive to reasons for applying it. What distinguishes moral wrongness as a *normative* concept, unlike yellowness, is that you can have the concept only if you are sensitive to reasons for the blame sentiment itself. It always makes sense to ask whether there are reasons to feel the blame sentiment; with the sensation of yellow there is no analogous question.

If the definability thesis were correct, we could draw the conclusion that anything normative our actual vocabulary allows us to say could be said in our language, with our actual vocabulary, while using only non-normative predicates and reason predicates. All normative content could be expressed that way. Other normative predicates would be expressively, if not practically, redundant.[3] If we have to supplement the definability thesis with the concept–possession thesis, as in the case of the moral concepts, the conclusion is somewhat different.

We can still ask whether it would be possible, without expressive restriction, not to have the term 'morally wrong' but only a word for the blame sentiment—'β'—plus a reason predicate that allowed one to distinguish between actions that provide sufficient reason for that response and actions which do not. Consider again the analogy with colour words. Would it be possible, without expressive restriction, to have no colour words but only colour–sensation words, and to talk only about the powers of objects to cause those sensations, and the grounds of those powers? This question should be distinguished from a question about the order of language learning, or of concept acquisition. Plausibly, the concept of a colour sensation is further on in that order than the concept of a colour, and it might well be argued that colour-sensation words cannot be grasped except through a prior grasp of colour vocabulary. However, this point about the order of learning would not show that a language which had colour-sensation words but no colour words would be *expressively restricted* in comparison to our actual language, as against user-unfriendly. Suppose 'Y' was the term referring to the sensation of yellow in that language. Semantically, if not learnably, a term referring to yellow could be introduced by description, as 'that feature which standardly causes Y in observers'. The same goes for the moral concepts. Moral terms may well lie earlier in the order of learning than terms for the blame sentiment, and that may well explain their semantic priority. So it may be possible to have the

---

[3] Of course if there is another way of reducing the normative predicates to a smaller number, not including the reason-predicates, then relative to that reduction the reason-predicates would themselves be expressively redundant.

concept *yellow*, or *morally wrong*, before one has the concept of a sensation of yellow, or a sentiment of blame. But that does not show that a language which included the reason predicates, and a term for the blame sentiment such as 'Ƅ', would be expressively restricted in comparison to the one we have. The claim would be that 'Ƅ-worthy in the absence of an excuse' (or the more complicated formulation of 12.2) expresses the same conceptual content as 'morally wrong'. A language which had this predicate but not our predicate 'morally wrong' would not be expressively restricted in comparison to ours.

These remarks assume that we can make relevant sense of the notion of 'saying the same thing', 'expressing the same content'. For that we need the notion of analytic equivalence, which will be discussed and defended in Chapter 7. Granting the assumption, however, the concept–possession thesis says that a concept, or proposition, is normative if it is expressible in some language by a normative predicate, or sentence containing such a predicate, whether or not it is so expressible in our language; and that a normative predicate is one definable in terms of the reason-predicates.

So stated, the concept–possession thesis presupposes that we have shown how to define what a normative predicate is in terms of the reason predicates. To this task we now turn.

4.2 Normative sentences and normative predicates

Stipulate, to begin with, that all sentences that predicate R, R_o or S are normative. On this basis we can define the class of *explicitly* normative sentences. Consider first sentences of the form:[4]

$R(\pi_i, t, d, x, \psi)$,
$R_o(\pi_i, t, d, x, \psi)$, or
$S(\pi_i, t, x, \psi)$.

Call such sentences *atomic* normative sentences, and define an *explicitly* normative sentence as one that is either:

(i) an atomic normative sentence

or

(ii) a sentence which is built from sentences which include at least one atomic normative sentence, by means of the connectives of propositional logic, quantifiers, and the truth operator ('it is true that').

Now define the class of normative sentences as follows.

(a) Any explicitly normative sentence is normative.
(b) Any sentence which has a normative sentence as a *definitional consequence* is normative.
(c) No other sentences are normative.

[4] For the case of epistemic reasons add 'e', ranging over epistemic fields.

'Definitional consequence' is to be understood as a narrower notion than that of analytic consequence in one standard, broad sense, i.e. derivability by principles of pure logic plus definitions. Definitional consequence is derivability by means of the natural deduction rules for conjunction and the universal quantifier alone, plus substitution of explicit definitions.

Psychological operators such as 'believes that', 'wonders whether', etc. are not included in the list given in (ii) above. Sentences such as 'Smith believes that there is reason to expect rain', or 'Smith is looking for a reason to sack me' are non-normative. What about sentences with a factive operator ('realizes that', 'knows that', etc.) in dominant scope, operating on a normative sentence? These are normative if they satisfy condition (b). So the question is, for example, whether 'p' is a definitional consequence of 'x knows that p'. If it is, then where 'p' is a normative sentence so is 'x knows that p'. On this view, to say that someone knows a normative truth is to make a partly normative claim.

Our definition of explicitly normative sentences commits us to counting the negation of a normative sentence as a normative sentence. Now the negation operator can occur within atomic normative sentences by occurring within one of their terms. That is, it can occur in one of the sentences in 'π_i', or in the verb, 'ψ', which denotes an act (one can have reason not to do something or to believe that something is not the case, or to have some feeling about something's not being so). There is no difficulty in the suggestion that a sentence of this kind, containing an internal negation, is normative. But what of the case where a whole atomic normative sentence is negated: '$\neg R(\pi_i, x, \psi, d, t)$', or '$\neg S(\pi_i, x, \psi, t)$'?

For simplicity I count these wide-scope negations as normative sentences. That is admittedly artificial, in that it's not obvious that the denial that there's a reason to ψ is itself a normative claim. After all, might that denial not come from a nihilist who holds that all normative propositions are false? Our definition attributes to the nihilist acceptance of some normative propositions as true. This is an awkwardness. But we can say that nihilism proper is the view that no atomic normative proposition is true. A nihilist is someone who takes no affirmative normative stance—he thinks there is no non-negative normative truth.

What now of conditional or disjunctive sentences formed from normative sentences? Here we come to an important point. Our definition commits us to counting a conditional with a normative antecedent or a normative consequent (or a disjunction with a normative disjunct) as a normative sentence. So consider 'If Michelangelo is not Italian, you should take up golf'. If we say that this conditional is normative, then the normative sentence it expresses can be deduced from non-normative sentences alone—in this case, from the non-normative sentence that Michelangelo is Italian. If instead we said that it is non-normative, a normative sentence would still be deducible from non-normative sentences alone. For this conditional, together with the non-normative premise that Michelangelo is not Italian, entails the normative conclusion that you should take up golf.[5]

---

[5] Cp. Prior 1960a. The same point applies to 'If Aunt Dahlia thinks that Bertie ought to marry Madeleine, then Bertie ought to marry Madeleine' (see Nelson 1995).

Given that all sentences are either normative or non-normative, the thesis that normative sentences cannot be deduced from non-normative sentences alone is false. However, we can maintain two truths that lie behind that thesis, and capture the proper force of the 'is/ought' or 'fact/value' distinction. The first truth is that there is no deductively valid argument from *true* non-normative premises alone to an *atomic* normative sentence, or negation thereof, as conclusion. This remains true on our account, which takes a conditional with a normative antecedent or a normative consequent, or a disjunction with a normative disjunct, to be normative. The second truth is that no normative sentence can be the *definitional consequence* of non-normative sentences alone. This follows from our definition of 'normative sentence', together with another claim we endorse, namely, that the reason predicates aren't *themselves* definable in non-normative terms. We can maintain this second truth because definitional consequence is narrower than deductive consequence. For example, a consequence drawn by or-introduction is not a *definitional* consequence.

It will also be useful to talk about predicates as well as sentences as normative. So let's say that any predicate formed from an explicitly normative sentence by dropping one or more singular terms is explicitly normative. A normative predicate is either explicitly normative or equivalent by definition to one that is explicitly normative. We can also say that a *wholly* normative sentence has no non-normative sentence as a definitional consequence, and a wholly normative predicate is one formed from a wholly normative sentence by replacing singular terms by variables. (So 'If Michelangelo is not Italian, you should take up golf' is wholly normative.)[6]

Lastly, take a normative proposition to be a proposition expressible by a normative sentence. A *wholly* normative proposition is one expressible by a wholly normative sentence. I shall also use the notion of a *purely* normative proposition: a purely normative proposition is a wholly normative proposition which no actual or possible facts give one reason to believe or disbelieve, whether or not there is outright reason to believe or disbelieve it. Thus, for example, the proposition that there is reason not to smoke is wholly but not purely normative, whereas the proposition that there is reason to accept the simplest explanation is wholly and purely normative.

4.3 Defining 'good'

To show that terms such as 'right', 'wrong', 'ought', 'should', 'good', 'bad', and others are normative, we must show that they are definitionally reducible to explicitly normative predicates. 'Right', 'wrong', 'ought' and 'should' have already been considered in 2.6. When they are used, in what I there called the 'designated' way, they are normative. So let us now consider the more contentious case of 'good' and 'bad'.

A number of philosophers have proposed definitions of goodness and badness in terms of attitudes—in favour and against—which it is correct, fitting, appropriate, or apt to take

---

[6] Our definition of 'normative' entails that 'Everything Aunt Dahlia believes is true' is a normative sentence, though not a wholly normative sentence.

towards a good or bad thing.[7] T. M. Scanlon recently revived this tradition, putting it explicitly in terms of reasons:

> To value something is to take oneself to have reasons for holding certain positive attitudes toward it and for acting in certain ways in regard to it.[8]

This, following Scanlon, is often called the 'buck-passing account'.[9] If, in particular, it is correct as an account of 'good', it shows 'good' to be a normative predicate by our definition.

Let's call the attitudes and actions in question pro-acts, or acts of favouring. The buck-passing thesis, as I want to propose it here, is then that 'y is a good F' means 'there is sufficient reason to favour y as an F'.

Since our aim is to define 'good' completely generally, we must give an account of what the pro-acts are that will adequately support that aim. A. C. Ewing, an early proponent of the buck-passing approach, gave some well-chosen examples: '"Pro-attitude"... covers, for instance, choice, desire, liking, pursuit, approval, admiration'.[10] His list, however, is oriented solely to the evaluative and practical domain. One can cavil with it even there: to approve something sounds very much like thinking it to be good. Yet we need an attitude that is appropriate to moral goodness. I don't think admiration is the attitude that is required; the appropriate attitude seems to me to be *respect* (which we shall come back to in discussing the moral sentiments in Chapter 15).

We also need an account of epistemic goodness. There can be good evidence, good arguments, and good reasons, as well as good policies and good performances. Good evidence for the proposition that p consists of accessible facts of which there is *sufficient reason* to believe that they constitute a *specific reason* to believe that p. Likewise with a good argument for the conclusion that p.[11] So favouring some particular evidence or argument for a proposition is believing that it provides some degree of reason for believing the proposition. How good the evidence or argument is depends on the degree of reason for belief that it provides. Finally, a 'good reason', in one main use of that phrase, is simply something that is genuinely a reason. For example, if one says 'There is no good reason to believe that' what one probably means is that any alleged reasons cited as counting in its favour are not actually reasons to believe, either because the purported facts don't actually obtain, or because they give no reason for the belief in question.

Provisionally, then, we have the following list of pro-acts: admiring; respecting; desiring; choosing; accepting as a reason. The term 'favouring' should be understood as a

---

[7] Rabinowicz and Rønnow-Rasmussen 2004, provide some earlier history.

[8] Scanlon, 1998: 96, etc.

[9] Rabinowicz and Rønnow-Rasmussen, 2004, call it the 'fitting-attitudes analysis'. As will emerge in later sections, I take it to be a correct account of evaluative terms in general.

[10] Ewing, *The Definition of Good*, 1947: 149. Ewing defines 'good' in terms of 'ought', rather than in terms of reasons, but he distinguishes various senses of 'ought', of which the relevant one for purposes of defining 'good' is that of 'fittingness' or 'reasonableness'. See also Ewing 1939 and 1959. I am grateful to Jonas Olson for pointing out to me these aspects of Ewing's view.

[11] The logician may use 'good argument' to refer to valid arguments. If validity is understood in terms of necessary truth-preservation, validity is a normative concept if necessity is. Chapter 8 will argue that it is.

disjunction of these. According to this list the good is the admirable, or the desirable, or the choice-worthy, or the respectable or respect-worthy, or the reason-conferring.[12]

With this account of acts of favouring to hand, let's turn to logical structure. Note first that 'good' and 'bad' are attributive adjectives—if a thing is said to be good or bad it makes sense to ask what it's good or bad *as*.[13] A good performance is good as a performance; a good hammer is good as a hammer; a good plan is good as a plan; good evidence is good as evidence, and so on. Moreover a thing can be good as an F and bad as a G. On a buck-passing account this attributive character is readily comprehensible. If I say that someone is a good athlete but a bad artist I mean, according to that account, that there is sufficient reason to admire them as an athlete and also sufficient reason to deplore them as an artist. The predicate qualified by 'good' or 'bad' will often indicate the appropriate standpoint of appraisal, but sometimes context will be required. Context may defeat initial appearances as to what standpoint of appraisal is in question; thus what looks like an epistemic standpoint may actually be evaluative—the argument may be good in that it's arresting, elegant, clever, etc., or it may be practical—the argument is good in that it will win the contract and thus should be used, even though it's neither sound nor particularly clever.

Note also that y may be good as an F to varying degrees; this reflects the fact that the appropriate pro-act may itself have varying degrees. One can have more or less admiration for something, be more or less moved to belief by some evidence or arguments, etc. To say that y is good to such-and-such a degree is to say that there's sufficient reason to favour it to such-and-such a degree. The degree qualifies the pro-act, not the reason—the reason is a *sufficient* reason, not itself a reason of degree. A good violin performance, say, is not just one that there's *some* reason to admire but one that there is sufficient reason to admire to some degree. The goodness of the performance varies with the degree of appropriate admiration.[14]

The word 'good' also occurs in the constructions 'good for x', and 'the good of x'. How should we approach these? Saying that something is good for x seems to come down to saying that it conduces to the goodness of x, or the good of x (as an F). Mowing is good for a lawn in that it conduces to the goodness of the lawn *qua* lawn. Regular practice is good for violinists: it conduces to their goodness as violinists. Oiling is good for locks, in that it maintains their goodness as locks—which in this case is functional goodness, to which we'll come in a moment. In all these cases saying that y is good for x as an F is saying that y would effect a change in x which is such as to constitute sufficient reason for increased favouring of x as an F.

What about the good for, or the good of, persons? Some classically-influenced philosophers incline to the idea that the good for a person, or a person's good, is what conduces

---

[12] A good judge is a judge there is reason to trust: i.e. one whose judgements give reason to believe the judgement true.

[13] Geach 1956. Some deny that 'good' is always attributive. I'm inclined to think it always is; at any rate our definition at least needs to take into account that it often is.

[14] If I say it was the best performance I mean it was the one there was sufficient reason to admire most. That's if 'best' means 'most good'. If 'best' means 'most good or least bad', then the best performance is the one there's sufficient reason to admire most or deplore least. (I take words like 'exceptional', 'outstanding', etc., when used to praise, to be abbreviations for 'exceptionally good', 'outstandingly good', etc.)

to the person's goodness as a person. I doubt whether this is what is normally meant by such phrases. Cod liver oil is good for you because it's good for your health: that is, it conduces to your good health. It is implicitly taken for granted that good health is functional for your good. But it is not taken for granted that your good is your goodness *as a person*. That would make your good a matter of your virtue, which cod liver oil may or may not be good for. Maybe virtue is a part of or the whole of your good, but that is a substantive ethical question. So what do we mean by a person's good? In Chapter 11 it will be argued that the good of a person comprises what there is sufficient reason for that person to desire, or what there would be such reason for them to desire if they were capable of sufficiently developed desires. Thus whether virtue is a part or the whole of your good depends on whether it is one of the things, or the only thing, that there is such reason for you to desire.

If this is correct, then the relevant pro-act is desiring, and the reason for favouring is agent-relative. (In all the other examples we've considered so far the reasons in question have been agent-neutral.) Hence also the good in this case is also agent-relative: when we talk of the good of x we mean whatever there is reason for that person, x, to desire. We also talk about the good of the country, the good of the club, etc. I suggest that that reduces to what there is reason for citizens of that country, or members of the club, to desire for their country or club.

A further case to consider is that of functional uses of the word 'good'. Suppose we are considering how well an object would perform the function of Q-ing; for example, how good a picnic table this tree stump would make. What is the buck-passing account of this? An obvious suggestion is that the object's goodness as a Q-er turns on how much reason there is to choose it for Q-ing. But there may be no reason to choose it for Q-ing, even though it would make a very good Q-er, because there is no reason to Q. The question, then, is whether *if* there's reason to Q there's reason to choose the given object to Q. To say that y is or would make a good Q-er (in contexts which determine the standpoint of appraisal as practical–functional) is to say that *if there's reason to Q then the fact that there's reason to Q is a specific reason to choose y for Q-ing*. A thing either is or would make a good picnic table if there's specific reason to choose it as a picnic table when there's reason to picnic, *because* there's reason to picnic. (There may of course be reasons to choose it or not to choose it which have nothing to do with its suitability or otherwise as a picnic table.) This batsman, bat or batting technique is a good run scorer if, when there's reason to score runs, the fact that there's reason to score runs is a specific reason to choose this one to score runs.[15]

This account applies to biological functions as well as artefacts. A good human heart, say, is a heart which circulates blood well when it's appropriately fitted in a human being. That is, it's a heart which there's reason to choose if one has reason to arrange for the circulation of blood in a human being. Similarly to say that a scorpion's sting is a good sting is to say that when it's in a scorpion it does some activity of Q-ing (such as defending against a predator) well: that is, that one would have reason to choose to have

---

[15] However, see Section 4 on reasons and cans.

it in a scorpion if one had reason to have Q-ing done in a scorpion. That can be true even though—as far as we're concerned—the fewer scorpions with good stings there are the better.

Finally we should note the various qualifications we can make in the way we talk about goodness. As well as asking what a thing is good *as*, we can ask in what *way* it is good *as* that. We can ask *how* good it is in some *respect*, and *how* good it is taking all relevant respects into account. I may say that the violin performance was good in respect of technical accomplishment but not so good in respect of musical sensitivity. I'm saying there's reason to admire y *as* a violin performance, in respect of its technical accomplishment, but less reason to admire it, *as* a violin performance, in respect of its musical sensitivity. These respects in which there is reason to admire become criteria of goodness (they could be given marks, for example). So we admire y as an F, in respect of C: when we ask *how* good y is, we're asking how much it should be admired in some respect C, or how much it should be admired taking all relevant respects C into account.

Putting all these points together gives us the following definitions:

> *y is a good F (in certain respects C, to degree d, at t) if and only if there is sufficient reason to favour y as an F (in those respects C, to degree d, as y is at t).*

The definition of 'good for x' will be:

> *y is good for x (as an F), (in certain respects C, to degree d, at t) if and only if y would maintain, promote, or enhance those features of x which make it a good F, or which partially constitute the good of x (as an F), (in those respects C, to degree d, as y is at t).*

The definition of the 'good of x' is:

> *y constitutes the good of x (in certain respects C, to degree d, at t) if and only if there's sufficient reason for x to desire y (in those respects C, to degree d, as y is at t).*[16]

And the definition in the functional case, 'good Q-er' is:

> *y is or would make a good Q-er (in certain respects C, to degree d, at t) if and only if, if there's reason to arrange that something Qs (in those respects C, to degree d, at t), then that fact is a specific reason to choose y to Q (in those respects C, to degree d, at t).*[17]

What about saying that something is bad? We may be saying that there is sufficient reason to 'con' it in some way. Or we may be saying that there is not sufficient reason to pro it in some way. In the epistemic case, when we say that y is a bad argument for the conclusion that p we're saying that there's no reason to believe that p in virtue of y. In the evaluative case when we say that y is bad we may be saying that there's sufficient reason to deplore or be averse to y. What about the practical case? Is saying that a choice or

---

[16] Or for the citizens, members, of x to desire y in virtue of being citizens, members.

[17] y_1 is better than y_2 if, given that there's reason to arrange that something Qs there is more reason to choose y_1 than y_2 to Q. Also, note that the definition of functional good extends the general favouring account. In general 'good' is understood in terms of what there is sufficient reason to favour. Here, on the other hand, we have conditional favouring and no reference to a sufficient reason.

policy is bad saying there's sufficient reason *not* to choose it? But it may be the least bad thing to do. So what we're saying is that it has features there is sufficient reason to avoid if possible. And what about a bad person? This question cannot be properly answered until we have considered the moral attitudes. To anticipate, by a 'bad person' we mean a person likely to do morally wrong things, and that in turn amounts (as will be argued in 12.1 and 12.2) to: a person likely to do things that there would be reason to blame him or her for doing.

4.4 Objections to the definition

Two significant kinds of objection face the buck-passing account.[18] It may be objected in the first place that the equivalences spelt out above fail to hold. And second, even if the equivalences hold it may be objected that the definition gets things the wrong way round. This second kind of objection raises the question of explanatory order. If there's sufficient reason to favour y as an F, it says, that's *because* y is a good F. I *explain* why there's reason to favour y by pointing out that the reason is that it's a good F. If saying that it was good just *was* saying that there's sufficient reason to pro it, the objection runs, that wouldn't be an explanation.

'Evil demon' examples illustrate why the equivalence may be thought to fail. Suppose the violin performance is not good, but the evil demon will punish me with eternal torture if I fail to admire it. Is that not sufficient reason for me to admire it, even though it's not good? Similarly, suppose that some purported evidence to the effect that p is not good evidence, but the evil demon will again punish me if I fail to believe that it probabilizes the conclusion that p. Is that not sufficient reason for me to believe that it does probabilize that conclusion, even though it's not good evidence?

In replying to this objection we should distinguish (as in 2.9) between reasons to believe or feel, on the one hand, and reasons to bring it about that one believes or feels, on the other. Thus although there is no sufficient reason for me to admire the performance, there certainly is sufficient reason for me to bring it about that I admire the performance, if I can. In other words, in this case there is reason for me to bring it about that I admire something which there is no reason for me to admire. Likewise: there is no sufficient reason for me to believe that this purported evidence to the effect that p probabilizes that conclusion, but there certainly is sufficient reason for me to bring it about that I believe it does, if I can. Bringing about these things is undoubtedly choice-worthy, if it is possible. It is important to specify what exactly it is that is good. Neither the performance nor the evidence is good; but the policy of making oneself believe that they are good *is* good. And that is what the buck-passing definition delivers. What is good in these cases, according to the definition, is the *policy* of (trying to) do whatever I can to make myself admire the performance, or believe the evidence to be probabilizing. But

---

[18] For objections of this kind, see Crisp 2000; D'Arms and Jacobson 2000 (especially Section IV); Rabinowicz and Rønnow-Rasmussen 2004.

because we can distinguish between practical reasons, on the one hand, and epistemic and evaluative reasons, on the other, it does not follow on the buck-passing analysis that the *performance* or the *evidence* itself is good.

Is this response as *ad hoc*?[19] I don't think so. The distinction between epistemic, evaluative, and practical reasons is independently based on what kind of act—belief, feeling, or action—a given reason is a reason for. So the response is just an automatic consequence of identifying what exact reason relation we are discussing.[20] In the case of the violin performance, the fact that the evil demon has his evil plans is a sufficient reason for me to *do* something—namely, bring it about that I admire the performance, if I can. In the circumstances, that would be a very good thing to bring about. Over and above that uncontroversial point, there is then the question of whether an evaluative reason relation also holds. Does the selfsame fact about the evil demon stand in that *distinct* reason relation to me and a certain feeling of mine, namely, *admiring the performance*? The two relations are distinct, since their *relata* are distinct. And once they have been distinguished, a case needs to be made for holding that the second relation holds as well as the first.

Take the case of belief. Someone may agree that there is a difference between epistemic reasons to believe and practical reasons to make yourself believe, or bring it about that you believe—but still insist that facts about the usefulness of believing that p are not just a reason to make yourself believe that p but *also* a reason to believe that p. That is a substantive, and contentious, proposal in normative epistemology, which it is not ad hoc to reject. Why should we posit this further epistemic reason to believe that p, on top of the acknowledged practical reason to make oneself believe that p? There seems to be nothing self-contradictory in saying that the utility of believing something—for example, that you will survive the dangerous mission—is a reason to *make* yourself believe it even it is *not* a reason to believe it. This point seems to me decisive against alleged 'pragmatic' as against 'evidential' epistemic reasons to believe. But suppose that it is denied. The denier would have to have an at least partly pragmatic theory of truth. It is a priori that a reason to believe that p is a reason to believe that it is true that p. Pragmatists about truth can happily accept that: they hold that the usefulness of believing a proposition is a priori indicative of the truth of that proposition. For them, therefore, the usefulness of believing that p is unproblematically both a reason to believe that p and a reason to believe that it is true that p. Suppose, in contrast, that one holds the truth of a proposition and the usefulness of believing it to be entirely distinct questions. How, in that case, can the usefulness of believing that p constitute, in and of itself, a reason to believe that it is true that p?

We shall argue in 7.5 for a minimalist view of truth which is incompatible with the pragmatic theory, and in 20.2 we shall have more to say in favour of the trichotomy of reasons. On closer consideration, however, we can for the moment sidestep these particular debates. Suppose we define evidence that p as consisting in any accessible facts

---

[19] As suggested by Rabinowicz and Rønnow-Rasmussen 2004: 412.
[20] I suspect, however, that one main reason why people reject the buck-passing story is that they don't believe there really are irreducible reasons for feeling, for affective responses. As a result, an irreducible category of ethical and aesthetic value plays, for them, the role in ethical and aesthetic cognition that propositions about evaluative reasons play for the buck-passer.

that give one reason to believe that p (cp 9.2). Then, on the pragmatist view, if I know that the demon will torture me unless I believe that he is God that *is* good evidence that he is God. Which leaves us with no objection to the buck-passing account of 'good evidence'. At this point the objector will seek to distinguish, among accessible facts that give one reason to believe that p, between those which are 'evidential' and those which are 'pragmatic'. Surely it is this distinction that seems *ad hoc*, compared to the distinction between reasons to believe and reasons to bring it about that one believes, which does equivalent work more naturally. In any case the distinction does not undermine the buck-passing account of epistemic goodness, it just complicates it. Good reasons to believe that p will be reasons to believe that p which there is sufficient reason to accept as reasons to believe that p, while good evidence that p will be the special case of reasons to believe that p that (i) satisfy some restriction on what reasons to believe that p count as *evidence*; and that (ii) there is sufficient reason to accept as reasons to believe that p.

The same response applies to alleged pragmatic reasons for admiration. If someone holds that the usefulness of admiring y really *is* a reason to admire y, and not just a reason for bringing it about that one admires it, then he has an unusual proposal to make in the substantive theory of evaluative reasons. On what principled basis can he refrain from an equally unusual theory of aesthetic value? If I'm threatened with torture unless I admire the violin performance, then on this theory the performance now becomes distinctly valuable for me.[21]

It may be replied that these responses beg the question, in that they presuppose the 'buck-passing' analysis of good evidence, good reason, and good performance. They do presuppose it, but I don't think they beg the question. The onus of proof is on the objector. He needs to justify a difference between two kinds of genuinely epistemic or evaluative reasons—evidential and pragmatic, or value relevant and pragmatic—and to show why we need it, given that all the relevant work can apparently be done by the unpuzzling distinction between epistemic or evaluative reasons, on the one hand, and practical reasons, on the other.

Let us turn to the second objection. Does our definition get things the wrong way round? I can *explain* why there's reason to favour something by pointing out that it's good. I don't *explain* why it's good by pointing out that there's reason to favour it.

Although a 'wrong way round' or 'cart before the horse' point of this kind can be a sound objection against a proposed definition based on an equivalence, in this case I do not think it is. Note first that there may be reason to favour a thing in one way because there's reason to favour it in some other way. Thus the reason to *choose* this CD performance may be that it's the best performance—the one there's most reason to admire. However, we might have reasons to choose this particular CD for reasons other than the quality of the performance: because it's cheap, for example. If we're working to a tight budget the cheapest CD performance may be the best choice, even though the performance

---

[21] i.e. there are patient-relative reasons for me to admire it (and not just agent-relative reasons for me to make myself admire it). But we think reasons for admiration are patient-neutral, not patient-relative.

is not the best. So it has genuine explanatory force to say that there's reason to choose the CD because it's contains the best performance.[22]

In contrast, to say only:

> (1) There's reason to favour the performance most because it is the best performance

has little explanatory force. Still, it doesn't sound positively odd, as does saying:

> (2) It's the best performance because it's the one there's reason to favour most.

But again I think this asymmetry arises because there can be reasons to favour a performance *other* than its quality as a performance. Remember that 'good' is attributive. The best performance is naturally understood as the performance that is best *as a performance*. There might be reason to favour a performance other than the fact that it's best *as a performance*. It might be best as a way of keeping the pigeons away, for example. So (1) can tell us something substantive, by eliminating possible reasons for favouring the performance other than its quality as a performance. In contrast, on the same natural understating of 'best performance' (2) would be false if the reason for favouring the performance most was that it was best at keeping the pigeons away. But if we clarify (2):

> (2*) It's the best performance as a performance because it's the one there's reason to favour most as a performance

then it seems to be at most a way of conveying the meaning of 'best'.

Further, how do we explain why something is a good F? We do so by pointing out the facts about it that make it good as an F. Those are the very facts that give one reason to favour it as an F. In that sense we do explain why it's a good F by stating the reasons for favouring it as an F. While we don't of course explain why a thing is good by simply saying *that* there are reasons to favour it, we do explain by saying what those reasons are. More generally, it is a virtue of the buck-passing view that it eliminates a factitious middleman. Consider the following three claims:

> (3) This pastime is pleasant.
> (4) This is a good pastime.
> (5) There's reason to favour this pastime.

On the non-reductive view of 'good', (5) holds in virtue of (4), and (4) holds in virtue of (3). Between the pleasantness of the pastime and its goodness there is a supervenience relation, and between its goodness and favouring it there's another relation: the reason relation. Thus we must add a further non-definitional step to (3) and (4):

> The fact that this is a good pastime is a reason to favour this pastime.

---

[22] You might have reason to choose a CD which has a bad performance just to illustrate in your consumer survey what poor value there is on the market. In this case the bad performance is a good choice. (Cp. Ewing 1959: 100. I owe this reference to Jonas Olson.)

And from that we get (5) by existential generalization:

(5*) (∃x)(x is a reason to favour this pastime).

On the buck-passing view, in contrast, it's the pleasantness of the pastime that is the reason to favour it:

(6) The fact that this is a pleasant pastime is a reason to favour this pastime.

For the buck-passer (4) and (5) are synonymous: so either is deducible from (6) by existential generalization. Whereas on the non-reductive view the 'supervenience' relation between pleasantness and goodness is distinct from the reason relation between goodness and favouring, on the buck-passing view the supervenience relation simply *is* the reason relation.

Obviously we still have to address questions about the epistemology and ontology of the reason relation itself. According to the Reasons thesis, the meta-theory of normativity reduces to these. In that light it is worth noting that we do not have to ask those same questions about another, supposedly distinct relation, that of normative supervenience.

The two objections that have been considered in this section, and our responses to them, are structurally symptomatic, in that they do not arise only for our analysis of 'good'. Analogous objections and responses can be made to all the other accounts of normative concepts in terms of reasons that will be made in this book. This applies especially to the 'cart before horse' objection. For beyond the points that have been made in reply to it in this section with respect to 'good', more general metaphysical questions arise, questions that we shall only reach in Part IV. We shall address them in 18.6, taking into account all the analyses of normative concepts that will by then have been offered in Parts I to III.

In the extensive literature that has built up about the buck-passing account of 'good' since Scanlon revived it in *What We Owe to Each Other*,[23] there are a number of objections which do not fall under the two structural ones that have been considered here. It would take us to far afield to consider them in detail; however, I believe that the following three general points of clarification are relevant to many of them.

First, remember that in 3.3 we took reasons to be *nominal* facts, that is, truths. Since there are normative as well as non-normative truths, our analysis of 'good' is no way entails that reasons must consist of non-normative as against normative truths. Furthermore the analysis is neutral as to whether all reasons must 'at bottom' come down to non-normative facts—on that question see 19.5.

Second, the buck-passing account, despite its biconditional form, does not entail that there are no 'purely deontological reasons'.[24] The fact that I have promised is, indeed, a

---

[23] See (for example) Bykvist 2009; Crisp 2005, 2006, 2008; Danielsson and Olson 2007; Väyrynen 2006. For a further sampling of recent work, see also *Ethical Theory and Moral Practice* 12, 2009 (4), edited by Kevin Mulligan and Wlodek Rabinowicz, is about value theory. Scanlon and Moore's views are compared in Stratton-Lake and Hooker 2006.

[24] As suggested by Roger Crisp (2008: 260).

reason to keep my promise; hence by the buck-passing analysis ('from right to left') it follows that keeping my promise is a good thing to do, at least in that respect. (It might be a bad thing to do in other respects; i.e. there might be reasons not to keep it.) However, why should this stop us from acknowledging that the duty to keep promises is a source of 'purely deontological reasons'? The reason to keep a promise is deontological in the sense that it arises solely from what the promisee can permissibly demand: it is an instance of what in Chapter 14 we shall call the Demand principle. This particular reason does not arise from the good consequences of keeping one's promises, or from any special 'value in itself' that keeping one's promise has. It is true that there are such deontological reasons, or so it seems to me. But it is also perfectly consistent with the buck-passing account. This account of 'good' is neutral on substantive ethical questions concerning deontology and teleology, just as it is neutral on whether all reasons 'at bottom' consist of non-normative facts.

Finally, a question we have not considered is whether *there is reason for x to ψ* entails *x can ψ*. I have no definite answer to this; on the face of it one could go either way.

Consider the following case:[25] the evil demon will punish you not only if you fail to admire the (worthless) violin performance, but also if you in any way seek to bring this admiration about. You will avoid punishment if and only if you admire the performance without in any way bringing it about that you admire it, making yourself admire it, or even trying to admire it.

Is this a case in which there is reason for you to admire the performance but no reason for you to make yourself admire it? On the account we have given, it is not a case in which there is reason for you to admire the performance. Whether there's reason for you to *do* anything is more debatable. It depends on whether there can be reason to do something that cannot be done—in this case, causing oneself to admire the performance without the demon knowing that one has done that. On the one hand, it might be argued that 'ought implies can' applies only to moral obligations, because it arises from the connection between moral obligation and blame. It does not apply to 'ought*' or to reasons. There can be reason to believe something that one cannot believe, so why can't there be reason to do something that one cannot do? On this view, to vary the example, if a billionaire offers me a million pounds for squaring a circle, that's a reason for me to square a circle—unfortunately it's impossible. If, alternatively, we take the view that there can be reason to (try to) do only what it is possible to do, then it follows there is no reason to (try to) square the circle, although there would be reason to (try to) do it if it were possible. It follows, on this latter view, that the buck-passing account must be formulated in terms of what there would be reason to do if it were possible to do it. For example, to say that there is a good picnic table in some inaccessible place is to say that there *would* be reason to use it for picnicking if it were possible to do so. I have ignored this complication in formulating the definitions in Section 3, but I do not thereby mean to assume that it is irrelevant.

---

[25] Put to me by Wlodek Rabinowicz.

4.5 Thick evaluative terms: (i) wholly normative

We have now considered the thin or topic-neutral normative terms that make up the central circle of normative vocabulary. We also have to consider the difficult and ramified outer circle. Significantly, many terms in this outer circle are in fact evaluative, having to do with reasons for feeling this or that—I will call them 'thick evaluative terms'.

When we say that something is good or right, we say there are reasons without saying what the facts are that constitute those reasons, or for what act or attitude they provide a reason. Thick evaluative terms impose tighter restrictions. How do they do that?

One way they might do so is by being more specific about what attitude there is reason for. Consider in particular predicates of the form:

A: $(\exists \pi_i) S(\pi_i, \phi(y))$

where 'ϕ' names some specific affective reaction. What they say about y is that there is sufficient reason to take attitude ϕ to y.[26] They say no more than that. However, that may tell us quite a lot. From our inner understanding of that particular reaction—admiration, say, or disgust—we can work out quite a bit, indirectly, about what sort of facts those facts must be, even though we are not told what specific facts obtain.

The number of potential practical–normative or epistemic–normative predicates is as large as the number of action and belief contents, i.e. indefinitely large. In the evaluative case the affective *attitudes*, as well as their contents, ramify indefinitely. Furthermore, and very importantly, evaluations of type A will not all be neatly classifiable as asserting that there is sufficient reason for a *pro* or *con* attitude toward the object, and thus, as implying that the object is good or bad in some respect. Does the fact that there is reason to be disturbed or shocked by a performance, for example, make it good or bad? That may well depend on context. Disgust is generally a con-attitude. But even this need not always be evident. An object may give sufficient reason to respond with a complex of attitudes of which disgust may be an element. Yet the overall complex may justify a pro-attitude. This openness between making a specific evaluation in terms of an affective attitude and determining whether that evaluation counts towards the goodness or badness of the object is one of the things that gives Critical discourse in the arts its depth, complexity, and elusiveness. Specific evaluations can be indefinitely subtle, quite informative (though inexplicitly) about the facts, and linked in no neat or simple way to an assessment of their objects as good or bad.

Does ordinary language contain any terms analysable as type A predicates? One set of candidates for the role consists of terms like 'admirable', 'lovable', 'enviable', 'desirable', and so on. Arguably, 'This is admirable' means 'there is sufficient reason to admire this'. If that is right, 'y is admirable' is a purely normative predicate.

It may be replied that predicates of this kind—'ϕ-able'—can have the non-normative meaning 'capable of inspiring admiration/desire/love'. Maybe they are useable in either

---

[26] This is the simplest case. Where the reason is relative to an agent the agent variable can come into play: there is reason for me but not for you to desire y. Where it is temporally relative the time variable will come into play: there was reason then, but there is no reason now, to hope that y would come.

or both ways, the normative and the non-normative. But we need not accept this. The appearance that such predicates have non-normative use may be explained away, by reference to their epistemology and their function. The fact that something does inspire admiration, desire, love, or whatever (lastingly, on reflection, after discussion) is the fundamental epistemic criterion for its being worthy of admiration, desire, love, etc. Now just because the fact that *p* is criterial for, that is, constitutes a defeasible sufficient reason for, the assertion that *q*, it does not follow that in asserting that *q* we are asserting that *p*. Nonetheless, when a proposition is very tightly tied to a dominant criterion, as in the case of these 'ϕ-able' predicates, it is easy to think (though strictly it is incorrect) that asserting the proposition is asserting that the criterion obtains. Furthermore, given the use of these predicates in criticism and persuasion, it is very natural, if one is challenged as to whether a performance is really admirable or a house is really desirable, to fall back on the fact that many people do admire it or desire it. But neither point shows that 'admirable' or 'desirable' have a non-normative meaning. So the view that these are purely normative predicates can be defended.

At first sight terms such as 'frightening', 'moving', 'boring', and so on seem more clearly to fall on both sides of the normative/non-normative border line. Again, however, one can argue by reference to their epistemology and their function that the appearance of non-normative content is misleading. Take 'frightening'. Can it *mean* 'fear-causing' as well as 'fear-worthy'? It is not easy in fact to come up with an example of a use that is definitely non-normative. Consider 'These steps would be very frightening to someone with poor balance and short sight'. 'Frightening' here could mean 'fear-causing', but it could also mean 'fear-worthy'. Or again: 'Spiders are frightening to many people but there's really nothing about them to be frightened of'. Is the first occurrence of 'frightening' in this sentence a non-normative use? Not necessarily. The sentence could mean 'Spiders seem to many people to be fear-worthy but they are not really'.

In the same vein, suppose I attend a lecture on quantum physics and find it boring. Note the typical locution: *finding* something boring, amusing, irritating, etc. This looks as though it might be factive, but it is not: from the fact that I found something boring it does not follow that it *is* boring. Rather, to say I found it boring is equivalent to saying that it seemed boring to me. Someone may reply 'It was not *really* boring—it is just that you do not know anything about the subject. The experts who were there found it really interesting'. Likewise, if one says that something was genuinely moving, or really or truly moving, one makes a contrast between what merely seems moving and what really is. How does the contrast between appearance and reality work here? It is not that something can seem to move me without really moving me. Rather, the contrast is between apparent and real normativity. When one is moved by something, a musical performance say, one doesn't simply experience an emotion, one experiences it as appropriate, fitting to its object. But it can happen that this normative dimension in one's feelings strikes one as misguided. I am moved by the performance, and that emotional reaction comes packaged, so to speak, with an impression of itself as reasonable—but at a level more detached from the reaction itself I think to myself that I am being sentimental. The performance was not genuinely, really, moving; I am just a sucker for that sugary kind of violin sound. So 'genuinely moving', 'truly moving' are normative.

So far, so good. Yet many terms used in ordinary language evaluative discourse *seem* normative even though they carry no connection to an affective reaction on their face. In aesthetic evaluation they abound: consider, for example, 'bizarre', 'beautiful', and 'sublime'.

Since our linguistic taxonomy of affective responses is less ramified than our taxonomy of evaluations one should expect difficulty in finding a word to characterize, for each evaluative predicate, the *specific* affective response that its application says there is sufficient reason for. Take the example of 'bizarre'. It has reference to some form of surprise. To say that something is bizarre is to say, according to the *Oxford English Dictionary*, that it is 'extravagant, whimsical, strange, odd, fantastic'. But also: 'At variance with the standard of ideal beauty or regular form; grotesque, irregular'.[27] In each case the surprise is justified by the fact that the item in question goes beyond what there is reason to expect from a 'regular' item of that kind. The whimsical, fantastic, etc. is surprising in *that* way; it gives reason for an attitude of surprise directed to *that* content. What content? Something that is grotesque, irregular, in a word, bizarre: something that occasions that specific kind of somewhat mocking, somewhat enjoyably supercilious, surprise. So it seems that we have the same circularity here as we found with 'morally wrong'. Even if the term is not definable in type A terms, because we have no term for the relevant ϕ which does not produce a circularity, the concept expressed is of type A. The difficulty of introducing a term to refer to it—as I suggested could be done for the blame sentiment—is compounded by the fact that there is no action (as against reaction) which is characteristically prompted by the surprise of the bizarre (or indeed by surprise in general). So one is reduced to explanation by paradigms of what merits it, and lame attempts to characterize it.

With the beautiful and the sublime we arrive at classical terms which have long been recognized as difficult to define. Many of the traditional discussions in aesthetics have actually been concerned with what *makes* a thing beautiful (in the sense in which one might discuss what makes a thing annoying). It seems uncontroversial that the beautiful is that which is admirable in a certain way. But what way? By giving a certain sort of pleasure, in virtue of a certain sort of rightness or grace of combination, of proportions, colour combinations, or whatever. So: if *y* is beautiful then *y* has properties combined in such a way as to give satisfaction or pleasure of the kind taken in this perceived *rightness* of combination, and in virtue of that pleasing combination, to give sufficient reason for admiration. (The concept of the sublime seems simpler in its logical structure: it is that which is uplifting, exalting, ennobling, awe-inspiring.) The properties of a beautiful thing have a rightness of combination, they combine as they should. And it is this rightness of combination that gives sufficient reason for delight and admiration. But what can it mean to talk about whether properties are combining as they should—how can the normative concept get an application here? Does it just mean that they combine in a way that gives

---

[27] The OED also has: 'At variance with recognized ideas of taste, departing from ordinary style or usage; eccentric...' But recognized ideas of taste, and ordinary style and usage, may themselves be bizarre, in which case the eccentric may precisely not be bizarre. None of these, of course, are strictly *definitions*.

reason for delight and admiration? Or does the concept of the beautiful involve a double layer of normativity: (i) properties combining as they should; and (ii) that fact constituting a reason for delight/admiration? It is tempting to think that a simulated functional assessment is involved in a judgement of beauty, captured in Kant's idea of 'purposiveness without a purpose'. We can say that an object with a function is working as it should, arranged as it should be, by reference to its function. But with beauty we have the appearance of rightness of arrangement without a function to underpin it. Thus in (i) we have seeming rather than real normativity: a *seeming* should, an *appearance* of rightness which constitutes the beautiful.

4.6 Thick evaluative terms: (ii) mixed

There might be terms that predicate both a non-normative property and a reason constituted by possession of that property. Where 'F' is the non-normative property in question, such terms would have the form:

B: S(the fact that Fy, $\phi(y)$).

Are there any such predicates?

We have just suggested that various predicates which may look as though they have this form don't really. Term like 'admirable' and 'boring' are wholly normative. It's true that the fact that something is boredom-causing is, epistemically speaking, a defeasible reason to believe it *is* boring, but that is a different point.

Then again, some predicates which may be thought to be mixed are probably not normative at all. Consider 'That was a cruel thing to do'. This means (at least) 'That was a hurtful action which showed in its motivation the presence of a substantive desire to inflict suffering'.[28] So the assertion makes a factual claim. But does it also, as part of its meaning, make a normative claim? That would make it a mixed predicate: e.g. 'y shows in its motivation the presence of a desire to inflict suffering, and that fact is a sufficient reason to disapprove of y'.

It is not clear to me that this is the right account. Is it self-contradictory to deny that there is reason to disapprove of cruelty? I think not: it is just false. Likewise with kindness, courage, resentfulness, laziness, arrogance, coldness, and so on. These are names of character traits which we take to be virtues or vices, excellences or defects, but it does not seem to me to be part of their meaning that that is what they are. Similarly with such terms as 'adultery': there seems to be nothing self-contradictory in saying that there is nothing wrong with adultery. (One might avoid that word, meaning to avoid unintended conversational implications, or one might choose it precisely to rid the word of those implications.)

But now consider 'murder'. To call something a murder is at least to say that it's an intentional killing with 'malice aforethought'. Is it a definitional truth that there is reason

---

[28] Can't one be unintentionally cruel? It seems to me that cruelty proper is more than unknowing hurtfulness, or callousness, or lack of care. 'It wasn't just thoughtless, brutal, stupid, reckless, etc.—it was cruel'.

to condemn murder? If it is, that's because *malicious* killing means (at least) 'killing there is reason to condemn in virtue of its motive'. Not every intentional killing is malicious, and it is at least not easy to narrow down the intentional killings that are malicious by a wholly non-normative criterion. Even if that can be done, it is surely not part of the semantics of 'murder'. Rather, 'murder' means something like 'intentional killing where the intention is of such a kind that there is sufficient reason to blame the person who does the act with that intention'.[29] In other words the relevant class of acts is picked out partly by a descriptive condition and partly by a normative condition. It does not give us a wholly *non-normative* characterization of the fact on which the blameworthiness supervenes, so it does not fit form B. It has this structure:

> y is an intentional killing of such a kind that there is sufficient reason to blame the person who does y.

Predicates with this structure have a non-normative component, but one that is not strong enough on its own to characterize the reason purely descriptively. Consider courtesy and discourtesy. Courtesy is a matter of paying due care to putting people at their ease in a social context where that is relevant. Discourtesy is giving insufficient attention to that. 'Insufficient' is normative: the attention (if any) the action showed to placing others at their ease was small enough to constitute sufficient reason for disapproval of that aspect of the action. So the predicate 'y is discourteous' has a reason predicate as a definitional consequence—'there is sufficient reason to disapprove of y'. But it is not possible to factor out a wholly non-normative component that expresses the sufficient reason for disapproval. We are assessing the action by reference to how much attention it showed, in its context, to putting others at their ease, and saying that it did not show enough. Saying that is assessing the action normatively. Equally if we say the action was courteous, we are assessing it in the same dimension and saying that it showed a degree of attention to putting people at their ease great enough to give sufficient reason for approval.

So what we are saying, in these two examples, is of the form:

> C: y has property F to a degree or in a way which is such as to give sufficient reason to $\phi(y)$.

Various other terms work like that: 'careless', 'reckless', 'negligent', 'inattentive', and 'overbearing'. We characterize the degree of care, attentiveness, etc. by saying that it is such as to satisfy a normatively expressed condition. So we cannot factor out a non-normative sentence which states the fact that constitutes the sufficient reason.

Thus we should agree with philosophers who hold that there are thick evaluative terms from which a reason-giving factual component is inextricable. We may not have a way of exactly characterizing just those facts that merit a particular attitude except by reference to the attitude in question. And we may not have neat vocabulary to characterize exactly the attitude in question. However, these points do not undermine the two

---

[29] There can of course be further distinctions, say between murder and culpable homicide, or murders of various degree.

truths which in Section 4.2 we noted as lying behind the is/ought distinction.[30] Nor are they in any way inconsistent with the Reasons thesis.

4.7 Functional goodness and cost-effectiveness

As noted in Section 4.3 functional goodness is a matter of cost-effectiveness. Consider a filleting knife. It's a good one, good as a filleting knife, if it can be used to cut large, neat, very thin slices while requiring, relatively to other possible tools for the job, less use of scarce resource. A good filleting knife requires relatively low levels of attention or expenditure of time for a given level of result, and less time on the part of the typical user: these, in this case, are the scarce resources. Aesthetic questions may come into one's appraisal of filleting knives. Tradition, appearance, the scope for demonstrating skill, etc. may influence one's judgements. But if filleting knives are considered purely functionally, in terms of what there's reason to choose for filleting alone, economy in the use of scarce resources is what matters. A good filleting knife is a cost-effective one: its use expends relatively little scarce resource, in comparison to other tools, for the required level of performance. In general, the fact that makes something good for Q-ing is that it Qs fairly cost-effectively; it is a fairly cost-effective way or means of, or tool for, Q-ing. It's the *best* Q-er if it's the most cost-effective one.

So instead of our definition of 'good' above can't we simply define a good Q-er as one which Qs cost-effectively—with a relatively low expenditure of scarce resource? And isn't that a definition of functional goodness which does not define that concept in terms of the reason relation? If so, we must either give up the Reasons thesis or concede that the concept of functional goodness is not normative.

Bear in mind that there can be reasons to use a Q-er that have nothing to do with its functional goodness as a Q-er. There might be reason to use this picnic table because your mother gave it to you and is coming to the picnic—but that does not, I think, affect the question of how good the table is as a picnic table, as against how good it is as a way of pleasing your mother. Call this the 'irrelevant reasons' point; it means that if we want our notion of cost-effectiveness to correlate with functional goodness, then the fact that using this particular picnic table would please your mother should be irrelevant to its cost-effectiveness as a picnic table, as well as to its functional goodness. It may be a cost-effective *picnic table*, without being the most cost-effective solution to your total decision problem when all your objectives are taken into account. And that seems right: the cost-effectiveness of this table as against others *as a picnic table* has to do with how cost-effective it is for picnicking. It is, in fact, just the notion of functional goodness in another guise. Now according to our definition of functional goodness, the goodness of a picnic table, as a picnic table, is a matter of how much reason there is to picnic off it, as against picnicking off something else, given

---

[30] There are many thick evaluative terms that one may eschew because of their 'in-group' significance. Consider: 'y is naff' = 'y has a style which merits a reaction of disdain'. But 'naff' is also a term use of which indicates membership of a group with attitude, an attitude that implies a belief in the superior taste of the group, and may carry an intention to insult. One may eschew it for these reasons, even while not disagreeing with what 'y is naff' literally says.

only that there is reason to picnic. We should define cost-effectiveness in the same way; the cost-effectiveness of a Q-er, as a Q-er, is defined as how much reason the fact that that there's reason to Q gives to use this Q-er, as against other Q-ers.

Furthermore, if we take the notion of cost-effectiveness as non-normative, and then seek to define functional goodness in terms of it, an open-question argument arises. Consider the inference from:

(7) y is or would make a good Q-er

to

(8) If there is reason to Q then there is reason to choose y for Q-ing.

I submit that this inference is analytic; and it does indeed come out as analytic by the definition of 'good' for the functional case given above. Contrast the inference from:

(9) y is or would make a cost-effective Q-er

to

(10) If there is reason to Q then there is reason to choose y for Q-ing.

What is the status of the inference from (9) to (10)? Is it analytic? Not if cost-effectiveness is a non-normative notion. In short if cost-effectiveness is a non-normative notion it cannot define functional goodness, whereas it if is, it is definable in terms of functional goodness, rather than *vice versa*.[31]

We should take it in the latter way, as identical to the normative concept of functional goodness. So understood it features in an important principle which we can call the *Transmission principle*, in that it transmits reasons from objectives to means.[32] This principle says that if there is reason to pursue an objective then there is reason to adopt some means of doing so—the strength of that reason being proportional to the strength of reason to pursue the objective, and the cost-effectiveness (functional goodness) of that particular means.

I shall claim that the Transmission principle is analytic (Section 4.9) whereas the Instrumental principle is false (10.4 and 10.5). First, however, we should examine how reason relations behave within conditionals; for there are some puzzles here that can easily mislead.

4.8 Reasons and conditionals

Consider the following conditional:

(11) If you should go to the lecture then you should get up now.

---

[31] Note further that since cost-effectiveness applies to choice under risk and uncertainty, a theory of cost-effectiveness is a theory of 'rational choice', and will thus involve normative principles, such as the Savage axioms or others, as discussed in Section 4.9.
[32] Cp. Joseph Raz's 'facilitative principle' (Raz 2005).

The lecture is taking place early in the morning; if you don't get up now you won't have time to get to it. So (11) seems true. Suppose it's also true that you should go to the lecture. It is false, however, that you're going to go to it, or have any intention whatsoever of doing so. In that case, is it true that you should get up now? Apparently not. In the circumstances getting up now will be rather pointless: there's nothing else for you to do other than going to the lecture, so you might as well stay in bed. On the basis of such examples, it may seem that the following form of argument is invalid:

(12) You should α_1.
(13) If you should α_1 then you should α_2.
(14) You should α_2.

Reading 'should' in the designated sense (2.6), what we have is:

(15) $S(you, \alpha_1)$.
(16) $S(you, \alpha_1) \rightarrow S(you, \alpha_2)$.
(17) $S(you, \alpha_2)$.

But this argument is a straightforward case of *modus ponens*. How can it be invalid?

Remember that S, the sufficient-reason relation, is a relation between agents, acts, and *sets of facts*. Whether there's sufficient reason for you to α, and thus whether you should α, depends on what facts obtain. So in assessing the validity of arguments involving S, like (15) to (17), we must hold the set of facts to which S is implicitly relative *constant* in all premises and in the conclusion.

In puzzling cases such as the one we are considering, context invites a shift in the set of facts relative to which the truth-values of premises and conclusion are assessed. In assessing whether you should go to the lecture, that you are *not* going to go to it is not taken as one of the given facts. But if indeed you are not going to go it, then, relative to the total set of facts which also includes that fact, it's true that you should stay in bed.

This basic line of thought is correct but two difficulties with it should be considered. First, how can it be relevant to distinguish between different sets of facts to which 'should' is relativized? If it's a fact that you are not going to go to the lecture, then doesn't the totality of facts include that fact? Second, relative to that totality it is false that you should get up now. And yet can it not also be true, given that very same totality, including the fact that you are not going to go to the lecture, that you *should* go to it? Surely you can't argue 'Well, I'm not going to go to the lecture, so it isn't true that I should go'?

It is crucial that whether or not you are going to go to the lecture is *up to you*. It follows that when we assess whether or not you should go to the lecture, we cannot regard it as a given that you are going to go, or that you are not going to go. That is, we cannot include either the fact that you are or the fact that you are not going to go in the set of facts relative to which the assessment is made. For the assessment is precisely an assessment of whether you should go. The general rule here is that when the truth-value of 'You should α' is being assessed, the fact that you will α (if you will) or that you will not (if you will not) cannot be included in the set of facts relative to which the assessment is being made.[33] By the very nature of premise (12), then, the set of facts relative to which its truth-value is assessed cannot include either the fact that you will or the fact that you will not perform α_1. Likewise, then, the set of facts relative to which (13) and (14) are assessed does not include either fact.

In particular, therefore, when we consider the truth-value of 'You should stay in bed' we cannot include the fact that you will or the fact that you won't stay in bed in the set of facts relative to which we make our assessment. However, if it's a fact that you are not going to go to the lecture we can certainly include that fact—it is quite obviously relevant. We can truly say:

(18) Given that you're not going to the lecture, you should stay in bed.

And we can also truly say:

(19) You should go to the lecture but if you are not going to go to the lecture you should stay in bed.

In (19) the set of facts relative to which the first 'should' is assessed does not include the fact that you are not going to go to the lecture, whereas the set of facts relative to which the second 'should' is assessed does. We can call shoulds of the second kind 'second-best counsel'.[34] For example, if the doctor tells me:

(20) You should give up all fatty foods but if you're not going to do that then at least you should give up crisps,

then here again the second 'should' is second-best counsel.

Does second-best counsel work in the same way in cases of moral obligation? Special issues arise in this case because non-compliance with *moral* obligation is blameworthy. Consider these two examples (where 'ought' is understood in the moral sense):

(21) You ought to go and visit your aunt but given that you're not going to do that at least you ought to ring her up for a chat.
(22) You ought not to murder your father, but given that you're going to murder him, you ought to do it as painlessly as possible.

Do (21) and (22) work in exactly the same way as (19) and (20)? I think they do. But while (21) constitutes a perfectly familiar kind of second-best moral counsel, most people would balk at issuing (22). It's not clear, however, that this is because (22) isn't true. It may rather be to do with the morality of giving second-best counsel. Perhaps the only counsel that it's permissible to give to an intending father-murderer is not to commit the murder. Giving second-best counsel in this case is too close to condoning the crime. (Compare 'You ought not rob the bank, but given that you're going to, you should force the window rather than the door'.)

---

[33] So facts consequent on what you will *in fact* do cannot be included either, though conditional facts about what would happen if you did this or that can be.
[34] Cp. Chisholm's 'contrary to duty imperatives' (Chisholm 1963, 1974). Also Greenspan 1975.

The degree of overall reason for you to α, and whether you should α, is relative to all the facts *except* the fact that you will, or the fact that you will not, α. Almost always, however, that totality will include many *other* facts about what you will or will not do. This point becomes important when we consider the role in practical reasoning of rules, commitments, ideals and the like (for example, in considering rule utilitarianism, 13.9 and 13.10).

We should also at this point consider the possibility of wide-scope readings of 'should' and 'ought', as in:

(23) You ought (if you intend to go to the lecture, get up now).[35]

In the framework we have developed, oughts and shoulds are not treated as operators on sentences, and thus *a fortiori* not as operators on conditionals. They are relations between facts, actors, and acts. So how should we understand this proposed wide-scope 'ought'? We must understand it as the 'ought' of rational requirement. It is not in the first instance directly about reasons, but rather about requirements or constraints formulated in terms of rational criticizability. If you don't do what you ought or should in this sense, you are criticizable in respect of rationality. For example, if you have an objective, believe a given action to be the only means to that objective, but fail to perform it, you are rationally criticizable. Why? Have you failed to do something you ought* to have done? Well, the following cannot all be true simultaneously:

(i) you had sufficient reason to pursue that objective,

(ii) you had sufficient reason to believe that this was the only way to do so,

(iii) you had no reason to adopt these means.

Similarly with the rational requirement that you ought, if you believe that p and that p implies q, believe that q. It cannot be true simultaneously that:

(i) you have sufficient reason to believe that p

(ii) you have sufficient reason to believe that p implies q, and

(iii) you do not have sufficient reason to believe that q.

So in both of these cases, and in all cases where you fail to meet a 'rational requirement', you do something which you had insufficient reason to do, or fail to do something which you had sufficient reason to do. This is the respect in which you are rationally criticizable: your failure to respond to some reason you have (though obviously there can be plenty of extenuating circumstances).

What kind of criticizability is this? We have moved in these examples to talking of the reasons you *have*: what I shall call, in the next chapter, your *warranted* reasons. We shall come back to the notion of rational criticizability there (5.11). As we shall see, what 'rational requirements' obtain depends on truths about reasons, not vice versa.

Meanwhile, we have shown how (12) to (14) and (15) to (17) can be regarded as straightforward instances of *modus ponens* argument. Genuine conditionals of the form of

---

[35] Cp. Broome 2000.

(11) work quite straightforwardly; we simply need to pay careful attention, where relevant, to holding the facts (and the time) to which an ought, or should, or sufficient reason is relative constant throughout the course of an argument.

4.9 The Transmission principle

To return now to the Transmission principle. We framed it in terms of the pursuit of objectives;[36] if there's reason to pursue an objective, there's reason to pursue it by cost-effective means:

> Transmission principle (TP): if there is reason of degree d for x to pursue O there is reason for x to adopt a means m to achieve O; the strength of that reason being proportional
> (a) to d
> (b) to the cost-effectiveness of m as a means to achieve O.

The Transmission principle is analytic.[37] 'Pursuing O' just *means* 'adopting a means to achieve O'; so 'there is reason of degree d to pursue O' means 'there is reason of degree d to adopt a means to the achievement of O'. Cost-effectiveness is by definition functional goodness; by definition of functional goodness and betterness, if m_1 and m_2 are equally functionally good in producing O, then the fact that there is reason to pursue O constitutes equal reason to adopt either of them, co-varying with the strength of d.

It is important, however, to distinguish the definition of functional goodness, or cost-effectiveness, from its normative theory. Ways and means of bringing about O can differ in their propensity to bring about O. I'm more likely to kill a bird with a gun than with a bow and arrow. The gun is a more effective means in the sense of being more likely to achieve the objective—but it may not be more *cost*-effective. It may be very expensive in comparison to a bow and arrow. And using it may have very bad side effects. It may also of course have good side effects, and all these side effects, good and bad, will each be more or less likely.

Plainly any measure of functional goodness must take into account chances or propensities as well as benefits. One well-established view of how to discount benefits by chances is 'expected'[38] utility theory. So we might measure functional goodness by saying that when degrees of reason for pursuing all objectives are held constant, the functional

---

[36] 'Objective' should be understood in a broader sense than 'end'. In 13.6 we shall distinguish between telic and non-telic reasons, where telic reasons are reasons to bring about a final end. Keeping a promise is not an end; if your reason for doing something is to keep a promise that is not a telic reason. Nevertheless, keeping the promise is the *objective* of your action.

[37] As explained in the previous section, when assessing the truth value of such a conditional the facts relative to which antecedent and consequent are being assessed must be held constant.

[38] I put 'expected' in quotes because we are talking about chances in this section, not epistemic probabilities (i.e. degrees of epistemic reasons relative to a field, see 9.6). The normative question we are considering is how chances (propensities, 'causal probabilities') determine practical reasons. There is a further question about how *epistemic* probabilities determine *warranted* practical reasons, but that is not the issue here, though it is certainly relevant to the theory of rational choice, since rational choice is a matter of the actor's warranted reasons (in the sense discussed in Chapter 5).

goodness of various means for pursuing a given objective O is measured by their expected utility.[39] This approach would require some way of screening out what we called irrelevant reasons—reasons for favouring a means other than its cost-effectiveness as a means of producing O. Suppose there is a way. It then still remains the case that making use of expected utility theory to measure the cost-effectiveness of ways and means is making use of one particular *normative* theory of practical reasons, a theory that rests on debatable normative axioms of 'rational choice'.[40] The same applies of course to any other theory of 'rational choice' that might be used to measure cost-effectiveness. The Transmission principle itself is analytic, but these theories, and hence claims about how to *measure* cost-effectiveness, are not.

4.10 Categorical and hypothetical

The Transmission principle, I claim, is the general principle of objectives/means reasoning. Yet many hold that the general principle of such reasoning takes a quite different form, which we can call the Instrumental principle:

> Instrumental principle (IP): if x has objective O, there is reason for x to adopt any means m for bringing about O, the strength of that reason being proportional
> (a) to the intensity of x's commitment to O
> (b) to the cost-effectiveness of m as a means to achieve O.

Here too a theory of how to measure cost-effectiveness will be a normative theory of practical reasons that incorporates chances. The difference is that IP focuses not on the objectives that there's reason for a person to pursue but on the objectives that person actually has. It asserts that the very fact that a person *has* an objective, whatever that objective may be, constitutes a reason to adopt any means to that objective, its strength corresponding to the intensity of that objective. A person's objectives are to be understood as the ultimate motivators of his actions, and the intensity of his commitment to them is measured by the degree of motivation they provide.

In one sense IP may seem more modest than TP: it does not assume that it's possible to assess how much reason there is for a person to pursue some particular ultimate objectives. But this dubious modesty is achieved by gross immodesty in another respect. For whereas TP merely analytically transmits reasons from objectives to means, IP puts forward a very strong, apparently substantive, normative thesis. It says that there's reason for a person to pursue an objective O if and only if their objective *is* O.

[39] Let d_i be the degree of specific reason, positive or negative, to bring about or avoid O_i under conditions of certainty. The utility of the various possible outcomes is measured by the degree of specific reason to bring them about. Let π_i measure, on a scale of 0 to 1, the causal probability that a given way or means, α, will bring about or avoid O_i. We can say that α *promotes* O_i to degree π_i. The expected utility of α-ing is the sum of $d_i\pi_i$.

[40] What is often called the 'sure-thing principle' is particularly controversial. See Skorupski 1999, Chapter 5, Appendix ('The Allais "Paradox"'). More basically, the expected utility approach assumes that d_i are continuous values. That is not an assumption we should make in the general case. For example, it should not be conceded that 'rationality' requires that adherence to moral obligations can be 'continuously traded-off' against other objectives.

Some philosophers hold that IP is the only reason-generating principle of practical reason. We can call this view *instrumentalism* about practical reasoning. It is a highly contestable view; in 10.4 and 10.5 I shall argue not merely that it is not the *only* principle of practical reason but that it is false. For the moment, however, we should note how the notion of second-best counsel can lend it a spurious plausibility.

Suppose it is simply *given* that a person is going to pursue objective O. And suppose that no moral prohibitions or requirements apply. Then it's perfectly true, relative to that set of facts, that there is reason for that person to pursue O in a cost-effective way. We may think he should not pursue O, but we can still give second-best counsel. Yet still this is not IP. In advising him as to what is best for him to do, we can and should take into account not only what the objective he is pursuing actually is, but also what other objectives he *should* have. For example, if he's going to smoke anyway he should at least do so in a way that diminishes the bad effects on his health—and we ought to point that out, where appropriate. Thus even with second-best counsel what the agent should do is determined by the reasons there are for him to pursue various objectives, rather than the mere intensities of the objectives he actually has.

Having made the distinction between the Transmission and the Instrumental principle we should consider its implication for Kant's famous contrast between categorical and hypothetical imperatives, which will be important in Part III.

There are various difficulties in understanding what Kant says about this contrast that we do not need to examine. Indeed it is not clear that he had a fully thought-out view. On the whole, however, it seems best to interpret what he means by a hypothetical imperative in terms of the Transmission principle, not the Instrumental principle. On this interpretation the form of a hypothetical imperative is:

> if there is specific reason to pursue O there is specific reason to adopt a means to achieve O, in proportion to the strength of reason to O and the cost-effectiveness of that means of achieving O.

Or in a formulation that is closer to Kant:

> if you ought* to pursue O then you ought* to adopt a means to achieve O.

Kant thinks the hypothetical interpretative is analytic,[41] and for reasons given in the previous section this principle is indeed analytic. Furthermore, this interpretation clarifies how hypothetical imperatives combine with categorical imperatives.

Categorical Imperatives state that there is reason to pursue an objective O, irrespective of what objectives the agent actually has, that is, what the agent wills. As Kant puts it, they say that 'I ought to act in such or such a way even though I have not willed anything else'.[42] They are (I agree with Kant) a priori, synthetic practical–normative truths which apply to the agent *whatever* the agent actually wills. By the Transmission principle, together with facts about means, Categorical Imperatives generate substantive reasons to

---

[41] e.g. *Groundwork* 4: 417, 419.
[42] *Groundwork* 4: 441.

adopt means. If there are reasons for action at all, there must be 'Categorical Imperatives' understood in this way.[43]

Correspondingly, if we explain the hypothetical imperative in terms of the Instrumental principle, we have two difficulties. First there is the question of status. I shall argue that IP is false; certainly it is not analytic. Second, on this interpretation we have a blatant lack of fit between hypothetical and Categorical Imperatives. Suppose x has objective O. In that case according to IP there is reason for x to adopt a means to achieve O, whether or not a Categorical Imperative says that x should pursue O. Suppose, on the other hand, that a Categorical Imperative states that x should pursue O, but O is not one of x's objectives. By what principle do we then get to the conclusion that there is reason for x to adopt a means to achieve O (if there is)? We can of course appeal to TP, but, in that case, why bring in IP in the first place?

Could we interpret hypothetical imperatives in terms of rational requirements taking wide scope? Thus: you are rationally required (if you have an objective O, and believe that there are means to achieve O, to adopt one those means). Two points about this. First, as noted in Section 4.8, this is in any case only true in virtue of the Transmission principle. Second, if we read *ought* as *rational requirement* we cannot deduce by basic logic, from the premise that you ought to pursue O together with the wide-scope principle, the conclusion that you ought to adopt a means to O. A special principle is required.[44] In contrast, given the Transmission principle this conclusion is a simple case of *modus ponens*.

The natural home for the Instrumental principle is a philosophy which denies that there are any Categorical Imperatives at all, holding instead that IP is the *sole* principle of practical reason. The Kantian view, in contrast, is best represented as combining Categorical Imperatives, in the sense of practical norms about sufficient reasons, with a purely analytic Transmission principle. To this we can add that on Kant's view to *will* an objective is to judge that there is reason to pursue it, and thus to be committed, by TP, to holding that there is reason to adopt means to it.

In fact Kant's basic conception of practical and epistemic reasons treats them in parallel. Just as there are synthetic a priori practical norms, so there are synthetic a priori epistemic norms. Just as willing is being committed to holding that there is sufficient reason to will, so believing is being committed to holding that there is sufficient reason to believe. I believe that this basic conception is sound—so far as it goes. What it leaves out, with hugely damaging consequences, is the whole domain of evaluative reasons. In Parts II and III we shall be developing the basic conception, but bringing evaluative reasons back in.

---

[43] Two factors complicate the situation. (1) Kant introduces a distinction between relative and absolute ends (4: 427–8). The former have value relative to our inclinations, the latter have value irrespective of inclinations. He does not explain how the notion of 'value relative to one's inclination' is supposed to work, but he says it can only support hypothetical imperatives. This confuses the categorical/hypothetical distinction with an alleged distinction between inclination-relative and absolute value. If there is such a distinction then there should be a corresponding distinction between relative and absolute categorical Imperatives. (2) In saying that if there are reasons there are Categorical Imperatives I am not endorsing Kant's identification of Categorical Imperatives with moral principles. This identification appeals to a notion of 'imperativeness' or 'practical necessitation' (moral obligation) that is stronger than the bare idea of practical normativity (the practical should*), as will be discussed in Chapters 12 and 15.

[44] Analogous to the modal principle $\Box p$, $\Box(p \to q) \vdash \Box q$. But note that when '$\Box$' is interpreted as the ought of 'rational requirement' that principle requires defence. Indeed the whole enterprise of treating rational requirement as an operator on propositions requires defence.

5

WARRANT

Self-determining actors can respond *from* reasons, as discussed in 3.1. To do so they must be able to know what reasons they have. They must be able to audit those reasons, to assess whether they have *warrant*, that is sufficient reason, to believe, to feel, or to act, or whether they have reason to investigate further in order to acquire warrant.

To define warrant we need to distinguish between two concepts of a reason. On one concept, which I shall refer to as the concept of *warranted reason*, actors can always in principle know what reasons they have, just by careful enough reflection. On the other concept that is not the case. There may be reasons for the actor to believe, do, or feel something of which the actor is unaware, and which he cannot come to know by reflection alone. The latter concept is the one we have been discussing so far: it is the basic concept. Warranted reasons, and warrant, can be defined in terms of it.

Warrant, we shall see, is a very strong notion. Going along with it is another very strong notion, a Kantian notion of autonomy: to act autonomously is to act from full normative insight into the reason relations underlying one's warrant. I take *self-determination* to be a weaker notion than that. So too rationality. You are not necessarily criticizable as failing in rationality just because you fail to recognize and act from a warrant. In assessing a person's rationality, or responsibility, we are interested in something else, which I shall call that person's *justification*. Then again we are also often interested in the *reliability* of a person's judgements as to reasons. Whether a person can be said to know a truth about reasons turns on how reliably based his belief is.

Our main task in this chapter is to clarify these basic notions, focusing particularly on the notion of warrant. We shall also set out the main points of a somewhat Kantian argument whose implications will be developed in the next chapter and in Part IV. Knowledge of reason relations must be a priori, if we can know what reasons we have. But self-determination requires that we can know that. So the possibility of self-determination requires that reason relations are a priori.

5.1 Self-accessibility and warrant

We talk about reasons in two ways, then, according to whether or not we are thinking of them as *self-accessible*. I shall often mark this contrast by distinguishing between:

(i) the reasons there *are* for a person to ψ

and

(ii) the reasons a person *has* to ψ.

The reasons there *are* for a person are not in general self-accessible. He may need to investigate his epistemic field to discover them, or they may lie outside his epistemic field. In contrast, the reasons a person *has* are self-accessible: if he has them he can know—recognize, tell—that he has them, solely by means of normative insight and self-examination, including attention to the way things seem to him. The levels of normative insight, cognitive competence and self-scrutiny needed may require time and capacities that he does not have: the point is that nothing else is required. When we talk in this sense about the reasons a person has to ψ at a given time we are referring to what there is sufficient reason for him to *believe* are the reasons for him to ψ, on the sole basis of facts knowable by self-scrutiny at that time, and normative reflection.

Of course we also talk about 'the reasons a person has' in other ways. Quite often, for example, we are not referring to a person's warranted reasons but to the reasons he *takes* himself to have. However, whenever I refer in this book to the reasons a person *has* without further qualification, I am referring to his *warranted* reasons.[1]

To illustrate. There is a reason for Mary to slow right down as she approaches this bend, over and above the usual reasons for caution around bends. A very large truck has broken down just the other side of it and is blocking the whole road. However, Mary cannot tell that that has happened until she has got far enough round the bend to see the truck, by which time it will be too late to avoid hitting it. It is only when she reaches that point, where she sees the truck, that she *has* a reason—a warranted reason—to slow right down. Even so, there *is* a reason for her to slow right down before she gets to that point; namely, the fact that a truck has broken down round the bend. This becomes a reason for her to slow down as soon as she gets to the earlier point at which slowing down is necessary to avoid hitting the truck. We could usefully put up a warning triangle at that point. If instead we put up a notice saying 'By the time you've read this notice there will be reason for you to slow right down', that statement would be perfectly true (though less useful).

The peculiar scratches on the window sill (1.3) may constitute a sufficient reason to conclude that the criminal escaped that way. But Watson hasn't noticed them, so he *has* no (warranted) reason to believe that the criminal escaped that way. The fact that your aunt is your great but secret benefactor is a reason for you to feel grateful to her. I might truly tell you, 'There is reason for you to feel great gratitude to a certain relative of yours, though I can't reveal who it is'. You don't *have* (warranted) reason to feel grateful to her, though there *is* reason for you to feel grateful to her.

Let us say that a person has a *warrant* to ψ if and only if that person has sufficient reason to ψ. Thus we are distinguishing between what you should* ψ (in the designated

---

[1] A person's warranted reasons belong among the facts that person has *sufficient reason to believe* obtain; the reasons he takes himself to have belong among the facts he *believes* obtain. In each case these are intentional objects: putative nominal facts which may or may not obtain. Note the implication: there can be warranted reason to ψ but no reason to ψ.

sense—2.6) and what you have warrant to ψ. Given the evidence available to him, Watson should* conclude that the criminal has escaped through the window. That is what there is sufficient reason for him to believe on that evidence. But given what he has actually noticed, he has no warrant for that conclusion: he does not have sufficient reason to believe it. You have a reason to ψ if and only if you have a warrant to believe that there is that reason for you to ψ; hence the term 'warranted reason'.

A person may have a reason to ψ and be unaware of it; equally, he may mistakenly take himself to have a reason that he does not have. Either can happen through inattention, haste, lack of reflection, lack of insight. It is the reasons a person *takes* himself to have that are relevant in explaining what he does. (His failure to grasp some warranted reasons may also of course call for explanation.) Such explanations in terms of reasons will be considered in Chapter 10. Here our concern is exclusively with the notion of a reason that is in play when we ask what reasons a person has for believing, doing, or feeling something, irrespective of what reasons he *takes* himself to have.[2]

One other point is important. A person may have a warrant to ψ, know that he does, and ψ—but not because he has that warrant. His ψ-ing is warranted but he doesn't ψ because he recognizes that he has that warrant. When a person ψs in virtue of recognizing that he has a warrant to ψ, I shall say that he ψs *from* that particular warrant. When I say only that his ψ-ing is warranted, or that he ψs with warrant, I mean that he has a warrant for ψ-ing, whether or not he ψs from that warrant or even realizes he has it. Further, when a person responds from what he *takes*, in the moment of acting, to be a warrant for the response he is *self-determining* (whether or not his assessment of what is warranted is correct). When he responds from genuine insight into, first-person *recognition* of, warrant, he acts *autonomously*. Autonomy is thus a special case of self-determination. An autonomous response is a response from warrant. And since self-determination *aims* at warrant it aspires, in that sense, at autonomy.

5.2 Epistemic self-audit

Self-determination and autonomy are pivotal concepts for the account of reasons developed in this book; we shall often be returning to them. The significance of warrant follows from them. It is indispensable to our thinking because we are self-determining, and in aspiration autonomous, actors.

People often assess what they have reason to believe, to do, or to feel. They may ask themselves whether, in the light of what they have reason to believe, they have reason to

---

[2] Cp. Allan Gibbard, 1990: 161–2. In his terminology the reasons there are for you are your 'potential reasons', the reasons you have are your 'available reasons', and the reasons you take yourself to have are your 'putative reasons'. For our purposes, however, these terms are somewhat misleading. A 'potential' reason sounds as though it is not actually a reason, and 'available reasons' sound like a subclass of potential reasons. On the contrary, however, as already noted, the warranted reasons you have to ψ are not a subclass of the reasons there *are* for you to ψ. You may have warranted reason to ψ when there is in fact no reason to ψ (Section 5.3). Furthermore, whereas reasons are facts warranted reasons are intentional objects: putative facts which you have sufficient reason to believe obtain, and which would be, if they obtained, reasons.

do this or feel that. They may also ask themselves what they have reason to believe. A typical result of this latter reflection is that the reflecting thinker sees the need to do some further inquiring. He realizes that he does not have sufficient reason to believe—has no warrant to believe—this rather than that about something that matters to him. By further inquiry, he may discover further reasons for belief, reasons which he did not already have.

You have a suspicion, say, that the garage is cheating you: they haven't carried out the service properly. But you don't yet have sufficient reason to believe that—you need to check out the facts carefully before you have sufficient reason to be annoyed with them, and to refuse to pay the bill. When you conclude that you do not have sufficient reason to believe, you do so just by reflective self-scrutiny. You reflect 'I don't have enough information on this to warrant a definite conclusion—if I'm going to make a complaint I'll need to inquire further into the facts'.

It must be possible for people to recognize in this way that they don't have sufficient reason for belief: just by self-examination and reflection without any further inquiry into the facts that goes beyond that. For suppose deciding the truth of this self-assessment— that you do or do not have sufficient reason to come to a conclusion—could itself require further inquiry into the facts. Then when the inquirer asks:

(i) Do I have a warrant to believe that p, or do I need to inquire further into the facts?

it could be that he cannot decide this question without further inquiry into the facts. He would have to ask:

(ii) Do I have a warranted answer to (i) or do I need to inquire further into the facts?

Answering this question could also require further inquiry into the facts. So he might have to ask:

(iii) Do I have a warranted answer to (ii) or do I need to inquire further into the facts?
...etc.

Undecidability at any level would infect all lower levels. If further inquiry were needed at every level, there would undecidability at every level; we could not know whether we had warrants for our beliefs.

But we think we can know that. Specifically, we think that we can always work out, simply by careful reflection on our warranted reasons, whether we have sufficient reason for a belief or need to inquire further. (This inquiry, of course, may or may not bring about success in achieving warrant, and in any case may or may not be worth pursuing in terms of our practical ends.) Given that this is possible it must always be possible to answer question (i) by self-scrutiny and reflection alone, though the answer may be vague, because 'sufficient reason to believe' is vague.[3] Call this process 'epistemic self-audit'. Self-audit in general is the capacity to appraise what one has reason believe, feel, or

---

[3] A sceptic might question whether an answer is ever available at any level in the (i); (ii); (iii)...sequence. This would be a new kind of scepticism—it would be saying, not that we never have sufficient reasons for belief, but that it is unanswerable whether or not we ever do. However, the Critical question is 'How is warrant possible?' We are accepting that it is possible and asking what must be the case if it is.

do; the special thing about epistemic self-audit is that it is required in evaluative and practical self-audit too. Self-determination presupposes the capacity to engage in self-audit. It thus requires possession of the concept of a warranted reason, for self-auditors are asking themselves about their warranted reasons. This point is of fundamental importance to the philosophy of reasons: we shall see that even though the concept of a reason is the definitionally primitive normative notion, the role it plays in the concept of *warrant* is the key to its philosophical significance.

Self-determination is responding from what one takes to be warrant. Autonomy is responding from recognition of warrant. Thus self-determination aims at autonomy. What sort of recognition does autonomy require? It requires (a) *knowledge* of the particular norms that, in combination with the actor's epistemic state, constitute the warrant; and (b) *normative competence*, the capacities involved in reasoning in accordance with relevant norms to arrive at knowledge of warrant: memory; deductive; and computational skills, etc. Recognition of warrant requires knowledge of norms and successful exercise of these capacities. But what is it to know the norms? As far as responding from warrant is concerned, it can be implicit knowledge; self-audit, however, may sometimes require making it explicit.

Warrant is a very strong notion. Your warranted reasons right now are those you could recognize now without further factual inquiry—if you had perfect normative insight and competence. Moreover, since (as I shall argue) warrant is closed under itself [4] completely autonomous actors would recognize all warranted consequences of warrants: they would recognize all the reasons they had. Obviously none of us can do that. Indeed it is a point of first importance that for us the normative, as it confronts us at a concrete time, is in many ways opaque. Even allowing for testimony-based warrant, real people, most of the time, do not and cannot penetrate deeply into many of their warrants.

For this reason the concept of warrant is not the only concept we need for appraising the quality of people's responses. Far from it. When our concern is to assess critically the rationality, or the due care, of a person in some particular case of judgement, action, or feeling three factors can be in play, of which their capacity for recognizing their warrants is only one. Also relevant are the time available to them, and the opportunity cost to them, in the particular case, of spending time on self-audit rather than acting directly or 'naïvely' on the appearances, factual and normative. Hence we need a concept of *justification* distinct from that of warrant, though related to it. It will take account of what normative features in a concrete situation in which someone finds themselves they could be *expected* to notice. For example, in a law court the jury may need to judge whether my beliefs on some matter were reasonable ones for me to have at the time in question. It is asking whether my beliefs were *justified*; its question is not settled by determining whether or not they were *warranted*. We come to the interplay between warrant and justification in Section 5.9.

---

[4] That is, if there is warrant to believe that p, and warrant to believe that p implies q, then there is warrant to believe that q. See Section 5.8.

5.3 Epistemic states

We want warranted reasons to be self-accessible, but we also want a definitional link between the notion of *having a reason* and that of *there being a reason*. Since our thesis is that the latter is the primitive normative concept we must define the former in terms of it, yet in such a way as not to lose the former's self-accessibility. How should we do that?

Is it that having a reason is recognizing that there *is* a reason—as is suggested by the example of Watson, who fails to notice the scratches on the window sill? That is too strong, in that it entails that you only *have* a reason if there *is* a reason. The concept of self-audit that we are exploring has to allow that you may have reason to believe that p even though it's not the case that there really *is* reason for you to believe that p. Suppose someone in the security office emails you that there is a primed bomb in the basement. You have reason to leave fast. But, though you have no reason to believe that it's a hoax, it is: there is no bomb in the basement, as you would easily discover if—unreasonably sceptical—you went down there to check. You *have* a reason to leave even though there *is* no reason to leave. So your warranted reasons, the reasons you have to ψ, are not a subclass of the reasons there are for you to ψ.

For a clear view we need the notion of an *epistemic state* as well as the notion of an *epistemic field*. Whether a person is warranted in believing something depends on the epistemic state he is in. Epistemic states are subsets of epistemic fields. We characterize the subset as follows: x's epistemic state at t, $s_{x,t}$, consists of the set of facts such that:

(1) The fact that p is in $s_{x,t}$ if and only if at time t it is in itself a sufficient reason for x to believe that p.

Now it is not in general true that the fact that p is a reason for x to believe that p—not even when the fact that p is in x's epistemic field. Suppose, however, that I have a sick feeling. Then the fact that I have is itself a sufficient reason for me to believe that I have.[5] Now suppose in contrast that there is a frog on the desk before me. I have sufficient reason to believe that there is because I can see it. The fact that there is is in my epistemic field. But it's not true that what gives me sufficient reason to believe that there is a frog on the desk is the fact that there is. I have sufficient reason to believe there is a frog on the desk because I have sufficient reason to believe that I *see* there is; what gives me sufficient reason to believe that I see there is, is that I seem to see there is. (This will be further argued in 9.1.) Finally, what gives me sufficient reason to believe that I seem to see there is just is that I seem to see there is. That fact in itself constitutes sufficient reason for the belief that it obtains. Hence the facts that there is a frog on the desk and that I see that there is are not in my epistemic state, though they are in my epistemic field, whereas the fact that I seem to see a frog on the desk *is* in my epistemic state, as is the fact that I have a sick feeling.

---

[5] I discuss the view that such beliefs cannot be said to be held for reasons, or to constitute knowledge, in 9.1. (It can, of course, be vague whether the feeling I have is properly called a *sick* feeling. I take it that in such a case it is vague whether (it is true that, a nominal fact that) I have a sick feeling, and thus vague whether I have sufficient reason to believe that I have a sick feeling.)

A fact belongs to your epistemic state just if it plays a specific epistemic–normative role in relation to you: it must itself constitute sufficient reason for you to believe that it obtains. Furthermore, since you must be able to recognize your warrants by attention and reflection alone, it must be the case that if a fact is in your epistemic state you must be able to know that it obtains solely by attending to it. Otherwise it could not play its role. However, we don't have to add this requirement to (1), since (as will be argued in Section 5.5) facts which satisfy (1) satisfy this requirement as well.

5.4 Having a reason

Since x's epistemic state at t is a subset of x's epistemic field at t, any fact present in the former belongs in the latter. We can thus ask (as above) whether in the epistemic field consisting solely of x's epistemic *state* at t there is reason, or indeed sufficient reason, for x to believe that p. A sufficiently competent self-auditor, x, will be able to answer this question for himself, without needing any capacities other than sufficient appropriately directed attention and normative insight.[6]

We can now define warranted reasons, for all the three types of reason, as follows:

> x has (specific, overall, sufficient) warranted reason to ψ at t if and only if $s_{x,t}$ gives x (specific, overall, sufficient) reason to believe that there is (specific, overall, sufficient) reason for x to ψ at t.

Our definition of warrant was that ψ-ing is warranted for a thinker just if that thinker has sufficient reason to ψ. These two definitions together give the following result:

> There is warrant for x to ψ at t if and only if $s_{x,t}$ gives x sufficient reason to believe that there is sufficient reason for x to ψ at t.[7]

Symbolizing 'x has a warrant to ψ at t' by '$W(t, x, \psi)$' we have:

$$W(t, x, \psi) \Leftrightarrow S\{s_{x,t}, \beta_x S(t, x, \psi)\}$$

Note the double-layer character of warranted reasons. A warranted reason for ψ-ing consists in sufficient reasons for believing that there are reasons to ψ; the belief that p is warranted for x if and only if there is sufficient reason in x's *epistemic state* for x to believe that there is sufficient reason to believe that p in x's *epistemic field*.

What a person believes from warrant is limited by how carefully he has investigated his epistemic field, whereas what there is sufficient reason for him to believe in his epistemic field is not. In some cases, of course, active investigation is not required—I don't need to do any detective work to be warranted in believing that I'm currently typing at a

---

[6] If we think of epistemic fields as tree structures (2.4) then epistemic states may have to be thought of in the same way, since a person cannot simultaneously attend to all the facts which, considered severally, satisfy (1).

[7] If $s_{x,t}$ gives x some reason but not sufficient reason to believe that there is reason to believe that p, or it gives x sufficient reason to believe that there is some reason but not sufficient reason to believe that p, then x has some reason to believe that p but is not warranted in believing that p.

computer. In other cases ingenious and diligent investigation of the epistemic field may be required to get a warrant for belief. Holmes (1.3) is warranted in his belief that the criminal escaped through the window, because of the unobvious facts he's noticed. But Watson has no warrant for that belief, even though he shares Holmes's epistemic field, because he hasn't looked hard enough. Furthermore, even though Holmes is warranted in his belief, there may nonetheless be no sufficient reason for it in his epistemic field, because the *prima facie* sufficient reason he has noted is defeated by other facts in the field which he hasn't noted.

5.5 Acting from a warrant: (i) knowledge of one's epistemic state

If you are auditing your warrants with a view to action, including further inquiry if necessary, you want to know what warrants you have. Your goal is to act from warrant; that is, from *knowledge* that you have a warrant. Merely having a warrant for thinking you have a warrant is not enough, since at any level you can have warrants without realizing that you have. Nor is believing that you have a warrant enough. Since your belief may be false, you may act from the belief that you have a warrant and yet still without warrant. Acting from a warrant requires recognition that you have it.

The recognition must be *de se* knowledge acquired in the first-person way. Thus in my own case, if I am to act from a warrant it is neither necessary nor sufficient that I know John Skorupski has it. I must know that *I* have it. I must also have acquired it in the first-person way, i.e. by my own attention to and reflection on my epistemic state. I may know *de se* that I have a warrant without knowing it in the first-person way.[8] Suppose, for example, that I have been authoritatively told that I have a warrant to ψ, without being told what it is. Nor am I able to work out (say, in the time available) what it is. In that case I cannot act from *that* warrant, the warrant I have been told I have.

To satisfy this condition, of being knowable in the first-person way, the facts in your present epistemic state must be facts you can come to know simply by attending to them: *de se* facts about your own present states. Only such facts can satisfy condition (1): that is, give you sufficient reason in themselves to believe that they themselves obtain. But not all facts about your present states—not even all facts about your present mental states—are in your *s*. The facts that your memory is unusually retentive this morning, or that you're jealous of your rival, can be said to be facts about your present mental states, but they do not satisfy (1). The fact that your memory is unusually retentive is not itself sufficient reason to believe that it is. You need evidence provided by present memory feats, plus information about how retentive your memory usually is, to have sufficient reason to believe that your memory is unusually retentive. Similarly with jealousy. You might suffer a pang of jealousy, and that fact would be in your *s*, but you could still ask yourself whether you are really jealous or whether this was just an aberrant pang. The facts in

---

[8] Equally I may know facts that are not *de se* in the first-person way. First-person knowledge requires first-person knowledge of *de se* facts but is not restricted to them.

your *s* must be facts that you can simply *attend* to, make the object of your attention, and neither of these facts is of that kind.[9]

Now the facts that satisfy condition (1) are facts that you can know just by attending to them. They are such facts as that you have a sick feeling, or that you seem to see a frog on the desk. To vary the example, suppose you have an ache in your knee. Suppose you come to believe that you have, by attending to it. (If you mistakenly think you have no ache in your knee you can correct that, or could have corrected it, by more careful attention alone. This can happen: 'How's your knee?'—'Fine...no, wait a minute, I do have a slight pain around the cartilege'.) Do you then know that you have an ache in your knee? Your belief is warranted;[10] furthermore, it is reliably and, as we can suppose, non-deviantly caused by the fact that warrants it *in virtue of that fact warranting it*. According to the analysis of knowledge to be adopted below (5.10) this means that you know that you have a pain in your knee.[11] In general, for any fact that is in your *s*, you can come to know in the first-person way, by attention alone, that that fact obtains.

5.6 Acting from a warrant: (ii) normative insight into complete reasons

If warranted reasons are to be self-accessible we must be able to know the facts that constitute them in the first-person way; we must also be able to know by reflection alone the reason relations in which those facts stand. Suppose some set of facts in *s*, π_i, warrants the belief that *p*. To know that by attention and reflection alone I must not only be able to tell in the first-person way that these facts obtain, I must also be able to tell in that way that they warrant the belief that *p*. Knowing the truth of a norm in the first-person way—having present insight into its truth—contrasts with knowing it on the basis solely of testimony or merely remembered insight. Call this reflective unmediated knowledge of reason relations *normative insight*.

If warranted reasons are to satisfy the self-accessibility requirement this insight must be a priori; which means that there must be normative propositions about the reason relations in which putative facts would stand that can be known to be true a priori. The nature of the a priori will be discussed in the next chapter. I shall argue that a priori knowledge is always of normative propositions—a priori knowledge just is normative insight, insight into normative, non-factual truths. Furthermore, a priori propositions are definable as propositions there is reason to believe outright, i.e. on the basis of no facts (2.5). So epistemic states contain no 'a priori facts'. They consist wholly of facts about oneself.

---

[9] Distinguish attending to a fact from attending to (= thinking about) the proposition that a fact obtains. You can of course attend to the proposition that your memory is unusually retentive, or that you are jealous.

[10] I'm construing 'knee ache' in such a way that you can have an ache in your knee even if you don't have a knee. (It's a phantom limb, but the pain still has that phenomenal location.) If this is objectionable, we must say that pain in the knee is not in your epistemic state, but having a pain that feels as though it is in your knee is.

[11] A fact that *p* that is in your epistemic state constitutes both a sufficient reason and a warranted reason for you to believe that *p*. In your *s*, your epistemic reasons and your warranted epistemic reasons coincide.

Obviously, however, not all propositions about reasons are a priori. Consider this example: the fact that the building is on fire is a reason for Smith to enter it. That could be true or it could be false, and we certainly can't tell which a priori. If Smith is just someone who works in the building it may be false, if Smith is a firefighter it may be true. Yet in all particular instances we could give a fuller statement, which could be known to be true a priori. If that was not the case, epistemic self-audit would be impossible: we could not know whether we had warrant to believe that there was reason for Smith to enter the building. This fuller statement might be long and complicated. It might, for example, be this:

> (2) The fact that Smith is voluntarily and non-exploitatively employed as a firefighter, that she's in that official role at the scene of a building in which a fire needs to be extinguished, that this role includes entering buildings and extinguishing fires when it is necessary and possible to do so, that it's possible for her to enter this building right now and extinguish the fire, and that she is asked by the fire officer in charge, on the basis of these facts, to do so, is a specific reason for Smith to enter the building right now.

I think I know a priori that those facts, if they obtain, give Smith a specific reason to enter the building. Of course there may well be specific reasons for Smith not to enter the building; perhaps, on the whole, she shouldn't enter the building. It may, for example, be too dangerous to do so. Irrespective of my knowledge of that, however, I know a priori that if these facts obtain they give Smith a specific reason to enter the building. My knowledge that these facts, if they obtain, give Smith reason to enter the building is not itself a further bit of factual knowledge. There are no further facts that I need to establish before I can judge the truth of this claim.

But perhaps collateral facts could 'silence' this reason?[12] Suppose that Smith's entering the building would precipitate an enormous human disaster. One view is that there is still a specific reason for Smith to enter the building, but an immensely stronger specific reason not to. Another is that when this second consideration obtains the first ceases to constitute a specific reason to enter the building. It is silenced. Nor—on this view—can such silencers be simply built into the complete statement of the specific reason. The question then arises whether we need to establish that no silencers obtain *before* we can warrantedly make the assertion about Smith. If we do, why can't that fact be built into the complete statement of the specific reason? If not, (2) will still be a priori, but it will be defeasible. Either way we can say that if propositions about specific reasons are ever warranted there must be sets of facts that constitute those reasons, and that our warrant for thinking that those facts constitute such reasons must be a priori, even if defeasible by 'silencers'.

In fact, however, I don't see a persuasive case for the existence of such silencers. True, there can be compelling reasons, or indeed moral obligations, not to advocate various options, not even to contemplate them—to rule them completely out of reflection and discussion. It does not follow that there are no specific reasons for them. A child points

---

[12] The terminology of 'silencing' is John McDowell's: 1998a: 17–18, 55–6, 90–3.

out that visiting a lonely old uncle is going to be very boring. Her parents might reply that she should not be thinking about that; what she should be thinking about is that it's his birthday, that there is an established family expectation that older relatives are visited on their birthdays, and, far from least, how happy he will be to see them. They may be right in their response. Thinking about the boredom is at best a waste of time, and at worst will lead astray. Still, the fact that the visit will be boring may be a specific reason for the child not to go nonetheless. In fact it seems a pious fiction to deny that it is. Or suppose that violence against innocent people would advance our noble cause. I may have a moral obligation not to consider that option, not to point it out to people, or in any way advocate it. It should be ruled off the agenda of deliberation. It still does not follow that it is not a reason for such violence.

Let us turn next to evaluative reasons. Consider this:

> (3) The fact that Fred failed to turn up for a meeting with Joan that he had agreed to come to, did not forget, could have warned Joan easily, but just couldn't be bothered either to come or to warn Joan of his not coming, is a specific reason for Joan to be annoyed with Fred.

Here again I believe I can know that a priori. What if Fred failed to turn up because he sincerely thought he had some good reason neither to come nor to warn? In that case it isn't true that he failed to turn up just because he couldn't be bothered. So whether there's a reason for Joan to be annoyed depends on what reasons Fred thought he had for failing to turn up without warning, and which of these thoughts were operative. Reasons for annoyance with Fred depend on Fred's reasons, in this sense, for what he did.

In the case of evaluative reasons, as in the case of practical reasons, there may be reasons stemming from morality, or ethical ideals, or prudence to try to ignore certain reasons for feeling—to bring it about that one does not consider them. If someone insults you there's reason to be resentful. But maybe there's reason to refrain from doing anything about it; maybe a Christian attitude of turning the other cheek is best. Yet if someone just doesn't see the reasons for resentment his practical wisdom is impaired. (The Christian attitude can slide into an exhortation to cultivate this deficiency.) Similarly, there can be very good reasons for jealousy. But maybe it's prudentially counterproductive, on the whole, to accede to jealousy—in which case there is practical reason to cultivate an attitude of not dwelling on such reasons.

Philosophers with various substantive theories of normative reasons may disagree with these particular examples. Neo-Humeans, for example, or internal reasons theorists, may think that practical reasons have to include facts about the actor's desires and motives. We shall discuss these views in Chapter 10, but at present they are not at issue. The present point is that any account, short of complete scepticism as to knowledge of reasons, must accept that some propositions about reasons are knowable a priori—that knowledge of their truth is not empirical knowledge but normative insight (for these propositions are not analytic truths). In general, then, I can know a priori the truth of some propositions of the form:

(4) If it is the case that Π_i, $R(\pi_i, t, d, x, \psi)$.[13]

A second claim now follows trivially: since what is knowable a priori is that any proposition falling under this schema is true, reasons are universal. The two points, about normative insight and universality, are closely connected: they capture the Kantian theme that normative insight is into universal truths.

We can call any set of facts π_i that—with appropriate assignments to the other variables[14]—produces an a priori truth of form (4) a *complete* specific reason. Complete specific reasons may be quite 'incomplete' and quite 'unspecific' in the sense of being very uninformative about the reason: for example, the fact that α-ing will cause me to suffer is a complete specific reason not to α, though this says nothing about *why* it will cause me to suffer. Nonetheless, 'complete' seems an appropriate word, in that if you give me a complete specific reason for ψ-ing—a set of facts, which when taken together constitute a complete reason—and I still ask 'Why is that a reason?' I am showing lack of normative insight rather than ignorance of relevant facts. Complete reasons to ψ are sets of facts of which it is knowable a priori, by pure normative insight, that they stand in the R relation to ψ.

To be clear, 'complete reason', unlike 'reason' is a technical term that we are introducing stipulatively.[15] Ordinary talk does not use the term 'reason' to mean 'complete reason'; it often describes some of the facts in a complete reason, but not others, as 'the' reasons to ψ. This seems heavily dependent on the context of inquiry, however. In some contexts, for example, the answer to 'What reason is there for Smith to enter the building?' might be that she is the only one able to, or come to that, that she is the only who isn't being exploited by her employers. And in an appropriate context the answer to 'Why climb Everest?' might be, as Hillary said, 'Because it is there'. Another relevant point, arising from our discussion of thick evaluative concepts in 4.5 and 4.6, is that it may be in practice impossible to *state* complete evaluative reasons in non-circular terms. What sets of facts are sufficient reason for boredom, or admiration? This is not a point about vagueness, or lack of agreement. Abstracting from these, when we discuss whether something is boring, or admirable, we hope to attain a right answer. Such an answer can only be achieved by purely normative insight into what, in the particular case under discussion (the way the play was acted, the way the story developed), constitutes a complete reason for boredom, or for admiration. But that does not commit us to

---

[13] 'Π' is a schematic letter replaceable by a declarative sentence; where 'Π' is replaced by a sentence that expresses a truth, 'π' refers to the corresponding nominal fact. Substitutions for 'Π' and correspondingly 'π' can contain 't', 'x'; replacements of these by singular terms must be uniform. This may produce universal but relative reasons in the sense of 3.4 and 3.5.

[14] Not including 'd'. We should allow that one can have a priori knowledge of (4) without knowing the strength of the specific reason in question. Consider, for example, the fact that it's in your best interest to α. Arguably that's a complete specific reason to α, in the sense defined—but you may not know how strong a reason, in the particular context, it is. It may depend, among other things, on how much in your interest the alternative actions are, and what other reasons there are to do them. However, whenever you can reach a reflective conclusion about the strength of your overall reason to α, compared to the strength of overall reasons to do alternative actions, some a priori ordering of strengths must be possible.

[15] Joseph Raz (2000) also uses the term 'complete reason' with (I think) the same basic idea in mind. Jonathan Dancy (2004: 97–8) gives a good objection to Raz's particular account of it, however, the objection does not apply to the account given here in terms of (4).

thinking that that complete answer can be spelt out in *non-normative* terms (other than by the artificial expedient of introducing a non-normative designator by means of a normative reference fixer).[16]

Given our definition of 'norm' as 'a priori true proposition about reasons', norms are complete reasons. The two norms so far considered, (2) and (3), were respectively practical and evaluative. How do we extend this to epistemic reasons, with their relativization to epistemic fields? Here too any account of knowledge of epistemic reasons, short of denial that there really is such knowledge, must accept that some propositions about epistemic reasons are known a priori. These propositions are *epistemic* norms. Such propositions will have the form:

(5) If it is knowable that E by x at t, $R(e_x, \pi_t, t, d, x, \beta(p))$

('E' schematizes some declarative sentences corresponding to e as Π corresponds to π.) here again propositions of that kind, when so stated as to be knowable by pure normative insight are universal. In the epistemic case, however, a priori knowledge of (5) is knowledge that some facts constitute a complete reason *in some epistemic field*. A stronger notion of completeness for epistemic reasons takes them to constitute a complete reason, absolutely, *in any epistemic field*. It follows that absolutely complete reasons are indefeasible.

This discussion has been framed in terms of knowledge of specific reasons. To complete it we should note that overall and sufficient reasons are fully determined—so far as they are determinate—by the totality of specific reasons, and that knowledge of these determining relations must also be a matter of a priori normative insight, and thus knowledge of something universal. Note also that 'a priori' can be understood here simply as 'non-empirical'. Non-cognitivists can agree that there must be such normative claims, which an actor must in some sense 'accept' a priori, and know that he does, to be self-determining. In taking it that these a priori claims are about the truth of purely normative *propositions* I anticipate the case for cognitivism that will be made in the next chapter and in Part IV.[17]

5.7 Apperception and independent objects

By our definition of 'epistemic state', (1), the fact that p belongs in x's epistemic state at t if and only if that fact is, at t, *in itself* a sufficient reason for x to believe that p: or as we can now say, if and only if it is an *absolutely complete* sufficient reason for x to believe that p. (Furthermore, if this condition holds then the fact that p is also a warrant for x to believe that p.) We shall say that x *apperceives* the fact that p. A fact is in x's epistemic state at t if and only if it is apperceived by x at t. From the discussion of Section 5 it follows that one

---

[16] Some neo-Humeans wish to distinguish between the facts that constitute a reason for x to α, and facts about x's desires in virtue of which those facts constitute a reason to α. See 10.4. On our definition of 'complete reason', and assuming for the sake of argument that the neo-Humean analysis of practical reasons is correct, both sets of facts will be included in a complete practical reason.

[17] The arguments for non-cognitivism, and our reasons for rejecting them, are summarized in 17.7.

apperceives only states of oneself. The existence of a state of affairs that is not a state of oneself, for example, that an apple is on a dish, may be perceivable but is not apperceivable. As with our characterization of 'epistemic state', this characterizes apperception in terms of its epistemic role, not its nature, what it is. The term usefully suggests a consciousness that may not involve attention or noticing.[18]

But what about states of oneself that involve relations to objects independent of oneself, objects that have properties that do not depend on one's existence? Can any states of oneself involving such independent objects be apperceived?

Suppose Marcel is thinking about Albertine; i.e. it is true of Albertine that Marcel is thinking about her. Does Marcel apperceive that he is thinking about Albertine? An apperceived fact that p is an absolutely complete sufficient reason for x to believe that p. In general of course, given the holism of epistemic reasons, a fact in an s constitutes a sufficient reason for a particular belief only relative to the other facts in s. It may not be an absolutely complete sufficient reason. Suppose again that I see a frog on the desk in front of me. In many cases in which I see it the fact that I *seem* to see it will be a complete sufficient reason, relative to my epistemic state, for me to believe that I see it. In those cases I have warrant to believe that I see a frog. However, that won't be true in all cases: there may be seeming memories in my s about the habitat of frogs, or about the effects of a drug I've taken, such that even though I seem to see a frog I don't have sufficient reason to believe that there is a frog there. So while the fact that I seem to see a frog can in a suitable s give me complete sufficient reason to believe that I see a frog it is not an absolutely complete sufficient reason.

This fact does, in contrast, give me absolutely complete sufficient reason to believe that I seem to see a frog. Whatever other facts are in my epistemic state, the fact that I seem to see a frog is sufficient reason to believe that I seem to see a frog. Or take the fact that I feel sick. Whatever other facts are in my epistemic state, this fact gives me sufficient reason to believe that I feel sick. We shall come back to this claim in Chapter 9.

But what now about *de re* thoughts? Can we say that the fact that you are thinking about y is an absolutely complete sufficient reason for you to believe that you are thinking about y? If so, does the fact that you are thinking about y give you absolutely complete sufficient reason to believe that y exists?

Suppose you're flying an aeroplane, and a moving speck in your eye causes you to think another aeroplane is coming from your right and will hit you. You think something which you express by saying 'That plane will hit us'. But there exists no plane to which 'that plane' refers. We have two options. One is to say that you had no singular or definite thought. You just had various indefinite thoughts (such as 'there's a plane on our right that will hit us') in virtue of which you said what you did. Those indefinite thoughts are your warrant for your assertion, but the assertion expresses no singular thought. It isn't even true that it *seemed* to you that you were thinking about that plane. The other, less popular, option is to say that you had a *de re* thought about a non-existent object: the

---

[18] We shall consider what kind of consciousness this is in 19.1. In using the word 'apperception' to refer to it I have Kant in mind, though this use of the term differs in significant ways from his use of it, as will be noted there.

plane you thought you saw, and that other people thought you saw. I shall explain and defend this ('Meinongian') option in Chapter 15. For the moment, however, the point to note is that on either option you have no absolutely complete sufficient reason to believe that you are thinking about an existent object. On the first option there has been no singular thought whose truth could provide such a reason. On the second option the fact that you are thinking about *y*, the plane you think is about to hit you, does not give you absolutely complete sufficient reason to think that the plane exists. The plane you think is about to hit you is not a mind-independent object. It could have no properties if it did not have the property of being the plane you thought you saw. Given our account of knowledge in Section 5.10, it follows that on either of these options *there is no apperceptual knowledge of mind-independent existents*.

In many cases, nonetheless, we can say that you know what independent object *y* you are thinking about just because you *are* thinking about it. In such cases it's the fact that you are thinking about *y* that constitutes sufficient reason for you to believe that you are. However, this sufficient reason is defeasible, and hence not absolutely complete: there are epistemic fields in which the fact that you are thinking about *y* is *not* a sufficient reason to believe that you are. This may be for two possible reasons: (i) it can be true that you are thinking about *y* but you may be unsure, unable to tell, what you are thinking about just by reflecting on it; and (ii) it can be true that you are thinking about *y* but the fact that you are thinking about *y* may not give you sufficient reason to believe that you are because of other facts in your epistemic field.

Suppose, for case (i), that Marcel is in fact thinking about Albertine. But he's not sure that he is. *Was* it Albertine he had that conversation in the park with, or might it have been Gilberte? His companion may reassure him that it is in fact Albertine he is thinking about. Here the fact that he is thinking about Albertine is not a sufficient reason on its own for him to believe that he is—he needs the supporting reason provided by his friend.

Next, suppose he is thinking about Albertine and has the clear impression that that is who he is thinking about. But his companion assures him that it must have been Gilberte, and points out some facts accessible to both of them that constitute very good reasons to believe that it was Gilberte that he was walking with in the park on that day—even though in fact it *was* Albertine. This is an example of case (ii). In this epistemic state there is not sufficient reason for Marcel to believe that it is Albertine he is thinking about, even though he has the definite impression that it is Albertine, and even though that impression is in fact quite correct.

5.8 Some theses about warrant

We can now set out some theses about warrant. In self-audit I form warranted beliefs about what reasons I have. Since norms are warranted outright, these higher-order warrants cannot involve any facts other than the facts that constitute the reasons. If in *s* some facts π_i warrant ψ-ing, then reflection on those facts alone should suffice for the self-auditing thinker to recognize they do, subject only to adequate normative competence and insight. In general, when I have a reason to ψ I have a warrant to believe that I have that reason to ψ (hence 'warranted reason'); in particular, when I have a warrant I have a warrant for thinking that I have that warrant. So we have:

> (6) If there is in an epistemic state s a warrant for ψ-ing then there is a warrant in s for the belief that ψ-ing is warranted in s.
>
> $W(s, ψ) \rightarrow W\{s, βW(s, ψ)\}$

What about the converse? Can it fail to hold? Warrant is not in general factive: it does not in general, follow from the fact that there is a warrant to believe that p that p. But we can still ask how I could have a warrant for the belief that I have a warrant to ψ, when I do not have a warrant to ψ. Can s warrant me in thinking that s warrants the belief that p, while yet at the same time s does *not* warrant the belief that p?

Testimony-based warrants might seem to show how this could be so. For example, mathematical friends might tell me that some mathematical claim, M, has been proved. Might I not be warranted in believing them, even though M has not been proved, and is in fact proveably false? In this case we apparently have testimony-based warrant in s for the belief that M is warranted, even though it is not. However, there is an equivocation here. The sense in which M is not warranted is that no a priori warrant can be found. I do have an a posteriori, testimony-based warrant for the belief that M is warranted, and in this case that is an a posteriori warrant for the belief that M is true.

But given that M is proveably false, do I also have an a priori warrant for the belief that it is false?

We can relativize warrants to the actor's normative powers or to the actor's epistemic state. Warrants in the latter case are those that could be recognized by an ideally normatively competent and insightful actor, with unrestricted capacity to remember his thinking and no restriction on time. With warrant so construed, we are in effect asking what *is* warranted in x's s, rather than what warrants a particular actor x could grasp in s. In this section we construe warrant in the former way: what *is* warranted in x's s. When warrant is so construed, there are no testimony-based warrants for a priori, as against a posteriori, truths.[19]

So we have:

> (7) If there is a warrant in s for the belief that ψ-ing is warranted in s then there is a warrant for ψ-ing in s.
>
> $W\{s, βW(s, ψ)\} \rightarrow W(s, ψ)$

Taking these together gives us the 'double W principle':

---

[19] Surely, however, even though I may not have been able to 'see for myself' the truth of some purely normative proposition, I may nonetheless come to know it through the testimony of trustworthy people. In that case, if I act from it, am I not acting from warrant? Presumably I am, and if so, then on a weaker reading of autonomy I am acting autonomously. Against this, a stronger notion of autonomy would require full personal insight into the norms that structure the warrant from which one acts—bracketing off what one has been told about norms (as against substantive facts) by others. It can seem that something like that is the Kantian conception of an ideally autonomous agent. The contrast becomes important in considering moral agency and moral integrity; we shall come back to in 15.8.

(8) $W\{s, \beta W(s, \psi)\} \leftrightarrow W(s, \psi)$

Or more briefly,

$W \leftrightarrow W\beta W$.[20]

It is a further question whether higher-order warrants are indefeasible. If in s I am warranted in thinking that ψ-ing is warranted in s, can a *strict improvement* on s, $s^\star$, remove my warrant for thinking that—namely, that ψ-ing is indeed warranted in s?

Strict improvements on an epistemic state or field are lossless enlargements of it. In the case of epistemic states, such enlargements rarely occur. Almost always some of the facts in s will have dropped out of apperceptual awareness altogether. However, it's still instructive to consider the case of strict improvement, since it also models improvements which are 'locally strict', i.e. in which the facts that have dropped out are irrelevant to the warrant in question.

It is true in general that a strict improvement on s can remove a warrant that obtained in s—i.e. the warrant to ψ that obtained in s no longer obtains in $s^\star$. That is a basic general truth about the defeasibility of warrants. But what about the defeasibility of *higher-order* warrants? Can the belief that ψ-ing is warranted in s ever be (a) warranted in s, but (b) not warranted in $s^\star$?

We can argue directly against this from the knowability of warrants. I can know all warrants in s solely on the basis of attention to what facts are in s plus sufficient normative competence. Since $s^\star$ contains all the facts that are in s, I will be able to know in $s^\star$ what warrants are available in s. Now assume that if I know that p, I have sufficient reason to believe that p. (More on this below.) So I will be warranted in believing that those warrants hold in s. Higher-order warrants are therefore indefeasible:

(9) If the belief that ψ-ing is warranted in s is warranted in s then every strictly improved epistemic state will warrant the belief that ψ-ing is warranted in s.

$W\{s, \beta W(s, \psi)\} \rightarrow (s^\star)W\{s^\star, \beta W(s, \psi)\}$[21]

Another noteworthy thesis is that warrant is closed under itself, relative to an epistemic state. If a conclusion follows by warranted reasoning in s from a proposition that is warranted in s then it is warranted in s:[22]

(10) $W_s p \,\&\, W_s(p \rightarrow q) \rightarrow W_s q$

This is a weaker thesis than the deductive closure of warrant, since the latter requires the further assumption that all deductively valid inferences are warranted, whereas this principle just requires that there is warrant to hold that *modus ponens* is valid.

---

[20] More generally we have the epistemic SS principle: $S\beta \leftrightarrow S\beta S\beta$. Note that we also have $\neg W\beta \leftrightarrow W\beta \neg W\beta$ and $\neg S\beta \leftrightarrow S\beta \neg S\beta$.

[21] More generally, by the knowledge principle we also have $W(s, \psi) \rightarrow (\forall s^\star)W\{s^\star, \beta W(s, \psi)\}$.

[22] A warranted proposition is a proposition belief in which is warranted. Closure under itself must also apply to *sufficient reason to believe*: $S_e p \,\&\, S_e(p \rightarrow q) \rightarrow S_e q$.

But it may still seem very strong. Remember, however, that we are unable to recognize most of our warrants most of the time. All that I have claimed is that all warrants are knowable given sufficient normative insight and competence. Furthermore, limitations of memory, short and long term, are important constraints on one's actual knowledge of warrants. If I forget a starting point or interim result in my reasoning, I lose knowledge of the warrants it provided. Even if I don't forget it, once it moves into memory out of present insight I must either refocus insightful attention on it or my warrant for it must rely on memory. I may or may not be warranted in believing, on the basis of apparent memory, that I found it warranted. Thus although the norms that hold in an epistemic state are warranted in that state, it is far from true, given these limitations, that I can know them all to be warranted. In saying that they can all be known to be warranted I am abstracting from all these limitations. All warrants in all epistemic states are knowable—by perfect normative insight and unlimited attention spans or perfect memory.

5.9 Warrant and justification

In the introductory remarks to this chapter I distinguished between 'warrant' and 'justification'. We should now consider this distinction.

Higher-order warrants are indefeasible, but that does not mean that a person's conclusions about what warrants they have are incorrigible. Mistakes can arise from insufficient attention to one's own epistemic state or insufficient reflection on the warranted reasons it yields. Yet the actor's belief, feeling, or action may still be *justified*. I shall take the term 'justification' to pertain to appraisal of the virtues of rationality in the actor, his or her rational ability and care in judging of reasons and acting on them. One's belief, action, or feeling is justified if, in the circumstances that prevail, it opens one to no criticism in respect of rationality—whether of competence or care. Justification, as against warrant, focuses on the person: it is the person who is either justified ('just', fault-free) or criticizable in holding a belief. Warrant, in contrast, is a relation between an epistemic state and a response. If one recognizes that one has a warrant for ψ-ing, then one is justifying in ψ-ing, but the converse does not hold.

We noted that this divergence can arise in two broad ways: from the depth and complexity of the normative; and from the fact that deliberation is typically subject to time constraints.

As to the first point: remember that warrant is closed under itself. That produces a vast class of warranted normative conclusions. But the task of establishing many of these warrants involves occurrent and remembered insight and reasoning by individual reasoners, discussion among them, and occurrent and remembered testimony. *Establishing* warrant is in practice a collective, archival process. The domain of reasons presents itself to any particular individual as something standing firm against him which his personal insight can penetrate only very partially—and yet ideally, as something which his insight *could* fully penetrate and make wholly his own. There are many purely normative propositions which there is warrant to believe, but which no one is justified in believing—and many more that this or that person is not justified in believing.

Then there is the quite fundamental point that deliberation and rational self-determination take place in time. Faulty belief and, equally, failure to have a warranted belief, may result from a perfectly justified allocation of time. Time is a scarce resource, while self-audit is not instantaneous, so in any given situation a question can be raised about how much time should be applied to investigating one's warrants rather than doing something else. Deciding what to attend to, and how much attention to give it, is a practical decision. There may be good practical reasons for not attending to the facts, or working through the norms, thoroughly enough to enable one to know that one is warranted in forming a particular belief. For example, if one has to decide, within 30 seconds, whether to sell or hold a particular investment, it may be best to think quickly and act on a hunch. Similarly if one has to decide whether the building is on fire, or on which flank the enemy will attack.

Now cases of the kind just mentioned are not, as a rule, cases of acting on a fully formed belief, but of deciding to act on a particular hunch or assumption. Nonetheless, a belief is involved. One believes that the assumption on which one acts is one on which it is *justified* to act, given the facts one has considered and the amount of reasoning one has been able to do in the time available.

Since the justification concerns a decision about the basis on which one should act, and not a conclusion about what one should believe, it is practical, not epistemic. Here too, however, we must distinguish between practical justification and practical warrant. To see this, distinguish between what x chooses to do and the *method* whereby x chooses what to do—where the method of choosing is itself something x may choose.

Suppose Napoleon has 30 seconds to decide whether to defend against an attack on the left or an attack on the right. One method of deciding which flank to defend would be to work out which if any defensive choice is *warranted*; that is, to work out whether his s gives him sufficient reason to believe that there is sufficient reason for him to defend on the left, or alternatively, to defend on the right. But to work that out might take much more than 30 seconds—he might have to trawl through his memory of previous attacks, try to work out a pattern, etc. And the eventual answer might in any case be that there is no warrant for one action rather than the other. In such circumstances working out whether he has a warrant for defending on the left or the right is not a warranted method of choosing what to do. Rather, given the time at Napoleon's disposal, choosing at random is warranted. But that does not mean that the action he takes as a result of choosing at random is itself warranted. It may or may not be.

Napoleon may realize that he is warranted in choosing at random, in which case both his method of choice and the action he chooses are justified. He is not criticizable in point of rationality on either score. But suppose he decides to defend the left flank on the basis of a hunch, because he has an unwarranted belief in the reliability of his hunches. He believes that his hunches are reliable, he fails to see that that belief is unwarranted, and, let us suppose, in the circumstances he is rationally criticizable for failure to see that. In that case the *basis* on which he chooses his method of choice is unjustified, the *choice* of method is unjustified, and the resulting *action* is unjustified. Nevertheless, the action might be warranted. It might be that if Napoleon had had time to think he would have seen that there was in fact warrant to expect the enemy to attack on the flank he actually chose to defend. And the choice of method might be warranted too, even though unjustified. Napoleon may have chosen it from an unjustified belief in the reliability of his hunches, but actually backing a hunch was in the circumstances the warranted way to randomize (he didn't have a coin to toss, he needed to impress his generals, etc.). Equally, we could easily spell out a case in which both the method of choice and the resulting action were justified, though neither was warranted.

Napoleon does not believe that the enemy will attack on the flank he chooses to defend. He just decides to work on that assumption. In a different but very common kind of case genuine belief is justified, whether or not it is warranted. The salient point in these cases is that deliberation is a fallible process. One can be justified in making a judgement even if one has not fully eliminated the epistemic possibility of oversight or error in examining one's epistemic state and its implications. Otherwise the standard for justification would be set too high. Though an error or oversight of this kind is always in principle detectable through sufficiently careful examination of one's epistemic state and one's reasoning from it, that does not mean that there is an effective procedure for detecting it, still less that the procedure must have been applied before we are justified in proceeding to judgement.

Take Jane, the director of a nuclear power station. She hears the fire alarm, forms the belief that a fire is being signalled and immediately presses the button for evacuation. She has forgotten that at the beginning of the month she ordered that the alarms should be tested this morning—by being rung at this precise time to a specific pattern, careful checks having previously been made to establish that there was no fire. She *hasn't* forgotten this in the sense that she is unable to recall it but only in the sense that she is preoccupied when the bell rings, and in her hurry to take prompt action 'fails to bring it to mind'. If she had recalled it she would have noted the ringing pattern and formed the belief that there was no fire. So in fact her epistemic state warrants the belief that it is most unlikely that there is a fire.

Was Jane's actual belief, that someone was indicating the presence of fire, justified? Or could we criticize her for carelessness or absence of mind? To answer that question, we would have to examine the actual circumstances in detail. One crucial issue would be how much else she had to think about, and how important it was. Again, did her secretary remind her that morning of her earlier decision? etc. If the circumstances were sufficiently pressured we might conclude that Jane's belief that a fire was being indicated was perfectly 'understandable'. She was not criticizable—in the circumstances, the memory lapse could easily have occurred to anyone.[23] In which case her belief was, in the present sense, justified though not warranted.

Or a belief may be justified though unwarranted because it rests on excusable errors of reasoning. Suppose someone has to decode a transmitted order in a limited period of

---

[23] So criticizability, and thus justification, is a matter of degree.

time. He gives it his full attention but he makes a small mistake which alters the sense of the whole message. The mistake was one which, in the actual circumstances, *any* trained decoder could have made. Then we can say that his belief as to what order has been transmitted is justified, thought it is both unwarranted and false.

These are cases in which there is justification without recognition of warrant. Indeed an act can be both justified and warranted, without being justified *because* its warrant is recognized. Suppose, for example, that the decoder makes two perfectly understandable mistakes which cancel each other out. Then his belief as to the content of the message is both justified and warranted, but not justified because he has duly identified the warrant. Or suppose the bell in the nuclear power station rings at the precise time in question, but *not* in the predetermined pattern. Jane's belief that a fire is being signalled is then warranted; and it is justified. But it is not justified *because* she has recognized the warrant: to recognize the warrant given by her epistemic state she would have to note that the bell is not ringing in the predetermined pattern, whereas she has simply had a momentary and 'understandable' failure of attention. She is justified in believing and also warranted, but not justified by virtue of recognizing the warrant.

Nonetheless, warrant, not justification, is what the self-determining actor aims at. Thus to be justified in believing I must also be justified in believing that I am warranted in believing. There is no inconsistency in this, for the higher-order belief, about being warranted, may of course be mistaken, though justified. A similar point holds for justified feeling: if I am justified in feeling ϕ I must also be justified in believing that I am warranted in feeling ϕ. But no similar point applies to action, as the Napoleon example shows. The most one can there say is that if I am justified in performing an action I must think that *my method of choosing it* is warranted, and be justified in that belief.

5.10 Reliability and knowledge

Now we should turn to the difference between warrant and knowledge. Unlike the notions of warrant and justification, the concept of knowledge plays a role only in the epistemic case. Beliefs, not actions or feelings, can constitute knowledge.[24] The same applies to the notion of reliability: we can talk about how reliable your judgements are, but not in the same way of the reliability of your actions or feelings—though we can ask how reliable your *judgements* as to what there is reason to do or feel are. And we are often more interested in the reliability of your judgement than in its warrant or justification.

Your reliability in a domain is a matter of how good a guide your sincere judgements are to the truth of the matter in that domain. We also talk about how *authoritative* your judgement is. Epistemic authority is a special case of reliability. Indicators, measures, gauges can be more or less reliable—they cannot be authoritative because they make no judgements. The reliability of a gauge, say, is a purely causal matter. But judgement

---

[24] Capacities can constitute knowing how.

always also involves responsiveness to norms. As a judge, your responsiveness to whatever norms bear on the particular judgement you are making may be more or less imperfect: however *this* responsiveness (unlike the responsiveness of a speedometer to the speed of a car) is not a causal matter, as I shall argue in Chapters 16 and 17. In terms of the Kantian contrast between spontaneity and receptivity it is a matter of pure spontaneity: talk of responsiveness to norms, or reasons, becomes misleading if it is thought to imply that such responsiveness involves any element of receptivity.

However, the core of the notion of reliability, including epistemic authority, is no more than *trustworthy indication*. X is a reliable guide to Y to the extent that its indications can be trusted. It is another question whether that must involve some notion of causal tracking, or of X receiving a signal of some kind from Y. Is your authority in normative judgements seriously explicable by supposing you to be a good receiver of signals from the normative domain? Cognitive irrealists about the normative will deny that it is. They will stress that the method whereby you acquire reliable normative beliefs can only be that of reflecting carefully, without preconceptions, etc., on the purely normative question in hand, examining what you are spontaneously inclined to think, and discussing it with others who are engaged in the same reflective process. What they do not deny is that there *is* such a thing as reliably acquired normative belief; on the contrary they hold that beliefs acquired by such reflection and discussion are trustworthy indicators of normative truth. Normative reliability is a notion that both irrealist and realist can appeal to.

With the broad notion of reliability, covering both the causal and the normative case, at our disposal, I propose the following thesis:

> (11) For all x's beliefs that p, x is warranted in believing that p only if x is warranted in believing that the means by which x's belief that p is produced is reliable.[25]

Consider, for example, the case of perceptual beliefs. If my perceptual state itself warrants the belief that there's something red there, it also warrants the belief that it is produced by something red being there. If it *didn't* warrant that belief how could it warrant the belief that there's something red there? Warrant requires a warranted belief in reliability, and in this case reliability involves causal tracking. If I acquired evidence that my colour experiences are very poorly cued by objective colours, or even evidence which showed that I could not assume them to be so cued, *then* an experience as of something red before me would not warrant the belief that there was something red there. Nonetheless, it is precisely that experience, the experience as of there being something red before me, that—in the absence of defeating information—warrants my judgement that I see something red there, that something red before me is producing that experience.

---

[25] This should be understood to mean that the means whereby the particular belief is on the particular occasion produced is reliable. If you are travelling through Barn County without realizing it (Goldman 1976) you may be warranted in your belief that you see a barn—because you are warranted in believing that seeing, right now, what looks just like a barn is a reliable indicator that you see a barn. But if you know that you are in Barn County, and that Barn County is littered with mere barn facades, you may not be warranted in believing that you see a barn, even if in fact you do. That is because in these particular circumstances trusting to your sight alone is not a reliable way of telling whether you're seeing a barn.

We are here broaching substantive issues of epistemology and metaphysics. How can an experience as such warrant a judgement about its origins? If a spontaneous disposition to take a colour perception as reliable is default-warranted (warranted in the absence of defeating information), would a spontaneous disposition to take apparent telepathic perception as reliable be equally default-warranted? Could one or both be default-warranted before we've settled *a posteriori* whether perception or telepathy works?

One could also ask about judgements made on the criterion of theoretical simplicity. If these are warranted, then are we also warranted in thinking that the method by which we arrive at them is reliable? That is, if we are warranted in believing that inference to the best explanation is a sound method, are we warranted in believing that our judgement, that it is, is reliable? Or consider aesthetic judgements. If I'm warranted in believing, say, that a particular musical performance is admirable, am I also warranted in believing that my judgement on this matter is reliable? Can this latter judgement, about my own normative judgement, be treated as default-warranted though defeasible, as in the colour perception case?

These questions raise fundamental issues about spontaneity, the relative priority of normative and factual judgement, and the scope of realism. They will be discussed in later chapters of this book (Chapters 9, 16, and 20). However, I believe thesis (11) survives discussion and should be accepted. We can then derive a conclusion about the connection between warrant and knowledge.

It does not follow from the fact that I'm warranted in believing that p that I know that p. But if I believe that p, and do so from recognition of a warrant to believe it, am I warranted in *believing* that I know that p? By (11), if I am warranted in believing that p, then I am warranted in believing that the means by which my belief is produced are reliable. And by (6), if I am warranted in believing something then I am warranted in believing that I am so warranted. So if I'm warranted in believing that p, I'm warranted in believing the three-way conjunction:

> p, I'm warranted in believing that p, and the means by which my belief that p is produced are reliable.

Would the truth of this conjunction suffice for my knowing that p? Not quite: it must be true that I believe that p and that I do so from recognition of my warrant to believe it. Plausibly, however, I know that p if and only if I truly believe that p because I recognize a warrant for believing that p, a warrant that is, in the actual circumstances, a reliable basis for the belief that p.[26] That being so, the following principle is true:

> (12) (*The WK principle*) if x is warranted in believing that p then, were x to recognize that warrant and on that basis believe that p, x would be warranted in believing that x knows that p.

---

[26] The analysis of 'know' is a highly contested subject. I am proposing an account that seems to me plausible and useful for our purposes—however, I accept that we may have more than one concept of knowledge, and that the application of any such concept is context-dependent. Our account has both 'internalist' elements (warrant) and 'externalist' elements (reliability). In virtue of its internalist element it implies that if x knows that p then x has warrant to believe that p. But we could drop the internalist element and still get to (12) from (11).

If one believes from warrant one is warranted in believing that one knows.[27]

5.11 Rational commitment and rationality

If I believe or feel something which I have no warrant to believe or feel, people can point that out and challenge me to find a warrant or give up the belief or feeling. In this sense, warrant is the proper object of rationality; we shall consider the question of why I should be, or seek to be, rational in the next section.

The case of action, as we saw, raises a special issue. Here I may need to adopt a *method of choosing* how to act (Section 5.9). In that case the question becomes whether the method I adopt, rather than the action I do, is warranted. The difference is that sometimes I have to do *something*, whereas I never in the same sense *have* to believe or feel something. (Giving verdicts—should BSE be pronounced infectious to humans?—and making working assumptions—are stock markets going to fall?—are in this respect actions rather than beliefs. We sometimes have to make them even if we have insufficient reason to believe the proposition that we assert in doing so.)

So let 'δ' range over believing that such-and-such, feeling that so-and-so, and adopting a method of choosing what to do—which we'll take to include just choosing what to do. Then one can say quite generally:

R1. If I δ I am rationally committed to the judgement that I am warranted in δ-ing.

But what does talk of 'rational commitment' mean? Consider:

(13) p but I have insufficient reason to believe that p.

That may be true, but you don't have a warrant to believe it. For if you have a warrant to believe that p, then the second conjunct of (13) is false. And if you have a warrant to believe the second conjunct, then you don't have a warrant to believe that p.[28] Furthermore, your lack of warrant for believing both conjuncts of (13) is sufficiently obvious to open you to rational criticism, i.e. criticism in respect of your rationality, if you do believe them both.

The same analysis holds for the other two cases—that of adopting a method of choosing and that of feeling. Since that's more obvious for the case of adopting a method than the case of feeling, let's consider the latter. Here R1 says, for example, that if I am grateful, or exasperated, then I'm committed to the belief that gratitude or exasperation is warranted. Now of course one can be exasperated without having any explicit belief

---

[27] This thesis, when combined with the principle that warrant is relative to knowable facts in one's s, produces an interplay between knowledge and warrant. In 9.2 we take evidence—and epistemic reasons in general—to consist in knowable facts (cp Williamson 2000). The concept of a warranted reason is in contrast an 'internalist' notion; nonetheless, warrant still presupposes a prior possibility of knowledge—of apperceptual facts which can be known by attention alone.

[28] This is obvious; however, in the terms discussed in this chapter it follows by the principle that $W\beta\neg W \to \neg W$.

about whether one's exasperation is warranted.[29] But if, having raised the question whether exasperation is warranted I am unable to conclude that it is, then I am open to rational criticism—describable as imperfectly rational, or even unreasonable—if I nonetheless remain exasperated.[30] In this sense my exasperation rationally commits me to the belief that exasperation is warranted.

The notion of rationality that is in play is the broad one set forth in Chapter 1: it pertains to feeling as well as action and belief. We do not, as noted there, choose what to feel—but neither do we choose what to believe. It does not follow that beliefs and feelings cannot be appraised as more or less rational, more or less justified, just as actions can be.

Next consider:

R2. If I judge that I'm warranted in δ-ing I'm rationally committed to δ-ing.

This may seem less obvious than R1. It is most plausible for the case of belief. If I judge that the belief that p is warranted but fail to believe that p, it's plausible to see that as a defect of rationality. It is less obvious for actions. If I judge that giving up smoking is warranted but fail to give up, it's not so obvious that that is a defect of *rationality*. And what if I judge that admiration for a performance is warranted but fail to admire it? Is that a defect of rationality? That is still less obvious.

The explanation, I think, is that one's feelings, and to a lesser degree one's actions, are more subject to non-rational causes than one's beliefs. In particular, to non-rational causes that intervene between the judgement that an action or feeling is warranted and the action or feeling itself. Thus even though I judge the performance was admirable I may be too depressed to admire it. And even though I judge that I should give up smoking I may be too addicted, or too keen on social smoking with my group of smoking friends. That is less common with belief, but it can happen even there. I may reluctantly believe that I have sufficient reason to believe that my girlfriend is cheating me, yet still find myself unable to believe it.

In these cases my failure to δ even though I judge that I have a warrant to δ stems from the intervention of non-rational causes. It's not, one may say, that my *rationality* is itself impaired or defective, it's just that non-rational factors got in the way. Rationality is the power to recognize warrants and believe, feel, or act on them. To criticize a person's rationality is to say that that power is defective in some respect. But even though rationality is an active power it may be blocked by other causes without being in any respect defective. (More on rationality as an active power in 19.4.)

We should also bear in mind the distinction between reasons to believe or feel, and reasons to bring it about that you believe or feel (11.9). Suppose the belief that p is warranted, but bringing it about that you do not believe that p is also warranted. Suppose that you can and do bring it about that you do not believe that p. In that case you have

---

[29] Although the disposition to feel φ normally does come with a *disposition* to think that one's feeling is warranted. (So too for actions and beliefs.)

[30] This doesn't necessarily mean that I'm blameworthy. Perhaps I couldn't help being irrational, or perhaps I had no obligation to be rational. Criticism in respect of rationality is not moral blame.

deteriorated your spontaneous rational power but you had good reason to do so. Similarly for the case of feelings.

To go back now to R2. If I judge that I'm warranted in δ-ing I am rationally committed to δ-ing in the following sense: if I fail to δ I am criticizable in respect of rationality *unless* (i) I justifiably judged myself to have sufficient reason to bring it about that I do not δ; or (ii) non-rational causes blocked my δ-ing. This covers the case of belief and feeling—in the case of action (i) drops out. So understood, R2 seems to me to be correct.

One could put this in terms of 'rational requirement', or what 'rationality requires': if I judge that I'm warranted in δ-ing I'm rationally required, or rationality requires me, to δ. For R1, however, this sounds too strong. It is too strong to hold that whenever I δ I am rationally required *to judge* that I am warranted in δ-ing. In this case, as noted above, I am rationally criticizable only if I positively disbelieve that I am warranted in δ-ing. Hence 'commitment' seems better than 'requirement'.

This characterizes rational commitment in terms of rationality. Rationality itself is characterized in terms of responsiveness to the reasons one has. It follows from our overall claim that reasons are primitive that it must be this way round. But further, it seems plausible anyway. If rationality is not responsiveness to one's warranted reasons what is it? How can rationality 'require' anything *except* by virtue of being a capacity to respond to warranted reasons?[31]

One may still ask what it is for a belief, a feeling, or an action to be rational. Since rationality is an active power, one may act *from* that power. We have just said that rationality is responsiveness to warranted reasons. However, as we often use the word 'rational', what rationality *directly* connects to is justification rather than to warrant: one acts from one's power of rationality when one acts because one justifiably believes that one is warranted. That may in many cases amount to acting from warrant; but not all mistakes about warrant impugn one's rationality. We have to take into account the practical limitations on thinking about warrants, which we discussed in discussing justification.

As well as considering whether some act was rational we can also ask whether it would be rational to do it. In that context I submit that the following applies:

> R3. It would be rational for x to δ if and only if x would be justified in thinking that δ-ing is warranted.

Thus what it would be rational to do is not the same as what one would be warranted in doing, nor of course the same as what one should* do. Rationality goes with justification, not directly with warranted reasons, and certainly not with reasons as such. To δ rationally is to δ with justification. Thus a response may be reason-supported for x, or even what x should* believe, feel or do, though x has no warrant to think so, and even though it would not be rational for x to respond that way.

---

[31] Contrast Broome 2000, 2004, and forthcoming; compare Kolodny 2005, 2008. See also 'Rationality' in Harman 1999, whose conception of rationality is (I believe) broadly similar to that given here.

Finally let me emphasize that the contrast between 'rational' and 'irrational' is not exhaustive.[32] Irrationality is more that just *any* degree of lack of rationality; it is a strong fault or defect, involving an incapacity to detect or act on very obvious warrants, even when there are no, or only very weak, blocking factors. 'Irrational' is thus far too strong as a description of most acts that fail to be rational. Nor should the notion of irrationality play much role in philosophical argument. For example, if an act-utilitarian thinks we should* maximize the impartially conceived good, it is no argument against him to say that people who fail to do so are not *irrational*.

5.12 Autonomy

Finally, to ask a very well-worn question, why try to act from warrant, autonomously? The tautologies that justified acts are justified, that warranted acts are warranted, and that acts that should* be done should* be are just that. However, it is not a tautology that one is warranted in seeking to respond only from warrants. That constitutes a practical project. Actually it may be an impossible project—so consider the project of seeking to respond from a warrant whenever possible. Clearly this project will involve effort, self-education and training that may have very high opportunity costs. Hence there is a genuine question about whether one is warranted in engaging in it. One can put it this way: is it warranted to try to be as autonomous as possible?

The answer depends on your theory of practical reasons. At one extreme, if the sole ultimate end there is reason to pursue is your own good, then how autonomous you should* try to be depends on how much effort in that direction maximizes your good. At another, less popular, extreme stands the idea that being as autonomous as possible is simply a Categorical Imperative which trumps all other considerations.

The same point applies to the question whether one is warranted in investigating further, when one recognizes that one has insufficient grounds to warrant a belief, action, or feeling. Investigation is an activity; so how far one is warranted in pursuing it likewise depends on one's theory of practical reasons.

If we set aside the view that maintaining autonomy as far as possible is simply a Categorical Imperative which trumps all other considerations, we are likely to find that it is only one project among others which can sometimes outweigh it. There may indeed be good reason to produce in oneself an unwarranted act, if one has the means to do so. If a billionaire will give me a million pounds if I admire his violin playing for a day—though there's nothing admirable about it—and I have some tablets which will cause me to admire it for that day, then that's a reason for me to swallow them. Likewise, if belief in God will make my life go better, and I have it in my power to cause myself to believe in God, then that's a reason to do so. It's a practical reason to cause myself to believe in him; it's not an epistemic reason to believe in him.

---

[32] Cp. Scanlon 1998: 26–7.

However, even if autonomy is not a Categorical Imperative, it can be an ideal, and it can also be in its own right an end. One thing that's rather off-putting about making yourself admire the billionaire's violin playing, or making yourself believe in God, is that you cause in yourself a sentiment or a belief which you can presently see to be unwarranted—and you can do that only by reducing your own capacity to recognize warrants. That may make you less admirable in your own eyes, and it conflicts with an ideal you may have: seeing things as they are, and affectively responding to them as thus seen. Maybe these responses are outweighed—a million pounds talks—but they're still there. And as Kant saw, they are linked to ideals of self-respect and dignity.

Of course these are arguments for autonomy from *within* substantive Normative views about practical reasons. That is necessarily so, insofar as these arguments advance reasons for seeking to be rational. There is, perhaps, still an itch to ask what's *wrong* with someone who doesn't care about being rational? That may be a medical question. But if it's a question of finding a way to *show* him that *he* should care, by showing him some deficit that he should care about, then as has often been pointed out, there may be no way.

We now turn to a fuller investigation of epistemic reasons. Epistemology is the substantive theory of epistemic reasons. But in Part II we shall not be primarily concerned with substantive theory. Our main task will be conceptual: to show that the basic concepts of *aprioricity, necessity, evidence,* and *probability* are all normative. Propositions about what is a priori, necessary, what the evidence is and what is probable are all propositions about reasons.

PART II

Epistemic Reasons

6

THE A PRIORI

In this chapter we begin to use the framework developed in Part I. I shall give an account of what it means to say of a proposition, of a warrant, and of knowledge that it is a priori.

On this account, to say that a proposition is a priori in an epistemic field is to say that there is outright reason to believe it in that field. It is to make a normative claim. As for a priori warrant and a priori knowledge, to say that someone has these is again to say something normative, but also to say more, about the state of mind and insight of the knower.

These claims are integral to the *Normative view*, the view being developed in this book as a whole. In the Introduction (1.9) I set the view out in the form of four claims. The first is that normative propositions are propositions about reason relations. This has been explained and argued in Part I. The remaining three claims were these:

- that there is a fundamental epistemological and ontological distinction between factual propositions and a priori propositions about reason relations
- that all synthetic a priori propositions are in the first place normative
- that reason relations are irreal objects of true and false thoughts.

We begin our defence of these three claims in this chapter; although the last, while presupposed here, will only be directly defended in Chapter 17.

According to the Normative standpoint a double relationship exists between apriority and normativity. First, to say that a proposition is a priori is to say something normative about it. And second, any proposition that is not strictly analytic, and of which this normative claim is true, must itself be either wholly normative or an offshoot of a proposition that is wholly normative. Either way, no such proposition is factual.

In developing this account we should keep in mind two other approaches to the a priori: *intuitionistic realism* about a priori propositions (*intuitionism* for short) and the *no-content view*, which holds that such propositions are all analytic. A crucial element in the argument will be what I shall call the 'Critical thesis'. This states that no cognition-independent fact can be known to obtain a priori. It will be discussed in Section 3. The no-content view and the Normative view accept it, while intuitionism rejects it. However, intuitionism and the no-content view agree that that all informative propositions are factual, while the Normative standpoint rejects that.

Kant's response to the Critical thesis—transcendental idealism—gives an account of some a priori propositions that differs in a distinctive way from all three of these approaches. We shall consider it at length only in Part IV. But I shall anticipate in this chapter some Kantian theses which will be more fully developed in Part IV: most importantly, that there is a fundamental epistemological contrast between spontaneity and receptivity. Our final assessment of aprioricity, factuality, and cognition-independence, and of the relations between the Normative view and Kantian idealism, will be reached in Chapter 20.

6.1 Three models of aprioricity

In more detail, the three models of the a priori that I have in mind are as follows.

(I) Intuitionism. This holds that a priori truths state substantial facts, and that we know these facts obtain by a receptive faculty of intuition.

Of course 'intuition' is a slippery philosophical term. The phrase 'intuitive knowledge' can be used just to mean 'underived a priori knowledge'; in this use 'intuition' is not being appealed to as an *explanation* of how such knowledge is possible. 'Intuition' can also be used, as by Sidgwick, to refer to a certain attitudinal response on one's part to a proposition, a response whose presence gives one defeasible reason to think one immediately knows the proposition to be true.[1] However, it can also be used, more ambitiously, to refer to a postulated receptive faculty, a faculty of intuition, that gives knowledge of facts whose existence is independent of that faculty: cognition-independent facts. *This is the sense in which I use the term 'intuition' in this book*. Realists about a priori truths are, we shall argue, committed to the existence of intuition in *this* sense: their model of knowledge must be that we have knowledge of the truth of a proposition insofar as we have receptive access to the fact that makes it true, or to some other facts from which it can be inferred that that fact obtains. Conversely, someone who claims that we have 'intuitive' knowledge of some class of propositions, but rejects the receptive-faculty model of intuition, is committed to rejecting realism, in the sense of this book, about that class of propositions.[2]

---

[1] Having noted that the term 'intuition' 'has sometimes been understood to imply that the judgement or apparent perception so designated is *true*', Sidgwick continues:

> I wish therefore to say expressly, that by calling any affirmation as to the rightness or wrongness of actions 'intuitive,' I do not mean to prejudge the question as to its ultimate validity, when philosophically considered: I only mean that its truth is apparently known immediately, and not as the result of reasoning. I admit the possibility that any such 'intuition' may turn out to have an element of error...Sidgwick 1981 (1907): 211.

See also his 'Incoherence of Empirical Philosophy' (1882) in Sidgwick 2000.

[2] Sidgwick seems not to have been a realist, in that sense. Cp Shaver 2000. A number of current writers who hold that a notion of 'intuition' can play an *explanatory* role in epistemology have taken it in something like Sidgwick's way. See Audi 2008 for discussion of some of the possibilities here. They may be 'intuitionists' in one or another sense, but insofar as they reject the receptive-faculty model, they are not intuitionists in the sense of this chapter (and they should reject realism about a priori propositions).

The familiar forms of receptive access are perception and memory; in the case of intuition receptive access must be via some receptive faculty which has the same power to give knowledge of cognition-independent facts that these have, but is neither perception nor memory. Perceptual knowledge is knowledge of the visible, audible, etc. facts—facts about the perceptible or sensible qualities of things. By analogy, a serious appeal to intuition must hold that intuitive knowledge is knowledge of the a priori intuitable qualities of things. As with perceptible facts, moreover, the facts accessible to intuition obtain independently of the powers of intuition that particular knowers may or may not have.

(II) The no-content view. I have in mind views that were influential in the first third of the twentieth century: Wittgenstein's Tractatus view of apriority as tautology, and then the conventionalism that is associated with Carnap and with Wittgenstein's Viennese years in the 1920s and 30s.

In these views, what traditional philosophers interpret as a priori knowledge is taken to be a linguistic phenomenon. A clean version of the no-content view entirely eliminates a priori knowledge. There are no a priori propositions to know; the sentences that seem to express them are empty of informative content and thus strictly speaking lack meaning. This way of putting it ties the notions of meaning and proposition tightly to the notion of informative content. It also makes it clear that the no-content view is a version of non-cognitivism. The 'a priori' sentences that lack informative content are actually expressions of rules, that is, of linguistic decisions.

It is convenient, however, to allow that non-informative sentences can have meaning, even if only in a derivative sense. Sentences that are empty of content can be said to have meaning by virtue of their inferential roles in the language. Since I am using the term 'proposition' in such a way that any declarative sentence that has meaning—that can be said to assert something—expresses a proposition (7.3), these sentences can be said to express propositions and those propositions can be said to be true or false a priori. Further, it is also convenient to say that we know an a priori truth or falsehood when we grasp that a sentence is analytically true or false ('incoherent') by virtue of understanding its compositional structure and the meaning of its constituent terms. In this usage, therefore, there can be contentless propositions, propositions that convey no informative content. This way of speaking allows smoother discussion of meaning, truth, and inference, even if from the no-content standpoint it is somewhat misleading.[3] In considering the notion of analyticity in the next chapter we shall follow it; we shall accept that there are some analytic truths and falsehoods, and that their truth or falsity is a priori. No-content views, in this way of putting it, hold that *all* a priori propositions are analytic propositions, rather than that there are no a priori propositions. But it must be remembered that the driving idea of the no-content view in its 'Viennese' version— non-cognitivist conventionalism—is best expressed in the latter way.

---

[3] From a Viennese point of view the objection to it is actually stronger: just as an expressivist about normative sentences encounters the 'Frege/Geach problem' so a pure conventionalist–expressivist about analytic sentences should encounter it too.

After Wittgenstein rejected the doctrines of the *Tractatus*[4] neither he nor Carnap accepted the correspondence theory of truth. But they could still give an epistemological as against a metaphysical characterization of the notion of 'fact'. Thus their view at this point was that 'analytic' sentences were empty of content, and merely expressive of linguistic rules, but that—these rules being fixed—all other declarative sentences had *factual* content. For this version of the no-content view, 'fact' is elucidated in terms of 'true factual statement', and factual propositions exist only within a fixed framework of linguistic conventions. They are expressed by the non-analytic sentences in a total scientific theory. No other sentences have genuinely truth-evaluable meaning. In general both Wittgenstein in this 'middle' period and the logical positivists were, as we can put it, global *factualists*, in that they held all content to be factual content, even if they were not *realists* inasmuch as they held an epistemic conception of factuality and thus rejected the cognition-independence of facts.

We shall consider the no-content view in more detail in Chapters 7 and 18. Our purpose here is to highlight how it differs from the Normative view which this book defends.

(III) The Normative view is cognitivist but irrealist. It agrees with Kant on two points. It holds that there is no receptive faculty of intuition ('intuition' in the sense of this book of course, not in Kant's sense). And it also holds that there are true synthetic propositions whose truth we can know a priori.

Given the Critical argument to be discussed in Section 6.3, it follows that these propositions are either not cognition-independent or they are not factual. In effect, Kant takes the first option with respect to a priori truths about space, time, and causation. He holds that no receptively-based knowledge is of cognition-independent facts; so he holds that knowledge of phenomena is not knowledge of cognition-independent facts. That is his transcendental idealist explanation of a priori truths about nature. But Kant does not take the same view with respect to pure rational requirements—of theoretical understanding or of practical reason. Our a priori knowledge of these has nothing to do with the necessary forms of our sensibility. It is not *receptively* based at all—it is based on pure spontaneity. For Kant that means that it cannot be factual knowledge, since factual knowledge always involves some receptivity. Thus he seems committed to holding that some synthetic a priori knowledge is factual but not cognition-independent, while some is not factual at all. He clearly recognizes the first commitment, but it is not clear that he recognizes the second.

The Normative view goes for the second option in *all* cases: no synthetic a priori proposition is factual. Our knowledge of the truth of synthetic a priori propositions is intuitive in the weak sense mentioned above; but since we're reserving 'intuition' for the strong sense, I shall speak instead of normative *insight*. Insight into the truth of an a priori proposition is not a quasi-perceptual receptive awareness of facts. Nor is it just knowledge of the meanings of words and sentences. Warrant for an a priori proposition is

---

[4] Some would argue that he didn't accept it in the *Tractatus* either. See, for example, Conant 2002, Diamond 1991. If persuaded by this, we would have to say that he never accepted the correspondence theory.

grasped by insight into and reflection on its substantive content, or by warranted inferences from proposition that are grasped in this way. Some a priori propositions are, in this sense, *self*-evident.[5] But how can they be so? How can one grasp that a proposition is warranted merely by understanding its content? The Normative view argues that this is possible only when the content of the proposition is purely normative. Only norms can be self-evident.

We call in aid realist-sounding metaphors even when we are not committed to any literal realism. This is a perennial source of unclarity, obscuring the real difference between (I) and (III). Take a statement like 'I know this proposition ("suffering is bad", "2 plus 2 = 4", etc.) to be true because I can just see that it is'. This explanation of my knowledge can be construed in the irrealist way—I can 'see' that it's true just by reflecting on its content. I have insight into its truth. Or it can be construed by analogy with 'I know the proposition that it's raining to be true because I can see that it is raining'. Construed in this realist way we have an explanation of my a priori knowledge which is clear enough in its outline, but incurs strong and obscure metaphysical commitments. Certainly, it offers the form of an explanation: my knowledge of the truth of the a priori proposition is being explained by reference to my acquaintance with, and thus linkage to, some corresponding fact, in exactly the same way as when I say that I know it's raining because I can see that it is, I'm saying that I know the proposition to be true because I'm perceptually aware of the fact that makes it true. In contrast, if we read the statement in the irrealist way, it involves no metaphysical inflation; but neither, it seems, does it offer any explanation. Rather it raises a question: how *can* one know the truth of a proposition just by reflecting on its content?

As the *Tractatus* puts it: 'A priori knowledge that a thought was true would be possible only if its truth were recognisable from the thought itself (without anything to compare it with)'.[6] This point leads Wittgenstein to his no-content view. But the alleged possibility he ironically refers to here is precisely the possibility (III) endorses. It says that there are thoughts whose truth one can recognize simply by grasping their content—without anything to 'compare' them with.

Where (II) holds that aprioricity is an aspect or offshoot of analyticity, (III) holds that it is an aspect or offshoot of normativity. On the Normative view, the perceptual model deployed by the intuitionist erroneously treats purely normative knowledge as though it were factual, and thus attempts to apply an epistemology appropriate to factual knowledge in an area where it has no place.

This view obviously raises a number of questions. In the first place there is the question of whether all the propositions we regard as a priori can really be regarded as normative.

---

[5] Consider Robert Audi's account of self-evidence: it is self-evident that p if and only if: (i) you can be justified in believing it just on the basis of adequately understanding it; and (ii) if you believe it on that basis you know it (Audi 2001: 265, note 27). We shall, in contrast, adopt a more minimal, Sidgwickian notion of self-evidence; that is, we drop (ii). A proposition is self-evident if and only if at least some people can be *warranted* in believing it just on the basis of adequately understanding it. Hence by the WK principle ((12) in 5.10), if the proposition that p is self-evident, and those people believe it just on the basis of understanding it, they have warrant to believe that they know that p. As to what it *is* to know it, however, that remains to be discussed in Section 6.10 and in Chapter 16.

[6] Wittgenstein, 1961 (1921), 3.05. Chapter 5.1363.

Does apriority reduce to normativity? That question is addressed in this chapter. But next, even if we grant that apriority is normativity, there is still the epistemological question. These normative propositions have substantive, non-analytic content. They are synthetic a priori. How *can* one know the truth of a substantive normative proposition just by reflecting on its content? In Part IV we shall develop an account of the epistemology of the normative based on Kantian ideas about receptivity and spontaneity. Only then shall we be able to develop the contrast between realist and irrealist views of the normative fully.

6.2 Intuitionism

Meanwhile, Part I has provided a framework within which we can at any rate *state* realist and irrealist views of the a priori. Consider first the view of intuitionistic realists. They model the epistemology of the a priori on the epistemology of perception. Now in the case of *apperceptual* facts, such as the apperceptual fact that I am right now thinking, we have argued that it is the apperceptual fact that p itself (for example, the fact that I am now thinking) that gives me sufficient reason to believe that p (that I am thinking):

(1) $S(e,$ the fact that $p, x, \beta p)$.

But the epistemology of perception differs. In the case of perceivable facts, we shall argue (9.1), it is the fact that *I perceive that p* that gives me reason to believe that p. Suppose, for example, that you're talking to someone on their mobile phone. You don't know where they are but they tell you that it's raining in London. You ask 'What reason do you have to believe that?' or more likely, 'How do you know that?' They answer 'I can see that it is'. This does not mean 'There's a possible world in which I see it'. It means 'I am so placed as to see that it is'. I'm in London and can see it with my own eyes—I'm not relying on a weather report, etc. In such cases perceiving is my reason for believing. Thus we have:

(2) $S(e, x$ perceives that $p, x, \beta p)$.

In either case, apperception and perception, it is a further question what *warrants x* in believing that p. The apperceptual fact that p itself warrants the belief that p. In the case of perceptual warrant, however, the warranting fact is the apperceptual fact in one's epistemic state that gives one sufficient reason to believe that one perceives that p. In general, and subject to defeating collateral information, that is simply the fact that one has an experience as of perceiving that p. What sort of fact that is—what it is to have an experience as of perceiving that p, an experience with that intentional content—will be discussed in 19.1. For the moment, however, it is the *structure* of perceptual warrant that concerns us. Perceptual warrant for the belief that the street is wet consists simply in the fact that one seems to perceive, in this case to see, that the street is wet. *That* one seems to perceive that is an apperceptual fact in one's epistemic state. And this fact gives one a warrant for the belief, of oneself, that one perceives that *p*—though it only does so, of course, if no other fact in one's epistemic state defeats it. But in any *s* in which it is undefeated we have:

(3) S(*s*, *x* seems to perceive that *p*, *x*, β(*x* perceives that *p*))

and by (2) this also constitutes a warrant for the belief that *p*. In general, I suggest, perceptual warrants have this (3)/(2) structure. You have a perceptual warrant for the belief that *p* if and only if in your epistemic state, *s*, your seeming to perceive that *p* is sufficient reason for you to believe that you perceive that *p*. If you have some other warrant for the belief that *p*,[7] such as testimony, that is not a *perceptual* warrant.

Now intuitionists, as we are understanding that position here, take seriously the analogy between the epistemology of perception and the epistemology of the a priori. So they apply this structure to intuition. Thus they holds that in the case of intuitable facts it is the fact that *x* intuits that *p* that gives *x* a priori reason to believe that *p*. And by analogy with (3) what gives *x* a priori *warrant* for the belief that *p* must be that *x* seems to intuit that *p*:

S(*s*, *x* seems to intuit that *p*, *x*, β(*x* intuits that *p*)).

On the intuitionist view, then, the class of a priori propositions is a class definable by the class of intuitable facts to which they correspond; and these in turn—like the class of visible or audible facts—are definable by reference to the faculty which uniquely accesses them. Likewise, an a priori warrant is a warrant based on an undefeated seeming intuition. On this view 'a priori' is not a normative notion, any more than 'visible' or 'audible' is.

As for a priori knowledge, that will be treated as analogous to perceptual knowledge. What constitutes perceptual knowledge is of course a tricky question. I shall take it that two necessary conditions of perceptual knowledge that *p* are (i) that one has a perceptual warrant for the belief that *p*; and (ii) that the seeming perception that *p*, which constitutes the warrant for that belief, is produced in an appropriate reliable way by the fact that *p*. Likewise, then, two necessary conditions for a priori knowledge that *p* are that one should have an a priori warrant for the belief that *p* and that the seeming intuition that *p*, which constitutes the warrant for that belief, should be appropriately produced by the fact that *p*.

Clearly this account cannot be endorsed by (II) and (III), since neither of these accepts that there *are* a priori (substantial) facts. But for the intuitionist, a priori knowledge *is* knowledge of substantial facts—facts that are cognition-independent in the way that we think the fact that it is raining is independent of my cognition that it is. This realist view is ruled out by the Critical claim that no cognition-independent factual proposition is a priori. So before we consider the irrealist account of apriority we should examine the argument for this claim.

---

[7] Or, come to that, for the belief that you can perceive that *p*.

6.3 The Critical argument

When I take a proposition that p to be true a priori, it does not seem to me that I have come to believe it in an arbitrary or inexplicable way—as though I somehow found myself believing, for no apparent reason, that aliens were approaching Earth. Rather, I feel myself to be *warranted* in the belief, at home with it. I might find it impossible to conceive or imagine how it could be false, for example. I have a strong disposition not just to believe it, but to believe that there is reason to believe it, that it's right to believe it. I come to believe it on the basis of attitudes of this kind to it. Both intuitionism and the Normative view hold that the fact that I have these attitudes can in and of itself give me a priori warrant for the belief that p.

The phenomenology of these attitudes will be discussed more fully (16.2 and 16.3). But there is clearly a general question, on *any* account, about how facts about any attitudes of mine to a proposition, whatever their character, can warrant me in believing the proposition. Since this question is epistemological, attitudes should be understood as apperceptual states; thus attitude A is distinct from attitude B if and only if a self-auditor can distinguish one from the other by attention alone.

Indeed this question is at the very heart of the disagreement between global realism and Critical philosophy. The Critical claim is that the question cannot be answered if we take a realist view of a priori propositions, that is, take them to be factual and take facts to be cognition-independent. So what is the argument for this claim?

The first premise is:

(A) A thinker can be warranted in judging that p on the basis of his attitudes towards the proposition that p only if he is warranted in believing that the fact that he has these attitudes towards the proposition is a reliable indicator of its truth.

This is an application of thesis (11) in 5.10, which is a general thesis about warrant. The next premise is specifically about *factual* propositions:

(B) Where the proposition in question is factual, the thinker's attitudes towards it can be a reliable indicator of its truth only if there is an information-transmitting causal link between the fact that p, or some facts from which the fact that p can be inferred, and the attitudes.[8]

I take it, for reasons to be discussed in a moment, that there is outright warrant for premise (B). Hence (by closure of warrant under itself—thesis (10) in 5.8):

(C) A thinker can be warranted in judging a factual proposition to be true on the basis of his attitudes to it only if he is warranted in thinking that such a link exists.

But, the Critical line of thought now proceeds:

(D) If the former warrant is to be a priori then so must the latter be.

---

[8] As explained in 17.3, 'cause' and 'produce' should be understood in a wide sense.

And now the final premise is:

(E) No warrant for thinking such a link exists can be a priori.

It follows that there cannot be an a priori warrant for *any* factual proposition. And we can safely take it that if a proposition is a priori it must be possible for a thinker to have an a priori warrant for believing it. Hence no factual proposition is a priori.

But why should (B) and (E) be accepted? Why, in the factual case, does reliable judgement require an information-transmitting causal link between some facts in the thinker's epistemic field and the thinker's attitudes towards the judgement? And why couldn't a belief in the existence of such an information-transmitting link be warranted a priori?

(B) and (E) are, I submit, simple corollaries of the notion of a substantial fact. It seems to me that cognition-independence is part of that very notion. Your attitudes towards some factual proposition that p are one thing—the fact that p, and the existence of a link between the fact that p and those attitudes, are another. They are, as Hume would say, distinct existences, and distinct existences are logically distinguishable.

This distinguishability thesis underlies the Critical argument. It does not say that all relations between distinct existents are *contingent*. I and my father, for example, are distinct existents even though I could not have existed if my father had not: being the son of that particular person is one of my essential properties. What the thesis says is that where x and y are distinct existents there is no relation R for which it's *a priori* that x has R to y. True, it is a priori that *if* your father is x then necessarily your father is x; but it is not a priori that you stand in that relation to any x. ('Your father' picks out its referent relationally, so it is analytic that if you have a father, he fathered you. But it is not a priori that you have a father.)

Since no relations hold a priori between any distinct existents x and y, the existence of y is not deducible from the existence of x. I am happy to accept this as a conceptual truth: a condition on *distinct existence*. There is thus outright warrant for premises (B) and (E): it is a conceptual truth that a fact can indicate the existence of a distinct fact only by means of some relation between them, and that the existence of such a relation cannot be a priori.

Two comments about this. First, to anticipate Chapter 17: I am talking here about substantial or real relations, not about nominal or irreal relations. Suppose your actual belief that p is warranted by your epistemic state, s. That is an a priori relation between distinct existents: s and your belief that p. But it is a nominal not a substantial relation.

But second, even with this qualification, is the distinguishability thesis too strong? It means, for example, that if it is a priori that $4>2$, then numbers are not distinct existents. In general, it entails that either there are no distinct existents or there is no a priori argument for the existence of anything. If there were sound a priori arguments for God, for example, then co-existence with God would be an a priori relation every existent stood in. Hence someone who takes the ontological argument to be sound must either deny the Critical thesis or accept that there is no existent genuinely distinct from God. Hence also Descartes' response to scepticism, insofar as it goes via the ontological argument, is incompatible with (E). But I shall argue in 17.4 that numbers are not existents at all, and

I am happy to reject the premise of the ontological argument (namely, that it is metaphysically possible that there is a necessarily existent being).

Given the distinguishability claim, we have the Critical thesis: no factual proposition is a priori. Is this thesis too strong even for Kant—doesn't he hold that some factual propositions such as the parallels postulate are synthetic a priori? His transcendental idealism allows for cognition-dependent *phenomenal* facts. In contrast, I have formulated (B) unrestrictedly because I take cognition-independence to be part of the very notion of a fact. If that is rejected we must restrict the scope of (B) to cognition-independent facts. Then if the other premises are accepted the conclusion is that no proposition stating that a *cognition-independent* fact obtains is a priori. Insofar as Kant takes the world of phenomena to be a world of fact, he must deny that those phenomenal facts are cognition-independent. The phenomena are not distinct from our cognition of them. That two straight lines do not enclose a space is on this view a fact—but not a cognition-independent fact. So there are both cognition-dependent facts (phenomena) and cognition-independent facts (noumena). Alternatively, Kant could be read as holding that while phenomena are cognition-dependent appearances-to-us, the true facts, the noumena, are unknowable just because they are cognition-independent. On any reading, however, Kant's 'Copernican' response to the Critical argument is not just that cognition-independent facts are not a priori, but that they are not knowable.

This last conclusion is very strong and surprising—does it flow from the Critical argument as such or from Kant's transcendental idealist response to it? We shall make a final assessment of these issues only in 20.4 to 20.8. Our eventual conclusion will be that the Normative standpoint, which accepts the Critical argument, does *not* imply this conclusion. The unknowability of cognition-independent facts arises from Kant's transcendental idealism, not from the Critical argument.[9]

6.4 Against intuitionism

Like any version of the Critical stance, the Normative standpoint holds that empirical knowledge is only possible within an a priori framework. Consider perceptual warrants again. Here the Normative view takes the following to be a priori: the fact that x seems to perceive that p is (default) sufficient reason for the belief that x perceives that p. In which case it's a priori that this same fact is sufficient reason for the belief that p and the belief that there's an information-transmitting causal link from the fact that p to the fact that x seems to perceive that p.[10] So doesn't it follow a priori that a causal link exists between the fact that x seems to perceive that p and the fact that p? But these are distinct existents, and thus the distinguishability thesis says that there is no a priori relation between them.

---

[9] Why should Kant's doctrine about the form of intuition not lead us to an error theory about intuition? (If the famous pink spectacles are glued to our nose, should we not form an error theory about appearances-to-us of pinkness?) If it is to lead, instead, to the conclusion that the parallels postulate is a priori we need to add, to the form of intuition doctrine, a doctrine of cognition-dependence for phenomenal facts.

[10] I take it that if the fact that p and your seeming to perceive that p are simply co-products of some third fact then you aren't perceiving that p. But it makes no essential difference to the argument if this is denied.

In a non-defeating epistemic field, the fact that you seem to perceive that p is indeed sufficient reason for you to believe that the fact that p is the cause of your seeming perception that p. That whole proposition is normative, and it is a priori. However, that does not imply that your warrant for the causal proposition itself is a priori. Since it is a fact about your seeming perceptions that gives you warrant to believe the causal proposition, the warrant is a posteriori. Furthermore, the fact that you are warranted in believing it is consistent with your belief being false; the existence of the causal relation is thus not *deducible* from the fact that you seem to perceive that p. Warrant is an a priori nominal relation between your epistemic state and a belief type or token; but, since you can be warranted in the belief that p even when it is not the case that p, it *not* an a priori substantial relation between your epistemic state and the fact that p.

But then why can't intuitionists say exactly the same about warrant for a priori propositions? On their model of intuition, your a priori warrant is also grounded in a fact about you, in this case about what you seem to intuit. What makes the warranted proposition a priori, they can say, is simply that it is warranted by intuition not perception. A priori warrant just *means* intuitively-based warrant. And if (E) does not rule out perceptual warrant, it does not rule out intuitive warrant. It either rules both out or it allows both. If there is an objection to intuition as against perception, it will have to arise from the difficulty of making intelligible what kind of information-transmitting link intuition could be—a powerful enough consideration in itself, to be sure.

Let us look at this more closely. Perceptual warrant requires that in epistemic states which contain no relevant defeaters, a seeming perception is sufficient reason to believe that one perceives. In particular in such an epistemic state, s_x,

(4) $S(s_x,$ the fact that x seems to perceive that p, x, $β$(the fact that p is the cause of x's seeming perception that p)).

The analogue for intuitive warrant would be that in states s_x which contain no relevant defeaters of the relevant intuition

(5) $S(s_x,$ the fact that x seems to intuit that p, x, $β$(the fact that p is the cause of x's seeming intuition that p)).

One might argue that (4) is an a posteriori proposition knowable on the basis of an inference to the best overall explanation of experience. That is not very plausible even for (4),[11] and it seems hardly possible for (5)—at least in the absence of a mechanism for intuitive receptivity that could be taken seriously. More plausibly, one could propose that (4) and (5) are both warranted a priori.

In that case, from the intuitionist's realist standpoint both these normative propositions, (4) and (5), state normative *facts*. They are also a priori; so to know them is to be intuitively aware of the facts they state. We can therefore apply (B) and (C) to them. In particular, x's seeming intuition that the fact asserted by (5) obtains can be an indicator that it does only if there is an appropriate link between the fact and the seeming intuition.

---

[11] See 9.5.

That there is this link is something for which the thinker must have intuitive warrant. And so on (apply (2) and (3) again). There is a regress. *Every* epistemic warrant, be it a posteriori or a priori, requires an infinite series of intuitions. Moreover this regress is vicious. We would reject an account of perception that said every perception involves an infinite number of perceptions, and we should reject an account of a priori intuition that says every intuition involves an infinite number of intuitions.

Contrast the Normative, irrealist, account of a priori warrant. On this view, (4) is a priori but it is *not* a factual claim. Hence (B) does not apply to it. As for (5), the question of its truth does not even arise, since from the Normative standpoint its realist notion of intuition is quite empty.

We can draw a powerful conclusion. *Intuitionistic realism cannot give an account of a priori warrant, or even of perceptual warrant.* If epistemic warrant is possible at all, an irrealist account of the a priori must be correct. That leaves three by now familiar views in play. There is Kantian transcendental idealism, according to which a priori knowledge of space and time is possible because spatio-temporal facts are not cognition-independent. There is non-cognitivism about the a priori as in the no-content view. And finally there is the Normative view, to which we now turn.

6.5 A priori propositions

Where the proposition that p is a priori, what then is my reason to believe it? It is not the fact that I can intuit that p, as the intuitionist holds. Nor can facts about my attitudes to the proposition constitute a reason for me to believe it. But nor does it seem perspicuous to say that I believe that p 'for no reason'. This does not distinguish between my belief that 2 plus 2 equals 4, and my belief that aliens are approaching the Earth. The former belief, unlike the latter, is *warranted*—and on our analysis, warrant involves the notion of a reason.

There is another possibility: that the reason to believe an a priori proposition is not identifiable with *any fact*. This must be the Normative view: a proposition is a priori when there is *outright* reason to believe it. Outright reasons, it will be remembered (2.5), are limiting cases in which there is reason in an epistemic field to believe a proposition, but that reason is not identifiable with any non-empty subset of the facts in the epistemic field. On the Normative view aprioricity is a pure concept of normative epistemology. A proposition is a priori in e if and only if there is outright sufficient reason to believe it in e (or to disbelieve it—I won't keep inserting this qualification).[12]

[12] This definition of a priori propositions can be compared to Hartry Field's definition of a '*weakly* a priori proposition as one that can be reasonably believed without empirical evidence' (Field 2000: 117). There are other overlaps between the Normative account of the a priori propounded in this chapter and Field's 'evaluatist' account. Normativism would agree, for example, that 'reasonableness does not *consist* in anything: it is not a factual property' (Field 2000: 127). However, it would not agree that what it is reasonable to believe without evidence—hence, what is (weakly) a priori—depends on our goals, since it holds that epistemic reasons are not dependent on practical reasons: they are not reasons to bring about beliefs. Cp. Field: 139–44. In this discussion it seems to me that Field ignores our actual epistemology of normative claims, which we come to in Chapter 16.

As this makes clear, there is no way of defining 'a priori' that is neutral as between intuitionism and the Normative view. Since we are taking the Normative view, it is the normative definition of 'a priori' that we now adopt.

Empiricists who take the no-content view can also agree with the normative definition of the a priori. Where there is outright reason to accept a claim their explanation is that the claim is analytic; it conveys no factual information but merely expresses a rule of the language. They can be factualists about content, but still agree with the Critical claim that no factual proposition is a priori. The Normative view, in contrast, holds that there are synthetic propositions that have *content* but are *non-factual*. Purely normative propositions fall within this class. Thus the way seems open for the idea that purely normative propositions are the basis of the a priori. On the face of it, neither of these views needs to makes any concession to transcendental idealism.

Not all wholly normative propositions are a priori, of course. Consider the proposition that everyone should keep fit. That proposition is wholly normative, but if it's true there are various facts in virtue of which it's true: for example, that people who keep fit lead more enjoyable lives than people who do not. To know the proposition to be true is to know that some such facts obtain, even if one doesn't know what they are. So this wholly normative proposition is a posteriori. But there are also wholly normative propositions that there is outright sufficient reason to believe. These, if true, are norms. The Normative view is that all a priori truths are norms, or, as will be explained below, non-factual offshoots of norms.

Now the definition of aprioricity in terms of outright reason to believe makes aprioricity relative to an epistemic field. That follows from our general account of epistemic reasons. It leaves open the possibility that a proposition that is a priori in one epistemic field—in that there is outright reason to believe it in that field—is not a priori in another. Furthermore, it does not in general follow from the fact that there's reason to believe a proposition, even sufficient reason, that it is true. So our definition leaves open the possibility that a proposition may be a priori in an epistemic field but not true.

Note also that outright reasons may be sufficient or of degree, and that in defining an a priori proposition as one that there is outright sufficient reason to believe, we have said nothing about the case where there is outright reason of degree. May there not be, in some cases, some degree of outright reason to believe a proposition, but not sufficient reason? Might there, for example, be *some* degree of outright reason to believe that there is no action at a distance? If so, that proposition would have a *degree* of aprioricity. That is: there would be *some degree* of outright reason to rule out a theory that postulates action at a distance—some a priori weighting against it—but this would not amount to sufficient reason. If the theory does enough explanatory work, there might be sufficient reason to adopt it. Our definition of aprioricity does well to leave possibilities of this kind open. We can allow for propositions that are more or less a priori in an epistemic field: where a proposition is a priori there is outright sufficient reason to believe it, where it is partly a priori there is only an outright reason of degree. Thus (with '∅' denoting the empty set and **R** standing in for any of the three reason relations) we can say that the proposition that *p has some degree of a priori support* in *e* if and only if:

$\mathbf{R}(e, \varnothing, \beta p)$.

It is *a priori in e* if and only if:

$\mathbf{S}(e, \varnothing, \beta p)$.

Some important questions remain to be resolved. In the first place, though we have defined what it is for a proposition to be a priori in an epistemic field, we have not yet considered what it is to have an a priori *warrant* for a belief, or to have a priori *knowledge*. Furthermore, many a priori propositions don't look normative and don't look analytic either—including such well-known examples as that nothing is both red and green all over, or that 5+7 = 12. What should we say about this? And what do we want to say about the defeasibility of a priori propositions? Can a proposition be a priori in an epistemic field but fail to be a priori in an improved epistemic field? Can there be sufficient reason in an improved epistemic field to believe it to be false? We turn to these questions in the next four sections.

6.6 A priori warrants

One may be warranted in believing an a priori proposition for a variety of reasons, including reasons based on testimony or empirical evidence. Though the proposition believed is a priori, the warrant for believing it may not be. To have an *a priori* warrant for believing a proposition is to have a warrant of a certain first-person kind. What sort of warrant is this?

It will consist in some form of apperception. If I have a priori warrant for the belief that *p* then some fact which I apperceive gives me sufficient reason to believe that there is outright sufficient reason in my epistemic field to believe that *p*. One has a warranted a priori reason for believing a proposition if one's epistemic *state* gives one reason to believe that there is outright reason to believe it in one's epistemic *field*. This follows directly from our definition of warrant together with the normative definition of a priori propositions given in the previous section. When *x* has an a priori warrant to believe that *p*, there are facts in *x*'s epistemic state which give *x* sufficient reason to believe that there's sufficient outright reason to believe that *p*.[13]

On the no-content view (II), a priori warrant will always consist solely in one's understanding of a language. To say that a person has an a priori warrant for the belief that all mothers are parents, for example, will be to say that that person is aware of the meaning of some sentence in some language that expresses that proposition, and just in virtue of that awareness grasps that the sentence in question is to be counted as analytic. So the warranting fact in that person's epistemic state will be the fact that he understands an appropriate sentence in a certain way: that he understands it in that way will be what he apperceives.

---

[13] Given the discussion of the previous section, there is the possibility that a warrant may be only in part a priori. That is as is should be, but for simplicity I'll ignore it, and assume that warrants are either entirely a priori or entirely a posteriori.

What of the Normative view? It accepts that there are synthetic a priori propositions; what account does it give of a priori warrant in these cases? On this view, a priori warrant for the belief that p can only consist of some attitude or attitudes that one apperceives oneself to have towards the proposition that p. (This is the basic case; one can also be warranted in thinking a proposition to be a priori on the basis of seeming to remember that one had that attitude towards it when one attended to it, or on the basis of inference or calculation involving propositions and principles of inference towards which one has that attitude, or on the basis of testimony. But though these are warrants for thinking the proposition to be a priori, they are not a priori warrants in the sense intended here.)

There may be various clusters of such attitudes—but the common element in them all will have to be that in one way or another they generate a spontaneous inclination to believe that there is outright reason, sufficient, or of degree, to believe the proposition, and that this spontaneous inclination, in the right circumstances, constitutes an a priori warrant.

A variety of attitudes can play this role. In the case of epistemic norms, for example, phenomenological limits on representation sometimes do so. By 'representation' I mean the capacity to represent to oneself 'from the inside' what it would be like for some state of affairs to obtain. For example, one can imagine from the inside what it would be like to see something as green or red, but when one tries to imagine oneself seeing something as simultaneously red and green imagination fails. Likewise when one tries to imagine seeing two straight-looking lines enclosing a space, or a way of partitioning three objects in an imagined space into two lots of two.[14] Such appeals to 'representability' obviously have their well-rehearsed limitations; but the relevant point for us is that they often do, in fact, generate in us spontaneous normative dispositions to think there is outright reason to believe.

In the case of practical or evaluative norms, in contrast, what seems central is that one considers how one would be disposed to act or feel in imagined situations. Take the proposition that there's reason to help others. If one thinks there's outright sufficient reason to believe that proposition, it's because of what one imagines oneself disposed to do, and to accept as a reason for doing, in cases where one can help another. Or consider the proposition that there's reason to be grateful for kindness shown. Again, if one thinks there's outright sufficient reason to believe that, it's in virtue of how one imagines oneself reacting, and what would seem a reason-supported reaction, where kindness is shown. The dispositions here are spontaneous dispositions of the will or the feelings, dispositions which are felt to have normative significance. Spontaneous dispositions to believe work similarly in the case of more purely methodological epistemic norms, such as enumerative induction, or inference to the best explanation, where no direct appeal to perceptual imagination is involved.

---

[14] In the relevant sense I *can* imagine seeing a 53-sided polygon. The fact that I couldn't see how many sides such a polygon would have 'just by looking' does not strike me as a difficulty about representing its existence—I can imagine constructing it by adding sides. Even in the case of action at a distance this kind of perceptual representability seems to be involved—one can't imagine the process involved in such action without spatio-temporal transmission. (Such points about representability contribute to the plausibility of transcendental idealism about space and time.)

Spontaneity, as in Kant's contrast between spontaneity and receptivity, is the notion that is crucial for the epistemology of the a priori. Whereas the intuitionist takes intuition to be a receptive faculty, the Normative view is that normative insight, and thus all a priori judgement, is an exercise of pure spontaneity.[15] We shall discuss this further in Chapter 16. For the moment we anticipate by saying that the attitude that can generate a priori warrants for the belief that p is that of *being spontaneously disposed to judge outright that p*, symbolizing 'x is spontaneously disposed to judge outright that p' as '$SD(x, p)$'.

Not every epistemic state of x that contains the fact that $SD(x, p)$ provides sufficient reason for x to believe that it is a priori that p. This fact is a *prima facie* sufficient reason for the belief but may not survive when all facts in s are considered. But, in an s in which it does give x sufficient reason to believe that there is sufficient outright reason to believe that p we have:

$$S\{s, SD(x, p), x, \beta S(e_x, \varnothing, \beta p)\}$$

When that is the case we can say x has *a priori warrant* in s for the belief that p.

This double layer of sufficient reasons is essential. Plainly, even a satisfactorily full phenomenology of a priori warrant will not make it plausible that phenomenological facts apperceivable to the thinker constitute sufficient reason, or any degree of reason, to believe the a priori proposition itself. How could they? What we should say is not that these facts are reasons to believe the proposition but that they are reasons to believe that the proposition is a priori—reasons to believe that there is outright sufficient reason to believe it. Thus, for example, I cannot give myself an imaginative representation of surfaces or volumes which are both red and green. These facts about the limits on what I can perceptually imagine spontaneously dispose me to believe, and thereby give me sufficient reason to believe, that there is outright sufficient reason to believe that nothing is both red and green—i.e. that that proposition is a priori.

But now consider that proposition—that nothing is both red and green—itself. The sentence that expresses it is not normative. Must we not conclude that the proposition is factual, and thus abandon the Critical thesis that no factual proposition is a priori?

6.7 The normativity of a priori propositions

We are working with two distinctions. One is a semantic distinction between normative and non-normative sentences, and the propositions they express, the other is an ontological distinction between factual and non-factual propositions. Wholly normative propositions (we shall argue in Chapter 17) are not factual. So an a priori proposition may be non-factual because it is synthetic but wholly normative. It may also be non-factual because it is analytic, as the no-content view proposes. Then there is also the possibility that some non-factual propositions are neither normative nor analytic—and are a priori in some cases and a posteriori others. 'Hesperus is Phosphorus' is an example of the

---

[15] This does not apply to Kant himself: given his doctrine in the Transcendental Aesthetic he cannot think that all a priori judgement rests on normative insight.

latter case. Bearing in mind the distinction between nominal and substantial fact, we can say that that proposition asserts no substantial fact, even though it is a posteriori. The only thing the Critical thesis *rules out* is that there should be a factual proposition that is a priori, where 'fact' is understood in the substantial way.

So let us consider 'Nothing is simultaneously wholly red and wholly green' within this framework. Our questions about it are whether it is a priori, whether it is analytic, and whether it is factual.

We can derive it from four premises:

(i) Red is not identical with green.

(ii) Red is a colour.

(iii) Green is a colour.

(iv) If c_1 and c_2 are non-identical colours then no object is both wholly c_1 and wholly c_2.[16]

Hence, no object is both wholly red and wholly green. Consider these in turn:

(i) is a statement of non-identity, and it has referential as against descriptive singular terms on both sides. I shall take it that a referential singular term, 'a', is one whose meaning is given simply, by the statement that 'a' refers to a (with appropriate modification for indexicals): it is not given descriptively, by a statement that says that 'a' refers to whatever object x uniquely satisfies a given descriptive condition. Let us call identities and non-identities of this kind—propositions expressed by sentences in which the identity predicate is flanked by referential singular terms and not by descriptive singular terms—*simple* identities and non-identities. (i) is a simple non-identity. For knowing the meaning of 'red' and 'green' consists simply in knowing that 'red' refers to red and that 'green' refers to green. It does not consist in knowing the truth of a conditionally stated semantic clause (that 'red' or 'green' refers to any object x that uniquely satisfies some descriptive condition).

Simple identities and non-identities are not analytic.[17] And they may not be a priori, even though they are necessary. In general, where 'a' and 'b' are referential singular terms, one can know what 'a' refers to and what 'b' refers to without knowing whether or not a = b. Establishing whether or not a = b may be a matter of empirical inquiry. This is especially clear where the singular terms refer to particulars: 'Tully is Cicero', 'William Shakespeare is not Francis Bacon'.

Can we say that (i) is a special case, so that just by knowing what its terms refer to we know that their referents are non-identical? If I know what 'red' and 'green' refer to I'm *thereby* in a position to know that they refer to distinct properties. That is because red and green are immediately perceptible qualities of objects. Thus if you show me the referent of 'red' and 'green' in a meaning-demonstrating way (a way that serves to convey their meaning, say by pointing to samples that do look red and green to me), then I can *just see* that red is not green.

---

[16] Colour terms can stand in the determinable/determinate relation—e.g. 'blue' and 'ultramarine'. An object can be wholly blue and wholly ultramarine. For present purposes let's stipulate that colours are to be understood as 'equal determinates'.

[17] Other than for the case 'a = a'. See 7.2.

Does this make (i) a priori? If I understand the word 'red' and 'green', I will have had perceptual impressions as of redness and greenness, and on that basis, I can immediately tell that red is not green. Similarly, I can immediately tell that having a backache is distinct from having a headache. Failure to know the truth-value of 'a = b' typically involves distinct modes of presentation associated with 'a' and 'b'. But red and green are given immediately, not by means of a mediate mode of presentation. Nothing corresponds to this immediate givenness in the case of particulars. Particulars are always given in a mediate mode of presentation—by reference to their properties, or by an inherently perspectival ostension. Even if you point to the particular over there and the particular over here it is not *given* that they are distinct. If time travel is possible than perhaps the particular over there *is* the particular over here.[18] In contrast, where 'a' and 'b' are referential singular terms referring to perceptible qualities, the explanations of how we might fail to know whether or not a = b while knowing what 'a' and 'b' refer to fail. Moreover we seem to know a priori, as a general truth about identity, that if a is not identical with b it could not be.

These simple identities and non-identities of perceptible qualities are not analytic, but they are a priori. However, I have already claimed that they are not factual. So their aprioricity is not incompatible with the Critical thesis (that no factual proposition is a priori). (ii) and iii) have a better claim to be analytic. Do I not, just by understanding 'red', 'green', and 'colour', know that 'red is a colour' and 'green is a colour' express truths? I dobut does this show that these sentences are analytic? In Chapter 7 we shall answer this question in the negative.

Next consider (iv). On the one hand, no model of analyticity considered in the next chapter would show it to be analytic. On the other, whereas red and green are immediately apprehended as distinct, that an object *cannot* be both is not something that can be immediately apprehended. What we do find, phenomenologically, is that we cannot perceptually imagine this (give ourselves a representation, in perceptual imagination, of an object which is both red and green). But there is the obvious question of how we can move from the fact that we cannot perceptually imagine it to the conclusion that it cannot be the case.

Can we present (iv) as a normative proposition? By definition, (iv) is normative if and only if the sentence that expresses it has a normative sentence as a definitional consequence. But it does not.[19] We must try another approach. Can (iv) be seen as the *offshoot*, in a certain sense, of a normative proposition?

---

[18] It's Dr Who over there and Dr Who over here. He's in two places at one time. (The question is not whether time travel really is possible but what this thought experiment shows about whether identity or distinctness of particulars, as against (ap)perceptible qualities, can be simply *given*.)

[19] See 4.2. What about:

> If there is reason to believe that c_1 and c_2 are distinct colours and there is reason to believe that x is c_1 then there is reason to believe that x is not c_2?

But this doesn't follow from (iv). Epistemic reasons are relative to an epistemic field. So this will only be true in *e* if there's sufficient reason to believe (iv) in *e*. What then about:

> If in *e* there is sufficient reason to believe that no object has two distinct colours, sufficient reason to believe that c_1 and c_2 are distinct colours, and sufficient reason to believe that x is c_1, then there is sufficient reason to believe that x is not c_2?

Does this follow from (iv)? Yes, inasmuch as it is a necessary truth. But it's not a *definitional* consequence.

6.8 Offshoots of normative propositions

A useful model is provided by systems of natural deduction in logic. A crucial point here is that the principles of inference in such a system govern not just deduction from what is believed but also deduction under supposition. I shall argue in Chapter 8 that logic is normative; but of course not *all* epistemic norms are deductive principles. Nonetheless, we can deploy epistemic norms in general to make *suppositions* about *arbitrary* objects, and reason *within our epistemic field* from these suppositions. (Supposition will be considered further in Chapter 8.) Consider, in this light, the following normative proposition:

> (N) If the fact that an arbitrary object x has colour c_1 is in *e* there is sufficient reason in *e* to believe that x does not (simultaneously, in the same place) have c_2, where $c_1 \neq c_2$.

This is to be understood as a norm governing reasoning under all suppositions (and thus, according to the account we shall give in 8.4, as a necessary truth). Under a given supposition that x has colour c_1 it licenses in *e* the inference to the conclusion that x does not have colour c_2. By analogy with systems of natural deduction, N can be represented thus:

$$x \text{ is } c_1, c_2 \neq c_2 \; \tau_e \; \neg x \text{ is } c_2 \quad [20]$$

We then have:

(6) x is c_1 (Supposition)

(7) $c_1 \neq c_2$ (Supposition)

(8) $\neg x$ is c_2 (By N on 6, 7)

(9) $c_1 \neq c_2 \rightarrow (x \text{ is } c_1 \rightarrow \neg x \text{ is } c_2)$ (By two steps of Conditional Proof on (6) and (7))

(10) $(x)(c_1 \neq c_2 \rightarrow (x \text{ is } c_1 \rightarrow \neg x \text{ is } c_2))$ (From (9) by generalization on an arbitrary case)

(11) $(x)(c_1 \neq c_2 \rightarrow \neg(x \text{ is } c_1 \; \& \; x \text{ is } c_2))$ (By $p \rightarrow \neg q \; \tau \neg (p \; \& \; q)$).

This reasoning involves no non-normative premises. It relies on a non-deductive application of the epistemic norm N at (8) together with principles of deduction (whose status will be discussed in the next two chapters).[21] The whole reasoning holds in relation to an epistemic field, *e*, so there's outright sufficient reason to accept its conclusion in that *e*. Specifically, since this reasoning works in *our e*, there is outright sufficient reason *for us* to believe (11), that is:

(12) $\tau_{our \, e} \, (x)(c_1 \neq c_2 \rightarrow \neg(x \text{ is } c_1 \; \& \; x \text{ is } c_2))$.

So (11) is a priori in our *e*.

(11) is not a normative sentence, by our definition of 'normative sentence'. Nor is it a *definitional consequence* of N. In particular, the move from (12), which is a norm established

---

[20] Read '$p_1,\ldots,p_n \, \tau_e \, q$' as: 'There is outright sufficient reason in *e*, given suppositions that $p_1,\ldots,p_n$, to infer that q', and '$\tau_e \, q$' as 'There is outright sufficient reason in *e* to believe that q'.

[21] Note that the application of Conditional Proof requires that we are warranted in believing that (N) holds for all *e* (see 20.5). By our analysis of necessity in Chapter 8 this entails that N is necessary as well as a priori.

by an argument from supposition, to endorsement of the non-normative (11), is not a deductive move at all. It involves the transition:

$$\frac{\tau_{our\,e}\,p}{p}$$

So N remains wholly normative, by our definition of wholly normative. Further, (11) is not an analytic truth. Our warrant for it is based on our a priori warrant for norm (N), and that norm (as we shall see in the next chapter) is not analytic. To be clear: warrant for (11) is based on warrant for (N), not vice versa. This claim is crucial to the Normative view. But it may well be asked, does it not put the cart before the horse? This type of question has already arisen in connection with the buck-passing accounts of 'good': we shall take general stock of it in 18.6.

Meanwhile, where does our analysis leave the Critical thesis that no factual proposition is a priori?

A Kantian account of (11) might say that it is factual, but not in a cognition-independent way. Its factuality is in some way conditioned by, or relative to, the limits of our capacity for perceptual representation; the fact in question is therefore a phenomenal fact, not a fact about things as they really are. In contrast the Normative view says that our capacities for perceptual representation do not bear directly on the facts but rather warrant us in accepting certain epistemic norms, such as N. This view says that propositions like (11), arrived at from epistemic norms in the manner illustrated above, are not analytic, not normative, but also not factual. They are *non-factual offshoots* of epistemic norms.[22] *Pure normativity* remains the sole basis of the synthetic a priori. This is the route that I advocate. It requires no distinction between phenomenal and noumenal facts. However, we shall need a further examination of the contrast between factuality and normativity (in 20.4 and 20.5) before we can make a final assessment.

6.9 Aprioricity and defeasibility

Our definition of aprioricity relativizes it to an epistemic field: a proposition is a priori in *e* if and only if in *e* there is outright sufficient reason to believe it. That is a special case of the general point that epistemic reasons are relative to an epistemic field. And the point applies to all a priori propositions, be they propositions about epistemic, practical, or evaluative reasons. At the same time, however, it is crucial to remember that where a proposition is about epistemic as against practical or evaluative reasons there will be a reference to epistemic fields in its *content* as well. To round off the picture we should therefore consider some further questions:

---

[22] It may be objected that to say that an object is red, or that it is green, is clearly to assert that a substantive fact obtains. So surely both the conjunctive proposition that this object is red and green, and its negation, must be factual? But if this was a good argument then we could equally argue from the factuality of 'He is a bachelor' and 'He is not married' to the factuality of 'He is a bachelor and he is not married'.

If there is a priori support for a proposition in e, is it a priori in e that there is a priori support for it in e?
If there is a priori support for it in e, is it a priori in all e that there is a priori support for it in e?
If there is a priori support for it in e, is there a priori support for it in all e?

These questions are analogous to the questions raised about warrant in 5.8. Consider the first. Could there be outright reason to believe a proposition but not outright sufficient reason to believe that there is? In that case it would be true that:

(13) $\mathbf{R}(e, \varnothing, \beta p)$

but false that

(14) $S(e, \varnothing, \beta \mathbf{R}(e, \varnothing, \beta p))$.

But if it is possible to recognize that (13) holds by pure reflection then it must possible to recognize, by pure reflection, that (14) does. This applies to both the cases of apriority that we have recognized: analyticity and pure normativity.[23] Thus we have:

$\mathbf{R}(e, \varnothing, \beta p) \rightarrow S(e, \varnothing, \beta \mathbf{R}(e, \varnothing, \beta p))$.

What about the other direction? Like warrant, sufficient reason, including outright sufficient reason, is not in general factive. But here we have a special case. How could there be outright sufficient reason in e for the belief that there is reason in e to believe that p, when there isn't? The issues about testimony-based higher-order warrants discussed in 5.8 do not arise here, since we are talking about *outright* sufficient reasons, and no testimony-based reasons are outright, precisely because they consist in the fact of testimony. Thus we have:

(15) $\mathbf{R}(e, \varnothing, \beta p) \leftrightarrow S(e, \varnothing, \mathbf{R}(e, \varnothing, \beta p))$.

There is a priori support for a proposition in e if and only if it is a priori in e that there is.

Let us turn to the other two questions. We should notice that some epistemic fields may be too poor for a proposition that is a priori in richer fields to be formulated relative to *these* fields at all. Consider, for example, the proposition that nothing is both red and green, and an epistemic field that contains no facts about visible properties. There isn't a priori reason, in that field, to believe the proposition or its negation.

We don't need to discuss this sort of case, however, because the interesting question is rather this: if there is a priori support for a proposition in e, is it a priori that there is in all *strict improvements* on e? In 5.8 we defined a strict improvement on an epistemic state s as an s^* which contains every fact in s and also some other facts; we can define a strict improvement on an epistemic field e in the same way, as an e^* which contains every fact in e and also some other facts. (As noted in 5.8, strict improvements can also model

---

[23] It is not a priori that any sentence has the meaning it does, and thus not a priori that a sentence expresses an analytic proposition, if it does. But *given* that it does, then it is a priori, of the proposition that it expresses, that that proposition has no content. There is outright sufficient reason to believe that it has no content, and outright sufficient reason to believe that that in turn is so.

improvements which are 'locally strict', i.e. in which the facts that have dropped out are irrelevant to the warrant in question.)

Now we ask:

(i) If there is a priori support for a proposition in e, is it a priori in all strict improvements on e that there is?

(ii) If there is a priori support for a proposition in e, is there a priori support for it in all strict improvements on e?

Clearly the answer to the first question is 'yes'. A proposition that has a priori support in e can be understood in all strict improvements on e, and that makes it possible to tell in any $e^\star$, by reflection on e, that it has a priori support in e. For reasons just discussed in connection with (15), this can be strengthened to a biconditional:

(16) $\mathbf{R}(e, \emptyset, \beta p) \leftrightarrow S(e^\star, \emptyset, \beta \mathbf{R}(e, \emptyset, \beta p))$.

However, the answer to (ii) is much less clear. The question here is whether:

$\mathbf{R}(e, \emptyset, \beta p) \rightarrow \mathbf{R}(e^\star, \emptyset, \beta p)$.

We cannot get to that result just from (15) and (16). And that is as it should be, because in general there can be sufficient reason, or some reason, to believe that p in e but insufficient reason or no reason to believe that p in $e^\star$. In e, for example, the scratches on the window may constitute sufficient reason to believe that the criminal escaped that way—but not in $e^\star$, which includes the fact that the scratches were there before the crime.

However, in the case of purely normative propositions the reason to believe them is outright. And if there is *outright* sufficient reason to believe a proposition in an epistemic field, then surely, it may be argued, there cannot fail to be outright sufficient reason to believe it in an improvement on that field? How can the *aprioricity* of propositions about reasons vary across epistemic fields?

Where the normative proposition in question is about evaluative or practical reasons this is immediately plausible, since the very same proposition is being considered in all these fields. But when the proposition is *itself* about epistemic reasons there is the complication that in this case the proposition will have reference to an epistemic field in its *content*: it will be some proposition about what reasons for belief there are in a particular e. Now if such a proposition is true in e then it is a priori true in all $e^\star$ that it's true in e, and that it is a priori in e. However, what we want to know is whether it follows from the truth of this proposition that the analogous but different proposition, about what reasons there are in $e^\star$, is true and a priori in $e^\star$? When we ask question (ii) about epistemic–normative propositions, we should understand it in this particular sense.

Consider, for example, Euclidean physical geometry. Was there outright reason, in the Greeks' epistemic field, to believe Euclidean physical geometry, including the parallels postulate? Did certain Greek geometers have an a priori warrant for believing it?

A case can be made for holding they had an a priori warrant for believing the parallels postulate; namely, that any plausible account of the phenomenological circumstances in which one has an a priori warrant will say that they had it. Both we and they are unable to represent a 'biangle' (a closed figure with two straight sides) to ourselves, in perceptual imagination—just as we are unable to represent to ourselves an object that is red and green all over. And the possibility that this phenomenological warrant might be defeated exists in both cases. Both seem open to indirect theoretical undermining, in that they are based on what we can represent to ourselves in perceptual imagination but apply beyond what we could perceive.[24] But in the Greeks' case the warrant was not defeated, whereas we, though we still (I believe) find the parallels postulate spontaneously evident, are warranted, via knowledge of current physics, in believing it false.

It doesn't follow from the Greeks having a warrant, even an a priori warrant, to believe the parallels postulate that the postulate is true. It doesn't even follow—for all we've said so far—that it was a priori in their epistemic field. There's the possibility of arguing that even though the Greeks had sufficient reason to believe it to be a priori, based on undefeated spontaneous dispositions which gave them an *a priori* warrant, the proposition was nevertheless not a priori in their epistemic field. In our improved *e* there is sufficient reason to reject the postulate; does that not also show that in our *e* there is sufficient reason to hold that the postulate was not a priori in their *e*?

This might be thought unpalatable. What more could the Greeks have done to see that the parallels postulate was *not* after all a priori in their epistemic field? They would be unable to tell that it was not, and warranted in believing that it was. We have no reason to fault their normative dispositions. To deny that the postulate was a priori in their epistemic field breaks the connection between a proposition being a priori and it being possible to know that it is. Surely if a proposition is or is not a priori in one's *e* one should be able to tell that it is or is not. We shall return to this point in the next section.

Yet if current views are right the parallels postulate is false.[25] Whatever proposition it is that's false, the Greeks certainly didn't know *that* proposition. But what is it exactly, that's false?

We can put the parallels postulate in indexical–normative form: the fact that a pair of lines intersects more than once is outright sufficient reason, in our *e*, for the belief that at least one of them is not straight. Since that is a proposition about reasons it is implicitly relative to an *e*—*our e*:

(17) a pair of lines intersects twice $\tau_{our\ e}$ at least one of them is not straight.

There is a *de se* reference in (17) to the asserter of the proposition; when (17) is asserted by us it is false.

But might it be true in the mouths of ancient Greeks? If it is then:

(18) If a pair of lines intersect twice one of them is not straight

---

[24] One applies to lines however long they may be, the other applies to extensions however small or distant they may be.
[25] I am taking it as a proposition of physical geometry, not as an axiom in an uninterpreted formal system of geometry.

is a priori in the Greeks' epistemic field. It is an offshoot, just like 'Nothing is red and green all over'. But whereas the Greeks had outright sufficient reason to believe it true, we do not. On the contrary, we have reason to believe it false. Nevertheless, we could still hold it to be true that:

(19) a pair of lines intersect twice $\tau_{\text{Greek } e}$ at least one of them is not straight.[26]

And that would be consistent with (15) and (16). On this view, then, the parallels postulate is a priori in the Greeks' epistemic field, normative for their theorizing, but false. In our own epistemic field (17) and (18) may have some a priori support but are not a priori: that is, there is no outright *sufficient* reason to believe them.

Thus the idea that we must take seriously is this: that the question of what there is *outright* sufficient reason to believe is not isolated from the available facts. What we know and could know in a given epistemic field contributes to determining what is a priori and a posteriori in that field. For anyone who knows only what the Greeks knew or could know, the fact that a pair of lines intersects more than once is outright sufficient reason for the belief that at least one of them is not straight. A theoretical revolution was required to achieve an epistemic field in which (17) could no longer be truly asserted.[27] If this view is correct the answer to question (ii) can be 'no'.

In summary, we have so far found no clear and general basis for an affirmative answer to question (ii). However, we have not yet finished with it. We shall return to it in 20.6, where we shall—contrary to the view just canvassed—endorse the affirmative answer. And this answer is relevant to how we analyse the notion of a priori *knowledge*.

6.10 A priori knowledge

Having a priori knowledge is more than just knowing, of an a priori proposition, that it is true. It consists in knowing the proposition to be true in virtue of recognizing its aprioricity in a certain way. And further, if one knows that it's true a priori solely by testimony—which is of course the way that one knows many propositions to be true a priori—then one still does not have a priori knowledge of the kind that we are interested in analysing in this section. One knows that it's true a priori, but in an a posteriori way.

What is it, then, to know a proposition to be true by virtue of recognizing its aprioricity in the way that we are interested in? It requires *insight* into its aprioricity. Our discussion so far has lead us to distinguish the following claims:

(i) x has a priori warrant in e for the belief that p

(ii) the proposition that p is a priori in e

(iii) the proposition that p is true.

---

[26] 'Greek e' refers to the epistemic field the Greeks were in.

[27] In virtue of the closure of warrant under itself the Greeks were warranted in thinking the parallels postulate is independent of the other Euclidean axioms (if Euclidean geometry is consistent). But it's arguable that that was not enough—a theoretical revolution in physics was also required.

Now if we could just assume that whenever a person has a priori warrant for the belief that p, the proposition that p is a priori in his epistemic field, and that whenever it is a priori that p in an epistemic field then it is true that p, then we could say that a person has a priori knowledge that p whenever he believes that p in virtue of recognizing that he has an a priori warrant to believe it. However, we cannot just assume that. For given the definitions we have given, (ii) is not *deducible* from (i), and (iii) is not *deducible* from (ii). Nor is (iii) deducible from (i). We need to consider the connections between (i), (ii), and (iii) in their own right.

First, then, there is the question of how (i) and (ii) are connected. It is certainly possible that it should seem to a person that he has an a priori warrant when he does not really have one. What this person thinks of as an a priori warrant may be simple prejudice, a mis-step in reasoning, a blindness to counter-examples or alternate possibilities which are obvious when pointed out. Furthermore, he may be justified (in the sense of 5.9) in thinking that he has an a priori warrant when he does not have one. Cases in which this is particularly obvious are those in which judgement is to the fore—as to whether a particular conclusion is justified on the evidence, for example, or what the right policy decision is, given the facts, or whether a specific evaluation of a performance or a work of art is sound. Non-convergence with others, or just greater experience, may warrant a person in concluding in such cases that his spontaneous judgement is defective.

However, the case that interests us is that in which a person does have a priori warrant—(i) is true. The epistemology of the normative, we shall argue in Chapter 16, involves nothing other than spontaneity educated by experience and discussion, plus appropriate sensitivity to defeating conditions. We shall examine normative dispositions—of which the dispositions underlying judgements that a proposition is a priori are a special case—and consider how they come to be judged reliable, when we consider the epistemology of the normative in detail in Chapter 16. But we can anticipate by endorsing the link, suggested in the previous section, between the aprioricity of a proposition and a priori warrant:

> (20) It is a priori in e that p if and only if thinkers relevantly informed as to the facts in e would have a priori warrant for the belief that p.

As just noted, (20)—which makes (i) and (ii) equivalent—is not a *logical* truth (i.e. one deducible from logic plus our definitions). However, I submit that it is a constitutive truth: this is what it is for a proposition to be a priori in e. What else could it be?

Now we can consider a priori knowledge. Following our discussion in 5.10 we have the following account:

> x has immediate (i.e. non-inferential) a priori knowledge that p if and only if
> (i) p
> (ii) x believes that p on the basis of normative dispositions to believe that p
> (iii) which are reliable.

Reliability, we noted (5.10), is trustworthy indication. In many cases a belief that p trustworthily indicates that p because a reliable information-transmitting link runs from the fact that *p* to the belief that *p*. With wholly normative beliefs (and their offshoots) that is not the case. Where these are based not on testimony or inference from other normative beliefs, but on first-person normative insight, the 'reliable means' can only consist in reliable normative dispositions to believe them. What then is it for these dispositions to be reliable?

We measure the reliability of a normative disposition by the degree to which it can be trusted to provide an epistemic basis for an a priori warrant. But now there is an apparent difficulty. For if this is how we measure the reliability of normative dispositions, then it seems that we are not measuring it, at least not directly, by the degree to which it indicates *truth*. Warrant is one thing, truth is another.

If we allow that a priori warrants are defeasible, this becomes a real, indeed decisive, difficulty. For suppose the ancient Greeks' normative dispositions *were* reliable, so that they *were* a priori warranted (relative to their *e*) in believing the parallels postulate. But their belief failed condition (i): they did not know the postulate to be true. An unbridgeable gap now opens between reliable indication of warrant and reliable indication of truth.

We shall in due course argue, however, that all outright epistemic reasons, and hence in particular a priori warrants, are indefeasible. If that is so, there can be no warranted counter-example to the equivalence of a priori warrant and a priori truth; there is no positive obstacle to accepting that a reliable indication that (ii) holds is a reliable indication that (iii) holds. It is an important point, however, that to accept this conclusion is not yet to *identify* a priori truth and a priori warrant. Indeed we should not do so. For we shall be defending a minimalist view of truth (7.4 and 17.5). On this minimalist view, the proposition that *it is true* that two straight lines never intersect twice is identical to the proposition that two straight lines never intersect twice. But it is *not* identical to the proposition that there is outright warrant to believe, in all *e*, that two straight lines never intersect twice.

Yet if a priori warrant and a priori truth are not identifiable, how can we be confident that they are equivalent? Our answer involves two steps. First, we have argued in this chapter that all non-analytic a priori knowledge is of purely normative propositions and their offshoots. It follows, then, that the basis of all synthetic a priori knowledge is knowledge of pure propositions about *reason relations*. Next will come a second, vital, step. In Part IV we shall argue that reason relations are objective (not mind-dependent), but *irreal*. If this is so, there may be no problem about how a priori warrant can be an indefeasible indicator of truth. For given the irreality of reason relations, the Critical argument raises no difficulty as to how we can have a priori knowledge of them. The basis of that argument (Section 6.3) was that no real relation holds between distinct *existents* a priori. If reason relations are irreal, the Critical argument does not apply to them. Nor does knowledge of them posit any *real* (as against nominal) relation to them.

This gives us the makings of a properly Critical account of synthetic a priori *knowledge*. Its basic claim is that in the case of purely normative, as against factual, propositions, a reliable criterion of a priori warrant is a reliable criterion of truth. It does not explain this claim by defining or 'modelling' a priori truth in terms of indefeasible outright warrant.[28] Knowledge, like truth, is not definable it terms of reasons. Its explanation turns rather on the link between the epistemology and ontology of reason relations.

But a full development of this account must await Part IV. In particular, we need to dig deeper into the claim that both a priori normative propositions and their offshoots (where these exist) are non-factual. Meanwhile, we turn in the following two chapters to analyticity and modality. One way in which a priori propositions can lack factual content is by being analytic, so we should take a closer look at the notion of analyticity, and consider whether it can explain a priori knowledge in general. And what is it to claim that a proposition is necessarily true or false? Is that a factual claim? Can we sometimes know it to be true a priori? If we can, how does that square with the Critical argument?

---

[28] Thus I am not claiming that truth is definable for the case of purely normative propositions in terms of any normative equivalent to Crispin Wright's notion of 'superassertibility', such as indefeasible warrant (Wright 1992). Nor that in the case of normative propositions truth *consists* in superassertibility. Truth, we shall argue in Chapter 17, is not a substantial property at all.

7

ANALYTICITY

This chapter has a twofold aim. In the first place, the Normative version of Critical philosophy requires its own account of analyticity. We shall give that account in this chapter. Second, we should review the concept of analyticity developed by what I called (in Chapter 1) the Viennese version of Critical philosophy—the ideas of Wittgenstein in his 'middle' period and the Vienna Circle. Since their ideas of analyticity were central to their Critical stance, it is important to take careful stock of them.

A new concept of analyticity was the basic tool deployed by these philosophers. By means of it they thought they could defend the apriority of logic and mathematics while still maintaining the traditional empiricist tenet that no proposition with substantial informative content is a priori. Logic and mathematics turn out to be empty of content. What was new in their view was not the no-content notion of analyticity as such; it was their new way of explaining it: the idea that analytic sentences lack content because they simply express 'grammatical' or 'syntactic' rules of a language. This greatly expanded the reach of the analytic. To work it out they needed a new model of meaning, and that was provided by verificationism.

In comparison the account of analyticity that I shall give in this chapter demotes its importance as a philosophical tool. We shall find that there is a perfectly good no-content notion of analyticity, but that it cannot begin to do the Critical work the Viennese wanted to do with it. For the purpose of understanding the a priori, analyticity is a marginal phenomenon. On an account of analyticity in which analytic propositions *genuinely* lack content, logic itself is synthetic. This conclusion, which had already been forcefully argued by John Stuart Mill, stands firm, despite the spirited Viennese attempt to show otherwise. The upshot, therefore, is that if we are to defend the apriority of logic no notion of analyticity will help us.

The ideas of the Viennese School are no longer influential—they have succumbed to powerful objections. However, there is danger in this. When views lose influence in philosophy they rapidly become poorly understood; in particular, the problems they were meant to solve are often ignored or unjustifiably depreciated. The Viennese School was a genuinely Critical response to problems that are real in at least the sense that they demand a serious philosophical response. After the failure of the Viennese response to them they remain untreated. The Normative view advocated in this book is a response to them which like the Viennese view seeks to dissolve them—to show that they are not real after all. In this respect both views belong to the Critical tradition.

Nonetheless the two approaches are quite distinct. The Normative view does not appeal to Viennese ideas about verification and 'grammar' or 'syntax'—or to any ideas about *language* at all. Nor does it agree that all informative propositions are factual. It holds that synthetic a priori propositions are in origin informative propositions purely about reasons, and that such propositions are not factual. Thus, on the one hand, it agrees with Kant that some propositions are both synthetic and a priori, while, on the other hand, it retains the empiricist thesis that no factual proposition is a priori. That is its spirit, though we shall have to come back to the status of those 'offshoots' of epistemic norms that were discussed in 6.6. They should be regarded, I claimed, as non-factual as well as non-normative. However, the notion of a factual proposition cannot be cut clearer than the substantial notion of factuality, and we shall only complete our discussion of this notion in 20.8.

Section 7.1 of this chapter sets out some important historical contrasts in the treatment of analyticity. Sections 7.2 to 7.4 give details of what I call the *empty-inference* approach to analyticity. I argue that this gives a perfectly viable, but very restricted account of that notion. Sections 7.5 and 7.6 review and criticize the Viennese approach, which approaches analyticity through the notion of *implicit definition*. Sections 7.7 and 7.8 consider some implications of the Kripkean distinction between fixing the reference of a term and giving its meaning.

7.1 Kant, Mill, Frege, and Vienna

In arguing against Kant that mathematics was analytic the Viennese were committed to working out a no-content model of analyticity broad enough to take in mathematics as a whole.

This project contrasts with that of Frege. Frege also holds, contra Kant, that arithmetic is analytic, but his disagreement with Kant is of a different nature. He does not adopt the no-content model of analyticity. He takes an analytic proposition to be one that is reducible to truths of logic with the help of definitions alone; his project is then to show that that can be done for arithmetic. He does not hold that logical truths have no content. As he acknowledges, a question can be raised about how we have knowledge of them. He answers that we know such truths via 'the logical source of knowledge', but shows little interest in explaining how this source of knowledge works. Insofar as he says anything about it, however, what he says sounds notably unlike the no-content view:

> I must...protest against the generality of KANT'S dictum: without sensibility no object would be given to us. Nought and one are objects which cannot be given to us in sensation...

> In arithmetic we are not concerned with objects which we come to know as something alien from without through the medium of our senses, but with objects given directly to our reason and, as its nearest kin, utterly transparent to it.
>
> And yet, or rather for that very reason, these objects are not subjective fantasies. There is nothing more objective than the laws of arithmetic.[1]

These are highly suggestive remarks. In what way, and to what extent, did Frege actually need to disagree with Kant's dictum? In what sense if any would Kant have denied that there are objects given directly to our reason and thus utterly transparent to it, even though they are not subjective fantasies? We shall come back to these questions in Chapter 17, where I shall argue that reason relations, and with them all abstract objects, are both *objective* (not mind-dependent) and *irreal*.

Frege does not develop answers to these questions; the epistemology of logic is not his topic:

> It is enough for us [as logicians] that we can grasp thoughts and recognize them to be true; how this takes place is a question in its own right.[2]

From the Critical standpoint, however, it is a crucial question. If logical and mathematical knowledge is not analytic in some no-content sense, then we must ask how such knowledge is possible. It does not emerge clearly in Kant that this question can be asked about logic as well as mathematics, because Kant's own account of analyticity is famously ambiguous—on the one hand, he seems to intend the no-content model of analyticity, on the other hand, he also seems to endorse the idea of analyticity as reducibility to logic. Presumably he did not consider the possibility that logic itself is synthetic, because he took it for granted that 'formal' logic is in some strong sense empty of content. (To say that it is empty of existential commitment would not be enough.) Nonetheless his Critical project mandates adherence to a no-content notion of analyticity. Whenever a proposition that has factual content is a priori, the question of how a priori knowledge of it is possible must arise for Kant. That will apply to truths of logic, if these have factual content and yet are a priori.[3]

Likewise, the logical empiricists could not simply take over Frege's notion of analyticity. To endorse it they had to show in some way that logic is empty of content—a challenge which they (somewhat waveringly) accepted. From both the empiricist and the Kantian perspective the vital point about a no-content notion of analyticity is that *it should make it completely perspicuous why knowledge of the truth of an analytic proposition*

---

[1] Frege 1953 (1884): 101, 115.

[2] Frege 1979: 145.

[3] As Burge points out, both Kant and Frege 'take analyticity to consist in being subject to analysis' ('Postscript to "Frege on Apriority"', Burge 2005: 389). Strictly speaking, on Frege's definition of 'analytic', logic is not itself analytic. Likewise, Kant did not take either the principle of non-contradiction or strict identities of the form $a = a$ to be analytic, since their truth was not demonstrable by *analysis*. But nor did he take these principles to be synthetic. He took it that strict identities have no factual content; his view of the principle of non-contradiction is moot. Burge suggests that he may have regarded basic logical principles as 'canons for regulation of good thinking' and, further, that he may not have regarded them 'in their basic form', as true or false. If that was Kant's view it would be comparable to the one I argue for in Chapter 7, viz., that logical principles are epistemic norms. However, this view would not require Kant to hold that they are neither true nor false.

raises no interesting, non-trivial, epistemological problem. A particularly important corollary is that if analyticity is to explain some or all a priori knowledge *it should not presuppose the possibility of a priori knowledge in a way that remains unexplained.*

We shall now examine two approaches to the no-content notion of analyticity. The first starts from the idea that an inference is analytic when its conclusion is already asserted in the premises. Analytic propositions are then defined in terms of that basic idea. I will call this the 'empty-inference' approach. This was the approach explored by Mill, who is perhaps the first philosopher to place it in the context of worked-out theory of meaning. The second, due to Wittgenstein and the Vienna Circle, approaches analyticity in terms of the idea of implicit definition; I will call it the 'implicit-definition' approach. This is the approach that was thought to offer the prospect of showing that logic and maths, and other supposed examples of the synthetic a priori, such as that nothing is red and green (simultaneously, in the same place), are analytic. Our overall conclusion will be that the implicit-definition approach does not satisfy the test that explanations of the a priori in terms of analyticity must pass: it does not explain a priori knowledge without either presupposing apriority in a way that remains unexplained, or relying on an untenable theory of meaning. On the other hand, the empty-inference approach, though it passes that test, does not show that even the most basic logic is analytic.

The upshot is that while Kant's Critical project relies on an untenable idealism, the Viennese Critical project relies on an untenable conception of meaning. The root problem is that neither project does justice to our common sense notion of the cognition-independence of facts.

7.2 The empty-inference approach

It should not be controversial that there are propositions that have no information content. They can be normative or non-normative. For example, 'Tomorrow is the day after today' is analytic and non-normative, whereas 'A mother should do anything that all parents should do' is analytic and normative. The important question is not whether the no-content notion of analyticity has instances but whether there is any illuminating philosophical work for it to do.

The empty-inference approach effectively shows why such examples are analytic. Its basic idea is that of an inference whose conclusion is already asserted in the premises. An inference that contains no assertion in the conclusion that is not already asserted in the premises is analytic: it conveys no information, infers no new thing. So the following inference is analytic:

(1) It will rain tomorrow
———————————
It will rain tomorrow.

Since a conditional, 'If p then q', can be read as 'The proposition that q is inferable from the proposition that p', the corresponding conditional of an analytic inference is analytic:

if it will rain tomorrow then it will rain tomorrow.

Substitution of synonymous terms preserves analyticity.[4] 'Tomorrow' is synonymous with 'the day after today', so both the following are analytic:

It will rain the day after today
―――――――――――――――――
It will rain tomorrow

and the corresponding conditional:

if it will rain the day after today then it will rain tomorrow.

So far this implements the no-content conception in a perspicuous way. I grasp the validity of inference (1) just by seeing that the premise and the conclusion are one and the same. Nothing new has been asserted in the conclusion so no question arises of how I can know the validity of the inference. Furthermore, anyone who understands the English words 'tomorrow' and 'the day after today' knows they are synonyms. We know that if it will rain tomorrow then it will rain the day after today, because we grasp the synonymy and can thus see that this proposition is true in virtue of being the corresponding conditional of an analytic inference.

So much should be uncontentious. True, if Quine's radical arguments against synonymy were sound, they would undermine the assumption that we can know the conclusion sentence of an inference to have the same meaning as a premise sentence. They would do so even in cases where the conclusion sentence is type-identical to the premise sentence—under radical indeterminacy of translation there would be no 'fact of the matter' as to whether these two token sentences had the same meaning. But I believe, as many others have argued, that Quine's arguments against the very idea of synonymy can be resisted. (Quine's criticisms of conventionalism are in contrast definitive, but these sound criticisms can be made without putting the notion of synonymy in question.)[5]

Thus the issue is not whether the empty-inference model gives us some genuine examples of analyticity in the no-content sense, but how much aprioricity it can explain. Let us see whether and how it can be extended.

What about:

(2) Tomorrow is tomorrow?

Intuitively, it conveys no information. But is it analytic on the empty-inference approach? On this approach an inference of the form 'Fa therefore Fb' is analytic where 'a' is synonymous with 'b'. We stipulate that if an inference of that form is analytic, then the corresponding identity, 'a = b', is analytic. Thus (2) is analytic because an inference of the

―――――――――――――――――
[4] This also applies to 'contextual' definitions: Bentham's paraphrases, or Russell's theory of descriptions.
[5] An early critique of Quine's view is Grice and Strawson 1956. Quine on analyticity: 'Two Dogmas of Empiricism' (1951), in Quine 1961. On conventionalism: 'Truth by Convention' (1935) and 'Carnap and Logical truth' (1954), both in Quine 1966.

form 'Fa ⊢Fa' is analytic. And 'Tomorrow is the day after today' is analytic since 'tomorrow' is synonymous with 'the day after today'.

It may be denied that (2) conveys no information. Doesn't it convey the information that:

(3) $(\exists x)(x = \text{tomorrow})$?[6]

Two points. First, in developing the empty-inference model we must not *assume* that all logical truths are analytic. (3) follows from (2) by ∃-introduction. The question is whether this deduction principle is analytic, on the empty-inference model? I shall argue in a moment that the answer may be 'no'. Second, for reasons to be considered in Chapter 17, I agree with logicians who deny that the 'existential' (or better, particular[7]) quantifier has existential force. There are many things that do not exist, among them, for example, Sherlock Holmes. Thus the following are all true: (i) Sherlock Holmes = Sherlock Holmes; (ii) Sherlock Holmes = Sherlock Holmes → $(\exists x)(x = \text{Sherlock Holmes})$; and (iii) Sherlock Holmes does not exist. If this is right, then even if we find a no-content model of analyticity that makes ∃-introduction and *modus ponens* analytic, it will still not be analytic that (2) has existential import.

As so far characterized, an empty inference has the form:

(I)

$p_1, \ldots, p_n$
___

$p_1, \ldots, p_i$

where p_i is a subset of p_n. Inferences reducible to this form by explicit definitions of terms are analytic, and analytic propositions are the corresponding conditionals or identities of such inferences. With regard to propositions and inferences that are analytic in this sense no question arises about how acceptance of them is justified, because there is no content, or no genuine cognitive move, there to justify.

This approach is in essentials due to Mill.[8] Its great virtue is that it really delivers on the 'no content' idea. (Hence Mill's terminology: instead of talking about 'analytic' and 'synthetic' he contrasts 'merely apparent' inferences and 'verbal' propositions with 'real' inferences and propositions. But he says that his distinction coincides with that of Kant.[9])

Just because Mill delivers on the no-content idea, his account renders most of logic as well as mathematics synthetic. It was his distinctive contribution to the empiricist tradition to point that out. *On any reasonable development of the empty-inference conception, we shall have to conclude that many purely logical truths are synthetic.* Thus we are owed an answer to the question, how is a priori knowledge of logical truths possible? If we want

---

[6] Likewise with (1).
[7] Graham Priest's term (which he took over from Richard Sylvan).
[8] See Skorupski (1989). Mill's semantics, with its distinction between denotation and connotation, is largely developed to underwrite it.
[9] Mill, (1963–91), vol. VII (*System of Logic*): 116.

to answer in terms of a Kantian framework pf transcendental idealism, it will turn out that we need a 'Copernican revolution' even for pure logic.

Is there an intuitive way of extending this notion of an empty inference? Mill's intuitive test for whether an inference $p \vdash q$ is empty is this: if it is asserted that p, has it literally been asserted that q? Pattern (I) certainly passes that test. However, Mill goes further. He holds that the assertion of a conjunction is the assertion of its conjuncts. So when I assert something of the form $p_1 \& \ldots \& p_n$ I assert p_1 and so on, through to the assertion that p_n. Conversely, when I make a string of assertions I assert their conjunction.

The narrowest empty-inference account of analyticity would exclude even this, on the grounds that it's not literally the case that in asserting a conjunction I assert the conjuncts, or vice versa. However, Mill's view feels right. If you assert that Smith, Bornholtz, and Sharif were there, you have literally asserted that Smith was there. And if you assert each of the propositions that Smith was there, that Bornholtz was there and that Sharif was there, you've asserted that Smith, Bornholtz, and Sharif were there. So let's allow as analytic the following inferences:

(II)

$$p_1 \& \ldots \& p_n$$

$$p_i$$

and

(III)

$$p_1, \ldots, p_n$$

$$p_1 \& \ldots \& p_n$$

That gives us &-introduction and elimination. Also, given the Millian reading of 'if p then q' as 'the proposition that p is inferable from the proposition that q', we can argue that Conditional Proof is empty. If I infer that q from the premise that p, Conditional Proof allows me to infer that if p then q—that is, that q is inferable from p. Conditional Proof consists in *stating* what the proof so far has shown. It seems reasonable to extend the notion of empty inference to this particular move: if I know that I have found a valid inference from p to q there is no non-trivial epistemological question as to how I *also* know that q is inferable from p. So we have:

(IV)

$$p_1, \ldots, p_n \vdash q$$

$$p_1, \ldots, p_n \rightarrow q$$

But what of other natural deduction principles, for implication, disjunction, negation, and the quantifiers? Can any of those be regarded as analytic by the intuitive Millian test?

By that intuitive test the answer must be 'no'. Consider *modus ponens*. Suppose I've asserted the proposition that *p* and also asserted that the proposition that *q* is inferable from the proposition that *p*. Have I asserted that *q*? I have not literally asserted that *q*; I've just said it is inferable from something I have asserted. It might be replied that if you've asserted that *p* and that *q* is inferable from *p* you've 'endorsed' the assertion that *q*. But to get from this 'endorsement' to the assertion that *q* you have to apply *modus ponens*.

Similarly with introduction and elimination principles for disjunction. If I assert that *p* have I asserted that *p* or *q*, for any *q*? If I assert that Mary is in the dining room, have I asserted that she is in the dining room or the kitchen? By the strict Millian test, the answer has to be 'no'. I said nothing at all about the proposition that Mary is in the kitchen. As for the elimination rule: if I assert that (i) she is either in the kitchen or in the dining room, that; (ii) if she is in the kitchen she is in the house; and (iii) if she is in the dining room she is in the house, have I asserted that she is in the house? Again the answer must be 'no'.

In the case of negation it is particularly clear that the introduction and elimination rules are non-empty. If I assert that *p* do I assert that it's not the case that not *p*? Or vice versa? We can grant, for the sake of argument, that grasping what is asserted by the assertion that *p* requires one to grasp what is not asserted. However, that is not to say that when one asserts that *p* one is *asserting* that it is not the case that not-p. One is simply not asserting that not-p. Equally, in denying that it is the case that not-p, one does not assert that *p*.[10]

Next consider the quantifiers. If the deduction principles for disjunction are synthetic then so too, presumably, are the introduction and elimination principles for '∃'. What about the universal quantifier?

Mill plays with both the idea that '(*x*)F*x*' is a conjunction, and the idea that it's a 'memorandum' that any assertion of the form F*x* is true—i.e. something like a schema. The first idea would clearly make the elimination rule analytic. But if I assert that all men are mortal I have not referred to the Duke of Wellington and asserted that he is mortal (Mill's example). So we have to reject it. The memorandum idea is more promising. Can we not expand the empty-inference idea this far? Think of the assertion that (*x*)F*x* as a schematic assertion of *anything of the form F*x*. (For the introduction rule, we can argue in the same spirit that reasoning with arbitrary names is already essentially universal.)

Suppose I say 'I hereby assert every proposition of the form F*x*' (for some predicate F). Have I asserted that F*a*? The obvious objection is that the inference from what I did assert to the conclusion that I asserted F*a* requires the premise that F*a* is of the form F*x*, and then applications of universal instantiation and *modus ponens*. However, we are not questioning the *truth* of the premise nor the *validity* of these principles, so the conclusion is sound: I have asserted F*a*. But wait—can I achieve the same trick of multiple assertion by saying 'I hereby assert every proposition that Genghis Khan asserted'? Surely not. So where do we draw a principled line? Evidently we cannot, quite generally, assert any proposition that has a certain property by simply referring to the property and announcing that we are doing so. But we *can* genuinely assert any proposition that has a certain

---

[10] Mill explicitly notes that the principles of bivalence and exclusion are not analytic (in his terms, 'verbal') in vol. VII: 277–8.

schematic form by announcing that we are doing so, as when we lay down an axiom schema. Apparently that is the function universality plays in reasoning: it licenses shifts between a *form* and an instance of the form.

So are the introduction and elimination rules for the universal quantifier empty? If we accept them as empty we get the notion of definitional deducibility invoked in 4.2. I shall not pursue the question of whether we should (though the answer, strictly speaking, seems to me to be negative). We shall touch on the issues again when discussing rule-following in Chapter 18. Here I simply conclude that the empty-inference account of analyticity allows the conjunction rules and Conditional Proof as analytic, that it is tempting to add the rules for the universal quantifier as analytic, but that in any case other natural deduction rules come out as synthetic by the empty-inference test.

Thus there *are* analytic deduction principles by this test, but not all natural deduction principles are analytic by this test. So if they are all a priori, some of them are synthetic a priori. And on the Normative view, that must mean they are either normative principles or offshoots thereof. But perhaps the Viennese account of analyticity can do better than the Millian account? Before we get to that question we must clarify our notion of a proposition, and then say some preliminary things about truth.

7.3 Sentence, proposition, and truth condition

We have been talking about *propositions* as analytic. That's fine on the empty-inference account: it takes the primary bearers of truth and falsity to be propositions, and treats inferability as a relation between propositions. Note, however, that since it takes the conditionals and identities that correspond to empty inferences to be propositions, it must also accept that a sentence with no informative content, e.g. 'If snow is white then snow is white', can express a proposition. Furthermore there are distinct analytic propositions, even though none of them have content. Thus analytic sentences, sentences that express analytic propositions, can differ in meaning even though they have no content. 'Mothers are parents' does not mean the same as 'Tomorrow is the day after today': these sentences express distinct propositions, as is clear from their different inferential roles.

The connections between sentence, meaning, proposition, content, inferential role, are debatable. We do not need to decide among options if they do not affect the argument of this book. The broad picture I am working with is the following (I discuss it further in Chapter 17).

Propositions, not sentences, are what is asserted, believed, considered, and hypothesized. And it is what is asserted, believed, considered, hypothesized, etc. that is true or false. To say that a *sentence* in a language L is true—on a particular occasion of use—is to say that what is said by its use in L in that context is true: the proposition is what is said. What you assert by uttering 'Mothers are parents', or 'Tomorrow is the day after today', is not the same, even though in neither case does your assertion convey any information. You can deduce by principles of pure logic that mothers should do what parents should do from the first proposition but not from the second.

Since what is said depends on context, the meaning of a sentence is a function from its contexts of use to the proposition asserted. Knowing the meaning is knowing the function, i.e. knowing what proposition the sentence can be used to assert on a given use-occasion. It follows that sentences have the same meaning just if they express the same proposition in the same contexts of use. Equally, the same sentence can express different propositions on different occasions: indexical sentences, for example, express different propositions on different occasions. If A and B both utter 'I am ill', the sentence they use has the same meaning in each context but the use-context differs and different propositions are asserted. I leave it open how to individuate 'contexts of use'. Obviously speaker, time, and place are among the relevant parameters.

I take this conception of meaning, sentence, and proposition to imply that if sentences in a thinker's language have the same meaning it must be possible for the thinker to know that a priori, by reflecting on their meaning. Since the meaning of sentence-constituents is their contribution to the meaning of sentences, the same applies to them. Given the connection I am making between a sentence's meaning and what proposition it expresses, this presupposes an epistemic conception of the proposition in the following sense: if a proposition expressed by sentence A in a speaker's language is the same proposition as that expressed by sentence B it must be possible for the thinker to know that a priori.[11] However, I am not saying that the thinker can know a priori that expressions in other people's mouths have the same meaning. Furthermore, in the twin Earth scenario described by Putnam I may be wrong in thinking that what twin-Earthers mean by 'water' is what I mean, even if to all appearances they do (and even if nothing 'in their heads' reveals they don't). So this epistemic conception does not imply that 'meanings are in the head'.[12]

The meaning of a sentence is given by its truth condition. As I shall use the term, a sentence's truth condition specifies its meaning, so that a systematic account of truth conditions for a given object language L is a theory of meaning for L. The truth condition of a sentence in L is a condition under which it is true in a use-context—hence 'truth condition'. Any sentence has many extensionally correct truth conditions, but *the* truth condition is the one whose correctness is deducible just from the conventions that fix meanings in L. Knowing this requirement, one knows that the truth conditions the theory gives for sentences in L give the meanings of those sentences—equivalently, give the propositions they express. We cannot talk meaningfully about the truth condition of a *proposition*, as against a *sentence*.

The term 'truth condition' can also be used in a referential way. Understood this way, a truth condition specifies how the truth-value of a sentence depends on the referents or semantic values of its constituents in all possible worlds. Sentences with different

---

[11] This is weaker, however, than the view that follows from Frege's theory of indirect reference, according to which if you can believe that *p* and fail to believe that *q*, then *p* is a different proposition to *q*.

[12] Putnam, 'The meaning of "meaning"', in Putnam 1975. Let's suppose they call that watery-looking stuff 'twater', and I come to use that word as well as water, thinking that twater is water. Nonetheless, I cannot rule out a priori the possibility that twater isn't water. It seems to me to follow that 'twater' does not mean the same as 'water', even if twater *is* water. (See §7 below.) In *this* sense meanings *are* in the head. (It's important that the twin-Earthers come from a historically distinct speech community to mine.)

meanings can have the same purely referential truth conditions. For example, the referential truth conditions for 'Hesperus is a planet' and 'Phosphorus is a planet' are the same. So too with 'There is water in the glass' and 'There is H$_2$O in the glass'. Thus you can have knowledge of the referential truth condition of a sentence without knowing its meaning, and thus without knowing what *proposition* the sentence expresses.

Finally I should emphasize that I am not identifying truth conditions with 'truth makers'. The latter notion presupposes a definite metaphysical stance, that of global realism, which the Normative view rejects. So it is obviously important for the purposes of this book to distinguish very carefully between the two notions.

7.4 Are the basic principles of truth analytic?

In Chapter 17 I shall endorse a 'minimalist' conception of truth[13], according to which the notion of truth is exhausted by the following three schematic principles:

(4) It is true that $p \leftrightarrow p$
(5) P is true $\rightarrow$ (P = the proposition that $p \rightarrow$ it is true that p)
(6) It is true that $p \rightarrow$ (P = the proposition that $p \rightarrow$ P is true)

where 'P' is a variable ranging over propositions, while 'p' is a schematic letter. What we can consider here is whether these principles are analytic. Let us first consider (4).

It seems plausible to hold that the proposition that p is identical with the proposition that it is true that p. What information do I convey in asserting one of these that I do not convey in asserting the other? What different inferential role do they play? An immediate consequence of this identity claim[14], given the empty-inference account of analyticity, is that (4) is analytic, since it conjoins two corresponding conditionals of empty inferences.

I find this identity claim extremely plausible—but it faces striking difficulties, which we should note. Consider, first, whether (4) requires us to accept bivalence. A simple argument seems to show that it does. Suppose that some proposition, the proposition that p, is neither true nor false. In that case it is false that it is true that p. Hence it is false that *it is true that $p \leftrightarrow p$*, since the propositions on either side of the biconditional do not have the same truth-value, and hence (4) has a counter-instance.

So is bivalence also an analytic truth?

We have just noted that if the proposition that p is neither true nor false, then it is false that it is true. However is this inference correct? We should distinguish two ways in which bivalence may fail. One possibility is that it is *true* of some proposition that it is neither true nor false. (4) rules out this possibility. Another possibility is that for some proposition

---

[13] See Horwich 1990: 7; he also calls it the deflationary conception. These terms do have the disadvantage of suggesting that there is some intelligible non-minimal and non-deflated concept of truth—I don't mean to imply that.

[14] Put forward by Frege: 'the sentence "I smell the scent of violets" has just the same content as the sentence "It is true that I smell the scent of violets". So it seems, then, that nothing is added to the thought by my ascribing to it the property of truth'. Frege 1977 (1919, 1923): 6.

that p it is neither determinately the case that p nor determinately the case that not-p. In that case it is not determinately the case that it is true that p and not determinately the case that it is false that p. On this view, if it is indeterminate that p then it is indeterminate that it is true (or that it is false) that p. In such an instance a truth-value cannot be assigned to either side of (4). However, if (4) is analytic because in every instance its two sides mean the same, then this instance of (4) should be assessed as true, not as indeterminate: it is true that an indeterminate proposition is identical with itself. What is less clear is the status of 'It is either true or false that p'. Perhaps we should say that it too is indeterminate.[15]

What is this notion of indeterminateness? In Chapter 16 we shall want to leave open the possibility that a purely normative proposition may be indeterminate in truth-value, even though it is not vague. A factual proposition may also, on the face of it, fail to be determinate; in this case because it is vague. Either the relation of the facts to the proposition is vague, or the facts themselves are vague. Suppose, for example, that the boundary between the Norwegian Sea and the North Sea has never been clearly defined. Now consider a point x in some ocean sector which is neither determinately Norwegian nor determinately North. We should accept that 'x is in the North Sea' expresses a proposition, since it is clearly meaningful—but that proposition is indeterminate with respect to truth-value. So we should not assert that x is in the North Sea, nor should we assert that it is not: neither of these assertions has a determinate truth-value. What about the proposition that it is either true or false that x is in the North Sea? Perhaps we should say that it is determinate that it is either true or false but not determinate which. Or perhaps we should say that it does not have a determinate truth-value either.

A difficulty of a different order is presented by the liar paradoxes. Consider the assertion *The proposition I am hereby asserting is false*. It does not, in combination with (5) and (6), generate a contradiction if we can say, plausibly enough, that it is indeterminate. But what now of the 'strengthened liar': *What I am saying is indeterminate*? If this assertion is indeterminate is it not true that it is? And if it is true, is it false? Still we could say, in reply, that if the proposition asserted is indeterminate it is indeterminate that it is true. That is forced by the identity claim (4). Presumably it is also indeterminate that it is false.[16]

There is a vast literature about both vagueness and the liar paradoxes. There seems to be no wholly intuitive account.[17] My point in this section is no more than that (4) is not obviously incompatible with indeterminacy, so that holding (4) to be an analytic truth is not obviously incompatible with it either.

So much by way of defending the claim that (4) is analytic by the strict 'empty-inference' test. But what of (5) and (6)?

---

[15] Though much discussion of these issues would oppose this conclusion—including 'epistemicist' defences of bivalence (Sorenson 1988; Williamson 1994) that deny that vagueness involves indeterminacy and supervaluationist treatments of vagueness-induced indeterminacy.

[16] In general, if it is indeterminate that p and indeterminate that q, then it is indeterminate that $p \rightarrow q$. However, given that we are reading this as 'q is inferable from p', we should accept that where the proposition that p = the proposition that q, the conditional is true: on the grounds that a proposition is unrestrictedly inferable from itself. So that saves (4).

[17] That also applies to the account in terms of indeterminacy. (Is it, for example, permissible to assert indeterminate, as against true, propositions? If not, then one should not assert that the 'liar' proposition is indeterminate ...)

If the predicate 'is true' could be explicitly defined in terms of the operator 'it is true that' the predicate could be eliminated. However that is not possible. What do we make of this? On the one hand, (5) and (6) look like mere devices for shifting from the truth operator to the truth predicate and back again. On the other hand, there is no explicit, eliminative, definition of the truth predicate. So do (5) and (6) commit us to the existence of a property, that of *being true*? How can it be analytic that such a property exists?

Can we say that in combination with (4), (5), and (6) *implicitly* define the truth predicate? That brings us to the Viennese account of analyticity.

7.5 Analyticity and implicit definition

The empty-inference approach gives a satisfactory 'no-content' test of analyticity, in that it shows clearly why some propositions are true through lack of content. However, these propositions turn out be a very restricted, uninteresting group. Viennese philosophy in the twentieth century had a much more ambitious programme for its no-content notion of analyticity. Let us see how this emerged.

A main source was some important thinking about the status of geometry done at the turn of the century, notably by Hilbert and Poincaré. Moritz Schlick was among the first to appreciate its full philosophical potential.

Hilbert[18] had provided a set of axioms for Euclidean geometry and suggested that the primitive terms used in them—'point', 'straight line', 'plane', 'between', 'outside of'— should be thought of as implicitly defined thereby. A definition of this kind is 'implicit' in that no explicit meta-linguistic stipulation about the meaning equivalence of two terms is made; whereas in a definition such as ' "Square" means "plane figure bounded by four equal rectilinear sides" ' we have an explicit stipulation of synonymy. Treating axiom-sentences as implicit definitions is directly stipulating that they are to be so understood as to be true.

An explicit definition is a rule of substitution, not a proposition, so it cannot play the role of premise or conclusion. In contrast, an implicit definition is a stipulation that a certain set of object language sentences is to be so understood as to be true. Such sentences can play a role as axioms, for example, in a formalized geometry. But what about the status of the logic by which the theorems of the formal system are derived? If the truths of its underlying logic are not contentless then neither is pure geometry. The answer is that we must reapply the same treatment to logic itself, treating its axiomatized principles as implicit definitions of the primitive logical constants. It seems that Schlick had something like this in mind when he said that the principles of contradiction and excluded middle 'merely determine the nature of negation' and 'may be looked upon as its definition'.[19]

In the 1920s this implicit-definition conception of analyticity begins to appear in the thinking of Wittgenstein and Carnap. Wittgenstein's *Tractatus* idea of aprioricity as tautology had been, at least in intention, in line with the empty-inference notion of analyticity. That is, it was meant to show rigorously that tautologous inference is empty of

---

[18] Hilbert 1971 (1899). [19] Schlick 1985 (1925): 64, cp. 337.

content, wholly non-instructive. True, it did so only on the assumption that bivalence and exclusion are empty of content. A Millian could justly point out that the *Tractatus* doctrine of 'bipolarity' as a condition of the sense of propositions takes that dogmatically for granted. But now, in his conversations with the Vienna Circle, Wittgenstein rejected the idea that tautology is the essence of the apriori:

> That inference is a priori means only that syntax decides whether an inference is correct or not. Tautologies are only one way of showing what is syntactical.[20]

He still held that such inferences are non-instructive, but the way in which this was now to be explained was much simpler. Analytic sentences have no content because they simply articulate rules of the language. The a priori is still the analytic, but we have a new view of what is analytic.

This new view is philosophically challenging in a way that the empty-inference criterion of analyticity is not. How can syntax 'decide' whether an inference is correct or not? Doesn't that depend on whether the inference is truth-preserving? Presumably the answer must be that syntax decides what is truth preserving. But the natural objection is that we can't just stipulate that a sentence is true, or an inference rule truth-preserving: truth is not up to us, it is not for us to stipulate it.

Let us go back to the case of geometry. What exactly is 'up to us' here?

(i) We can freely lay down uninterpreted axiom-sentences and analyse their formal consequences. The question of the truth of axiom-sentences does not then arise.

(ii) We can stipulate that the terms occurring in the axiom-sentences are to be understood to have referents which are such as to make these sentences express truths.

Certainly (ii) is up to us. But does this activity of ours suffice to confer meaning on the sentences? Only, according to the natural objection, if it determines a unique set of referents of which the sentences are true. For if more than one interpretation makes the axioms true then we haven't—simply by means of our stipulation—specified what referents are intended. And if no interpretation makes them true then we haven't found an interpretation at all. It follows that stipulation, as in (ii), only gives us conditional metalinguistic knowledge: it tells us the axioms express something or other that's true, *if* they express anything at all. To know *what* the axioms say—that is, what propositions they express—and that *these* propositions are true, we need more knowledge. Either we must have a specification of what objects are intended, in which case we must know that those intended objects satisfy the axioms. Or we must know that a unique set of referents satisfies the axioms. Either way, this auxiliary knowledge may be a priori or a posteriori. And either way, it is not the stipulation that delivers it.

Stipulation at most gives us a constraint on how certain words are going to be used. We only have a priori knowledge that the propositions expressed by the axioms are true if the auxiliary knowledge we require is itself a priori. Furthermore, we only have a priori knowledge that the formal consequences of these axioms are true if we know a priori that our rules of inference are valid. It seems then that the notion of an implicit

---

[20] Wittgenstein 1979: 92.

definition cannot explain the nature of a priori knowledge. An implicit definition yields a priori knowledge only if we already have a priori knowledge.

The point applies wherever we are considering an implicit-definition approach—be it the theory of logic or the theory of phlogiston. One can stipulate that certain sentences containing the word 'not', or the word 'phlogiston', are to be so understood as to express true propositions. But only if the world co-operates does that confer meaning on them. Take the sentence:

Phlogiston is driven off whenever a metal or combustible material is heated.

We could, first of all, approach this as a good old-fashioned explicit definition:

Phlogiston $=_{df}$ the substance x that is driven off whenever a metal or combustible material is heated.

It is then a posteriori that phlogiston exists. Or we could simply stipulate that some sentences of phlogiston theory and their consequences are true. What is stipulated, to put it more carefully, is that either the terms in these sentences have referents that make them true or they have no referents. So we do not know a priori that there is a true proposition to the effect that phlogiston is driven off whenever a metal or combustible material is heated. The question whether 'phlogiston' has a referent is a posteriori. (And the a posteriori answer is that it does not.)

Exactly the same points hold if we apply the implicit-definition approach to logic itself. Suppose we stipulate that 'not both p and not p', and 'either p or not p' are to be so understood as to be true. What is a priori, on this stipulation, is that either 'not', 'and', and 'or' have referents that make these sentences true or they lack a referent. It does not follow from this alone that any true propositions are expressed by 'not both p and not p', and 'either p or not p'. If we have a priori knowledge of the truth of such propositions it is not the implicit-definition account of analyticity that gives it to us. To have that a priori knowledge we must know a priori that there is an object, in this case a truth function, that satisfies the stipulated condition. This is just another way of saying that we must know a priori that bivalence and exclusion hold. So the implicit definition presupposes that these can be known a priori rather than demonstrating that they are a priori because analytic. The same applies to the two principles of truth, (5) and (6), in the previous section.

According to this objection the only way to show an inference to be analytic would be the Millian way. The objection seems decisive. But the logical positivists did not accept it. Their view rested on a rethinking of language, truth, and logic which was truly revolutionary and would, if sound, refute it.

7.6 Verificationism and its difficulties

It is natural to think that particular languages are merely contingent vehicles for the expression of thought. Thoughts themselves are a language-independent domain about which there are language-independent truths. The picture of propositions (thought contents) I drew in Section 7.3 is consistent with this.

As noted in the Introduction (1.4) the Vienna School rejected this picture. There is no such domain of thought contents. On the Viennese view there are no language-independent facts or norms; there are only rules of particular languages and facts expressible by true sentences in a particular language. The notion of a linguistic rule elucidates, or better, just replaces the classical philosophical notion of the a priori.

The meaning of a sentence is determined by the conditions in which it is assertible, and this determination occurs only in the framework of language rules. 'Verificationism' is the familiar name for this. The essential point is that the meaning and thus truth-value of a sentence is internal to a framework of linguistic conventions.[21] There is nothing beyond or outside these conventions. There are no extra linguistic, non-conventional, norms. 'There are only empirical facts and decisions'. And just as *truth* is internal to the conventions, so is *existence*.

We can now see the Viennese reply to the natural objection mentioned earlier in this section. It is a generalization of Schlick's treatment of definitions. Once geometrical axioms have been set down and co-ordinated with experience by ostensive and metric conventions, there is no further question about the unique existence of appropriate geometrical objects. A priori knowledge is knowledge of the rules—and that can include existential knowledge, since existence is internal to the rules. Likewise, if we simply stipulate that phlogiston is driven off whenever a metal or combustible material is heated, there is no further question about whether phlogiston exists. And in the case of logic itself the same point applies. The only questions concern the pragmatic convenience of this or that language. These points were explicitly made by Wittgenstein and Carnap:

> Can an ostensive definition come into collision with the other rules for the use of a word?—It might appear so; but rules can't collide, unless they contradict each other. That aside, it is they that determine a meaning; there isn't a meaning that they are answerable to and could contradict.
> Grammar is not accountable to any reality. It is grammatical rules that determine meaning (constitute it) and so they themselves are not answerable to any meaning and to that extent are arbitrary.[22]
> In logic, there are no morals. Everyone is at liberty to build up his own logic, i.e. his own form of language, as he wishes. All that is required of him is that, if he wishes to discuss it, he must state his methods clearly, and give syntactical rules instead of philosophical arguments.[23]

The application to mathematics now looks simple: it is simply that mathematics as a whole belongs to the framework.[24] Where Mill is forced by his narrow empty-inference

---

[21] A survey of these issues, including the connection between an epistemic conception of meaning and an epistemic conception of truth, can be found in Skorupski 1997a. Carnap gives an account of his evolving views on truth in Carnap 1963.

[22] Wittgenstein 1974: 184. See the application to the meaning of 'not' which follows, and the whole discussion of convention and arbitrariness in Section X.

[23] Carnap 1937 (1934): 52.

[24] Wittgenstein alludes to this point, 'the paradox that mathematics consists of rules', in a marginal MS comment quoted in the note on p. 184 of Wittgenstein 1974.

criterion of analyticity to treat logic and mathematics as a posteriori, this linguistic turn preserves empiricism, allows that all aprioricity reduces to analyticity, and yet includes all logic and mathematics within the a priori.

But now let's turn to some formidable difficulties. They can be considered under three headings:

(i) How do we tell whether a sentence expresses a linguistic rule or conveys an empirical assertion? I.e. whether it is analytic or synthetic?

(ii) Can mathematics be shown to be part of the linguistic framework?

(iii) Is it true that 'There are only empirical facts and (linguistic) decisions'?

In response to (i), Carnap insists that 'analytic in L' was only definable relative to a clearly specified framework L. True, as Quine points out, any language that is actually used is always stretched and restretched on an inextricable mix of experience, theory, and convention. But still Carnap can answer that that is merely a practical point. What he is interested in is the *possibility* of specifying a linguistic framework.

Now however question (ii) arises: can mathematics be part of the linguistic framework, even in an ideal language? *Prima facie*, the framework of such a language should be specified by individual stipulation of each sentence or inference rule contained in it. But if all logic and mathematics is to be included in the framework this cannot be done. It is not even possible to specify a procedure that effectively decides whether any given sentence belongs to the framework.

What about giving an effective axiomatization of the framework, that is, stipulating that any theorem of the axiom system is to be counted a convention? With a fully determinate meta-logic we would have a fully determinate specification of the analytic sentences in the object language—so this would answer question (ii) as well as question (i). But this approach gives rise to deep questions.

What is the status of the meta-logic? Consider a sentence to the effect that an object language sentence is derivable in the system. Is it itself part of the framework? Presumably it has to be, on pain of allowing that there really are non-conventional, and thus non-analytic, logical truths. The point at stake is not merely that the meta-logic itself must be regarded as a set of conventions. Consider the metalanguage sentence 'Given the meta-logic we have stipulated, sentence S is derivable in the object language.' Does *this* sentence express a stipulation? It seems that the only possible answer for the logical positivist is that it does—this is the view that Michael Dummett called 'full-blooded conventionalism'.[25] The only alternative available within logical positivism would be the thesis that the sentence in question is an empirical sentence—for example, a sentence to the effect that members of the speech community would accept the derivation. But that idea would undermine the framework/empirical—content distinction. What belongs to the framework would become an empirical matter; but empirical matters are supposed to be determinate only in the context of a determinate framework. Yet the radical conventionalist

---

[25] Dummett 1978: 170. (The essay is his 1959 review: 'Wittgenstein's Philosophy of Mathematics'.)

answer also puts in question the determinacy of the framework. There are, on this view, no rails to guide us; at every step, in applying 'the' framework we make new decisions. The framework cannot be specified 'in advance', indeed no unique framework is 'given' at any time.[26]

The framework idea seems to call for a radical conventionalism which accepts that the framework is always 'open', or 'in process of construction'. But does such radical conventionalism make sense? Is every application of a convention just a further 'decision' or does that undermine the very idea of an 'application'? If we accept that there are truths about the right way to apply a convention we must give a negative answer to question (iii). This is the deepest issue, brought out in Wittgenstein's discussion of rule-following. I shall argue in Chapter 18 that there are epistemic norms which hold neither in virtue of empirical facts nor in virtue of linguistic decisions. Every application of a linguistic rule to a new case involves a normative judgement.[27]

But if the language-relative view of existence is abandoned then the Viennese notion that aprioricity reduces to analyticity succumbs to the fundamental objection we have considered in the previous section. For the Viennese defence against that objection crucially depended on the idea that truth and existence are themselves internal to a language framework. Without that assumption we have not shown that logic and maths are a priori and necessary *because they are analytic*.[28]

7.7 Fixing a reference and aprioricity

'Implicit definitions' cannot do what the Viennese wanted them to do. Existence is not internal to a language framework. We cannot stipulate phlogiston into existence. Nonetheless, we can stipulate the following:

> If phlogiston exists then it is a substance driven off in combustion.

We can similarly stipulate that:

> If there are numbers then they satisfy the Peano postulates.

or

> If there is a truth property then it satisfies (5) and (6).

---

[26] Also noteworthy in this context is Godel's incompleteness theorem of 1931: true non-provable propositions can be formulated within the language of any consistent, effectively specified axiomatization of arithmetic. It reinforces—in a highly unexpected way—the general point that language frameworks as envisaged by logical positivism cannot be formally specified.

[27] I believe that this is the origin of Wittgenstein's discussion of rules in his later work. See 18.2.

[28] There has recently been renewed interest in the implicit-definition notion of analyticity. See e.g. Hale and Wright (2000). It seems to me that this notion presupposes either the Viennese account of existence as internal to the language framework, and thus something like the Viennese account of meaning, or alternatively, an irrealist account of reference of the kind that will be given in Chapter 18.

Such stipulation can fix the reference of terms subject where necessary to an assumption of unique existence. In terms of Saul Kripke's distinction they fix their reference rather than 'giving their meaning'.[29] Here is a simple example.

Suppose the police are looking for a murderer. They think the murder has been committed by a single person, though they've no idea who he or she is. However, they come to talk about that person as 'Charlie'. Now consider the sentence:

(7) If there exists a single murderer, then Charlie is the murderer.

It is plausible that (7) expresses an a priori truth. Yet 'Charlie' has not been *defined* as meaning the same as 'the murderer'. It's just the nickname the police have come to use. (7) fixes the reference of 'Charlie', but does not give its meaning. That is, (7) is not synonymous with:

(8) If there is a single murderer, then the murderer is the murderer.

Furthermore, unlike (8), (7) is contingent. Suppose there is in fact a single murderer. Then it follows by (7) that that murderer is Charlie. But there are possible worlds with respect to which the proposition that Charlie did not commit the murder is true.

Should we then classify (7) as analytic or synthetic? Let's ask first whether, if there is no single murderer, (7) expresses a proposition. On the view of propositions that we have taken, it seems trivially true that it does: for surely someone who asserts it says something, and the proposition is what he says. However, two steps would lead us to the conclusion that it does not:

(i) names denote simply

(ii) names denote existents.

(i) is Mill's view. He puts it by saying that although names *denote* they do not do so by virtue of *connoting* any attribute of the denoted object. They have no connotation. It does not follow that they have no meaning; they have meaning in virtue of contributing to the meaning of sentences in which they appear, and they contribute by having a denotation.

So if a number of names denote the same object do they all have the same meaning? A Millian view can deny that. Take Mill's example of 'Tully' and 'Cicero'. To say that 'Tully' denotes *simply* is to say that the right semantic axiom for it is:

(9) 'Tully' denotes Tully.

If 'Tully' connoted some set of attributes C, the right axiom would be:

(10) 'Tully' denotes the x that uniquely satisfies condition C.

In that case 'Tully' would denote Tully *conditionally*, i.e. by virtue of satisfying a stipulated condition. It would then be analytic that if there is a denoted object it satisfies that condition.

---

[29] Kripke 1981 (1972).

Names that denote the same object can differ in meaning, even if they denote simply.[30] What we understand, in knowing that 'Tully' is a name, is that:

'Tully' denotes Tully.

Even though that's true if and only if 'Tully' denotes Cicero, we don't know that by our grasp of meanings alone. And the same holds, of course, for our understanding of 'Cicero'. We know that:

'Cicero' denotes Cicero.

Again, however, we cannot deduce from this semantic knowledge that 'Cicero' denotes Tully. We need to know that Cicero *is* Tully. Thus 'Tully' and 'Cicero' have different meanings, the sentences 'Tully was an orator' and 'Cicero was an orator' have different meanings, and the propositions they express are distinct. You cannot know a priori that Cicero was Tully, because the semantic clauses for 'Cicero' and 'Tully' differ. So the Millian view that these names denote simply does not infringe our requirement, that where two expressions or sentences have the *same* meaning it must be possible for someone who understands both to know they have the same meaning a priori, by reflecting on their meaning.

In the same way, the meaning of 'Charlie' is given by:

'Charlie' denotes Charlie.

But what if there exists no single murderer? Does it follow that 'Charlie' has no meaning?

If 'Charlie' has no denotation, (7) expresses no proposition. However, there is a further question: does denotation require existence? On the view I shall argue for in Chapter 17, it does not. The police have in mind a putative single murderer. That is what they are talking about when they talk about Charlie (and wonder who he is). Their discourse adequately *anchors* the denotation of 'Charlie' (as I shall put it): Charlie is the putative single murderer. It's another question whether the putative single murderer exists.[31]

In contrast, on the common view that denotation requires existence (7) (i.e. the sentence) expresses a proposition—has a meaning—just if there exists a single murderer. That is a difficulty for the common view. But we can put this issue to one side for present purposes, since on either view we can ask whether the proposition expressed, where a proposition *is* expressed, is analytic.

(7) is not analytic by the empty-inference test. Furthermore, as we noted, (7) is contingent. Specifically, whether it's necessary or contingent *is not something we can know just from grasping the meanings of words*. We have to know whether being the murderer is an essential property of Charlie. However, the proposition expressed by a sentence is analytic

---

[30] Here I follow McDowell 1977.
[31] On this view there are objects of shared thought and discourse that do not exist, and truths about these objects. I shall maintain in Chapter 17 that the truth property is one of these. So are propositions; hence nominalistic objections to unreduced talk of propositions are misguided. Where existence is not in play implicit definitions *can* be given. Thus the truth predicate can be implicitly defined by (5) and (6).

if and only if it is possible to tell the modal status of the proposition just by grasping the meaning of the sentence. That fits with the empty-inference criterion, but it makes (7) synthetic.

Alternatively, we could say that (7) is analytic because its aprioricity arises from a feature of the sentence that expresses it: the way the reference of 'Charlie' is fixed. This would be an additional criterion of analyticity, separate to the empty-inference test, for the inference from 'F(the murderer)' to 'F(Charlie)' is not empty. The case for counting it as analytic would be that this kind of aprioricity is 'purely linguistic'. But what is meant by saying it is 'purely linguistic'?

7.8 Propositions and content

How names in actual languages function is an empirical question. On the Millian view, they simply denote. That view seems correct, and so does the idea that to describe our linguistic practice we need a distinction between fixing a reference and giving a meaning. I have been discussing in the previous section how our account of analyticity should take account of these points about actual language. But note that it does not matter for our overall argument whether the Millian view of names is correct of our actual language, or the distinction between fixing a reference and giving a meaning applies to it. It does not matter whether actual names denote simply or whether, like other singular terms, they denote conditionally.

It is enough that a language is *possible* in which some terms denote simply. Let's imagine that (7) is a sentence in a language L constituted by a set of conventions which allow for simple denotation. Now suppose:

(i) By convention in L, the proposition expressed by sentence (7) is true.
(ii) No convention in L determines whether the proposition expressed by sentence (7) is necessarily true.

These two together constitute a reference-fixing convention for 'Charlie'. Among the axioms of the semantics for L will be: 'Charlie' denotes Charlie. From these the truth conditions for sentences in L are deducible, including the following:

(iii) 'If Charlie exists then Charlie is the murderer' is true in L iff Charlie exists then Charlie is the murderer.

Since the truth condition states the proposition expressed by the sentence, from the conventions of L we can deduce:

(iv) The proposition expressed in L by 'If Charlie exists then Charlie is the murderer' is the proposition that if Charlie exists then Charlie is the murderer.

Hence from (i) and (iv) we have:

(v) The proposition that if Charlie exists then Charlie is the murderer is true.

We know a priori that the conventions constituting L are a possible set, so we know (v) a priori, purely on the basis of knowledge of conventions.

This explains the sense in which the aprioricity of proposition (7) is purely linguistic. Should we describe it on that basis as analytic? At this point we must remember that we want a no-content notion of analyticity because we are attracted to the thesis that no factual proposition is a priori. Can we say that (7) has no content, is non-factual?

The only fact you need to know, to know that Charlie is the murderer, is that Charlie exists. Thus to know that (7) holds you need to know nothing, so (7) has no factual content. We can, if we like, count propositions that are a priori in virtue of reference-fixing stipulations, such as (7), as analytic—even though they are contingent.

Importantly, however, 'analyticity' of this kind explains some cases of aprioricity but no cases of a priori necessity. It does not enable us to explain the philosophically problematic cases of *apriori necessity* by appeal to their analyticity. The propositions that $7 + 5 = 12$ or that whatever is green is coloured are not just a priori but necessarily true. We seem to see a priori not just that they are true but that they must be true.

Examples of apriori necessity such as these cannot be explained by reference to analyticity, even in the extended sense. True, the distinction between stating a meaning and fixing a reference gives us a distinct linguistic source of aprioricity without requiring verificationism. But it cannot play the role in Critical philosophy that the verificationist version of implicit definition played. Can the Normative view do better? Can it give an account of a priori necessity? An account of the notion of necessity is our next task.

8

MODALITY

The concept of necessity is only to be found in our reason, as a formal condition of thought; it does not allow of being hypostatised as a material condition of existence.[1]

When we assert a necessity are we making a factual claim? I argue that we are not. The aim of this chapter is to establish the first step of the argument, by showing that modal 'musts' are analysable in term of epistemic reasons: specifically, reasons to exclude and include suppositions in the course of eliminative inquiry.

All 'musts' are analysable in terms of reasons: I shall argue in Chapter 12 that the moral or deontic 'must', the 'must' of moral obligation, is analysable in terms of evaluative reasons. Both modal and moral musts convey something categorical or unconditional.[2] In the case of modality it is a question of what should, unconditionally, be ruled in or out of inquiry; in the case of moral obligation, it is a question of what should, unconditionally, be done or not done. An analysis in terms of reasons must capture this unconditional character, and it can do so.

In neither case, modality or morality, are we dealing with a substantial factual domain of modal or moral facts, which we know by some special receptive faculty of intuition. Showing that modal and moral musts can be analysed in terms of reasons is a step on the road to showing that this is so, for in Part IV we shall show that pure propositions about reasons are not factual and are not known by any such receptive faculty.

Our task in this chapter, then, is to show that modal concepts are analysable in terms of reasons for epistemic acts. But a little more will have to be said about the particular inquiry that we call logic.

You can't do more to refute a view than show its logical impossibility. 'If sheer logic is not conclusive, what is?'[3] But what about impossibilities other than logical impossibilities?

---

[1] Kant, *Critique of Pure Reason*, A620/B648.
[2] Further, all musts are reducible to the modal or moral. 'To get to the station you must turn right'. That is a modal must. The basis may be natural necessity: given the facts and necessary limits on your motion (such as that you can't fly), turning right is the only way. Or it may be the 'must' of compliance: the only way to comply with the traffic rules is to turn right. Here the underlying necessity is modal, in this case logical. (There may of course also be a moral obligation to comply with the traffic rules.)
[3] Quine 1970: 81.

Is logical impossibility a harder kind of 'must'? Is it a special *kind* of 'must'?[4] Radical empiricists about logic, such as Mill and Quine say that the necessity involved in logical deduction is simply the necessity we discover when we discover any law of nature. They add that our knowledge of the laws of logic is no different in kind to our knowledge of other laws of nature. It is empirical knowledge; it has no special a priori status.

This is a strong and attractively simple pair of theses. Call the first, which says that one and the same notion of necessity features in common sense, science, mathematics, and logic, the *uniformity thesis*. Take, for example, the following impossibilities: it is not possible for a mass to approach another mass without mutual gravitational attraction; it is not possible for a proposition and its negation to be both true. The uniformity thesis says that the same kind of impossibility applies in both cases. The second, empiricist, thesis says that our knowledge of these impossibilities is in both cases empirical.

I do not defend the second thesis. There might, nonetheless, be an important element of truth in it. A priori support for a proposition is, we argued in Chapter 6, relative to an epistemic field. Where there is outright reason to believe a proposition, the strength of that reason, comparatively to other reasons, may vary. In improved epistemic fields the degree of a priori support for a proposition may diminish, or indeed there may be warrant to hold it false. Radical empiricism about logic says that that applies to the propositions of logic as to others.

Still, even radical empiricists would be wise to accept that logic has *some* a priori basis, even if it is defeasible. One might think that that already implies that logical necessity is in some way distinct from and higher than the necessity involved in any 'natural' law. We shall see that that is a mistake. The uniformity thesis is correct. Though some necessities that govern thinking are a priori and some are not, the nature of the necessity involved is the same. The special 'hardness' of logic is not due to its being made (so to speak) out of a different kind of metaphysical metal.

8.1 Logic

If necessity of the modal kind is univocal, what marks out the subject matter of logic? Granting that logic is a priori we can say that purely logical deduction is a priori as well as necessary:

(1) Y is deducible from X only if it is a priori that Y necessarily follows from X.

But this is not a sufficient condition on deducibility, or *logical* implication, because on most conceptions of logic proper ('formal logic'), the class of inferences that satisfy (1) is wider than the class of inferences of pure logic. There are the familiar examples, such as:

---

[4] Wittgenstein on the 'hardness of the logical "must"'—Wittgenstein 1978 (1956): 352 (VI.49). Cp. McDowell 1998b: 215–16. I agree with McDowell in taking a view of both the moral and the modal 'must' which is neither non-cognitivist nor 'descriptivist'. However, for reasons that will emerge in Chapters 16 and 17, I don't think it a good idea to call this position 'a species of platonism' (McDowell: 215), even with his reservations.

>   (2) It is red all over, therefore it is not green all over.

Consider also examples such as this:

>   (3) This action will cause undeserved suffering against the sufferer's will, therefore there is some reason not to do it.

(2) and (3) satisfy the necessary condition for deducibility given in (1); but they would not be said to be inferences of pure logic. We need a broader term to cover all cases in which (i) it's impossible that p is true and q is false; and (ii) that that is so is knowable a priori. I shall say that in this case the proposition that p *entails* the proposition that q. In (2) and (3) the premise entails the conclusion.

Entailment is wider than logical deducibility,[5] so whether or not you are an empiricist there is a demarcation issue about where to draw the line around pure logic as such. How should that be done?

The idea that what makes the aprioricity and necessity of logic special is that it arises from the fact that logic is analytic—not just in the Fregean sense in which that is trivially true, but in the no-content sense—still remains powerful. If true, it would certainly make logic special. But we have seen in the previous chapter that it is not true.

One can fall back on the vaguer idea that logic consists of conceptual truths—these being understood in some terms other than the no-content notion of analyticity. We shall discuss in 18.5 whether there is a philosophically interesting notion of conceptual, as against analytic truth. Concepts can be thought of as constituted by certain epistemic norms and these constitutive norms can be called conceptual truths. However, conceptual truth in this sense differs radically from analyticity; it is not a linguistic notion and it does not deliver a no-content notion of aprioricity which would *explain* why conceptual truths are a priori necessary. Analyticity is meant to be a way of explaining this. In contrast, to say that a norm is a conceptual truth does not *explain* how it is a priori; it presupposes that it is. In any case conceptual truth does not demarcate logic, because there are many conceptual truths beyond the truths of what we call logic. Analytic truth is too narrow to capture logic, conceptual truth is too wide.

Of course if different kinds of necessity are at stake, as between say the necessity of *modus ponens* and the necessities involved in (2) and (3), then these different kinds of necessity can do the demarcating. In contrast, however, if the uniformity thesis is correct the demarcation issue loses a lot of its philosophical interest. Logic is what logicians do, physics is what physicists do, and ethics is what moral philosophers (or just human beings) do. All these inquiries aim to discover necessary truths: logic and ethics belong to philosophy because they inquire into *a priori* necessary truths.

This is the standpoint taken here. If we still seek to demarcate logic it will have to be as the set of truths in which only a fixed list of terms appears essentially—the terms that by general agreement are 'logical'. Similarly with ethics. However, demarcating logic and

---

[5] I am treating entailment as strict implication. If this is questioned, the term 'strict implication' will do just as well. I do not mean to take sides in that debate.

characterizing thereby a strictly logical notion of deducibility is not essential to our main purpose. Our question is about the nature of modality in general, and about how it is that some modalities are known a priori while others are only known a posteriori.

To that end we can focus first on the concept of impossibility. The idea I want to develop is the following: the impossible is that which there is sufficient reason to exclude from all suppositions in what I shall call the *maximal epistemic field*.

8.2 Acts of inquiry and epistemic reasons

When we engage in inquiry we typically proceed by making suppositions. Thus Sherlock Holmes might think to himself:

> Suppose the criminal escaped through the window. If he did he must have left scratches like these on the sill, and prints in the flower bed below. However I can see (looking outside) that there are no prints—and the scratches could have been there before the crime. We should ask the housekeeper about that, and we should ask the gardener whether he raked the flower bed this morning, and if so whether he saw prints.

He interviews the housekeeper. If he finds that the scratches were indeed there before the crime, he eliminates the window supposition: there would have had to be *another* set of scratches. But if he finds that they were not there, he goes on to interview the gardener. If he finds that the gardener did rake the bed, and saw some prints, the window supposition stays alive and gets some confirmation by way of inference to the best explanation (which we'll consider in the next chapter). If the gardener raked the bed without noticing whether there were prints or not, it stays alive with less support. If the gardener definitely saw no prints, it dies. For a supposition Holmes does *not* consider is that the criminal levitated over the flower bed. He knows that is impossible: he can exclude, rule out, disallow, it.

Holmes is proceeding by elimination. Note the occurrence of modal concepts in his thinking. In this type of eliminative inquiry suppositions are put up with a view to investigating whether or not they should be ruled out. You have a tree of supposition-branches; you investigate each supposition-branch to see whether it should be ruled out—'lopped off'—in the light of what you (take yourself to) know. Some branches can be lopped off more or less quickly. In other cases further investigation is needed: you should follow the supposition-branch to see where it goes. The window supposition may be eliminated at the housekeeper stage, or at the gardener stage. Or it may be eliminated further down the branch, e.g. by discovering that it was impossible for the criminal to have got from the window to the road without being seen.

Eliminative inquiry, the method of supposition and elimination, require an initial boundary premise as to what the possibilities are. Your underlying epistemic state generates a warrant for that premise. The results of your eliminating and supposing may lead you to revise your initial boundary assumption, together with anything you initially take yourself to know. As Holmes famously said, when you have eliminated the possible only the impossible remains. He meant (to labour a point) that when you have eliminated all the suppositions that you thought were possible, you must reconsider the ones you initially ruled out—change your boundary assumptions. Nonetheless, any eliminative inquiry has to be bounded by prior *prima facie* warranted beliefs to work. That goes for a criminal inquiry or an inquiry into the causes of a disease. Elimination can sometimes get you all the way, leaving you with just one possibility. In which case that must be what occurred, or will occur. But it may be impossible to narrow down to a single possibility. If you conclude that a number of mutually exclusive suppositions remain open, the case has not been closed. (You may have some probabilities, but we leave that to the next chapter.)

Now we come to an important question. When we say that a supposition should or should not be ruled out, what is the sense of 'should'? Although 'including' and 'excluding' are acts, this 'should' is epistemic: it refers to sufficient epistemic reasons. How can this be, if epistemic reasons are reasons to *believe*? How can there be epistemic as against practical reasons for acts of including and excluding?

The Critical point is that inquiry is internal to judgement: it is the dynamic procedure that effects transitions from one set of judgements to another, readjusting them in a holistic way, allowing for switches into reverse gear that revise the initial judgements that we bring to it. These dynamics can be represented abstractly as procedures consisting of suppositions and inferences leading to inclusions and exclusions in a tree structure. Note that even at this abstract level the process has to be thought of dualistically, as involving *premises* and *assumptions* in the one hand, and, on the other, *steps* transforming these into conclusions. What is being abstractly represented in this procedure is a self-governing agent who does not statically grasp warrants but has to establish them by inquiries that involve suppositions, inferences, and revisions. Any agential cognition has to be represented in this dual way: it is not just acceptance of a set of beliefs but a set of transformative acts on beliefs.[6] Both the beliefs and the inquiries are reason-responsive. In both cases the norms involved are *epistemic* because both are part of thinking: reaching reason-responsive beliefs by reason-responsive procedures which determine what there is reason to believe. Thus also reasons for these transformative cognitive acts are relative to an epistemic field, just as reasons for beliefs are.

Of course real-time cognition takes place as a concrete sequence of actions that have opportunity costs. Therefore whether you have reasons to engage in such an inquiry in the first place, and how carefully you should pursue it, are clearly practical questions about practical reasons. When we think about inquiry purely in the abstract, however, we abstract from these practical questions: the reasons internal to the inquiry for taking this or that step remain epistemic reasons. A full implementation of the method might show that there is not sufficient epistemic reason to exclude some supposition; yet you might be *practically* warranted in not following it fully through, because you are practically warranted in not seeking to achieve full epistemic warrant, as against something less, such as a rough *prima facie* estimate of likelihoods. However in this chapter we are considering

---

[6] This is one moral of Lewis Carroll's discussion between Achilles and the tortoise.

inquiry purely as an abstract sequence directed to answering questions about epistemic warrant, subject to epistemic considerations alone.

8.3 The dynamics of supposition

Central to eliminative inquiry is the following principle:

> In considering whether you have sufficient reason to believe that p, you should consider whether you have sufficient reason to rule out suppositions incompatible with it's being the case that p. If you do not, then you do not have sufficient reason to believe that p, though you may have some degree of reason.[7]

This principle employs a normative distinction between propositions that you do and do not *have sufficient reason to exclude as suppositions* in a particular process of inquiry. I am going to argue that the modal notions of possibility, impossibility, necessity, and entailment can be analysed in terms of this distinction, and thus turn out to be normative.

We should distinguish, to begin with, between impossibility that is conditional on some facts and unconditional impossibility. The former always presupposes the latter. Suppose we're considering the supposition that Fiona had lunch in London on the relevant day. Someone tells us that at lunchtime she was in Edinburgh. Given that fact, it's impossible that she had lunch in London. That is a conditional impossibility. It relies on an unconditional impossibility: you cannot be in two places at one time. In contrast, Sherlock Holmes directly asserts an unconditional impossibility when he rules out the supposition that the criminal levitated over the flower bed. From now on when I refer without qualification to possibilities, impossibilities, and necessities I shall mean *unconditional* possibilities, impossibilities, and necessities.

Corresponding to this distinction we can distinguish between conditional and unconditional inclusion and exclusion. When an inquirer engages in a supposition-procedure he takes himself to know certain modal and non-modal facts already, independently of that procedure. Starting from these he branches out some alternative suppositions for purposes of inquiry. *Conditional* inclusion of a proposition is inclusion in a supposition-branch, either (i) because the inquirer takes himself to know the truth of the proposition independently of the supposition-procedure; or (ii) because the inquirer is supposing the proposition to be true within the particular supposition-branch being investigated, without thinking that it should be included in all supposition-branches whatever. He argues (say) 'Let's *suppose* that p; *given* that it's also the case that q then so-and-so'. Here both the propositions that p and that q are included conditionally. Such suppositions may be counterfactual, typically in an inquiry into causes: even if the train had been travelling much more slowly it would still have gone of the rails; if there had been no paper in the room the fire would not have taken hold.

---

[7] The role this principle plays in sceptical arguments is considered in 20.7. For the moment note that there are non-eliminative forms of reasoning about the facts. Inference to the best explanation, for example, is *not* as such a form of eliminative inquiry. You do not, in general, have to *eliminate* all other hypotheses to have some reason to believe a good one.

Unconditional inclusion is inclusion in all supposition-branches, not conditional on either (i) or (ii). In the same way we have conditional and unconditional *exclusion*: unconditional exclusion is exclusion from all supposition-branches, where the basis of exclusion is neither (i) what the inquirer takes himself to know to be the non-modal facts nor (ii) what the inquirer is supposing to be facts within a particular supposition-branch being investigated.

Suppose we take ourselves to know that Fiona is in Edinburgh, and are considering whether she could make it in time to the meeting here. Then we will include the proposition that she is in Edinburgh in all supposition-branches. Likewise, we will exclude the proposition that she is not in Edinburgh from all supposition-branches. Neither of these is unconditional. We include the proposition that she is in Edinburgh in all supposition-branches because we take ourselves to know that she is. We then exclude the proposition that she is not in Edinburgh from all branches because we take ourselves to be warranted in *unconditionally* excluding the pair of propositions (she is in Edinburgh, she is not in Edinburgh). In similar fashion, when Sherlock Holmes is considering whether the criminal escaped through the window he takes himself to be warranted in *unconditionally* excluding the proposition that the criminal levitated over the garden. There is indeed a difference between these two unconditional exclusions, namely, that the first is warranted a priori while the second is warranted a posteriori. However both exclusions are unconditional. Holmes excludes the proposition that the criminal levitated over the garden neither because he happens to know that it is false, as he might happen to know that the scratches on the window were there before the crime, nor because he is supposing, in the particular supposition-branch he is following, that it is false, but because he knows, independently of the supposition-procedure, that he has sufficient reason to exclude it unconditionally—the impossibility of levitation is a boundary condition on the problem.

The eliminative procedure we are considering is a method of arriving at epistemic warrants for beliefs about what is the case—about the world as it is, including hypothetical consequences (as in 'If this happened then that happened', or 'if you do that so-and-so will follow'). This is what I mean by eliminative inquiry. Inclusion and exclusion should be understood specifically as acts in a process of eliminative inquiry. We can also of course make suppositions for various other purposes, for example, to write a science fiction story about a world in which gravitation is cancelled, or to study para-consistent logic. For those purposes we can suppose that gravitation does not hold, or that non-contradiction does not obtain. We may nonetheless be epistemically warranted in excluding these suppositions for the purpose of *eliminative* inquiry. It is this notion of inclusion and exclusion in an eliminative inquiry that we need in order to analyse modality.

8.4 Modality as unconditional exclusion and inclusion

So now can the notion of impossibility be analysed in terms of *unconditional exclusion*?

What you should include or exclude in an inquiry is relative to your epistemic field. In contrast, what is impossible is not. Possibility and impossibility do not depend on what you know or on what you, as you are placed, could discover. Remember, however, that the epistemic reasons that obtain in a given epistemic field are thinker-invariant (abstracting from cognitive internalism—3.9). So we can think simply in terms of the epistemic reasons that exist in particular fields of facts, without reference to particular inquirers. Next we take an important step. We form the notion of what epistemic reasons exist in the *maximal field*, consisting of *all the facts*. And now our proposal is that 'It is unconditionally impossible that p' means 'There is sufficient reason to unconditionally exclude the supposition that p in the maximal field'.

Modal facts should not be included in this notion of 'all the facts'. If my argument that modal propositions are normative and that normative propositions are not factual is correct, then there *are* no modal facts (in the substantial sense of fact). That leaves us with the required notion: all the (substantial) facts. If this notion were thought questionable on finitistic grounds, we would have to consider how much could be done with a constructive notion of *all the facts*. However, the arguments of this book do not depend on any form of finitism, and I am going to assume that there is nothing wrong with a non-constructive notion of *all the facts*.

Consider then the maximal field, μ—the epistemic field consisting of all the facts. I submit that the following equivalence holds:

> It's impossible that p if and only if there is sufficient epistemic reason in μ to exclude unconditionally the proposition that p.

Note that we are referring to *unconditional* exclusion. This equivalence does not make anything that is not the case unconditionally impossible. True, in μ there is sufficient reason to exclude anything that is not the case *conditionally* from all supposition-branches. As noted above, however, excluding not p conditionally on the known fact that p relies on unconditional exclusion of the proposition that p *and not-p*. And in μ there is sufficient reason to exclude that proposition unconditionally (or there is if dialetheism is necessarily false).

I shall take it that the equivalence gives a definition of unconditional impossibility. Let 'E' abbreviate the phrase 'to exclude unconditionally the proposition that'. Then the proposal is this:

(4) It is impossible that $p =_{Df} S_\mu Ep$.

Note that S here refers to an *epistemic* sufficient reason even though it governs an act of inquiry: as discussed in the previous section, inquiry involves the idea of epistemic reasons for epistemic acts as well as premises and conclusions. Nonetheless, this proposal may seem puzzling. What would be the point of supposition for a being whose epistemic field was μ?

That, however, is a question about what the *practical* point of inquiry would be for such a being. There would be it seems no point; it is hard to see how such a being could even exist, or at least act, in the world of space–time in which we exist.[8] It seems that it would

---

[8] See Dummett, 'Bringing about the past' (1964), in Dummett 1978.

have no practical use for inquiry and hence no practical use for the distinction between necessary and contingent facts.

However, there is no need to speculate about beings that know all the facts. The only assumption we require is that there is some determinate truth about what suppositions should* be unconditionally excluded in any epistemic field, and hence in particular in μ. That determinate truth, however far it extends, will also determine what the modal facts are. The claim is that there is nothing more to impossibility than warranted unconditional exclusion in μ.

Now let's consider the definition of possibility and necessity. Possibility is straightforwardly definable in terms of impossibility:

It is possible that $p =_{Df}$ it is not impossible that p.

Thus to say that it's *possible* that p is to say that it is not unconditionally excludable that p:

(5) It is possible that $p =_{Df} \neg S_\mu E p$.

What about necessity? We have:

(6) It is necessary that p if and only if it is impossible that not p.

Should we, however, regard this as true by definition? Intuitively, to say that it is necessary that p is to say something about what should be *included*:

(7) It is necessary that p if and only if in μ there is sufficient reason unconditionally to *include* the proposition that p.

If we took (6) to be true by definition, then saying that it is necessary that p would only be saying that there is sufficient epistemic reason in μ to *exclude* unconditionally the supposition that not-p. To get to (7) we would need the principle:

If there is sufficient reason in μ to exclude unconditionally the proposition that not-p, then there is sufficient reason in μ to include unconditionally the proposition that p.

This principle is by no means true by definition; nor is its converse. Both can be derived from the purely normative proposition that one but not both of the suppositions, that p, and that not-p, should be included in every supposition-branch.[9] This is the normative foundation of classical logic, whence:

(8) $S_\mu E \neg p \leftrightarrow S_\mu I p$

We may hold that classical logic is true a priori, but it is not true by definition. So we should define necessity directly in terms of (7):

(9) $\Box p =_{Df} S_\mu I p$

---

[9] Think in abstract terms of complete supposition-branches. Of course we know in practice that many propositions are simply irrelevant to a particular process of inquiry—it's not necessary to consider separately the supposition-branch in which they are included and the supposition-branch in which their negation is included. So we do not in practice bother to include them or their negations in our suppositions.

On this account of modality, subjunctive conditionals become normative propositions, propositions about what propositions should be supposed in a supposition-branch if other propositions are supposed in it.

8.5 Normative interpretation of modal logic

I will refer to this analysis as the normative analysis of modality (in parallel with the normative analysis of aprioricity). If it is correct, modal propositions are wholly normative propositions about the maximal epistemic field. What modal principles obtain on this analysis?

The most evident and uncontested modal principle says *if it is so, it is possible*:

$p \to \Diamond p$

On the normative analysis, this says that if p then there is not sufficient epistemic reason in μ to exclude unconditionally the proposition that p. Or a little more succinctly:

(10) If p then in μ the proposition that p should not be unconditionally excluded.

That is clearly correct, for if p then the fact that p is in μ. And what is knowably the case may certainly be included in supposition-branches in an eliminative inquiry.

What of the principle that *if it is necessary, it is so*:

$\Box p \to p$?

We can get to this conclusion from (10) by (8), and (9). What is says, by our definition of necessity, (9), is:

(11) If in μ the proposition that p should be unconditionally included then p.

The argument to it relies on classical principles (contraposition and the negation rules). It might be objected that (11) is evident *irrespective* of classical logic: it is evident in its own right, whether or not we accept excluded middle and non-contradiction. If non-contradiction fails, then we cannot infer the proposition that $\neg\neg p$ from the proposition that $\Box p$, but we can surely still infer the proposition that p! On this view (11) is a pure epistemic norm that is evident in its own right. That seems right: it is evident that if in μ the proposition that p should be unconditionally included then it is included in the particular supposition-branch that coincides with how things are.

The Normative view provides an interpretation of modal logic that validates the system known as S5. We get this system by adding the following modal principles to classical propositional logic:

Axioms:

$\Box p \to p$

$\Box(p \to q) \to (\Box p \to \Box q)$

$\Diamond p \to \Box \Diamond p$

Necessitation Rule: If A is a theorem, then so is □A.

The first axiom has already been considered. On the normative interpretation the second asserts the closure of S under itself. We argued for that in Chapter 5, and we now extend it to acts of exclusion and inclusion in μ:

$$S_\mu I(p \to q) \to (S_\mu Ip \to S_\mu Iq)$$

The third asserts that:

$$\neg S_\mu Ep \to S_\mu I \neg S_\mu Ep$$

We can get this by another extension of epistemic principles to epistemic acts, in this case the epistemic SS principle, in the version in which it says $\neg S\beta \leftrightarrow S\beta \neg S\beta$ (see 5.8, footnote 21). Extending this to epistemic acts, we have $\neg S_\mu Ep \to S_\mu I \neg S_\mu Ep$.

Finally we must consider the Necessitation Rule. On the normative interpretation it says that any theorem of S5, i.e. of propositional logic augmented by the above axioms, should be unconditionally included in μ. Since we can see a priori that the principles of propositional logic plus the further principles just considered should be unconditionally included in all suppositions, we can see that the Necessitation Rule is correct.

We should also consider necessities of identity and origin:

$$x = y \to \Box x = y$$

and

The origin of x is $o \to \Box$ the origin of x is o.

What these respectively say is that:

If $x = y$ then in μ the supposition that $x = y$ should be unconditionally included,

and

If the origin of x is o then in μ the supposition that the origin of x is o is to be unconditionally included.[10]

What about a priori contingents? Consider again the proposition that Charlie is the murderer, which we discussed in 7.7. The police know a priori that if any one person is the murderer it's Charlie, but that proposition is contingent.

Yet can't the police unconditionally include, in all suppositions, the proposition that the murderer is Charlie? They can and do. But the question is whether it should be unconditionally included in μ. Suppose there is no one murderer. Then the proposition is not true, and certainly should not be unconditionally included in μ. Suppose, on the other hand, that there is just one murderer and the murderer is x. Then Charlie = x. The proposition that Charlie = x should be unconditionally included in μ. But the propositions that

---

[10] So if x's origin is o we should rule out or 'close off' the counterfactual supposition that it is not (that supposition leads to a *reductio*).

Charlie is the murderer, and that x is the murderer, will only be conditionally included in μ. There can be suppositions—contrary to fact suppositions—from which they are excluded. 'If someone else had been the murderer, would the police have found that out—or were they just acting on an unreliable prejudice which turned out luckily?'

If the police suppose that Charlie is y (where y ≠ x), and work through that supposition tree, they are making a supposition which in μ should be unconditionally excluded. That is, it is necessarily false. Perhaps it should be unconditionally excluded relative to their epistemic field *e*, because the facts in *e* suffice to show that it is false, and therefore necessarily false. But the police haven't yet worked that out, so they are perfectly right to pursue the supposition until they can exclude it.[11]

'Possible worlds' are ways of modelling maximal supposition-branches. Which ones we should consider—how far we should branch out in our inquiry—depends on our inquiry's goal. If the goal is to find out what is (was, will be) the case, we should exclude all suppositions we are warranted in thinking unconditionally excludable: in other words, exclude *every* world that we have sufficient reason to believe impossible. That is trivially true, since the notion of unconditional exclusion was defined with reference to that goal, and then impossibility was defined in terms of it.

But the goal may be more theoretical; our inquiry may be into what *is* possible or impossible, or into some question that involves modal notions, such as what powers or capacities some object has. In some cases, such an inquiry is a priori; even then we may need to consider a world which turns out to be a priori impossible, for example, for purposes of *reductio*. In other cases it is a posteriori; inquiries into natural impossibilities require inductive inquiries (whose guiding norms will be considered in the next chapter). These too may involve supposing what *turns out* to be impossible: for example, finding out that something is impossible by supposing it possible and trying to do it, or testing a consequence that would obtain if it was possible. As inductive inquiries get more global they may lead to a reconsideration of *prima facie* a priori warrants. It is debatable, for example, to what extent the impossibility of action at a distance is a priori, at least in some epistemic fields. However, in most cases inductive inquiry into natural necessities assumes that a priori impossibilities are held constant. This generates a felt difference between a priori and a posteriori impossibilities, but it does not show that the impossibility itself is different. Only a theory of the a priori which gives a priori knowable truths some *metaphysical* standing that no a posteriori truth has can do that. Intuitionist realism has this character, the normative account does not.

To sum up: the method of inquiry we have focused on in analysing modality is eliminative inquiry into the facts as they are. Of course our inquiries may have various other goals. We may want to explore alternative logics, or alternative ethics, or a semantics that

---

[11] One other example. Consider S: 'If it's actually the case that *p* then *p*'. The 'actually' operator assigns in all possible worlds the truth value to a proposition that it actually has. So S is a priori true, and its antecedent is necessarily true. But S may not be necessarily true, since it may be a contingent truth that *p*. Assuming that it is, I can make the contrary to fact supposition: 'Even though it is actually the case that *p*, let's suppose that not *p*'. (Suppose the murderer had not been x—would the police have caught him?) So S should not be unconditionally included in μ, since that (in combination with unconditional inclusion of its antecedent) would rule out such suppositions.

requires us to postulate impossible worlds, or we may simply want to work out a fairy story or a science fiction in a cogent way. There can be many reasons for branching into suppositions that for purposes of *eliminative inquiry* should be unconditionally excluded.

8.6 Modal knowledge and fallibilism

Bounded, situated actors—actors who make practical plans in a world within which they and their actions are located and which they only partially know—must make eliminative inquiries. To put the same point in the modal way, situated actors need modal beliefs—as a 'formal condition of thought', in Kant's words. But now there is the old question: how can knowledge of what is actually the case ever give one knowledge of what could or could not be the case? How can a priori reflection and a posteriori induction lead to modal conclusions?

The normative analysis makes this question more tractable. It says that modal propositions are normative propositions about what should be unconditionally included or excluded in μ. How we can know such propositions to be true, therefore becomes a special case of the general question we shall be concerned with in Part IV: how can we know truths about reasons? Our account of normative knowledge in Chapters 16 and 17 will be cognitivist but irrealist. Since modal knowledge is normative knowledge, and normative knowledge is not knowledge of a special domain of facts, the resulting overall account of modality will therefore at least remove one apparently insoluble question: how knowledge of one set of facts—the non-modal facts—could possibly give one knowledge of a distinct set of facts—the modal facts. There *are* no modal facts, in the substantial sense of fact. Modal knowledge requires knowledge of epistemic norms, not of modal facts.

However, that leaves us with another question which should be addressed here. What S relations obtain on μ is a priori. Hence if one knew what set of facts constitute μ, one could infer all impossibilities and necessities (in part by means of inductive epistemic norms of the kind considered in the next chapter). But we cannot do that because we don't know, and could not know, what those facts—all the facts—are.

How then can a limited epistemic field, that is not identical with μ, give us a posteriori sufficient reason for modal beliefs, if these beliefs are about what suppositions should* be unconditionally included/excluded in μ? On the Normative view, the question of how specifically *modal* knowledge is possible comes down to this.

The fact that a proposition should* be believed in *e*, whether on a priori or a posteriori grounds, never *logically* implies that it should* be believed in every strict improvement on *e*. This is the thesis of fallibilism, taken to apply to a priori as well as a posteriori epistemic reasons.[12] Fallibilism, note, is not scepticism; it does not deny that there are epistemic warrants. And it applies to unconditional inclusions and exclusions: the fact that a proposition should be unconditionally included or excluded in *e* never *logically* implies that it should be so in every strict improvement on *e*. For example, unconditional inclusion of

---

[12] Fallibilism is further discussed in 9.4 and 20.6.

the parallels postulate was warranted in the ancient Greek epistemic field, but it is not warranted in our epistemic field.

In particular, then, the fact that in our epistemic field a proposition should be unconditionally included or excluded does not logically imply that it should be unconditionally included or excluded in μ. Fallibilism denies that the following conditional is a logical truth:

(11) $Sp \to S_\mu p$

Contrast

(12) $p \to S_\mu p$

This is an analytic truth. By definition, for any fact in any epistemic field there is sufficient reason in that field to believe that it obtains. Since μ consists of all the facts it includes the fact that p, hence $S_\mu p$.

There is outright sufficient reason to believe (12), and so by closure of S under itself[13] we have:

(13) $Sp \to SS_\mu p$

Given sufficient reason to believe that p, there is sufficient reason to believe that in μ there is sufficient reason to believe that p. Put it this way: if we have sufficient reason to believe that p we have sufficient reason to believe that if all the facts were knowable there would be sufficient reason to believe that p.

Now let's consider the case of unconditional exclusion (the same points will apply to unconditional inclusion). Here too, in parallel with (11), fallibilism denies that the following is a logical truth:

(14) $SEp \to S_\mu Ep$

But what about the analogue of (13)? This will be:

(15) $SEp \to SS_\mu Ep$

Here 'Ep' does not stand in for a proposition but refers to a cognitive act (whereas 'Sp' is as usual short for 'There is sufficient reason to believe that p'). So we cannot get to (15) by substituting 'Ep' for 'p' in (12). We have to accept (15) as a basic principle.

This raises some elusive points. (13) says that the facts available to us can give us sufficient reason to believe that p only if they also give us sufficient reason to believe that *were all the facts knowable* there would be sufficient reason to believe that p. Likewise (15) says that the facts available to us give us sufficient reason to unconditionally exclude the supposition that p only if they also give us sufficient reason to believe that *were all the facts knowable* there would be sufficient reason to do so.

In both cases there is the same element of, as it were, 'extrapolation' of one's warrant from its home field into the field of *all* the facts. This kind of extrapolation is not some-

---

[13] See 5.8. We have $S(p \to S_\mu p)$. By closure, $Sp, S(p \to S_\mu p) \vdash SS_\mu p$. So $Sp \to SS_\mu p$.

thing thought can avoid. For it arises from an act that is essential to rationality: namely, the move from coming to believe that S(e, ψ), where e is recognized as one's own epistemic field and ψ is a cognitive act, to the act of ψ-ing. Note the character of this move. The fact that S(e, ψ) is not itself a reason to ψ. Rather, failure to move from recognition that S(e, ψ) to the act of ψ-ing opens one to criticism in respect of rationality (5.11). In that sense one can say that the move is 'rationally required', or that it is essential to rational thought.

Where ψ-ing is believing that is particularly clear, in the light of (12). I come to believe that there is sufficient reason to believe that p. Being rational I thus believe that p, and so by (12) I am committed to believing that $S_\mu p$. But the point holds for all cognitive acts. In moving from believing that S(e, ψ) to ψ-ing I make the extrapolating move: I take it that were *all* the relevant facts knowable there would be sufficient reason for me to ψ. Mentally removing, so to speak, the restriction to my limited epistemic field I take my reason to be a reason in the light of the *facts as such* and I go ahead and ψ. Thus we have:

(16) $S\psi \rightarrow S\beta S_\mu \psi$[14]

Adnittedly, this seems very strong. Suppose someone says: 'OK, but I don't *know* whether ψ-ing would be warranted if I knew all the relevant facts. I don't have sufficient reason to believe anything about *that*. So by (16) there is not, after all, sufficient reason for me to ψ.'

Fallibilism is distinct from scepticism because it resists this *modus tollens* argument. It holds that the sceptic's claim that $\neg S\beta S_\mu \psi$ is warranted only if one has specific defeaters for the claim that $S\beta S_\mu \psi$—reasons to *deny* that $S_\mu \psi$. We shall pursue this contrast between fallibilism and scepticism in 20.7. But we can return now to our question: how can our limited epistemic field give us warrant for modal beliefs, if these beliefs are about what unconditional inclusions and exclusions are warranted in μ?

Whatever in our epistemic field constitutes sufficient reason to unconditionally exclude the proposition that p, thereby also constitutes sufficient reason to believe that given all the facts there is sufficient reason to unconditionally exclude the proposition that p. Hence, by our definition, it gives us sufficient reason to believe that it is impossible that p. Furthermore, the fallibilist's rejection of unrestricted *modus tollens* arguments based on (16) allows that there *can* be sufficient reason to unconditionally exclude a proposition, even in a limited epistemic field.

8.7 Modality and normativity: cart and horse

We have analysed modality in terms of normativity. There is an objection to this way of proceeding that the reader may well have had in mind for some time. Consider again (4), our definition of impossibility:

---

[14] There are acts one should* do precisely because of limitations in one's epistemic field, i.e. where the facts that constitute the sufficient reason *include* the fact that one's epistemic field is limited. The principle can be said to hold for these too, in the following way. Let p = given the limitations on my current epistemic state, and given my practical reasons, I should* find out whether it will snow. Here the fact that p does *not* entail that I should* believe that in μ I should* find out whether it will snow. However, it's still true that if Sp then $SS_\mu p$.

It is impossible that $p =_{Df} S_\mu Ep$

Two kinds of objection can be made to this. We can, in the first place, ask whether the underlying equivalence:

$$\neg \Diamond p \leftrightarrow S_\mu Ep$$

is correct and if so whether it's a priori. Suppose it is. Second, we can ask whether it's analytic, and whether, if so, that is because the left-hand side is definable in terms of the right-hand side as (4) proposes. The objection is that (4) puts the cart before the horse. It's *because* it is impossible that p that there is sufficient reason in μ to exclude the supposition that p. The impossibility *justifies* the unconditional exclusion. Hence, we cannot define the former in terms of the latter.

This objection has a general form that can arise with respect to all the normative analyses given in this book. We have encountered it already in 4.4, in connection with the buck-passing analysis of 'good'. It could be raised against our analysis of aprioricity, and it will come up with respect to our analyses of probability, of moral wrongness, and of rights. Underlying it, in each case, is a realist intuition—to the effect that we are analysing out a genuinely explanatory property. Thus in the case of 'good' the intuition is that goodness is a property of an object *in virtue* of which reasons to favour the object arise. In the case of modality the intuition is that impossibility is a property of a proposition *in virtue* of which reasons to unconditionally exclude the proposition arise. The reasons supervene on the property and so the property cannot be defined in terms of the reasons.

Before we can consider this 'cart and horse' objection in general terms we need a discussion of what realism encompasses, and how it stands in relation to the Normative view. We shall consider the objection generally in 18.6. I shall there argue that the realist impulse arises—across the board—from a tendency of thought to reify its own normative categories. That of course is exactly the diagnosis one can expect from any Critical stance—the quotation from Kant that provides the motto for this chapter is an instance of it. For the moment, however, we should consider some points about the objection that specifically arise with respect to modal concepts.

The objection starts from a point that is not in dispute: if there is sufficient reason to exclude unconditionally the supposition that p that is *because* it is impossible that p. This point alone does not undermine (4). For what it means, according to (4), is that if there is sufficient reason to exclude unconditionally the supposition that p that's *because* there is sufficient reason to exclude it unconditionally in μ. And this can be read, on the normative analysis, as saying that the data that give us sufficient reason for the exclusion only do so *insofar as they give us sufficient reason to believe* that there would be sufficient reason for the exclusion if all (relevant) facts were known. If they didn't give us sufficient reason to believe that, they wouldn't give us sufficient reason for the exclusion. That is just what (15) asserts.

However, can we not still ask why there is sufficient reason to exclude the supposition unconditionally in μ? Here there is clear disagreement. On the normative analysis it is because there are facts in μ which constitute sufficient reason to exclude it. There is no further, distinct, and irreducibly modal, fact which 'makes it true' that there is sufficient reason to exclude it. Thus on the Normative view we have:

(i) $S_\mu\, Ep$

and

(ii) $\neg\Diamond p$

but *not*

(iii) $S_\mu Ep$ because $\neg\Diamond p$

at least if (iii) is thought of as having genuine explanatory force. The fact that $\neg\Diamond p$ is not a fact about some 'modal reality' independent of the domain of reasons. It is not distinct from the fact that $S_\mu\, Ep$, and so cannot be an 'explanation' of that fact.

The modal realist's putative explanation of (i) imposes an intuitionist epistemology of modal knowledge. We must be equipped with a faculty that is receptive to the alleged ontological domain of modal facts. The Normative view says that no non-metaphorical account of any such faculty exists or can be given. If we look seriously at *how* we achieve modal knowledge, all we find are spontaneous dispositions to make judgements about what suppositions should or should not be excluded in eliminative inquiry—spontaneous judgements based on knowledge of *actual* facts. Even if, *per impossibile*, there was some domain of 'modal reality' we would know nothing of it and its existence would make no difference to our actual modal judgements and their warrants.[15]

From the Normative standpoint, the basic phenomenon to focus on in understanding modality is apriority: in particular, the role of the a priori in determining what suppositions to include or exclude in eliminative inquiry.

Synthetic a priori judgements, based on the spontaneous dispositions mentioned in 6.5, provide the initial structure of our world view, the governing inclusions and exclusions. We fill in, and sometimes revise, this structure by means of inductive inquiry. The methods of inductive inquiry are themselves a priori; they yield generalizations which we are a posteriori warranted in thinking hold for all the facts. By a further a priori step we take these universal generalizations to hold necessarily: to ground unconditional exclusions and inclusions. Thus the totality of facts fixes the totality of modal truths a priori. It makes no sense to speculate that there might be modal facts unknowable in μ, or that some modal propositions which there is sufficient reason to believe in μ might yet be false. Reading supervenience as the S relation, we can say that necessity and possibility supervene on the actual facts.

Finally, this Normative view of modality fits with our overall picture of the situated agent as a self-determiner in the domain of reasons. Situated self-determiners need modal beliefs. Modal concepts have a role in self-determining cognition through their use in

---

[15] Could God alter the modal facts that constitute this reality, while leaving the actual facts unchanged? If not, why not? And what difference would it make if he did? How do we know he's not doing it all the time?

eliminative inquiry as to the actual facts. This role—their use in generating warrants for beliefs about what is actually the case—exhausts their content.

8.8 Factualism versus the normativity of logic

The cart/horse issue that we have just been considering is also the heart of a dispute between factualist and normative conceptions of logic.

A factualist view of logic takes it to consist, like any other science, of universal non-normative factual truths. Logic is the most comprehensive science because its truths are the most comprehensive of such truths: in Frege's nice phrase, they are the laws of truth itself. Principles of logical inference hold in virtue of universal logical truths:

(17) $p_1,...,p_n \vdash c$ is a deductively valid rule of inference because whenever it's the case that some propositions of form $p_1,...,p_n$ are true a proposition of form c is true.

Logical truths are not, on this view, about reasons to believe; the question of how they generate reasons to believe is a separate issue. The factualist will add that logical truths are necessary, and may add that they are a priori. Intuitionism about logic is a form of factualism which adds both. Empiricist factualism, if it adds anything, adds only necessity.

The normative analysis of logic is quite different. It holds that logic is in its very essence normative: that it is fundamentally a set of propositions about epistemic reasons. Non-normatively stated logical truths are offshoots of these fundamental propositions about reasons, namely, principles of unconditional inclusion and exclusion of the form:

(18) $p_1,...,p_n \tau_\mu c$: there is outright sufficient reason in μ to unconditionally include a supposition of the form c in all suppositions that include suppositions of the form $p_1,...,p_n$.

From (18) we get

$$\Box(p_1,...,p_n \rightarrow c)$$

and

$$p_1,...,p_n \vdash c$$

On the normative analysis, to say that logic is a priori is to say that logical norms of form (18) are warranted outright in our epistemic field.

In contrasting the Normative view of logic with factualism I am anticipating what I will argue in Part IV: that purely normative propositions are not factual. A position which accepted the analysis of modality in this chapter, and the other analyses in terms of reasons given in this book, might still deny that. Such intuitionism about normativity itself would say that *normative* propositions are factual propositions about a special domain of fact, facts about reasons, to which we have intuitive access.

Arguments against this view will be given in Chapter 18. The Normative view which we shall argue for is cognitivist and irrealist: it takes logic to be a priori, normative, and non-factual. Let us now complete our discussion of modality by comparing this Normative view with empiricism.

8.9 Empiricism and reasons

An empiricist should, it seems, be a factualist. He should agree with (17). The truths of logic are universal a posteriori truths. But then what should he say about their modal status? Can he take the Mill/Quine view that all necessities are a posteriori? What about their ontology? Should he say that modal propositions are propositions about modal facts? If modal claims are propositions about a special domain of modal fact, how does, say, the fact that p relate to the fact that $\Diamond p$? Is the fact that $p \rightarrow \Diamond p$ a further fact, a fact that we discover by a posteriori inquiry? That seems particularly unviable.

However, on the account given in this chapter he may seem to have another option: to hold that modal propositions are normative, non-factual—and always a posteriori. This would be a limiting case of the Normative view: 'Normative empiricism'. It would say that modal claims are propositions about epistemic reasons, as argued in this chapter—but that these propositions are all a posteriori.

Against this arises a fundamental objection: norms are knowable by self-determiners. It is this Critical point that places limits on empiricism. Self-determiners must be able to perform epistemic self-audits; to do so they must be able to recognize the reasons they have. That, however, is possible only if a priori insight into some epistemic norms is possible. This was argued in Chapter 5. Furthermore, our discussion of analyticity in Chapter 7 clearly showed that epistemic norms are not analytic (in the relevant, 'no-content' sense). Yet first-person knowledge of warrants *is* possible. Hence general empiricism, the view that no truth is synthetic a priori, must be false. That much must be granted to the Critical perspective.

What about the necessity, as against the aprioricity, of epistemic norms? If we have sufficient reason to take a proposition about reasons as an epistemic norm, there is outright sufficient reason to include it in every supposition and hence (by (15) together with our definition of necessity) outright sufficient reason to *regard* it as necessary. More: I shall argue in 20.6 that epistemic norms are indefeasible, and that entails that they *are* necessary. Epistemic norms are both a priori and necessary.

These points might be accepted ('quasi-accepted') by a non-cognitivist who proposes a non-cognitive or 'projective' account of claims about reasons. That is a potential option for an empiricist; however, I shall argue in Part IV that if irrealist cognitivism about reasons is viable, non-cognitivism about them is redundant.

The other option to which an empiricist may be driven is simply to deny that there are epistemic norms. Reasons for belief reduce to practical reasons. If you want to believe the true, or the true in some area that interests you, then there is reason for you to believe that p just if it is true that p. And what is the status of these practical reasons?

Here the response is an instrumentalist account of practical reasons, together with the claim that instrumentalism is analytic.

Now I have already argued that instrumentalism is not just not analytic, but false (4.9 and 4.10). But even if the instrumentalist thesis were an analytic truth, that would not help. For this response still runs up the preconditions for self-determination. It disastrously fails to explain what *warrant* we ever have to believe anything. Thus suppose (a) I want to believe the true; and (b) it's raining in Mogadishu. In that case, on this instrumentalist view, there *is* reason for me to believe that it raining in Mogadishu. But what reason do I *have* to believe there is? That is, what warrants me in thinking there is a reason to believe that? No account has been given of how I know what reason there is to believe anything.

Actually it's not even true, strictly speaking, that on this account there are any reasons for me to believe anything. There are only practical reasons for me to bring it about that I believe this or that. It can be true (granting instrumentalism for the sake of the argument) that there is reason for me to cause myself to believe that it is raining in Mogadishu. But since epistemic reasons are relative to epistemic fields it does not follow that there *is* reason for me to believe it, still less that I have warranted reason to believe it. (We shall come back to these points in 20.2.)

These considerations are meant to refute a global empiricism, one that asserts that there are no synthetic a priori truths. They do not refute empiricism about logic in particular. for an empiricist about logic might agree that *inductive* norms, of the kind discussed in the next chapter, are a priori. Mill, it is true, seems to disagree:

> Principles of Evidence and Theories of Method are not to be constructed *a priori*. The laws of our rational faculty, like those of every other natural agency, are only learnt by seeing the agent at work.[16]

However, it is arguable that the dispute is terminological. Mill directs his argument at intuitionism. He does not deny that our rational faculty has normative laws. The 'evidence' he offers for these laws is that they are epistemically grounded in our actual, spontaneous, cognitive dispositions. The thrust of his discussion of the 'inductive process' in the *System of Logic* is then to show how, starting from the basic norms that are in practice accepted by 'the agent at work,' and their success in discovering rough-cut empirical generalizations, powerful tools of eliminative inquiry can be constructed 'a posteriori'. All this is perfectly consistent with the epistemology of the a priori that I shall describe in Chapter 16.

However, is empiricism about logic coherent? What account can it give of the notion of consistency, as that appears, for example, in the requirement that a hypothesis should be consistent with the data?[17] Suppose I believe that $h \rightarrow p$ and that $\neg p$. Am I required to reject h? In what sense am I required? Does empiricism about logic say that this is just another empirical question?

---

[16] Mill (1963–91) vol. VIII: 833. There is some further discussion of this Millian epistemology in 11.3.
[17] Cp. Wright 1986.

At this point we should bear in mind the difference between reasons and rational requirements. To say that I am rationally required to reject h is not to assert a further fact. It is not to assert that:

$$\Box\{((h\to p)\&\neg p)\to\neg h\}$$

if that is understood as a further *fact*. We need a normative formulation:[18]

> (19) There is sufficient reason to reject unconditionally any supposition in which h, h implies p and $\neg p$

Now suppose you have warrant to accept this proposition about reasons. That being so, if you make the supposition that h implies p and that $\neg p$, then you are criticizable in respect of rationality if in that supposition-branch you fail to reject the supposition that h. You fail to reject something you have sufficient reason to reject. That being so, and in the light of our discussion of rational requirement in 5.11, we can say that it is a rational requirement, if you suppose that h implies p and that $\neg p$, that you reject the supposition that h. And this applies irrespective of whether your warrant for (19) is a priori or a posteriori. Empiricism about logic can cope perfectly well with the rational requirement of consistency. It can accept that the truths of logic may be formulated as propositions about reasons. Its only claim is that that these truths are posteriori.

However, although empiricism about logic in particular (as against epistemic norms in general) is coherent, I believe that the Normative view removes the need for it. Two insights of radical empiricism in the tradition of Mill and Quine hold fast. The first is the uniformity thesis: there is no necessity which is somehow metaphysically 'higher' than the necessity possessed by laws of nature. The second is fallibilism about logic, mathematics, and science. However warranted we may be in accepting universal non-normative principles in any of these domains, including the purely logical, we cannot deduce that any of them are empirically indefeasible.[19] Furthermore the Normative view agrees with empiricism insofar as it rejects intuitionist realism and holds that all *factual* propositions are a posteriori. And it provides an epistemology of the a priori that bases it on our spontaneous dispositions. One may well urge that all the good insights of empiricism are captured by these points.

---

[18] Achilles and the Tortoise again: reasoning requires norms as well as facts.

[19] However, this is not the same as saying that the epistemic norms which (on the Normative view) *underlie* the non-normatively stated principles are indefeasible. See 20.6.

9

NON-MONOTONIC NORMS

We have now given normative definitions of aprioricity and necessity. As far as the purely definitional part of our account of normative epistemic concepts is concerned, the task that remains is to give definitions of evidence and probability. However, we should also sketch an account of the epistemic norms—a priori truths about epistemic reasons—that govern a posteriori warrants and non-deductive reasoning. They include norms of apperception and what I shall call receptivity—perception, memory, empathy with or understanding of the inner states of others, and perhaps testimony. They also include norms of induction and probability. A distinctive feature of all these norms, other than the norm of apperception, is that they are not monotonic. In that respect they differ from norms of deduction. The notion of monotonicity is explained in Section 9.4.

It is not the aim of this chapter to give fully worked out formulations of these non-monotonic norms, or to defend particular suggestions as to what they are against others. It is enough for our purposes to take a broad-church approach, indicating how various views can be characterized within our basic normative framework. I shall sometimes indicate my preferred options but keep track of how other options can fit in.

We should start from the contrast between apperception and perception.

9.1 Apperceptual and perceptual reasons

In 5.7 I introduced the notion of apperception and characterized it in epistemological terms. You apperceive the fact that *p* if and only if that fact is in your epistemic state: that is, if and only if that fact is a complete sufficient reason for you to believe that *p*. We noted that it also follows, given this characterization, that if you apperceive the fact that *p* you are warranted in believing that *p*; and further, that if you believe that *p* on the basis of apperceiving that *p* you know that *p*.

Wittgenstein thought that one cannot be said to *know* these apperceptual facts about oneself. I think he would also have claimed that one cannot be said to have *reason* to believe that they obtain; even that one cannot be said to *believe* that they do. These were claims about what he called the 'logical grammar' of the language game of avowals.[1] We shall not follow him. True—it is otiose to ask a person what reason he has for thinking he is thinking, or that he is in pain. But that is because the reason is obvious. If you think you are thinking, or in pain, you think so because it is so. It is, I submit, perfectly true, though usually pointless, to say that your reason for thinking you are in pain is that you are in pain. Likewise, it true to say, though usually pointless, that when you're in pain you usually know it. (Though you might be so distracted by something that is going on, such as the match you're taking part in, as to fail to realize it, etc.)

However, it is a good and important point that the question *how* you know—'how do you know you are in pain?', 'how do you know you are thinking?'—makes no sense, at least in ordinary contexts. There isn't a *way* in which you 'learn' of your pain, or of your thinking.[2] In contrast, it makes perfectly good sense to ask how you know it's raining. One way you might know it is by seeing that it is, another way is by feeling it on your skin, another is by hearing it on the roof, another is by being told that it is. It would be a basic error to think of apperception on this model, as though it was another *way* of knowing in this sense—a kind of perception of internal states of oneself. A fact that is apperceived is *not* perceived. When a fact is perceived there are two facts: the fact perceived, and the fact that it is perceived. There is a causal link from the former to the latter. In apperception that is not so. The apperceptual state may draw attention to itself, as in the case of a sudden pain, but attention is not a form of perception. Apperceptual knowledge is perception*less* knowledge: there is no way, no mode, by which you know yourself to be in the apperceptual state, though you may need to attend to it to know it.

The key is that apperceiving a state is just *being* in that state. Being in pain is apperceiving that I am in pain; thinking is apperceiving that I am thinking. With such states *esse* is *appercipi*. Their property of being apperceived is their essential property. There is, however, no class of objects of which it is true that *esse* is *percipi*, for apperception is not inner *perception*. These points will be discussed in 19.1[3]; in this chapter I shall simply assume that there are states of the self that fit the apperceptual epistemic—normative role: such facts as that I have an itch in my back, that I am getting hungry or that I am thinking about my lecture.

Apperceptual reasons are reasons for beliefs about one's current apperceptual states, and they consist of those very states. Contrast perceptual reasons. Suppose that the street

---

[1] 'It can't be said of me at all (except perhaps as a joke) that I *know* I am in pain. What is it supposed to mean—except perhaps that I *am* in pain?' Wittgenstein 1958a, §246. Compare p. 222:

I can know what someone else is thinking, not what I am thinking.
It is correct to say 'I know what you are thinking', and wrong to say 'I know what I am thinking'.
(A whole cloud of philosophy condensed into a drop of grammar.)

[2] Wittgenstein continues, in §246, 'Other people cannot be said to learn of my sensations *only* from my behaviour,—for I cannot be said to learn of them. I *have* them.'

[3] In defending them we must distinguish conceptual and pre-conceptual self-awareness. To have conceptual awareness of one's thinking is more than merely apperceiving it, in that it links conscious thinking to abilities to apply concepts. *Judgements* concerning apperceptual reasons, as against apperception itself, require concepts.

is wet, and that I can come to see that it is, for example, by walking over to the window and looking. On the assumption that if I can see that something is the case is then I can know that it is I can come to know in this way that the street is wet. Thus my epistemic field contains:

(i) the fact that the street is wet.

The assumption is not unrestrictedly true; there can be cases in which I am able to see that the street is wet but not able to know that it is. In such cases I am in fact seeing that the street is wet, but I have epistemic warrants that defeat my reason for thinking that I see it. Where that applies my epistemic field does not contain (i). Although I am seeing that the street is wet I cannot know that I am. Granting, however, that familiar purely sceptical arguments about perception lack force, there is indeed a broad range of normal cases in which seeing is knowing.

When I see that the street is wet, I have a visual experience as of seeing that the street is wet. Since this is an apperceptual state my epistemic field contains:

(ii) the fact that I have a visual experience as of seeing that the street is wet.

Furthermore, in the broad range of normal cases just mentioned my epistemic field also contains

(iii) the fact that I see the street is wet.

Which of these three facts gives me perceptual reason to believe that the street is wet? Going by what we would ordinarily say, it looks most implausible to claim that it's (i), the fact that the street is wet. If someone asks you how you know the street is wet, or what reason you have to think that it is, you wouldn't say 'Well, it *is* wet'. It would also be distinctly bizarre to answer with (ii)—'I have a visual experience as of seeing that the street is wet'. The fact that you *see* that it is, (iii), is a much more plausible candidate than either of these. You might well answer either question by saying 'I can see that it is wet'. The answer to either question might have been that you have been told, or that you can hear it raining, or that someone has just come in with a wet umbrella, etc.; in actual fact, however, you know it's wet because you can see it is.[4]

The perceptual reason for you to believe that the street is wet is the fact that you see it to be wet. There is, further, reason for you to believe that *you see it to be wet*: that reason is (in normal epistemic states) the apperceptual fact that you have a visual experience as of seeing that it's wet. To generalize: the fact that x perceives that p is sufficient reason for x to believe that p; if x has a perceptual experience as of perceiving that p, there is (in normal epistemic states) sufficient reason for x to believe that x perceives that p. A normal epistemic state, in this context, is a state which contains no epistemic warrants that defeat

---

[4] In many cases of course the very fact that you're being asked these questions might itself make you doubt whether you really can see that the street is wet. So imagine that you are being asked on the telephone, by someone who doesn't know that you're in a room with a window onto the street, who expects the street to be dry, and is very concerned to establish that it is. He might well ask you to state your reason for thinking it's wet.

x's reason for thinking that x perceives that p. (Perceptual experience is 'innocent unless proved guilty'—we shall come back to this.) So in these normal states x is warranted in believing that p, because warranted in believing that he perceives that p. He is so warranted even if in fact he does not perceive that p, so that there *is* no reason for him to believe that p. That is just a particular instance of the general point that a person can have a warrantable reason when there is no reason.[5]

Both perception and apperception that p can be termed 'direct awareness' that p. However, when I apperceive that p the fact that p itself gives me reason to believe that p, whereas when I perceive that p it is not the fact that p *itself* that gives me reason to believe that p. It is, rather, the fact that I perceive that p. But this contrast turns out to be not quite as sharp as it seems, once we take into account that apperceiving a state, such as that one has a seeming perception of rain, is identical with being in that state. This being so, we can say that the fact that gives me apperceptual reason to believe that p is indeed the fact that I apperceive that p—i.e. the fact that p.

9.2 Evidence and reasons to believe

Some of our beliefs are based on evidence. The evidence gives us reason to believe. Clearly the two epistemic concepts, *evidence that p* and *reason to believe that p*, are closely related; they are, nevertheless, not the same.

Evidence is evidence for the truth of a factual proposition. It is evidence that some fact obtains. We talk about evidence that the Earth is warming, that the crime was committed by Smith, and so on. It sounds slightly odd to talk about evidence for the *belief* that the Earth is warming; however, we naturally talk about evidence for the *conclusion* that the Earth is warming, or evidence in favour of a *hypothesis*. Both evidence and reasons to believe consist of facts. In the case of evidence the basic construction is *the fact that q is evidence that p*, while in the case of reasons it is *the fact that q is reason to believe that p*. So a pleasingly simple definition would be that a fact constitutes evidence that p if and only if it is reason to believe that p.

However that is too simple. There are, first, many cases in which it is correct to say that a fact is a reason to believe that p but not correct to say that it is *evidence* that p. For example, if there is sufficient reason to believe that that a proposition follows from some propositions there is sufficient reason to believe, then that is sufficient reason to believe it. It is not *evidence* that it's true. Again, we do not talk about *evidence* for normative conclusions. For example, the fact that an action causes suffering may give one reason to believe that it is wrong, but it is not *evidence* that it is wrong.[6] In the case of true purely normative

---

[5] Equally, if he perceives that p, but is not warranted in thinking that he does, then there *is* sufficient reason for him to believe that p even if he does not *have* sufficient reason. (This is worth noting before one engages in 'internalist' versus 'externalist' controversies about perceptual reasons.)

[6] Mill famously says that the fact that something is desired is evidence that it is desirable. He does so to avoid saying that it *proves* it's desirable; but this way of putting it is odd, and has caused much misunderstanding. What is true is that the fact that something is desired gives one some *prima facie* reason to think it desirable.

propositions (norms) there is outright reason to believe them; i.e. no fact constitutes the reason to believe them. *A fortiori*, one cannot say there is *evidence* for them.

It is even more important to take account of how the notion of evidence relates to apperception, perception, memory, and perhaps testimony. I have urged that it is perfectly correct to say that you can have beliefs about your own current apperceptual states and reasons for those beliefs. But it is not correct to say that what you think about those current states is based on *evidence*. Say that you are thinking about holidaying in Italy. You believe that you are, and your reason for your belief just is the fact that that is what you are thinking about. It rings false, however, to say that it is your *evidence*. That would be saying that the fact that you are thinking about holidaying in Italy is evidence of itself: evidence that you are thinking about holidaying in Italy. It can be evidence of something else, for example, that you are getting bored with the committee meeting, but it cannot be evidence of itself. Others may have evidence that that is what you are thinking about (you're looking at brochures, and so on), you do not.

It also sounds odd to say that the fact that I seem to perceive that p is evidence (for me) that I perceive that p; and equally odd to say that the fact that I perceive that p is (for me) evidence that p. These facts may, it seems, be evidence for other people, but *for me* the reason relations involved are not evidential relations.[7]

With memory and testimony it seems to get hazier. Here again, that you seem to remember that the street was wet is a reason for you to think that you do remember that (as ever in many but not all epistemic fields); that you remember that it was is a sufficient reason for you (or anyone) to think it was. In the case of memory, however, it seems less inappropriate to talk about evidence: it doesn't seem wrong, at least to me, to say that the fact that you seem to remember the street being wet is evidence that it was, for you as for others. In the case of testimony there is I think the same uncertainty. The fact that a friend has told me that Fiona is in Edinburgh may well be a reason to believe she is. Is it *evidence* that she is? We'll come back to these cases.

Evidence involves the notion of inference, and in particular, *a posteriori* inference. My seeming to see that the street is wet is not for me evidence that the street is wet, because it is (at least normally) wrong to say that I *infer* from my seeming to see to the conclusion that I see. The point is not that I don't infer it as a matter of fact; it's rather that normative reconstruction of what reason there is for me to believe the street is wet does not write in an inference at this point. Likewise in the case of memory, perception, and testimony: whether their deliverances constitute evidence turns on whether beliefs based on them are *inferred* from them.

---

[7] 'The situation in which I would properly be said to have *evidence* for the statement that some animal is a pig is that, for example, in which the beast itself is not actually on view, but I can see plenty of pig-like marks on the ground outside its retreat. If I find a few buckets of pig-food, that's a bit more evidence, and the noises and the smell may provide better evidence still. But if the animal then emerges and stands there plainly in view, there is no longer any question of collecting evidence; its coming into view doesn't provide me with more *evidence* that it's a pig, I can now just *see* that it is.' Austin 1962: 115 (quoted in Kelly 2008, §3). Austin notes that we do talk about the evidence of my own eyes, but holds that 'the point of this trope is exactly that it does *not* illustrate the ordinary use of "evidence"—that I *don't* have evidence in the ordinary sense'.

Nor do we say (usually) that a fact is evidence for a conclusion when it *entails* that conclusion. The fact that *p* is not *evidence* for the conclusion that *p or q*, for example, because that inference is a deductive inference. Taking these various points into account, can we characterize evidence in the following way?

    (1) The fact that *q* is evidence that $p =_{df}$ the fact that *q* constitutes a non-deductive inference-based reason to believe that *p*.

If so, then evidence is a species of epistemic reason.

However, this is not the only way we use the term 'evidence'. It seems that evidence that *p* can exist even when there *is* no reason to believe that *p*. Suppose marks on the bark of a tree are evidence of a certain disease in trees of that kind. Now suppose that one of those trees exists at a time before humans evolved, or in an area of space too far away for us to reach, and that it has those marks. Then it seems true that the marks on the bark of *that* tree are evidence that it has the disease. Yet this fact about its bark is not a reason for us to believe anything about the tree in question, since no facts about the tree, including this one, are in our epistemic field. On the basis of this kind of example it seems that evidence is not relativized to an epistemic field, whereas reasons to believe are.

Furthermore, even if the tree were in our epistemic field the marks on its bark might not constitute a reason to believe that it had the disease. They would be so only if the fact that these marks were often or always caused by the disease were also in our field. Thus the marks on the bark would be a reason to believe that the tree had the disease only where there was evidence for that generalization.

Compare the way we use 'evidence' when we say that the fact that all the swans in an epistemic field are white is evidence that all swans are white. It is evidence for that conclusion in *that* field; it is not evidence in epistemic fields which also contains non-white swans. Whether or not a fact constitutes evidence of this kind for a conclusion is relative an epistemic field.

Let us call the first kind of evidence, the kind that is unrelativized to an epistemic field, *indicative* evidence. Facts are indicative evidence that *p* if and only if they indicate that *p* in the sense of 2.5. An indicator is an effect of what it indicates, or it is an effect of a cause of what it indicates. Either way there is a causal connection between the indicator and what it indicates. So indicative evidence, or indication, is factive. For example, the fact that there's a footprint on the window sill is *indicative* evidence that the criminal went that way only if he caused it.

Let us call the second kind of evidence, the kind that is relativized to an epistemic field, *inductive evidence*. (1) will be our definition of *inductive evidence*. Thus the fact that all swans in an epistemic field are white is inductive evidence in that field that all swans are white.

We could say that inductive evidence, defined in terms of epistemic reasons, is the core notion; the appropriateness of the term 'evidence' in the indicative case still traces back to a connection with reasons: a fact is appropriately described as an *indicator*, or *indicative evidence*, that *p* only because there are epistemic fields in which it would be a reason to believe that *p*, based on inductive evidence. These epistemic fields are not constrained by location (where in space we could be). But they *are* relative to our receptive powers (together with extensions of them by means of detecting instruments). A sound that dogs can hear but we can't isn't evidence for us. On the other hand, the dog's ears pricking may be evidence for us. Thus it seems that indicators must be facts to which we would be receptive if we were in the right spatial position equipped with the right instruments.

9.3 Inductive evidence

One or both of two kinds of 'upward' inductive evidence to generalizations is usually recognized: enumerative inductive inference and hypothetical inference, 'inference to the best explanation'. Some philosophers have argued that only the first kind of inference is legitimate, others have argued that only the second kind is. We assume for present purposes that both are, and refer to *both* types of inference as inductive.

The basic idea of enumerative induction is that where a given proportion of the As in an epistemic field are Bs, that proportion of all As are Bs. But the epistemic field may also contain facts which imply that the given proportion is accidental, or remove the warrant for thinking that it is significant. Call such facts defeaters; then when the field contains no defeaters it is a *non-defeating* field. Now we can characterize the norm of enumerative inductive inference as follows:

(2) The fact that m/n (most, many, few) of the As in e are B is a specific reason, when e is non-defeating, to believe that m/n (most, many, few) of As are Bs.[8]

Following Reichenbach we can call this the *straight norm of induction*.[9] Note that (2) does not say how strong the specific reason is. Presumably—though this is not uncontroversial—in some cases it can become a sufficient reason. In any case it is a striking fact that inductions that match in formal respects, including their sample size, can generate very different degrees of reason to believe.[10] Plainly a reason based on the straight norm strengthens not just with the size of the sample but also with the variety of conditions in which the As occur, because that increases the probability that it is significant. Furthermore it is affected by the context of background theory, which may reduce the significance of the observed proportion or defeat it completely. There are plenty of other issues (for example, 'A' and 'B' should be 'projectible', so a question arises about how to characterize projectibility). We do not need to raise them here. (2), as it stands, is a good enough formulation for the questions we aim to discuss.

The principle of inference to the best explanation is:

---

[8] (10), below, refines this.

[9] Reichenbach 1948 (1935). I am calling it the straight norm, not the straight *rule*, because I take it to be an a priori true normative proposition. From the Normative standpoint there is a sharp distinction between norms and rules—see Chapter 18.

[10] This, not the issue of inductive scepticism, was the 'problem of induction' Mill sought to solve in the *System of Logic*.

(3) Where hypothesis h is the best explanation of some facts $p_i...p_n$ in e—taking account of all relevant facts in e—that is reason in e to believe h.

Now given our buck-passing account of 'good', this says that where h is the explanation that there is most reason to believe in e there is reason to believe it. However, a sceptic can argue that there is never any reason to believe any explanation, and so never any such thing as the 'best' explanation.

We may take it, on the contrary, that there is *some* reason to believe *any* candidate explanation that is empirically adequate, i.e. that would explain all the facts and contains no explanatorily redundant premises. A candidate explanation must posit some underlying causal powers or propensities and show how the *explanandum* flows from, or at least is probabilized by, these. Whatever the right way to spell this out may be, however, there must be criteria of what explanations are belief-worthy beyond mere predictive adequacy. Let's assume that these involve notions of simplicity and comprehensiveness plus some principle of conservative holism (requiring due weight to be given to what there is existing reason to believe). There may also be a priori or at least 'contextually a priori' constraints on what causal mechanisms there can be, e.g. principles of continuity and conservation, the principle that there is no action at a distance, or that nothing can travel faster than light. The best explanation—i.e. the one there is most reason to believe—is the one that most closely meets the criteria, taking into account their relative importance.

A belief-worthy explanation must be empirically adequate. However an *investigation*-worthy explanation need not be. There can be reason to investigate explanations that are promising by criteria other than empirical adequacy. A hypothesis with strong enough merits of simplicity and comprehensiveness can be worth investigating even if fails the adequacy criterion; and if it eventually passes it, it can outweigh the conservative criterion.

An enumerative induction that is *significant* is one that gives reason to believe that some underlying causal mechanism is involved. Where that is unknown we tend to treat the enumeratively-based generalization as at best a working hypothesis. An inference to an explanation appeals to the nature of things, observable and unobservable—to the way these things must work in virtue of their nature, the causal powers they have. In either case if we think there's sufficient reason to believe the inferred generalizations we think there is sufficient reason to include them in all suppositions; that is, we take them to be necessary. *Inductive inference is inference to necessary truths.* That is integral to our empirical realism about the world.

9.4 Defeasibility and monotonicity

Upward inductive evidence in general is field-relative, holistic, and defeasible; its governing principles are a priori non-monotonic norms. This is a convenient point to consider in more detail the concepts of defeasibility and monotonicity, and in particular distinguish the question whether a norm is monotonic from the question whether it is indefeasible.

Think of evaluative and practical norms as having the structure $\mathbf{R}(\pi_i, \psi)$, where π_i is a complete reason to ψ, and $\mathbf{R} = R$, R_o or S.[11] Let 'π_i+' refer to the union of π_i with any other facts. Then the evaluative or practical norm $\mathbf{R}(\pi_i, \psi)$ is monotonic if it entails that $\mathbf{R}(\pi_i+, \psi)$.

By this criterion all practical and evaluative norms are monotonic. Given that π_i is a complete reason to ψ, so is π_i+.[12] However, the case of epistemic norms is more complicated, because epistemic reasons are relative to epistemic fields. Think of them as having the structure $\mathbf{R}(<\pi_i, e>, \beta p)$, where '$<\pi_i, e>$' is a pair consisting of the facts that constitute the complete reason and a field in which they do.[13] Now consider these two claims:

(i) If $\mathbf{R}(<\pi_i, e>, \beta p)$ it follows that $\mathbf{R}(<\pi_i+, e>, \beta p)$, where the facts added to π_i in π_i+ are facts that are in e.

(ii) If $\mathbf{R}(<\pi_i, e>, \beta p)$ it follows that $\mathbf{R}(<\pi_i, e^*>, \beta p)$, where e^* is a strict improvement on e.

Since norms state complete reasons (i) is always true; (ii) may be false. It is (ii) that is relevant. An epistemic norm is monotonic if and only if (ii) is necessarily true. Ignoring the possibility that an epistemic norm, $\mathbf{R}(<\pi_i, e>, \beta p)$, may fail to apply in a sufficiently impoverished epistemic field, we can say it is monotonic if it is a necessary truth that for all e in which π_i obtain, $\mathbf{R}(<\pi_i, e>, \beta p)$.

Some epistemic norms are monotonic.[14] Apperceptual norms are: if the fact that p is an apperceptual fact then it follows from:

$\mathbf{R}(<\text{the fact that } p, e>, \beta p)$

that

$\mathbf{R}(<\text{the fact that } p, e^*>, \beta p)$.

If you apperceive that p that is a sufficient reason to believe that p whatever other facts obtain in your epistemic field, and so long as you apperceive that p that remains a sufficient reason, however we expand your field. So are deductive norms. Given, for example, that $\mathbf{R}(<\text{the fact that } p, e>, \beta(p \vee q))$ it follows that $\mathbf{R}(<\text{the fact that } p, e^*>, \beta(p \vee q))$. For this reason deductive norms support universal non-normative offshoots: if p then p or q. Logic can be expressed in the universal-factual mode because logical norms are monotonic.[15]

In contrast, inductive norms are non-monotonic. Thus take (2), enumerative induction. That is a non-monotonic norm, because it can be true that:

$\mathbf{R}(<\text{All As in e are Bs}, e>, \beta(\text{All As are Bs}))$

but false that

---

[11] Strictly speaking, the norm, i.e. the *a priori* truth, has the form 'If it is the case that Π_i then $\mathbf{R}(\pi_i, \psi)$'. See 5.6. But we can ignore that here.
[12] In saying this I am disallowing the possibility that complete reasons can be 'silenced'. See 5.6.
[13] Strictly speaking, again, where Π_j are the propositions whose truth would constitute $<\pi_i, e>$, the norm is: if it's the case that Π_j, then $\mathbf{R}(<\pi_i, e>, \beta p)$.
[14] Which is not to say, of course, that people who apply them never make mistakes.
[15] See 8.9. The point will come up again in 20.5.

R(<All As in e are Bs, $e^\star$>, β(All As are Bs).

For example, $e^\star$ may contain an A that is not B (a black swan).

Hypothetical inference is also non-monotonic. Suppose I observe that the audience at a lecture is yawning. Is that a reason to believe they're bored? I reasonably take it to be such because given the available data, that is a good explanation. But now you tell me that the people in this audience have had no sleep for a week and that you know them to be very interested in the subject which the lecture concerns. Of course, a lecture may be boring even though the topic is interesting, so the probability that the audience is very tired does not preclude the possibility that they are also bored. Nevertheless, given this information I would no longer be warranted in taking the fact that they're yawning to be a reason to believe they're bored. Two explanations of why they are yawning are now available: that they are bored; and that they are tired.

The distinction between monotonicity and non-monotonicity applies to norms. We can derivatively apply it to reasons: those that instantiate monotonic norms are monotonic, while those that instantiate non-monotonic norms are non-monotonic. Thus apperceptual reasons are monotonic, as are reasons that instantiate deductive norms. (Of course a deduction may lead one to reject a conclusion and hence a premise. What we are talking about here is whether a valid deduction from some *facts* is defeasible.)

We should distinguish between the monotonicity or non-monotonicity of a norm and its defeasibility or indefeasibility. Since norms are a priori, reasons to believe them are outright reasons. But we have seen that outright reasons too are relative to an epistemic field. Thus we can ask, of any ostensible norm **N** which there is outright reason to believe in our *e*, whether it follows that there would be outright reason to believe it in any $e^\star$. That is, whether:

R(<∅, *e*>, β**N**) entails that **R**(<∅, $e^\star$>, β**N**)

If it does not, then **N** is defeasible, whether or not it is monotonic. (Because the higher-order norm, **R**(<∅, *e*>, β**N**), is non-monotonic.)

We noted in 5.8 that higher-order warrants are indefeasible. That is, if in *e* the belief that **R**(β**N**) is warranted, it is warranted in all $e^\star$ that that belief is warranted in *e*. It does not follow that the belief that **R**(β**N**) is warranted in $e^\star$. The indefeasibility of higher-order warrants leaves open the possibility that norms are defeasible. It remains possible that we may be warranted in *e* in believing that some norm obtains, but not warranted in believing that in some $e^\star$.

Applying these points about defeasibility to epistemic reasons, we see that *prima facie* an epistemic reason is defeasible in two ways: (i) because it is non-monotonic; and (ii) because the norm it instantiates is defeasible. The most radical fallibilism would say that all norms, as well as all factual propositions, are defeasible. That is very strong; too strong, I shall maintain in 20.6: norms, whether monotonic or non-monotonic, are indefeasible. If the argument there is sound, then for *reasons* (as against norms) defeasibility and non-monotonicity come down to the same thing. But for now let us return to another class of epistemic norms.

9.5 Non-inductive, non-monotonic norms: norms of receptivity

Induction can warrant factual beliefs only if some factual beliefs are warranted in another way. Thus if we have factual warrants at all some must be non-inductive.

Apperceptual warrants are the clearest case. If apperceptual plus inductive epistemic norms are the only ones, then all our factual warrants must be based on explanatory inferences from the apperceived facts. On this account, the fabric of our factual beliefs gets its ultimate support from the normative pillars of (i) apperception; and (ii) inference to the best explanation alone. That has a certain elegant economy to it, but it seems a very implausible view. So are there other non-inductive factual warrants? The most plausible candidates are those based on putative norms of perception and memory. Let us see what these norms might be.

Suppose I seem to see a red surface. Then (in most epistemic fields) there's reason for me to believe that I see a red surface. Not in every field: in some fields there are facts which give me sufficient reason to believe that I am not or may not be perceiving a red surface: for example, that there isn't one there or that my visual impression is not being caused by any such surface. Similar principles govern the other modes of perception. In general, an epistemic field in which x has the perceptual impression that p may contain facts which give reason to believe that x's perceptual impression is not, or may not be, caused by the fact that p. If these reasons are strong enough to defeat x's *prima facie* perceptual warrant for the belief that p, they are defeaters.[16] So like the norm of enumerative induction the norm of perception must refer to *non-defeating* fields:

> (4) The fact that x has a perceptual impression as of seeing that p is sufficient reason in a non-defeating e to believe that x perceives that p.

I am placing no constraints on the content of perceptual impressions other than those entailed by the possibilities of perception itself. Thus one can have a perceptual impression that the front of the cathedral is lopsided, that a bell of a certain timbre and pitch is tolling a particular rhythm behind one to the left, or that there is a smell of a certain kind and strength in a certain location. (But one can't have a perceptual impression that 16 times 20 is 320, that a particular response is irritating, or that it's time to leave.) A being's perceptual impressions can have highly complex contents even if it does not have the conceptual resources to describe those contents—though it must have those conceptual resources to respond to the *norm* such. Or rather, having the conceptual resources *is* being able to respond to the norm as such, as will be discussed in Chapter 18.

Now we can have:

> $R(<x$ has a perceptual impression that $p, e>, \beta(x$ perceives that $p))$

---

[16] In a defeating e x's perceptual impression may or may not still constitute some degree of reason to believe that x perceives that p. For example, if x is taking in part in some laboratory experiment on perception, and knows it, it may constitute no reason at all.

but it may nonetheless fail to be true that

> **R**(<x has a perceptual impression that p, $e^\star$>, β(x perceives that p))

since $e^\star$ may contain all the relevant facts contained in e, but some defeaters as well.

So if this is a norm, it is both a non-inductive and a non-monotonic norm. But is it a norm—an a priori truth? Seeing a red surface is a causal process, in which a red surface causes visual impressions in the perceiver. Hence if my perceptual impression gives me reason to believe that there is a red surface there before me, it gives me reason to believe that that surface is causing in me a visual impression. Am I non-inductively warranted in thinking this? Or does my visual impression constitute a warrant for the perceptual judgement only in epistemic states in which there is also warrant for an appropriate theory of perception, grounded in an inference to best explanation? That is, only if I have theory-based warrant to treat the visual impression as indicative evidence?

This is a very big question, which for our purposes we do not need to resolve. Still, it seems implausible that induction could carry this much weight. As already noted, we don't think of the belief that I see a red surface as an *inference-based* belief on my part, or of my visual impression as *evidence* to *me* that I am seeing.

It is even more implausible in the case of memory. It seems quite implausible to think of memory-based warrants as requiring an egocentric explanatory inference from my apperceptual states now. There is, rather, a *norm* of memory:

> (5) The fact that x has an impression as of remembering that p is sufficient reason, in a non-defeating e, to believe that x remembers that p.

We are thus led to the idea that there are non-monotonic norms of perception and memory which hold in their own right, and provide a context *within which* inductive norms operate. Can we add any others?

Two traditional, more contestable, candidates that present themselves concern other minds and testimony. Suppose, to take the first of these, that you touch a very hot surface, leap back, cry out, clutch your hand. These observable facts are reasons for onlookers to believe that you're in pain. Is it appropriate to call them *evidence* that you're in pain? The same issues arise. Do we *infer* from them, by an explanatory inference, that you are in pain? Or do we just *see* that you are in pain, where seeing involves a sense or insight that we have for the subjectivity, the thoughts and feelings, of our fellows, grounded in their behaviour and expression?[17] We *see* that you are happy, irritated, taken aback, puzzled. We *hear* the tension in your voice. Let's call this ability to sense what others are feeling and thinking on the basis of perceiving their behaviour empathy. We then have the following putative norm:

> (6) The fact that x has an empathetic impression that p is sufficient reason in a non-defeating e to believe that x is empathetically aware that p.

---

[17] Compare McDowell 1998b, Chapter 17, 'Criteria, Defeasibility, and Knowledge', and on testimony, Chapter 19, 'Knowledge by Hearsay'.

Behaviour and expression is the medium in which I see that you are happy, embarrassed, distracted. And again this empathetic awareness is a causal process.

The lesser plausibility stems not from any difference in the normative structure but from the fact that behaviour and expression are often enigmatic. One is often unsure what they signify. In contrast perceptual impressions are almost always transparent. But still this seems a matter of degree not of kind. In perception too, one may not be sure what one is seeing—it's distance, size, etc.—while with empathy one often distinctly senses what a person is thinking or feeling without being at all conscious of the *way* in which one does. In either case, when transparency fails, the medium obtrudes, and becomes the opaque object of attention.

Testimony can be fitted into this framework. Thomas Reid's 'principle of credulity'[18] can be treated as a non-inductive norm:

> (7) The fact that x is told that p is sufficient reason in e to believe that x can know by testimony that p unless there are defeaters—facts in e which give reason to believe that what x is told does not reliably originate from the fact that p.

In this case the medium is not perception, memory, or empathy, but testimony, being told that.

Let's generalize. Let $I_x p$ be an operator on the proposition that p that says that x is in one of these putatively receptive or information-receiving states, where the putative information is that p. Then the general norm is the *norm of receptivity*:

> (8) The fact that $I_x p$ is sufficient reason in a non-defeating e to believe that x knows that p.

Whichever specific cases—perception, memory, empathy, and testimony—we include, the general norm can be thought of in three ways.

- There is first the *purely inductive* view. Here the medium—perceptual and memory impressions, expressive behaviour, telling—is thought of as indicative evidence, whose status as such we know by inference to the best explanation. So there is no norm of receptivity as such. There are only inductive norms.

- Then there is the *a priori evidence* view. Here too the medium is thought of as indicative evidence. But we do not identify it as indicative evidence by inductive methods. There is a norm which gives it a priori standing as such; it defeasibly warrants the claim that $I_x p$ is indicative evidence that p. Thus the norm of receptivity takes the form:

    S(the fact that $I_x p$, non-defeating e, β(the fact that $I_x p$ is indicative evidence that p).

- Finally there is the *transparent medium* view. Here the medium—perceptual or empathetic impression, another's telling—is not thought of as indicative *evidence* from which

---

[18] 'a disposition to confide in the veracity of others, and to believe what they tell us'. Reid 1817 (1764): 353–4 (Chapter VI, sect. 24.) For the way in which norms like (7) are based on spontaneous dispositions see Chapter 16.

one *infers*. It is 'transparent': we, so to speak, see through it to the facts themselves. Here too the norm of receptivity applies; but this view insists that the medium whereby we know (when we do know) is not best thought of as *evidence*.

Each of these approaches involve appeal to epistemic norms. The purely inductive view requires no non-monotonic epistemic norms beyond those involved in induction; but as I noted, it seems very implausible on its own—though it can still have a role in strengthening the degree of overall reason to believe propositions which get their primary epistemic support from the norm of receptivity.

So we are led to one of the other views. The distance between them is small compared to the distance between them and the purely inductive view. Both appeal to non-inductive, non-monotonic norms; it is a matter of which formulation best captures our thinking. I think the transparent medium view captures it best. It's not just that we do not actually *infer*, even a priori, to what we see from our seeming seeings. We do not think of it even in principle as an inferential move, or of seeming seeings as evidence—even though we think they can be defeated. Of course, this view must allow that we can detach from the medium, in order to consider its reliability on a particular occasion, or more radical hypotheses. It is via such detachment that we are led to think of perception, and receptivity in general, as a causal process. Detachment involves a shift to a third-personal stance: an empirically realist view of one's own receptive powers. The shift facilitates scientific inquiry, while at the epistemological level it tends to push towards either scepticism or the purely inductive view. But that push can and should be resisted.

9.6 Probability, frequency, and propensity

The final set of epistemic norms I want to consider are those involved in probabilistic reasoning.

How do propositions about probability relate to propositions about epistemic reasons? By now in our study an attractively simple view offers itself: they *are* propositions about epistemic reasons. Talk of probabilities is talk of epistemic reasons. 'It's probable that p' means 'There's some degree of reason to believe that p'. 'There's an m/n probability that p' means 'There's a reason of m/n degree to believe that p'. 'π_i probabilizes the proposition that p to degree m/n' means 'π_i is a specific reason of degree m/n to believe that p'. This normative definition, we shall argue, is correct. It makes immediate sense of two important points. First, both propositions about probability and propositions about epistemic reasons assert some relation between a proposition and an epistemic field. Second, an assessment of overall degree of probability, like an assessment of overall reason to believe, must take into account all relevant facts in the field.[19] The epistemic field that is being referred can vary; but I take it that in normal contexts an assumption of adequate knowledge is involved. That is, if I *tell* a person, without qualification, what the probability of something is I am

---

[19] Carnap's requirement of total evidence again, mentioned in Chapter 2, footnote 13.

implicitly indicating that I have *adequate* knowledge of the relevant facts, and if I *ask* a person what it is, I am implicitly assuming that they have adequate knowledge. If they think they do not, their answer should be that they don't know, or it should at least be qualified by explicit reference to their epistemic field. We shall come back to this.

But first we must take into account some different, non-normative, interpretations of the probability concept. Some probability theorists hold that when we talk of probabilities we are referring to frequencies of some kind. Others hold that when we talk of probabilities we are at least sometimes referring to chances or propensities, understood non-epistemically as determinate dispositions or tendencies of objects or states of affairs. Let us consider these views in turn.

Observable frequencies constitute inductive evidence for propositions about probability. They are better or worse evidence depending on their diversity and size. However, that does not show that probability propositions *refer* to frequencies. The difficulties that arise if one tries to give a frequency interpretation of the *meaning* of 'probable' are telling. The reference cannot be to finite frequencies, since it's possible that the probability of an outcome differs from the frequency of the outcome in any finite set of instances. It cannot be to limiting frequencies in an actual infinite sequence of instances, since such infinite sequences may not actually exist. So should we define 'probable' in terms of limiting frequencies in a *hypothetical* infinite sequence conducted under 'laboratory conditions'? Suppose the probability that a specific die will fall on one of its faces is 1/6. Does it follow, deductively, that if it were thrown an infinite number of times in those conditions (without any change to the underlying properties of the die, the throw and the environment) it would fall on that face with a frequency of 1/6? I don't believe it does. What is true is that the fact that the probability is 1/6 is sufficient *reason* to believe that it would: to believe that that would be the limiting frequency. That is one of the norms determining the concept of probability. Consider also the converse: suppose it true that if this die were thrown in these conditions an infinite number of times it would fall on the given face with a frequency of 1/6. Does it follow deductively that the probability of it falling on that face on this throw is 1/6? Again it seems not. Once again, it is just that if that counterfactual fact could be in an *e* it would constitute sufficient reason to believe that the probability is 1/6.

We take the probability to depend on the die's propensity. We think the die has a propensity, a necessary tendency, to fall on any given face, supervening by natural necessity on the die's fundamental properties—or just *being* one of its fundamental properties (as the indeterministic propensity of a radioactive mass to emit particles might be one of its fundamental properties). Given the straight norm of induction, frequencies are evidence of propensities. Knowledge of propensities, in turn, warrants expectations about frequencies. This too holds in virtue of norms of probability. Thus, for example, if we take the die to have a propensity to fall on a given face 1/6 of the time (other things equal) we are warranted, absent defeating information, in expecting it to fall that way with a limiting relative frequency of 1/6.

Suppose I say that there's an even chance the bull in this field will charge at interlopers—what is it I'm saying? I may be saying that relative to my epistemic field there is a 0.5 degree of overall reason to think that it will charge at anyone who enters the field and a

0.5 degree overall reason to think it will not. I will base my actions on that. Or I may be attributing to it a 0.5 propensity to charge. That is a property it has, supervening by natural necessity on its fundamental properties. (We can also talk about the propensity of the actual bull-in-field situation, as against the bull.)

Propensities exist, whether they all arise from initial conditions by deterministic laws, or whether some are fundamentally indeterministic. Or rather, we have no reason to deny they do, given our concerns in this book. Our question, granting that the notion of propensity is cogent, is whether *any* sense, *the* sense, or *one* sense, of 'probable' is definable by propensity.

Propensity cannot be the only sense of probability. When we talk about the probability of a hypothesis, an explanation, we are not talking about propensities. We are talking about how much reason there is to believe it. Is there then more than one sense of 'probable'—a normative sense and a propensity sense?

If the bull has a 0.5 propensity to charge, that fact, in an e in which there are no other relevant knowable facts, constitutes an overall reason of degree 0.5 to expect it to charge. Relevant facts are facts which give one greater reason to believe that it will charge than its propensity as such would give, such as that it is being goaded, or which give one reason to believe that its propensity is blocked or impeded, such as that it is tethered or sedated. The probability that it will charge is altered by these other facts, which should all be taken into consideration insofar as they are in e.

Thus we have the following *propensity* norm of probability:

(9) In a non-defeating e the fact that y has an m/n propensity to ξ in c is an m/n overall reason to believe that y will ξ in c.

On the normative definition of 'probable', this is the same as:

(9*) In a non-defeating e the fact that y has an m/n propensity to ξ in c gives an m/n probability that y will ξ in c.

The relationship between propensity and probability is captured by this norm; we do not need to introduce a special propensity sense of 'probable'.

Indeed rather than analysing probability in terms of propensity it is more plausible to fix the reference of 'propensity' in terms of probability and thus in terms of epistemic reasons. To say that y has an m/n propensity to ξ in c is to say that y has some property F in virtue of which, when no facts other than it's being F are taken into account, there is an m/n probability that it will ξ in c.[20] On this account propensities are second-order properties of objects: epistemic reason-giving properties of the objects' properties. The task of inquiry is to discover their ground—the property F.

But what if we have no idea of propensities, but know something of frequencies? That brings us back to the straight norm, (2); but we should now take into account Hempel's

---

[20] Of course in a defeating field the fact that y has an m/n propensity to ξ in c may or may not constitute a specific reason to believe that y will ξ in c. If we know that the bull is tethered the fact that it has that propensity to charge is no reason to expect that it will charge at all.

'requirement of maximal specificity'. This says that to determine on the basis of purely statistical information what degree of overall reason there is in *e* to believe of a particular *y* that it's a B we must place it in its narrowest 'reference class'.[21] Consider all those generalizations in *e* whose consequents are 'is a B', and under which *y* falls; take the probability that *y* is B to be that given by the most specific of these. (The characterization AC is more specific than A, and so on.) We then have the following refinement of the straight norm:

> (10) In a non-defeating *e* in which A is the maximally specific characterization with respect to B, and there is sufficient reason to believe that m/n As are Bs, that fact gives a specific reason of m/n degree to believe that if *y* is A, *y* is B.[22]

y may fall under non-overlapping generalizations: n% of As are Bs, and m% of Cs are Bs. In such situations there is, arguably, no usefully stateable general norm for judging overall degree of reason on the basis of specific reasons. (The same, as we shall see, applies to practical reasons.)

So far we have been considering probabilities relative to propensities or frequencies in an *e*. But propositions about propensities and frequencies will themselves be more or less probable, and so will propositions about what descriptions objects fall under. These probabilities will themselves be relative to an epistemic field. Thus we have to work out the probability of an outcome in *e*—the degree of overall reason to expect it in *e*—from probabilities of frequencies or propensities, and probabilities that the objects fall under the frequencies or propensities. How we do this depends on a calculus of probabilities. But what is the right calculus? Do probabilities as epistemic reasons satisfy the standard Kolmogorov calculus?

9.7 Do epistemic reasons satisfy the probability calculus?

Formulations of this calculus vary. For our purposes we can state its three basic axioms: *non-negativity*; *normalization*; and *additivity*, as follows. Non-negativity says that the probability of any proposition is greater or equal to zero. Normalization says that the probability of analytic truths is one. Additivity says that if the probability that P&Q is zero the probability that PvQ is the probability that P plus the probability that Q.

An intuitively helpful model of the probability calculus is provided by the notion of proportion: take the probability of A to be that proportion of some whole, total, or set, which is A. However, this model does not tell us what probability actually is. For example, the probability of a hypothesis has nothing to do with any notion of proportion, but does have to do with how much reason there is, overall, to believe it. Similarly with an apperceptually grounded proposition. Furthermore, I have argued that 'probable' is not an

---

[21] Hempel 1965: 399–401.
[22] It's quite plausible to hold that what the straight norm actually governs is evidence of propensities—necessary tendencies—rather than degrees of epistemic reason as such. On that formulation we would get to (10) indirectly, via (9).

ambiguous term but has just the one normative meaning: probability is degree of overall epistemic reason. Thus the question should be whether the standard probability calculus fits our normative definition of probability rather than *vice versa*.

So can we interpret the standard axioms in terms of epistemic reasons? We must first accept that probability (unlike propensity) is relative to an epistemic field. We then read 'The probability that p in e' as 'The degree of overall reason to believe that p in e'. On this interpretation non-negativity says that there cannot be *less* reason in any e to believe a proposition than no reason at all. Normalization serves two functions: it provides a benchmark maximum value (there cannot be greater overall reason to believe anything than there is to believe an analytic truth); and it lays down the maximum value as 1. This raises a question: does it make sense to think of overall epistemic reasons as having a maximal value?

Since we are taking epistemic reasons to be relations to facts in an epistemic field, the possibility that degrees of *subjective certainty* can rise without limit is irrelevant. I propose that we take *sufficient reasons* as the upper limit on overall degrees of reason to believe. That is, a probability with the value 1 is a sufficient reason, which is an overall reason of degree of 1. There is outright sufficient reason to believe an analytic truth. There is outright sufficient reason to believe norms (a priori normative truths). There can be a posteriori sufficient reason to believe a proposition, such as that it is raining.

But can't propositions which there is *sufficient* reason to believe differ in the *overall degree* of reason to believe them? That is, can there not be sufficient reason to believe that p and sufficient reason to believe that q but more reason to believe that p than to believe that q? There is, for example, sufficient reason for me to believe that $2 + 2 = 4$, and sufficient reason to believe that I've ordered a taxi, but can't there be more reason for me to believe the one than the other?

If the normative interpretation of probability is to satisfy the standard calculus the answer must be negative. It may help to make this reply plausible if we note that there is a difference between the probability a proposition has in a field and the probability, in that field, that it will be defeated in an enlarged field. Thus we can have:

(11) There is some degree, d_1, of overall reason in e to believe that p.

(12) There is some degree, d_2, of overall reason in e to believe that $\neg(\exists e^*)(\neg Sp \text{ in } e^*)$.

d_1 can differ from d_2. Furthermore, there can be sufficient reason to believe that p ($d_1 = 1$), even if $d_2 > 0$.[23] True, there can be 'downward leakage' from (12) to (11). If, for example, I have sufficient experience of my apparent memories being wrong, my apparent memory of having ordered a taxi may cease to be a sufficient reason for the belief that I have. But downward leakage is not automatic. There can be more reason for me to believe that my belief that $2 + 2 = 4$ will not be defeated than for me to believe that my belief that I have ordered a taxi will not be defeated, but still equal overall reason for me to believe both these propositions. If in each case that is a sufficient reason, then there is equal overall reason to believe each.

---

[23] It will still be the case that $Sp \rightarrow SS_\mu p$, as claimed in 8.6 (see (13) there).

What about additivity? A first question here, of course, is whether degrees of epistemic reason can be placed on an additive scale at all. We should not exclude the possibility that they cannot be. But then that applies to probability as well. It is far from clear that all probability judgements can be represented by an additive scale. We may simply have no idea what the probability of, or overall degree of reason to believe, a proposition is, or only a very vague or rough idea. Then there is the possibility of incommensurable or discontinuous probabilities. On the normative interpretation, the first point refers to the possibility that we may have no *warranted* reason for any belief about what the overall degree of reason to believe a proposition relative to our e is. If we needed to aquire a warranted belief about probabilities, we would have to do some inquiring. As to the second point, incommensurability or discontinuity of probabilities amount to incommensurability or discontinuity of epistemic reasons. But while practical and evaluative reasons may exhibit these features (14.4), I must say that I find no intuitive examples for the case of *overall* epistemic reasons. There can be discontinuity between overall and sufficient reasons: the strength of an overall reason can approach indefinitely close to 1, so you can always have a stronger overall reason without ever getting a sufficient reason, as in the stadium example below. There might also be incommensurabilities between different kinds of specific epistemic reason. But what we are interested in is whether degrees of *overall* reason can be added. Some idealization is involved; but we can still ask whether probabilities/degrees of overall reason can be represented by real numbers which satisfy the probability calculus.

Let's assume such idealization is useful enough to make the question worth asking. It then seems unproblematic to hold that degrees of overall reasons cannot add up to more than 1. But can they add up to less than 1? May there not be no overall reason (or very little reason) to believe that p *and* no overall reason (or very little reason) to believe that $\neg p$, even though there's sufficient reason to believe that p $\vee$ $\neg p$?

Take a two-horse race. Might it not be the case, for some epistemic fields, that there's *no* reason to believe Dobbin will win and *no* reason to believe that Neddy will win, even though there is sufficient reason to believe that one of them will win? But if we agreed that there is no reason to believe that Dobbin will win, our interpretation of the probability calculus would require us to hold that there is sufficient reason to believe that Dobbin will *not* win—a clearly false conclusion. If overall reasons are to model the calculus, we must say that since there is equal reason to believe that Dobbin will win and that Neddy will win, and sufficient reason to believe that one of them will, the degree of overall reason to believe of either one of them that it will win = 0.5.

When I say that I have no reason to believe that Dobbin will win, or lose, I think I mean that I have no *specific* reason. I am aware of no facts, such as previous form, which provide evidence that he will win, or that he will lose. Is this consistent with holding that my degree of *overall* reason = 0.5?[24]

---

[24] I am now putting this in terms of warranted reasons, so we are asking about probabilities on my s. We could equally put it in terms of e. The same principles apply.

Suppose you have a set of n mutually incompatible propositions of which you know that one is true. But you have no more reason to believe that any one of them is true than any other. You know, for example, that Fred is in a European capital but you have absolutely no idea which one.

There is a sense in which you have no reason to believe that Fred is in Bucharest: you have no *specific* reason to believe that he is. Yet there is a sense in which you *do* have *some* reason to believe that he is in Bucharest: he is in a European capital and Bucharest is one of them. If someone asked you whether you had any reason to think he was in Bucharest, you might answer yes or no depending on what that person could already be assumed to know. Or you might say, 'Well, I know that he is in one of the European capitals, but I have no specific reason to think it is Bucharest'. The point of the first part of this answer is to give your questioner a relevant piece of information: relevant in that it gives *some* reason to think that Fred is or 'may be' in Bucharest (but definitely not in Dijon).

Since there is sufficient reason to believe that $p \vee \neg p$, the probability that $p \vee \neg p = 1$. By the probability calculus, since $\text{prob}(p \& \neg p) = 0$, $\text{prob}(p) + \text{prob}(\neg p) = 1$. True, if someone asked you whether there is any reason to believe that p, it would be very odd to tell him it was 0.5 just because excluded middle applies, and because you have no specific reason to believe that p rather than that *not-p*. But then it would be equally odd to give that answer if they asked you whether there was any probability that p. Your answer is correct relative to your epistemic state, but they are not asking you about your epistemic state. As noted above, to give information about probabilities is to imply contextually that one has knowledge of relevant facts. You are being asked whether there is any degree of overall reason to believe that p under the assumption that you have or may have that relevant knowledge.[25]

Suppose now that the situation is as follows. Either it's the case that p, in which case damaging consequences will follow against which you can insure, or it's the case that $\neg p$, in which case other damaging consequences will follow against which you can also insure. You have no specific reason to believe that p, and no specific reason to believe that $\neg p$. If that literally meant that you had *no* reason to believe either proposition, you would have no reason to take out insurance against either set of consequences. But clearly you do have reason to take out insurance against each eventuality. You should decide what insurance to take in light of the fact that you have overall reason of 0.5 degree to expect each.

Thus we are led to the following norm, the norm of *indifference*:

> (13) If in e there is sufficient reason to believe that one of p_n mutually exclusive propositions is true, and the degree of overall reason to believe that p_i = the degree of overall reason to believe that p_j, then the degree of overall reason to believe any proposition in $p_n = 1/n$

This, on our interpretation, is the distinctive norm that underlies the probability calculus. It determines degrees of overall reason to believe even when no specific reasons are available.

---

[25] Similarly, if someone asks you what the best way out of the forest is, and you have no idea, you should say that you don't know, rather than saying that the best way is to follow a random straight line.

This norm has also sometimes been called the *principle of insufficient reason*; that name fits our normative interpretation of probability very well. The principle says that where there is *insufficient* reason to differentiate degrees of *overall* reason there is *sufficient* reason to consider them equal.

Consider, finally, the stadium puzzle: n people have entered the stadium but we know that only m ($m < n$) have gone through the turnstile and paid. In the absence of any other information, the higher n is and the lower m is the higher the probability that any one of these people did not pay. But there is a reluctance to believe that this probability can ever constitute sufficient reason to believe that each one of them did not pay. This is consistent with our interpretation: the degree of overall reason approaches 1 without ever getting there. But what is behind this: why don't we think such probabilistic evidence can ever constitute sufficient reason to believe any given individual did not pay? Because sufficient a posteriori reason, in this case at least, requires specific reason—indicative evidence. For example, a piece of fabric left on a spike on the wall which matches a tear in someone's suit and thus identifies that particular person. Thus in criminal courts, where the standard of proof applied is 'beyond reasonable doubt', what is wanted is sufficient reason to believe that the accused is guilty, and that requires specific reasons, not just a 'balance of probabilities'.

It is illuminating to consider this in the light of the WK principle (5.10): if one's belief is warranted one is warranted in believing that one knows. To believe that p from warrant is to believe that there is sufficient reason in one's s for the belief that there is sufficient reason in e to believe that p. One's belief that p is warranted only if one is warranted in believing that one *knows* that p. But the mere fact that there is a very high probability, for any given individual, that he did not come through the turnstile cannot give one knowledge that he did not, whereas specific indicative evidence that picks him out can do so.

All this is consistent with the indifference norm. Indifference is the distinctive norm of probability but not the *only* norm that governs probability propositions. Since probability propositions are propositions about overall epistemic reasons, the other epistemic norms we have been considering all bear on them. Each of them can be the source of a probability judgement. The probability calculus only comes in when we have, in one way or another, estimated the strengths of overall reasons.

9.8 Bayesianism

The normative interpretation is much closer to Bayesianism than to the frequency and propensity views, but it differs in two respects. The first, in some ways less important, is that the Normative view does not postulate degrees of belief, as against degrees of reason to believe. Bayesianism takes the opposite line: it postulates degrees of belief, and 'rational constraints' on degrees of believe provided by the probability calculus, but no epistemic reasons. The second difference is that the normative interpretation, unlike the most common versions of Bayesianism, is neither subjectivist nor non-cognitivist about probability propositions.

The idea of a degree of belief is obscure. Belief, unlike feeling, does not come in degrees. One can feel more or less strongly, but one cannot believe more or less strongly. It makes sense to say that there is *sufficient* reason to feel a *little* grateful; what could it mean to say that there is sufficient reason to believe a *little*?[26] True, we can be more or less sure: more or less strongly *inclined* or *disposed* to believe. The strength of a belief disposition might be measured by how hard it would be to remove or block it; we can also often tell its strength in a first-person way. But the important point is that belief dispositions and reasons to believe don't invariably correlate; the strength of one's disposition to believe often diverges from what one thinks to be the strength of reason to believe, and certainly from the actual strength of reason to believe. I may be strongly disposed to believe something while holding that there is not much reason to believe it. Nor am I contradicting myself if I say that I 'can't help' being strongly inclined to believe something even though I realize it is not probable.

Furthermore when I have no warrant to make a judgement that I need for action, even though I am strongly inclined to believe it—for example, when the issue is whether a student is cheating in an examination—it is never the case that I should act on my brute dispositions to believe, and often not the case that I should act on the probabilities relative to my s. What is often true is that I should inquire further. In general, unless I simply want to enjoy a gamble, and subject to opportunity cost, I should seek to act (i.e. am warranted in seeking to act) on the best available information, estimating probabilities relative to that. The decision problem for me in a particular case is whether I am warranted in seeking further information. The 'in principle' answer is determined by applying the correct theory of rational choice—expected utility or some other—to my pure practical reasons and my warranted probabilities, i.e. the probabilities relative to my s. (There are puzzling questions about 'second-best' strategies when the 'in principle' answer is unavailable, but we can ignore them here.)

Thus when I make a judgement about probabilities I am never making a judgement about the strength of my dispositions to believe. I am making a judgement about the strength of my epistemic reasons relative to one or another field.

Bayesianism starts from the wrong place—the actor's dispositions to believe. Dispositions are indeed relevant to the *epistemology* of epistemic norms, as dispositions to act are relevant to the epistemology of practical reasons, and dispositions to feel to the epistemology of evaluative reasons. We shall consider the epistemology of reasons in Chapter 16. But they are not what probability judgements are *about*. Having started from the wrong place Bayesianism then inserts a correction designed to get it back to a more plausible position. The correction identifies probabilities with 'rational' degrees of belief—degrees of belief consistent with the probability calculus. But from its own subjectivist starting point this constraint is arbitrary, while from a more plausible

---

[26] There is the usage 'I strongly believe that'. This was discussed in Chapter 2, footnote 21.

standpoint it is too weak. I can have crazy degrees of belief, and still be consistent with the probability calculus.[27] These degrees of belief have nothing to do with what the probabilities for me are. That is a normative question: it depends on what there is reason to believe relative to my epistemic field.

What you should* believe about probabilities is determined by the epistemic reasons in your epistemic *field*, while what you are warranted in believing is determined by the epistemic reasons in your epistemic *state*. Since epistemic reasons satisfy the probability calculus either way, so should your beliefs about probabilities. Insofar as your beliefs about probabilities stray *unjustifiably* (in the sense of 5.9 to 5.11) from the warranted probabilities, you are open to rational criticism.

But why, on a subjectivist Bayesian account, should people conform their beliefs about probabilities to the probability calculus? Here we need to distinguish some positions, since what is meant by 'Bayesian' is vague. There is a view which differs from the Normative view I have laid out only at the meta-normative level. While the view of reasons propounded in this book is cognitivist this view is non-cognitivist. Our standpoint on probability claims is that they express normative propositions which may be true or false, but which correspond to no facts. The non-cognitivist view is that claims about probability should not be thought of as assertions of propositions but in another way. These meta-normative issues will be discussed in Part IV, so I leave the discussion until then. The presently relevant point is that *both* these views accept that claims about epistemic reasons are legitimate and that it makes sense to discuss their correctness or incorrectness. Both accept that one should justify the probability calculus by defending first-order claims about what epistemic norms there are.

In contrast what I have been taking to be Bayesianism proper eschews talk of epistemic reasons, or seeks to reduce it to talk about 'rationally' constrained degrees of belief. Either way it does not put forward first-order claims about epistemic norms. On this approach the epistemic–normative justification of the probability calculus that I have given is not available.

So why should you conform your degrees of belief to the calculus? In the absence of an epistemic–normative answer, Bayesians invoke the Dutch book argument. If you do not, a Dutch book can be made against you (a set of bets whose outcome is that you will lose whatever happens), whereas if you do, that cannot be done. However, this argument is unpersuasive. Suppose I am certain that either Dobbin or Neddy will win the race but have no 'degree of belief' (inclination to believe) that Dobbin will or won't or that Neddy will or won't. If probabilities are degrees of belief, then mine are out of line with the probability calculus. So can you make a Dutch book against me? You certainly can if I am prepared to put money on Dobbin losing, Neddy losing, and also on it turning out that one of them wins. But why on earth should I be? Given my state of belief I'll bet that one of them will win, but I won't be prepared to put money either on Dobbin or on Neddy.

---

[27] Bayesians have a story, based on Bayes' theorem, about how degrees of belief that are consistent with the probability calculus converge in response to new information. But this doesn't address the basic point.

I just don't have any degree of belief that either will win, *or* that it will lose, so I'm not going to bet on it. What then if I *have* to place a bet on one of the horses? An *independent* justification of the probability calculus, such as the indifference norm, will tell me what specific bets I should place. If that is unavailable, as Bayesians think, I am still warranted in following a method of choice that picks one of the horses at random, in the manner of 5.9. However, nothing now tells me what specific bets I should place and what specific bets I should refuse.

Apart from these points, consider the form of the Dutch book argument. If it worked, it would give you a practical reason for behaving as though you believed the probability calculus. However, what we wanted to know is whether there is any reason to believe that the axioms of the calculus are true. The Bayesian must hold that it basically makes no sense to ask whether the axioms are *true*; all that can be said is that there is sufficient *practical* reason to act as though they were. This line of thought must come from meta-normative considerations. From the meta-normative standpoint of this book, there is no reason to deny that there are epistemic reasons and hence no reason to invoke the Dutch book argument. Bayesianism about probability is an unnecessary response to undue scepticism about epistemic reason. This conclusion will be further argued in Part IV.

9.9 The dynamics of inquiry

The normative account of probability answers some important questions about it. Probabilities are relations to epistemic fields; the normative basis of the probability calculus is the norm of indifference (13). Epistemic fields are sets of facts; so probabilities are grounded in the facts, not in our beliefs about them, or even our warranted beliefs about them. There may be probabilities that are unknowable in all humanly attainable epistemic fields. All of that is consistent with analysing 'probable' in terms of degrees of overall epistemic reason.

If probability is analysable in this way then it is a normative concept. I argue in Part IV that purely normative propositions do not state facts. This being so one cannot identify a probability with any substantial property (such as a counterfactual limiting frequency, or a propensity). One can say that probabilities *supervene* on substantial facts: what this means is that those facts in an epistemic field constitute overall degrees of reason to believe.

However, it is important to remember at this point that inquiry is a dynamic process taking place in time. (A point that Bayesianism rightly highlights.) In reasoning with epistemic norms we apply them to the facts as we take them to be at the given stage of inquiry: that is, to the epistemic field we take ourselves to be in. The flow of information, when apperceptual and non-monotonic norms are applied to it, produces an ongoing process of updating, leading to continuous revision of our judgements as to the facts. At any stage this updating is 'innocent until proved guilty'. It is the presumptive truth—what we are warranted in believing – even though we are aware that improved epistemic states may defeat it. Non-monotonic norms give inquirers warrants for belief so long as their epistemic state gives no warrants for thinking that defeaters exist. There do not have to be warrants for thinking there are no defeaters. Indeed this is an inevitable feature of the dynamics of inquiry: without it, you could never depart from square one, since you would first have to prove a negative about how the facts stand outside your epistemic state.

Our aim has been to present an overall picture of epistemic normativity, and of how it drives the dynamics of inquiry, rather than to go into detailed questions of first-order epistemology. The broad picture of epistemic norms that we have presented identifies monotonic norms of *apperception* and *deduction*, and non-monotonic norms of *receptivity*, *induction* and *probability*. The aim has been to sketch the domain of epistemic reasons only so far as will be required for our purposes in Part IV.

We now turn, in Part III, to practical and evaluative reasons, where our aim will be the same. Yet here this task, though still limited, is inevitably a good deal more controversial. The first-order normative discussion is more contested, in much more fundamental ways. There is wide disagreement about what the norms of practical and evaluative reason are, and how they fit together. There is a further layer of disagreement about the nature of morality, and about how it relates to practical and evaluative reasons. It will be necessary to go into more depth and detail about what the normative sources of practical reason are, and how moral sentiment and judgement are connected to them.

PART III

Evaluative and Practical Reasons

10

RATIONAL EXPLANATION: BELIEF, FEELING, AND WILL

Will is a kind of causality belonging to living beings so far as they are rational.[1]

The explanation of why you believe may simply be that you realize you have sufficient reason. You believe you're due at the hospital because you see a note of the appointment in your diary. You are warranted in thinking the note accurate unless you know of some defeating evidence; since you know of no such evidence you take it to be accurate.

In this example, you believe in virtue of recognizing the belief to be warranted: *from warrant*, as I earlier put it.[2] The same can be true for feelings and actions. In all such cases, the explanation of your response is simply that it is warranted and that you respond to that warrant. Spelling out the explanation may not be easy. It may not be apparent what the warrant was, or whether it was a warrant, and if so why. Importantly however, in cases in which you respond from warrant no further explanation of the response[3] is required. To explain what the warrant was is enough. I will call explanations of this kind *rational explanations*—this is to be understood as short for *explanations which explain an actor's response by showing that it proceeded from the actor's recognition that it was warranted*. A rational explanation explains a person's response (belief, feeling, action) as proceeding from warrant. It imputes autonomy.

Rational explanation raises questions at the philosophical level. What connection must hold between your response and the facts that warrant it, for you to be said to respond from that warrant? What is it to be aware of, to recognize, a warrant? Do you have to *believe* that you have a warrant? Do you have to have the *concept* of a reason, or of warrant? Another group of question asks what must be the case, at the sub-personal level of description of an entity, for that entity to be said to act from reasons at all. A third asks

---

[1] Kant, *Groundwork* IV: 446.
[2] In 5.1, where we contrasted acting from warrant and acting in accordance with warrant.
[3] Of the response: one might still want explanations at other levels, or of other things; for example of why, given that you are usually so ditzy, you managed to get your act together on this particular occasion.

about the ontology and epistemology of rational explanation: is normative knowledge, knowledge of some class of normative facts, and if so how does one get to know them?

These questions will be addressed in Part IV. The aim of this chapter is to describe the *form* of rational explanations, and to show that exactly the same form of explanation applies to beliefs, actions, and feelings. Rational explanation has the same structure in all three cases; in all three cases it explains the act in terms of the actor's factual and normative beliefs. This may seem most plausible in the case of beliefs and least plausible in the case of actions. Because there has been so much discussion of the explanation of action in particular, I shall pay most attention in this chapter to it. We shall be led back to the thesis of cognitive internalism, already considered in 3.9; and we shall consider in what way the *will* differentiates between explanations of action and explanations of feelings and belief. The results of our discussion will provide us with a framework for the other chapters of Part III.

10.1 Explaining belief, feeling, and action

Since rational explanation explains a response as springing from the recognition of warrant, many responses will not be rationally explicable—because many do not spring from warrant. In some of these cases you may think you have a warrant when you do not. You could be making some error of reasoning; failing to attend properly to your epistemic state; failing to grasp a relevant normative truth. Or there could be more to it: you might be in the grip of some distorting emotion, delusion, or prejudice which inclines you wrongly to accept something as a warrant. In other possible cases there is warrant for what you do, but you don't do it from that warrant. The approach of the enemy may be good reason to run away, given the weapons he is carrying; but you just run from sheer panic. Or you realize you have a warrant, but wrongly think you are acting from it. You are deceiving yourself: the real causes of your response have nothing to do with what you rightly take to be your warrant. Much of the time you may be well aware that you are responding without warrant. For example, you can't help believing something even though you realize full well that you don't have sufficient reason to believe. Or you get angry even though you realize there is no warrant for that. Alternatively, the appropriate belief, feeling, or action simply may not come, even if you realize it is warranted—perhaps because of depression, tiredness, or weakness of will.

Responses that are not rationally explicable may or may not still be explicable at the personal level of explanation, that is, in terms of acts and states of mind expressed by predicates that range over persons. Let us call explanations at this 'personal' level *interpretative*; they offer understanding of the person. Interpretative explanation includes rational explanation, but is wider. For example, the fact that you can't believe your admired and beloved brother to be the murderer, despite the compelling evidence, is interpretatively understandable. Though it is not necessarily excusable just because it is understandable—*tout comprendre* is not *tout pardonner*—it may still mitigate blame for some of the things it makes you do. Admiration and love are attitudes hard to reconcile with facts that give reason for contempt and hatred, but also hard to give up. Indeed it may seem disloyal to give them up, since they involve trust, and that too is interpretatively understandable. It is understandable that you think you have reason to doubt the evidence, however compelling it seems.

In many ways, however, your responses will not be understandable at the personal, interpretative level, at all. That may be the case with humdrum mistakes you make in calculations, or in overlooking possibilities, or failing to remember something. They may be very understandable in the sense of being quite normal, but nonetheless not explicable at the interpretative level. You simply fail to remember an appointment: why you failed, in that particular case, is a matter of memory malfunction and may not be explicable in terms of *any* mental states attributable to you. More radically, your conviction that you are made of glass may not be interpretatively understandable, despite the best efforts of interpretative psychiatrists. Or take the desire some people have, when they look over the parapet of a tower, to throw themselves over it. One may be able, in a way, to 'understand' that strange temptation, and presumably there is some explanation for it—but we would have to go to a different level, beyond interpretation, to find it.

So we can distinguish between interpretative and non-interpretative explanations, with rational explanations as a special case of the former. In Chapter 5 I distinguished between warrant and the distinct category of justification. Whether in everyday cases or in historical studies, we often want to know whether an act was *justified*. However, we also try to understand unjustified responses interpretatively, not just for prediction, or for assessing how far we can get on with the other, but for the satisfaction of empathetic insight as such. If we weren't interested in such insight for its own sake, a lot of novels would remain unread. And in all cases, including those in which the response is not justified, *interpretative* explanation of the act involves attributing putative normative reasons to the actor in one way or another, and not just causes.

Rational explanation is the special case of interpretative explanation in which a response is explained as flowing from warrant. Thus the *explanans* in a rational explanation need attribute only cognitive states to the actor: apperceptual awareness and beliefs. One's response is explained by showing that one acted from recognition that one had sufficient reason so to respond, in the light of factual and normative beliefs which one could see to be warranted by one's epistemic state.

As I noted, this may seem most plausible in the case of beliefs. Does rational explanation apply to feelings at all? Non-normative causes *may* play a bigger role in the case of feelings, though one should not underestimate the power of non-normative causes in determining beliefs and actions as well. However, even if rational explanation applies less often to feelings, it can still apply, and when it does it has the same form: a rational explanation of why a person feels something explains how his feeling springs from warrant. I am, for example, annoyed with the garage because, as I can see, I have sufficient reason to believe they have cheated me, and thus sufficient reason to be annoyed. (As we have noted from time to time, there may be good reason to control one's feelings even when they're fully warranted, or to cause in oneself unwarranted feelings. Rational explanation of attempts to suppress one's feelings, or to cause oneself to have them, should not be confused with rational explanation of feelings as such.)

But what about explanation of action? Does it fit the cognitive model of rational explanation that I have proposed?

Actions, unlike beliefs and feelings, require motives. In every case the interpretative explanation of an intentional action combines motives with appropriately matching beliefs. What is called 'Humean' or 'desire–belief' psychology, a widely influential position, says that motives always include some affective state: a passion; inclination; desire, which in combination with appropriate beliefs causes the action. If this is correct, then either rational explanation is on its own insufficient to explain actions, or rational explanation of action is not purely cognitive.

Defenders of desire–belief psychology typically assert the latter alternative; they do not deny that actions are often explicable in terms of reasons; what they deny is that such explanation of action refers only to cognitive states.[4] They hold that any *warrant* for an action must comprise a relevant desire as well as relevant warranted beliefs. Since many writers have criticized this group of views effectively,[5] I do not propose to investigate the arguments and counter-arguments in detail. However, it is relevant to spell out in outline some of the ways in which the Humean idea can be developed, and to see why, when seen from the standpoint on reasons propounded in this book, they fail.

Arguments for desire–belief psychology can be divided into the psychological and the philosophical. The psychological arguments attempt to make an empirical case for 'desire–belief psychology'. The philosophical arguments are twofold, and in responding to them we shall bring together some themes from other chapters. There is, in the first place, an epistemological argument from Hume's thesis that all propositions concern either 'matters of fact and existence'[6] knowable only by empirical evidence or 'relations of ideas'. In the terms of this book, this is the empiricist thesis that all propositions are either factual and knowable only a posteriori, or are analytic. Then there is a metaphysical argument from global realism. Both arguments invoke an 'open-question' premise. We consider the psychological argument in the next section and the philosophical arguments in Section 10.3. We then consider the instrumentalist view of practical reasons (Section 10.4) and Williams' theory of internal reasons (Section 10.5). These positions have been independently influential in ways that do not depend, at least explicitly, on the psychological and philosophical arguments considered in the next two sections.

---

[4] Hume himself may be an exception. It's not clear that he makes room for *any* normative explanation, whether for action, belief, or feeling. One way of reading him is that he denies, at least while in the study, that there are reasons.
[5] See, for example, Korsgaard 1986; Scanlon 1998: 33–41; Schueler 1995. Recent defences of the Humean view include: Smith, M. 1994; Schroeder 2007; Svavarsdóttir 1999.
[6] See e.g. *Treatise*, III, i, i; *Enquiry Concerning the Principles of Morals*, Appendix I.

10.2 Cognitive and non-cognitive models of motivation: psychological arguments

We should first consider what is meant by 'desire'. 'Desire' can be used, and often is, in a narrow way. In this narrow usage, I may choose to go and visit a very boring relative, living on his own, because I think I ought to do so, even though I don't have the slightest desire to do so. The fact that I lack any desire to visit him may well be something I'm not very proud of, but being honest with myself, I have to admit that it is so. In general, it can be the case that I do something because I think I should, for a variety of reasons, moral and non-moral, without feeling any desire to do so. In this quite ordinary sense I can choose not to do what I most desire to do. On the contrary I may choose to do what I don't have the slightest desire to do. The thought of doing it may bore me, or even fill me with fear and loathing, but I may still do it, and do it for what strike me as good reasons. I shall refer to this as the *substantive* sense of 'desire'. 'Want' can also be used in this substantive sense: I really don't want to visit him, but I think I should.

Another perfectly ordinary usage, of 'want' in particular, though also of 'desire' is what can be called the 'aim-eliciting' use.[7] I can in this sense ask 'Why do you want to do that?' or 'Why did you want to do that?' meaning to ask you for your aim, purpose, or intention in doing it. The question is typically asked, for example, where a person tried but failed to do something, or is trying or meaning to do it without having yet done it, or has it as a standing project to do it some time. In asking you the question I am asking about your aims, objectives, purposes, or projects—why you have or had this particular thing on your list of things to be done, if possible and opportune. Or I may ask what you want, what you would you like, to ascertain your request or command. (As in the French 'Monsieur désire?') If you've actually *done* something, then we can straightforwardly ask why you did it. Nevertheless, it will still be true in this sense of 'want' that when you did something intentionally you wanted to do it. That just says that when you act intentionally you have some objective, purpose, project, or in many cases no more than some fleeting intention, based on a passing impulse, in mind.[8]

Because there can be intermediate aims, aims one has in order to achieve further aims, there can also be instrumental desires in the *aim-eliciting* sense. One can want to do this in order to achieve something else that one wants to achieve. In contrast, there are no instrumental desires in the substantive sense of desire. The distinction between instrumental and final reasons has no application to evaluative reasons, any more than it does to epistemic reasons. Just as there is no such thing as an instrumental reason or

---

[7] Cp. Schueler 1995: 29–38 ("Two Senses of "Desire"").

[8] In some of the more primitive cases it's natural enough to say there was no reason why one did the thing. I am in my hotel room, after an exhausting day, surfing the television. If you ask why I'm doing it, I may reply: 'no special reason, I'm just killing time'. What I mean is that I had no further purpose or intention in mind. Even more primitively, you might ask why I'm flexing my shoulders as I work at the computer. To which I might reply 'I wasn't even aware of doing that—I suppose I'm trying to stop feeling stiff'. You could still say: he just wants to kill time, or: he wants to stop feeling stiff. Citing what a person wants in the aim-eliciting sense is appropriate across the whole gamut of actions, intentions, and plans, from the most primitive action or impulse to the most deliberated and distant purpose.

a final reason to believe something, so there is no such thing as an instrumental or a final reason to admire, hate, love, or desire something. If I think that some action is a means to something I fervently desire, I may well do it with a good deal of eagerness; it remains true, however, that the action itself is not something I substantively desire to do; my eagerness stems from anticipation of that which I substantively desire. (There is also the psychological phenomenon of goal displacement, but where that occurs what started as an intermediate aim comes itself to be substantively desired, and thus becomes a final aim.)

Any spelt-out explanation of an intentional action will refer to the intention, or purpose, or aim, or desire, or normative belief, from which it sprang. This can be presented in the form of a belief–desire explanatory schema, if 'desire' is taken in the aim-eliciting sense. However, it is then perfectly possible that the aim being elicited is constituted by a normative belief about what one has reason to do; so it would be less misleading to talk of a 'factual belief–motive' schema. A motive is whatever can be adduced, in our everyday explanations of intentional action, as explaining (in combination with a person's factual beliefs) why the person did an action. The belief–motive schema is neutral between cognitive and affective models of motivation. It says nothing of whether substantive desires must play a role in motivation or whether, on the contrary, practical–normative beliefs can play a motivating role without assistance or mediation from any substantive desire. As Prichard nicely put it:

> At bottom... we mean by a motive what moves us to act; a sense of obligation does sometimes move us to act; and in our ordinary consciousness we should not hesitate to allow that the action we were considering might have had as its motive a sense of obligation. Desire and the sense of obligation are co-ordinate forms or species of motive.[9]

Suppose someone believes that he's just trodden on your toe and believes that that's a reason to apologize. Because he believe these things, he apologizes, for example by saying 'Sorry!' The belief that treading on a person's toe gives one reason to apologize was his motive for saying 'sorry': it is what explains his action, in combination with his factual beliefs. It's irrelevant whether he actually *felt* sorry. His motive was the conviction that, irrespective of his feelings, it was appropriate to apologize. In the ordinary, substantive, sense of the term 'desire', he apologized because he thought he had reason to do so, whether or not he desired to do so.

The Humean view, however, is that every motive must involve a desire, whatever the appearances. For a Humean, the essential points are that desire is an affective and not a purely cognitive state, and that only a motive which includes an affective state is capable of triggering action. Hence, according to the Humean, if A apologizes there must have been some desire, that is, affective state, or in Hume's word, 'passion', which caused him to do so. Some Humeans might agree with Prichard that a sense of obligation can on its own move one to act, but they would argue that the sense of obligation can only have this

---

[9] Prichard, 2002 ('Does Moral philosophy rest on a mistake?', 1912): 15.

practical power if it is *itself* an affective state. Having a practical–normative commitment *is* (in whole or part) having a desire or 'pro-affect' of some sort.[10]

Suppose you apologized because you believed that you should, even though (as you would say) you had no desire at all to do so. According to the Humean there must nevertheless have been some affective state of desire that caused you to act.

It is good enough, I believe, to reply that common experience shows the opposite. You may have a motivating reason to visit your uncle, or to apologize, without have any substantive desire to do so, or to achieve something that you think can only be achieved by doing so; nor does experience support the idea that the 'sense of obligation' motivating you is itself a desire. But Humeans may find this too brusque. Hume himself would have replied that you have a 'calm' but strong passion to apologize, or pay the visit (stronger than any more 'violent' passions you may have).[11] As it stands, this is a rather transparently question-begging claim. Modern Humeans, in contrast, are likely to be less transparent. They may say that the hypothesis that every motive includes a desire is to be regarded not as a low-level empirical generalization but as an a priori postulate of desire–belief psychology.

This move implicitly defines 'desire' as that putative psychological state, whatever it may be, that satisfies *all* the defining Humean theses. So 'desire', on this definition, does not have its uncontentious purely aim-eliciting sense, because it is a key postulate of Humean theory that desire is an affective and not a purely cognitive state. The question then arises whether belief–desire psychology so conceived is a good empirical theory considered as a whole. We should assess it against other empirical theories: for example, the traditionally well-established alternative view that introduces three categories of mental phenomena into motivation rather than two—the will as well as belief and desire (in the substantive sense). If this more complex theory is a better empirical theory, a theory that better fits the facts of experience, as I shall claim in Section 10, then we have no reason to accept that the implicitly defined Humean theoretical term, 'desire', has any referent.[12] And if Humeanism is treated as unfalsifiable, rather than as an empirical theory, then the content of its term 'desire' simply becomes unclear.

Can we find some way to strengthen the case for the belief–desire theory? The main argument put for it requires a determinist assumption at the interpretative level of explanation. What, it is asked, other than the presence or absence of a pertinent desire–affect, could explain why beliefs (including normative beliefs) sometimes cause and sometimes do not?

This argument is very weak. Suppose I'm driving along the motorway and I notice from the fuel gauge that my petrol is low. I think to myself 'I should stop at the next petrol station'—and almost immediately I see a turn-off to a petrol station. In scenario A I pull into it. In scenario B I fail to slow down, and drive past, possibly thinking 'Damn it! I should

---

[10] This is one route by which Simon Blackburn arrives at his expressivism, projectivism, or quasi-realism. As he says, it commits one to accepting expressivism about any normative commitment which can in and of itself motivate. Blackburn 1984: 187–8; 1998: 4–8.

[11] *Treatise*, II, iii, iv.

[12] See the discussion of implicit definition and reference fixing in Chapter 6.

have stopped at that one'. Any number of differentiating causal antecedents could explain this. They may take the form of states describable at the personal level, such as irresolution, or they may not. There is no reason to think that the difference between the two scenarios is that in one case I wanted to stop and in the other I did not. In general I have a disposition to do what I take myself to have most reason to do (in this case, pull into the station). I can have that disposition—that pathway from beliefs about what I should do to motor responses—in *both* scenarios. But the pathway may be only statistically effective. Or it may be blocked, for example, by an inertial disposition caused by the time I've spent at the wheel. In any case there is no a priori reason to assume determinism at the level of interpretative explanation, even if we assume determinism at a deeper-down physiological level. A normative belief may cause an action or may not, just as a desire may cause an action or may not. There may be no *interpretative* explanation of the difference.

There is, it is true, a dualism in the rational explanation of action. A motive combined with a pertinent belief gives rise to a disposition to action. But nothing has yet been said to show that this is a dualism of belief and affect. It may be simply a special case of the dualism in *all* rational explanation: in such explanations a factual belief combines with a normative belief to explain a belief, feeling, or action. In all these cases there must be an appropriate combination between factual beliefs and states of you that are not factual beliefs; it is the *combination* that disposes you to act.[13] This is not because of some mysterious limitation on the causal powers of cognitive as against affective states, but simply in virtue of the very structure of self-determination, which requires receptivity to facts and responsiveness to norms. To act from reasons is to recognize that one has reason to believe that some facts obtain and that they give one reason to act.

10.3 Cognitive and non-cognitive models of motivation: philosophical arguments

To avoid begging questions while we consider the philosophical arguments let me put this dualism in rational explanations as a dualism between factual beliefs and normative commitments. On the meta-theory of reasons defended in this book, normative commitments are just further beliefs. Psychological arguments, we have seen, do not undermine the cognitive model of rational explanation, and hence do not, at least by that route, undermine cognitivism about normative commitments. But there are also arguments that go in the opposite direction. They cast doubt on cognitivism about normative commitments, and thereby cast doubt on the cognitive model of rational explanation.

A thesis that plays a decisive role in Hume's own discussion is his empiricism, mentioned above: the thesis that a proposition either concerns an a posteriori 'matter of fact and existence' or is analytic. If normative commitments are to be understood as propositions about reasons, down which of these forking roads can they go?

---

[13] A priori beliefs are a special case. Here the normative explanation of the belief need invoke no factual beliefs.

They are clearly not (in general) analytic. So either they are not propositions at all, or they must be propositions about empirical facts. There are traces of both ideas in Hume's discussion—a non-cognitivist strand, but also subjectivist and dispositionalist strands:

> Our decisions concerning moral rectitude and depravity are evidently perceptions; and as all perceptions are either impressions or ideas, the exclusion of the one is a convincing argument for the other. Morality, therefore, is more properly felt than judg'd of; tho' this feeling or sentiment is commonly so soft and gentle, that we are apt to confound it with an idea...
>
> To have the sense of virtue is nothing but to *feel* a satisfaction of a particular kind from the contemplation of a character. The very *feeling* constitutes our praise or admiration... We do not infer a character to be virtuous, because it pleases: But in feeling that it pleases after such a particular manner, we in effect feel that it is virtuous.
>
> The vice entirely escapes you, as long as you consider the object. You never can find it, until you turn your reflexion into your own breast, and find a sentiment of approbation, which arises in you, towards this action. Here is a matter of fact; but 'tis the object of feeling, not of reason. It lies in yourself, not in the object. So that when you pronounce any action or character to be vicious, you mean nothing, but that from the constitution of your nature you have a feeling or sentiment of blame from the contemplation of it.
>
> The hypothesis which we embrace is plain. It maintains that morality is determined by sentiment. It defines virtue to be *whatever mental action or quality gives to a spectator the pleasing sentiment of approbation*; and vice the contrary.[14]

These well-known passages are rather indefinite; it is a scholarly question how best to interpret them within Hume's philosophy taken overall. Still, the first two may seem to point in a non-cognitivist direction, while the second two seem to point towards a subjectivist or dispositionalist view.

We could apply the dispositionalist view to the concept of a practical reason by 'defining' it, for example, as follows:

π_i are a reason for x to $\psi \leftrightarrow \pi_i$, if known to x, would dispose x to ψ.

Within Hume's empiricist framework, however, this naturalistic reduction (and every other more complicated one) seems untenable, whatever Hume's own view might be. For, on the one hand, it faces a simple open-question challenge: neither side of this biconditional analytically implies the other, whereas that is the only kind of 'relation of ideas' that Hume's fork allows. Yet suppose, on the other hand, that we do accept the biconditional as analytic. In that case we have to accept that all propositions about reasons are a posteriori. But we showed in 5.6 that the possibility of self-determination requires that some claims about reasons are neither analytic nor a posteriori. That being so, given the empiricist framework they cannot be assertions of propositions at all: non-cognitivism about these claims is forced. (See 17.7 for further discussion.)

---

[14] Hume 1968 (1739): 470–71 (III, 1, ii), 468–9 (III, 2, i); 1902 (1777): 289 (App. I).

Given this non-cognitivism, we can now derive a non-cognitive model of rational explanation from the normative–factual dualism of rational explanation. And note how general this line of thought is: it would apply not just to reasons for action but to all reasons, and thus to all rational explanations.[15]

The argument works if one accepts the empiricist premise; but it does not work within the framework of this book. For we rejected empiricism in Chapter 6, and retained only the Critical thesis that no synthetic *factual* proposition is a priori. Synthetic a priori propositions, we claimed, are normative; and we shall argue in Part IV that purely normative propositions are not factual.

So is there another philosophical argument to the non-cognitive model of rational explanation, which does not require the empiricist premise?

Suppose there is a strong form of the open-question challenge whose upshot is that no wholly normative claim expresses a substantial fact. This challenge will work against any form of factualism about the normative, be it naturalistic or non-naturalistic. But in that case—*given* factualism about propositional content—we again have to conclude that normative claims are not assertions of propositions at all, and cannot be said to be true or false. And again we get to a non-cognitive model of motivation via the dualism of rational explanation. This argument again applies globally: rational explanation will have to have a non-cognitive element in all cases, whether it be of actions, beliefs, or feelings.

We shall defend one of pillar of this argument—the strong open-question challenge—in 18.4. This challenge is deep and far-reaching. However, it only forces non-cognitivism about normative commitments when combined with factualism, and (as just mentioned) we shall argue that factualism about propositional content should be rejected. The case for rejecting it turns on the nature of truth and the ontology of reasons relations; it will be made in Chapter 17. If it is sound, the open-question argument does not force non-cognitivism about normative claims. It simply forces a fundamental distinction between the normative and the factual: wholly normative propositions cannot be factual.

Realists about normative propositions—naturalistic or non-naturalistic—will reject this line of thought. Suppose for the moment that they are right to do so. In that case a realist account of normative beliefs can be given, and there is no threat to the cognitive model of rational explanation. On this view normative commitments are beliefs, and they come together with non-normative beliefs in rational explanation. In general, a cognitivist account of normative claims, whether realist or irrealist, provides no support for a non-cognitive model of rational explanation.

I conclude that philosophical arguments for the non-cognitive model require rather special premises: either empiricism, or a combination of factualism with the strong open-question argument. And if they are sound, they refute the cognitive model of rational explanation right across the board—for beliefs and feelings as well as for action.[16]

---

[15] Hume seems to take a non-cognitivist view of epistemic reasons as well as practical ones (Hume 1968, 1739): 'all probable reasoning is nothing but a species of sensation' p. 103 (I, 3. viii), *"belief is more properly an act of the sensitive, than of the cogitative part of our nature"*, p. 103 (I.4, i).

[16] The arguments for non-cognitivism about normativity mentioned in this section are considered further in 17.7.

10.4 Instrumentalism

The philosophical arguments considered in the previous section require premises that are rejected in this book. The psychological arguments are unconvincing. So far then the view that rational explanation applies uniformly to all three cases of belief, feeling, and action, and in all cases is purely cognitive, remains in place.

We cannot quite leave the issue there, however. There is a position in the theory of practical reasons which may derive from an underlying empiricism, but is in any case highly influential in its own right—instrumentalism. If true, it has implications for our account of rational explanation at least in the case of explanation of actions.

Instrumentalism has already been introduced in Chapter 4, where I contrasted it with what I called the Transmission principle (4.9 and 4.10). It says that there's reason for a person to pursue an action if and only if doing so serves one of his ultimate aims or objectives. It also says that a person's ultimate aims or objectives are not cognitive states. They may consist in substantive desires he actually has or—in voluntarist or existentialist versions of instrumentalism—they may consist in ultimate choices, commitments or projects; or perhaps they consist in a combination of the two: for example, ultimate aims are those substantive desires 'endorsed' by a pure volition. In all cases, the important instrumentalist claim is that one cannot assess whether *there is reason* for a person to have the particular ultimate aims he has.

If one could, instrumentalism would commit one to holding that the existence or otherwise of reasons for a person's ultimate aims in no way affects how much reason there is for him to pursue them. That would be an implausible position compared to the Transmission principle. If the rationality of ultimate aims *can* be assessed, then clearly how much reason there is to do something must depend in part on how much reason there is to have the ultimate aim in pursuit of which it is done, as the Transmission principle suggests.

Suppose that there can be reasons for substantive desires. That is, we can ask whether there is *reason* for you to substantively desire something, such as pleasure or knowledge or whatever, and the question is one to which there can be an answer. Suppose next that if there is reason for you to substantively desire some object then there is reason for you to pursue it. Both these claims will be defended in the next chapter. If they are correct, then achieving the object is an ultimate aim which there is non-instrumental practical reason for you to pursue—a reason-supported practical aim—and thus one to which the Transmission principle can be applied.

In contrast, instrumentalism either denies that there are evaluative reasons, or denies that they generate reason-supported practical aims. So we should examine it with some care.

Let us first consider its status. Is it a constitutive view, about what it is for a fact to be a practical reason? Or is it a normative thesis, about the norm that governs all practical reasons?

The constitutive version of instrumentalism asserts an identity of facts. Consider the following biconditional:

(1) π_i are at t a reason for x to α ⟺ at t x has an objective o such that, given π_i, α-ing has a propensity to realize o.[17]

Constitutive instrumentalism is the view (i) that the propositions left and right of the biconditional are both factual; and (ii) that the fact expressed by the proposition on the left is identical to the fact expressed by the proposition on the right. Notice that this is distinct from the thesis that *reasons* are facts, which we have endorsed. Suppose, for example, that the fact that you will be killed unless you run is a reason for you to run. According to constitutive instrumentalism, there is a further *fact*, namely, the fact *that the fact that you will be killed unless you run is a reason for you to run*, and *that* fact just is *the fact that given that you will be killed unless you run, running has a propensity to realize one of your objectives*.

Constitutive instrumentalism says that facts about practical reasons are facts that can also be said to obtain by assertion of a non-normative proposition; so it is an instance of the reductive approach to normative propositions. We shall defend a strong open-question argument against all such reductive 'normative and non-normative' identities (synthetic as well as analytic) in Chapter 18.[18] But here we should also consider instrumentalism as a normative thesis.

The Normative version of instrumentalism can be put as follows:

(2) (i) The fact that x has an objective o at t which is such that α-ing has a propensity to realize o is, at t, a reason for x to α.
(ii) No other facts are reasons for action.

The Normative version clearly does not entail the constitutive version, for normative instrumentalism takes no meta-normative stand about the truth or otherwise of normative and non-normative identities. Less obviously, the constitutive thesis does not entail the normative thesis. (1) does not imply that the reason for x to α is the fact expressed on its right-hand side. The reason to α, according to (1), is the facts in π_i. That is not what (2(i)) says is the reason.

This observation may be important to philosophers who want to make a 'backgrounding' point—namely, that the constitutive thesis leaves undecided a wide variety of normative propositions about what facts π_i are reasons for action.[19] Suppose you think that the constitutive thesis can be supported on philosophical or psychological grounds, but you want to get away from what you find to be the implausible normative claim (2(i)). You can point out that it's not, say, the fact that I want to help the oppressed (that psychological fact about me) that gives me reason to help the oppressed; it's the fact that they're oppressed that gives me reason to help them. But you can still hold that what makes that *whole normative proposition true* is the fact that I want to help the oppressed. The difference

---

[17] I omit reference to the degree of strength of the reason here, and in (2) and (3) below. It will presumably depend on how strongly x adheres to objective o, and how cost-effective α-ing is. As noted in 4.7, there is substantive disagreement about the theory of cost-effectiveness; instrumentalists can differ on this point. In contrast, the reference to *time* is essential to instrumentalism; the only reason-giving objectives at t are those the agent has at t.

[18] Agreeing in this respect with Blackburn 1993a. (In general, the Normative view endorses the arguments against all forms of realism about the normative that are put forward by expressivists; it just rejects the need for expressivism.)

[19] See Pettit and Smith 2004; Schroeder 2007.

is the difference between the particular fact that gives me a reason and the fact which makes it true that that particular fact gives me a reason.

In one or another version, constitutive or normative, or both, instrumentalism is attractive to many philosophers and perhaps even more so to many theorists in social sciences that have a normative–explanatory frontier. It tends to be backed by the apparently simple thought, 'Well, what *else* could practical reasons be?' But the thought is only apparently simple. It probably gets some of its power from inexplicit reliance on background philosophical convictions, such as empiricism, or a combination of global realism with naturalism; these have already been discussed. Another part of its power is the idea that the normative and the descriptive study of action must be closely linked. If people only ever act to pursue their actual objectives then surely only those can *be* reasons for acting; and only *present* objectives can be reasons for *present* action.

In the broad sense of 'aim' and 'objective' that is in play, it's true that people only ever act in pursuit of their aims and objectives. (The sense is broad: acting out of duty also counts as pursuing an aim.) But that does not vindicate the core instrumentalist claim, that ultimate aims cannot be rationally assessed. If they can be then, as already pointed out, the plausible view must be that it is the aims there is reason for one to pursue that give one reason to act, not the aims that one actually has. To this we should add two points. First, any agent is committed to holding that his aims *are* aims there's sufficient reason for him to have—he is irrational if he both denies that and still pursues them (5.11). So within the first-person perspective the aims I have will typically, if not invariably, be taken by me to be aims there is reason for me to have. Second, it is true that facts to the effect that *x* desires something, or would desire it in certain circumstances, or that people like *x* desire it, are the only *criteria* for holding that that thing is desirable for *x*, that there's reason for *x* to desire it. So what a person wants (or what other people like him want) is often a good way of telling what there is reason for him to want, and thus what there is reason for him to aim for. In this sense it is perfectly true that the normative and the descriptive study of action must be closely linked: the former is closely linked epistemically to the latter. There is however, no entailment from what a person does desire to what there is reason for him to desire.[20]

10.5 Against instrumentalism

Constitutive instrumentalism is compatible with the cognitive model of rational explanation; in fact it entails it. The rational explanation of an action will still consist entirely of beliefs: the belief that an action will promote an objective one believes one has together with a normative belief that instantiates 2(i). One can be mistaken in one's beliefs about one's own ultimate objectives—you think you want something but you don't really. If you are mistaken in that way, you may act to achieve this objective even though you actually have no desire for it.

---

[20] For further discussion see 11.3.

We should also note that non-cognitivism about reasons is *in*compatible with constitutive instrumentalism, since the latter provides a factual truth condition for propositions about practical reasons. It is a species of normative realism. However, non-cognitivists could still endorse *normative* instrumentalism. They could interpret that view in an expressivist way: one is expressing a pro-attitude towards people who pursue their objectives in proportion to the strength of their desire for attainment of those objectives. (Though why should I have this odd pro-attitude?)

Since constitutive instrumentalism is a species of normative realism, the open-question arguments of Chapter 18 will apply to it. But what of normative instrumentalism in the form of (2)? To this there are familiar counter-examples—consider Williams' despairing teenager, Susan, who attempts to commit suicide.[21] Even though she can see, in a way, that things will be fine in three months time, she doesn't care. According to (ii), if her only aim in her state of despair is to commit suicide, then that is the only thing there is reason for her to do.

The backgrounding move considered earlier does not help in this case. It helped to deny the implausible claim that only the fact that *I want* to help the oppressed (that psychological fact about me) gives me reason to help the oppressed. But it still delivers the wrong result about Susan. If her objective is to commit suicide, then on the backgrounding view the fact that this drug is deadly is a reason for her to take it. On the contrary, however, it is not a reason for her to take it. Indeed if she will soon recover and live a happy life that is a reason for her not to take it, *whatever* she feels now. If that is true, normative instrumentalism is false.

More generally, on this approach the normative truths in the foreground (e.g. that the fact that someone is oppressed is a reason to help them) are neither necessarily true nor universalizable over all agents, whereas instrumentalism, in the shape of thesis (1), is. Foreground principles will hold only for those who have the appropriate ultimate aims. If we want to make them complete, fully universalizable norms in the sense of 5.6 we shall have to incorporate the fact that the agent has those aims into the reason-giving facts, π_i. But that undercuts the foreground/background distinction, and makes all practical–normative truths agent-relative. So if there are universalizable agent-neutral practical–normative truths, as we shall argue in the following chapters of Part III that there are, instrumentalism is false.[22]

10.6 Williams on internal reasons

Bernard Williams' claim that there are only 'internal' reasons is, on the face of it, a version of instrumentalism; but it turns out to have a rather curious distinguishing feature. Williams also advances an important argument for his view that should be considered here, since it raises an important question which takes us back to the cognitive internalism considered in 3.8 and 3.9. The two issues are discussed in this section and the next.

---

[21] Williams, B. 1985: 41–3.
[22] Schroeder 2007 attempts to deal with these points; for critical discussion see Price 2009.

What, then, is this view of reasons? Williams says that sentences of the form '*A* has a reason to ϕ', or 'There is a reason for *A* to ϕ'[23] might be interpreted in two ways:

> On the first, the truth of the sentence implies, very roughly, that *A* has some motive which will be served or furthered by his ϕ-ing... On the second interpretation... the reason-sentence will not be falsified by the absence of an appropriate motive.

The first interpretation takes these sentences about reasons to express what Williams calls *internal* reasons. The second allows that they may express what he calls *external* reasons. Internal reasons always display a relativity to the agent A's 'subjective motivational set', which Williams labels 'S', and which comprises A's existing motivational states: 'An internal reason statement is falsified by the absence of some appropriate element from S'.[24] Elsewhere he also holds that such a statement is *verified* by the presence of an appropriate element in S.

Williams does not deny that we sometimes talk as though there were external reasons—as though agents could have reasons which weren't relative to the motives in their S—but he denies that this talk has any clear meaning. The only clear notion of a reason is the internal notion: A has a reason to α if and only if A has some motive which will be served or furthered by his α-ing.

However, some motives are based on false beliefs about the facts. Williams imagines someone who wants a gin and tonic and believes the stuff in this bottle to be gin, whereas in fact it is petrol.[25] Is there any reason for him to mix the stuff in this bottle with tonic and drink it? He probably thinks there is, but if he does then as Williams says, he is wrong. (Assuming there is no other reason to drink it.) This agent wants to drink gin and he also wants to drink the stuff in this bottle. The first motivational state, let's assume, is not based on a false belief about the facts, whereas the second is—and that strips it of reason-giving force. So we should restrict S to motives whose reason-giving force is not vitiated by dint of their resting on false beliefs about the facts.[26] Then we can put Williams' view, that all reasons are internal reasons, in a nicely succinct way:

> (3) There is reason for A to α if and only if α-ing would serve a motive in A's S.[27]

As in our discussion of instrumentalism, we can ask whether Williams intends this as a constitutive or a normative truth. T. M. Scanlon suggests the latter reading in a lucid discussion of Williams' view, but I think Williams intends the former.[28] He rests his case for internalism on an analysis of what it is for something to be a reason, and as we have seen,

---

[23] He makes no systematic distinction between these formulations, as I do in this book.
[24] The quotations are from Williams, B. 1981: 101–2.
[25] Williams, B. 1981: 102.
[26] This is a slight modification of what Williams says: he includes such motives in S but says they give no reasons. Williams, B. 1981: 103.
[27] Williams also often puts his view in a rather different way, which appeals to whether there is a 'sound deliberative route' by which A could reach the conclusion to ϕ. But I think that Williams intends it to agree with (3), and that obscurities to which it gives rise can be clarified by reference to (3).
[28] Scanlon 1998: 365. However, Williams' view need not be read as a *definition* of the meaning of statements about reasons. It can be understood as offering a 'deeper-down' account of their conceptual content (and thus not a substantive, normative thesis).

he questions the *intelligibility* of external reason statements. In 'Internal reasons and the obscurity of blame' he asks 'What are the truth-conditions for statements of the form "A has a reason to ɸ"?'[29] and advances internalism (in the 'sound deliberative route' version) as the right answer. He is making a philosophical case against the very possibility of external reasons.

At the same time, however, he wants to be 'more liberal than some theorists have been about the possible elements in S'. He is willing, he says, to use the term 'desire' 'formally', for all these elements, noting that desire must then be understood to include 'dispositions of evaluation, patterns of emotional reaction, personal loyalties, and various projects embodying commitments of the agent'.[30] This looks like what we called the aim-eliciting sense of desire. The point is even clearer when Williams asks:

> Does believing that a particular consideration is a reason to act in a particular way provide, or indeed constitute, a motivation to act?...Let us grant that it does—this claim indeed seems plausible, so long at least as the connexion between such beliefs and the disposition to act is not tightened to that unnecessary degree which excludes *akrasia*. The claim is in fact *so* plausible, that this agent, with this belief, appears to be one about whom, now, an *internal* reason statement could truly be made: he is one with an appropriate motivation in his S.[31]

Williams agrees here, as it seems to me quite rightly, that a belief on A's part about reasons—for example, his belief that treading on your toe is a reason for him to apologize—can 'provide, or indeed constitute, a motivation to act'. In allowing that, and thus including the belief in A's S, he seems to depart from Humeanism about motivation. And this also looks like a departure from instrumentalism, inasmuch as instrumentalism holds that there can be no rational assessment of a person's ultimate objectives. Ultimate objectives are not reason-supportable states, according to the instrumentalist. In contrast, A's belief that he has reason to apologize is something that can be rationally assessed. As with other beliefs, one can ask what reason there is to hold it.

This departure has a peculiar consequence. For given (3) it now seems to follow in general—for *any* belief I have about what there is reason for me to do—that so long as the belief has motivating force it's true. If the belief that I have reason to α is in my S then it is a motive which would be 'served' by ɸ-ing.[32] So by (3) the '*internal* reason statement' that I have reason to α can truly be made about me.

Can this be right? I can certainly have false beliefs about what reasons I have to act; Williams does not dispute that.[33] And surely such beliefs can be false even if they *do* have motivating force. Williams could accept this in part too: he could answer that beliefs about reasons can be excluded from the agent's S when they are based on false beliefs about the facts. That would simply be an application of the general point that motives based on false factual beliefs can be excluded from S. But what, now, of *fundamental* beliefs about reasons—that

---

[29] Williams, B. 1995a: 35.   [30] Williams, B. 1981: 105   [31] Williams, B. 1981: 107.
[32] Take it that the belief that one has reason to ɸ is 'served' by ɸ-ing.
[33] See e.g. Williams, B. 1981: 103—point (iii)(a).

is, beliefs about reasons for action which are themselves ultimate, and not derived in part from factual beliefs? If these motivate a believer they will be in his or her S, and so, by (3) they will be true. Thus all of an agent's fundamental, motivating beliefs about reasons will be true.

We could avoid this result by excluding A's beliefs about what A has reason to do from A's S. If that is done, the internalist analysis of reasons will say that A's belief that he has reason to α can be true only if there is some motive for α-ing, *which is not itself a fundamental belief that there is reason to α*, in A's S: and this, presumably, will be a desire, in the sense of an affective rather than a cognitive attitude.

That pushes in the Humean direction. But Williams says things that pull in a non-Humean direction. Notably, there is his intriguing suggestion that Kant, who to some people's minds would be a paradigm *externalist*, is best treated as an internalist:

> Kant thought that a person would recognize the demands of morality if he or she deliberated correctly from his or her existing S, whatever that S might be, but he thought this because he took those demands to be implicit in a conception of practical reason which he could show to apply to *any rational deliberator as such*. I think that it best preserves the point of the internalism/externalism distinction to see this as a limiting case of internalism.[34]

Williams does not think this Kantian argument can be sustained, but he does on this basis accept that Kant is to be classified as an internalist. So in principle there can be motives which are not desires, for on the Kantian view under consideration, an agent can arrive at his moral obligations by a process of reflection on what is involved in his having reasons at all, and will then be motivated by his conclusions about those obligations; that is, motivated by a purely cognitive process. By (3), this agent has an internal reason to carry out the obligations he believes he has.

So Williams' view could be read as a version of subjectivism about fundamental practical norms: the ones that hold for you are the ones you really accept, in the sense that they really motivate you. This view is genuinely distinct from a Humean expressivism based on desire–belief psychology, and from instrumentalism. So interpreted, it can resist the challenge to instrumentalism outlined above. Scanlon puts a version of the challenge when he says that Williams':

> internalism seems to force on us the conclusion that our own reasons ... are all contingent on the presence of appropriate elements in our subjective motivational sets. This rings false and is, I believe, an important source of the widespread resistance to Williams' claims.[35]

Williams can parry this by means of the backgrounding move we considered above (though with the same limitations as before). A person's fundamental practical norms do

---

[34] Williams, B. 1995c: 220, footnote 3. (Williams is responding to Martin Hollis's view that Kant should be classified as an externalist about reasons, and agreeing with Christine Korsgaard's internalist reading of Kant (Korsgaard 1986)—cp. Williams, B. 1995a: 44, footnote 3).
[35] Cp. Scanlon 1998: 367.

not involve *reference* to that person's subjective motivational set; rather, if they really are *his* norms they will be in it. Yet Williams' view, understood in this way, has a very significant disadvantage: it implies an implausibly individualistic form of relativism about practical norms.

10.7 The requirement of effectiveness

Williams challenges the external reasons theorist to explain the content of propositions about reasons in a way which shows how *external* reasons can exist:

> What is it the agent comes to believe when he comes to believe he has a reason to φ? If he becomes persuaded of this supposedly external truth, so that the reason does then enter his S, what is that he has come to believe? This question presents a challenge to the externalist theorist.[36]

The challenge looks question begging:[37] it is a demand to provide a truth condition for propositions about reasons which does not *itself* deploy the concept of a reason. We have argued that the concept of a reason is primitive with respect to other normative concepts; and we shall argue for a non-reductive account of normative propositions. On this view there is no answer to Williams' question, other than that what 'the agent comes to believe' is just that: that he has a reason to φ. When I consider my belief that if I have inconvenienced someone I have reason to apologize, or my belief that if someone has done me a good turn I have reason to show gratitude, their content seems perfectly clear. It does not cry out for analysis in terms which eliminate the concept of a *reason*.

It is true, indeed truistic, that a person can only come to appreciate a reason for acting if they have the existing capacity to do so. A new belief must emerge from an existing belief-forming capacity. Since a capacity to recognize reasons is not in itself a motive, this truism provides no support for (3). It may, however, provide leverage for a form of internalism somewhat different to these. This will become clearer if we consider Williams' other and more challenging argument against external reasons.

It starts from what I shall call the requirement of effectiveness. This is a thesis, Williams says, about 'the interrelation of explanatory and normative reasons':

> If it is true that A has a reason to φ, then it must be possible that he should φ for that reason.[38]

Observe that particularization to the agent is important: if *this* agent has a particular reason to φ then it must be possible that *this* agent should φ for *this particular* reason. Imagine that Tom simply has no sense of gratitude. It's not just that he subscribes to a no-nonsense ethical ideal which regards gratitude as a futile emotion to be suppressed, even though, if he were honest with himself, he would see that he does feel it. He simply never feels it,

---

[36] Williams, B. 1995a: 39. Cp Williams, B. 1981: 109. [37] As noted in Hooker 1987.
[38] Williams, B. 1995a: 38–9.

never expects it—he just doesn't see what this thing called gratitude is about. So when Mary goes out of her way to help him, it's not possible that he should thank her for *that* reason, that is, simply and solely because he sees for himself that gratitude is appropriate. (He may of course recognize prudential reasons to observe the social conventions he's been told about, etc.) Does it follow that that particular fact—that she has gone out of her way to help him—is *not* a reason for him to thank her?

The issue this question raises concerns what in 3.9 I called *cognitive* internalism. If we say that Tom has no reason to thank Mary, the thought that moves us is that a fact cannot *be* a reason for an agent to α if it cannot be recognized as such by him. The thought concerns not the agent's knowledge of the reason-giving facts but his ability to recognize them as reason giving. It is a thesis about all reasons, epistemic, evaluative, and practical. The actor must be able to see for himself, know in the first-person way, that a fact or combination of facts *as such*, were it to obtain, would indeed be a reason to ψ:

(4) Its being the case that Π_i is a possible reason for x to ψ only if x has the ability to recognize that were it to be the case that Π_i, that would be a reason for x to ψ.

In other words, whether some facts π_i are a reason for x to ψ depends on whether x could recognize them as such. We shall consider the crucial question of what *recognition* of a reason requires later.[39] The point for the moment is that (4) is distinct from (3). Just because A has the ability to recognize that its being the case that Π_i would be a reason to ψ it does not follow that he actually believes it would be. He may not even have thought about it. In the case of practical reasons, as we've noted, an existing capacity to recognize a reason for acting cannot be described as an existing *motive*. So (4) does not sustain the view that A has a reason to α only if α-ing would serve a motive in A's S.[40] (4) allows that in Williams' sense of 'external reasons' there can be external reasons.

Nonetheless, there is still a point in calling this view 'internalism'. For (4) says that only considerations which an actor has the ability to recognize, for him or herself, 'from within', *as* reasons, can *be* reasons for that actor. Moreover it is a version of the requirement of effectiveness, which Williams regards as crucial. If an agent simply lacks the ability to recognize a type of consideration as a reason for ψ-ing, then it is not possible that he should ψ for *that* reason, and so, by the requirement of effectiveness, this cannot be a reason for that agent, even if *we* would regard it as a reason. In contrast, if the agent *can* recognize the consideration as a reason to ψ, then ψ-ing for that very reason opens up as an option for him. It becomes possible that he should do so.[41] Cognitive internalism is consistent with the view that beliefs about reasons can themselves motivate. And Kant can certainly be classed as a cognitive internalist: indeed (4) is simply a corollary of his central ideas about reason and autonomy. Autonomy, for Kant, is the capacity to see

---

[39] In Chapter 12, where the issue will become important (12.5, 14.6).

[40] And of course it's quite consistent with denying the converse: that if α-ing would serve a motive in A's S then A has a reason to α.

[41] Note, though, that it may not follow from your having the ability to do something that it's possible for you to do it- depending on how we interpret 'possible'. (You have the ability to walk a tightrope but I'm going to distract you whenever you try.) Williams' requirement of effectiveness should be so understood as not to fall to this kind of point.

reasons for yourself and respond to them, and only autonomous agents can be said to have reasons. Moreover cognitive internalism has bite, as we shall see in Chapter 12. In particular, it has many of the implications for the scope of blame which Williams believes his internalism to have. If we view Williams' critique of modern assumptions about morality from this standpoint, it retains its interest even for those who are unimpressed by Humeanism or instrumentalism about practical reasons.

10.8 Cognitive internalism and the range of practical reasons

In 3.9 I suggested that we don't have a clear-cut response as to the truth of cognitive internalism. Consider again Tom, who is subject to a psychological syndrome that makes him incapable of experiencing or understanding feelings like gratitude. Can we say there *is* nonetheless reason for Tom to be grateful to Mary? Can we say that there is *that* reason—that he has reason to be grateful—for Tom to thank Mary? (Exclude again the indirect reasons he may have, such as reasons of prudence to conform to what he can see are the prevailing social conventions.)

One might say 'there is great reason for him to be grateful to Mary—if only he could see it'. Does this mean that there actually is reason, reason for him, to be grateful, even though he can't see it—or just that there *would* be that reason for him if only he could see it? One could similarly say that there's reason for the wounded bird to thank the gardener who looks after it with loving care—if only it could see it. Or that there's reason for the cat not to torture the mouse, if only it could see it. In saying that we are not, I think, literally ascribing these reasons to the bird or the cat; we are making a roundabout point about the goodwill of the gardener or the badness for the mouse of what the cat does to it.

What would count in favour of ascribing a normative reason to agents who are quite impervious to that particular reason? It may be thought that the universality of reasons pushes in that direction.[42] Surely anyone has reason to thank a person who has helped them. True—but does 'anyone' include Tom? If this seems evasive remember that 'anyone' plainly does not include the wounded bird, or the cat. Whether it includes Tom is precisely the question.

Reasons are universal in the sense that a complete reason can be stated as a universal schema, in the way discussed in 5.6. But who or what falls under the schema? What is its domain? The universality of reasons tells us that reasons of gratitude are universal, but not over what domain they are. If any x has reason to thank a person who has helped them, then every x has; but that does not include the wounded bird, so the wounded bird does not fall within the scope of this class of reasons, and thus within the range of 'x'. The cognitive internalist explains this by invoking the obvious fact that the bird is not an agent capable of appreciating considerations of gratitude and their reason-giving force. It falls outside the range of 'x' because the range of 'x' is constrained by (4). On this

---

[42] As suggested in Scanlon 1998: 367, 372.

explanation it follows that if Tom is *really* incapable of understanding or feeling gratitude then he too falls outside the range of x, as far as reasons of gratitude are concerned. If we find this disconcerting, it is because we don't want to believe that someone in other respects so like us could be quite incapable of appreciating a class of reasons that we find obvious. Or more generally, because we want to get all human beings into the scope of all reasons.

Reality is more complex than the stark example of Tom. There is wide variation in, and a thick margin of unclarity about, the degree to which people are able to appreciate all the variety of types of reason. Furthermore, the degree and extent to which a person has the ability can vary greatly depending on the circumstances. People can suffer a temporary blockage on their ability to see a reason, or they can have an ability that has not yet developed. We can then talk about reasons that apply to them, even though they're unable to see their reason-giving force, or are not yet able see it—because we take as our benchmark their normal ability or the ability that they have a determinate potential to develop.[43]

Williams' despairing teenager, Susan, could be an example. Let's assume that for the moment she just can't see the fact that things will be better in three months time as a reason not to commit suicide. Her inability is caused by the very depth of her despair. In this case one can truly say 'Look, there really is reason for you not to do this. You will feel much better in three months, and that really is a reason. You're not in a state to appreciate that just now, but believe me it's true, and you'll agree with me later'. We reconcile that ascription of reasons to Susan, even in her suicidal state, with (4) by relying on her ability to appreciate these reasons when she is in her normal state.

Now consider some little boys playing a game of running across a railway track at the very last moment in front of an oncoming train. It's not that they don't appreciate the danger—on the contrary, the danger is the whole point. Rather they don't value the benefits of the life before them above the benefits of the glory and respect they gain from their gang right now. They really subscribe to the ideal of bravery and cool, and regard prudential considerations as beneath them. Can we say that they have more reason to avoid playing this game than they appreciate? We may think that we can; in which case we may reconcile our response with (4) by appealing to the assessment they will make when their capacity to appreciate and weigh reasons has matured.

But suppose that this kind of prudence is just not in their nature. They will always rate glamour and cool above everything else. Can we in *this* case say that they have more reason to avoid the game than they appreciate? They appreciate all the facts; they just cannot accept that they generate the balance of reasons that we think they do. We and they appreciate both reasons of glamour and reasons of prudence. But they, even 'in the full maturity of their faculties', give the former a degree of strength relative to the latter

---

[43] 'Determinate potential' raises tricky questions, of course. How determinate? If there's reason to think capital punishment is wrong is there reason for a two-year old with strong moral potential to think so? If not, what development of potential is required? Note also the difference between realizing the potential to grasp a reason and being merely indoctrinated into counting it as one.

which we think to be misguided. Yet surely if reasons universalize, so too does the strength of reasons.

However, in talking about glamour we are talking about *ideals*. The reason-giving force of ideals depends, at least within limits, on what matters to a person—what comes home to that person as worthy of pursuit. So if the ideal of glory is more important to a worldly hero than to an other-worldly ascetic, there *is* more reason for the hero to follow the risky path of glory than the ascetic. That is consistent with the universality of reasons, because what ideals matter to a person (stably, without self-deception, etc.) is written into the facts which generate the reasons.[44] True, a difference of ideals is the very thing that's most commonly experienced as a difference about what's important, and it's natural to put this as a difference about what the balance of reasons 'really' is. Natural, but indefensible: for as between competing, universally intelligible, ideals it can happen that there *is* no 'real', interpersonally invariant, balance of reasons. What ideals have reason-giving force for you depends on your temperament and the way it shapes your outlook; in the case of ideals we expect to find a variety of human temperaments.

In contrast, however, we do not think that how much reason you have to take moral considerations into account depends on your particular temperament. Moral considerations have a reason-giving force which does not vary with the particularities which differentiate one temperament from another. One can't just say 'I can see that doing your duty is admirable, and why there's reason for some people to do it—but I'm not that kind of person'. It seems, then, that with moral obligations, as against ideals, we have universality without subjective conditions. Nonetheless, in both cases—the reason-giving force of ideals and the reason-giving force of moral obligations—(4) can still be held to apply. It's just that with moral obligations, as against ideals, you cannot consistently accept that a moral obligation has reason-giving force for others without also recognizing its reason-giving force in your own case. But now what if you just can't see that some putative moral considerations have reason-giving force at all, for anyone—it's not in your nature to see it?[45] In that case (4) says that these considerations give you no reason to act. And hence if moral obligations are categorical, as I shall argue, these considerations give you no moral obligation. We shall consider these consequences of cognitive internalism in Chapter 12.

10.9 Reason, feeling, and autonomy

As noted in Section 10.1, many acts not rationally explicable are still intelligible, that is, open to interpretative explanation. These explanations provide intelligibility by attributing, in one way or another, normative reasons to the actor. The *attributed* reasons, however, may not *be* reasons for the act that is being explained. The point is worth dwelling on.

---

[44] As 'subjective conditions' in Scanlon's phrase (1998: 367).
[45] Or, perhaps, the circumstances of your social context prevent you from seeing it? Does this count as removing your ability, for purposes of (4)? I don't believe it does, but we can waive the question here.

Interpretative explanation can apply to involuntary behaviour as well as to intentional acts, and to the borders between the two. How then do normative reasons come into play in these cases? Consider some examples:

(i) You scream out because you are frightened; you are frightened because you believe you've seen a masked intruder on the stairs.
(ii) You curse the nail because you're angry with it: it bent when you hit it, which it was not supposed to do.
(iii) Someone cuts you out of a parking spot: you wait until they've left and then you let their tyres down.

You did not scream intentionally; you screamed involuntarily. You did let the tyres down intentionally. Cursing the nail comes somewhere on the borders; it may not be quite right either to say that it was involuntary or to say that it was intentional. In each case we know the reasons *why*: why you screamed; cursed; and let the tyres down. Were these reasons reasons *to* scream, curse, let the tyres down?

There was a reason to let the tyres down: the other driver had acted in a way that merited resentment. But that, someone might say, was no reason to let his tyres down! It was certainly not a sufficient reason—however, it would be merely pious to deny that it was *any* reason at all. Given what he did, there was reason for you to retaliate. As a measure of that, note that provocation mitigates blame. Suppose you remonstrated with him, and he treated your protest with cool contempt. That strengthens your reason to take retaliatory action. Your action was still unwarranted, no doubt—dignity, not getting involved, not acting for reasons on which morality frowns, all count against.

What about cursing the nail? Here there was a kind of reason to curse it: there was reason to be angry with it because it was misbehaving, and cursing it expressed your anger. Against that, surely there is never any reason to be angry with inanimate objects. To be angry at something is to see in it a criticizable intention or failure of expectable performance or care (as with the driver who cuts you out). Yet there is still a kind of reason by extension, from the case where a person or animal fails to do what they are supposed to do. The nail failed to do what *it* was supposed to do. This extension of a normative reason makes your anger, and your cursing as an expression of it, intelligible. (Many symbolic actions are intelligible in this extended kind of way.)

Your scream, however, was completely involuntary—an uncontrolled reaction, not an action. You didn't act for a reason, such as drawing attention to your plight. We cannot ask 'what did you scream for?' as against 'Why did you scream?' Normative practical reasons do not apply, since practical reasons are reasons for intentional actions. Yet that does not mean that normative considerations are not in play. We can ask whether there was reason to be frightened. There may not have been, if there was no intruder there. But if your impression that there was had been correct, there would certainly have been reason to be frightened. That is what makes the scream intelligible: it was a manifestation of understandable fear, and the fear was understandable because there is reason to fear masked intruders.

In all three examples behaviour is explained in terms of feeling, and is *intelligible* because there is reason for that explaining feeling. But in none of them is the behaviour open to rational explanation, because in none of them were you acting from warrant. In many other cases where we interpret an unwarranted act, evaluative reasons are in play. Take again the case where you believe your admired and beloved brother to be innocent, despite the compelling evidence. You are moved by admiration and love. It is (let us suppose) understandable that you should feel that way about this brother of yours and understandable that it should seem disloyal to entertain the thought that he might be the murderer, since it implies a failure of trust. These are reason-supported feelings.

Interpretation explains in terms of feelings for which there are reasons; it does not, and cannot while remaining interpretative, explain in terms of feelings that are completely unsupported by reasons. Rational explanation can also explain in terms of feelings. The point of saying that rational explanation is cognitive is not that it excludes feeling but that the feelings it deals with arise from warrant. You thank from a feeling of gratitude; you feel grateful because you see that this was a generous act. Here the feeling causes the action, but the feeling itself proceeds from warrant: that is what makes the explanation as a whole a rational explanation.

Let us now go back to the notion of autonomy. There is an old cluster of ideas in moral philosophy: full freedom, in a certain important sense of freedom, is autonomy; autonomy is reason; reason—autonomy, freedom—is threatened by the passions. I shall defend the equation of freedom in this sense ('positive freedom') with autonomy in 19.5. What truth is there then in the contrast between reason and the passions? Three points seem relevant.

A. Since we have defined autonomy as acting from warrant and accepted that rational explanation can cover feeling as well as belief and action, it follows that autonomy is a property of feelings as well as beliefs and actions. The fact that autonomy is a matter of feeling as well as action and belief is of first importance. It underlies liberal theory about the aesthetic education of man, in Schiller's phrase. You lose positive freedom when your feelings are unguided by developed insight into evaluative reasons. The greatest obstacle in the way of this notion of self-development is the rationalistic distortion of reasons that eliminates evaluative reasons. There is also a more subtle intellectualist distortion: acting from warrant in this case, as in the case of action and belief, should not be over-intellectualized. You look after your children because you love them. You do not normally question whether your love is warranted; you are naturally aware that it is. It is a sad day if something happens that forces you to ask whether they deserve your love; it is sad too if the circumstances of your life make you ask whether your warranted love for them warrants you in looking after them, as against undertaking some other duty.[46]

B. But granting that rationalistic and intellectualist distortions devastate a proper understanding of the place of feeling in autonomy, there is still obvious truth in the idea

---

[46] Which is not to deny that when affection fails the disinterested motive of justice may have to take over. Cp. Waldron 1993.

that autonomy can be undermined by passion. You can fail in autonomy through misperception of warrant, or through failing to act on a warrant correctly perceived. In both cases there may be no interpretative explanation of the failure. But when your failure is intelligible at all, it will often be explicable in terms of some interfering feeling. In these cases, willpower may be needed, not just in doing the warranted thing, but also in suppressing or at least disabling an unwarranted belief or feeling, or making yourself believe or feel something warranted.

C. That in turn will raise the question whether 'making yourself do it'—if you can—is warranted. Is it worth the effort in a particular case? Where it isn't, you may lack autonomy whatever you do. The same will hold if there can be situations where there is warrant to make yourself feel or believe what there is no warrant to feel or believe. And such cases are likely to arise in any theory of practical reasons which does not make autonomy the be-all and end-all of action. But a theory that does do that seems too extreme to be plausible. So one can autonomously give up some autonomy.

10.10 The will: *Wille* and *Willkür*

Belief and feeling are not actions. What then distinguishes action? One obvious contender is the will. Belief and feeling are not actions because we cannot believe or feel at will. We can decide, often with some effect, whether to let ourselves believe or feel, or try to stop ourselves from believing or feeling. That, however, is not believing or feeling at will; it is deciding what to do, or to try to do, about our beliefs and feelings. So what is the will?

One view is that 'willing' or 'volition' is an act that causes acts. Acts other than volitions are voluntary actions when they are caused by a volition. (Voluntary action in this sense contrasts with involuntary acts, not with coerced action.) In most cases we seem to be able to tell whether our behaviour was voluntary; for example, I know whether I screamed voluntarily or involuntarily. One can also discover that one can or cannot do something voluntarily, for example, wiggle one's ears. On this view when we know that our action was voluntary we know it was caused by a volition, and when we discover that we can do something voluntarily ('at will') we are discovering in which cases volition is effective.

However, even if this thesis is correct, it does not explain what differentiates action from belief or feeling. On the one hand, if volitions are actions (such as deciding or choosing) we still haven't given a *general* explanation of the difference between action and belief or feeling. Furthermore, if volition itself is action it becomes fruitless to postulate volition in order to explain why accepting a reason to act sometimes causes action and sometimes does not. We merely push back the question to why reason-acceptance sometimes causes this particular action—volition—and sometimes does not. On the other hand, it seems uncomfortably vacuous to postulate a mental event of volition which is not itself an action, but differentiates voluntary action from involuntary behaviour by causing the former. This postulated event does no other explanatory work. In particular, if we think it is required to explain how reason-acceptance triggers action, why isn't some similar event required to explain how reason-acceptance triggers belief or feeling?

In reality, there is no general problem about how believing that you are warranted in ψ-ing can cause you to ψ, be it in the case of action, belief, or feeling. In a certain sense, nothing can be more intelligible. True, you might be surprised that I managed to act rationally on this particular occasion when I so often fail, and you might seek an explanation. Usually, however, what requires interpretative explanation is the opposite: why a person failed to ψ, when they thought they had warrant to ψ. Either way, as noted above, we should not assume determinism at the level of interpretation, and so we should be prepared to find no *interpretative* explanation at all.

To have a will is simply to have the power of acting from what one takes to be reasons for the action. Accepting something as a reason for action and being disposed by this acceptance to act (immediately or as a standing disposition) are so closely connected as to be separable only through interfering causes (including inertial causes).[47] But since there can be reasons for and against an action, there can be conflicting dispositions of the will to act.

Even if no special mental act of volition underlies all voluntary behaviour, however, the phenomenon of *willpower* exists. A disposition of the will is a disposition to act from a reason-acceptance. But there can be dispositions to act that are not dispositions of the will—promptings of passion. Thus the strength of inclinations to act can diverge from the perceived strength of the reasons for action. The strongest total inclination to act may not coincide with accepted warrant. This is where willpower, or resolve, comes in.

We occasionally have to make ourselves do something we are not inclined, or positively disinclined, to do, or stop ourselves from doing something we are inclined to do. This may involve an effort of the will, or it may just require careful attention. For example: you are not naturally inclined to thank people, or compliment them, but you pay careful attention to doing so at the appropriate moments. (It may or may not come across successfully...) Another, familiar, example: you have to make a tremendous effort to get out of bed in the morning when you know you should. But in this case mere attention to the need to do so is not enough. You have to promise yourself that you'll get out of bed on the count of ten...or twenty...and then positively *throw yourself* out of bed. Let's include intentional attention, as well as intentional effort, under the heading of 'willpower'. Intentional attention and intentional effort are actions; they are, however, auxiliaries that are absent from most actions. Mostly, one acts or refrains from acting without having to exercise careful attention or effort. One simply accepts that there is good reason to do something and does it.

---

[47] 'Deviant causal chains' likewise involve mediation by interfering causes. In these cases one's action is caused by one's acceptance of some reasons, but one does not act *from, in virtue of,* that acceptance.

You can also exercise willpower to stop involuntary behaviour, or to do something intentionally that is normally involuntary. You may be able to stop yourself belching, coughing, screaming, or yawning: just by attending to the task, or by effort. You can try to see, for example, whether you can cry or whistle at will. It may require attention (whistling) or effort (crying). Finally your ability to exercise willpower can vary. It may be overwhelmed by passion, or undermined by tiredness.

Can willpower produce or prevent belief or feeling? The question is not whether you can bring it about that you believe or feel, cause yourself to believe or feel, by *indirect* means; but whether you can make yourself or stop yourself from believing or feeling directly, by attention to the task and effort, as in the case of crying or sneezing. It seems that you cannot make yourself believe or feel by willpower alone; it's not so clear that you cannot *stop* yourself believing or feeling by willpower alone. What you certainly can do by willpower is to unlink a belief or feeling from action. You can also exercise willpower—attention and/or effort, to overcome a desire to avoid inconvenient evidence, or to avoid scrutinizing a possible warrant too deeply. You can keep reminding yourself of some compelling evidence, or that there really isn't sufficient reason, say, to get annoyed. In these ways you can effectively school your beliefs and feelings. What you cannot do is believe or feel at will, where that means using only willpower, and no indirect or roundabout means. It seems that we are designed to take over motor control of our actions by willpower, in cases where spontaneous response to reason-acceptance is inadequate. This motor control involves the redirection of energy and effort and is thus costly on the resources of the organism overall. But the same mechanism of direct control of our beliefs and feelings—by an intentional switching-in of willpower—does not exist. Why the difference? It seems that the most important thing for the organism is to get *action* right (which makes evolutionary sense). Action is normally determined directly by belief, or by belief and feeling. However, where warranted belief and feeling is insufficient to determine action, or unwarranted belief and feeling threatens to determine it, a corrective mechanism is required. Given that this mechanism exists, and is linked to the capacity to assess warrants for belief and feeling, a further mechanism for correcting belief and feeling by direct effort is redundant.

This discussion provides a model for Kant's distinction between *Wille* and *Willkür*. *Wille* is simply practical reason, reason in its practical function: it is the power of recognizing and acting from reasons. *Willkür* in the narrow sense is a kind of special resource within this executive power; an effort which switches in when *Wille* is resisted.

Kant is one of those who identify freedom (in the 'positive' sense) with autonomy: positively free acts are those driven by reason-recognition as such, undistorted either at the point where reasons are recognized, or at the point where recognition causes action, by any alien causes, that is, causes irrelevant to warrant, causes which do not contribute to recognition of warrant. In 1.7 I criticized Kant for failing to recognize that feelings, as well as beliefs and action, have their reasons. They too can be warranted or unwarranted; a warranted feeling is not an alien cause. When such a feeling gives rise to an appropriate action—warranted gratitude, say, to thanks—that too is autonomy. I feel grateful, and I (rightly) take that feeling to be warranted: that is why I give thanks. Still, so long as it's granted that feelings, far from being 'alien', can enter the realm of autonomy in this way, Kant's assertion remains true:

> Will is a kind of causality belonging to living beings so far as they are rational. *Freedom* would then be the property this causality has of being able to work independently of *determination* by alien causes...[48]

We shall return to this idea in 19.4.

[48] *Groundwork*, IV, 446.

11

REASONS AND FEELINGS: (I) THE BRIDGE PRINCIPLE AND THE CONCEPT OF A PERSON'S GOOD

Having discussed the character of rational and, more generally, interpretative explanation, we turn in this and the next four chapters to the normative theory of evaluative and practical reasons. As in the discussion of epistemic reasons in Part II, our interest will be in the salient features that must appear in any reasonably comprehensive picture of this domain of reasons, the evaluative and practical: its distinctive normative concepts and its normative sources. What these are is in itself controversial, of course—considerably more so, it seems, than in the epistemic case.

In the course of the previous chapter, we rejected instrumentalism and motivational internalism as theories of practical reason. When these Procrustean theories are put aside, we discover a number of normative sources, each of which has served as a basis for ethical theorizing in the past. In fact our eventual conclusion will be that practical reasons have three irreducible normative sources, which I shall call the *Bridge* principle, the principle of *Good* and the *Demand* principle.

Many practical reasons arise from evaluative reasons: there is a reason for a person to do something because there is reason for them to feel something. The Bridge principle is the principle under which these practical reasons fall. It is therefore the essential component in a sentimentalist account of the connection between value and practical reasons. Important concepts that belong within this account are the concept of a person's good, and the concept of personal ideals. These concepts, together with the Bridge principle itself, are the main topics of this chapter.

Another main topic in Part III as a whole is moral obligation. There is a sentimentalist tradition among the British moralists (notably Smith, Hume, Bentham, and Mill) which gives an account of the moral concepts in terms of the sentiment of blame. Chapter 12 will show in detail that such an account of all the moral concepts can indeed be given. (Our touchstones will be Smith and Mill rather than Hume.) It will also show that this sentimentalist account is consistent with, and indeed entails, the categoricity of moral obligation: i.e. that if a person has a moral obligation to do something then that is what they have uniquely sufficient reason to do.

However, these conclusions leave two important questions unanswered. In the first place, although moral obligation is categorical in the sense just given, it does not follow that one has sufficient reason do an action that is moral obligatory *because* it is moral obligatory, i.e. that the fact that it is morally obligatory constitutes a reason to do it. That is not so. On the contrary, where an action is morally obligatory it is the specific considerations that warrant the action, whatever these are, that also makes it morally obligatory. Moral obligation is not as such an a priori source of practical reasons, though for some people it can become a source.

So what role does moral judgement, judgement as to what is morally obligatory or morally wrong, play in practical reasoning? Before we can address that question in Chapter 15 we need a comprehensive picture of practical reason's normative sources. Sentimentalism, we shall see, cannot give an adequate account of the normative role that *impartiality* plays in practical reason, whether it appears in the form of an appeal to impartial good, or to rights. The principles underlying these domains are the principles of Good and Demand. They are the topic of Chapter 13 and 14.

The other important question is about the nature of blame. The British moralists, mentioned above, were right to conceive moral wrongness in terms of blame, but mistaken, or at best impoverished, in their ideas of what blame, and thus morality, is. On the whole, we get little sense from their writings of the personal and anthropological significance of the moral. (Smith and Mill are substantially more forthcoming in this respect than are Hume and Bentham, but the point still applies.) For greater stimulus we must turn to a more phenomenological and hermeneutic tradition—that of German idealism: specifically, to some of its key ethical ideas: recognition; its withdrawal; ethical punishment; atonement; moral; or 'positive' freedom. These are the ideas from which to start an account of the emotional significance of the moral and its role in human life—though we shall develop them in our own way.

In this chapter, however, we are concerned with those reasons for action that fall under the Bridge principle, and with personal good and personal ideals.

11.1 Sentimentalism: the Bridge principle

Sentimentalism, as we shall understand it here, can come in a weaker and a stronger form.[1] In its weaker form it is the view (i) that there are irreducible reasons to feel, and (ii) that value is analysable in terms of these reasons to feel.

The weaker thesis, *sentimentalism about value*, is a pillar of this book. There is, we hold, an immanent rationality of the feelings—evaluative reasons are both conceptually and epistemically irreducible: their nature and strength can be assessed only from within, in

---

[1] D'Arms and Jacobson 2000 call it *neo-sentimentalism*. But the view that sentiments may be apt, proper, fitting to their object, correct in relation to it etc. is not new but old: it is the standard position, one can say, of the sentimentalist tradition in ethics—to which Hume was a conscious exception.

their own hermeneutic terms. Consider again the examples at the beginning of Chapter 1. We *understand* that when you win the match despite all the pressure, you have reason to be proud—that when someone who is supposed to be doing a job for you fails yet again to turn up you have reason to be annoyed—that you have good reason to be grateful to someone who helps you out of a very tight corner—and no reason to feel ashamed of yourself just because you made a very understandable mistake in reading the navigation chart. This is hermeneutic or interpretative understanding, an understanding that stems from our first-person acquaintance with those feelings. Its epistemological foundations will be explored in Chapter 16.[2]

We have argued that all value terms can be analysed in terms of reasons. Not all of them are analysable in terms of *evaluative* reasons, but sentimentalists are not claiming that they are. They are not saying that you should analyse what good evidence is, or what a good power drill is, in terms of evaluative reasons. Value terms span the whole tripartite field of reasons. Often, however, when we talk about *value* we have in mind a notion that does not include epistemic or practical value. We have in mind aesthetic and ethical value in the broadest sense—all those value terms that are analysable in terms of *evaluative* reasons. From now on we shall use the term 'value' in this narrower way.

In its stronger form, sentimentalism adds a thesis about practical reasons: (iii) that all practical reasons are in one way or another grounded in evaluative reasons. We shall not defend this *universal* sentimentalism about practical reasons. On the contrary, in Chapters 13 and 14 it will be claimed that there is such a thing as impartial or disinterested practical reason. Thus while we are committed to defending sentimentalism about value together with its dependent practical reasons, we shall reject thesis (iii).

Nonetheless it remains true, and important, that very many practical reasons are indeed grounded in evaluative reasons. By what logic? If at least some practical reasons are somehow grounded in evaluative reasons, there must be some principle or principles that bridge the gap from propositions about evaluative reasons to propositions about practical reasons. There is, I propose, at least one such principle; we can call it 'the Bridge principle'.

All feelings tend to manifest in characteristic behaviour. In particular, many feelings dispose to *intentional actions* that are distinctive to the particular feeling. This does not apply to all feelings; joy, for example, doesn't seem to prompt to any characteristic *action*, as against involuntary behavioural expression. The Bridge principle applies to that narrower class of feelings which have a characteristic propensity to prompt one to some type of intentional action.[3] A first stab at it is this:

(1) If there's reason for x to feel ϕ there's reason for x to do what feeling ϕ characteristically disposes one to do—the 'ϕ-prompted action'.

---

[2] Contrast evolutionary explanations of why we have the feelings we do. They have no direct bearing on interpretative understanding or normative assessment of evaluative reasons, though they might in principle bear on whether there is practical reason to foster some type of feeling or to attempt to control and reduce it.

[3] Comments by Ingmar Persson have helped me to clarify what I mean by the Bridge principle.

Here are some examples. Out of sheer goodness of heart, someone does me an unrequested good turn. That fact certainly gives me reason to feel grateful. And because I have reason to feel grateful to him for his good turn, I have reason to act from that gratitude, for example, by thanking him or giving him a present or by returning the favour. These are various forms of the characteristic intentional action to which gratitude prompts. Suppose, on the other hand, that he did me some undeserved harm. In that case I have good reason to feel resentful. And because I have reason to feel resentment I have reason to express that resentment, by recrimination, insistence on apology, or even by seeking amends. Likewise, if there's reason to be frightened of something then there's reason to avoid it; if there's reason to be bored by something then there's reason not to attend to it. Flight and attention-withdrawal are the characteristic actions prompted by fear and boredom. Fear may also root one to the spot, boredom may make one yawn; but these are involuntary responses, not intentional actions. (Yawning intentionally would be an action for which there might be reason, such as drawing attention, somewhat discourteously, to the fact that one is bored. But that is not a practical reason generated by the Bridge principle for boredom.)

Note that the Bridge principle is stated in terms of specific reasons, not overall or sufficient reasons. It's certainly not true, for example, that if there is sufficient reason to be frightened there is sufficient reason to run away. There may be all sorts of other reasons not to run away. Equally, there may also be reasons to do the ϕ-prompted action other than the one captured by the Bridge principle. For example, there is often reason to thank just because thanking is an 'expression' of gratitude. It is not true, by contrast, that there is a reason to run away because running away is an 'expression' of fear. Running away is not usually an expression of fear, in this sense of 'expression'. That is, it is not done in order to convey to others that one is afraid. The extra reason, in the case of gratitude, is that *conveying* that one feels the sentiment can be an appropriate thing to do in its own right—an important part of social reciprocity and co-operation. In the case of resentment, or boredom, the very same consideration may give reason *not* to express, show, what one feels. In all cases, however, the reason that comes via the Bridge principle remains.

(1) Is a conditional. It does not entail.

(1a) The fact that there's reason for x to feel ϕ is itself a reason for x to do what feeling ϕ prompts one to do.

Is this stronger claim true? Consider Tom, the 'gratitude-blind' person (10.7). Cognitive internalism (3.9) implies that there is no reason for him to feel gratitude. If there is no reason for him to feel gratitude, is there, nevertheless, reason for him to do a gratitude-prompted thing? There might be other reasons, for example, of prudence, but if cognitive internalism is right there would not be *that*, Bridge-based, reason. The existence of *that* reason is dependent on the existence of the evaluative reason. There is Bridge-based reason to thank because, in virtue of there being, reason to feel grateful. However, that is not quite captured by (1a). It is not, for example, the mere existential fact that *there is reason for me to feel grateful* that constitutes a reason for me to say thank you. Rather, the fact that you have done me a good turn is both a reason to feel grateful and a reason to thank you. The fact that *is* a reason to feel ϕ, whatever that fact may be, is always also a reason to do the ϕ-prompted action; but it is a reason to do that action in virtue of being a reason to feel ϕ. Thus we have the following statement of the Bridge principle:

> (2) (*Bridge principle*): Whatever facts give x reason to feel ϕ give x reason to do the ϕ-prompted action, in virtue of being a reason to feel ϕ.

(2) entails (1) but not vice versa. According to (2) the facts in question would not be a Bridge-based reason for x to do a ϕ-prompted action if they were not a reason for x to feel ϕ. They constitute the practical reason in virtue of constituting the evaluative reason. In general a Bridge-based practical reason exists in virtue of the existence of an underlying evaluative reason.[4]

What is the status of the Bridge principle? I submit that it is a priori but I do not claim that it is true by any definition. Rather, for each action-prompting feeling or sentiment, ϕ, to grasp the nature of ϕ, in particular its proper intentional object, is to grasp the truth of the principle for that instance. Our understanding of the nature of feelings is ineliminably, though of course not wholly, normative. Emotions have their own hermeneutic principles, constitutively linking the reasons for them and for the actions they prompt with their intentional objects. By a hermeneutic principle I mean a principle whose truth one can see for oneself (as against learning of its truth by testimony) only by experiencing and apprehending in one's imagination the emotion which it concerns.[5] It is, for example, by grasping in one's experience and imagination what it is to feel grateful that one understands the link between gratitude's intentional object and the action to which it prompts. A gratitude-blind person could not grasp that link.

This is how practical reasons are grounded in evaluative reasons (when they are). One knows that these facts are a reason to thank someone by understanding what gratitude *is*, hence knowing them to be reasons to feel grateful and understanding the link between gratitude and thanks. What we discuss when we discuss Bridge-based practical reasons is not the Bridge principle—that is too obvious to interest us; what interests us, typically, is exactly what there *is* reason to feel.

11.2 The concept of a person's good

We stated in 4.3 that a person's good consists in the realization of whatever there's reason for that person to desire. A state of affairs is part of a person's good if and only if there is

---

[4] 'In virtue of' is not a new primitive. The Bridge principle could be put thus:

> Whatever fact gives x reason to feel ϕ gives x reason to do the ϕ-prompted action, and the reason it does is that it is a reason to feel ϕ.

Here too, then, the supervenience relation is just the reason relation. See also 18.6.

[5] I assume that one cannot apprehend in imagination an emotion one has no capacity to experience. But if that is false imaginative apprehension is enough.

reason for this person to desire what it obtains. One can also say that a person's good consists in the realization of whatever is desirable for that person, using this phrase to mean whatever there's reason for that person to desire.

We are talking about substantive desires. As noted in Chapter 10, substantive desire should be placed with the feelings, not with the will. Hence when we assess whether there's reason for a person substantively to desire something we're assessing an evaluative, not a practical reason. The facts which constitute a reason to desire something are the facts which make it desirable, just as the facts which constitute a reason to admire something are the facts which make it admirable. Remember also (10.2) that the distinction between instrumental and final reasons has no application to evaluative reasons, any more than it does to epistemic reasons. Just as there is no such thing as an instrumental reason or a final reason to believe something, so there is no such thing as an instrumental or a final reason to admire, hate, love—or desire something.

There may of course be an instrumental *practical* reason to bring it about that one believes something or desires something, so far as one has the power to do that. There are the all-too-well-discussed types of case in which, for example, one is offered a million pounds if one believes that there are Martians amongst us or if one desires to sleep in a cesspit. In these cases one has instrumental practical reason to *bring it about* that one desires, but no evaluative reason to desire. There's no reason to desire to sleep in a cesspit, at least for most of us who don't have kinky sources of enjoyment. On the contrary, for most of us there's reason to desire not to. So sleeping in a cesspit is not for most of us a part of our good. Nonetheless, if you're offered a million pounds for desiring to do that, then there's good practical reason to try to make yourself desire it. A million pounds would get you a lot of things that there is indeed reason for you to desire, so that desiring to sleep in the cess-pit (if you can somehow bring about in yourself such a desire) will be instrumental to your good, even though it is no *part* of your good.

Thus when we say that a person's good is what there is reason for that person to desire, we are not talking about a practical reason to bring it about that one desires something but about an evaluative reason to desire it, a reason which admits no distinction between 'instrumental' and 'final'. The proposal is that an object contributes to a person's good if and only if there is *evaluative* reason for that person to desire it *substantively*. This is an application of the sentimentalist account of value to the notion of a person's good.

It is indeed a proposal, in part reconstructive. For it is not clear that there is a single distinct and prevailing notion of a person's good in non-philosophical discourse. We talk about what would be good for a person, what would be in their best interest, what would conduce to their welfare or well-being. These are plainly important ethical concepts, but it is not clear that they exactly converge on a single concept. To that extent the concept of a person's good is something that one needs to articulate and justify philosophically and not simply to describe.

We should not assume that it is exactly captured by 'what conduces to a person's *well-being*', or 'what is *good for* a person', at least in the usual meanings of these phrases. In this area it is worth paying attention to small ordinary language distinctions. The term 'well-being' has a strongly established ordinary use in which it refers narrowly to a person's physical and psychological well-being, or flourishing; his fitness, well-functioning, 'sense of well-being'. Well-being or flourishing in this sense is an empirical quality of a person which we may need the help of doctors and psychologists to characterize. It's certainly very plausible, at the substantive normative level, that well-being in this sense is an important part of a person's good—but it is not clear that it is the only part. Conceivably your overall good is better served if you let your well-being in this sense slip somewhat, by accepting the neuralgia and depressions involved in finishing your great novel. You might give short shrift to any doctors or clinical psychologists who tell you otherwise, thinking to yourself that they are going beyond their area of special expertise.

The phrase 'what is good for x' also has a distinctive ordinary use. As noted in 4.3, it expresses a general notion that applies more widely than to persons. There is what is good for the lawn; what is good for the bicycle; what is good for sharks or spiders. In general, what is good for an F is what tends to produce a good F, an F there is reason to favour as a specimen of its kind. What is good for the lawn is what tends to produce a lawn that there's reason to admire as a lawn. What is good for the bicycle is what tends to produce a cycle that there's reason to choose for cycling, if one has reason to cycle (at least if one is leaving aside the aesthetics of bicycles). By this reckoning, if it makes sense to apply this notion to a person, then what is good for a person is what makes him or her a good specimen of a person. Perfectionists, who may be influenced by ancient ethics, may hold that what is good for a person is what conduces to their being a good, an excellent, person. We shall return to perfectionism in Section 11.9. On a more down-to-earth understanding, what is good for a person consists in what maintains or promotes their sense of physical and mental well-being. This seems to me closer to what we ordinarily mean when we talk about what is good for you (as in 'Exercise is good for you').[6]

In any case, however, we should distinguish between formal theses about, and substantive theories of, a person's good. We can no doubt agree that a person's physical and mental well-being is likely to be, other things equal, something there is reason for that person to desire. It will be a part of their good.[7] And we can agree that for many people at any rate, their excellence as persons is a desirable end. But neither of these claims is true by definition. The truth of perfectionism, hedonism, or any other substantive conception of the human good is a substantive ethical question. Our definition leaves open that question. The case for it is that it is the right characterization of a notion that is crucially important for many if not all ethical theories; the one we require for a variety of Critical purposes in ethical thought.

---

[6] There is also an emerging, and as it seems to me, semi-technical use of 'what is good for a person' to mean what conduces to their good, in *whatever* way the latter is characterized. See, for example, Kraut 2007. The question is whether that use gives us leverage on the notion of personal good, or whether it's the other way round.

[7] It is also the part of a person's good that it is often easiest, or indeed appropriate, to focus on for policy purposes. That is relevant for policy, but shouldn't give it an undue salience for ethical theory.

11.3 Desire and reason to desire

But how do I tell what there is *reason* for me or anyone else to desire? Can it differ from what I actually do desire? What sort of Critical inquiry are we undertaking when we ask, in particular, whether there's reason for a person to desire something which they do not desire, or whether there's no reason for them to desire something which they do desire? How does this sort of gap open up?

The only way to tell what there is reason for a person to desire, what is desirable for that person, consists in evidence as to what they desire, or what people like them desire. This was John Stuart Mill's point in that famous passage of *Utilitarianism*:

> The only proof capable of being given that an object is visible, is that people actually see it. The only proof that a sound is audible is that people hear it: and so of the other sources of our experience. In like manner, I apprehend, *the sole evidence it is possible to produce that anything is desirable, is that people do actually desire it.*

Mill's analogy with 'visible' and 'audible' got him into well-deserved hot water;[8] nonetheless the italicized sentence—given its sly switch from 'proof' to 'evidence'—is sound. For our purposes, however, elucidation is required. We should distinguish between (i) evidence as to what *is* really, substantively, desired; and (ii) the more puzzling idea that facts about what is so desired are 'evidence' of what there is reason to desire.

It is not always easy to discover what is really desired, whether in others' case or in one's own. Desire is, so to speak, affectively and motivationally real—but it is by no means transparent to self-consciousness. On the contrary, it can be very hard to tell what you really want. A character in a novel, for example, might meet a former lover unexpectedly, and ask himself, 'Do I still feel any desire for her?' He might find that a very difficult question to answer. And one can easily imagine ways in which the answer might be important to him. He might regret later, for example, getting the answer wrong. And getting it right might have important consequences for his well-being. If only, he might think to himself later, I'd realized that I still wanted her (or come to that, that I no longer did).

It can sometimes actually be easier to see what other people really want than to know what one wants oneself, but for the most part it is even harder. What end a person pursues *ex ante* and how content they are with achieving it *ex post* (before and after they've got it) is the basic evidence. On that basis we can start forming hypotheses about what they want, in the aim-eliciting sense of want, or would want if they had more information as to the facts, or if they had other beliefs about their obligations, etc. Out of that information about their ends we still have to extract hypotheses about their substantive desires. Obviously it is relevant to ask them, and also relevant to consider what other people like them in age, character, or circumstances are found to desire. It remains that

---

[8] Though in the light of the enormous literature on this passage it is curious to see how little weight he placed on it. See his letter to his German translator, Theodore Gomperz in Mill (1963–91), vol. XVI: 1391. The passage itself is at vol. X: 234 (*Utilitarianism* Chapter. 4. para. 3).

knowing what a person really wants, and even more, knowing whether doing what they substantively want now will get them what they substantively want (are content with) when they get it, especially in the case of very big choices, is notoriously difficult.

So if people's substantive desires are the only evidence of their good, they are pretty obscure evidence. That is no objection, since what constitutes a person's good *is* often itself obscure. We are all aware, in our own case let alone that of our children say, or come to that our ageing parents, how hard it is to know, most of the time and particularly in important cases, what is really best for anyone. These difficulties go well beyond the problems of identifying probable outcomes or best means. They should be faithfully captured by the epistemology of personal good, since they really are there.

So much as to (i), evidence of substantive desire. What about (ii), evidence as to the desirable? The facts as to what someone substantively desires are *criteria* of what there is reason for them to desire. A criterion for a proposition is an a priori but potentially defeasible sufficient reason for believing that proposition. In that sense, facts about what people desire can be criteria for what is desirable, and are in the end the only criteria. This is a particular case of the epistemology of normative, as against factual, propositions—a topic to be considered more generally in Chapter 16.

Is it, however, appropriate to regard facts about people's desires as 'evidence' of what there is reason for them to desire? We are not dealing here with (say) behavioural criteria of psychological states, such as amusement or pain. Such criteria can be regarded, from one point of view, as the media in which one 'sees' the others' state of mind, but also from another, as indicative evidence of that state of mind (9.5). The normative case is different. It does not involve the idea of evidence, indicative, or inductive. Nonetheless, the fact that you substantively desire something can, in an appropriate epistemic field, be a reason to believe that there is reason (for you) to desire it.

This lack of connection with either the indicative or the inductive notion of evidence is what makes it somewhat odd to describe the fact that you desire O as *evidence* that there is reason for you to desire O. However, Mill's aim in using the word 'evidence' is to avoid the implication that propositions about what people desire *entail* propositions about what is desirable. And to that extent he is right: the relation between them is a criterial relation, not a relation of entailment.

So how can a gap open up between what you desire and what there is reason for you to desire?

An obvious way is through lack of knowledge. You may fail to desire something there is reason for you to desire because you lack relevant knowledge. For the same reason you may desire something there is really no reason for you to desire. Evaluative reasons are not in general determined by what you believe, or even what there's good reason for you to believe. So, for example, if someone is spreading malicious lies about you behind your back then there's reason for you to be angry with them even if you are unaware that there is. Equally if they're doing you an anonymous good turn then there's reason for you to feel grateful to them even if you don't know it. Similarly with desire. For example, the fact that you'll enjoy something is a reason for you to desire it, even if you don't know that you'll enjoy it. Equally, if you desire something in virtue of thinking it will be pleasurable, but your belief that it will be pleasurable is false, there may be no reason for you to desire it. Even if you wanted something in advance, and go on wanting it when you have it, that might be because of false beliefs you have about it, or ignorance about some aspects of it. The gap between desire and reason to desire can open up in this simple way.

Can it open up in other ways? Can there be a gap that is not explicable in terms of false factual beliefs or absence of true ones? There are other kinds of defeaters, which raise more complex questions. Perhaps you want the object only because you've been brought up in a way that stunts or limits your emotional potential. Is it in that case a part of your good to have it? It may or may not be: we can't answer without further investigation. Or your desires and lack of desires might reflect interfering factors such as depression, distraction, prejudice, preconception, and so forth. There is the extreme case of Susan considered in the previous chapter (10.5). Her only substantive desire is to commit suicide, but there is no reason for her to desire to do that. Again, as a matter of course desires can become ingrained: you have decided to give up smoking, and you have taken a pill that will make smoking a cigarette thoroughly unpleasant, so you know you won't like smoking it even as you light up; yet you still desire to light up.

So desire can be disqualified as evidence of desirability in various ways that are not related to inadequate *factual* knowledge. I want to draw particular attention to the fact that *normative* discussion about what is desirable, and in general comparison with the normative attitudes of other people, can kill or create desires. This can be a helpful process, if it kills desires there's no reason for you to have, and gives rise to desires there is reason for you to have. It can also be unhelpful. You may, for example, pick up distorting ideals or self-images from your peer group. You come to desire things that will give you no satisfaction (that you won't really want when you have them). Not that this *entails* that there was no reason for you to desire these things. You may have changed in the interim between desiring it and achieving it. That raises a general point that we should consider.

11.4 The irreducibility of reasons to desire

Desires are criteria of desirability: here as everywhere however we take the concept of a reason, in this case of a reason to desire, to be primitive, in the sense that the reason relation is not identifiable with any non-normatively characterized relation. As will be argued in Chapter 18, where we discuss the 'open-question' argument, this would be so even if an a priori biconditional could be given. Suppose, for example, that hedonism were true. In that case it would be true that an object satisfies 'there is reason for x to desire y (in the substantive sense of desire)' if and only if it satisfies 'y would please x'. But this would not show that the two predicates pick out the same property.

However, it is still interesting to ask whether an a priori true biconditional, linking desirability to hypothetical desire, can be produced. We might, for example, think in terms of interfering factors that cause in you desires that are distorted and thus do not qualify as evidence of desirability, or alternatively prevent you from developing desires in a way that would qualify those desires as evidence of desirability. Can we say that there is reason for you to desire O if and only if you would desire O in the absence of interfering factors?

Attempts to do this will encounter some familiar difficulties. In the first place this biconditional, even if true, would be non-circular only if we had way of listing what the interfering factors are that did not depend, explicitly or implicitly, on prior identification of what there is reason to desire.

Furthermore, it is highly likely that there are objects, there is actually reason for you to desire just *because* you are affected by interfering factors. Suppose you and your friends are greatly impressed by some flashy but minor piece of skill—long-distance accurate spitting, say. In your peer group this skill counts for a lot. On this basis you conceive a strong desire to master it, and having mastered it you get a lot of satisfaction from it. Were you to mix with a wider circle of people and develop your ideas of what is worthwhile—or just get a bit older—you would come to think that you were wasting your time mastering this, and that the admiration of your little group was silly. Spitting skills would give you no satisfaction, and you would lose the desire to have them. Your natural bent towards competitive physical achievement would instead develop into a desire to compete in some complex, taxing sport, such as pentathlon. Is there, as things are, reason for you to desire to perfect your spitting skills? Or is there reason for you to seek instead a wider experience that will promote a deeper insight into what it is worth your while doing?

No doubt both. The desire to be spitting champion is transiently reason-supported but in due course loses its support. Suppose, however, that some external interfering factors prevent you from widening your experience and knowledge in the required way. Then it remains the case there is reason for you to desire to be a great spitter, even though the widening process would remove the desire. This is a normative structure in which there is reason for you to desire something just *because* the presence of interfering factors prevents you from widening your experience and insight in a way which would remove the relevant desire. So it cannot be that what there is reason for you to desire is what there would be reason for you to desire if all interfering factors were removed.

This example touches the epistemological issues raised by Mill's famous distinction between higher and lower pleasures. In non-hedonistic terms, the distinction is between higher and lower personal goods: the claim is that there are more and less fulfilling ways of life open to you, and there is reason for you to desire to achieve those more fulfilling ways of life. How can we tell that one way is more fulfilling than another? Mill is quite right to think that there is no test, or criterion, other than what is desired by competent judges in non-misleading circumstances. The question is not whether there is an epistemic circle here—there is. We test what is more or less fulfilling by the judgements of competent judges and we test the competence of the judges by their judgements of what is more fulfilling. Furthermore, the mere fact that they have experienced both say, spitting and pentathlon, is not enough, unless 'experiencing' means experiencing properly, fully, etc.—and how do we know that they have experienced fully? This epistemic circle exists with all judgements of value; ultimately with all normative judgements. The question is whether it is a vicious circle, or as one might put it, a virtuous spiral.

Suppose you have an accident that arrests you at the skilful spitting stage. You will be well looked after and happy with what you have. Isn't that, nevertheless, a severe blow to your good? We can tell stories in which it might not be; in which, for example, if you developed a capacity to access higher goods that capacity would be inextricably accompanied by great mental anguish. If we set these aside, however, how many people feel that they do not really know whether such an accident in their earlier lives would have damaged their good? They take themselves to be perfectly competent to judge that it would have done, and they are right.[9]

But we must leave fuller discussion of the epistemology of normative judgements to Chapter 16. The point for the moment is that while what a person desires, and would desire under various conditions, is a *criterion* of what there is reason for them to desire—it does not *constitute* what there is reason for them to desire. As we shall argue in Part IV, nothing *constitutes* what there is reason to desire, because in general nothing *constitutes* reason relations. They do not have a 'constitution'.

11.5 Categorial and particular desires

Another point that plays an important role in Mill's discussion is that objects are desired under a conception of them as having a desirable characteristic. He uses this as part of his defence of hedonism, but it is important irrespective of that argument.

Mill wants to accept a claim made by critics, namely, that people desire things other than their happiness:

> it is palpable that [people] do desire things which, in common language, are decidedly distinguished from happiness. They desire, for example, virtue, and the absence of vice, no less really than pleasure and the absence of pain. The desire of virtue is not as universal, but it is as authentic a fact, as the desire of happiness. And hence the opponents of the utilitarian standard deem that there are other ends of human action besides happiness, and that happiness is not the standard of approbation and disapprobation.[10]

Mill agrees that virtue is desired by many people, but argues that insofar as they desire virtue they desire it as a 'part' or 'ingredient' of their own happiness. The point of this odd language is to highlight that if you want something under the idea of it as pleasant it does not follow that you want it as a *means* to your pleasure or enjoyment. He then concludes that:

---

[9] If we think it damages your good then, by our definition as it stands, there is reason for you to desire to play pentathlon even though you are blocked from developing in the way that would give rise to that desire. That looks rather implausible; so perhaps we should refine our definition: your good includes what there is reason for you to desire and what there would be reason for you to desire if blockages in the natural development of your desires were removed. Let's leave that open (but see the end of the next section).

[10] Mill (1963–91), vol. X: 234–5 (*Utilitarianism* 4.3).

there is in reality nothing desired except happiness. Whatever is desired otherwise than as a means to some end beyond itself, and ultimately to happiness, is desired as itself a part of happiness, and is not desired for itself until has become so. Those who desire virtue for its own sake, desire it either because the consciousness of it is a pleasure, or because the consciousness of being without it is a pain, or for both reasons united... If one of these gave him no pleasure, and the other no pain, he would not love or desire virtue...[11]

Let us put this in our terms. We have distinguished between what is substantively desired and what is 'desired', in the sense of aimed at, as a means to some objective beyond itself. Now, using the term 'desire' to refer to substantive desires, we distinguish the *particular* desire for some O, in this case virtue, with the *categorial* desire for pleasure. The object of the particular desire is O, the object of the categorial desire is pleasure. Even if O is desired under the idea of it as pleasant, it is still distinct from the categorial desire for pleasure. Mill could have said that the desire to act virtuously is a substantive desire in its own right; its object is virtuous action. His empirical claim would be that all substantive desires other than the desire for pleasure and the aversion to pain are desires for a particular object under the idea of it as pleasant or aversions to a particular object under the idea of it as painful.[12] If he were right in this empirical claim, that would be good enough to show that only pleasure and the absence of pain is desirable. It would be so even if people never categorially desired pleasure and the absence of pain *as such*.

Suppose I want to go to the pub because I expect to meet friends there, have a drink and a chat. What I substantively desire—under the idea of it as a pleasant thing to do—is a chat with friends over a drink. This is not a means to something else I substantively desire—pleasure—it *is* the object of my desire. Particular desires are not fungible: that is, if you stop me meeting my friends at the pub, and give me something else just as pleasant, you haven't satisfied my substantive desire, as you would have done if the only substantive desire in play was a desire for pleasure. I could truly protest 'Yes—but that's not what I *wanted* to do'.

One may or not have a categorial desire for pleasure as such, as against particular desires for objects under the idea of pleasure. A categorial desire for pleasure involves some effort of abstraction. It is at work, for example, when one thinks: I want to enjoy myself tonight. Let's see—what shall I do? Or you agree to a surprise that someone promises you, something they say you will enjoy, without revealing what it is. In this case you have the categorial desire for enjoyment without a desire for any object in particular under the idea of it as enjoyable.[13]

---

[11] Ibid., p. 237 (4.7).

[12] 'The ingredients of happiness are very various, and each of them is desirable in itself and not merely when considered as swelling an aggregate.' Ibid., p. 235 (4.5).

[13] You may also want something under the idea of it as pleasant even though you do not really believe it will be pleasant. Suppose you have always enjoyed doing high ridge walks in the mountains. But as you've got older, you've started to get vertigo, and these walks are no longer pleasant. Yet you still want to do them. Insofar as you want to go on that sort of walk you're thinking of it as pleasant, even though you know it won't be. That is a clear case of a substantive desire that is no longer reason-supported. You are perfectly aware of that, and so you have no plans to go on any more high ridge walks.

Let's go back to the case of virtue. Suppose Mary joins a group of car owners who ferry people who cannot make their own way to the local hospital in their cars. She joins because she wants to help others. If someone asked her why she joined she could truly say 'because I enjoy making myself useful'. She could equally well answer by explaining why it's useful to have an organized group providing ferry services to the hospital with their cars.

She is contributing to the car service because it is helpful. She thinks that is a reason to help, and she is right. It is *also* true, as she says, that she is contributing because she enjoys being helpful. That enjoyment *does* enter into the explanation of why she acts, just as your expectation that meeting your friends for a drink will be enjoyable enters into the explanation of your act. But it is incorrect to say that she acts *in order to get* the enjoyment of making herself useful. Her desire is non-fungible; doing something else that was just as enjoyable, such as reading a detective story, would not satisfy it. The correct account of her motives is not that she has a desire for her own enjoyment that combines with a belief that helping others will prove to be enjoyable. It is *service to others* that features in the content of the desire, not her own enjoyment.[14]

Where Mill goes wrong is not in his epistemological method but in his empirical claim. If this claim were right, pleasure and absence of pain would be established as *the* desirable feature that an object must have to be itself desirable, and hence to contribute to one's good. It would be the only 'categorial desirable'. But pleasure is not the only characteristic under which we desire objects (though it has the advantage that virtually no one seriously rejects it). There are others, such as knowledge of one's situation, worthwhile contribution, personal independence. I may want to know that I have a terminal illness, if I do. I may want it because I want to know how things are with me, not because I will enjoy knowing, or because I need to know in order to settle some obligations. I may be willing to reduce my total of pleasure in order to achieve this knowledge, even though my knowledge will benefit no one else. The idea under which I have this particular desire is 'knowledge of my situation'. Likewise I may want to make a contribution that others rightly regard as worthwhile. Similarly I may just want to get on with things in my own way: personal independence is the desirable category here. We are willing to sacrifice some pleasure to achieve these desired ends.

What categorial desirables there are is an important issue that can and should be philosophically discussed.[15] However, this is not to say that a person's good can be assessed against an 'objective list' of such desirables.[16] In the first place we should accept that such categories vary in their desirability for different people. There is a diversity of human ends, and divergence in what ends are desirable for different people. In the second place such assessment would be too abstract, even given the particular profile of desirable

---

[14] In a similar way, when a person acts from duty it can be misleading to say that he acts *in order to bring it about that* he has done his duty, even though it *is* because he thinks this is his duty that he acts. The formulation may suggest a moral narcissism that isn't there, or a wish to get the duty out of the way. The doctor who tends you is doing it because that's his duty—not because, for example, you are a personal friend he wants to help. But to say that he's doing it in order to discharge his duty suggests, for example, that he's accumulating moral points, or in a hurry to get home.

[15] Cp. e.g. Griffin 1986, Chapter 4, §3.

[16] Cp. Parfit 1984: 493ff.

categories that matter to a specific person. A person's good is constructive: we need to know the particular desires that have in fact developed under these categorial desires. And finally, there are reason-supported particular desires that do not seem to fall under any categorial desires.

Consider a discussion of whether achievement or knowledge are worthwhile. How might this discussion go? Jim says that he wants to make a contribution to his subject. Obviously he wants it to be well known: he wants to achieve something which will command the respect of people able to appreciate it, even if that only happens after he is dead. Ruth wants to find out what happened to her grandfather in a concentration camp. She devotes as much time as she can to this search. Her object is to find out something about her own family, and thus, to arrive at knowledge of her own situation, in the broadest sense, the sense in which an interest in philosophy, or the history of one's country, could fall under that. Colin does not see the point of these quests; that is, he does not see the desirability of the category under which they are desired. What is the point, he asks, of posthumous deserved respect when you won't be around to appreciate it? Or of knowledge about yourself, your relatives, or your world that makes no difference to the practical business of life? What happened to your grandfather in the concentration camp is all past history—why should it matter to you now? Nonetheless. if he comes to see that these are categories under which people do resiliently desire things, and to fix clearly what the categories desired are, he should accept that they are indeed categorial desirables for many people. They may become desirable for him when he has fully grasped them—or they may not. If he does come to desire things under this category, those desires are reason-supported for him. But if he does *not* come to desire them, then it is false that there is reason for *him* to desire them.

Thinking about your categorial desires can contribute to your reflection about what there is reason to desire. They can vindicate an existing particular desire as reason-supported. They can also show that a particular desire that you do not have would be reason-supported if you had it. Suppose you are an achievement-oriented person, who has just been made redundant. You feel frustrated and aimless. You are quite versatile, so there is a wide variety of things you could do that would give you satisfaction as achievements. At the moment you have not acquired a particular desire to do any one of them. You just think that you would like some project that you could bring to a worthwhile and satisfying conclusion. However, were you to pursue any one of these possible projects you would soon acquire a particular desire to bring that particular one to a worthwhile conclusion. You decide to write a book about mediaeval weaponry. Soon you are quite involved. You work hard to produce a really path-breaking, worthwhile book.

Should we say that there was reason for you to desire *all* of the achievement-oriented particular desires that you would have acquired had you chosen to pursue the particular achievement in question? Consider the similar question for pleasures. There are many activities that have never even occurred to you that you would enjoy if you did them, from listening to some world music you've never heard of to taking up tiddlywinks. Should we say that there is reason for you to desire any of the enjoyment-driven particular desires that you would in fact acquire if you chose to pursue the activity in question? It seems to me that that it is more natural to say that there is reason for you to desire achievement, and reason for you to desire pleasure—but that a particular desire for an object under that category is reason-supported only if you acquire it and it will in fact satisfy that category. If so, your good shapes itself not unspecifically around the categories that are desirable for you, but specifically around the particular reason-supported desires that you do in fact acquire. You don't have to think, as you write your book about mediaeval weaponry, 'Gosh! There's just as much reason for me to want to write a book about toadstools, and hence (*ceteris paribus*) just as much reason to write it'. The book you want to write is about mediaeval weaponry. Given the way your choices have gone, there is no reason for you to want to write a book about toadstools, useful achievement as such a book would be.

Finally, do all desires fall under some desirable category? If so we could say that your good is what satisfies your reason-supported categorial desires (your categorial desirables), taking into account the particular shaping they have acquired through your life. However, some desires seem to be radically particular. The most plausible cases arise from friendship and love. These are particularistic attachments falling under no category. If you are asked what fact about X gives you reason to love them, to desire to be with them, you might be stumped for an answer. 'I don't know why I love her—I just do.' True, one might say that the categorial desire under which the particular desires to be with friends and lovers, help them, share with them, etc., fall is something like 'deep personal relationships' or 'having someone to love'. And the fact that one cannot satisfy the *particular* desires involved by simply substituting one friend or lover for another equally good one could be explained in terms of the non-fungibility of particular objects of desire that we have already noted. Thus a lonely person may have the categorial without the particular desire: they strongly want to find someone to love, just because they do not have someone.

These observations are indeed true. Nonetheless, it seems odd to say that when one loves someone one loves them under the categorial idea of having someone to love. It is more plausible to say that love for a particular person or object is itself the category under which one desires this or that. You want to do something for a person because you love them. You want to find some safe place to keep the letters you had from them when they were still alive. Each of these desires arises in virtue of the emotional significance *this* person has for you. One could say that he or she is the categorial desirable under which these particular desires fall.

11.6 How a person's good can expand

It is not particularly controversial to assert that if something is part of my good there is reason for me to desire it. But many would say that there can be reason for me to desire an object even though it's no part of my good. If that is right, then defining personal good in terms of what there is reason for a person to desire is too broad.

People desire many things such as the good of others, or states of affairs whose coming to pass they will not aware of, and perhaps couldn't be—for example, because they'll be dead by that time. One view is that these desires are not reason-supported. Another is that they are but that achieving them is not a part of one's good. The second view is incompatible with our definition, since on that definition the good of these others, and the existence of these states of affairs, is a part of your good. But I want to argue that this is the right view to take, so that our definition of a person's good is not too broad.

We can learn from the idealist tradition of moral philosophy in our understanding of a person's good. What a person 'really' or 'truly' desires—to use the language of T. H. Green[17]—involves some combination of what he's like and what path he chooses. As already noted, there are some potentials that are determinate at the beginning, and some that are determined by basic life choices and also just by the accidents of life. In particular there will be determination from the ties and commitments in which the person comes to be contained, by choice or otherwise. Putting it another way, there is an important self-constructive element in a person's good.

Suppose an art collector, caught in his burning house, shouts out to us 'Don't worry about me, save my art collection'. One could certainly describe him as caring more about his art collection than his own well-being. But one could also say that the fate of his art collection has become a part of his good.

The art collector may have perfectly good reason to care more about his art collection than about his personal flourishing. He has spent a lifetime on it, he has put most of himself into it, and he quite reasonably wants to pass it on to others. This is a substantive desire, which turns on his love for the pictures, his project of benefiting others in the particular way he can, and his ambition to be recognized as a great collector. If it is a reason-supported desire, then on our definition saving the art collection contributes *pro tanto* to his good. It's even possible that in this desperate situation, where either he burns or his art collection does, saving his art collection contributes *more* to his good, though obviously not to his physical and mental flourishing, than saving him. That would be so if there is sufficient reason for him to desire the saving of the art collection more strongly than the saving of his own life.

The same may go for a drowning mother who desires more strongly that her drowning children be saved than that she should be. That can be a reason-supported state of desire. If it is, then the good of her children has become a more important part of her good than her own flourishing, in the narrow sense referred to above.

To say this is not to confuse the good of a person with what is good 'from their point of view'. The latter phrase, if it means anything clear, means what they believe to be good. No doubt the mother thinks that the saving of her children is good. We think that too. But it is also, for her, a part of *her* good. As for the art collector, he thinks his collection is valuable, and that saving it is good. But his relation to that good is different to ours. Because the collection is valuable, and a value made by his life-time efforts, its preservation has become part of *his* good. A deep feature of the good of human individuals is that human beings are able to achieve this kind of self-enlargement by identifying with other objects, people, causes, and assimilating the good of those 'significant others' into their

---

[17] In Green 2004 (1883). For discussion of Green see Brink 2003, and his introduction to Green 2004. See also Nicholson 1990. I discuss Green's notion of a person's good in Skorupski 2006b (from which I have borrowed some examples here).

own good. Human beings are by nature a kind of being whose good can transcend its own physical and mental flourishing.

We can say, it is true, that the art collector and the mother sacrifice themselves. But that does not show, it seems to me, that what they do is not a part of their good. Someone may go to civic meetings which she has no desire at all to go to, out of pure conscientiousness. She may be said to 'sacrifice herself'. What then of someone who has become thoroughly identified with the town, enjoys making himself useful, and goes for that reason? Does he sacrifice himself? He wants to go and his desire to go is reason-supported, even if he's going to find this particular meeting boring. He wouldn't say he was sacrificing himself. Contributing to the good of the town has become a part of his good. All the same, at the end of his civic career, he deserves thanks for the sacrifices of time and energy that he's made. He was giving up, for the good of the town, something rightly considered as precious—his time and energy—which he was entitled to use as he thought fit. It would be a misconceived response to say 'Well, he only did it because he felt like doing it'. Pursuing something as a part of your good is not necessarily acting selfishly or self-interestedly in any normal sense. On the contrary, making the good of the town a part of your own good is in itself admirable, and something that deserves thanks.[18]

So it seems to me that this expansive and pluralist account of a person's good is defensible in its own right.[19] However, it is a substantive theory about what constitutes a person's good, not a definitional thesis. Perfectionism, hedonism, and so on, are substantive theories; this is another. How then do we settle which one is right?

Someone who takes the notion of a person's good to be a primitive concept may want to answer that we must do so by direct exercise of intuition. On my definition, however, the way to settle which is right is by considering what there is reason for a person to desire. And that doesn't simply transfer the input of intuition to another point. Consideration of what there is reason for a person to desire will be based, in line with

---

[18] I agree with many of the points T. M. Scanlon makes about a person's good, or in his terms, well-being (Scanlon, 1998); in particular that it is an 'inclusive' good, that it is often more important from the standpoint of the benefactor that that of the agent, and that it can have 'surprisingly little role to play in the thinking of the rational individual whose life is in question' (p. 109). But my notion of categorial ends is narrower than his notion of rational aims. I do not agree that 'success in one's rational aims' is a 'component of well-being' (p. 123). This is too broad, at least if 'rational' here means 'reason-supported'. There can be sufficient reason for you to pursue various aims whose achievement would not contribute to your well-being, even pro tanto. The person who attends civic meetings out of pure conscientiousness has a rational aim, but attendance is not a part of their well-being. Helping them to attend might make their dutiful action less burdensome but would not necessarily promote their good in any other way.

[19] It is defended by idealists but one doesn't have to be an idealist to defend it. Peter Railton makes the point eloquently:

> When one studies relationships of deep commitment—of parent to child, or wife to husband—at close range, it becomes artificial to impose a dichotomy between what is done for the self and what is done for the other. We cannot decompose such relationships into a vector of self-concern and a vector of other-concern, even though concern for the self and the other are both present. The other has come to figure in the self in a fundamental way—or, perhaps a better way of putting it, the other has become a reference point of the self. If it is part of one's identity to be the parent of Jill or the husband of Linda, then the self has reference points beyond the ego, and that which affects these reference points may affect the self in an unmediated way (Railton 2003: 176).

These 'relationships of deep commitment' can be to things and causes as well as people, of course.

Mill's epistemology, on what ends that person really, substantively, desires or would in epistemically revealing circumstances desire, both before getting it and after.

We can go on the offensive by asking: if some substantive desires are nothing to do with one's good, what is the difference between those that are and those that are not? If it is too broad to characterize a person's good as that which there is reason for that person to desire, how should one characterize it more narrowly?[20] And furthermore, once we've acknowledged that not all motivation is desire-based, what motivates the posited further distinction between desires for my own good and desires for other things? What is its ethical point?

A wide range of ethical positions gives an important role to the notion of a person's good. They hold that my own good, or that of people I care for, or that of people in general, is something I should in one way or another take account of. Now suppose our definition is wrong. In that case what contributes to a person's good and what there is reason for that person to desire can diverge. If this divergence arises, then, what should I be taking account of—the good of the person in question, or what there is reason for them to desire? If an outcome promotes a person's good, but is not an outcome that there is reason for the person to desire, does that give me reason to produce the outcome—for that person's sake? Or, *vice versa*, if it promotes an outcome that there is reason for them to desire, but does not promote their good? It is hard to see what normative authority the notion of a person's good can have, if it diverges in this way from what there is reason for the person to desire, or what criterion could be used to determine the extent of the divergence.

Go back to the case of the collector, who wants us to save his collection rather than himself. Suppose the collection really is a valuable one, as he thinks—he's not just deluding himself. It really will be something people will want to see and something that he will be remembered by. These are things that he really cares about, much more than he cares about the enjoyments that still remain to him in life. His desire that his art collection rather than he should be saved is reasonable. In that case it seems to me that the best thing to do—for *his* sake, with *his* best interests in mind—may be to rescue the art collection.[21]

It might instead be held to be the best thing to do because one should respect a responsible person's self-regarding choices, even if they are not in his best interest. There can be cases of that kind; however, the thesis we are putting in the described case is that saving the art collector's collection rather than him *is* in his best interest—it is what advances his

---

[20] It may be suggested that satisfaction of a desire contributes to one's good only if the desire has some reference to oneself in it. A mother wants *her* children to be saved. The art lover wants *his* collection to be saved. But is this always significant? Rahul desires the success of an athlete he greatly admires, Jane desires the long-term regeneration of the Caledonian forest. These are objects with which, in T. H. Green's terms, they identify themselves. If they could do something to advance the satisfaction of their desires they would do so; but that does not mean that the object of Rahul's desire is that *he* should help the athlete to success, or of Jane's that *she* should save the Caledonian forest.

[21] I am not saying that it's what the fire brigade should do, even if it's the best thing to do. That is a more complex question, involving, for example, what realistic, comprehensible, 'best-overall' standing instructions the fire brigade should have.

good. As a matter of fact, these two views are not so easy to distinguish in practice, since the requirement that one should respect a person's self-regarding choices if the person is in a responsible frame of mind is trivially satisfied if he is *not* in a responsible frame of mind, and the nature of his choice may itself show that he is not. Nevertheless, the two approaches differ. If, for example, the art collector is romantically deluded about the value to him of his art collection as against his life, so that saving the art collection is not in his best interest, the respect-for-self-regarding-choices principle may point to saving the art collection, whereas the best-interest principle will not.

Another view is that it might be best to save the art collection because the gain to other people might outweigh the loss to the art collector, in other words, even though it's *not* best for him. But then it sounds as though we're sacrificing him for the sake of others. If that's the right decision then it might be right in a different case, in which a collector with an equally valuable collection cares, very reasonably, more for his own survival than for the survival of his collection. This other collector cares more about the enjoyments still left to him than about the fate of his collection. It is, to put it mildly, by no means obvious that we should save this other collector's collection, leaving him to die. For in this other case we are overriding the collector's reason-supported desires for the sake of the art collection, and its value to others. Whereas in the first case it is the survival of the collection that the collector really cares about. He identifies his good with the survival of the collection, and it is no way foolish on his part to do so.

11.7 Personal good and rational care: acting for someone's sake

Our account of a person's good fits it into the analysis of normative concepts presented in this book, according to which all normative concepts can be analysed in terms of the concept of a reason. Of course it has to be defensible in its own right, as we have tried to show it is. However, it is also worth comparing it with another account that analyses the notion of a person's good in terms of reasons: Stephen Darwall's 'rational care theory of welfare', according to which a person's good or welfare comprises anything that '*one ought to desire and promote insofar as one cares for him*' or that 'it would be rational to want for him for his sake'.[22]

Darwall does not think the mere fact that I do care for a person in the right way—that is, for their sake—gives me reason to benefit the person. They must be worthy of care. He assumes (not very plausibly, perhaps) that if I do care for someone I must think them worthy of care; but he considers it a conceptual possibility that a person may be unworthy of care, and in that case, he thinks, considerations of their good provide no normative reasons for acting whatsoever, whether for the person himself or for anyone else: 'it is a person's being worthy of concern...that makes considerations of his welfare into reasons'.[23] In particular, Darwall thinks it conceptually possible that one has no reason to pursue or even to care about one's own good.

[22] Darwall 2003: 7, 9.
[23] Ibid: 6.

Now whether it is a conceptual truth that one has reason to *pursue* one's own good depends, according to the account given in this chapter, on whether the Bridge principle is a conceptual truth. We can at least agree with Darwall that it is not an *analytic* truth that one has reason to pursue one's own ends. However, Darwall would also deny that it's an analytic truth that one has reason to *desire* the things that would constitute, be ingredients or parts of, one's good. Whether one has reason to desire those things depends, in his view, in part on whether one is worthy of concern. Furthermore, on his view one may have reason to desire things other than those that one has reason to desire for one's own sake. For both reasons a person's good cannot be defined in terms of what there is reason for that person to desire.

For reasons given above we can also agree that it is not a conceptual truth that there's reason for me to desire my 'well-being' or what is 'good for me', in the common or ordinary understandings of those terms. It is a substantive, not a conceptual, truth that my well-being, or what is good for me, understood in those standard ways, is a part of my good. There is a similar common understanding of 'welfare', in which it refers narrowly to a person's mental and physical flourishing. To identify a person's good with welfare in this sense would be a substantive normative doctrine. However, Darwall is not using the term 'welfare' in that substantive sense, but in the formal sense that equates to the general notion of a person's good. In that formal sense we are committed to holding that a person has reason to desire his own good, irrespective of whether he is worthy of concern, and that that is indeed an analytic truth. To hold that there is no reason for me to desire anything (as against reason to desire nothingness) would be to hold that there is no such thing as my good.

Given that Darwall allows the conceptual possibility that a person may be unworthy of care, his definition must be hypothetical: a person's welfare must consist in what there is or would be reason to promote for their sake if there is or were reason to care for them for their sake. This produces the kind of problem that counterfactuals have a way of generating. Suppose someone is unworthy of care. Presumably, then, he'd have to be different to be worthy of care. In which case his welfare might also be different. So what determines what his welfare actually is? The importance of this issue does not emerge clearly in Darwall's discussion, because he often underplays the hypothetical character of his definition, in effect assuming that there always *is* reason to care for people for their sake, or alternatively that for any person there always *is* something that 'it would be rational to want for him for his sake'. That seems right: however benighted a person may be there are still things there's reason to do *for his sake* (for example, help him to be less benighted).[24] But it's not clear that it is right on Darwall's analysis.

Taking Darwall's characterization of a person's good in this non-hypothetical way, then, there is a case for thinking it to be true a priori: in the terms of this book, a person's good comprises those things that there is reason do for him for his sake. Note the scope of the phrase 'for his sake'. We are quite familiar with the idea of looking after a person's

---

[24] 'Do' rather than 'want': there may be no reason for me to *desire* your good, or care for you, because I don't stand in that kind of affective relationship to you; but the fact that an action will contribute to your good is still a reason to do it.

art collection, or their children, after they have died—*for that person's sake*. (The children themselves might be rather appalling.) We may have reason to do so for their sake, or insofar we care for them. 'If you care for me, look after my art collection.' 'Look after my children for me—do it for me, for my sake.' So the integrity of an art collection, or the interests of children, can on Darwall's criterion be a part of a person's good even after their death. We can accept that in looking after the children, or the art collection, one is promoting the person's good. It is plausible just because one is promoting something that there was reason for that person to desire. Contrast the phrases 'doing it for his sake' and 'doing it in his memory'. If we put up a plaque in your memory we are not doing it *for your sake*. To do it for your sake would imply that a plaque in your memory was something you wanted put up after your death (and with reason).

So Darwall's characterization of a person's good, taken non-hypothetically, seems to be a priori correct. Can it be taken as a definition? There are two reasons to think not.

In the first place, it is a substantive normative truth that there is reason to do things for other people's sake. A person who denies it may be wrong, but is not misusing words. Do we want to say that such a person is denying that there is any such thing as personal good? I don't think so. True, one can equally ask whether a person who denies that there is any reason to desire anything is denying that there is such a thing as personal good. However in this case it seems plausible that that is exactly what he is denying. He need not be denying that there is such a thing as person's welfare, or what is good for a person, in the naturalistic medical sense. But he *is* denying that there is such a thing as a person's good in that sense in which ethical theories that require concern with one's own or other people's good hold that there is.[25]

We can also ask whether Darwall's definition gets things the right way round. Should we define a person's welfare in terms of caring for them for their own sake, or should we rather define caring for them for their own sake in terms of having their *welfare* at heart because it's *theirs*, and not for some other reason? Darwall's response to this obvious worry is ingenious:

> we need not define care ... if it is something like a psychological natural kind. Just as we can use a term like 'water' without a prior definition to refer to the natural stuff in rivers and lakes ... so likewise might we refer to care for purposes of a meta-ethical theory of welfare if it is a natural kind.[26]

However, even if 'care' refers to a natural kind, that does not show it has no definable descriptive content. 'H_2O' refers to a natural kind but has descriptive content nonetheless. So perhaps 'care' does too, and perhaps the concept of welfare features in that content. More generally, suppose care is a natural kind, the kind psychologists or neurophysiologists will pick out in due course as 'XYZ'. Still, to grasp Darwall's definition of welfare we

---

[25] What if we amend the definition to make a person's good what there would be reason to do for his sake *if one cared for him*? It seems to me that this would make no difference. What there is reason to do for a person *for his sake*, if anything, is unaffected by whether or not one cares for him.

[26] Darwall 2003: 50.

have to grasp the *concept* of care, which is not the same as the concept of XYZ. I am not convinced that we can explain the concept of caring for someone, in the sense of wanting things for *their* sake, without assuming a grasp of the concept of a person's good. Darwall distinguishes at the outset[27] between desiring intrinsically that another's good be satisfied and desiring this for *his* sake. If there's a difference, it must be that the latter concept is stronger than the former. Caring for you is not just desiring your good non-instrumentally, but desiring it that way because it's *your* good. Likewise, wanting something for your sake is wanting it because it will promote your *good*, and because it will promote *your* good. If this is right, the notion of wanting something 'for your sake' contains an implicit reference to your good, and thus does not throw independent light on it.

In sum, although Darwall's characterization of a person's good may well be correct a priori, I suggest that our account has a better case to be regarded as a *definition*.

11.8 Egoism

The Bridge principle combines with our analysis of personal good to generate formally egoistic reasons. However, it is not altogether straightforward to distinguish these from other reasons. Consider the claim:

> (3) If an action would promote x's good that would be a reason for x to do that action.

If (3) is true a priori—as we shall argue in a moment—then any fact that entails that an action will promote the agent's good is a *formally egoistic* reason for the agent to do that action. Note that for formally egoistic reasons to exist it is not enough that (3) should be true. Consider in particular such abstract but still a posteriori descriptions as 'human being', 'sentient being'. A utilitarian would hold that the fact that an action will promote the good of any human being, or sentient being, is a reason for anyone to do that action, and hence that if x falls under these categories (3) is true. That is a utilitarian, nor a formally egoistic reason for the agent to promote his own good. The basic idea of a formally egoistic reason is that the mere fact that an action will promote the *agent's* good constitutes a reason for the agent do it, whatever else is true about the agent: in other words, that that is a *complete* reason. The force of this reason does not depend on any description of the agent, even one so abstract as 'sentient being'.

Philosophical egoism is the view that all reasons for action are formally egoistic. I have been adding the word 'formally', which I will drop from now on, to highlight that such reasons need not in any ordinary sense be selfish. That should be clear from some of our examples in previous sections. Philosophical or formal egoism is not the view that one should always act *selfishly*. It is the view that the only practical norm determining reasons for action is (3). That, for example, is what eudaimonists like T. H. Green think. But they combine it with a broad account of a person's good, such as the one we have defended here.

[27] Ibid: 1–2.

Our definition of a person's good, together with the Bridge principle, entails that there are egoistic reasons. Through the Bridge principle one's good becomes an *independent source* of practical reasons. For the action prompted by the desire to (have) O is pursuit of O. Thus we have the following implication from the Bridge principle:

If there's reason for x to desire O then there's reason for x to pursue O.

Since by definition O is a part of my good just if there is reason for me to desire O, we can substitute into this implication, producing the following result:

If O is a part of x's good then there's reason for x to pursue O.

The Bridge principle, because it is a priori, gives it a priori status. Also, since the action prompted by desiring O is pursuit of O, the strengthened version of the Bridge principle, (2), gives us:

Whatever gives x reason to desire O gives x reason to pursue O, in virtue of being a reason to desire O.

So:

whatever fact makes O a part of x's good gives x reason to pursue O, in virtue of its making O a part of x's good.

Any fact that makes O a part of the agent's good gives the agent reason to pursue O.

Reasons of this kind, derived from Bridge, are egoistic; but what *egoism* says is that there are no others. That is not true. As we have already noted, there may be reason to *do* something, even though there's no reason to *desire* to do it. I have an aunt and an uncle, let's say. My aunt is a highly amusing gossip and a good cook, whereas my uncle has become a tedious curmudgeon. Thus there's good reason to desire the company of the first, but no good reason to desire the company of the second. Yet if I don't visit my uncle no one else will. So that's a good reason to visit him. I probably should do it. But this is a non-egoistic reason, and so if it is a reason, egoism is false. There may be reason to *pursue* something, even though there's no reason to *desire* it. Thus, for example, there's some reason to pursue the well-being of anyone at all, as will be proposed in Chapter 13, but it doesn't follow that there's reason to *desire* the well-being of anyone at all. When it comes to the well-being of most individuals on this planet, we can quite reasonably fail to have any desires whatsoever on the matter. The people whose well-being we substantively desire are people with whom we are affectively involved, in one way or another. As regards others most of us simply wish them well, or rather *will* them well, where 'willing them well' refers to a standing disposition of goodwill manifested in something like a readiness to help whenever it's reasonable and possible to do so.[28]

---

[28] That is what I am likely to feel towards Parfit's stranger on the train: Parfit 1984: 494. (We shall consider the disinterested will in Chapters 13 and 14.) However, if I really do get emotionally involved, developing, from a generous heart, a substantive desire for the stranger's recovery, then (for the period of that desire) their recovery becomes a part of my good, since if I do have this desire it is reason-supported. So too we can get genuinely emotionally involved in the project of reducing human misery, in which case progress in that direction becomes part of our good. But it is also possible to acknowledge it as a choice-worthy aim, and act on it, without a *substantive desire* for it. 'Niggardly nature' may have left me without those generous desires.

So the truth in egoism is that there is a special sort of reason to pursue one's own good; and this follows from the definition of a person's good together with the Bridge principle. That, I suggest, is the right location for it on the map of practical reasons.

It is also a good illustration of how important evaluative reasons are in deliberation. The interesting issue, and the one we all spend much the most time on, is not whether if there's reason to desire something there is reason to pursue it, but rather, what there *is* reason to desire. Of course once we have settled that to our satisfaction, and thus settled what egoistic reasons we have, we still have another question that can be very difficult: how these egoistic reasons stand in relation to other, non-egoistic practical reasons that may bear on our decision.

However, not all reasons generated by the Bridge principle are egoistic. Feelings other than desire prompt actions. When the feeling in question is reason-supported, then so is the prompted action.[29] This leads us to a sentimentalist account of a distinct and important class of values that generate reasons for action: ideals.

11.9 Ideals and practical necessity

Ideals can be seen as one of four fundamental ethical categories, of which the other three are personal good; morality; and impartial practical reason. Morality and impartial reason will be considered in the next four chapters, and we shall come back to ideals in connection with morality. Here we should consider how ideals relate to personal good.

Ideals are conceptions of what constitutes an admirable activity or way of life, an activity or a life that one can be proud of, find dignity, self-respect, significance, or importance in. The primitive basis of this contrast between personal good and ideals lies in the difference between desire and admiration. The philosophical theory of a person's good is the theory of what is truly, genuinely desirable for that person; the philosophical theory of ideals is the theory of what is truly, genuinely admirable.

Note an immediate contrast here: reasons to desire are patient-relative; they involve a fact about the way in which the desired object is related under some desirable category to me, or about my identification with another, such as love, followership, commitment. Reasons to admire are, as noted in 3.4, patient-neutral. If a violin performance is admirable there is reason for everyone to admire it. If a life of dedication to helping others is admirable, there is reason for everyone to admire it. In each case the facts that are reasons to admire will not be facts that refer back to the admirer in the patient-relative way.

The fact that you will enjoy an object is a patient-relative reason for you to desire the object. It is not a reason for others to desire the object. What gives a person pleasure may

---

[29] I do not say that when the feeling is reason-supported, so is the substantive *desire* to do the prompted action. If confronted by something there is reason to fear, a fearless man has reason to flee. But if, being fearless, he has no desire to flee, it is not obvious that he has reason to *desire* to flee. This point has theoretical significance, in that it allows that the Bridge principle generates practical reasons that are not egoistic, as well as egoistic ones.

be more or less admirable. But we don't hold that there is anything admirable in itself about a pleasant life. Thus a pleasant life is for us a part of our good but not an ideal, although ideals affect our admiration or otherwise of people as they figure through their pleasures.

If, in contrast, the ascetic ideal—the life of personal austerity and mental concentration on ultimate things—is indeed admirable, then we all have reason to admire it. We can of course discuss whether it is really admirable. The disagreement is illuminating, in that it shows what is at stake in valuing an ideal. Critics of the ascetic life see it as a form of self-repression, perhaps concealing some element of sado-masochism or will to power, while admirers see it as an aesthetically pure and clean renunciation of inessentials, freeing one to a disciplined focus on essentials. This is a dispute about whether the unsublimated psychological sources of the ascetic life are on inspection truly admirable (and possibly about whether it matters what the *unsublimated* sources are).

How do ideals generate practical as against evaluative reasons? Given that they rest on what there is reason to admire, they generate practical reasons by way of the Bridge principle applied to the case of admiration. The admiration-prompted action is *support*. This may take the form of attention and applause, or can extend to more extensive support in the form of private or public patronage, relief from duties, defence against criticism, and so on. What the Bridge principle does not provide is reasons to *emulate* the thing that is admired. Support and emulation are distinct. The fact that I correctly find a way of life admirable is not in itself, in other words via the Bridge principle, a reason to try to live like that. The fact that a sportsman's performance admirable is via Bridge a reason to support it in one way or another, but not thereby a reason to seek to emulate it oneself.

Admiration may or may not lead to desire. I can find a way of life admirable without desiring to lead a life like that. I may admire the ease and grace of an athlete or violinist, the dedication of a scientist, the vision and courage of a politician, without desiring to emulate them. I may be perfectly content to get on with my own comfortable life. Nor does the fact that all those qualities are genuinely admirable entail that there is *reason* for me to desire to attain them, whether or not I actually do. The connection between the admirable and the desirable is contingent. It rests on the fact that admiration sometimes but not always leads to desire, and desire of the strongest kind. How this happens is elusive. One way it happens is through the categorial desire for achievement, respect, meaning; but that does not explain why this desire is triggered by some objects that strike a person as admirable and not by others. The mere fact that an ideal is worthwhile and that I could attain it does not seem to be enough. It has to inspire me personally, to become something that I desire to attain in my own life.

Once this has happened an equally interesting phenomenon sometimes comes into play: ideals can *grip* you. Pursuit of an ideal can come to be felt as mandatory, a 'practical necessity', a path you just have to follow, a goal you *must* achieve. This may be associated with moral convictions, or convictions of honour, about the right way to live (as when someone cannot tell a lie), but it need not be, and it useful to consider cases where it is not. So let us suppose that a person comes to have this sense of practical necessity about preserving and regenerating a beautiful valley, or about becoming an outstanding tennis player who can hold his or her own against the best in the world. What kind of state of the feelings is this? It involves extreme aversion to activity that gets in the way of whatever is necessary to pursue the ideal, shame or self-disgust at failure.

This psychology, the psychology of vocation, has normative significance: we make due allowance for someone gripped by an ideal we regard as worthy. For example, we may excuse them, if we're sufficiently persuaded of their sincerity and rationality, from obligations we might otherwise think they had. This is an illustration of the connection between admiration and support. We are also prone to feel a certain lack of respect for those with no ideals at all, for whom making something worthwhile of their life has little or no importance—though such responses take us onto dangerous and delicate territory.

So does my feeling that 'I must do this' in itself give me a reason to do it? No—it only does so if the underlying desire is reason-supported, because the project is indeed admirable. It has to be true that it is a good thing for me to do this; if the perception that it is produces in me a desire to do it, then it is also true that it is part of my good to do it.

This discussion enables us to draw some conclusions about the ethical standpoint known as perfectionism. What is correct in perfectionism is that the admirable is a source of value distinct from the desirable, that it can be hugely important to us, and can shape our lives. But it is false that the fact that something is admirable is in and of itself a reason to achieve it, as against just supporting it. To give a person reason to pursue it, the admirable object has to become desirable to that person. This psychology, whereby the admirable can become the desired, underlies the Aristotelian and Millian principle that only the fullest self-development of one's potential gives access to the highest forms of human happiness or satisfaction. Potential means potential to realize an ideal in one's life. But ideals are not a source of reasons for this kind of personal pursuit until they are taken up and incorporated in this way.[30]

---

[30] So this is a rejection of the 'perfectionist ideal', as Thomas Hurka characterizes it (1993: 17)—pursuing an admirable way of life is not a *Categorical* Imperative.

12

REASONS AND FEELINGS: (II) MORAL CONCEPTS

Suppose in the street someone sinks to their knees, apparently in severe pain. I realize they may be dangerously ill; I have a mobile phone on which I could ring for emergency services. There isn't anyone else around. However, I'm late for a film I want to see, and I don't want to miss the beginning of it. I hurry past.

You might well say that in the circumstances I had an obligation to stop. Let's suppose that it was not illegal not to stop; further, that I am not employed to attend to people who are taken ill in the local streets. Despite that, you might still think that I had an obligation at least to stop and check what the problem was, and if necessary ring for an ambulance. You do not mean that I had a legal obligation or a contractual obligation. You do not mean that it was impolite of me not to stop. You mean that I had a *moral* obligation.

Yet moral obligation has become a problematic concept, at least in contemporary philosophical discussion and perhaps beyond. I do not mean that the experience of moral obligation is unfamiliar to most people. I mean that there is uncertainty about what to make of it. This uncertainty extends to the whole distinctive circle of moral concepts: moral wrongness; permissibility; obligation; conscience; blame; guilt; and remorse. Just because it is such a distinct and internally interrelated circle, it can seem detachable. One could be confident that there are valuable ends, great ideals, good ways of living, while remaining sceptical about whether *moral* concepts in particular retain a clear standing. This 'post-moral' attitude has a complex root system, ranging from Nietzschean and Freudian liberationist self-images, through incompatibilist ideas about responsibility, to ethical systems, such as utilitarianism, which present well-developed theories of the good within which moral concepts have no intrinsic place.

A brusque reply to these concerns would be simply this: you are right to think I had a moral obligation to stop, so there are moral obligations. It is a perfectly sound reply. However, there is a task of vindicating it, or even more modestly, understanding it. In asking how morality is possible we are asking a Critical not a sceptical question; yet in the case of morality the question has become pressing in a way that understanding the possibility of knowledge is not. People are confused about what morality is in a way that worries them. They may well be confused about what knowledge is, but if they are that does not worry them: they *know* there is knowledge.

It is thoroughly unhelpful bluntly to assert, at this point, the unique and indefinable nature of moral obligation, as some intuitionists have been known to do. Making a hard stand on this line of defence only adds to the air of mystery: to the idea that morality is a strange discourse about *sui generis* 'moral intuitions' which could simply be in wholesale error, like talk about supposed insights into magical powers. On the contrary, moral judgement is inherent in personal and social life—inextricably woven into it. A picture of our personal and social world that does not clearly show this is oversimple, or positively confusing.

How then to draw an adequate picture? In part with the tools of conceptual analysis, but mostly through the exercise of interpretative imagination and understanding. We must give an analysis of the moral concepts that shows how moral judgements are connected to evaluative and practical reasons. But we must also understand the moral emotions from within: their immanent rationality; their objects; their connection with personal integrity; and the social actions to which they dispose—and also their liabilities to distortion and dysfunction. Only in that way can we grasp how moral judgement fits into the domain of reasons.

We shall approach the task in two stages. Conceptual analysis is the task of this chapter. As to the hermeneutics of moral judgement, we shall address that in Chapter 15, after we have continued, in Chapters 13 and 14, our account of the fundamental norms governing practical reasons. Thus, this chapter is primarily concerned with conceptual preliminaries; our discussion of morality will be complete only at the end of Chapter 15.

Our starting point is the claim that moral judgement is judgement about *evaluative* reasons; specifically, that the sentiment that allows us to understand the distinctively moral concepts is that of blame. As noted in 4.1, to make this claim we must identify, without circularity and in sufficient depth, the sentiment of blame and the actions to which it disposes. In this chapter, however, our account of the action to which moral blame disposes—*withdrawal of recognition*—will be preliminary. Filling it out will be one of the tasks of Chapter 15. Here our task will be to consider how blameworthiness connects to practical reasons, and then to indicate how the whole range of moral concepts, including those that are based on the concept of a right, can fit this approach.

12.1 Wrongness and blameworthiness

Saying that x has a moral obligation to α is clearly not identical in meaning to saying either that x should* α (i.e. that there is sufficient reason for x to α (11.6)) or that x has a warrant to α. It can be true that you should* α, true that you have a warrant to α, but false that you have a moral obligation to α. The converse is less plain: can it be true that you have a moral obligation to α but false that you should* α or that you have a warrant to α? We shall answer that question.

To say that you have a moral obligation to α is to say that it would be morally wrong for you not to α. What then, in the first place, is the connection between moral wrongness and blameworthiness? I take it to be as follows:

> (1) It is morally wrong for x to α if and only if, were x to α from the beliefs that are warranted in x's epistemic state then either x would be blameworthy for α-ing or extenuating circumstances would apply to x's α-ing.

This of course requires explanation. Extenuating circumstances remove or diminish blame that would otherwise have been appropriate. The reference to action from the actor's *actually* warranted beliefs will be explained and defended in the next section. But first let us consider what 'blameworthy' means.

There is a causal meaning of 'blame' in which one can blame the dud calculator batteries for a mistake in the bill, blame the weather for the train delay, etc. Saying that they are to blame is just saying that they are the proximate cause of the unfortunate result. It is not this causal sense of 'blame' that is in play in (1). There is also a moral sense. One can say, for example, both that Mary was to blame for the misunderstanding, and that she should not actually be *blamed*—she was justifiably attending to something else that was happening. She was to blame in the causal sense, but not in the moral sense. Blame in (1) is to be understood in the moral sense.

Now when we talk of blaming someone in this sense we are normally referring to a judgement, or an action that is the expression of that judgement. The judgement is a judgement about the appropriateness of a sentiment—the feeling or sentiment of blame. To judge that someone is morally blameworthy is to judge that the blame feeling towards them is reason-supported, that there is sufficient reason for it, whether or not one actually feels it. The act of blaming is the act of expressing that judgement. For convenience however, I am going to use the term 'blame' to refer to the judgement, and sometimes directly to the feeling. Thus in (1) 'blameworthy' means 'blame-feeling-worthy': there is sufficient reason for the sentiment of blame.

It may happen, for a variety of reasons, that though the blame feeling is reason-supported and the judgement that it is is warranted, it should not be expressed. It may be counterproductive to do so, for example, in getting someone to change their ways. It is thus important to keep clear the distinction between the sentiment and the act of blame. It is also important in other, more theoretical, ways. When Mill gives his definition of moral wrongness in Chapter 5 of *Utilitarianism*, it is unfortunately not clear whether he is concerning himself with the sentiment or the act of blame.[1] However, inasmuch as he commits himself in theory at least to assessing the appropriateness of blame by utilitarian standards, he must be interpreted as referring to the *act*. For utilitarianism is a view

---

[1] Mill 1963–91, vol. X: 246: 'We do not call anything wrong, unless we mean to imply that a person ought to be punished in some way or other for doing it; if not by law, by the opinion of his fellow creatures; if not by opinion, by the reproaches of his own conscience... There are other things... which we wish that people should do, which we like or admire them for doing, but yet admit that they are not bound to do; it is not a case of moral obligation; we do not blame them, that is, we do not think that they are proper objects of punishment...' Allan Gibbard develops a definition in the spirit of Mill (Gibbard 1990: 40–5), specifically however, in terms of what it would be 'rational' to *feel* about the agent.

about practical reasons, reasons for actions, not about evaluative reasons, reasons for feeling. Insofar as some utilitarians elide this point they do so because they do not really believe in evaluative reasons, or assimilate them to practical reasons. In reality, however, when we assess whether the *sentiment* of blame is reason-supported in a particular case we are not considering the expediency of the *act* of blame. Properly moral judgement is, rather, a special case of our general evaluative capacity to assess reasons for feelings as such. In that respect our view will be more like Adam Smith's than Mill's, in that Smith takes the 'propriety' of feelings in general to be determined by their objects, not by the utility of the actions to which they dispose.[2] We shall see that this divergence makes a very big difference.

Granted these elucidations, I claim that (1) is a priori. However in 4.1, we noted a 'cart and horse' objection to any proposed definition of moral wrongness in terms of the blame feeling. (1), it may be granted, is an a priori truth; but it is so by definition of 'blame' not by definition of 'morally wrong'. Blame in the moral sense is defined as that sentiment which there is reason to feel towards something that is morally wrong. So (1) is true by definition—but by definition of 'blame'. 'Morally wrong' is semantically primitive in the sense that it is indefinable.

We accepted the objection as a point, so to speak, about the lexicon of English, but left open the possibility that the *concept* of the morally wrong could nonetheless be characterized in terms of the concept of an evaluative reason for blame. This broader approach draws on the idea that we can elucidate a concept by saying what is required for possession of the concept, rather than by the semantic route of explicit definition within the existing resources of a language. What distinguishes moral wrongness as a *normative* concept is that you have the concept only if you are sensitive to reasons for the blame sentiment.

On this approach we cannot appeal to a definition of 'blame sentiment' as 'that sentiment which there is reason to feel towards something that is morally wrong'. To be fruitful, this approach must characterize the blame sentiment without appealing to the notion of moral wrongness. How to do this?

In general, we characterize emotions by the objects that arouse them and the actions which they prompt. We may indicate the objects by showing exemplary cases, and where possible, by stating some general condition on the objects. Thus we could fix the blame feeling by saying that it is what one is disposed to feel towards an agent in a variety of sufficiently well-described cases, for example, towards the agent who ignores the person who has fallen ill in the street. Furthermore, a general condition will be important (Section 12.2): the object of the blame feeling must be something which we think the agent had warranted reason not to do, and which we think the agent could have refrained from doing. This is of course not sufficient: the nature of the reasons matters. It is the fact that the agent did the thing, despite *those* reasons, that gives sufficient reason for responding with the sentiment of blame. The next chapters will discuss what kinds of practical reasons there are. But they will not attempt to give an account of when mixes of those

---

[2] Smith, A. 1984 (1759), Part I, Section 1; Chapter iii and Part II.

various kinds of reasons become morally significant in a particular case, in the sense that failure to respond to them comes to attract reason-supported blame. That would be a substantive, and an endless, task. It is, as will be discussed in Chapter 15, the role of *moral judgement* to perform that task in specific cases.

12.2 Blame as withdrawal of recognition

What then is the sentiment we have summarily described as the 'blame feeling'? Our best fix on it comes from another direction—from the characteristic action which it prompts.

Blame does not prompt, like anger, towards attack, or like fear, towards flight. It is not (*pace* Adam Smith) resentment, because resentment is specifically occasioned by what is taken as injury or insult to oneself. Resentment is the opposite of gratitude, one may say: if gratitude is reason-supported then there is reason to give thanks or reciprocate with a favour; if resentment is reason-supported then there is reason to demand apology, the expression of regret, or even compensation.[3] Gratitude and resentment are patient-relative feelings, constituting the realm of benefits and torts, whereas the blame feeling is patient-neutral and constitutes the realm of right and wrong. If there is reason for anyone to feel it towards the object, there is reason for everyone to feel it. Its characteristic behavioural quality is a chilliness, or a shrinking away, or withdrawal rather than aggression. This is particularly clear in one's own case, in the experience of self-blame or guilt—which could hardly be resentment directed against oneself, but is indeed a shrinking from oneself. (The resentment view must make guilt something different to blame: fear of the resentment and retaliation of others, for example.)

Indignation, it is true, 'righteous indignation', is also patient-neutral: it is occasioned by what is taken to be wrongdoing, whether or not it involves injury to oneself. Yet it is a mistake to make it the emotional core of blame, even though wrongdoing is its object. To be righteously indignant about an action one must first find it blameworthy. But the sentiment of blame itself need involve no indignation—one may blame with disappointment, sadness, or regret. The difference between indignation and the blame feeling then lies not in their object but in the action to which they characteristically dispose.

Blame disposes to *withdrawal of recognition*. To withdraw, withhold, or refuse recognition is to cut off relations or refuse to enter into them, to exclude, in however partial and temporary a way; in more extreme cases it leads to ostracism, casting out, outlawing. Like fear, blame disposes to the creation of distance between oneself and the object; but the difference is that the disposition of fear is to fly, whereas the disposition of blame is to cut off, exclude. Guilt, self-blame, is the withdrawal of recognition from oneself. (Hence 'I couldn't live with myself if I did that'.)

---

[3] If we understand *envy* as resentment of a person purely for their achievement or good fortune then it is never reason-supported. There is reason to resent another's behaviour only if it is belittling, or shows insufficient consideration, and to resent their success only if it is inconsiderately or exploitatively achieved at one's own expense. The envious person thinks himself belittled by another's success; this type of resentment is Nietzsche's *'ressentiment'*.

This account of the blame sentiment will be fleshed out in Chapter 15. Let us draw in advance on that fuller account and assume that it fixes the sentiment clearly enough to allow non-question-begging introduction of a term that denotes it: 'ƃ', as suggested in 4.1. The reference of 'ƃ' is the sentiment that is (i) the appropriate response to certain representative examples of belief and action;[4] and that (ii) prompts a characteristic-type of action, namely, withdrawal of recognition. We then have:

> (1ª) It is morally wrong for x to α $=_{Df}$ were x to α from the beliefs that are warranted in x's epistemic state, and without any extenuating circumstances, there would be sufficient reason to ƃ x for α-ing.

From now on we shall understand 'It is blameworthy of x to α' to mean 'There is sufficient reason to ƃ x for α-ing'. Thus (1) should be understood as saying exactly what (1ª) says.

12.3 Morality, blame, and practical reasons

If I blame someone for doing something I must think he had a reason not to do it. That, though not sufficient, is necessary: if you show that he had no reason not to act as he did you refute the charge of blameworthiness. There can be no reason to blame someone who *had no reason not to do* what he did.[5]

I have put this in terms of reasons a person has. In 5.1 we attached a special meaning to the phrase 'reason a person has', meaning by it a warranted reason. However, this is not what it means here. As we noted there, when we talk of the reasons a person has we can mean a number of things. We can, for example, mean the reasons he *took* himself to have. But another thing we can mean is this: the reasons there would be for him if his factual beliefs were true. Let us call them the agent's belief-relative reasons.[6] Belief-relative reasons are not reasons in the primitive sense. But when it comes to blameworthiness it is these 'reasons' that are especially relevant.

Blame is concerned with the agent's belief-relative reasons. It does not follow reasons as such. Suppose you have just inadvertently taken poison. There is reason to ring for an ambulance. But I am not blameworthy for failing to call an ambulance if I have no warranted reason to believe that you have taken poison, and thus fail to believe that you have.

Nor, however, does blame follow warranted reasons. Suppose that I have warrant to believe that you've just swallowed poison, but, failing to recognize that warrant, I fail to believe that you have, and do nothing. In this case I am not blameworthy unless I could have been expected to recognize that warrant for belief. If my failure to recognize the warrant is negligent, then I may be blameworthy; the blame attaches to the failure to

---

[4] The reference fixer is something like: 'Blame is that feeling that there's usually reason to feel towards a person who knowingly hurts another just for the sake of hurting them, who misleads people for his own advantage, etc'.
[5] Cp. Shafer Landau 2003: 181–3; Darwall 2006: 28, 98.
[6] Note the restriction to factual beliefs. False purely normative beliefs can sometimes excuse or remove a person from blame; in the following examples I am abstracting from such issues.

recognize the warrant, not to the failure to help you. Note that this failure is still practical: it is a failure to think carefully enough, for example, about what was in that packet, and that is a failure to do something: 'you didn't think'. If, however, in the circumstances I could *not* have been expected to recognize the warrant—there was no negligent failure to think—then I am not blameworthy. My failure to believe was not *unjustified*, in the sense of 5.9.

Now, in contrast, suppose that I believe, but with neither justification nor warrant, that you have taken poison, and I do nothing. Am I blameworthy? Yes. We could quite naturally say that given that belief I had reason to call an ambulance, and here the sense of 'had reason' is the belief-relative sense mentioned above: there would have been reason for me to call an ambulance if my beliefs were true.

Next, suppose you administer a drug that you are warranted in thinking is a cure, but that you unwarrantedly believe to be a poison.[7] You took yourself to be poisoning the patient; in fact you cured him. Let us further suppose that other facts that you believe to obtain would not, if they did, give you sufficient reason to poison the patient (for example, you do not believe him to be Hitler, etc.). Are you blameworthy? You are, just because you believed yourself to be poisoning the patient. So either that was what you intended to do, or you didn't care that that would be (as you thought) the effect of your action. Either way you are blameworthy; yet there was no *warranted* reason for you not to administer the drug. Because blame follows the beliefs under which you acted, it follows neither the reasons there were for you, nor the warranted reasons there were for you, but your belief-relative reasons. In this case there was belief-relative reason for you not to administer the drug.

Thus we have:

(2) If x's α-ing is blameworthy, then if x's factual beliefs were true there would be reason for x not to α.

This feature of blame, its connection to belief-relative reasons, is inherent in the sentiment itself: one grasps it in understanding the sentiment of blame and thus understanding what can constitute an intelligible object of the sentiment. It makes no sense, lacks reason, to blame people for doing what they had no belief-relative reason not to do—though they may still be blameworthy for having the beliefs they have. It makes no sense to blame in such cases, in the way that it makes no sense, lacks reason, to resent a good turn without in any way thinking it to be maliciously meant, patronizing, etc. Someone who resents a good turn has to read malice or slight into the other's action, and similarly, someone who feels the sentiment of blame towards the other for what he did must read some belief-relative reason for not acting into the other's state of belief, or some epistemic negligence ('He knew, *really*'; 'he *should* have realized', etc.)

So far we have been considering blameworthiness, not moral wrongness. Blame connects to belief-relative reasons; thesis (1) however, connects moral wrongness to *warranted* beliefs about the facts.

---

[7] The example (and the term 'belief-relative') is adapted from Parfit (forthcoming), Section 21.

I submit that the actual beliefs from which an action was done are relevant to its blameworthiness but not in general to its moral permissibility or wrongness.[8] Say you administer the drug when you have warrant to believe that it will cure the patient, but from the *unwarranted* belief that it will poison him. In that case your action is blameworthy (absent extenuation), but according to (1) it is *not* morally wrong. Had your belief been warranted you would have been doing something morally wrong. In fact it wasn't, so although you acted with a blameworthy intention the action itself wasn't morally wrong. That remains the case even if, despite the fact that you have warrant to believe the drug will cure the patient, the drug actually kills him. So you intended to kill him, and you killed him: even so—though you are much to blame for what you did—what you did, given your epistemic state, was not morally wrong. Given what you had warrant to believe, what you did was actually the morally right thing to do.[9]

Moral wrongness turns neither on the agent's actual beliefs, nor on the facts, but on the beliefs warranted in the agent's epistemic state. Although blame, in contrast, is primarily concerned with the actual beliefs under which you acted, there is nonetheless a connection between blameworthiness and warranted reasons, as follows:

> (3) If, were x to α from the beliefs that are warranted in x's s, either x would be blameworthy for α-ing or extenuating circumstances would apply to x's α-ing, then x has warranted reason not to α.

Suppose, first, that x would be blameworthy for α-ing. Then by (2) x's factual beliefs must be such that if they are true there is reason for x not to α. Now suppose those factual beliefs that x has are warranted; then x has warranted reason not to α. We get to this conclusion from the self-determining nature of moral agency (to be discussed in Section 4): if some facts would constitute a reason for a self-determining agent x not to α, x can tell by reflection alone that they would. Thus if he is warranted in believing that they obtain, he has warrant to believe that there is reason for him not to α, that is, he has a warranted reason not to α. (2), we claimed is something that one knows just on the basis of understanding the blame sentiment. So if x's factual beliefs are warranted and x is blameworthy for acting from them, x must have warrant for the belief that there is reason not to α.

Suppose, second, that extenuating circumstances apply to x's α-ing. Extenuation exists when an action which would normally be blameworthy is excusable. It may be excusable *either* because you excusably failed to become aware of warranted reasons not to do the action *or* through some excusable failure to act on those reasons, even though you were aware of them (for example, the understandable emotional turmoil you were in). These alternatives cover large categories. The first, in particular, may involve something as simple as that there was a great need for haste and you excusably failed to consider a possible consequence, or as complex and hard to evaluate as that in the society in which you live

---

[8] If I believe that an action is morally wrong it does not follow that it is. But, depending on my actual factual and normative beliefs, it may be blameworthy on my part to do it, even if it is not morally wrong. However, a further point is that conscientious conviction can itself affect moral permissibility—see 14.8.

[9] I am grateful to David Copp for very helpful discussion of this point (about which we disagree).

298   The Domain of Reasons

you could not be expected to grasp the reasons not to do what you did. But given that this is the overall shape of extenuation, to say that extenuating circumstances apply to a person's action implies that there *was* warranted reason for that person not to do the action. Thus we arrive at (3).

From (1) and (3) we conclude:

(4) If it is morally wrong for x to α then x has warranted reason not to α.[10]

I suggest, further, that (3) can be strengthened. Can there be reason to blame a person who, acting from warranted beliefs about the facts, does what they were warranted in doing? Surely not. You cannot be blameworthy for doing what you had sufficient reason to do because you correctly saw that you had sufficient reason to do it: an action done from warrant cannot be blameworthy. This gives us:

(5) If, were x to α from warranted factual beliefs, either x would be blameworthy for α-ing or extenuating circumstances would apply to x's α-ing, then x has no warrant to α.

(5) arises, again, from the nature of the blame feeling—like (2) it is a principle internal to the sentiment of blame, a principle governing the intelligibility of that sentiment. How could there be reason to blame you for acting from warrant—doing what you had most reason to do because it *was* what you had most reason to do? What is there for blame to latch on to? You could *reasonably* be blamed only if you could and should have believed that there was more reason for you to do something else, that is, that there was warrant not to do what you did. So, for example, suppose it were true that you always have sufficient reason to do what you warrantedly believe is best for you—as egoism says. Then it could not be *blameworthy* for you to do that.

By a similar argument to the one just given (5) yields:

(6) If it is morally wrong for x to α then x has no warrant to α.

Since it is morally obligatory not to α if and only if it is morally wrong to α, we can conclude from (4):

(7) If it is morally obligatory for x not to α then has reason not to α

and from (6):

---

[10] This argument has the following form:

(1) $m \rightarrow (a \rightarrow (b \vee e))$
(2) $(a \rightarrow (b \vee e)) \rightarrow r$

Therefore:

(3) $m \rightarrow r$

m: it is morally wrong for x to α
a: x αs from factual beliefs that are warranted in x's s
b: x is blameworthy for α-ing
e: extenuating circumstances apply to x's α-ing
r: x has warranted reason not to α.

(8) If it is morally obligatory for x not to α then x has no warrant to α.

Can we further deduce that x has warrant not to α? If (acting from warranted factual beliefs) you were either blameworthy for α-ing or extenuation applied, you must have had warranted sufficient reason to believe that there was sufficient reason not to α.[11] I.e. you must have had warrant not to α. So as well as (8) we have:

(9) If it is morally obligatory for x not to α then x has warrant not to α.

(8) and (9) taken together say that moral obligation is *categorical*, in the sense of being inescapable and supreme.[12] That is, if you have a moral obligation to do something (not to omit doing it) you have sufficient reason to do that and no other thing.

This conclusion is striking: not merely is the categoricity of morality *consistent* with a sentimentalist account of moral concepts in terms of reasons to blame—it actually follows from it. The mistake of some varieties of sentimentalism is not to acknowledge sufficiently clearly that there are *reasons* to blame: the key to moral categoricity lies in the hermeneutics of the blame sentiment. A moral obligation to α exists *in virtue of the nature of the warrant to α*. It is because of the kind of warrant you have for doing the thing that it is morally obligatory to do it. The reasons constituting the warrant are reasons it would be blameworthy to ignore (absent extenuation).

The connection made in (1) and (3) is between moral wrongness and warranted reasons. This implies that moral obligation, like warrant and warranted reason, is an epistemic notion relativized to epistemic states. Should we have formulated (1) and (2) with a non-epistemic notion of obligation instead, as some would suggest? Thus:

(1*) It is morally wrong for x to α if and only if, were x to α from knowledge of the relevant facts then either x would be blameworthy for α-ing or extenuating circumstances would apply to x's α-ing.

(3*) If, were x to α from knowledge of the relevant facts, either x would be blameworthy for α-ing or extenuating circumstances would apply to x's α-ing, then there is reason for x not to α.

On the epistemic account, I may have a moral obligation to α even though there *is* no reason for me to α. On the non-epistemic account, in contrast, the connection would be between moral obligation, reasons, and *ought**; with corresponding changes to (7) and (9):

(7*) If it is morally obligatory for x not to α then there is reason for x not to α.

(9*) If it is morally obligatory for x not to α then there is sufficient reason for x not to α.

On the whole (despite some conflicting evidence) it seems to me that the epistemic account of moral obligation is the best account of that concept. We can confirm that, in

---

[11] i.e., not just *insufficient* reason to believe that there was sufficient reason to α (which would also entail absence of warrant to α).

[12] David Brink's terminology (1997).

the first place, by examples. There is the example already mentioned: if I have sufficient reason to believe you have unwittingly taken poison then I have a moral obligation to ring for the ambulance. That is so, even if in fact you have not taken poison.[13] In contrast, if you have unwittingly taken poison but I have no reason to believe this, then I have no moral obligation to ring for an ambulance: I do not act morally wrongly if I do not do so.

Consider next the case of the intended poisoning that cures. Here moral wrongness and blameworthiness intelligibly diverge. Suppose the agent had warrant to believe that administering the drug would cure the patient; in that case, I argued, it was not morally wrong to administer it (even if in fact it would kill the patient). That conclusion remains true even if the agent *unwarrantedly* believed that the drug would poison the patient and was thus blameworthy for administering it. Symmetrically, if the agent had warrant to believe that the drug would poison the patient, it was morally wrong to administer it, even if in fact it would cure the patient.

True, if you are offering me moral advice you might well say to me 'It would be morally wrong to do that' and then mention some facts—which I could not otherwise have known—that (as we would naturally say) *make* it morally wrong. Thus it seems that what makes an action morally wrong is the facts, not the agent's warranted beliefs about the facts.

Here we need to consider the requirements of advice. When I ask for advice about what I ought to do I *may* be asking what I am warranted in doing in my actual epistemic state. This is so, for example, if I know that you and I are in the same epistemic state. Or if I am in a group who share an epistemic state, my question 'What ought we to do?' is the question what we are *warranted* in doing. But if I ask someone who knows more, then I am asking for advice in the light of what *they* know. Thus in Alan Gibbard's forest example, if I ask a forester what we ought to do to get out of the forest I ask because I hope he knows the best way. If he does, it would be wholly inappropriate for him to tell me to take a straight line and stick to it, even though that is what I am currently warranted in doing in my present state of ignorance.[14] He should be helping me by advising me in the light of what he knows, not what I know. Exactly the same applies if your advice is about the moral aspects of my decision. You should be advising me about those aspects in the light of what *you* know, not what I know.

Speaking on the basis of what he knows, the forester might simply say 'This is the best way out', without telling me why. In telling me that, he would not be implying that I already had a warrant for thinking this is the best way out. But at this point a contrast emerges. What if you said 'This is what you have a moral obligation to do', without telling me why? Strictly speaking, that would be true only if I *already* had a warrant for thinking I had that moral obligation. If you were basing yourself on facts I did not know, you should make that clear.

---

[13] True, if you do not die people would not in practice feel the sentiment of blame as strongly as if you had. That is a significant point about moral luck; however, I think the general view would still be that I had a moral obligation to act and was blameworthy not to have acted.

[14] As Gibbard points out (1990: 19).

Suppose, however, that for one reason or another, confidentiality perhaps, you are unable to tell me the relevant facts. What you could still say is 'If you knew the relevant facts you would have such-and-such a moral obligation'. Next, suppose I am warranted in thinking that you are reliable. In general, agents have a moral obligation to do that which someone they are warranted in regarding as reliable assures them they would have a moral obligation to do, if they knew the facts. The obligation arises because, in virtue of what the reliable person has said, they now have sufficient reason to believe that the facts are such as to constitute sufficient reason to do the thing—a reason moreover, that it would be blameworthy to ignore if they knew what it was. It is surely blameworthy not to act on such a warrant.

For these reasons and others it is natural to formulate moral principles in terms of the facts: 'if a person has taken poison you ought to call an ambulance', not 'if you have sufficient reason to believe that a person has taken poison you ought to call an ambulance'. When we formulate them in this way we are spelling out the reasons which, if you know of them, it is blameworthy on your part to ignore. It is in this sense that moral wrongness supervenes on the facts.

12.4 Morality, self-determination, and autonomy

A survey of our judgements about moral obligation and blame tells in favour of the epistemic account of moral obligation. But there is also a more general consideration. Moral obligations, like rational requirements (5.11), follow *warrant*, not *ought**, because self-determining actors must be able to *act* from them. Moral agency is self-determining, and this requires that actors can reflectively recognize what moral obligations they have in a concrete situation, just as rational self-determination requires that they can reflectively recognize what specific warrants obtain. So also the connection between failure to comply with a moral obligation and moral criticizability is like that between failure to comply with a warrant and rational criticizability. In both cases we need to know the actor's warrants, actual beliefs, and excuses. We can ask what a person was either *rationally* or *morally* required to do given the factual beliefs they actually held, and we can ask whether they had warrant for their factual beliefs. We can also ask whether they were rationally or morally required, in the circumstances, to pay more attention than they did to establishing warrants. In short, the notions of moral obligation and rational requirement occupy analogous role positions in the pattern of normative assessment.

In 5.1 we distinguished between self-determination and autonomy proper. Self-determination consists in recognizing what one has sufficient reason to do relative to one's acceptance of certain normative tenets, and acting from that recognition. I am self-determining if I determine myself by normative tenets which I accept—even if I accept those tenets themselves on authority, on trust, or by my own *fiat*, and whether or not I have personal insight into their truth, indeed even if they cannot be said to *be* true or false. I can determine myself, in that I am able to audit my epistemic state, determine what warrants I have *given* acceptance of those normative propositions or commitments, and act from them. The same distinction applies in the moral case. I am morally self-determining if I am able to audit my epistemic state, determine the concrete moral obligations I have *given* acceptance of certain moral tenets, and act from them. I can have this ability even if I have no personal insight into moral truths, and even if there are no moral truths. What is required is that I am able to audit what concrete moral obligations I have (relative to the moral tenets I accept) from within my epistemic state.[15]

That moral agency, with its links to blame, is self-determining is inherent in the idea of the moral as such. It follows that the notion of self-determination is present wherever moral concepts are found. The idea of moral *autonomy*, however, is stronger. Moral autonomy is more than self-determination; it is self-determination grounded in personal moral insight, i.e. in the ability to recognize, by one's own lights, true moral propositions as true. The same can be said of rational autonomy; it is self-determination grounded in personal insight into reason relations as such, i.e. the ability to recognize personally the truth of norms.

We have weaker or stronger notions of rational and moral agency depending on whether we think of these forms of agency as merely self-determining or as requiring full autonomy. The stronger notion, that of autonomy, assumes a meta-normative conception in which normative tenets are indeed *propositions*, capable of truth and falsity, and in which their truth and falsity is knowable by personal insight. I will call the principle of moral or rational insight that is involved in this notion of autonomy the (moral or rational) *Insight principle*. For the moral case it can be put as follows:

(10) (*Insight principle*) morally autonomous agents can know their concrete moral obligations by means of their own insight into them.

For rational autonomy exactly the same can be said, putting 'rationally autonomous' for 'morally autonomous', and 'warrants' for 'moral obligations'. Autonomy in both cases is a matter of degree, depending on how much insight actors have, and how much control over their acts.

Rational autonomy can furthermore be understood broadly or narrowly. The broad understanding takes it to include grasp of evaluative reason relations. The narrow understanding takes it to include only epistemic and practical reason relations. Since rational autonomy consists in (the ideal case) of first-person insight into *all* reason relations, if we accept that there are evaluative reasons we must understand it in the broad way. Only then is moral autonomy a special case of rational autonomy; for it calls on broad, not narrow, rationality. It is insight into reason relations, but the reasons relations involved include evaluative relations of blame. We can agree with Kant, then, that moral agency is a form of rational agency. Yet the gulf remains great, in that Kant does not accept that there are evaluative reasons at all. Further, and connectedly, he treats moral norms ('the moral law') as though they were simply co-extensive with practical norms: that is, as

---

[15] Also, in 5.11, we took ordinary uses of 'rational' to connect with justification rather than warrant. Does the same apply to moral obligation, or does justified failure to perceive warrant simply extenuate, rather than altering moral obligation itself? I leave this question open.

though morality and pure practical reason were identical. On the account of moral obligation given here, that is by no means the case. Failure to recognize evaluative reasons is the fateful flaw in Kant's ethics (and aesthetics).

Irrespective of that however, the Kantian idea that human beings are autonomous fundamentally shapes modern ethical and political ideas. Particularly influential is an *egalitarianism of autonomy*, according to which all human beings are equally autonomous; and this is especially held to apply to *moral* autonomy. Nothing in the ethical legacy of Kant and Rousseau is more influential than this: the idea that what sets all human beings apart is their equal capacity for moral agency, and that their equal status and dignity as ends in themselves is founded on that capacity.

Kant's moral philosophy brings this idea into unprecedentedly sharp focus. Equal capacity for autonomy is not a question of equal calculative or computational skills, or equal experience. What Kant asserts is the equal *normative insight* of all humans, and on that basis their equal *positive freedom*. This proudly humanist doctrine is protected by Kant's transcendentalism about rational agency. Human beings are set apart from nature by their rationality. In principle, it seems, Kant's doctrine is that every rational being, through its own inherent spontaneity—through the causality of freedom—has insight into all purely normative knowledge. Quite clearly, however what specially matters to Kant is an egalitarianism of pure *moral* insight. It drives Kant's insistence that morality is accessible to everyone, that arriving personally at a correct moral judgement is open to the simplest human being. Every human being merits absolute respect, because every human being has absolute moral insight.

Shorn of the transcendental backing Kant provides for it, egalitarianism about autonomy is an empirical thesis. It is much stronger than the claim that moral agents must be self-determining. True, reason relations of any kind can only be known, in the first instance, by personal insight. However, that does not entail that everyone must know them in that way. For all the epistemology tells us it may be that some, perhaps many, can know, or truly believe, or just accept, only through trust, on authority, or from desire or fear. And while the very idea of moral agency requires self-determination, it is not obvious that that very idea of moral agency requires autonomy.

If the capacity for autonomous moral insight varies, we are left with three possibilities. The first is to say that the Insight principle, (10), does not apply to everyone because not everyone is autonomous. Moral norms, however, *do* apply to everyone; but some people must discover from others what some of their moral obligations are. They are self-determining, but they are not autonomous.

This is a view that has been taken for granted in many societies at many times. The notion that the gods or God tell us the moral law is a version of it—for the gods usually have authoritative priestly interpreters. But now such a hierarchy of moral authority sticks in many people's gullets. There are then two other options. Of these the first, historically very important over the last century or so, subverts the notion of autonomy from within. From the egalitarianism of autonomy it retains only the negative claim that no one is better placed to judge of fundamental normative claims than anyone else is. That, it says, is because we cannot justify the degree of objectivity in moral judgement that talk of greater or less moral insight assumes. It agrees that your moral obligations are those given by your own conscientious judgement; but it does not claim that conscience is a faculty of knowledge. Authenticity of conviction still matters—but not because authentic conviction as against inauthentic acceptance delivers moral truth; instead authenticity, understood as deciding sincerely or 'authentically' for oneself as against being led by others, becomes a peculiar, legitimacy-conferring, modern virtue of the person, though bereft of any epistemological foundation. We 'respect' the authentic person's moral judgement not because it is 'right' but because it *their* judgement. This is an ideal of self-governance without autonomy and without moral objectivity.

The second alternative option preserves autonomy, the Insight principle and the unity and objectivity of morality. But it holds that those who lack insight into some moral norm do not have the moral obligations associated with that norm. For if the Insight principle applies to them, but they cannot tell for themselves that they have a certain moral obligation, then they do not have it. In a specious sense, this preserves the thesis of equal autonomy: everyone is equally capable of recognizing what reasons and moral obligations there are *for them*. But not everyone is equally capable of telling what reasons and moral obligations there would be for them if only they were capable of the necessary insight: in that, more obvious, sense not everyone is equally autonomous. Furthermore, on this view not everyone has the same moral obligations. On this view the standards of moral obligation are higher for the more insightful, and thus more autonomous, than for the less. While this view preserves autonomy and moral objectivity it gives up egalitarianism about autonomy: it is the standpoint of moral autonomy *without* egalitarianism.

We can throw further light on this standpoint by noting how it sustains a critique of common moral assumptions analogous to that which Bernard Williams offers on the basis of his internal theory of reasons.

12.5 Cognitive internalism and autonomy

Morality is linked to reasons for action by the crucial implications stated in (6) and (7). Those implications can be contraposed. If the agent has no warranted reason not to α then it is not morally wrong for him to α. Thus a theory of reasons can shape one's views of moral obligation. That obviously applies to egoistic and instrumentalist theories of reasons. It also applies to Bernard Williams' 'internal' theory of reasons. It is in fact a main source of his critique of morality—as he notes, for example, in the following passage:

> Blame rests, in part, on a fiction; the idea that ethical reasons, in particular the special kind of ethical reasons that are obligations, must, really, be available to the blamed agent... *He ought to have done it*, as moral blame uses that phrase, implies *there was reason for him to have done it*, and this certainly intends more than the thought that we had a reason to want him to do it. It hopes to say, rather, that he had a reason to do it. But this may well be untrue: it was not in fact a reason for him,

or at least not enough of a reason. Under this fiction, a continuous attempt is made to recruit people into a deliberative community that shares ethical reasons... But the device can do this only because it is understood not as a device, but as connected with justification and with reasons that the agent might have had; and it can be understood in this way only because, much of the time, it is indeed connected with those things.[16]

When Williams says 'He ought to have done it, as moral blame uses that phrase, implies *there was reason for him to have done it*' he is assenting to something like (7).[17] To that he adds his motivational internalism, which says that there is reason for x to α only if α-ing will serve a motive in x's S. Combining these two theses, it follows that if α-ing *doesn't* serve a motive in x's S it won't be true that x ought to have α-ed, 'as moral blame uses that phrase'. The fiction we are then led into, Williams says, is that of treating x as though he really *did* have the relevant ethical reasons.

We are led into it, Williams suggests, because (sometimes, or often) we want to blame people who—by these internalist standards—simply do not have these ethical reasons. We want *everyone* to fall within the scope of blame. But suppose there are people who just don't have certain morally salient reasons, because these reasons have no grounding in their S. In that case we must either resort to fiction or accept that we cannot have what we want. Either we fantasize that these people really do have reasons which in fact they simply do not have—'recruit' them into sharing *our* reasons—or we accept that they have no such reasons and thus do not fall within the scope of blame.

We discussed and rejected Williams' motivational internalism in 10.6. Contrary to that view, ordinary morality holds that a person can have a moral obligation to do something whether or not carrying out the obligation will serve any of that person's existing motives. Williams makes an ingenious attempt to meet this point by invoking a 'desire to be respected by people whom, in turn, one respects'. Blaming a person who has that desire but otherwise has no motivation to avoid some particular moral wrong is 'as it were, a proleptic invocation of a reason'.[18] It *makes* it true that he has a reason to avoid it, in virtue of his desire to avoid blame when it comes from people he respects. For example, even if I don't have a desire to thank you for your good turn, I nevertheless have reason to do so, because another desire in my S is a desire for the respect of respectable people, and I won't get it if I don't thank you.

The desire for others' respect is an important human constant. But it cannot be invoked for Williams' purpose. If the respect sought is to be relevant to moral motivation, then it has to be respect for others as judges of when there is reason to blame. If I seek your respect because I respect you as a good judge of what's cool or macho, say, that doesn't necessarily give me anything much related to a moral motivation—on the contrary, this

---

[16] Williams, B. 1995b: 16.
[17] Something like (7), because his account on the whole seems to generate a connection between moral obligation and reasons as such, rather than warranted reasons. However, Williams does not discuss this issue, and it does not affect the question we are about to consider.
[18] Williams, B. 1995a: 41.

may cut across moral motivation. What then about the hard cases who, though they may seek various kind of respect from various kinds of peer groups, do not care a jot about others' responses of moral blame? Williams says they are beyond blame.[19] But this is clearly a mistaken criterion of moral agency. It is not the desire to earn respect that makes one a moral agent.

What makes one a moral agent is at minimum the capacity to know what moral obligations one has in the sense required for self-determination. On the view that moral agency is autonomous agency, however, the criterion of what makes one a moral agent is stronger—it is the capacity to recognize morally salient reasons as such, in the first-person way. This view—like Williams'—is still internalist about reasons, but the internalism is now cognitive not motivational. It is a special case of the cognitive internalism about reasons discussed in 3.9.

An autonomous moral agent subject to a moral obligation must be capable of personal insight into that obligation. Conversely, then, if such an agent cannot know by personal insight that they are thus subject, then they are not. To know in the first-person way that they are subject to a moral obligation they must be able to recognize, in that way, not only the relevant practical reasons but also that failure to act in accord with them will give sufficient reason for guilt and others' blame.

We argued in Chapter 10 that Williams' requirement of effectiveness (see (4) in 10.7) supports cognitive internalism, not motivational internalism. We can add that *motivational* internalism is responsible for the elements in Williams' critique of modern morality that ring false. This doctrine is a wrong turning, but that does not mean that there is nothing to Williams' critique of morality. Cognitive internalism has the implications for morality that interest Williams—and what is more it is indisputably an important part of modern morality in the shape of a doctrine of self-government by conscience, according to which people's moral obligations depend on what they can recognize by autonomous insight or accept by authentic conviction. The modern moralist cannot set it aside as easily as motivational internalism, or as an instrumentalist aberration. To criticize modern moral conceptions from the standpoint of cognitive internalism is to criticize it on the basis of its own commitments. If you cannot autonomously recognize or authentically endorse a moral obligation you do not have it.

It is unsurprising that philosophical possibilities which provide an a priori guarantee both that moral agency is self-governing agency and that everyone is equally a moral agent should be tempting. These are (a) to reaffirm Kant's transcendentalism about autonomy (the 'causality of freedom'); (b) to gravitate from the objective egalitarianism of autonomy to the subjective egalitarianism of authenticity (authenticity of existential choice). And the popularity of (b) is a testament to the desire to maintain an egalitarianism about moral agency, even when transcendental doctrines underpinning it have collapsed.[20]

---

[19] Williams, B. 1995a: 43.

[20] Probably the most common reaction, however, is to finesse the empirical question by a thesis of presumptive moral egalitarianism, according to which we can all be assumed to be fully competent moral agents unless shown to be otherwise. But if that assumption has to give way a lot of the time, what is accomplished by making it?

If we reject both (a) and (b), as we must, what line should we take? Should we accept moral autonomy and resign ourselves to its inequality—the standpoint of moral autonomy without egalitarianism? (In that case we should not base civic and political doctrines of equal worth on it.) Or should we fall back, in our conception of moral agency, from autonomy to self-determination and give up the Insight principle? Moral agency, that is, requires knowledge of moral norms which may be conveyed by others, not personal insight into them. Or, again, should we give up on (2), the connection between blameworthiness and reasons, and thus on the categoricity of moral obligation, so that we can say that someone is blameworthy for doing something even if they had no reason not to do it? But that seems incompatible with what we have said about the hermeneutics of blame. Should we then give up on cognitive internalism about reasons and say that they *had* sufficient reason to do it even though they were incapable of first-person insight into that reason? (We 'provide' them with a reason, as Nietzsche might say.)

We shall pursue these pressing questions in Chapter 15. But here we should complete our account of moral concepts and their connection with the concept of a reason. For we have yet to consider the concepts of rights, justice, fairness, and desert.

12.6 Rights and duties of right

Moral agency must be self-determining agency—and that entails, we have just argued, that agents' concrete moral obligations must depend on their epistemic state, just as their warrants do. In each case one must be able to tell one's moral obligations, or warrants, just by reflection on one's epistemic state. However, there is a very large and important part of moral discourse that we have not yet fitted into this picture: namely, the discourse of rights.

Suppose you've made a promise to me that you have, through no fault of yours, completely forgotten. You have no reason to believe you made it. Do you have a moral obligation to keep it? On the epistemic account you do not. But surely I still have a right to have the promise kept, reminding you of it if necessary? And if I have a right, must there not be some sort of corresponding onus on you?

It seems to me incorrect to say, of a person who has failed to carry out a promise he has blamelessly forgotten, that he has done something morally wrong. Yet we want to preserve the principle that where there's a right there's a duty. We can do so by distinguishing between the agent's *duties of right*, which arise from the rights of others, and his *moral obligations*. If A has a right that B do something, then B has a duty of right to do it; but if B is blamelessly ignorant of the fact his failure to perform is not morally wrong.[21]

---

[21] In referring to duties of right, and not simply duties, I mean to emphasize that 'duty' as used here is defined in terms of rights (as below). I am not implying that there are duties that are not duties of right. Role or office-based duties are duties of right. Suppose that I am the safety officer for the building, but through an attack of amnesia that I could not help have clean forgotten that fact. It remains true that I have a duty to check the building, and that performance of that duty can be demanded of me as of right, but false, given my amnesia, that I have a moral obligation to do so, unless I am reminded.

Suppose a lost will instructs that an estate should be left to a particular person. The executors have no idea of its existence. It is one of those situations from a Victorian novel: the will has fallen down the back of a very heave mahogany sideboard and the legitimate heir is languishing in some distant part of the world. Nonetheless, that particular person has a right to the estate, and hence the executors have a corresponding duty of right to make it over to him or her. They have that duty of right even while they are ignorant of it. But since their ignorance is entirely innocent they transgress no moral obligation, do nothing morally wrong, in failing to carry it out. Nonetheless, if they find the will they then have a moral obligation to make good the situation by carrying out its terms.[22]

If you have sufficient reason to believe you made a promise then you have a *prima facie* moral obligation to fulfil the promise that you have reason to believe you made. (It is *prima facie* in that *prima facie* obligations, like *prima facie* reasons, may turn out *not* to be obligations when all the facts you are warranted in believing are taken into account.[23]) In contrast, you have a right-based duty to fulfil the promise if and only if you've made it. In general the link between moral obligations and duties of right is that one has a *prima facie* moral obligation to fulfil duties of right that one has sufficient reason to believe that one has.

Not all moral obligations arise from duties of right. It is possible to think, as Kant thought, that we have a moral obligation to improve ourselves, without thinking that this involves a right on anyone's part. True or false, this is a coherent position. Furthermore, there can be a moral obligation to help someone who has no actual right to our help: a moral obligation but not a duty of right.

The difference I have in mind is sometimes phrased as that between perfect and imperfect obligation. However, this terminology runs the danger of conflating three distinctions: (i) between moral obligations and duties of right; (ii) between moral obligations based on duties of right and those not so based; and (iii) between morally obligatory acts and acts which are admirable but supererogatory. Kant's distinction between the doctrine of right and that of virtue provides apter terminology.[24] There is, it is true, no supererogation in the domain of rights; it is also true that how far a non-right-based moral obligation goes can sometimes be 'a matter of conscience', in the sense of turning on what one personally feels one must do. It does not follow that there are no clear-cut moral obligations outside the domain of right. For example, a clear-cut moral obligation of gratitude need not correspond to any right on the part of the person to whom gratitude is due.

---

[22] There may well also be moral obligations arising to the persons in *de facto* possession, in virtue of the legitimate expectations they have developed, even though they have (as it turns out) no rights as legatees.

[23] Cp. 2.3. However the relativity of moral obligation is to an epistemic state, not a field, since in talking about moral obligations we are in the domain of *warranted* reasons.

[24] He thus distinguishes Parts I and II of *The Metaphysics of Morals*; he distinguishes perfect and imperfect moral obligations in the *Groundwork* (4:421 ff.). Mill also refers to the distinction, but regards these expressions as 'ill-chosen', preferring the 'more precise language of philosophic jurists', in which:

duties of perfect obligation are those duties in virtue of which a correlative *right* resides in some person or persons; duties of imperfect obligation are those moral obligations which do not give birth to any right. Mill (1963–91), vol. X: 247 (*Utilitarianism* 5.15).

Note the switch from 'duties' to 'moral obligations', which registers the sense that 'duties of imperfect obligation' are 'only' moral obligations.

If you do me a good turn you don't have a *right* to my thanks. It is not a conceptual truth that every moral obligation is rights-based; nor is it a conceptual truth that outside the domain of rights no clear (as against precise) distinction can be made between obligation and supererogation.

Nonetheless, the concept of a right is clearly a normative moral concept (I am not talking about legal rights), so our general project requires an account of it in terms of reasons.

A definition of rights that would do the trick comes from Mill. In his words:

> When we call anything a person's right, we mean that he has a valid claim on society to protect him in the possession of it, either by the force of law, or by that of education and opinion. If he has what we consider a sufficient claim, on whatever account, to have something guaranteed to him by society, we say that he has a right to it...
>
> To have a right, then, is, I conceive, to have something which society ought to defend me in the possession of.[25]

According to this definition persons have a moral right to something if and only if there is a moral obligation on society to defend them in their possession of that thing, or to guarantee it to them. Mill gives this definition as the middle link in a chain of definitions: he defines justice in terms of rights, rights in terms of moral obligations, and moral obligation, as we have seen, in terms of there being reason to apply sanctions for non-compliance.

This general sequence—defining concepts of justice in terms of rights, rights in terms of moral concepts, moral concepts in terms of reasons—seems to me to be correct. It is the sequence we are following in this chapter (although, as already noted, we probably differ from Mill in taking moral concepts to be characterizable in terms of evaluative, not practical reasons). Unfortunately, Mill's specific definition of 'right' is unconvincing. H. L. A. Hart objected that an obligation on society to protect a person in the possession of something, or guarantee it to them, cannot define 'right' since the relevant obligation on society exists *in virtue* of the existence of the right. Mill's definition, he says, 'puts the cart before the horse'.[26] The objection is sound: for while we can explain why society has an obligation by appealing to the existence of a right, there may also be other explanations. It is not logically contradictory, as Mill's definition would imply, to say that society should guarantee x to y even if x has no right to y. The fact that x has a *right* to it is only one possible reason for guaranteeing it to him. There may be good reasons, even a moral obligation, to guarantee something to people with a threat advantage, but that does not show they have a right, a 'valid claim', to it.

Suppose a blackmailer credibly threatens some enormous damage to innocent parties unless we guarantee him a lifelong pension, in some irreversible way. We may have an

---

[25] X, 250 (*Utilitarianism* 5.24 and 5.25).
[26] Hart 1982: 103. This type of objection, which I call, after Hart, a 'cart and horse' objection, has application to many of the normative analyses in this book. Sometimes it works, sometimes it doesn't. See 18.6 for a general discussion.

obligation to guarantee it to him, even though he does not have a right to it. Even if we promise it to him he does not have a right to it, since the promise is given under duress. It is not the blackmailer's right to a pension that explains our obligation to guarantee it; this particular obligation does not arise from a duty of right to him.

The point we should focus on is that rights give rise to morally permissible *demands*. In this context moral permissibility must be understood non-epistemically, as moral permissibility relative to the facts, i.e. under the assumption that the relevant facts are known. Suppose, for example, that this is your computer and you have not given me permission to use it. If I know that, I have a moral obligation not to use it without asking you. Relative to those facts, i.e. assuming you to know they obtain, it is morally permissible for you to *demand* that I do not use it without asking you. (Absent special circumstances—I shall take this constant qualification for granted, so as to not to keep sprinkling it in the text.) Likewise, when I have promised to meet you at a given time, you are permitted to *demand* that I do. Suppose, in contrast, that you would like me to meet you even though I have not agreed to do so (and I am not your employee, etc.). You are permitted to request but not permitted to demand that I do. Or suppose that your computer has broken down and I happen to know how to mend it. In some circumstances, where your need is great and the distraction from my own projects small, I may even have a moral obligation of assistance to come over and mend it. But most of us would say that you are not permitted to *demand*, as against request, that I do. To claim a right where the other has at most a moral obligation is, precisely, presumptuous: presuming to something you do not have.

A demand is something stronger than a mere request. Demand is conceptually linked to the permissibility of some form of compulsion or exaction: a permissible demand is a request that it is morally permissible to enforce. I do not mean that it is actually possible to enforce it; we may intelligibly demand the return of hostages even if we have no power to enforce it. And of course enforcement, compulsion, exaction don't necessarily take the form of physical coercion. Even to say that you demand something is already to exercise a certain degree of exaction; demand is a form of command. You don't demand, as against request, things in polite company, even when you have a right to do so. To demand is to imply that enforcement would, if necessary be permissible; that given that it's been requested, it is something the other person has no moral option but to do.

Permissible enforcement must be proportionate to the seriousness of a right-infringement. Hence, just because demanding is already a form of enforcement, when a right is sufficiently trivial it may be disproportionate even to make demands. Suppose that we have previously agreed to have lunch together—and you have not pressured me unacceptably into that agreement. Then you have a right to expect me to be there, a right to be told in advance (if possible) that I can't come, and a right to remonstrate if I fail to turn up without bothering to tell you and without any excusing reasons. But, as often with small rights, it might well be foolish or petty-minded to act on these rights, by actually remonstrating, let alone demanding compensation.

Notice, next, that where harm or damage is caused to the right-holder by an infringement it is permissible for the right-holder to demand or enforce compensation. The sense of compensation that I have in mind is the broad sense of 'making up for loss' not the narrow, responsibility-accepting, 'making amends for loss because you have caused it'. I can be said to compensate you in the broad sense if I make up in some way for a setback, injury, or interference you have suffered. The act of compensation in this broad sense implies no fault on my part. I might compensate you out of the goodness of my heart for the flood damage to your house even if the flooding is not my fault and I have no obligation to do so. I might do so while disclaiming all responsibility. Furthermore, I may have a moral obligation to compensate even where there is no fault, and in particular no rights-infringement, on my part. We can, for example, have a communal obligation to compensate very hard-pressed people for the flood damage to their house, although we had no part in causing it. Where there has been a damaging infringement of a right, however, there is not just a moral obligation to compensate on the part of the infringer (if that is called for by the right-holder); it is, further, morally permissible for the right-holder to *demand* compensation from the infringer for the damage caused. Here too, of course, the damage may be so small as to make any demand for damages disproportionate.

It is the right-holder who in the first instance is morally permitted to demand compliance and compensation, and thus, where necessary and possible, proportionately to enforce it. (As ever, such permissibility is subject to defeat by weightier moral grounds, and what is permissible is proportionate enforcement of proportionate compensation, taking into account the circumstances of the infringer.) A further point, however, is that the right-holder may not be capable of issuing demands: infants, people with certain kinds of mental illness, and animals are not able to do so. It seems specious to say that they are still morally permitted to issue demands, though incapable of doing so; yet we surely do not want to deny that they have rights solely in virtue of that point.

A right-holder may empower an agent (another person, an institution) to issue, on his behalf, the demands he is permitted to make. Where the right-holder is not capable of doing so (an orphan infant, for example), 'society', in Mill's word, can empower an agent to act on his, her, or its behalf. Moreover, for traditional reasons arising from the overall desirability of an impersonal rule of law, society may under certain circumstances impose rules of enforcement, indeed it may take over and exercise the right-holder's permission to enforce, insofar as enforcement goes beyond mere demand. This is a case in which permission to enforce is overridden by weightier moral factors. However, to override is not to cancel. We should not simply say, in this case, that the right-holder has permission to demand but no permission to enforce. The permission remains latent, as can be seen from the fact that if society is unable to act as the right-holder's agent (for example, in situations requiring immediate self-defence) moral permission to enforce becomes live again. We can say that the State can legitimately forbid me from exercising that permission in person, so long as it exercises it effectively on my behalf.

With these points in place we define rights as follows:

(10) x has a right to y against z if and only if it is *prima facie* morally permissible (relative to the facts) for x or x's agent to demand that z does not take y from x, or does not prevent x from doing y, or delivers y to x (as appropriate), and to

demand compensation for x from z in the event of damage resulting from z's non-compliance.[27]

We can also define a *duty of right*:

> z has a duty of right to x in regard to y if and only if x has a right to y against z.

Thus z's duty is a duty not to take y from x, or not to prevent x from doing y, or to deliver y to x, as appropriate.

I should explain the occurrence of the word *prima facie* in (10). It can be permissible to infringe a right. For example, I may have to seize your bicycle without your permission in order to alert the local rescue service to a disaster that has occurred on the mountain. It is debatable whether we should say that in such cases the rights in question are not violated but legitimately infringed, or that they, together with corresponding duties of right, lapse in the face of emergency. Our definition takes the former option. So when it is permissible to infringe a right, it is not, all things considered, permissible for the right-holder to demand that it be observed. However, there may still be a duty of right to compensate you for the inconvenience you suffered in being unable to use your bike. You have a right to be compensated for inconvenience, even though you have no right to refuse use of your bike.[28]

(10) can replace the Millian definition in Mill's general sequence. It is consistent with the 'explanatory' aspect of rights noted by Hart. For z's moral obligation to provide, or not to interfere or take away, can be *explained* in terms of x's right: that is, in terms of the existence of a right-constituting normative relation between x, y and z, consisting in a moral permission for x to freely make appropriate demands of compliance and compensation to z in regard to y. The explanation assumes that if x is morally permitted to demand something of z then z has a moral obligation to provide it: we shall be taking this to be a substantive principle in the morality of rights (the Demand principle in 14.2). The existence of that right-constituting relation is then in turn explained by means of something else, such as a previously made promise, a duly acquired possession, or a liberty.

Moral permission to demand is what is special about rights. We may have a very strong moral obligation, for example, an obligation of assistance, to help people who have fallen into dire need through flooding. But if the flooding is caused by us then it is not, or not only, an obligation of assistance. In that case, the obligation to compensate arises from a *right* on the part of those flooded against us, a right not to have their environment degraded by us, and a *duty of right* on our part to them. They can legitimately *demand* compensation.

---

[27] In this definition what it is morally permissible to demand refers to what it is morally permissible *freely* to demand. The impermissible may become permissible under coercion. So, for example, it may be morally permissible to lie or break a promise under coercion. Thus suppose the hostage-taker forces his hostage to demand that the government releases some prisoners. It is morally permissible for the hostage to make that demand, but the hostage is acting under coercion, not freely. So it does not follow that it is the hostage's *right* that the government should release the prisoners, nor that the government has a duty of right to the hostage to release the prisoners. (I owe the example to Allan Gibbard, and I have benefitted from discussion of the definition itself with Antony Duff.)

[28] Cp. Thomson, 1990: 98 ff. As she points out, the scale of compensation depends on the nature of the emergency. You may have an obligation to shoulder some proportion of the cost of the rescue, rather than placing the whole cost on me.

Suppose there is flooding in village A, caused by our negligence, and also flooding in village B, which produces greater need in B than A, but is not caused by us in any way. It is permissible for the victims in village A to enforce compensation on us, and for others to help them enforce it if they lack the power to do so themselves. Compensation proportionate to our share in damaging them is their just due. The villagers in B have no comparable right, assuming we have made them no promises. Moreover it seems to me, as a moral matter, that we ought to duly compensate the villagers in A before we get round to assisting those in B. To bring this point home, suppose the villagers in A are unfortunately powerless to enforce compensation from us. If we know that, is it morally acceptable for us to distribute aid purely in proportion to *need* as between A and B, even though our resources will not then enable us to compensate village A in proportion to our fault and the damage caused by us in A? I believe that village A would have a just grievance if we did that. Village B, in contrast, would have no reasonable grievance if we duly compensated A before working out how much we could help B.

To take another example, if some group or tribe A loses their food sources as a result of a pollution of their territory that is caused by us, we have a right-based duty to them to compensate them. If another group or tribe B loses theirs through some natural disaster in no way caused by us, or through over-hunting (that does not result from a need for food that is itself caused by us), we do not have a duty of right to compensate them, though we may well have a moral obligation to do so. In this example, again it seems that the duty to compensate A must take precedence over obligations we have to help B.

It is likewise plausible that there are cases of need in which a sufferer can permissibly demand assistance from us. In such cases, arguably, the sufferer has a need-based *right* of assistance from us. In the examples above, if B's need is dire and A's is not, then B may have a need-based right of assistance against both us *and* A.

This discussion of our definition of rights has involved not just the definition but also some substantive claims about the content of rights. I have tried to keep these fairly uncontroversial, but the scope of rights is inescapably controversial. The point here has not been to enter the controversy, but to highlight the centrality to rights discourse of the notion of *morally permissible demand*.

12.7 Justice, desert, and fairness

To reject Mill's definition of rights is not to reject his definition of justice in terms of rights:

> Justice implies something which it is not only right to do, and wrong not to do, but which some individual person can claim from us as his moral right...Whenever there is a right, the case is one of justice...[29]

The same connection between justice and rights is found in Kant, in the form of his already mentioned distinction between the doctrine of right and the doctrine of virtue.

---

[29] Mill (1963–91), vol. X: 247 (*Utilitarianism* 5.15).

It seems to me to be correct (with the qualification that entities other than individual persons can have rights). We can *demand* justice—and as we have seen, permissible demand is the core of the notion of a right. A substantive theory of justice is a substantive theory of what rights people have and why.

But the substantive theory is not germane to our discussion. Our concern is the normativity of justice concepts; that is, showing how they can be analysed in terms of reasons. To recapitulate the overall picture I am proposing: justice is characterizable in terms of rights, rights in terms of moral permissibility, and moral permissibility in terms of reasons for blame. It remains to consider how certain concepts central to justice—desert, fairness, impartiality—feature in this picture.

The concept of desert plays a role in several contexts: (i) evaluation of persons; (ii) advantageous and disadvantageous responses by others; (iii) remuneration; and (iv) punishment. Of these only (iv) is clearly and entirely a matter of justice. With the others, as we should expect, the question turns on whether and how rights are involved.

(i) Most fundamentally, desert consists in evaluative reasons for a certain class of sentiments directed at persons. We can say that a person deserves gratitude, admiration, respect, contempt, dislike, or blame. We mean simply that there is sufficient reason for these feelings. In contrast, it is odd to say that anger, boredom, desire, or fear are deserved, even when there is sufficient reason for them. One can be angry with someone or bored by someone for good reason; we do not, however, say that they *deserve* anger or boredom, although we can say of a person who is often irritating or boring that he is for that reason deservedly disliked or despised. We feel admiration or contempt for a person, we admire, respect, despise, or dislike that person, feel grateful to that person. These are all person-focused evaluations of the goodness or badness of the person in some character, performance or role. (Not necessarily *moral* goodness of badness of course. A boring or irritating person is a bad companion, but not thereby a bad person.)

There is a difference, in respect of justice, between positive and negative evaluations of this kind. Admiration or gratitude may be undeserved, but it is not plausible to say (except in special contexts) that if undeserved they are unfair or unjust. With negative evaluations, on the contrary, when they are undeserved they can be said to be unfair or unjust. A person may be *unfairly* disliked or *unjustly* despised.

Positive evaluation is not a matter of justice because it is not clear that gratitude, admiration, etc. can be *demanded*—they are no one's *right*. In contrast, if people's negative attitudes towards you are unfair or unjust, you have a right to complain about them, and to demand that they change their attitude. That, I think, is because everyone has a right to a certain social standing or reputation unless they deservedly lose it. So too respect, in a civic sense connected to standing or reputation, can be demanded.

(ii) Given (i), it follows by the Bridge principle that where the underlying evaluation is deserved there is reason for the relevant prompted actions—thanks, rewards, tokens of honour, or avoidance, condemnation, ostracism. It does *not* follow by the Bridge principle that that there is sufficient reason for them. When we say that such actions. are *deserved*, it seems to me that what we are saying is that *there is sufficient reason for the underlying evaluation*, not that there is sufficient reason for the action it prompts. For example, avoidance may be what crass and boring people deserve, but it may nevertheless, for a variety of reasons, be wrong to avoid them. However, if an undeserved negative evaluation is unjust, it also follows that an action prompted by an undeserved negative evaluation is unjust.

Inasmuch as it not generally true that anyone can demand *positive* evaluation it is likewise not generally true that deserved thanks, rewards, etc. are required as a matter of justice. There are special contexts. We can say that a novelist's achievements have been unjustly ignored because she has not received the admiration and recognition she deserves. Here we appeal to an underlying context that makes due recognition a duty of right, at least for some people—critics, say. Whether anyone has such a duty is debatable. It becomes clearer if we make the context a competition, such as a literature prize. She should have received the Nobel Prize for literature long ago. Still, did successive juries have a duty of right to award it to her; did she or people acting on her behalf have a right to *demand* it?

Suppose it is found that there has been a conspiracy to prevent this novelist's name from being discussed, or that jury selection has been influenced by publishers' bribery. At this point, one might say, real injustice is involved. Legitimate demands can now be made, for example, to have the competition rerun, or the winner disqualified. The same applies if it can be shown that the jury was negligent in its duties, or biased. In contrast, wrong decisions by the jury made in good faith do not, it may be said, raise questions of injustice, only questions about the jury-members' aesthetic competence. On this view, if the novelist fails to get the recognition she deserves because people have in good faith underestimated her achievement, no injustice has been done. The alternative view is that although the jury, having acted in good faith, was blameless, it nevertheless failed to discharge its duty of right. Given her achievement, the novelist had a *right* to the prize.

(iii) We talk about what reward, in the sense of remuneration, a job deserves. It is not clear whether this is a separate context to (ii). If we mean that work should be remunerated in proportion to how much the contribution it makes deserves admiration, respect or gratitude it reduces to (ii). The question is then as before: whether such remuneration can legitimately be demanded. (I am talking here about morally permissible unconditional demand, not conditional 'demands' in the sense of conditions one puts forward prior to agreeing a contract.) Given the discussion hitherto, it seems that the answer is 'no'. Thus while one can require payment for a visiting lecture as a condition of giving it, one cannot, having given it, unconditionally demand an honorarium in proportion to its excellence.

Quite often, however, when people talk about what pay is 'deserved' they have cost-effectiveness in mind. Deserved pay is what on grounds of efficiency there is sufficient reason to pay; it is undeserved only if it rises above the value (in the economist's sense) that is added by the work. The two views can and do blend. They can also combine without blending. So, for example, one might have medals, bonuses, etc. for employees whose admirable effort deserves recognition, while also determining their salaries by the economic value they add. Insofar as the concept of desert is functioning purely as cost-effectiveness it is not functioning as genuine desert, and *a fortiori* not as a concept of justice as desert. In determining remuneration by cost-effectiveness, the evaluative emotions which lie at the heart of desert are not engaged.

(iv) A pure desert theory of punishment says that the severity of punishment that there is reason to demand and that it is morally permissible to demand (other things equal), is proportionate to the gravity of the crime. Who is permitted to make the demand is a matter of debate for desert theorists; a common view is that everyone is—not just the victim—but that the state permissibly takes over enforcement of the demand. Here again, then, desert is linked to justice through rights.

It is plausible to think that the desert theory of punishment is an instance of the Bridge principle: i.e. that it holds because punishment is an expression of deserved blame. By the discussion in (i), the degree of blame that is deserved is the degree for which there is sufficient reason, and that degree is assessed, other things equal (such as degree of responsibility compared to others), in proportion to the gravity of the wrongdoing. The deserved punishment is then the punishment that expresses the degree of blame for which there is sufficient reason. But as noted in (ii), it does not follow from the fact that a certain degree of punishment is deserved that it is the punishment for which there is sufficient reason. Other considerations may be relevant, and so the desert theory should not be pure; it should agree there may be other reasons to consider.

In any case this account, though on the right lines, is too simple. The direct expression of blame is not punishment but exclusion. How these are connected will be considered in 15.4. I shall argue there that we have a right to withdraw recognition from the wrongdoer, and to restore it only in the presence of remorse and atonement, i.e. *self*-punishment. This still leaves the question of why *we* have a right to impose punishment: an important question in the philosophy of punishment, but not one that we need to pursue.

In general then *desert* always comes down to reasons for certain person-evaluating feelings. It engages with *justice* where rights are involved. Desert becomes justice when someone can permissibly demand it. One way in which this can happen is through interaction with fairness, to which we briefly turn.

Fairness pertains to allocation or distribution of something within a relevant group of people each of whom has a right-based claim; impartial distribution is distribution within the relevant group in proportion to such claims. An act or process of distribution is impartial if the distribution it makes is driven solely by fairness.

Where it is a matter of desert-based rights, fair distribution is in proportion to desert. That applies to blame, for example; it can also apply in specific contexts to positive evaluations. Given the role of teacher or parent, failure to praise a child as it deserves in relation to others may well be unfair. Similarly with school prizes, sports prizes, and the like. However, fair distribution need not always be desert-based. Take the distribution of burdens within a group engaged in some collective task; of taxes; of a collectively owned windfall; of joint assets after a marriage breakdown (in which it's controversial whether desert should be involved); of compensation, for example, for creditors, employees, etc. after a bankruptcy. A variety of factors can be in play (skills, ability to pay, previous commitments given), and the task of a substantive account of fairness would be to sort them out. But the relevant point from our point of view is that a fair distribution is a distribution proportionate to what can permissibly be demanded. A theory of fairness is a theory of what distributions are in that way proportionate.

12.8 The epistemology of blame

We now have definitions of the moral concepts in terms of the basic concept of moral wrongness.[30] And we have outlined how moral wrongness can be characterized in terms of reasons for the sentiment of blame. It will be useful, in conclusion, to review some epistemological and conceptual issues about the predicate, concept, and property of moral wrongness.

Consider again our definition of moral wrongness:

> (1ª) It is morally wrong for x to α =Df were x to α from the beliefs that are warranted in x's epistemic state, and without any extenuating circumstances, there would be sufficient reason to β x for α-ing.

As already noted in 5.1, in giving this definition we are *not* claiming that people who learn the term 'morally wrong' as part of their first language, first learn a term, 'β', for the blame sentiment and then use (1a) to get to the sense of 'morally wrong'. Nor need they have the *concept* of the blame sentiment. Rather, they are presented with actions that they are told are morally wrong; by and large they spontaneously respond to them with the blame sentiment. They then classify further cases of action as morally wrong, relying on their spontaneous blame feelings. In the course of that learning process they have to negotiate their way through the complexity captured in (1ª); that is, come to grasp the difference between saying that something is blameworthy and saying that it is morally wrong. Only then do they attain the concept of the morally wrong.

The criterion of blameworthiness (and hence of morally wrongness) is the blame feeling itself. That is, the disposition to blame is a defeasible ground for the belief that there is reason to blame, thus for the judgement of blameworthiness. This is no more than a special case of the general epistemology of reasons to be discussed in Chapter 16.

As in all these cases of evaluative reason, however, the first-person disposition can be defeated by further reflection and discussion. *Internal* defeat appeals to nothing other than careful discussion and reflection on the hermeneutics of the feeling. Where value concepts are purely affect-dependent in their epistemology, internal defeat is the only kind: consider 'boring' or 'funny'. All you have to learn, to master the difference between 'I am bored' and 'This is boring', is that your judgement as to what is boring or funny may be defeated by further experience and non-convergence with the judgements of others.

Crucially, blameworthiness is more complex. This concept leaves open the possibility of an external as well as an internal defeater, through the principle that an action is blameworthy

---

[30] Not of all the concepts relevant to moral appraisal, of course—I suggested in Chapter 4 that some terms of key significance for moral discourse, such as 'cruel', 'kind' are not even normative. On this view it is a substantive, though obvious, normative claim that cruelty is a vice, i.e. a disposition to act from motives that are blameworthy, while kindness is a virtue, a disposition that there is reason to admire and love.

only if there was belief-relative reason not to do it. Since blameworthiness and moral wrongness are connected, the principle generates an external defeater for judgements of moral wrongness too. (These points were discussed in Section 12.3.) Thus we can argue about whether an action is blameworthy, and whether it is morally wrong, not just from our dispositions to blame but also from our views about practical reasons. And in the next two chapters we shall examine and endorse some such views, which go beyond the Bridge principle.

A theory that gives necessary as well as sufficient conditions for practical reasons might in principle, if correct, defeat the internal criterion completely. That is, it could entail via (2) that there is never evaluative reason to blame. If, for example, we became convinced that egoism is true we might become convinced that the blame feeling is never reason-supported. That would be because, on the one hand, a failure to act egoistically is not, by the internal criterion of blameworthiness, a reason for the blame. On the other hand, since there is no reason for you not to lie, cheat, and so on when it's in your interest to do so, the claim that you are blameworthy in such cases would be defeated. In our spontaneous responses of blame towards cheating we certainly do not excuse people who cheat from self-interest. But if egoism is true this internal criterion of blame is defeated—and it is not clear what undefeated judgement of blameworthiness remains. It might be the judgement that serious imprudence is blameworthy, if indeed we spontaneously blame such imprudence. The mere fact that a theory of practical reasons generates sufficient reason for a type of action will not entail that failure to do that type of action is *blameworthy*, as against unwarranted. Of course even if we have to conclude, as egoists, that no self-interested action is blameworthy, we might also conclude, by a Hobbesian argument, that positive sanctions against cheating should be instituted. That conclusion, however, does not tell us that there is (evaluative) reason to blame cheating, as against (practical) reason to penalize people who cheat—and perhaps practical reason to cause everyone to believe that there is evaluative reason to blame cheating.

Can discussion and deliberation about how people should* act in practice work to attach the blame response to new cases, as well as detaching it from old ones? That is not a simple question. Certainly judgements of blameworthiness can change over time in both ways; but this might be by 'immanent critique'—that is by appeal to the wider or deeper implications of existing *moral* convictions. We shall return to this question of 'ethical theory' versus 'immanent critique' in Chapter 15. My point here is that blameworthiness, and hence moral wrongness, is not a pure affect-dependent concept. In principle it could turn out, despite our spontaneous blame responses, that nothing is blameworthy or morally wrong, just as in principle it could turn out that, despite appearances, nothing is yellow. That does not apply to a pure affect-dependent concept, such as *boring*.

12.9 Moral wrongness: predicate, property, and concept

We have been discussing the epistemology of moral wrongness. But what *is* the property of moral wrongness?

Consider three claims about an agent and an action. The first two are:

- Were x to α from the beliefs that are warranted in x's epistemic state, and without any extenuating circumstances, then there would be sufficient reason to b x for α-ing—$B(x, \alpha)$.
- It would be morally wrong for x to α—Wrong (x, α).

When the first relation holds there must be some facts about x and α in virtue of which it does. That is, there must be some facts which would constitute sufficient reason to blame x for α-ing, were x to α. For example, the fact that x has warrant to think that α-ing would break a promise, etc., or that α-ing would cause unnecessary harm, etc. Now consider the complete disjunction of propositions that assert such facts—call it 'D':

- $F_1(x, \alpha)$ v ... v $F_n(x, \alpha)$—$D(x, \alpha)$.

Each of these three expresses a relation between x and α:

(a) $B(x, \alpha)$
(b) Wrong (x, α)
(c) $D(x, \alpha)$.

It is natural to say that these are downwardly dependent: '$B(x, \alpha)$' holds because 'Wrong (x, α)' holds, and 'Wrong (x, α)' holds because '$D(x, \alpha)$' holds.

Natural, but on our account misleading, insofar as it suggests a 'three-layer model' according to which there are three *distinct* relations, related in a uniform way by supervenience: (a) obtains *in virtue of the fact that* (b) obtains, and (b) obtains *in virtue of the fact that* (c) obtains. We have argued, on the contrary, that (a) and (b) are by definition one and the same relation. This *single* relation 'supervenes' on D. What that means, on our account of normative supervenience (2.10), is simply that if any disjunct in D obtains, the fact that it does is sufficient reason to blame x for α-ing, were he to α (with the other conditions applying). Saying that the fact that Wrong (x, α) supervenes on the fact that $D(x, \alpha)$ is saying just that.

The arguments here are like those we have already considered in discussing the buck-passing account of good. In effect, we are proposing a 'buck-passing' analysis of moral wrongness.[31] In discussing good we rejected the idea that there is a distinct property of goodness that constitutes a 'middle man' between facts and reasons (4.4); in this case we should reject the idea that there is a distinct property of wrongness that constitutes a middle man between facts and reasons. In doing so we can in both cases identify the relation of normative supervenience on the facts with S, the sufficient-reason relation. A moral obligation to do something exists in virtue of the kind of warrant there is for doing it. The reasons that constitute that warrant are what make the action morally obligatory. The moral obligation is not itself a further reason to do the action.

---

[31] I differ here from Scanlon (1998); and Darwall (2006).

The 'three-layer model', according to which there are three distinct relations, faces some challenging questions, as it did in the case of goodness. What is the distinct relation of wrongness? What is the supervenience relation between D and this relation, and then between this relation and B? Suppose some people were equipped only with the concept of blameworthiness and the concepts involved in D. What would they be missing? Would there be some property they simply had no notion of? Would they lack reasons to judge that some actions were blameworthy?

To sharpen the contrast between our account and the three-layer model, compare the following two claims:

(11) The fact that x does something it is morally wrong for x to do, without any extenuating circumstances, is sufficient reason to b x for doing that action.

(12) If x does something it is morally wrong for x to do, without any extenuating circumstances, there is sufficient reason to b x for doing that action.

On our account (11) is strictly false, while (12) is analytically true; on the three-layer model both are true, but neither is analytically true. (11) is false, on our account, because it is not the fact that the action is morally wrong that constitutes sufficient reason for blame, but rather the facts in virtue of which the action is moral wrong that constitute sufficient reasons. Those facts are sufficient reason not to do the action, and those reasons are ones which it is blameworthy (absent extenuation) to ignore. The moral wrongness of the action is not (as such and in general) a *further* reason not to do it. If we say that a person is blameworthy *in virtue* of having done something morally wrong, we are saying that he is blameworthy in virtue of ignoring some warranted reasons not to do the action which—absent extenuation—it is blameworthy to ignore. This statement is not analytic, because there might have been extenuation. Likewise we could say that he isn't blameworthy, even though he did something morally wrong—that would be because there was extenuation.

What is true, and lends colour to the idea that blameworthiness supervenes on moral wrongness, is the fact that English '(morally) wrong' is not *definable* in terms of English '(moral) blame'. In English it's the other way round. But we have already discussed that point.[32]

Finally we should note that there is, *prima facie*, another way to eliminate the middleman. It is to identify moral wrongness not with B but with D, the disjunctive relation. One version of this view might say that the B relation is the reference fixer for moral wrongness. Moral wrongness is then that property of x's action α in virtue of which B(x, α)—that property in turn is identical with D. So on this view wrongness does not supervene on D, it *is* D; but blameworthiness does supervene on wrongness.

We shall return to these issues in Chapter 18, where we consider the 'open-question' argument against reductive versions of realism.

[32] 4.1 and 12.2.

13

IMPARTIALITY: (I) THE PRINCIPLE OF GOOD

We have given a sentimentalist account of personal good in Chapter 11, and of moral attitudes in Chapter 12. Is it possible, then, to develop a sentimentalist account of all the sources of practical reasons? In this chapter and the next, we shall see that the answer is 'no'.

A purely sentimentalist account of practical reasons would treat them *all* as instances of the Bridge principle (11.1). On this view, whenever there is a reason to do something it can be traced back, via Bridge, to something there is reason to feel. If this were so, then the epistemic basis of our knowledge of practical as well as evaluative reasons would be our affective dispositions.[1] For in the first place, our knowledge of *evaluative* reasons is so based. Furthermore, understanding a feeling includes understanding what actions it prompts. The Bridge principle channels normative knowledge from feelings to actions: in virtue of knowing that there is a reason to feel something one knows there is a reason to do the thing prompted by that feeling. In this way, on a purely sentimentalist account, the affective dispositions become the sole *epistemic basis* of practical as well as of evaluative reasons. Furthermore, evaluative reasons become, via the Bridge principle, the sole *normative source* of practical reasons: practical reasons exist solely in virtue of the existence of some underlying evaluative reasons.

We shall argue, however, that critics of sentimentalism have been right in one important respect. Sentimentalism gives no satisfactory account of the various ways in which requirements of *impartiality* enter into practical reason. These requirements can take various forms, for example, through doctrines of impersonal good and doctrines of universal rights. What is their epistemic basis? It consists, we shall argue, in dispositions of the will, not dispositions of the feelings. Dispositions of the will stand to practical reasons as affective dispositions stand to evaluative reasons. In neither case is this a species of intuitionism, as will be explained in Sections 13.3 and 13.4.

Overall, we shall see, there are three normative sources of practical reasons. One has already been discussed. It is provided by evaluative reasons via the Bridge principle; its

---

[1] How spontaneous dispositions provide the epistemic basis for normative knowledge is discussed in 16.2 and 16.5.

epistemic basis is the affective dispositions. The other two underlie impartial good and impartial right. I shall call them the principle of *Good* and the *Demand* principle. The epistemic basis of these two principles is the dispositions of the disinterested will. In this chapter our concern is the principle of Good; the Demand principle is the topic of the next chapter, Chapter 14.

How do these three principles hang together as sources of practical reasons? Or do they fail to hang together? And how do they underlie moral obligation? These questions will be discussed at the end of Chapter 14 and in Chapter 15.

13.1 The limits of sentimentalism

The discussion of Chapter 12 showed that the sentiment and disposition of blame constitute the core of the moral concepts. But it did not discuss either the epistemic basis or the normative source of those reasons which morality singles out, by blaming failures to respond to them. Can a sentimentalist account of these moral reasons be given?

Consider again the person who falls ill in the street (mentioned in the introductory remarks to Chapter 12). A tempting account, for a sentimentalist, of the reason for stopping to help would be that it arises from the substantive desire to help, or from the substantive desire to avoid blame. Depending on what sort of person you are, there certainly may be reason for you to want to help, and/or reason for you to want to avoid blame, and that will yield a reason to help, or to avoid blame by helping, via the Bridge principle. Over and above such reasons, however, you have reason to help. You have that reason whether or not you desire to help, and whether or not there is reason for you to desire to. Likewise with the desire to avoid blame. You have reason to help whether or not you desire to avoid blame, and whether or not there is reason for you to desire to avoid blame. This applies to all moral obligations. Where there is a moral obligation there is a warrant for action irrespective of what there is reason for you to *desire*.

If you walk on by, your blameworthiness arises from the fact that you knew the situation, had sufficient reason to help, but did not. Of course it is the specific *nature* of that reason, not merely its sufficiency, that matters. Blame picks out failures to act on certain reasons, not on all; it singles out a proper subset of reasons as morally significant. Yet to say that it singles them out is not to say that it generates them. They were already there to be singled out. The only practical reason inherently generated by reason-supported blame is a Bridge-based reason to do what it prompts: withhold recognition.

If the reasons blame singles out as moral obligations pre-exist blame can they nonetheless be accounted for in a sentimentalist way? It seems plausible that some of them have a sentimental source: gratitude; love; and empathy. Thus to blame someone for their rank ingratitude, for example, is to blame them for failing to act where reasons of gratitude require them to act; and these reasons are generated from evaluative reasons via the Bridge principle. The same seems plausible for obligations of family or of friendship.

But morality also contains impartial principles. For example, our ordinary conception of rights includes universal rights that hold against everyone, whatever their relation to the right-holder. The duty of right not to torture a person, or to arbitrarily damage what is theirs, does not rest on ties of feeling to that person. It is hard to see how it could be generated from evaluative reasons.

Might we generate it from resentment and regret? Suppose you take something of mine without asking permission. That is a reason for me to feel resentful. It is likewise a reason for you to feel regret and (via the Bridge principle) a reason to apologize and perhaps compensate. But my reason for feeling resentful, and your reason to feel regret, is that you had no *right* to take it without asking my permission. These evaluative reasons presuppose that right; they are not its normative source. The right consists in a moral permission to demand that others respect my things. The permissible demand applies unless waived, and entails that there is reason for you not to take my things unless I let you. The underlying norm is that the existence of a permissible demand that x αs is a reason for x to α. This norm, as we shall see in the next chapter, is fundamental to the logic of authority and rights, thus to a very extensive part of morality ('the doctrine of right'). It does not lend itself to a sentimentalist account.

These are impartial principles *within* morality. But a wide range of moral philosophers, Kantians and utilitarians among them, think not merely that some principles within morality involve impartiality but that there is an impartial standpoint that stands outside morality, or that in some way governs it, or both. The content of this standpoint varies; for Kant it is the Categorical Imperative, for utilitarians it is an impersonal conception of the good.

Sentimentalists have always had trouble with impartiality. Sympathy is not impartial, however wide. Impartiality involves agent-neutral reasons: for example, that there is reason not to injure anyone, not to treat anyone merely as a means, to promote the good of anyone—irrespective of that person's relation to oneself.[2] Not that sentimentalism excludes agent-neutral reasons as such: patient-neutral sentiments, such as admiration and blame, for example, give rise to agent-neutral practical reasons via the Bridge principle. It makes sense to talk about impartial admiration, and impartial blame, and the requirement that practices of reward and punishment should be impartial is founded on the patient-neutrality of these evaluative reasons (12.7). The difficulty is, rather, that the impartial standpoints of the Kantian or the utilitarian—universal and impartial respect, or concern—do not seem to be underpinned by any such patient-neutral sentiment.

It is in impartial standpoints such as these that rationalism is at its strongest. That impartiality features in our moral thinking is undeniable. Fixing its exact role is a more debateable matter. A possible route for the sentimentalist is to argue that impartial principles are not fundamental. Whereas Kantians and utilitarians envisage getting to morality from an agent-neutral starting point, a sentimentalist might deny that any such starting point exists. That must be the view of anyone who says that the sole source of practical reasons is a person's reason-supported desires. On the expansive account of a person's good that I have defended

---

[2] I have put this in terms of persons, and will continue to do so. Some ethical stances bring entities other than persons (animals, nature itself) into the scope of their agent-neutral principles. I do not mean to exclude these—what classes of beings or entities have intrinsic and agent-neutral ethical standing is a question I am not addressing here; the view that all persons have such standing is already inconsistent with purely agent-relative accounts.

in Chapter 11, this is a formally egoist position. It makes all complete practical reasons agent-relative. Impartial, agent-neutral reasons must then be introduced at a derived level, through a contractarian or eudaimonist route. The contractarian line of thought would be that it is in everyone's interests to agree to abide by impartial principles. The eudaimonist line of thought is that to be good is at least a part, if not the whole, of one's good.

Formally egoistic contractarianism encounters familiar and (to my mind) fatal freerider problems. In particular, even if it is best for us to believe certain impartial norms, and even if we can all simultaneously do something that would cause every one of us to believe them, it does not follow that they are true, or that we have reason to believe that they are, as against making ourselves believe that they are. Thus if contractualism is based on a formally egoistic premise it does not actually yield a reason for acting impartially, as against making oneself believe things that will cause one to act impartially.

This criticism does not apply to forms of contractualism, such as T. M. Scanlon's, which in effect build in a requirement of impartiality in from the start, in their notion of what is *reasonable*. However, just because they build impartiality in from the start, they cannot be used to justify impartial principles on the basis that no one could reasonably disagree with them.[3]

Eudaimonism likewise seems open to this cart-and-horse objection, to which we keep returning. A eudaimonist account does yield a genuine reason to do the impartial thing. The desire for moral integrity, personal at oneness, is a reason-supported desire, and by the Bridge principle gives reason to do the morally right thing, including the impartial thing, where that is morally required.

However, if this is advanced as an account of what reason there is to do the right thing (a formally egoistic reason), we can point out that it does not explain moral categoricity, unless one's good consists *entirely* in being good. If doing the right thing is only a part of one's good, the specific practical reasons that it generates may be outweighed by reasons stemming from other parts of one's good, unless the former can be shown in some way to have lexical priority over the latter (which indeed may not be so implausible). More fundamentally, there is the cart and horse point: doing the impartial thing is part of one's good *because* there is pre-existing reason to do it, and a virtuous person who ignores that kind of reason diminishes his own good.

These very briefly sketched difficulties strongly suggest that reasons of impartiality must have their source in some fundamental norms that are agent-neutral. But what are these, and what is their epistemic basis?

13.2 Impartiality and autonomy

Kant attempted to establish the impartial standpoint from the very idea of autonomy. And indeed there is something plausible in the idea that autonomous thinking and acting acknowledges constraints of impartiality, *just in virtue* of its autonomy. Let us see whether that can be spelt out.

---

[3] This is not necessarily a criticism, in that these models of impartiality are not necessarily trying to *justify* impartiality.

The Categorical Imperative incorporates a requirement of impartiality, as is particularly clear in the Formulation of Humanity—which for many people is its most resonant and inspiring version. This formulation requires us to treat *all* rational beings, impartially, as ends and not merely as means:

> Act in such a way that you always treat humanity, whether in your own person, or in the person of any other, never simply as a means, but always at the same time as an end.[4]

Of course there is more to the Categorical Imperative, as Kant envisages it, than just a requirement of impartiality. Impartiality can be upheld in various ways in otherwise very different moral schemes, whereas Kant claims that a rather distinct and definite moral scheme is implicit in the Categorical Imperative. Many present day moral philosophers influenced by Kant are primarily interested in that moral scheme. In particular they have typically wanted to distinguish their view from utilitarianism; showing the moral difference, it may be said, between impartial *respect* and impartial *concern*. Among these philosophers, some take the Categorical Imperative to be *the* supreme principle of morality in the way that Kant intended—while abandoning the claim that it can be derived from autonomy. Others make a more modest claim, though still an interesting one—that the Categorical Imperative should be seen as being a highly general principle *within* morality, with far-reaching implications to be sure, but not one that on its own generates the whole of morality.

While these philosophers are interested in the potential moral implications of the Categorical Imperative, they are less interested, and often quite sceptical about, the Kantian move from autonomy to the Categorical Imperative. However, it is this move that concerns us. Let me say straightaway that I do not believe you can get the rich moral doctrine that Kant thinks is contained in the Categorical Imperative from autonomy alone. Kantians interested in that rich doctrine are right to downplay the move from autonomy to the Categorical Imperative. The question is whether we can get *impartiality*, as against the whole set of moral doctrines we think of as Kantian ethics, from autonomy.

At this point we should remember a point already discussed, in connection with Sidgwick, in 3.6: you cannot get to a requirement of impartiality from the mere universality of reasons.[5] The case of rational egoism illustrates that; the rational egoist's principle is agent-relative but universal: everyone should always do the action that is best for them.

Impartiality requires not just the universality of reasons but also the existence of agent-neutral reasons. If our substantive insight into practical reasons reveals to us that all or some reasons are agent-neutral, what it reveals is a substantive normative truth. This

---

[4] *Groundwork* IV: 429. Although in this formulation Kant refers to 'humanity' he means 'rational nature': 'man, and in general every rational being, exists as an end in itself...' (IV: 428); "Rational nature exists as an end in itself" (IV: 429).
[5] Sidgwick 1981 (1907): 208–10, 420–1, 497–8. Sidgwick's point is directed at Mill's 'proof' of the principle of utility as much as at Kant.

substantive insight is not analytically derivable from the very notion of a reason. So if we interpret Kant as arguing to impartiality from the sound formal point that reasons are universal, we have to conclude that his argument is fallacious.

Let us turn instead to a promising observation made by Henry Allison.[6] Recognizing the force of the Sidgwickian objection, Allison acknowledges that no impartial principle can be deduced from the universality of reasons alone. However he denies that, that is Kant's intention. Instead he points out that Kant means to derive impartiality from *autonomy*: that is, from the idea of acting solely from recognition of what one should do.

Acting thus means that one accepts no aim for one's action, and no constraint on it, unless one sees reason to pursue that aim or observe that constraint. Anyone who accepts an aim or a constraint which they see no reason to accept is not acting from reason-responsiveness alone; they are being driven heteronomously by non-rational factors, 'alien causes' in Kant's words. This is an important feature of Kant's account. It generates (as we have already in effect argued in 10.5) a sound objection to an instrumental, means-objective conception of rationality, according to which rationality consists in adopting efficient means to one's objectives. Against this conception we can ask: why should we pursue our objectives if there *is* no reason to pursue them? This may be your or my objective, but it remains an open question whether it should be. Strictly speaking, in fact, one should deny that an instrumental conception of rationality is a conception of *rationality*, the capacity to come to a purely reason-responsive conclusion about what one should do, at all. Rationality is the capacity for free and unconstrained rational deliberation. Such deliberation requires that we should be able to pursue reasons all the way down, never accepting a positive end or constraint simply as given: there must be no positive end, no constraint, that practical reason cannot put in question, by asking and answering whether there is reason to accept it.

This is a plausible interpretation of Kant's notion of autonomy, and of why he thought it so important. The possibility of autonomy entails the existence of categorical, not merely hypothetical, imperatives. It is the crucial thing an instrumental conception of rationality omits. The objection to instrumentalism is not that it cannot be universalized, for it can be: 'everyone should act in a way that most efficiently advances whatever objectives they seek to advance'. The objection is that this principle simply takes objectives for granted, without asking whether they should be adopted in the first place, and so cannot be the principle of an autonomous, fully free rational agent.

The instrumentalist conception of practical reason is agent-relative, and is ruled out by the 'open-question' requirements of autonomy. Obviously it does not follow that *all* agent-relative principles are ruled out by autonomy. In particular, rational egoists do not hold that you cannot deliberate about ends. They hold that there is reason for everyone to pursue their own good and they deliberate about what constitutes that good; thus (on our account) about what there is reason to desire. They can accept that autonomy requires recognition of 'Categorical Imperatives' in the very thin sense of practical norms; they

---

[6] Allison 1990: 204–10. See also Hill 1985.

think pursuit of one's own good is *the* practical norm. For all that mere analysis of the notion of autonomy can tell us, personal good may be the only rational end; it may be that for each person their own good is the only final and unconditional end. In which case a rational egoist acts autonomously.

13.3 Impartial good and the disinterested will

The Universal Law Formulation contains a famously suggestive idea that may help us. It is the idea of what you *can will*:

> Act only on that maxim through which you can at the same time will that it should become a universal law.[7]

Is this idea meant to rule out only those maxims that we cannot will to be universal laws because they cannot, as a matter of logic, be *formulated* as universal laws? Or is it saying something stronger than that: is it meant to cut out some universalizable maxims because although they can indeed be universalized without self-contradiction we cannot *will* them in their universalized form? Presumably the latter. But in that case how does one defend it? Let us first consider what Kant says.

Kant holds that the inference from autonomy to morality is analytic: 'if freedom of the will is presupposed, morality, together with its principle, follows by mere analysis of the concept of freedom'.[8] A natural explanation of why he holds this would be that he thinks it is morally permissible to act on any maxim that is not self-contradictory when universalized—in the strict sense of 'self-contradictory' in which a self-contradictory proposition must be false. The thought would be that any maxim is an application to oneself of some universal normative proposition about what should be done; if the underlying universal proposition is literally self-contradictory then it is false. Hence you cannot rationally will it to be a universal law: where willing it to be a universal law means something like accepting its truth or correctness, accepting it as a norm. If morality were simply the rejection of such maxims, it would follow analytically from autonomy.

This is quite obviously far too weak to yield morality, however, and Kant does not pursue it. The most one can say is that his interest in the notion of a maxim being 'self-contradictory' when universalized may well arise from the idea that morality follows analytically from freedom. In practice he works with a looser notion of contradiction, in which a maxim is 'self-contradictory' when it is impossible for everyone to act on it. To introduce this new sense is to abandon the project of showing that morality follows *analytically* from autonomy; it presents a stronger reading of the Universal Law Formulation, which brings in a new idea.

Furthermore it is open to familiar difficulties, at least so long as we see it as a way of getting to morality from autonomy alone. It is, for example, not *impossible* that everyone

---

[7] *Groundwork* IV: 421.
[8] Ibid IV: 447. Compare the *Critique of Practical Reason*, V: 31. (Full freedom of the will is autonomy.)

should act on the maxim 'Break your promise when it is to your advantage to do so'. True, in our actual world, and given human nature, it is very unlikely that disadvantageous promises could always be broken without people knowing, and hence if everyone tried to act on that maxim the institution of promises might well cease to be taken seriously. But this is clearly a matter of our social circumstances, not of logic, whereas the universal law of reason is meant to hold for all rational beings in all possible worlds. There certainly are logically possible worlds in which everyone follows the promise-breaking maxim; for example, they may not believe that everyone else is doing so too, or immediately forget, or do so only when no one else could know. And finally, it is quite obvious that the egoist's universalized maxim is not impossible for everyone to act on.

These points refute any attempt to derive morality 'analytically' from the very idea of autonomy. Of course they fall away as irrelevant if one thinks that the Categorical Imperative is simply a test of fairness, and that we have a pre-existing obligation to act fairly. Given that obligation, we can bring in the idea of what I can will in the way that it is often brought in, and which Kant often seems to intend: as a way of testing whether our maxim is fair. I can ask myself whether, given my necessary needs and limitations as a human being, I can will a society in which everyone cheats whenever they can get away with it, in which there is no mutual aid, and so on. If I would not want everyone to do that kind of thing, because of the bad consequences such behaviour would have for me, or for people in general, then I am taking unfair advantage of others if I do it myself. I am using them. This is a sound appeal to the obligation of fairness; but it makes no attempt to derive the obligation of fairness from autonomy. Nor does it show any other way in which pure practical reason itself can be said to bring fairness, or even impartiality, onto the scene.

So is there a way in which one might show a connection between autonomy and impartiality by considering the idea of what can be willed by an autonomous will, solely in virtue of its autonomy? This idea remains intriguing. So far we have considered two options:

(i) Derive the Categorical Imperative from the very idea of autonomy. That is, show it to be an analytic truth that if a being has the capacity of autonomy the Categorical Imperative applies to it, so that when that being acts autonomously it is acting in a way that acknowledges that Imperative. (*The 'analytic' interpretation.*)
(ii) Present it as a very general moral principle—perhaps not the only one, perhaps not one that all rational beings would accept, whatever their interests and needs—but one that human beings (or we modern people with our morality, etc.) on reflection accept. (*The 'moral intuitionist' interpretation.*)

(i) is what Kant says is his view. (ii) gives up on the idea of deriving impartiality from autonomy. Can we find materials for a view that is closer to Kant's ambitions than is (ii), without claiming that impartiality follows analytically from autonomy? That is, without claiming it to be an *analytic* truth that a person acting autonomously duly observes whatever requirements of impartiality arise? Our guideline is to find a line of thought between (i) and (ii), as it were—neither analytic nor intuitionist.

The challenge is to derive impartiality as a constraint which any being capable of autonomy wills ('gives itself as a law') so far as it is thinking and acting autonomously.

We can approach this challenge by asking whether there is anything, and if so what, that a being can will inasmuch as it wills autonomously but without knowledge of the *content* of reason-supported ends, its own or those of others, to work on. If there is something that would be willed in these circumstances, then it would still be willed by anyone who wills autonomously, even when knowledge of their particular reason-supported ends is fed back in. Call this *the 'disinterested' interpretation*.

The question can be illustrated by a thought experiment. You are contemplating a world of people that does not include you. All you know about them is that they are pursuing some objectives they know they should pursue, in ways they know they should follow. (So by the categoricity of morality, already established in the previous chapter, they are not seeking to do anything morally wrong.) You have some green buttons you can press, one per person, to assist them to achieve their ends. You have some red buttons you can press, one per person, to frustrate their pursuit. Pressing any of these buttons has no other effect. You know nothing else; in particular you know nothing about who these people are or any relation they might have to you, or about your own current inclinations. Is there anything you can autonomously will? That is, is there anything there is still *reason* for you to will?

I think there is a spontaneous disposition to press as many green buttons as you can, chosen at random if you can't press them all, and not to press any red buttons. Furthermore this disposition is in harmony with a corresponding normative disposition—to take that as what there is *reason* to do. This is the kind of normative harmony that will be discussed in 16.2 and 16.3, where we shall argue that it constitutes warrant for a normative claim—in this case the claim that there is reason to press the green buttons and not the red ones.

If this is so, then that is what an autonomous will can will *purely* as autonomous, before any further material is brought in that might give it further reasons for action. Putting it another way, the autonomous will accepts that achievement by anyone of their reason-supported goals has value not just for them, agent-relative value, but agent-neutral value, value 'in itself'. It is good in itself that people should achieve their reason-supported goals. There is agent-neutral reason to press the green buttons, chosen impartially.

On this account everyone's reason-supported ends have standing as agent-neutral ends to be considered impartially by the autonomous will.[9] Rational egoists deny that. In this thought experiment, they will say, there is no reason for you to press any buttons at all, green or red. They agree, to be sure, that your interests have no special importance just

---

[9] Kant says something similar at IV: 428, 'Now I say that the human being, and in general every rational being *exists* as an end in itself...'. However, he seems to conflate two things (i) having unconditional worth; (ii) having agent-neutral worth. It is true that autonomy requires that there be something that has unconditional worth; but a clear-headed rational egoist will say that his own good is for him an end in itself in the sense that it has unconditional worth for him—but is not an end in itself in the sense of being an *agent-neutral* end, which is what Kant clearly intends.

because they are yours. But that is because they deny that anything has importance in this sense—an importance that is not agent-relative. Your interests have rational importance for you; my interests have rational importance for me. There are no agent-neutral ends.

If, contrary to the rational egoist, we accept the account we have certainly not shown that reasons must be agent-neutral just by deriving that conclusion from the notion of a reason. Nor have we shown that *all* reasons must be agent-neutral. Once you bring knowledge about your inclinations and relations to other people back into the picture, you may well bring back agent-relative reasons. The claim is not that the autonomous will can *only* will agent-neutral ends. The claim is that when we focus on whether there is anything that an autonomous will can will purely in virtue of its property of autonomy, without reference to further facts about its own evaluative reasons—and how these generate practical reasons via Bridge—we find that there is indeed still something it can will, and that something is the achievement of any being's reason-supported ends as such. This is what it is still disposed to will when it abstracts from its own partial concerns.[10] The moment of impartiality that is (on this view) contained in the will exercises a constraint or counter-influence of some form on our pursuit of our other reason-supported ends.

Our thought experiment exhibits the epistemic basis of a principle of impartial good, as consisting in the dispositions of a disinterested autonomous will. Notice, however, that it does not show that the disinterested will, qua disinterested, has no *other* disposition. We shall see in the next chapter that a distinct principle underlying rights also has the same epistemic basis. But here we should take initial account of some questions about the epistemology of this appeal to the disinterested will; and of some similarities and differences between Kant's account of will, practical reason; and morality and ours.

13.4 Practical reason and the will

Doesn't the appeal to a disinterested will just get us back to a form of moral intuitionism? What is the difference between it and (ii) in the last section, the moral intuitionist interpretation? Two distinct points can be made.

First the word 'moral' does not fit. Moral intuitionism is a standpoint that works from within morality, holding certain *moral* propositions to be intuitively known. But moral concepts did not enter our thought experiment. For all that has been said, it may be that morality proper has sources not only in impartiality but also in the feelings, so that only when you bring these back in, and join them to purely rational constraints of impartiality, do you get morality proper.

---

[10] Note that the thought experiment is not an appeal to what a rational agent would choose behind a veil of ignorance. It directly elicits a conative disposition. We could call it the disposition of benevolence, understanding 'benevolence' literally as a disposition of the good *will*, and thus as distinct from sympathy, which is a disposition of the feelings. But it is probably too late to rescue 'benevolence' for this use.

Nonetheless, can't the account given in the previous section, of how autonomy and impartiality are connected, be described as a form of *normative*, if not moral, intuitionism? This leads us to a second point.

As discussed in 6.1, we should distinguish between self-evidence and intuition. A self-evident proposition is one whose truth can be known a priori without deriving it from some other propositions; we argued in Chapter 6 that such propositions are normative, or offshoots of normative propositions. In this sense of 'self-evident' a philosopher who holds that there is normative knowledge must accept that there is self-evident normative knowledge—knowledge grounded in normative insight alone.

Intuitionism in contrast says more than that: it understands intuition as a form of receptivity. Intuitionists hold that there is a world of normative facts that we know by normative intuition, in the way that we know the world of space and time by spatio-temporal perception. Thus intuition is not self-evidence; it is a purported *explanation* of self-evidence. Self-evidence is a formal notion that can be shared by all normative cognitivists; intuition is a substantive notion belonging to a realist metaphysics of the normative. Furthermore this realist explanation of normative knowledge implies a separation between practical–normative knowledge and dispositions of the will. First we have knowledge of normative facts, then we choose what to do.

For Kant there is no such separation. Indeed rejection of intuitionism is basic to any Critical philosophy. Kant's view is that the epistemic basis of judgements of pure practical reason is not any form of receptivity but pure spontaneity of the will. As I understand this view, it means that the epistemic basis of these practical–normative judgements is the *spontaneous dispositions of the will*. Practical reason is practical—i.e. gives rise to action via the causality of freedom—just because it has this basis. Theoretical reason, i.e. cognition of epistemic reasons, likewise originates in spontaneity, in this case spontaneous dispositions to believe; hence it too can give rise to beliefs, again through the causality of freedom.

There is no appeal, in either case, to any intuitionist notion of receptivity to explain these spontaneous dispositions. There is nothing beyond them, epistemically speaking. They are basic. I agree with Kant's epistemology of reason, so interpreted, and shall defend it in Chapter 16.

Now if this is Kant's account of the epistemology of reason, how should we interpret his claim that the inference from autonomy to the Categorical Imperative is analytic?

Kant denies the feelings any epistemic role in determining the content of moral obligation. He does hold that it is in virtue of our emotional nature that we experience the universal law of reason as a Categorical *Imperative*. This view to some extent parallels the sentimentalist account of moral obligation that we gave in the last chapter; we shall come back to it in 15.5. However, the *content* of morality, according to Kant, consists entirely and exclusively of whatever is required by 'pure practical reason'. These requirements apply as much to the Holy Will, which does not experience them as Categorical Imperatives, as to us, who do.

When Kant affirms that there are *pure* principles of practical reason he means two things, which he does not distinguish. One is that these principles are a priori truths, the other is that their epistemic basis is spontaneity of the *will alone*. They have nothing to do with the sentiments. Thus 'pure practical reason' consists in a priori truths about practical reasons whose epistemic basis in no way involves a disposition of the sentiments. Furthermore, all practical reasons have this epistemic basis: a spontaneous disposition of the will alone. When stated as complete reasons they are all in that strong sense pure.

The will is completely free, or autonomous, when it responds only to its own spontaneity, unaffected by any other, 'alien', causes—in particular the sentiments. That, for Kant, is true by definition. Thus such a will is by definition disinterested, in the sense that it is not affected by particularity—the particular interests or inclinations of the agent. Hence its dispositions (assuming that it has some) are disinterested dispositions. And these are the epistemic basis of the requirement of impartiality.

It is this Rousseauesque conception of the completely free will that seems to me to underlie Kant's claim that the Categorical Imperative follows by analysis alone from freedom.

Indeed, Kant has so little to say about this claim that it seems he took it as obvious. It is telling that his emphasis in both the *Groundwork* and in the *Critique of Practical Reason* is on something else: how we can be justified in thinking of ourselves as capable of autonomy, and thus as falling under the moral law. In the former he attempts to justify it by a famous 'transcendental deduction' from the fact that whenever we deliberate we have to think of ourselves as free. In the latter he appeals to the notorious 'fact of reason'.[11] These two approaches appeal to the two sides of the reciprocity thesis: that we are free if and only if we are under the moral law.

However, it is only because Kant is an incompatibilist about freedom that the question of how we can be justified in thinking of ourselves to be free moral agents becomes crucial. Kant thinks he can only 'solve' or at least bypass the 'empirical' incompatibility of freedom and determinism by appeal to transcendental idealism. This makes the crucial question unanswerable. The *Groundwork* effectively admits as much. As for the 'fact of reason'—the fact that we are immediately aware of being under moral obligation—that is indeed a fact: but it could not be if will were noumenal. So here Kant appeals to something that is true but incompatible with his framework. But the problem does not arise from his analysis of autonomy. It arises from his attempted solution to the supposed problem of freedom and determinism. It is perfectly tenable to accept that an autonomous response is a response from warrant, while denying that there is any problem about the very possibility (as against the frequent difficulty) of such a response, or about how we can know that our response is from warrant. Here to it may sometimes be very difficult to identify the real reasons from which one acted, but it is certainly not impossible.

So let us return to the claim that the transition from autonomy to impartiality is analytic. This remains a mistake: the problem, as so often, is that an illicit existence assumption has been made. All that is true analytically is that *if* an autonomous will has any disposition at all it is a disinterested disposition. That it does have such dispositions is not an analytic truth.

---

[11] See Chapter 1, footnote 11.

But it is, I claim, a truth; and it is also true that the epistemic basis of practical reason is the spontaneous dispositions of an autonomous will—the dispositions of a will unaffected by alien causes.

These conclusions are somewhat Kantian. But we diverge from Kant in another important way. Kant rightly, holds that brute inclinations, inclinations unsupported by reasons, are alien causes. However, contrary to Kant, feelings themselves can be supported by reasons, and reason-supported feelings are not alien. By the Bridge principle they generate practical reasons; and the autonomous will is a will that responds to practical reasons. As for the epistemic basis of the Bridge principle, that is a disposition to will whatever action the *feeling* one is disposed to prompts.

Sentimentalists about practical reason deny that there are any principles whose epistemic basis is the will alone. For them the epistemic basis of all practical norms is the affective dispositions. Via Bridge, a spontaneous disposition to feel gives rise to a spontaneous disposition to will. One could not grasp the practical reason without grasping the evaluative reason. Thus they deny that there is, in the stronger Kantian sense, such a thing as pure practical reason. Kant, in contrast, holds that *all* a priori principles of practical reason are pure in the stronger sense. Instead of taking one of these extreme positions, we should accept that both kinds of principle exist. Some practical norms have their basis in the sentiments—but there are impartial principles whose epistemic basis is the will alone.

Among the spontaneous dispositions of an autonomous will there are disinterested dispositions which structure or frame all other practical dispositions. That, we can now say, is the sense in which we should ask whether we *can will* our maxim to be a universal law: we are asking whether we can will it in the presence of those pure or disinterested dispositions, which are the spontaneous dispositions of autonomy itself.

13.5 Good and rights

In considering the argument from autonomy to impartiality we abstracted from the contrast between 'concern' and 'respect'. But now consider the following two principles:

> *The principle of impartial good*: the fact that achieving o promotes x's good is a reason for anyone to help x to achieve o.
>
> *The principle of impartial right*: the fact that x has the capacity for self-determination is a reason for anyone to respect (not interfere with) x's self-determinations—unless these themselves constitute interferences with the self-determinations of others.

Each principle is impartial in that it is universal and agent-neutral. Each is a substantive principle of practical reason; hence neither is derivable merely by analysis from the concept of autonomy. Each must be regarded as self-evident by proponents who consider it a fundamental principle of practical reason.

Impartial right requires some articulation in a theory of rights, which fleshes out the idea of respecting a person's self-determinations. Something like it exists in a variety of ethical standpoints, not least because the capacity of an agent for self-determination, and still more for autonomy, has to be a significant moral consideration in any serious ethical view.

One can try to capture the principle in a Millian way, for example, in the form of a liberty principle founded, as he famously argued, on utility 'in the largest sense'.[12] Or one can regard it as a first principle—basing it, as we have based impartial good, directly on the dispositions of the disinterested will. To base impartial right, rather than impartial good, on the disinterested will clearly gets closer to Kant. Not that it fully captures Kant's ethical stance, since it fails to account, for example, for his theory of duties to oneself, or of duties to promote the happiness of others; yet these duties are supposed to be somehow implicit in the Kantian ethical idea of 'respect for persons'. However, it is not our plan here to pursue Kantian normative ethics; our aim is to consider the contrast between the two principles, of good and right, as such.

The thought experiment of the previous section seems to me to support the principle of impartial good. Yet something similar might be said about rights: they too might be epistemically grounded in the dispositions of the disinterested will. We shall consider how this can be so in the next chapter. Our eventual conclusion will be that both a principle of impartial good and an principle of impartial right should be recognized as fundamental. In the rest of this chapter, however, we shall explore the scope and force of impartial good.

13.6 Telic reasons

For this it will be useful to introduce some terms.

An *end* is a state of affairs which there is (neutral or relative) reason to 'promote'—i.e. to produce, bring about, maintain, protect. If the fact that an action will promote a state of affairs is a complete reason to do it, that state of affairs is a *final end*. Where the final end is a state of affairs that can be said to hold more or less, to a greater or lesser amount, degree, extent, etc. then by definition of 'final end' there is more reason, *pro tanto*, to promote a greater amount than a lesser. Thus if happiness (be it yours, or everyone's) is a final end, there is specific reason to produce more rather than less. Finally, the fact that an action will promote a final end is a *telic* reason to do it.

Not all reasons are telic. Consider saying thank you, or clapping. There can be a complete specific reason to thank or clap, even if there is no reason to do so in order to promote some state of affairs. Suppose I clap simply to convey my admiration, and there is indeed reason to admire. Then that is a complete reason to clap but not a telic reason. I am not clapping in order to bring about the final end of my having expressed my admiration, any more than when I do something to keep a promise I am doing it to promote the final end of my having kept a promise. There *can* be telic reasons to clap: I might clap because your parents will reward me if they hear me clapping your performance, and

---

[12] Mill 1963–91, vol. XVIII: 224 (*Liberty* 1.11).

being rewarded by them contributes to one of my final ends. Or again I might clap in order to make someone happy, that being my final end.[13]

There are other significant examples of non-telic reasons. An action done purely out of respect for others' rights is done for a non-telic reason. Respect for others' rights is not, in the sense we have just introduced, based on an *end*; it is, as will be argued in the next chapter, based on a *demand*. True, I may do or avoid doing something in order not to violate a right; but I don't thereby do it in order to bring about the end state of *my not violating a right*.[14] An agent may have telic reasons not to violate rights: for example, I might be trying to show you that I'm capable of not violating some particular right, in order to promote some end I have. But respect for rights as such is not a telic reason.

Bridge-based reasons can be telic or non-telic. The Bridge-based reason to clap is non-telic; but a Bridge-based reason to seek the satisfaction of one's reason-supported desires is telic. Reason-supported desires generate final ends that there is agent-relative, end directed reason to pursue, so these are telic reasons.

By the buck-passing account of goodness, states of affairs that constitute final ends are goods. Not all good things are final ends, however. A picture, a burglar, a screw-driver, an argument may be good without being an end; i.e. without it being true that there is reason to do something in order to 'promote' them in any sense. We also say that a work of art is good 'in itself', in the sense that its goodness is aesthetic goodness not functional goodness, goodness for a purpose. Again it does not follow that it is an end in itself in the sense of constituting a final end. To hold that there is reason to promote aesthetic goodness as a final end is a substantive thesis.

So let's say that states of affairs that do constitute final ends are *telic* goods.[15] Thus the theory of final ends is the theory of telic reasons, or of telic goods. It is a theory of the telic goodness of states of affairs in general, whether or not they result from human actions; how good a state of affairs is, is a function of how much reason to produce or avoid it there would be if we could do so.

Since we have allowed that there may be non-telic reasons we cannot assume that a theory of telic goods is a complete theory of practical reasons. But clearly some account of telic goods is important for any such theory unless it actually denies that there are any

---

[13] Could we say that clapping (e.g.) is bringing about the state of oneself clapping, and that whenever one claps intentionally, one does it in order to bring about that state? It is false that α-ing is bringing about the state of oneself α-ing. Suppose I push a button which activates a mechanism that causes me to clap, in order to bring about the state of myself clapping. That action (pushing the button) is not redescribable as clapping. As the example indicates, bringing about a state is doing something that causes that state to obtain. But clapping is *not* doing something that causes the state of oneself clapping to obtain. Furthermore, even if one allowed the identity assumption (clapping = doing something that causes one to clap) it would still not follow that reason to clap is reason to bring it about that one is clapping, since 'there is reason to α' is an intensional context.

[14] We can say that my 'objective' is to avoid violating a right. Every action has an objective, in that neutral sense, even though not every action (*pace* Aristotle) is done 'for the sake of some end'. My objective in clapping is to convey my admiration; it is not done (usually) in order to bring about the state of my having conveyed my admiration.

[15] I am not calling these goods final goods, because that would raise the misleading suggestion that non-final goods are instrumental goods. A great work of art is neither a telic nor an instrumental good.

telic reasons. No serious ethics can take that view.[16] However, there are serious ethical views that deny the existence of non-telic reasons. Such views must argue that apparently non-telic reasons, such as rights-based reasons, turn out to be telic when stated in complete form. Utilitarianism, on standard accounts of it, is one such view. In the rest of this chapter we consider it more closely.

13.7 Utilitarianism

For brevity let's call the system of agent-neutral final ends, that is, of agent-neutral telic reasons and their strengths, *the Good*. In calling it a system I assume no more than that some states of affairs are *better* than others, i.e. that total incommensurability does not prevail, and that that is often enough true to make evaluating the relative overall Goodness of outcomes a frequently important element in practical deliberation, rather than always a pointless one. In other words, I assume that possible outcomes of actions fall often enough into an ordering by their Goodness to affect what one should do.

A *welfarist view of Good* states that the good of any individual is an agent-neutral final end. Welfarism further holds that a state is a final end *only* if it is good for someone that it be realized. Adding this to impartial good we get a welfarist conception of Good:

> The fact that achieving x's objective, o, promotes x's good is an agent-neutral telic reason for anyone to help x to achieve o, and there are no other agent-neutral telic reasons.

This should be understood imparitally (we argued that agent-neutral partiality is irrational in 3.6).

The welfarist doctrine of the Good is (I believe) the really plausible core of the utilitarian tradition.[17] To be sure, when we seek to fill it out, things get more controversial. There are various views of the substantive content of personal good, and various accounts of how the strength of welfarist reasons is determined. Impartiality does not dictate any one particular distributive structure. Welfarism only says that Good is some positive function of the good of all individuals and of nothing else. It accomodates a broad class of positions. For example, a welfarist version of Rawls's leximin idea[18] fits it just as well as the total-maximizing view of standard utilitarianism.

It is of course a substantive view which can be contested: one might hold, for example, that the preservation of great works of art or of natural beauty is a final end, irrespective

---

[16] Kant's 'ends in themselves' are not final ends in my sense. (It doesn't make sense to say that a person is a final end in our sense, since a person is not a state of affairs.) However, his ethics commits him to holding that there are final ends in our sense: one's own perfection, and reward of moral goodness and punishment of moral evil, are in that sense respectively agent-relative and agent-neutral final ends.

[17] Mill, for example, would have lost little that mattered to his ethics (as against his historical and political self-image) had he explicitly given up the hedonist and total-maximizing elements of his position. But he would have been a very different kind of moral philosopher if he had given up a welfarist idea of the Good—or the specifically utilitarian conception of the role of the Good in practical reason that we are about to consider.

[18] Rawls 1971: 83.

of the good of individuals. Or that excellence is. To me, however, such views seem implausible once the distinctions of the previous section have been made. Works of art, works of nature, human beings, can be admirable by virtue of their beauty or excellence. They are then admirable in themselves, irrespective of any contribution they make to other valuable things. If a thing is admirable there is reason to admire it. That generates reasons to act appropriately via the Bridge principle. It does not follow that it generates any final ends. Beauty, as against the experience of beauty, is not a final end. Excellence is admirable, but we have argued in 11.9 that unless it becomes desirable there is no telic reason to pursue it.

Thus a welfarist conception of the Good seems to me to be correct, and firmly founded in the disinterested disposition of goodwill. But our aim in this chapter does not require us to accept or reject it.[19] The aim is to consider in *general* terms the role of the Good within the domain of practical reasons, and its relation to moral obligation. For this purpose we shall not need to retain a welfarist point of reference. We can abstract from questions about the nature of the Good. All that is essential is that there is such a thing—i.e. that there *is* a system of agent-neutral final ends.

So it will be convenient to use the term *utilitarianism* in a similarly abstract way. Utilitarians agree that:

(i) There is a system of agent-neutral final ends (the Good).

They then add some of the following theses:

(ii) There are no complete agent-relative telic reasons.
(iii) There are no complete non-telic reasons.
(iv) Agent-neutral telic reasons are dominant.

We can call a position that endorses (i)–(iii) *pure* utilitarianism.

Now we state the principle of Good:

> (1) (*Principle of Good*) the fact that α promotes Good is a complete specific reason to α, proportionate in strength to the degree to which α promotes Good.

I take this principle to be, along with the Bridge principle, one of the basic normative sources of practical reasons. (This assumes, of course, that Good has some definite substantive content, but we are not concerned with that here.)

Pure utilitarianism says more than (1). It adds:

> (2) No other fact is a complete reason to α.

Thus it holds that the principle of Good (in some concrete version of it or another) is the *one and only* normative source of practical reasons. It entails:

---

[19] The discussion of this chapter is also neutral between experience-based and person-based welfarism, where the latter holds that the only good is the good of actual present and future people. (I discussed the content and distributive structure of Good in Skorupski 1999, Part II.)

(3) The sole fact that gives sufficient reason to α is that α-ing promotes most Good.

So the best action—the most choice-worthy, the action one should* do—is the one that promotes most Good, taking into account objective propensities if these exist, in whatever is the right way to do so (and allowing that there may be more than one best action).

This very strong view says that all practical reasons are Good-based, that is, that when spelled out they are instances of the principle of Good. We have in fact already disagreed with it, by accepting that some practical reasons are Bridge-based. So we should consider some weakening of this very strong view. Must Good *monopolize* practical reason, or may it simply dominate it? There is a possible view which does not deny that there are reasons other than Good-based reasons but says only that reasons of Good are dominant—that is, that they beat others. Call it 'dominance utilitarianism':

(4) (*Dominance utilitarianism*) if there is more Good-based reason to α than β, then the presence of other reasons cannot give one more overall reason or even equally strong overall reason to β.

Dominance utilitarianism endorses (i) and (iv), but does not deny the existence of practical reasons other than agent-neutral telic ones. (Pure utilitarianism also endorses (iv), but one can endorse (iv) without endorsing (ii) and (iii), i.e. without endorsing pure utilitarianism.)

Dominance utilitarianism shares the essential utilitarian spirit, namely, the very powerful teleological thought that *nothing can ultimately beat the practical–normative force of Good*. It is weaker than pure utilitarianism; yet it still remains, of course, a very strong doctrine. It means that reasons not based on Good, however strong, cannot outweigh Good-based reasons, however weak. So we should also consider weaker views which endorse a *Weak Dominance principle of Good*:

(5) However strong the reasons that are not Good-based against doing some action α may be, there can always be a Good-based reason strong enough to outweigh them.

Obviously the force of this principle is moot—it depends how strong Good-based reasons have to be to dominate. To know how strong the principle is we have to have some idea of the trade-offs between Good-based and other reasons. The stronger Good-based reasons have to be to dominate others, the weaker the principle. A wide range of views would agree with sufficiently weak versions of it, though there are some that would not. (For example, an absolute ban on killing the innocent; though proponents of such absolutist views have a tendency to shrink from considering extreme or 'outlandish' cases at all, which is in itself interesting.)

Of the classical utilitarians, Sidgwick is the only one who is clearly not a pure utilitarian: he rejects at least (2). It is debatable whether he rejects (3); we shall consider this further in 14.1. Mill, on the other hand, is a pure utilitarian: he says that the principle of utility is 'the ultimate principle of teleology', that is, of:

the Doctrine of Ends; which, borrowing the language of German metaphysicians, may also be termed, not improperly, the principles of Practical Reason.

This is a clear and clearly intended statement of pure utilitarianism: the utility principle is *the* principle of practical reason as such, regulating all its sub-departments (which Mill here describes as 'Morality, Prudence or Policy, and Aesthetics; the Right, the Expedient, and the Beautiful or Noble, in human conduct and works'[20]).

Pure utilitarianism, as we have characterized it, is a substantive theory of practical reasons. But we should remember, of course, that utilitarianism is usually presented as a theory of *morality*. So how does one derive moral obligations within a pure utilitarian theory of practical reasons?

13.8 Utilitarianism and moral obligation

Moral obligation is not identifiable with ought* in the designated sense. So we cannot derive a moral theory, a theory of moral obligation, from a theory of practical reasons, without some linking principles that contain the concept of moral obligation as well as the concept of a practical reason.

On the account of moral obligation that we have given such linking principles could not be true by definition. Moral concepts, we argued, should be understood in terms of blameworthiness—where this in turn is understood in terms of sufficient reason for the sentiment of blame. Blameworthiness consists not in sufficient practical reason for the action of blame but in sufficient evaluative reason for the blame sentiment. From this account we were able to derive the principle of moral categoricity: if you have a moral obligation to α then you have sufficient reason to α. Using that principle, a theory of practical reasons might tell us that an action is *not* morally obligatory; what it cannot tell us is when an action *is* morally obligatory. It can never be true *by definition* that if a person fails to act in accordance with some practical reasons there is evaluative reason to blame him.

So utilitarianism considered purely as a theory of practical reasons can determine what there is most reason to do, but not whether it's morally obligatory to do something. It may, it is true, give us a theory of when there is sufficient reason to try to *make* oneself or other people feel the blame sentiment, but that is not a theory of reasons for blame, given that blame refers to the sentiment, not the action.

It is not clear, as noted in 12.1, whether Mill was fully alive to this distinction. But suppose that we interpret Mill's blameworthiness account of moral wrongness not in the sentimentalist way, but in terms of the practical appropriateness of sanctions. Then by definition an action is morally wrong just if (subject to conditions) there is sufficient reason to *do* something—express blame, punish, etc. Mill can now deploy his pure utilitarianism to determine whether there is a sufficient reason.

On this practical as against evaluative conception of blameworthiness moral obligation is derivable (with empirical premises) from utilitarianism alone. However, it is not categorical. On this conception, it does not follow from the fact that an action is morally obligatory

---

[20] Mill 1963–91, vol. VIII: 232 (*System of Logic*).

for a person that there is sufficient reason, or any reason, for that person to do it. That is because it does not follow from the fact that it is Best to blame anyone who does this action that it is Best for this person to do it. It may both be Best for him to do it, and Best to blame him for doing it. (By the 'Best' action I mean the one most productive of Good. It is a substantive question whether the Best action is best in the sense of most choice-worthy, the one there is most reason to do; utilitarianism takes it that it always is.)

In contrast, on the sentimentalist conception of blameworthiness moral obligation is categorical but not derivable from utilitarianism alone. A substantive linking premise must be added. That linking premise cannot be analytic; it therefore seems that it must be a substantive moral claim. What might this be?

Moral agency, as noted in 12.4, is self-determining agency. Moral agents must be able to tell by reflection what concrete moral obligations they have. Thus moral obligation connects to warranted reasons, not reasons *per se*: to be relevant to moral conclusions Good-based reasons must feature as contents of warranted beliefs.

A principle that meets this requirement and links utilitarianism to moral obligation is 'warranted act utilitarianism':

> WAU: it is morally obligatory to do one of the actions one has warrant to think Best.

This cannot be a definition. It must be regarded as itself a moral doctrine, to be assessed by moral insight. But—with some idealization—it is consistent with moral self-determination. What about taking it as a moral principle in its own right?

There are some old and good objections to this. On many occasions you have no warrant to think that *any* action is Best, but you can still know what you have a moral obligation to do. Another decisive objection is that WAU is inconsistent with supererogation, and supererogation is a basic feature of moral common sense. Does anyone think that people are blameworthy whenever they fail to do the warranted Best thing? If common sense is right, WAU is false.

The immediately relevant question, however, is whether WAU would follow from pure utilitarianism with true empirical premises, plus a definition of moral wrongness in terms of practical blameworthiness. It is pretty obviously counterproductive to blame people (in the practical sense of blame) for failing to do the warrantedly Best thing. So a utilitarian with a practical as against an evaluative conception of blameworthiness would have sufficient reason not to do so. Thus WAU seems false, whether one takes it from the standpoint of common sense or from the standpoint of a utilitarian theory of practical blameworthiness.

13.9 Rule utilitarianism

Rule utilitarianism offers the prospect of a much better fit with common sense morality. Assume for the sake of argument that there is some one system of rules of conduct whose acceptance by everyone would be Best.[21] This is the ideal code of conduct. Now the rule utilitarian proposition is that the morally obligatory is that which is required by the ideal code.

What is the status of this proposition? Once again it cannot be true by definition if our account of moral wrongness in terms of evaluative reasons for blame is correct. One could still claim that it is the basic principle of morality, i.e. that it is a substantive moral proposition. Yet that is very implausible. Does morality have a master principle *within* it that says that we have a moral obligation to do whatever is required by the ideal code? It doesn't seem to contain any references to ideal codes. The rule-utilitarian proposition sounds like a philosophical gloss on moral convictions, rather than a moral conviction.

However, we could also combine rule utilitarianism with the practical as against the evaluative definition of moral wrongness. On this combined account rule utilitarianism says that an action is morally obligatory if and only if it is required by a code non-compliance with which there is sufficient practical reason to sanction by means of practical blame. Suppose the rule utilitarian offered that as the definition of 'morally obligatory' (on our account of morality and blame it would be an incorrect one, of course). The criterion of what the code of rules should be would then be whether a general practice of blaming non-compliance with those rules is Best.

This account assumes that there is such an action as 'sanctioning a set of rules by means of a practice of blame'. It is consistent with the self-determining character of moral agency only if the rules in question are somehow known as moral (i.e. sanctionable) rules by moral agents. And it is inconsistent with moral autonomy, as against moral self-determination, because the former assumes the Insight principle (11.4), according to which autonomous moral agents know their concrete moral obligations by means of their own insight into them. But no one can know, by conscientious reflection alone, what concrete-obligation-delivering rules are contained in the ideal code.

Well, perhaps we should give up on moral autonomy. But that highlights an important point. Rule utilitarianism may seem to align with common sense, but it remains an inherently revolutionary and centralizing doctrine. Underlying the rule-utilitarian model of morality is the implicit assumption that there can be an effective rule giver, empirically knowledgeable enough to determine the Best rules and communicate them to moral agents. If there is no such knowledgeable rule giver, rule utilitarianism makes moral obligation unknowable. So if this rule giver isn't God, who is it? Should it be a committee of sufficiently well-informed legislators? If so, how would we know they've got the rules right? And even if we knew they had, what would be the reason to comply with those rules—from the standpoint of the principle of Good?

But before addressing this second question, we should consider a third tack rule-utilitarians may take. They may say that their thesis is intended neither as a moral proposition nor as a definition, but as part of an 'explanation' of morality.

---

[21] Obviously there are questions about whether the criterion should be 'acceptance by everyone', and about whether, on the most suitable criterion, we can assume that there will only be one such system. I ignore them here. See Hooker 2000. (I have been greatly helped in this section by discussions with Brad Hooker.)

What sort of explanation is intended? Perhaps we can appeal to theoretical reduction in science as a model. We know the observable properties of some natural kinds; these properties are then redescribed at an underlying level of theory and derived from that reducing theory's laws. We initially know these properties by their characterization in observational terms; we then accept the reducing theory on the basis of an inference to the best explanation. So while the reducing theory has priority in the explanatory order, priority in the epistemic order goes to the observable data, although some correction of apparently observed data by the theory may be allowed if the theory has enough explanatory power.

Does this kind of theoretical explanation in science provide a model for 'explaining' morality in terms of the principle of Good?

The analogy would run as follows. Just as we have observational knowledge of some empirical truths, so we know by direct moral insight, though perhaps in rough form, the truths of morality, for example, that you have a duty to pay your debts, or that it is wrong to hurt others when there's no reason to do so other than your own enjoyment. From these known moral truths we then infer to the best explanation of their truth, allowing again, perhaps, for some correction to our *prima facie* moral knowledge in the light of the reducing theory, if that theory has enough explanatory power. The explanatory theory will involve a redescription of moral properties in terms of utilitarian vocabulary. Moral wrongness, for example, turns out to be identical with inconsistency with the ideal utilitarian code. Moral obligatoriness is the property of being required by the ideal utilitarian moral code. So the moral truths are 'explained' by deducing them from welfarism, empirical facts, and the theoretical identities that identify moral properties in the vocabulary of the reducing welfarist theory.

What about the epistemology of this model? By analogy, again, with theoretical explanation in science, it will hold that while we do have broadly correct *direct* knowledge of moral truths, our knowledge of the utilitarian theory by which the moral truths are 'explained' is only inferential. The good news—at first sight—is that this picture is compatible with self-determination, and indeed autonomy. Since it allows that we have direct knowledge of the moral truths it can accept that anyone who has a moral obligation in a given situation can tell for themselves that they have. The bad news is that it does not explain how knowledge of such moral truths is possible in the first place.

By hypothesis, we do not know the moral truths by deducing them from the underlying utilitarian theory. We can know our moral obligations even though we don't know they satisfy their utilitarian descriptions, so there is a disconnection between our knowledge of these moral truths and what, according to this utilitarian account, makes them true. How then do we know them?

We have a story about how we know that something is water, and the story incidentally tells us how we can know (in most cases) that it *is* water without knowing that it is H_2O. One property of H_2O is that it can give rise to the watery appearance by which we identify something as water. What analogous story could there be about our moral knowledge? Semantically, the reference of 'water' is fixed as *that stuff, whatever it is, that appears to us in a watery way*. I can know what water looks like without knowing what water is. Science then discovers that that stuff is H_2O. Does the analogous semantics hold for 'moral wrongness'? Is its reference fixed as that property, whatever it is, that causes feelings of blame in us? Can I know what moral wrongness feels like ('blamey') without knowing what moral wrongness is? That can't be right, because it loses the normativity of moral wrongness. The morally wrong is not that which *causes* blame feelings, but that which is blame*worthy*.

To say that an action is morally wrong is to say that there is sufficient reason to blame anyone who does it from warranted beliefs and without extenuation (12.1). That is, the action has some property which constitutes that sufficient reason. Can this property be the property of being inconsistent with the ideal welfarist code? *Being inconsistent with the code* is, on this account, the property of an action that constitutes sufficient reason to blame anyone who does it from relevant warranted beliefs and without extentuation. It is the essence of moral wrongness, as being H_2O is the essence of water.

There is a disanalogy, however. Whereas the scientific theory of the nature of water includes an account of how we know stuff to *be* water even when we don't know what *makes* it water, this theory of moral wrongness offers no account of how we know something to be wrong without knowing what makes it wrong. It has to assume that we know some moral truths, but then leaves a mystery as to *how* we know them. Furthermore, we do seem to know, by moral insight alone, just what properties of an action make it blameworthy. They vary from case to case; but if, for example, I'm asked to explain why it is blameworthy to torture people, I'll probably say that it's an assault, causes them intense agony, that it's unacceptable to do that just to extract information, and so on. *That* explains why it's blameworthy. That is what makes it morally wrong.

No gap is apparent for further explanation to fill. Yet this account asks us to accept, on the basis of an inference to the best explanation, that there is after all a deeper wrongness-maker—one that we do not know by moral insight alone. We know it only by empirical and philosophical inference from the content of morality. If that is so, then we must conclude either that pre-theoretical moral thought does not *really* know that torture is wrong or that it knows it to be wrong without knowing what *really* makes it wrong.[22]

These conclusions are incompatible with moral autonomy. In the case of physics, much about the nature of things is hidden from the scientific inquirer's perceptions and can be discovered only by theoretical inference. Perception can tell us that something is water without being able to tell us what *makes* it water. The physical theory itself explains why that is so. In contrast, rule utilitarianism does not explain how essential aspects of the moral can be hidden from the agent's moral insight and discovered only by theoretical inference. Nor could it, if we accept moral autonomy. For by this principle no moral

---

[22] Evolutionary explanations are irrelevant. Let's suppose that human beings have come to have a genetically inherited tendency to blame certain actions because blaming them is conducive to general welfare, and because doing things that are conducive to general welfare increases survivability. This may explain why we innately blame certain actions. But it does not, as far as I can see, explain why they are blame*worthy* or how we *know* them to be blameworthy.

truth is inaccessible to moral insight: moral insight penetrates to the very essence of moral wrongness. In morality, nothing is hidden.

None of this shows that the rule-utilitarian proposition is false. It cannot be a definition, a moral truth, or a theoretical identity, but it might still be an empirical truth. The code that is ideal from the standpoint of Good *might* be materially equivalent to the most plausible immanent formulation of ordinary morality. Whether that is so is, to say the least, a highly elusive empirical question. And even if it were true it would not give the ideal code any normative standing in its own right. That is, it would not follow from the fact that the ideal code requires an action that there was reason to do it. The reason to do the action would still have to derive from the reasons recognized by ordinary morality.

An important attraction of rule utilitarianism is that it claims to offer an 'indirect' *justification* of, more or less, ordinary moral principles of conduct, based on a utilitarian theory of reasons. A justification in the sense, I mean, would consist in showing that there is sufficient reason for people to obey those principles. If the theory of reasons in question is pure utilitarianism, the justification would consist in showing why from the standpoint of pure utilitarianism there is sufficient reason to do, by and large, what ordinary morality requires, including its agent-relative and non-telic moral requirements.

But none of the strategies we have considered does that. True, if a pure utilitarian could flick a button or waive a wand, which would make people obey the rules that constitute the ideal code it would be Best for him to do so. It does *not* follow, however, that there is Good-based reason for anyone to follow the rules. Should we perhaps postulate a further fundamental practical–normative principle, over and above the principle of Good: the fact that α is prescribed by the ideal code is a reason to α? But where does this come from? As a fundamental principle of practical reason it has no plausibility.

A rule-utilitarian view that is based on pure (or dominance) utilitarianism leaves it an open question whether there is reason for an individual to comply with the rules on any particular occasion. That depends on whether it is Best on that particular occasion to do so. Rule utilitarians could, indeed, abandon the project of *justifying* compliance to people and devote themselves instead to making, or letting, people believe that they have reason to follow the rules even when that is false—or simply to imposing sufficient sanctions to cause them to follow them (if we make the big assumption that that would not be counterproductive). By the time they have reached this point they have given up moral autonomy, the Insight principle and the categoricity of morality. And they have accepted a very strong esotericism in their moral philosophy. This last point will be pursued in the next chapter (14.5, 14.6, and 14.7).

13.10 Other indirect options

Are there other options for a utilitarian—options that maintain (at least broadly) the principle that one is warranted in doing the morally obligatory thing?

A relevant empirical claim would be that common sense is not a bad utilitarian guide, in that simply following common sense moral obligations is usually more productive of

Good than deliberating as to what is Best. Furthermore in most cases the agent does not know, and within the constraints of the situation cannot feasibly tell, whether common sense principles beat deliberation or not. This calls for a strategy, in the sense of 5.9. So by pure utilitarianism an agent may usually be *justified*, even if not warranted, in following common sense. Furthermore, given that he has resolved to do so, second-best counsel as regards his subsequent acts takes into account his resolve, in the manner explained in 4.8. Thus while in cases where he can clearly see that a departure from common sense is warranted he has warrant to depart from it, in other cases he has warrant, relative to the fact of his strategic resolve, to do what common sense morality requires.

This seems the most attractive position for a pure utilitarian, assuming its empirical premise to be correct. And obviously there are also good utilitarian grounds for social and political action designed to move common sense principles, so far as necessary and possible, in the direction of making the premise correct.

But what should this strategic utilitarian say about moral obligation? There are two options. The first is to reject morality altogether. The second is to reject the idea that moral obligation can be *derived* from the good and to accept that common sense moral principles have standing in their own right. That requires rejection of pure utilitarianism in favour of the dominance version.

On the first option, a pure utilitarian would give up the project of deriving moral truths altogether and simply deny that there are any. There are, that is, no truths about moral obligation and moral wrongness, although there are truths about what one should* do. Utilitarianism can lead one to this view, as we noted in the introductory remarks to Chapter 12.[23] In contrast I believe that there are moral truths, and am more convinced of some of these moral truths than of the truth of pure utilitarianism. More to the point, however, our guideline in this book is to understand how the normative concepts we actually have function. This is not meant to *rule out* in advance the possibility that some normative concepts, even those that are as deeply ingrained in human life as the moral concepts, are confused or just redundant; but we start from the provisional assumption that that is not so. We shall come back to the role and vindication of morality in Chapter 15. But what about the second option?

This gives up pure utilitarianism in favour of the Dominance view. Suppose we combine the Dominance view with acceptance that common sense moral obligations have some normative standing in their own right, a standing that derives in part from normative sources other than the principle of Good (for example, from the Bridge principle). On this view, we have:

> When warranted Good-based reasons to α outweigh, overall, warranted reasons not to α (including warranted reasons that are not Good-based) it is not morally wrong to α.

This follows from moral categoricity: if there is warrant to believe that there is insufficient reason to α, then it is not morally obligatory to α.

---

[23] See e.g. Norcross 2006. Something like this view is also defended in Crisp 2006.

Such a position has some significant attractions. Given Bridge, we can already see that pure utilitarianism is false; but Bridge is compatible with the Dominance view. Furthermore, we can maintain the principle of moral insight that is so important to ordinary morality. What this view proposes is 'insightful' normative adherence to common sense morality (as against merely strategic adherence), but with a standing readiness for defeat by strong enough Good-based reasons.

Consider a familiar example. You are in a trench with your fellow soldiers, taking part in a just war against an evil enemy. The enemy lobs in a grenade. Common sense morality, we can suppose, says that you have an obligation not run away; hence it is committed by categoricity to holding that there is not most reason to run away. On the Dominance view falling on the grenade is warrantedly Best, since you are warranted in thinking that that action will save more people than any other. (You know that your comrades won't fall on it but won't run away either.) Furthermore the Dominance view agrees that there is not most reason, and thus (as we are using 'sufficient') insufficient reason to run away.

Common sense morality does not say that you have a moral obligation to fall on the grenade—it regards that as supererogatory. The only thing it insists on is that you have an obligation not to run away—you are permitted to take avoiding action.[24] But it is willing to concede, it seems, that there is more reason overall to fall on the grenade than just to take avoiding action, even though either is morally permissible. This is debatable, obviously—yet if falling on the grenade isn't what there's more overall reason to do, what is so admirable about doing it? If it isn't what there's most reason to do then the people who took avoiding action did something there was just as much—or more?—overall reason to do. Arguably, then, in the Grenade example, Dominance and Morality say the same thing.

However, many people would say that there are occasions on which you have a moral obligation *not* to do that which is warrantedly Best, and that on these occasions doing what is warrantedly Best—what you are warranted in thinking will produce the Best outcome—is *not* what you have most reason to do. That is inconsistent with Dominance utilitarianism. Is it a firm deliverance of common sense morality? If so, common sense morality is incompatible with utilitarianism of either kind, dominance as well as pure. We shall come back to this in the next chapter, after we have considered the Demand principle.

---

[24] We can say that you are morally obliged either to take avoiding action without running away or to fall on the grenade. Certainly you discharge your moral obligation either way. It does not follow that you have sufficient (and thus equal) reason to do either of those actions. Moral categoricity must be understood as saying that if you are morally obliged to do one of a number of things there is at least one of them you have sufficient reason to do.

14

IMPARTIALITY: (II) THE DEMAND PRINCIPLE

The epistemic ground of a practical norm is people's spontaneous practical dispositions. Dispositions to action can arise from affective dispositions, which prompt to actions by giving rise to feelings. Corresponding at the normative level to this psychological sequence we have the Bridge principle. If there are other practical norms, norms that escape a sentimentalist account, their epistemic basis can only be the spontaneous dispositions of a will insofar as it is not influenced by sentiment.

I argued in Chapter 10 that normative beliefs can be operative motives for action just as much as desires. Acceptance of such norms can give rise to action through the will, without the causal influence of sentiment. Sentimentalists may agree with that and still rightly argue that most agent-relative norms can be explained in their terms. Indeed we showed how to argue precisely that in Chapter 11. Thus sentimentalism about practical reasons need not rest on the view that every action is driven by sentiment. As we have characterized it, it simply claims that the Bridge principle is the only normative source of practical reasons.

We have shown how agent-relative interests derive their normative authority: they derive from evaluative reasons that work their way through the Bridge principle. That being so, we can also postulate that they have no *other* normative source. Hence a will uninfluenced by Bridge-based reasons would be a disinterested will. It would abstract from agent-relative interests.

But can there be such a will? This issue is a real turning point for ethics. Many philosophers deny such a possibility, some vehemently. But we claimed in the previous chapter that the disinterested will exists. And we argued that it provides epistemic ground for the principle of Good. We defended this principle, distinguishing it from the varieties of utilitarianism.

The main aim of this chapter is to introduce a third and final principle of practical reason: the Demand principle. It too is an impartial principle, epistemically based on the disinterested will. It is the normative source of the theory of rights. The Demand principle says that if it is morally permissible for a person to demand that others act in a certain way that very fact is a reason for them to do so, unless they have the person's permission not to.

If this principle is accepted we have three practical norms in play, and so the question naturally arises of how they interact. We should not *assume* that there must be some further principle that determines how they do. That would be a 'rationalistic conception of rationality', to quote Bernard Williams.[1] And in fact I believe that no such principle can be found. No higher combinatory principle regulates how the three normative sources, on any particular occasion, consolidate into a conclusion about what there is sufficient reason to do. *A fortiori*, there is no higher principle by which they combine to generate moral obligation. Familiar default moral norms can be stated—the principles of moral common sense—but in the end this combinatory task remains the task of *moral judgement*, the topic of the next chapter.

It is, no doubt, impossible to refute in general terms the possibility that there is some unifying higher principle. All one can do is, on the one hand, exhibit the implausibility of particular attempts to produce it and, on the other, consider how moral judgement actually operates on the three underlying practical norms. Given our interest in unravelling the domain of reasons, the latter question must interest us: the question of how moral judgement plays on the norms of practical reason. We shall start to consider it in this chapter, by considering a putative counter-example to dominance utilitarianism. At this stage in our discussion, dominance utilitarianism still remains in play; for while acceptance of the Bridge and Demand principles is inconsistent with pure utilitarianism, it is not inconsistent with dominance utilitarianism. Nor will our putative counter-example *refute* it. It will, however, lead us to an analysis of conscience, common sense, and moral esotericism, which Chapter 15 will then broaden by considering the nature, force, and role of moral judgement. It will become evident, I think, that 'refutation' is not the right way of describing what moral judgement can do.

Insofar as our account of the practical domain has, to this point, evolved around the Bridge principle, the principle of Good and common sense morality, it has affinities that are worth considering to Sidgwick's famous discussion of his three methods of ethics. Sidgwick's discussion, despite its comprehensiveness, is limited by failure to recognize the third practical norm, the subject of this chapter: the Demand principle. But it is a much more comprehensive discussion of ethics than most, and raises issues which can serve us as a starting point.

14.1 Sidgwick's three methods of ethics

Sidgwick's methods of ethics respectively study the implications of egoism, utilitarianism, and 'dogmatic intuitionism', i.e. intuitive common sense morality. Why 'methods'? A natural interpretation is that Sidgwick sees each one of these methods as an attempt to identify distinctive practical norms on which it builds an ethical theory. The question would then be how, in Sidgwick's view, these normative sources combine. However, this

---

[1] The conception that 'two considerations cannot be rationally weighed against each other unless there is a common consideration in terms of which they can be compared' (Williams, B. 1985: 17–18.)

is not how Sidgwick's discussion goes. There turn out to be two striking puzzles. The first concerns how Sidgwick sees the relationship between egoism and utilitarianism. The second concerns whether he sees morality as a fundamental normative source at all.

Utilitarianism's principle is the principle of Good. *Utilitarianism* says that this is the only principle of practical reasons. Sidgwick understands Good in a hedonist and aggregative way, but if we abstract from that then the 'method' of utilitarianism amounts to what I have called pure utilitarianism. As for egoism, its principle says that the fact that an action promotes a person's good is a reason for that person to do it, corresponding in strength to the degree to which it promotes that person's good. And again, *egoism* as such says that this is the only practical principle.

Sidgwick thinks the egoist *principle* and the utilitarian *principle* are both self-evident, and he seems committed to holding that they are both correct. If only this is said, there is no inconsistency; there is just the question of how they combine in generating practical conclusions about what a person should do. What is puzzling is that Sidgwick thinks not only that each principle is correct but that egoism and utilitarianism themselves are individually self-evident. This leads him to his famous dualism of practical reason: unless the egoist principle and the utilitarian principle taken individually always prescribe one and the same action there is a contradiction. But this famous conclusion completely understates the difficulty. The two positions just are contradictory, even if they never prescribe incompatible actions.[2]

So far as this first puzzle is concerned, we could simply drop the idea that egoism and utilitarianism are both self-evident, retaining only the claim that their *principles* are. That is what a number of philosophers influenced by Sidgwick have done.[3] That view is structurally similar to the position we have reached so far—allowing for the difference between the egoist principle and the Bridge principle. As we saw in 11.8, the egoist *principle*, as against egoism, follows from Bridge when combined with a definition of personal good in terms of reason-supported desire. So every formally egoistic reason is a Bridge-based reason. The converse does not by any means hold, even on the wide construal of a person's good that I have argued for. Nevertheless our position so far is structurally similar to that of these philosophers, in that we have two distinct sources of practical reasons, which have to be reconciled on particular occasions of decision—not just about what one has warrant to do but about what if anything one has a moral obligation to do.

The second puzzle in Sidgwick's treatment is that he proclaims three methods but seems to think there are just two normative sources: utilitarianism; and egoism. Hence the 'dualism of practical reason'. Morality, it seems, has no normative sources of its own. If it did have, there would be not just a dualism of practical reason but a three-way tension.

There are two aspects to this. In the first place it is not quite clear from Sidgwick's discussion whether he thinks that 'dogmatic intuitionism' identifies independently

---

[2] As I have stated the positions the point is obvious. Thus this way of stating it may be thought unfair to Sidgwick. But I have argued elsewhere that no tenable reading of Sidgwick's view rescues 'the dualism of practical reason' from outright contradiction. See Skorupski 2001, 2008.

[3] For example, Crisp (2006) and Parfit (2007).

self-evident principles, as egoism and utilitarianism do. In the second place it is not clear whether he thinks that moral principles independently generate reasons for action.

A 'method of ethics' sounds like a method of deciding what should be done. So one might expect dogmatic intuitionism to identify moral principles that tell us what we have a moral obligation to do, and therefore a warrant to do. But that does not mean that it generates practical reasons in its own right. That cannot be so, if the only two practical-normative sources are the egoist principle (or come to that the Bridge principle) and the principle of Good. Suppose that 'dogmatic intuitionism' *does* identify some self-evident moral principles, and that these determine on some particular occasions what there is a moral obligation to do. The question then arises what reason there is to do it. And the answer (for Sidgwick) can only be supplied by the egoist's and the utilitarian's principles. Hence, given the a priori connection between moral obligations and practical reasons, no principle of moral obligation can be in its own right a priori, for if it was there would be a source of practical reasons other than egoism and utilitarianism. The task of moral judgement can only be to determine how independently given principles of practical reason combine in particular cases to provide reasons for action that it is blameworthy to ignore.

Our account of moral obligation agrees with Sidgwick on this point: the fact that an action is morally obligatory never itself constitutes a complete reason to do it. Rather, if an action is morally obligatory then there will be some sufficient reason to do it on which its moral obligatoriness supervenes. In the good-Samaritan case of Chapter 12, for example, there is sufficient reason to blame the person who fails to help because he *had* sufficient reason to help. It is not the blameworthiness that generates the reason to help. The failure to help was blameworthy, because there was reason to help of a certain kind and urgency that it was blameworthy to ignore. Blame *singles out* the reason as morally significant; it does not create it. It serves to highlight, emphasize, certain practical reasons; it does not generate practical reasons (other than reason to do that to which it disposes—withdrawal of recognition, via Bridge).

One can say that a practical reason (or combination of reasons) becomes a morally salient reason when it is blameworthy not to act on it. If Bridge and Good are the only two normative sources, all practical reasons must come from them. Or if there is another practical norm, the principle of Demand, they must come from these three.

Bridge and Good cover quite a few morally salient reasons. In the case of Bridge, consider gratitude. The Bridge principle generates reasons to express gratitude, let us say by thanking someone; moral judgement highlights cases in which failing to respond to that reason becomes blameworthy. The same account could be given for obligations of care, friendship, or loyalty. The reason to stand by someone may arise via Bridge from the reason there is to love him, or admire him, or have faith and trust in him; moral judgement determines when a particular failure to respond to that reason becomes a blameworthy betrayal. Moral categories, such as lack of consideration; lack of appreciation; lack of commitment to dependants, also sound as though they are directed to failures to act on Bridge-based reasons. (I am not saying that morality requires us to feel these sentiments on pain of blame: remember that you don't have to feel a sentiment to grasp that there is reason to feel it.)[4]

Other morally salient reasons are plausibly traced back to Good. Take the case of the person taken ill in the street. Perhaps you stop to help despite irritation at the delay. Your own particular ends give you reason to go on via the Bridge principle. Yet you see, despite your irritation, that there is reason to help him. This is not a reason generated by who in particular he is; there would be the same reason to help anyone in his plight. Good is the normative source of this particular reason. Morality then judges that a failure to respond to it in this particular case, despite the countervailing reasons, is blameworthy.

14.2 The Demand principle

But while this dual approach covers many of the reasons moral judgement highlights, it does not cover them all. For we have yet to consider the fundamental moral category of *rights*.

Consider the obligation to keep a promise. What reason is there to keep a promise—the reason to keep it which makes failure to keep it blameworthy? What is its source? Let us take it that the practical norm involved is the following:

> *Promise*: the fact that you've freely promised to α, where (i) it is not morally wrong for you to promise to α; and (ii) there are no facts which had you known them would have made it morally wrong for you to α, is a specific reason to α.

Reasons that fit this schema are *promise-keeping reasons*. Where (i) or (ii) fails to hold, no promise-keeping reason exists. Thus the fact that you've promised to do something you could tell was morally wrong is not a reason to do that thing. (You may well be blameworthy for having done so.) Furthermore, if you've promised to do something in ignorance of facts which, if you knew them, would make the promised action morally wrong, there is no reason to do that thing. Suppose you've promised some friends to be somewhere and do something that seems innocent enough and which you happen to be well-placed to do. In fact, in doing this thing you are assisting in a crime. If that is the situation there is no reason for you to keep the promise, and if you come to know that that is the situation you come to know that you have no reason to keep it.

Promise constitutes a sufficient reason unless there are strong enough counter-reasons to outweigh it. It is a morally salient reason: when you are warranted in believing that you have made a promise to α and that, together with your warrants overall, generates a warranted sufficient reason to α, failure to α incurs blame.

---

[4] And of course in all cases we can dig deeper. Take gratitude: an expression of gratitude acknowledges what the other person has done for you; if the acknowledgement is not freely given, there is reason for the other person to feel disappointment. Yet it is not that you should express gratitude *because* the other person will be disappointed if you do, as the principle of Good might suggest. Nor is it that the other has a *right* to your thanks; so it doesn't stem from the Demand principle. It is simply that thanking *is* the right thing to do: a free acknowledgement of a freely given benefit. All this, together with the reaction of blame towards the ingrate, is still within the domain of the Bridge principle.

But where does *Promise* come from?

The fact that someone is relying on what you will do is a reason to do it. That reason falls under Good: if you don't do it, the other person will be disappointed in their plans. However, this Good-based reason obtains irrespective of whether you've promised. If the other person has simply come to rely on your being there, the Good-based reason for being there obtains, but no promise-based reason obtains. The other person has no *right* to expect you to be there. Where promising is involved, the notion of a right comes in.

We have analysed moral rights in terms of morally permissible demands (12.6). Where a promise has been made it is morally permissible for the promissee to make certain demands—that the promise should be kept, and if it isn't kept, that apology/compensation should be made. This may apply even if there was sufficient reason for the promise to be broken—in that case the promissee can't demand that the promise be kept, but it can still be permissible to demand apology/compensation.

The underlying normative source here, the norm under which Promise holds, we can call the *Demand principle*:

> (Demand principle) if it is morally permissible for x to demand that y αs, the fact that it is is a complete specific reason for y not to fail to α without x's permission.

We can broaden this to the case of authority. Authority is a right to command. x has authority over y within a given domain if and only if x has a right to be obeyed within that domain, i.e. it is morally permissible for x to demand that his commands are obeyed. This generates a reason to obey the command via the Demand principle:

> If it is morally permissible for x to demand that y obeys x's command to α, the fact that it is, is a complete specific reason for y not to fail to obey x's command to α (i.e. to α) without x's permission.[5]

It is important that the reason-giving force of a command is stronger than that of a request (12.6). A simple request usually has reason-giving force, and indeed at least *prima facie* content-independent force. The mere fact that someone asks you to do something is usually a reason of some degree to do it. But it is not strictly a reason in itself. The request has reason-giving force because one assumes that it is made in good faith, i.e. because it will be permissible and useful to do the thing requested. This can be therefore be traced back to Good. (Or because there's good reason to desire stay on good terms, or because the request comes from a friend, etc., so then to Bridge.) But unlike a request, an authoritative command is something the commander may permissibly *demand* is obeyed, and permissible demandability is in itself a reason to obey, irrespective of whether obeying will do good.

There is (it seems to me) a remarkable degree of system, clarity, and convergence in our underlying convictions about what rights people have. This substantive system of

---

[5] Thus the authority to command generates content-independent reasons to obey the authority's command, as Raz has pointed out (Raz 1979, 1990: 35–84). The demand-based reason for obeying an authority's command is simply the fact of the command, rather than (within the limits of the authority) facts about the action commanded.

rights is an extremely important part, though by no means the whole, of ordinary morality. It is a substantive set of principles about what people may permissibly demand of others, which joins with the Demand principle to produce a concrete set of rights. Though it is not pertinent to our task here to articulate that system substantively; it is certainly pertinent to be aware of its normative strength and importance.[6]

But does Demand provide an *independent* normative source of practical reasons? That it's not derived from Bridge is obvious: we can see by inspection that it does not have the right form. Could it, however, be derived from Good?

People living together are better off as a whole if they mutually limit their freedom by a system of rights. However, the fact that people would be better off if they generally acted on the Demand principle does not entail the Demand principle. This is a special case of the general point about rule utilitarianism that we noted in the last chapter: to say that there would be Good consequences if people in general followed a rule is not to say that there is reason for them—in particular a Good-based reason—to follow the rule.

Also to be noted, however, is the distinction between a rights violation and rights infringement (12.6). A *prima facie* rights violation is a permissible infringement, not a violation, when there are sufficiently strong Bridge-based or Good-based reasons for it. It seems to me plausible that no right is strictly absolute, in the sense that it is *never* permissible to infringe it (perhaps with compensation). However, this does not subordinate the Demand principle to the other two. Demand-based reasons may be outweighed in specific cases by Bridge or Good-based reasons; in most normal cases, however, they outweigh them. Furthermore they cannot be derived from Good or Bridge-based reasons. The principle underlying rights—Demand—is distinct from the principle of Good and the Bridge principle. It is a practical–normative source in its own right.

14.3 Demand and the disinterested will

It is possible that the reason-giving force of the three norms taken together always combines to yield consistent and determinate strengths of overall reason for all actions in any choice set of any person. Not only is it possible, it is what our conception of the relation between specific and overall reasons entails. Thus—although this is a stronger claim—there may be an ordering of the goodness (as against Goodness) of actions for a person, i.e. their *choice-worthiness* for that person, that can be represented by a utility function. But even if they can be so represented, representation is not philosophical theory. It is not a demonstration, in any interesting philosophical sense, that practical reason is purely teleological (let alone agent-neutral).

The right way to see the situation, philosophically, is to accept that there are three independent normative sources of practical reasons: Bridge; Good; and Demand. But now if Demand is an independent normative source, what is its epistemic basis?

---

[6] See, for example, Thomson 1990. I outline a sketch of the substantive system of moral rights in Skorupski 2010a.

Demand falls outside the scope of sentimentalism, just as Good does.[7] Its epistemic basis, as with Good, lies in the phenomenology of the will; specifically, in the existence of a disinterested will. But whereas the epistemic basis of Good is a disinterested will to act in certain ways, the basis of Demand is a disinterested will that everyone act in certain ways.

Spontaneous dispositions of will are the criterion of what there is *reason* to will. Hence of practical reasons: for what there is reason to will and what there is reason to do are one and the same. Also, reasons are universalizable. But that does not mean that reference to everyone gets into the *content* of what is willed, i.e. that any disposition of the will is a will that *everyone* does something.

For example, a spontaneous disposition to seek one's own happiness provides an epistemic basis for the belief that there is outright reason to seek one's own happiness. To think that there is outright reason to seek one's own happiness is to think that (x) (there is reason for x to seek x's happiness). In this sense one can say that spontaneous willing is universally normative: it is the epistemic basis for a universalisable practical norm.

One could put this in a Kantian way: the epistemic basis for practical principles is what 'I can will to be a universal law'. But this Kantian formulation can easily mislead us when we consider the special nature of *Demand*. In the example just considered, I do will to seek my happiness, I do *not* will that everyone seeks their happiness. Other people do not enter into the content of my will. It's just that if this disposition gives me ground to hold that I have reason to seek my happiness, then it *ipso facto* gives me ground to hold that everyone has reason to seek theirs. It is only in this weak sense that *all* willing is universal willing.

To get to Demand we need a strong notion of willing something to be a universal law: the idea of a will whose content is that people in general do something. To will is to be disposed to act; to will that people in general do something is to be disposed to *make them* act. (Consider 'willing someone on'.) It is a disposition to will, in *this* sense, that everyone αs that provides the epistemic basis for principles specifying reasons to make others α—that is, reasons to *demand* that others α. Such principles will be of the form (x) (there is reason for x to demand that everyone αs).

What then is our epistemic basis for principles about what it is permissible to demand that other do? And how do such principles give rise to reason for them to do it? How does a permissible demand with respect to others' actions become normative for them?

As with the move from personal to impartial good this is accomplished through the moment of disinterestedness that is one of the dispositions of our will.

In the case of Good, Bridge-based dispositions of the will give way to a disinterested will to pursue the good of anyone, impartially, and this moment provides the epistemic basis for the principle of Good. The epistemic basis for the Demand principle involves the same moment of disinterestedness, of detachment from the standpoint of one's

---

[7] Although as ever, demand-based reasons can be the *object* of reason-supported sentiments. If the garage has failed to comply with the terms of its servicing contract there's reason for me to be annoyed with it. It has failed to do something there was demand-based reason for it to do. That does not derive their demand-based reason from my reason to be annoyed: the latter presupposes the former.

sentiments. It detaches from the disposition to pursue Bridge-dependent reasons (including one's own good). In this moment there is no demand from the standpoint of your *sentiments* to will that this or that person does something, or that people in general do something. Yet there remains a disinterested will, disposed to issue a general demand.

It is a second-order demand: a demand that people do not make certain demands. This second-order demand is suspended only when, in virtue of some facts about a person, the person's demand that others do something is a sufficient reason for them to do it. When that is so the disinterested will demands that everyone does what the person in question demands, unless that person allows them not to. For example, the fact that this is your computer disposes the disinterested will to accept your demand that others don't use it without asking you, and to will that everyone complies with your demand.

So where x and y are distinct individuals, we have:

(i) A disinterested will that x does not demand that y αs except in certain circumstances, $C(x)$.
(ii) A disinterested will that everyone αs when $C(x)$ unless x refrains from demanding that they α.
(iii) A disinterested will to α, given a disinterested will that everyone αs.

These disinterested dispositions are the epistemic basis of Demand. Specifically, a disinterested will that everyone αs is the epistemic ground for the claim that there is sufficient reason for everyone to demand that everyone αs.

Next, I claim that a demand on anyone's part is morally permissible if and only if there is sufficient reason for everyone to demand that it be obeyed. (This is not a definition; it is a substantive moral claim.) Disposition (i) is then the basis for:

x is not morally permitted to demand that y αs except in $C(x)$.

Dispositions (ii) and (iii) yield:

If, when $C(x)$, x is morally permitted to demand that y αs then when $C(x)$ there is sufficient reason for y to α, unless x refrains from the demand.[8]

Now rights are defined in terms of *prima facie* morally permissible demands. Thus if it is x's right that y αs, there is *prima facie* sufficient reason for y to α unless x refrains from demanding that y αs. A substantive theory of rights is a theory of what circumstances constitute C.

Whereas moral obligations do not themselves constitute reasons, I am taking it that rights do. Moral obligations belong at the level of warrant; they enter into consideration when the agent assesses the moral salience of independently present warranted reasons for and against an action. They are not themselves reason-givers. Rights, however, belong at the level of reasons, not warranted reasons; they enter into practical deliberation as

---

[8] Where it is permissible for a person to demand something, *refraining* from demanding is often what requires positive expression. Thus, in the case of your computer, you do not need to express the demand that I don't take it, but if you want to permit me to take it you must express that permission.

reason-givers. It is the fact that you can permissibly demand that I do something that gives me sufficient reason to do it.[9] That fact may itself be explained: for example, I have promised you to do it, or the computer is yours and I can't just take it. These explanations work by identifying what right is involved. So a promise, other things equal, creates a right in the promissee, and ownership other things equal, creates a right to refuse use.

In a broader sense of ownership we could say that a person 'owns' those actions of others that he can permissibly demand: it is for him to choose whether or not to demand them. Let's say that x is normatively free to α just if no one is permitted to demand that x does not α. The disinterested will impartially wills equal normative freedom for all. The substantive theory of rights fills out the content of that normative freedom.

Thus the disinterested will is the epistemic basis of *both* Good and Right. The construction of both a system of Good and a system of Right must assume, for its epistemic grounding, that in its disinterested moment the will still retains dispositions. However, I am certainly not claiming that substantive systems can be built just from the very idea of a disinterested will. Both the construction of Good and the construction of Right must make assumptions about human psychology, for example, about the human desire for close personal relations, for security, for a territory and boundaries against others.

14.4 On the mutual relations of the sources of practical reasons

I submit that Bridge, Good, and Demand are the only normative sources. If I am right, two questions arise:

> How do they combine to produce overall reasons for action?
> How do they give rise, in combination with reasons for blame, to moral obligations?

Given the categoricity of moral obligation these questions cannot be sharply separated. But let us begin in this section with some points about the first.

As already noted, we cannot assume that it can be answered by stating a *principle* that regulates how the three normative sources, on any particular occasion, consolidate into a conclusion about what a person should* do. In fact such an assumption appears obviously false. We cannot even assume that what a person should* do in various possible choice sets can be represented by a utility function.[10]

There are some limiting possibilities. For example, the three normative sources could be completely incommensurable; if so the strength of a reason from one source would never be rankable against the strength of a reason from another. When they conflicted there would simply be no truth as to what there was either overall reason or sufficient reason to do. That seems clearly false; still, there could be more local incommensurabilities. They could exist as between reasons from different normative sources or—in the

---

[9] Remember also that the moral permissibility of a demand is relative to the facts, not to epistemic states (12.6).
[10] Preferences must satisfy certain conditions to be so representable. It's not obvious that a preference ordering generated by a correct account of a person's practical reasons would do so. Whether it would is a substantive ethical question.

case of the Bridge principle and the Demand principle—between reasons from within the same broad source.

Alternatively, it might be that there are no incommensurabilities at all. Many of the dilemmas that make one reach for the idea of incommensurability actually collapse on careful scrutiny into what James Griffin calls 'rough equality'.[11] In these cases the difficulty of decision, when there is difficulty, may be simply the difficulty people often experience when they have to make a criterionless choice. In another class of cases the decision is difficult because the reasons are so disparate—but one still feels there is a right answer. Take a judgement, within the domain of the Bridge principle, as to the correct balance between reasons of prudence and reasons of honour. In principle these two kinds of reason might be incommensurable, even though both are Bridge-based. But the fact that people agonize about such conflicts suggests they don't think these reasons are literally incommensurable—at least if what they are agonizing about (and asking advice about) is *what is the right thing to do*. If in such a dilemma there was clearly no such thing as *the* right thing to do what would there be to agonize about? One would still feel mortified at having either to swallow one's pride or accept a setback to one's interests. Yet the right advice would still be: just pick one—do what you feel like, or if that doesn't resolve it, toss a coin. However, that is not how this kind of problem usually feels. I ask myself is it *really* acceptable to put up with this humiliation just because it's in my interests to do so? On our account the right answer may well be very specific to me, to my personality and the ends and ideals it gives me reason to accept—to things I am still discovering about myself. But that is not the same as saying there is no right answer.

Perhaps what cases like this illustrate is not incommensurability but particularism. Particularity and incommensurability are theoretically distinct, in that the former supports universalizable judgements (however fact-specific) about what there is sufficient reason to do while the latter does not. Our account of practical reasons is not meant to rule either of these possibilities out—or in.

We can find cases in which reasons of any one of the three kinds seem to be outweighed, in many people's judgement, by reasons of one or both of the other kinds. Considerations stemming from Good or from Demand can certainly outweigh Bridge-based reasons—for example, reasons stemming solely from what is best for you or for members of your family. On the other hand, common sense seems to say that Bridge-based reasons can outweigh Good-based ones. Many would say, for example, that parental love and commitment is mostly reason-supported and may be the source of sufficient reason to protect one's own children in some cases where doing so fails to produce most Good. Similarly, many would say that there are cases in which Demand-based reasons do exactly the same—in which Right trumps Good. We shall discuss a putative case of this kind in the next section.

---

[11] Griffin 1986: 80–1. Note that we are discussing genuine incommensurability. I think it's quite plausible that there are what he calls discontinuities (85 ff). And of course we are not here considering the daunting *epistemic* difficulties of making a choice in circumstances in which we simply do not know enough about the relevant facts.

In a certain sense, it is true, Demand-based reasons cannot be outweighed: because only a *permissible* demand constitutes a reason. However, that is only because the weighing of reasons must have already been done in the assessment of the permissibility. It is, for example, not permissible for me to demand that you do not take my bike—even though it is mine, not yours—if you need it for an urgent rescue mission. Thus the existence of a *permissible* demand to α entails a sufficient reason to α (absent permission not to), whatever reasons there may be not to α.

Furthermore, a permissible demand made on me is not just a sufficient reason for me to act but always a morally salient one. When one is warranted in thinking that a permissible demand exists it is morally wrong to ignore it. Nonetheless, simple personal inconvenience can defeat the permissibility of a demand; the defeater does not have to be some countervailing *moral* consideration. If you have promised to meet me for lunch but you find that the only way you can keep your promise, through no fault of your own, is by hiring a private jet, it would very likely not be permissible for me to demand that you keep it (assuming you're not a billionaire). Your only duties of right are to ring me up to explain the situation, perhaps to apologize.

Demand has special connections with morality that the other two sources do not have—but that does not mean that we can give a full account of morality appealing only to the Demand principle. And if a purely Demand-based theory of morality is inadequate, it is still more obvious that a purely Demand-based theory of practical reasons is. Quite obviously not all my practical reasons arise from other people's permissible demands. In contrast, many people do not find it so obvious that they do not arise purely from Good, or purely via Bridge. Utilitarianism and sentimentalism have strong attractions as comprehensive theories of practical reasons.

Let's come back to the case of utilitarianism. The utilitarian's teleological idea is that the best action—in the sense of the one there is most reason to do—must be the Best in the sense of producing the Best outcome. This is an attractive idea; even if pure utilitarianism is untenable dominance utilitarianism might still implement it. Surely the fact that α produces the Best outcome is sufficient reason to α, whatever reasons not to α apply. If so, an argument from what action is Best always defeats Bridge-based reasons. And it always defeats the *prima facie* permissibility of a demand that α should not be done. Remember that dominance utilitarianism is a thesis about practical reasons, not about moral obligation. The soldier who falls on the grenade to save lives had no moral obligation to do so; but the question is whether, given the appropriate supporting facts, he did what there was most reason for him to do. The answer may well be that he did.

Yet attractive as this idea is there is no compelling case for it. The history of ethics, and a string of familiar counter-examples, should have made that clear by now, even if they themselves fall short of being compelling.

Some of these counter-examples at least suggest that doing the Best thing is sometimes morally wrong. If so, it also follows that in those cases it is not what there is most reason to do; in which case dominance utilitarianism falls and the attractive teleological idea is unsustainable. My own view is that it does fall. (Even if it does, of course, there is still the question of *how* strong the appeal to Good is, in relation to Bridge and Demand.)

However, I am not going to make a case for this view. What we shall do in the next section is to take a counter-example of this kind and examine what it shows us about how moral judgement, when it works properly, addresses and tries to resolve such issues: to put it Sidgwick's terms, what the *method* of 'dogmatic intuitionism', or rather, moral common sense, is. Rather than addressing substantive questions about moral obligation directly, our task (continued in the next chapter) will be to show how, when moral common sense addresses them, it both makes space for conscience and limits that space.

Our overall aim is to examine the structure and epistemology of practical normativity; we enter into substantive ethical theory only so far as seems necessary given this aim.

14.5 Can it be wrong to pursue the Good?

Consider Galahad. He works in a fairly averagely paid job as a technician specializing in electronic control systems. He is known for his probity and uprightness, and his dedication to good causes. He is so known from his actions, not from sermons that he gives to other people. He is a rather quiet, modest person. He has no expensive commitments, such as to children or to undertakings, that he has an obligation to fulfil. He lives on his own in a decent but inexpensive flat. He has no elderly relatives that he must look after. Some time ago, in fact, his father died in a hospice run by a charity.

For Galahad, that was quite a transformative experience. He was impressed by the affection and care with which the nurses in the hospice looked after his dad, and saddened by their terrible lack of resources. He saw quite clearly and correctly that they were doing much real good, and that they could and would do even more with any money he could contribute to their voluntary fund. He looked into this very carefully and realistically, and quite rightly concluded that his contributions would definitely produce real good, and would not have bad side effects. They would, for example, have no tendency to reduce the amount of funding to these charities coming from the public purse. (Perhaps the public funding is done on a 50% top-up basis.)

On the basis of this very conscientious investigation Galahad contributes all that he can to these hospices, as well as smaller amounts to a selection of other respectable charities. He is not a fanatic—he leaves himself enough to live a modestly decent life and continue with his ordinary job.

But further: because of his specialist software and hardware skills, Galahad has noticed a simple and totally foolproof method of cheating with his City Transport Travel Card. There is no possibility of being discovered, nor does he need to tell anyone at all about it. He travels for nothing on City Transport but he puts the money he has thus saved by cheating into the amount he regularly sends to the hospice fund. He does this because—again quite realistically—he thinks that the disbenefits caused by his cheating are negligibly close to zero, whereas the benefits are, over time, significant.

Clearly it would be dangerous, for more than one reason, for Galahad to discuss this policy with other people. Apart from anything else he's aware that if many other people did the same thing the outcome would not be good. What he is doing is right, he thinks, but to do anything that might encourage other people to cheat with their Travel Cards would be wrong. So he keeps what he is doing completely secret, and as a result the only person he can discuss his action with is himself.

Is he doing what there is most reason for him to do? Is his action morally permissible? If it is not morally permissible then by categoricity it is not what he has sufficient reason to do. Yet it does not follow that dominance utilitarianism is false. For remember that this principle is cast in terms of should*, whereas categoricity is cast in terms of warrant. It may be that it is morally wrong for Galahad to act as he does, even though he should*. It may also be the case that it is morally permissible for him to act as he does, or that he is not blameworthy for doing so, though he should* not do so.

Of course some may simply say that Galahad's action is morally wrong because—as he is quite capable of knowing—it violates the rights of others (including those who make their contribution to the transport company's costs in good faith). But suppose one is not convinced of that, perhaps because one thinks that given the Good he produces by his action, and its very small cost, he is only infringing, rather than violating, others' rights. Nonetheless what Galahad does is clearly controversial (as he knows). Does Galahad's sincere conviction that he is doing the right thing make his action morally permissible just because it is his sincere conviction?

Let us consider a view that argues his action is wrong irrespective of his sincerity *and* irrespective of the underlying balance between Good and Demand.

What Galahad does is wrong, it says, because his action is arrogant.[12] He arrogantly assumes, without justification, that he knows the best thing to do. Now, of course, it does not immediately follow from the fact that an action shows arrogance that it's morally wrong. Morally obligatory or permissible actions can be done in arrogant ways. We shall have to consider that point further. But first let's ask why his action should be thought arrogant.

Galahad, this objector says, takes it for granted that *he* knows that secretly cheating City Transport is the right thing for him to do, even though he knows very well that others would disagree, and without discussing it with them. It is not that he relies on his own analysis of likely outcomes. We often have to rely on our own analysis of outcomes, and we can assume that no particular intellectual overconfidence is involved in this case. The point is that he relies on his own moral assessment, despite knowing that others would strongly disagree. He is morally arrogant.

Yet, sometimes one ought to do what one conscientiously believes is the right thing, even though others disagree. It need not be arrogance to act on one's conscience in such cases. Moreover we all take this point to be *important*: the moral authority of conscience has been a prime tenet of modern morality. So what is the accusation of arrogance based on here?

Sidgwick famously observed that:

---

[12] I am grateful to Stephen Darwall for suggesting this particular line of thought to me.

the Utilitarian conclusion, carefully stated, would seem to be this; that the opinion that secrecy may render an action right which would not otherwise be so should itself be kept comparatively secret; and similarly it seems expedient that the doctrine that esoteric morality is expedient should itself be kept esoteric. Or if this concealment be difficult to maintain, it may be desirable that Common Sense should repudiate the doctrines which it is expedient to confine to an enlightened few.[13]

That is also Galahad's conclusion. He thinks there are occasions on which it is Best that most people do not do what there is in fact most reason for each of them individually to do. This fact, however, is itself Best kept secret. So he is prepared to lie about what he is doing, and indeed about the beliefs behind his action, in order to maintain total secrecy. He does not reveal what he is doing and why, and one of his reasons for not doing so is that he thinks it desirable that common sense should maintain some doctrines which are in fact false.

The arrogance charge is not that he acts from his own conviction of what is morally right, even though he knows that others would disagree. That in itself does not make him arrogant. It is rather that he is arrogant in his assumption that he knows what is morally right, when he has not properly discussed it with other people. Here too there may be cases in which I rightly take myself to know the right thing to do, even though I have not discussed it with others, and even though I have to act secretly—without any accusation of arrogance being appropriate. But these will be cases in which the relevant moral assessment is uncontroversial and known by me to be so. For example, I secretly help a person who desperately needs help, because I know that if he knew about it he would feel compelled by misguided notions of honour to refuse.

But what if Galahad has formed his view partly through going to moral philosophy seminars in which abstract issues of moral principle, and hypothetical examples, have been discussed?[14] The proponent of the arrogance objection may think this is not enough. It fails to take into account the concrete social *embeddedness* of moral knowledge. Suppose Galahad has an aunt, an untheoretical person of old-fashioned probity and considerable moral wisdom. He does not discuss his plan with her, perhaps because he fears that her old-fashioned probity might make her inform the police. Yet if he had confidentially discussed his plan with her, not as an abstract example but as a concrete intention, she might well have fixed him with a mild but nonetheless somewhat steely look and said simply 'Galahad—that would be *cheating*'. If Galahad is a morally open-minded person, this might well have made him think again, in a way quite different to abstract seminar discussions.

14.6 Hegel on conscience

One of the most impressive discussions of these issues is the section on Good and Conscience in Hegel's *Philosophy of Right*.[15] Hegel seeks to reconcile three things. On the one hand, he accepts what he thinks of as a distinctly modern conception of the moral

---

[13] Sidgwick 1981 (1907): 490. [14] A question pressed on me by Tom Hurka.
[15] Hegel 1991 (1821), Part II, *Moralität*, Section 3, The Good and the Conscience, pp. 129–41.

authority of conscience—which he refers to as 'the right of the subjective will'. He thinks it a major achievement of modern morality, a step towards freedom. It is in fact the Insight principle of 12.4. That principle, as we saw, is a corollary of the thesis that moral agency requires autonomy (and not just self-determination). On the other hand, Hegel argues that morality is not derivable from abstract principles and that is not possible to have private moral knowledge. These 'anti-abstraction' and 'anti-individualist' currents lead him to a contrast between two conceptions of morality, and associated ways of life: Hegel calls them *Moralität* and *Sittlichkeit*.

Sittlicheit, often translated as 'ethics' or 'ethical life', refers to the moral convictions and practices of a shared tradition—the inherited, shared, and immanently rethought morality of a community. I shall refer to it as the morality of *common* sense, or moral common sense, or where the emphasis is on the common practices lived within the ambit of those share moral convictions, as *moral life*. *Moralität*, often translated as 'morality' or the 'moral point of view', is a certain modern conception of moral life, an interpretation of the right of the subjective will which assumes that moral obligations are derivable by conscientious private reflection on abstract principles; thus it distances itself epistemically, and perhaps practically, from the shared moral tradition. It is the object of Hegel's anti-abstractionist and anti-individualist critique. Nonetheless, Hegel agrees that modern as against traditional *Sittlichkeit* must find a place for autonomy, with its insistence that moral agents act not just from principles they have in some way received and accepted but from their personal insight into these principles as normative sources of practical reasons.

In pursuing these themes Hegel makes his famous criticisms of Kant's Categorical Imperative. What is of interest to us is the balance he strikes:

> However essential it may be to emphasize the pure and unconditional self-determination of the will as the root of duty—for knowledge of the will first gained a firm foundation and point of departure in the philosophy of Kant, through the thought of its infinite autonomy... to cling on to a merely moral point of view [*Moralität*] without making the transition to the concept of ethics [*Sittlichkeit*] reduces this gain to an *empty formalism*, and moral science to an empty rhetoric of *duty for duty's sake*. From this point of view no immanent theory of duties is possible...[16]

The object of criticism here is neither the idea of acting for duty's sake nor the idea that freedom—'infinite autonomy'—consists in acting from duty. Far from it:

> I should do my duty for its own sake, and it is in the true sense my own objectivity that I bring to fulfilment in doing so. In doing my duty, I am at home with myself (*bei mir selbst*) and free. The merit and exalted viewpoint of Kant's moral philosophy are that it has emphasized this significance of duty.[17]

Hegel's criticism is directed at Kant's idea of how one can *know* one's duty. It is Kant's epistemology of moral knowledge that reduces 'knowledge of the will' to an 'empty rhetoric of duty for duty's sake'.

---

[16] Hegel 1991 (1821), Part II, *Moralität*, Section 3, The Good and the Conscience, 135, remark.
[17] Ibid: 133, addition.

We have argued that the epistemic basis of practical principles of good and right is the dispositions of a disinterested will. Hegel could agree with that. His point is that the mere idea of disinterested willing cannot yield *substantive moral* knowledge. The idea of autonomy cannot provide an abstract route from impartiality into moral knowledge. This is sound criticism, and important because its target is so attractive to modern ethical and political ideals. Instead of 'dogmatic' moral assertions, the Categorical Imperative purports to get morality solely out of the deeply attractive self-image of ourselves as fundamentally and ultimately, metaphysically, free. It has woven its spell from Kant to Sartrian existentialism, and remains deeply beguiling.

But while rejecting (with some scorn) the notion that the idea of autonomy can, through the Categorical Imperative, deliver moral norms, Hegel by no means rejects autonomy itself, and the moral authority it gives to conscience. He gives it many eloquent formulations:

> *Conscience* expresses the absolute authority of subjective self-consciousness, namely, to know what is right and obligatory both *within oneself* and *as proceeding from oneself*, and to recognize nothing other than what it thus knows as good; also the authority to claim that what it thus knows and wills is in *truth* right and obligatory[18]

Given that I have a moral obligation if and only if I can personally know it, it follows that I may reject any putative moral obligation whose normative force I cannot see. Hegel is well aware of the potentially anarchic effects of that, but thinks they arise from a one-sidedly individualistic understanding. The principle of moral insight says that you can tell for yourself what is morally right. It does not say that you can tell *by* yourself. And of course it does not say that you have a moral obligation if and only if you believe sufficiently strongly that you have. Conscience is the final source of moral knowledge, but its true voice cannot be recognized in a purely private way.

You can have first-person knowledge of moral obligation only when you are freely and critically engaged in open discussion within a shared moral tradition. You may in the end reject some aspect of that tradition, and you may be right to do so. But without that social dimension you lose the possibility of reliably distinguishing between warranted and unwarranted conviction, between what seems to you right and what is right:

> The right to recognize nothing that my insight does not perceive as rational is the highest right of the subject, but by virtue of its subjective determination, it is at the same time *formal*; on the other hand, *the right of the rational*—as the objective—over the subject remains firmly established.

---

[18] Ibid: 137, remark (I have drawn on both the Knox and the Nisbet translation)—'*within oneself* and *as proceeding from oneself*': i.e. one personally recognizes the right and obligatory, and freely accepts it, 'gives' it to oneself as law.) Compare:

> As conscience, the human being is no longer bound by the ends of particularity, so that conscience represents an exalted point of view, a point of view of the modern world, which has for the first time attained this consciousness, this descent into the self. Earlier and more sensuous ages have before them something external and given, whether this be religion or right; but [my] conscience knows itself as thought, and that this thought of mine is my sole source of obligation. p. 136 addition.

Compare p. 148.

> The objective ethical order...[consists of laws and institutions which] give the ethical a fixed *content*...whose existence is exalted above subjective opinions and preferences...[19]

By analogy with Wittgenstein's private language argument, I shall call this Hegel's private morality argument. It is, I believe, more than an analogy. Both Wittgenstein's and Hegel's arguments turn on the dialogical epistemology of normative judgement—though the Hegelian doctrine that morality is essentially *social* also has important aspects that go beyond this point and will be explored in the next chapter. In both cases the capacity for normative judgement requires that one must be able to recognize for oneself, by one's own insight, what is normatively required in concrete situations, yet in both cases normative competence is impossible in isolation from discussion within a community. Wittgenstein thinks that this epistemology of the normative means that language is inherently shared, Hegel thinks it means that morality is inherently shared. In each case the normative judgements required, for linguistic or moral practice, cannot be purely private.

Or one might better say, they cannot be esoteric. We can put this, for the case of morality, in the form of an *exoteric* principle:

> You cannot know what is morally right without engaging in a discussion with others that takes serious account of their voice.

This should be understood to encompass, in principle at least, *everyone's* voice. You should ideally pay careful attention to everyone's sincere moral conviction. It is not a mere matter of courtesy, civic equality, or democratic 'consultation'; it is an epistemological *desideratum*. Of course it does not mean that in the end you have to agree with others as to what is right. The right of conscience, to borrow Hegel's phrase, also 'remains firmly established'.

14.7 Esotericism and abstraction

I think the exoteric principle captures precisely what is off-putting in that famous passage from Sidgwick. The objection to utilitarian esotericism is not that it is elitist. Some people are morally more penetrating, wiser, in their concrete moral judgements than others; they have an obligation to give a lead. This may be 'elitism'; at any rate it is no doubt true. The objection to esotericism, however, is that it underestimates the epistemic dangers of esoteric moral discussion. Sidgwick may seem to think that a utilitarian elite can come to know what is morally right while systematically excluding the generality of people from the discussion—excluding, that is, 'the moral consciousness of a plain man'. The objection is at least epistemological: moral convictions cannot be guaranteed to constitute knowledge if some voices are in that way systematically excluded. Under these conditions of

---

[19] Hegel 1991 (1821), Part II, *Moralität*, Section 3, The Good and the Conscience, 132, remark; 144.

exclusion, moral discussion becomes an unreliable, one-sided thing. If morality is also social in some other important ways, there may be other objections to follow.

Of course the difficulty in applying the exoteric principle to Galahad lies in the inevitable vagueness of the principle. Granting the epistemic indispensability of discussion, how much discussion? With whom? With how many people? How often? About what? Suppose Galahad does have a confidential chat with his aunt. She might earnestly say to him 'You really should talk about this with some people you trust, Gally'. The question of arrogance is the question of how seriously he should take such advice.

Suppose first that Galahad's underlying view is the Weak Dominance principle ((5) in 13.7). He may think, rightly, that this is not a very controversial principle in the abstract. On its basis he thinks that his Travel Card ploy is justified. He accepts that there are reasons against it not based on Good, for example, that it forces him into deception, and into breaking a contract with the City Transport Corporation. But he thinks that the Good-based reasons are strong enough to outweigh.

In reality, while many people might agree with the abstract principle, many would strongly disagree with Galahad's concrete application of it. How, *in practice*, does one know who's right? When the case is put in this way the exoteric principle of moral knowledge begins to look quite persuasive. One asks, in some concrete case such as Galahad's, whether Good-based reasons are strong enough to outweigh other considerations, and thus generate sufficient reason to act on them. To be warranted in thinking they do, is to be warranted in thinking the action is morally permissible. But is this a warrant one can have purely on the basis of a private or esoteric judgement? Doesn't communal judgement have some real epistemic authority here?

What if Galahad's underlying conviction is stronger—either the Dominance view or pure utilitarianism? If either of these views is correct, no casuistical question arises. It clearly follows from either of them that Galahad's policy of altruistic cheating is correct. Might one not hold that such abstract principles are for moral specialists, and that—although knowledge of them remains, to be sure, dialogical—the necessary discussion can be accomplished through philosophy seminars? Why in that case should there be any arrogance in coming to a conviction about them on the basis of such discussion, and then going out and applying one's conviction in life?

However hard it may often be to estimate consequences, or to determine what gives people happiness, etc., a utilitarianism based on a substantive account of Good, such as welfarism, by no means lacks moral implications. As Galahad's case shows, it can have quite definite concrete implications, subversive to received moral ideas. It cannot be accused of *empty* abstraction. It thus escapes Hegel's too-convenient dichotomy between the empty path of 'subjective' abstraction, epitomized by Kant's Categorical Imperative, and the path of Critical engagement with the common moral notions of the community: Hegel's favoured modern version of *Sittlichkeit*.

Nonetheless there is still an 'abstraction' criticism that can be levelled at utilitarianism, when this is conceived as a theory of practical reasons. The point now will be that moral convictions can be criticized only from the perspective of moral convictions—immanently. We have seen how this applies to utilitarianism: to reach moral conclusions it requires a moral premise. The argument against utilitarianism would now be that if it is presented solely as a theory of practical reasons it does not have moral standing and thus cannot have force against considered moral convictions ('from this point of view no immanent theory of duties is possible'). Considered as itself a *moral* assertion, on the other hand, it is highly implausible.

But though utilitarianism cannot produce an 'immanent theory of duties' it can have negative force against moral common sense: not immanently, but from the outside. It can have that force in virtue of the categoricity of morality. For if it is a priori that a morally wrong action is unwarranted, then a warranted action cannot be morally wrong. And a utilitarian account of practical reasons says that Galahad's action is warranted. In this context, which view wins? Can Galahad be certain that dominance utilitarianism is correct, just from abstract discussion and reflection? Can he be sure that it is not the mere neatness of the idea that is simply carrying him away? He needs to test it against concrete cases, but at this point his judgement of these concrete cases also needs to be tested through discussion with others. If he proposes to put these abstract principles, which so strongly conflict with common moral notions, into practice, then going to seminars and reading books is not enough. An abstract principle like the dominance principle has to be tested within communal moral life. The question is what degree of resistance or acceptance ongoing moral life puts up to the abstract principle that is proposed to it. These points obviously apply even more strongly to pure utilitarianism, since the idea that all normative reasons are Good-based reasons seems wildly out of line with most people's spontaneous assumptions about what reasons for action there are.

Moral judgement is judgement about whether an action is blameworthy given the pattern of warranted practical reasons available to the agent. That in turn requires underlying views about practical reasons. Clearly abstract considerations about practical reasons are relevant to this. If the premises of an abstract theory of practical reasons turn out to be incompatible with considered commitments of the moral community, which should give way? It seems to me that no definite answer can be given in advance. Abstraction and concrete insight are interactive. It is certainly possible, even likely, that in the long run of discussion abstract premises can shape considered communal commitments.

14.8 The principles of safety and conscience

Even if we agree that there is an element of moral arrogance in Galahad's conviction that he is doing the right thing, it does not follow that his belief is false. The points about moral epistemology that underlie the arrogance claim could at most show that he does not know that his belief is true. *For all he knows*, what he is doing is wrong. Can we move from this to the conclusion that what he does is morally wrong?

The connection must be via some such principle as this (call it the *Safety principle*):

> (*Safety*) when you have insufficient justification for the belief that your action is morally permissible, it is not morally permissible for you to do it.

This principle turns not on warrant but on justification in the sense of Chapter 5. There might be warrant for you to think the action morally permissible, but your belief that it is might still be unjustified.

The insufficiency can arise from an uncertainty as to the facts. Suppose you have a feeling that you promised to meet a friend today. As a matter of fact you haven't, but you're not sufficiently certain that you haven't. In this situation it might well be wrong to stay at home and read, at least without ringing him up to check. It would be a case of taking insufficient care. Due diligence requires that you check.

That is uncertainty as to the facts. However, there can also be insufficient justification to trust one's own moral judgement, and the Safety principle also covers that case. What most people do when they're unsure what judgement to make, or unsure about whether to trust the judgement they are inclined to make, is to cast around for opinions and advice. But there is also the case in which someone is unjustifiably *sure*. Galahad, the objection goes, is confident that his action is morally permissible, or even, just confident that there is a sufficient probability that it is[20]—the trouble is that he does not have sufficient reason for this confidence. He has not exercised due diligence. Hence by the Safety principle his action is wrong.[21]

When you are aware that there is a serious and widespread opinion that holds your proposed action to be morally wrong, you should reflect on it. That is especially so when there is no plausible undermining explanation of why serious people think the action wrong. In cases of this kind, asking them why they think it wrong is a necessary precaution. When it comes to radical divergences from common sense morality proper discussion is a condition of safety—hence not paying for his tickets, under Galahad's *actual* conditions, would be wrong. Galahad's arrogance lies in placing such confidence in his view that he thinks he can discount the sharp disagreement of others without discussing it with them. And this leads him to override the Safety principle.

All this said, it does not follow that anyone who acts from conscience against the communal voice, even without consulting it, is arrogant. It does not follow that he is wrong in his conviction, and even if he is, it does not follow that he is blameworthy. There is a principle of conscience as well as a principle of safety:

> (*Conscience*) if, after due diligence, you conclude that you have a moral obligation to do something then you are not blameworthy if you do it.

We put this in terms of blameworthiness. A stronger version of the principle of conscience would say: if, after due diligence you sincerely conclude that you have an obligation to α, you have an obligation to α. However, that is too strong. It would

---

[20] Versions of the Safety principle, cast in terms of probabilities, have long been discussed by moral theologians. (For Hegel's somewhat glib discussion of 'probabilism' see p. 140, remark.)

[21] There is a possibility of moral dilemma (pointed out to me by Toby Ord): if you have insufficient justification to think that doing something is permissible, and insufficient justification to think not doing it is permissible, does it follow that both doing it and not doing it are morally wrong? This is an interesting question in its own right, which may well show that the Safety principle as I have stated it is too simple. However, in the example under discussion everyone, including Galahad, agrees that Galahad would *not* be acting wrongly if he paid for his Travel Card; no one questions whether *that* belief is justified.

imply that if you have considered with due diligence and concluded that you have an obligation to a you have a warrant to α. But you may not have; your conclusions, however diligent and sincere, may be false. So a possible verdict is that Galahad's action is morally wrong, but that he is not blameworthy.

No doubt Galahad thinks that he has exercised due diligence and that his action is morally permissible. His critics may reply that what constitutes due diligence is itself something you cannot privately or esoterically know, as Galahad should realize; so they may deny that the Conscience principle releases him from blame.

But it is not obvious that they are right. None of the above *proves* that Galahad is arrogant, or that his action is wrong. It simply locates the objection. Although the frontier between unsafe arrogance and a true conscience standing out against the crowd is sadly unmarked, the objection says that Galahad has overstepped it.

Of course these considerations about safety and the epistemic requirement of discussion apply to common opinion just as much as they apply to Galahad. Perhaps moral common opinion would and should be shaken out of its conformism by a serious encounter with Galahad and other such thinkers. However, this would have to be tested against concrete life and decision, not in an abstract discussion. Suppose, for example, that Galahad is, contrary to expectations, detected and arrested. How do people react to his very conscientious explanation of his reasons? Do they find him blameworthy? Do they think his action morally wrong? What if instead of cheating on City Transport his pursuit of the Good lead him to assassinate a politician? And so on.

These remarks and questions are not meant to point in a strongly anti-theoretical direction. I do not doubt that ethical theory is a needed part of common ethical reflection. Utilitarianism has made an impressive contribution in just that way: it has changed common sense in healthy directions even as common sense has resisted it. At the same time, by going boldly forth into the public domain, it has exposed itself to the weight of common moral judgement. I do not myself think it survives that judgement in either its pure or its dominance form: it can be wrong to pursue the Good. Be that as it may, however, the important point is not to succumb to esoteric temptation, whether by oneself or in a coterie. An ethical theory that confines itself to ever finer esoteric discussions among its acolytes may be a fascinating pursuit, but fatally undermines its own epistemic credentials. Yet by the same token, a dogmatic conception of public moral discussion which ruled ethical theories (however comprehensive and metaphysical) off the agenda would epistemically undermine itself.

It is time to turn to this crucial thing: common moral judgement.

15

MORAL JUDGEMENT AND FEELING

a sentiment of the understanding, or...a perception of the heart[1]

We began our discussion of the normative sources of practical reason in Chapter 11. There we saw how reasons for feeling generate practical reasons through the Bridge principle. Chapter 12 gave a sentimentalist analysis of the moral concepts. Chapters 13 and 14 went beyond sentimentalism about practical reasons by introducing two other sources of practical reason, Good and Demand, whose epistemic basis is the disinterested will. The three principles thus identified—Bridge, Good, and Demand—constitute, I have suggested, the complete framework within which all practical reasons can be specified.

Moral obligation is not itself a further normative source. It is categorical, but not in its own right reason-providing (12.3). The fact that an action is morally obligatory does not itself give reason to do it—rather, if an action is morally obligatory there is some sufficient reason to do it, arising from the three normative sources, of such a kind as to make it morally obligatory. But why, in that case, is morality needed? What, a post-moralist might ask, is it for—what does it do? Is it redundant, rather than supervenient? Might it be better to stop moralizing, and try to school oneself out of the feelings which morality mobilizes?[2] Our discussion in Part III will be incomplete without examination of this question.

The question to be considered in this chapter is not about the truth-aptness of moral propositions. We have already determined the truth conditions of moral propositions in terms of reasons for blame (12.2); meta-questions about normativity in general will be taken up in Part IV. Our question in this chapter is about the authority and role of moral judgement: this sentiment of the understanding, or perception of the heart, as Butler so well described it. Why do we engage in moral judgement, as well as practical judgements about what to do?

---

[1] Butler 1970 (1736): 148.
[2] A point attractively put by Nietzsche: 'It goes without saying that I do not deny—unless I am a fool—that many actions called immoral ought to be avoided and resisted, or that many called moral ought to be done and encouraged—but I think that the one should be encouraged and the other avoided *for other reasons than hitherto*. We have *to learn to think differently*—in order at last, perhaps very late on, to attain even more: *to feel differently*.' (Nietzsche 1982 (1881): 103).

Moral judgement regulates the life of a community; for many it also shapes personal life as the ground of an ideal. It frames the constitution of social relations yet at the same time provides the basis for conscientious dissent. These roles of moral judgement are related, as we have already begun to discuss (14.6 to 14.8). They are strongly present in modern secular societies, despite the by now long history in these societies of morality-critique. Without understanding how moral judgement does what it does and why it is needed, we cannot draw a full picture of the domain of reasons.

To understand the role of moral judgement we must deepen our understanding of the moral emotions. The account of moral concepts in Chapter 12 defined them in terms of reasons for the sentiment of blame: on that account, therefore, the distinctively *moral* emotions are those that enter into or are in some other way associated with blame.[3] This 'blameworthiness' account of moral wrongness has a way of arousing strong opposite reactions. Some recoil from it as making morality too dark and threatening—others seem positively attracted to it for that very reason. Either way, such responses are superficial. They might arise, in the first place, from oversimple assumptions about the connection between blame and punishment. These are certainly connected, but the connection is not simple, as we shall see.

It is also true, however, that morality as an actual communal practice always has threatening potentials for corruption, distortion, moral panic, imposition of conformity. These potentials arise from the very nature of the moral emotions; they too must therefore be part of our picture. But before rushing to these dysfunctions we must grasp what the moral emotions are, and what they do when they play the role they can play and that we should let them play: how they can be catalysts in the formation and reformation of moral personality and the renewal of a moral community, why moral integrity is so important an aspect of self-realization for many people, an aspect that cannot be cut off from the other elements of a rewarding personal life.

The moral emotions have great powers for good and ill. They should not be understood one-sidedly. We must attend to the whole pattern of feelings involved in blame and 'ethical punishment' (as I shall call it)—blame, guilt, remorse, repentance, forgiveness, and reconciliation.

15.1 British sentimentalism and German idealism

Prototypes of Chapter 12's account of moral concepts can be found in a number of 'British moralists', including Hume, Smith, Bentham, and Mill; I have been taking Smith and Mill as particular touchstones. This 'British' sentimentalist[4] account of morality has a basic soundness and strength. It also has weaknesses.

Mill, as we saw, has an incisive few paragraphs defining morality in terms of sanction. But he does not clearly distinguish blame as a feeling, and evaluative reasons for that feeling, from blame as an action, and practical reasons for that action. Thus he seems

---

[3] Of course many other valuing emotions are important to living together—love, trust, admiration, respect, gratitude...I am talking about the emotions that *distinctively* characterize *morality*.

[4] One could say Scottish, but I won't pursue that tempting hare.

satisfied with a utilitarian account of reasons for blame, understood as practical sanction. In various places we get sudden penetrating insights into the emotional significance of moral judgement, for example, in his brief remarks on conscience, or on virtue as a part of happiness, or on the sentiments involved in justice—but as so often with Mill they are frustratingly brief, coming from a hinterland which he does not bring to the fore. He never delves into the normative structure of reasons for feeling and for action, and of how one gives rise to the other. Nor does he have anything to say about the proper *object* of blame, namely, the crucial fact that blame is directed to failure to act on certain reasons that the agent had, should have recognized as sufficient, and acted on.

To be fair to Mill, his concerns predominantly lie elsewhere. For him analysis and interpretation of moral concepts primarily subserves reforming moral and political teaching. Smith, in contrast, is first and foremost an analyst and interpreter, though with plenty of enjoyably urbane incidental moral commentary. Smith's subject is the *theory* of moral sentiments, and he supplies a rich stock of resources. Importantly, from our point of view, he has a conception of evaluative reasons, in the shape of his notion of the propriety of a sentiment, that is, of what kind of object properly gives rise to it. His main concern is to give an account of the mechanism by which we make such judgements of propriety—an account in which sympathetic simulation of what one would oneself feel in a situation plays a leading role. To that account it is quite easy to attach an epistemology of evaluative reasons: we can simply note that what we can imagine feeling on the basis of sympathetic simulation is our main epistemic criterion for what it is 'proper'—what there is reason—to feel. Smith also explicitly distances himself from the idea that utility is the explanation (and implicitly) the appropriate criterion for judgements of approbation and disapprobation:

> the usefulness of any disposition of mind is seldom the first ground of our approbation...the sentiment of approbation always involves in it a sense of propriety quite distinct from the perception of utility.[5]

Smith has the elements of an account of the connections between evaluative and practical reasons: 'whatever appears to be the proper object of gratitude appears to deserve reward; and...in the same manner, whatever appears to be the proper object of resentment, appears to deserve punishment'.[6] This can be seen as a particular application of the general Bridge principle (even if the connection between punishment and *resentment* is mistaken). Furthermore Smith also has the elements for an account of the other important connection between reasons for blame and practical reasons, which goes via the object of blame. He holds that the proper object of 'disapprobation' is an action which is itself improper: i.e. was not as it should have been.

In these ways the sentimentalist approach to morality which we have outlined can be thought of as loosely Smithian: it develops conceptual connections that are germinally present in his theory of the moral sentiments.[7]

---

[5] Smith, A. 1984 (1759): 188.   [6] Ibid: 67.

[7] Moreover Smith makes room for impartiality. Note that the famous impartial spectator is not a hypothetical construct but the 'imagined man within'. This is, in effect, a departure from sentimentalism close to that we have made. A disinterested will is brought into play by one's own impartial or detached reflection: 'the imagined man within' is oneself.

If Smith does not develop them himself that is because his main interest lies elsewhere: in psychological observation and explanation, rather than in conceptual analysis of moral and normative concepts. But a weakness arises just here: at the descriptive rather than the conceptual level. Smith and Mill are penetrating moral psychologists full of often acute, often subtle, particular observations. However, their concern with naturalistic explanation pulls them towards oversimple explanations that distort the facts. If the aim is to contribute to pioneering work in the scientific psychology of morals this need not be a criticism: from that point of view simplistic models can be a perfectly reasonable first stage in producing something better. However, scientific psychology is not our concern. For our purpose, we need an accurate description of the moral phenomena presented in a way appropriate to our philosophical questions. We must positively avoid explanations that too simply model the facts, and thus obscure the phenomenology—however dialectically useful such models may be for scientific progress. In particular, our question is not whether blame in some sense causally 'derives' from this, that, or the other, be it some simpler emotions, or some evolutionary sequence. Our question is what it is, as it *is*, and what it does. There can, it is true, be genealogies that are genuinely subversive, and thus relevant to normative theory, in that they show that our reasons for some judgement or feeling are not what we think they are, or even that there *can* be no reasons for it. That was important to Mill, as to Marx or Nietzsche. But the first thing to be sure of is that these are *accurate* explanations.

A good example is Smith's idea that blame is sympathetic resentment. This could be a causal theory: blame originates in this way—or it could be a description: blame is a form of resentment. In fact it seems to be both, given Smith's account of sympathy. Understood in the first way, it lacks evidence; understood in the second way it is misleading as well as false. The descriptive and the explanatory claim shadily support each other.[8] A subversive explanation hovers (I am not attributing it to Smith): blame is really 'just' resentment, and 'thus' mostly irrational fear or anger. Yet it is simply false to describe blame as a form of resentment. Gratitude and resentment are important reactive feelings; as noted in 12.2 they have their reasons, or proper objects, and they give reason for appropriate actions of thanks, or demand for apology and compensation. But this system of feelings and reasons is distinct from the system of moral respect and blame.

Nietzsche evidently relished the 'English psychologists' somewhat saturnine take on morality; what Bernard Williams praised as their 'realism'.[9] Realism in this sense certainly requires one to recognize the enormous force of resentment. It can burst out of its normative limits and overpower and suborn the moral emotions. But it is not realism to confuse the patient with the patient's disease.

---

[8] Sympathy in Smith's theory could be understood as the psychological faculty that allows us to simulate another's feelings and assess whether they are reason-supported. So understood, sympathetic resentment cannot *be* blame. The latter is rather a sentiment towards a person that often *arises* from sympathetic recognition that there is sufficient reason for a third party to resent that person's actions. But in any case we should not assume that all blame arises in that way.

[9] Nietzsche on the 'English psychologists', Nietzsche 1998 (1887): 9. Williams, B. 1995c: 204. Both Nietzsche and Williams illuminatingly, but in my view one-sidedly, discuss this dark side of morality.

I believe that we can deepen our account of moral sentiments by drawing also on a different tradition, that of German idealism (Kant, Fichte, and Hegel). This tradition, in the first place, reasserted and explained the role played by will and practical reason in motivating and justifying moral action, against those who think that will and practical reason are fictions. We agreed with that tradition's view of the will in Chapter 10, and in Chapters 13 and 14 we also examined how dispositions of the disinterested will epistemically underpin appeals to impartial good and rights.

What is especially important for our purposes in this chapter is the materials Kant, Fichte, and Hegel provided for an account of what moral valuations are and the emotional role they play in individual and communal life. Their contribution was to focus attention on various forms of recognition and their presuppositions. In particular, Hegel gives an insightful account of punishment in terms of withdrawal of recognition and reconciliation. This is not the place for a detailed interpretation and critique of their ideas, however—interesting as that would be. Rather, we shall draw on them freely in developing our own account.

15.2 Moral recognition

Recognition is recognition of another as, in some way, an *other* of the kind *I* am; specifically one that can, like me, address others, including me, and enter with others into a relationship of mutual recognition. It is, in Butler's language, as much a 'sentiment' as a 'perception', an affective attitude, a feeling of reciprocity, of a common nature of one or another kind.

It is a wide, generic notion—*moral* recognition is one kind. We have already invoked moral recognition in distinguishing blame from anger, resentment, and fear (12.2). One may blame with disappointment, sadness, regret—the blamed person may be feared, pitied, or both, or neither. Blame disposes neither to aggression nor to flight, but to withdrawal of recognition.

To pick out moral recognition in particular we can distinguish two other forms of recognition that are relevant to morality. Each involves a certain reciprocation: I recognize the other as one that is able to recognize me as an other that can be addressed in the relevant way (and thus conceive myself as one who can be addressed in that way).

(i) Summons. A being may be able to 'call on' or 'summon' others. I recognize it as, like me, a being with concerns it can call on me to respond to.

This is a primitive relationship that can exist with animals as well as people (though it can no doubt be sentimentally exaggerated as well). An animal can issue an appeal by looking at me, for example, if it is injured, or if it is expecting a command, or by coming up to me in a certain way, as in an appeal to come and play. It can appeal to me by bringing me a gift (a dead mouse)—the call is to a reciprocal relationship. The call places an onus on the called; it calls for recognition—one can't help feeling that to turn it down requires some 'explanation' or at least show of feeling. The natural response is a desire to help, co-operate, take part, reciprocate, console, and this gives rise to a Bridge-based reason. The animal that looks at one in pain is effectively saying 'Help me please'. The natural, reason-supported, response is solicitude, which prompts help. There is also at least some element of reciprocity here: to the degree an animal can genuinely issue such a summons it can in some degree recognize me as a potential summoner and respond to my summons.

(ii) Demand. The other may issue a *demand* to me, in the sense already considered in Chapter 14. This is stronger than a summons in the sense of (i). Demand is command. Here I recognize the other as a *right-holder*, or the agent of a right-holder. Contrast the case of gratitude. A good turn can have the nature of a summons; for just that reason you may prefer to help me anonymously, because you are *not* seeking recognition, wanting to address me in *that* way: 'I wasn't looking for thanks'. Gift exchanges are important in many societies. But we don't, I think, want to say that someone who does you a good turn automatically acquires a right. A rights-oriented society finds gift exchange as way of structuring role relations at least embarrassing: gifts should belong to the private or at least informal sphere.

Here again there is reciprocity. I recognize the other as someone who (or whose agents or representatives) may make demands of some kind of me. They recognize me as someone to whom those demands may be made. To demand is to recognize the other as capable of responding to a demand, thus as capable of recognizing the demand as a reason to act. In demanding, I take it that I give the other a reason. I take it that a demand from another can be a reason to act. We are in the world of Hegel's Abstract Right, whose principle is 'Be a person [i.e. act as a being that has rights] and respect others as persons'.

(iii) Finally we have moral recognition, the form of recognition whose withdrawal is at stake in blame, and which we are concerned with in this chapter. It is recognition of the other as a *responsible moral* agent, i.e. one who possesses the subjectivity and moral insight of a moral agent, and can be relied on, and if necessary called on, to act on it. My main model for moral recognition will be Hegel's account of the way punishment figures in the transition from 'Abstract Right' to '*Moralität*' in the *Philosophy of Right*.[10]

Fichte's notion of recognition (*Anerkennung*) corresponds best to the form of recognition that I am calling *demand*, and thus to the mutual recognition of persons as right-holders. However, reciprocal attitudes of demand are too narrow to capture the *generic* notion of mutual recognition—of various forms of mutual 'second-person' relations, in Stephen Darwall's phrase.[11] These can involve mutual recognition of vulnerability, and of moral responsibility, as well as of rights. Connectedly—although I agree with Darwall on

---

[10] Hegel 1991 (1821): 90–104. (Thus not his discussion of the 'master–slave dialectic' in the *Phenomenology of Spirit*.) The quasi-historical or developmental aspect of Hegel's account will not matter to us here, and I am not endorsing it (though I think it still deserves careful consideration). I take moral recognition to be involved in any form of *Sittlichkeit*, primitive or modern. For discussion of the relationship between Fichte and Hegel on recognition, see Clarke 2009, Neuhouser 2000, Williams R. 1992.

[11] Darwall 2006. Note that if the class of second-personal attitudes is understood as always involving some form of mutual *recognition* it is narrower than Strawson's broad category of 'reactive attitudes' (Strawson 1962). Mutual contempt, for example, is not a form of mutual recognition in the present sense; it need not involve the possibility of any kind of call on the other—on the contrary.

many points regarding moral agency and obligation—his Fichtean focus on the notion of demand seems to me too narrow an account of the second-personal relations involved in moral recognition: it builds in a bias to a rights-based conception of morality. There is, importantly, a *difference* between what we have a moral obligation to do and what anyone, including the 'community', can permissibly demand of us. (Consider obligations of gratitude, of loyalty in friendship, of tact; moral obligations to oneself, if there are such.) The moral obligation to do something arises from the nature of the reasons for doing it: the specific facts which both give one reason to do it, and make it morally obligatory to do it. Those facts may or may not comprise facts about someone's rights. Moral obligation does not always arise from any individual's or collectivity's permissible demands; there is a doctrine of virtue as well as a doctrine of right.

We can distinguish the capacities and actions that may be required to attain a certain standing—the factual basis, 'credentials', or 'entry-requirement'—from the bestowal of that standing. In some cases bestowal of a standing need involve no credentials in this sense; where it does not we have a pure 'club' model, in which no reasons for bestowal of standing have to be given. Who is recognized as a member of the club is a matter of choice on the part of the existing members. In other cases there is an entry requirement which, if satisfied, compels recognition as of right, for example, in the case of citizenship. And there are intermediate cases, such as learned societies or honourable companies in which recognition of someone as 'one of us' by the members must be based on recognition of that person's achievements, but yet a person who has those achievements cannot demand recognition as of right.

Moral recognition has a factual basis which compels recognition as of right. The factual basis is moral agency—in the narrow sense in which moral agency is self-determining action that actually does respond to and accord with moral norms. A capacity for moral agency in this sense is not itself moral agency. However, an agent who has the capacity is either responsible (answerable) or irresponsible; one who does not have it is non-responsible.

Moral recognition then consists in the first place in the expectation that the other is responsible—that is, can account for his or her actions in accord with moral norms that should be accepted in common. The mutual address it grounds assumes that we both respond to moral norms, can enter into discussion of what they are, and can justify our actions and judge those of others in those terms. Withdrawal of moral recognition is not refusal to recognize that the other has the *capacity* for moral agency. On the contrary, it makes sense only with respect to agents who have that capacity. It is a withholding of standing, one may say suspension of membership of, or conditional expulsion from, the moral community of responsible agents. Moral recognition involves openness to certain interactions with the other; withdrawal of recognition is the withholding of those interactions.

What are they? Withdrawal of moral recognition is not withdrawal of solicitude, nor necessarily of sanctuary. The interests of wrongdoers should be impartially considered with those of all others. Furthermore wrongdoers retain certain rights. Yet a wide variety of interactions is cut off. There is a withholding of association, trust, co-operation in voluntarily assumed common projects, willingness to engage in dialogue on moral questions ('There's nothing more to discuss until you acknowledge you were in the wrong.') The communal nature of this withholding is central to its force. And just as recognition is the right of a responsible agent, so withdrawal of recognition is our right in face of a wrongdoer.

Moral recognition, not least of oneself by oneself as well as by others, gives dignity, value and structure to a life, a confidence in one's independent standing among others. The moral sentiments, the sentiments underlying recognition and its withdrawal, are correspondingly powerful. That is also why, when they are coldly manipulated, or taken over by resentment, rage, moral panic, they can be truly frightening.

So let us make our picture of these feelings more precise.

15.3 Blame and avoidability

Withdrawal of recognition, we have noted, is not a matter of ceasing to treat a wrongdoer as a being capable of moral agency, of consigning them, so to speak, to the realm of wild things. In terms of this metaphor, the moral outlaw exists in a liminal field which is neither the village nor the wilderness (bush, forest), even though it is to the wilderness that he has been literally or metaphorically expelled.

Blame puts in question the wrongdoer's membership of a community in which people can live with each other in uncoerced relations. It puts it in question but it does *not* close routes to an affirmative answer. The action to which it prompts is not a final and irreversible exclusion, but a conditional one that leaves open the possibility of reconciliation, restoration—given a change of heart on the part of the wrongdoer. This possibility of reconciliation explains why a blameworthy action must have been an avoidable action, one that the agent had the power not to do, and can therefore resolve not to do in future.[12] Blame presupposes the capacity for moral agency: specifically, the ability to see that what one did was *morally* wrong—hence, the ability to recognize when self-blame is warranted. (You can only blame those who can blame themselves.) To be effective the process of repentance must give rise to a change in the disposition of the will: a new resolve not to do again what one *could* have resolved not to do in the first place, to *be* guided by those morally salient reasons which one was able to see as such but which one did not try hard enough to see, or set aside. This condition of the self—moral resolve—is required for true reconciliation, and it provides the basic logic of ethical punishment, which will be discussed in the next section.

Two close kindred of blame and guilt (much closer than resentment) are a kind of horror or disgust, and contempt, disdain. In each case the key difference is that the rejection to which these dispose does not, as does that involved in blame, inherently posit the

---

[12] Avoidability and voluntariness are not quite the same. Involuntary actions may be blameworthy if avoidable. Consider yawning when it was important that you should not, and could have refrained. (You could have voluntarily refrained—but you did not voluntarily omit to refrain.) Similarly with thoughtlessness.

possibility of restoration of standing. Unlike blame, these emotions do not presuppose that the properties of the agent which give rise to them are avoidable properties.

Horror and disgust, it has been plausibly argued, is a species of rejection directed at that which transgresses boundaries.[13] These feelings treat the transgressive item as a polluting impurity or uncleanness. Where no clear distinction is made between moral and metaphysical boundaries a magical identification of guilt with impurity can arise.[14] In this pattern of thought guilt, or sin, may be transferable from the polluted transgressor through rituals of cleansing, such as the scapegoat carrying its burden of transferred evil into the wilderness. If however pollution is irremovable, the polluted transgressor must be permanently excluded. Even when this pattern of feeling is in abeyance it remains latent and can still influence ideas of the moral. Horror and disgust can be important elements in one's emotional attitude towards someone, including oneself, who does a serious moral wrong. But the magical identification of moral wrongdoing with impurity cannot be seriously sustained, and when it is dismissed the essential point about blame, that it excludes but holds out the possibility of restoration given moral resolve, stands out more clearly.[15]

One can feel horror or self-disgust at one's wrongdoing; one can feel ashamed of it. But remorse is distinct from shame, self-contempt, or self-disdain; so too is blame from contempt or disdain. Again the key point is that blame assumes avoidability. It can thus hold out the prospect of reconciliation, given a newly forged resolve, whereas disdain and shame do not.[16] Central to the latter feelings is the notion of honour: personal standing, status, or rank. The behaviour to which disdain disposes is not exclusion but demotion, not withdrawal of recognition as such but loss of respect. Shame is the experience of diminished standing in one's own eyes.

If shame and guilt are related in this way, as demotion to expulsion, it is also understandable that they should blend. With shame, however, there is no analogue to repentance and reconciliation. Standing requires honour-worthy properties of the self which go

---

[13] Mary Douglas, *Purity and Danger*. See also Haidt and Graham 2007, on purity as one of what they take to be five foundations of morality.

[14] The gods may show themselves to be above boundaries by doing polluting things without being polluted. There is also the idea that to the pure—who effectively become gods—all things are pure.

[15] Christianity's doctrine of sin contains many elements of purity and danger. Thus original sin is a transgressive pollution transmitted down the generations irrespective of answerability. Then there is the 'immaculate conception' (pollution-free conception) of the mother of Christ, and Christ's atonement for original sin, with its model of the scapegoat lamb. Hell is a clear survival of the idea of pollution: Christianity, to its honour, teaches the moral importance of remorseful change of heart, yet it reserves a place for the morally atrocious idea of final exclusion without the possibility of a reconciling change of heart.

[16] My account of withdrawal of moral recognition overlaps to some considerable degree with Scanlon's 2008 account of the 'impairment of relations' that is involved in blame, however I don't agree with him that blame does not presuppose avoidability. Unfortunately Scanlon's admirable discussion appeared to late for me to take it as much into account as I would have liked; still, as regards this point it seems to me that it assimilates withdrawal of recognition rather too much to withdrawal of friendship, and the sentiment of blame too much to sentiments like dislike, contempt, disdain. But recognition is a right, friendship is not. Connectedly, Scanlon seems to me to pay insufficient attention to the presuppositions and significance of remorse and resolve. Forgiveness is no more a right than friendship is; but *reconciliation*, in the sense of restoration of recognition, of standing as a responsible, 'answerable', moral agent, can be. By the same token, someone who lacked control of their actions in the first place is not properly blamed (unless for getting into that state, or not making efforts to get out of it).

beyond (may not even include) any required disposition of the will. A shameful defect is not necessarily or even typically a defect of the will, and it may not be possible to remedy it by effort. I may be ashamed of my ugliness; inability to stand my ground; inability to catch a ball; or lack of wit, but it makes no sense to repent of them.

The intermixture of honour codes with morality is characteristic of aristocratic or caste society; their radical differentiation and the downgrading of shame and disdain as disciplinary categories is characteristic of modern liberal individualism.[17] This broadly fits the general Weberian phenomenon whereby modernity differentiates, rationalizes and disenchants. Our tendency is to eradicate pollution-horror and to moralize shame. We think that 'there is nothing to be ashamed of' in being unable to catch a ball, or come up with a quick and clever response—in general, we want to think that there is nothing to be ashamed of about incapacities that are not subject to the will. We replace shame with the weaker, more acceptable notion of 'embarrassment'. The only thing, we tend to think, that should make us feel badly of ourselves is moral fault. And yet we know, implicitly, what humiliation is; how torturers, for example, can make it work for them.

15.4 Ethical punishment as atonement

Blame is the withdrawal of recognition; guilt, self-blame, is withdrawal of recognition from oneself. Restoration is accomplished through what I shall call the dialectic of ethical punishment.

Ethical punishment is free self-punishment; we shall come back to how it relates to punishment in the usual 'external', legal, or institutional sense. It comprises the processes of guilt, remorse, repentance, and reconciliation. It is an inner travail to be voluntarily undertaken and communally recognized. Its effect is reconciliation with oneself and others. It is thus atonement—the bringing about of the condition of being at one.[18]

In what way are wrongdoers divided within themselves as well as from others? Freedom requires the power to act from warrant, even when the warranted action does not correspond to that which one is most strongly disposed by desire to do. This is 'will-power' (10.10). There are cases in which you lose that power. In those circumstances you are unfree, and you are excused blame for what you do in that state, if not for getting into it. We can also accept that there are many cases in which willpower and thus responsibility is reduced to varying degrees, in various ways. Nonetheless in some cases you act wrongly even though you retain the capacity to act from warrant. You act from something

---

[17] But we shall see that Kant makes the ideal of *equal* respect, understood as an honour concept, central to moral standing. (In a way that is characteristic, perhaps, of early, still aristocratically-oriented, liberalism.)

[18] Originally 'atonement' referred to the condition of at oneness itself, but its meaning has shifted to refer to the travail that restores that condition, namely, the transgressor's *work* of atonement. In saying that ethical punishment is atonement, I use it in the latter sense. Other patterns or metaphors associated with ethical punishment include (i) redemption: redeeming an obligation 'owed' to society and which puts one in bondage until redeemed; (ii) propitiation: calming the wrath of the gods by gifts. These appeal to an emotional logic distinct from that of the dialectic of atonement, and to my mind less fundamental. Redemption makes the idea of an undischarged debt particularly prominent; propitiation has a magico-religious connection with pollution.

you take as a reason, perhaps in the moment of action letting yourself take it as a warrant, even though you really know that it is not. In these cases your wrongdoing is free but heteronomous. These are cases of *divided*, not overpowered or limited, will.[19]

In such cases one may on occasion be ashamed of oneself, angry with oneself and so on. I smoked that cigarette, kidding myself it would be the last. Or one may simply note the failure to do what one believed best and resolve to do better next time. In contrast, if I have done some moral wrong, there is something inadequate in a response that *merely* resolves to do better, as one might resolve not to raid the fridge again. Why is that not enough? A narrowly rationalist view of moral wrongdoing has no answer. For the answer clearly centres on sentiment, on the connection between moral wrongness and deserved *blame*: on the special kind of dividedness—withdrawal of recognition from oneself—that guilt involves. On our account it thus arises from the very nature of moral wrongdoing. Moral wrongdoing warrants guilt, and thus by the Bridge principle (other things equal), self-exclusion. Division of the will is division of the self.

A wrongdoer is capable of moral agency, and a being capable of moral agency can know the moral law as a moral law: i.e. as something to which it is blameworthy not to conform. The first step in ethical punishment is the real, not merely notional, acknowledgement of one's own blameworthiness, the *feeling* of guilt, and consequent withdrawal of recognition from oneself plus acknowledgement of the justice of others' withdrawal. In this the idea of a moral community is crucial. But because the idea of atonement is the idea of *deserved* reconciliation, with *oneself* as well as with others, it leaves scope for the idea of community to be more or less idealized, and correspondingly, as we shall see, more individualist or more communitarian.

In more detail, ethical punishment can be seen as the pivotal element in a process comprising the moments of (i) transgression and expulsion; (ii) liminality and repentance; and finally (iii) atonement through annulment: 'at-one-ment' of the self with itself and with the community. Thus we have:

(i) Withdrawal of recognition. The expelled wrongdoer enters a liminal position, neither in the community of moral agents nor in the wilderness to which the law is not promulgated.

(ii) Liminality and repentance. A transgressor recognizes the moral law as their moral law, which they know and will, and thus their own dividedness. He or she suffers through this recognition, through the split in themselves which it forces them to acknowledge, and through the process required to restore wholeness: recognizing the transgressing self as oneself but at the same time going on from it or beyond it—'superseding' it. This suffering is proportionate to the wrongdoing.

---

[19] In some cases but not all you can be blamed for being thoughtless: failing to realise when you should have realized. For example, you thoughtlessly leave your mobile phone on. We blame you to the extent that we think you 'must have' or at least 'should have' realized that this was a time to check your phone. You should have realized, but couldn't be bothered to think. I include these cases under 'divided will'. Cases of complete forgetting (you're sure you've left your phone at home) do not involve the will and are not blameworthy—though they may be highly embarrassing.

(iii) Atonement, return to the community by means of this suffering. 'At-one-ment' with the community is also 'at-one-ment' of the self: re-identification of the individual's particular will with the moral will, return to an undivided self.

But why does (iii) require (ii)—why does atonement require the suffering of repentance? Why must it involve not just a *resolve* to do better but a particular sort of suffering, often expressed in a freely undertaken work of repentance proportionate to the seriousness of what one has done? (Guilt goes beyond simple self-blame just because of this connection with repentance.)

The freely accepted suffering of repentance annuls the wrongdoing. Hegel's formula of punishment as the 'negation of the negation' captures it neatly:[20] in wrongdoing the will denies or negates the moral law, in accepting punishment it negates that negation. We can accept that this indicates a real emotional dialectic—even if we cannot accept it as an explanation relying on something called 'speculative logic'. The freely embraced pain of repentance is the condition for atonement, reconciliation.

What kind of explanation is this? What we are looking for is more like a justification. Pain is bad, so must it not be outweighed by a compensating good? And if the compensating good is restored recognition (by self and community), would it not be better if that could be achieved without the pain, for example, by a simple, painless but effective, resolution, communicated to others? Why shouldn't that be enough to restore recognition?

But we can ask similar questions about regret and grief. Why, if one has grievously injured someone is it necessary to *feel* sorry—that is, to undergo that particular emotional pain—both for one's own peace of mind (not to feel it would be at least alarming) and to be reconciled with the other? Why is coldly offered compensation not enough? Cold compensation can close the rupture in one way, i.e. pacify aggression; but true sorrow is necessary for true forgiveness: the closure of an emotionally disrupted state. And with the true sorrow of regret it is the *effort* of compensation that counts in closing the emotional rupture. Consider the rich man who pays you anything you want but couldn't care less about the injury. He compensates in the sense of making the injured party as well off as before, but he does not make up, in the sense of restoring good relations through reciprocity of amends and forgiveness.

Similarly, why is the pain of grief necessary for recovery after the loss of a loved relative or friend? Why do people not just experience grief but feel the need to experience it, so that they are so to speak locked in and unable to move on and beyond if, for example, the body is lost and cannot be buried? Here again we can answer that the emotional pain is necessary for the closure of a disrupting state. It is necessary not least because it is warranted. It would not be better for us if we could simply switch off the pain and get on with our lives.

So too with ethical punishment: it closes the disrupted state, heals the self, reforges through pain the disrupture of the moral will.

---

[20] Hegel 1991 (1821): 82, 104.

In none of these cases is our attitude to the suffering instrumental, a case of taking your medicine because no less painful remedy is available. Grief and penitence are particularly comparable in this respect. Each is accepted for itself, not as an instrument but as a friend, and each restores wholeness by annealment. Repentance identifies with the transgressing self as oneself but at the same time goes on from it or beyond it, grief at the loss of another identifies with that other as a part of oneself but at the same time goes on from it or beyond it. At this point explanation, at any rate at the hermeneutic level, has to stop. It is a fact about us that repentance, regret, grief are ways of restoring ourselves with ourselves and others, and that we find them good.

In this dialectic ethical punishment is located in (ii): it is the work of penitence, whose emotional logic requires a suffering proportionate to the wrongdoing in order to achieve atonement. This is the degree of suffering that gives sufficient reason to restore recognition. It is the sentimental basis of the idea of desert, and hence of the desert theory of punishment.

The act of blame can hurt the wrongdoer. If he desires to maintain recognition (by himself and others) it has the effect of a penalty inasmuch as it declares the existence of a *right* to withdraw something whose restoration is conditional on ethical punishment. The declaration can be more or less public and formal. And just because the very hurtfulness of public blame can exceed any deserved punishment in unimportant cases, there is a proper reluctance to blame.[21] Nonetheless blame is not itself punishment, nor is exclusion, the action to which it prompts.[22] Of course exclusion can also be very painful. Nonetheless the moment of punishment is the moment of atonement—the atoning travail.

The dialectic of ethical punishment lies at the heart of punishment in the legal or institutional sense: it is the rational core of the 'retributive' element that is essential to punishment properly so-called. I should stress, however, that an account of ethical punishment does not justify fully retributivist theories, and that it cannot give us a full philosophy of punishment in the legal or institutional sense. In the first place, legal punishment has to deal also with people who don't care about being moral agents, who don't desire recognition, or whose responsibility is limited—the hardened criminals, the people living 'outside' society, and those who don't see that what they do is morally wrong. These are people whom ethical punishment cannot reach. Connectedly, the main question about institutional punishment is what right we have to *enforce* hard treatment on wrongdoers. From the standpoint of ethical punishment, we have a right to withdraw recognition—and an obligation to be reconciled given due penitence. Neither of these entails that we have a right to *enforce* the due penitence required: atonement is the right of the transgressor, not a duty we can enforce. The dialectic of ethical punishment does not tell us what right we have to enforce hard treatment, as against insisting on voluntary acceptance of due penitence before we are ready to be reconciled.

---

[21] Furthermore blame chills other relationships that one may want to maintain. For these good reasons, and other less good ones, we often want to bypass, soft-pedal, duck past the judicial element in blame, staying on equal, good terms with the other, being 'non-judgemental'.

[22] I have profited here from discussion with Tim Scanlon.

But of course there is the obvious point that criminals are people who unjustly put others in danger, cause them suffering, or at least impose unjust costs on them. It is our right to prevent and deter them from doing so. It thus seems inevitable that our best accounts of institutional punishment will be an amalgam of disparate considerations. On the one hand, the dialectic of ethical punishment takes the criminal to be a moral agent, who can see the rightness of a punishment proportioned to the wrong done, and voluntarily accepts it as route 'back to society'. In that sense, as Hegel famously said, punishment is a right (or law) of the criminal. It is not, as he also said, about threatening a dog with a stick.[23] It declares the law, and enacts due repentance even if the repentance isn't there. On the other hand, institutional punishment clearly does involve considerations of prevention and deterrence, and these can be justified in part as stemming from the right of self-defence. If this is our justifying basis, we do not need to assume that the criminal, or rather the threat, is a moral agent. The relevant criterion for preventive detention is minimum necessary force—a criterion quite different to that of what punitive treatment is deserved. Bear in mind also, however, that the right to exclude is not the right to abandon: the transgressor remains an object of moral concern, and we may have a duty of care. When we combine this duty with the need for self-defence, it may turn out that it can only be discharged in ways that require indefinite incarceration. Nonetheless, we still want the institutions of the law to *declare* the ethical basis of the law to the criminal and to others as moral agents, and this seems to require release of the criminal when desert is done. Between the logic of ethical punishment, the logic of self-defence, and the logic of deterrence there can be real tensions—but this is where legal punishment is placed.[24]

15.5 Recognition and respect

As noted at the beginning, we tend to recoil from the emotions involved in ethical punishment—guilt, remorse, repentance. Ethical standpoints that are roughly-speaking 'rationalist' and 'individualist' are likely to recoil most strongly. But these emotions are in no way inherently irrational. They may be misplaced or exaggerated, like any other feelings, or they may be based on sufficient reasons. Still, even though blindness to the rationality of emotions is a perennial source of weakness in ethics, it is not I think what mainly causes this particular recoil. Rather, there seems to be something primitive and frightening about *these* emotions, with their reference to community and exclusion. The anxiety remains even if we distinguish moral ideas clearly from the invidious notions of purity and pollution.

This anxiety is not misplaced, but that does not mean that we can or should remove its source. A way to see this is to contrast the notion of recognition that we have been

---

[23] Hegel 1991 (1821): 100, 99, addition.

[24] We also say the criminal has 'paid his debt' to society. The redemption metaphor is tempting just because repayment of a debt may permissibly be enforced when it is not made voluntarily; but the metaphor explains neither the desert nor the self-defence and deterrence elements in institutional punishment.

developing with the Kantian notion of respect, which for many provides a kind of sanitized surrogate.

For Kant respect plays a number of roles: it is basic to the modern civic ideal of equal dignity and respect due to every human being; it provides a substantive foundation for morality as such—for never treating persons merely as means; and it provides a way of formally characterizing what morality *is*. In the effort of sustaining these theses, Kant transforms respect into a metaphysical concept. Nonetheless, it is empirically based in an important and recognizable human feeling. This feeling is a constituent of the civic ideal of equal freedom and dignity, and hence rightly important. But I do not believe that it can get to the roots of what morality is.

Kant appeals to respect in at least three ways.

(i) There is the idea of respect or reverence (*Achtung*) as the distinctive attitude that is appropriate towards 'the moral law'.

(ii) There is the idea of respect as the distinctive attitude that is appropriate towards any being that has the capacity to make and act on moral valuations—which Kant thinks all human beings equally have:

> a human being regarded as a *person*, that is, as the subject of a morally practical reason, is exalted above any price; for as a person (*homo noumenon*) he is not to be valued merely as a means to the ends of others or even to his own ends, but as an end in itself, that is, he possesses a *dignity* (an absolute inner worth) by which he exacts *respect* for himself from all other rational beings in the world. He can measure himself with every other being of this kind and value himself on a footing of equality with them.[25]

(iii) There is the idea of respect as the distinctive attitude that is proper towards someone who does his or her duty, observes the imperatives of morality.[26]

Respect in sense (ii) cannot lend itself to characterizing what morality *is*. That is because the kind of respect, if any, that is called forth simply by the *capacity* for making and acting on moral valuations as such is called forth independently of how well or badly, in moral terms, the person who has the capacity acts. The point does not apply to the notion of respect involved in (iii). If we can identify an attitude that is appropriate just to those who carry out their moral obligations, then it may be possible to characterize moral obligation in terms of it. A moral obligation, we could say, is a type of warrant compliance with which gives sufficient reason for that attitude towards the person who complies. Likewise with (i): if there is a distinctive sentiment, *Achtung*, that is called forth just by those warrants that are moral obligations, then we can say that a moral obligation is that towards which *Achtung* is properly felt.

Let us consider the latter suggestion first. For Kant moral obligation is a relational notion: it presents or identifies categorical practical principles by reference to the

---

[25] Kant, *Metaphysics of Morals*, 6: 434–5.
[26] Compare Stephen Darwall's distinction between 'appraisal' and 'recognition respect' (Darwall 1977)—though for my purposes I am contrasting respect and recognition.

distinctive impact they make on *our* affective nature. He does not think that a Holy Will experiences practical laws as *moral obligations*. The Holy Will does not feel the sentiment of respect or reverence for the moral law; it is finite sensuous beings who experience practical laws as moral obligations, proper objects of the feeling of respect or reverence.

Kant provides an insightful phenomenology of this feeling. Respect for the moral law reduces the influence of self-love and:

> *strikes down* self-conceit altogether, since all claims to esteem for oneself that precede accord with the moral law are null and quite unwarranted because certainty of a disposition in accord with this law is the first condition of any worth of a person...[27]

Reverence for the law is thus connected with self-respect: in the absence of a reliably moral disposition other bases of self-esteem fall away. Furthermore, while Kant thinks that experiencing the law-giving of our own reason, that is, its imperatival effect on us, is elevating, he also thinks that it necessarily contains an element of burdensomeness or constraint: 'we stand under a *discipline* of reason' though it is 'our own reason' that gives it.[28] To imagine that we humans, with our sensuousness and our finite rationality, could transcend the moment of constraining discipline contained in the experience of moral obligation is, according to Kant, to think that we could be holy beings who do not experience practical oughts as moral imperatives at all, but simply and readily act on them. It is to usher in '*moral enthusiasm* instead of a sober but wise moral discipline'.[29]

This account presents reverence for the moral law as basic, respect for others and oneself as subsidiary. To experience a warrant as a moral obligation is to experience it as something one cannot violate on pain of loss of self-respect. Or: a moral obligation is a warrant acting from which merits such respect. Non-compliance—acting morally wrongly—removes merited respect; in other words, it merits *loss of respect* (in sense (iii)).

How different is this to our characterization in terms of withdrawal of recognition? Kant characterizes moral obligation in terms of the sentiment it arouses: characterizing a principle of practical reason as a *moral law* is saying that it appropriately gives rise to the distinctive sentiments towards it, oneself and others which we have just been considering. He thinks that the principle itself applies categorically, irrespective of that experience of it. We can agree with that, for we have argued that the reasons for doing something that is morally obligatory exist independently of its characterization as morally obligatory. It is their specific nature that make the action morally obligatory, an action that it is blameworthy not to do.

The difference that remains between our view and Kant's is thus the difference between respect and recognition and their respective loss in one's own eyes and others. Two differences should be highlighted in particular. (i) The Kantian idea of respect treats morality as an honour code which it seeks to transmute into a universal ideal: self-respect is derived from one's affiliation to a code that commands respect, and the degree to which one lives up to that code. In contrast, morality is more fundamental than any ideal. You do not

---

[27] Kant, *Critique of Practical Reason*, 5:73.   [28] Ibid, 5:82.   [29] Ibid, 5:86.

shrink from moral wrongdoing because it is *beneath* you, you shrink from it because it is wrong. (ii) The recognition model is more communally grounded. It connects moral knowledge and agency to recognition within a determinate community and its historically evolved morality, rather than to the individualistic metaphysical picture of a finite being's profoundly personal encounter with a noumenal realm of moral law.

15.6 Respect and honour

An honour code associates noble action with honour, esteem and pride, ignoble action with dishonour, contempt and shame. Much of what Kant says about servility and self-respect mobilizes these feelings, while detaching nobility of character from the idea of social rank that goes with them in their aristocratic version. He invokes an honour code for Everyman—every person, moral subject, representative of humanity:

> A human being can...be an object of my love, fear or admiration even to amazement and yet not be an object of respect. His jocular humour, his courage and strength, the power he has by his rank among others, could inspire me with feelings of this kind even though inner respect toward him is lacking. Fontenelle says '*I bow before an eminent man, but my spirit does not bow.*' I can add: before a humble common man in whom I perceive uprightness of character in a higher degree than I am aware of in myself *my spirit bows*, whether I want it or whether I do not and hold my head ever so high, that he may not overlook my superior position...*Respect* is a *tribute* that we cannot refuse to pay to merit, whether we want to or not; we may indeed withhold it outwardly but we still cannot help feeling it inwardly.[30]

This is moving and true. The respect that is due to moral merit, uprightness of character—and that is explicitly what Kant has in mind here—is distinguishable from all questions of rank, and from all other excellence. Respect of this most fundamental kind is due to any person who grasps their moral obligations and acts, even in adverse circumstances, on what they grasp. It is the due attitude towards people of moral integrity.

Now consider the use Kant makes of this attitude of respect in his advocacy of morality. Honour codes confer self-respect on the basis of one's status and one's ability to live up to it. In the ideal type of an aristocratic ethic, the self-respect that distinguished status confers arises not just from *having* that status but from *living up* to its obligations. Essential to the point is that these are obligations that those who don't have the status don't have—as Nietzsche emphasized, the meaning or self-worth conferred by an honour code presupposes the 'pathos of distance'. What then creates the distance for Kant? It is our standing as moral beings *in comparison with the rest of nature*, and our success in living up to that standing. Respect in sense (ii) is thus related to respect in sense (iii), in exactly the way that an honour code links a status to success in living up to that status. Honour, or respect, results from living up to one's standing, shame and disgrace are the sanctions.

[30] Ibid, 5:77.

Kant connects the two forms of respect—(ii) and (iii)—in this way in his fascinating discussion of servility in *Metaphysics of Morals*:

> This duty with reference to the dignity of humanity within us, and so to ourselves, can be recognised, more or less, in the following examples. Be no man's lackey.—Do not let others tread with impunity on your rights.—Contract no debt for which you cannot give full security.—Do not accept favours you could do without, and do not be a parasite or a flatterer or (what really differs from these only in degree) a beggar. Be thrifty, then, so that you will not become destitute.—Complaining and whining, even crying out in bodily pain, is unworthy of you, especially if you are aware of having deserved it; thus a criminal's death may be ennobled (its disgrace averted) by the resoluteness with which he dies.—Kneeling down or prostrating oneself on the ground, even to show your veneration for heavenly objects, is contrary to the dignity of humanity... one who makes himself a worm cannot complain afterwards if people step on him.[31]

The distinctions Kant makes here, between humility and servility, arrogance, and self-respect, appeal to a discipline and ideal of the noble. In a group regulated by an honour code, the code is the fundamental object of reverence. Self-respect is founded on the degree to which one knows oneself to have lived up to it, humility on the fact that one can never do so fully. One measures oneself only by the code to which one is bound.

Kant writes about morality in the same vein. Humility, he says, as against servility, arises not from comparing ourselves to other people but from judging ourselves by the moral law. Arrogance involves inappropriate comparison of oneself with others, self-respect, the judgement that one has succeeded in following the code.[32] His strategy of persuasion is to put every person, every representative of humanity, on their mettle by appeal to an honour code that gives to all the 'sublime vocation' of rational beings. Mere nobility of birth or social power become utterly irrelevant. *All* of us are placed distantly above—incommensurably above—the merely natural domain. This is Kant's ideal, or honour code of Humanity.

There is a good deal more to Kant's ethics than this, and which need not depend on this; yet the honour code of Humanity is a vital part of its appeal. For within modern ethics there is a current of individualist humanism, a commitment to the dignity of all human beings simply as human beings. Kantian transcendentalism provides this humanism with a cosmic setting which can have genuinely inspiring effects, though it can also seem hollow or quixotic. But the important point to grasp is that neither this ideal, with or without transcendentalism, nor *any* honour code, however universal, could accomplish

---

[31] Kant, *Metaphysics of Morals*, 6:436–7. Compare 6:463: 'I cannot deny all respect to even a vicious man as a man; I cannot withdraw at least the respect that belongs to him in his quality as a man, even though by his deeds *he makes himself unworthy* of it' (my emphasis). Kant proceeds to condemn certain punishments as disgraceful because they 'dishonour humanity itself'. Similarly, an aristocratic society will hold that an aristocrat deserves a certain respect just in virtue of his status as an aristocrat, despite his wrongdoing, and shield him from certain punishments on the grounds that they would dishonour the aristocratic status itself.

[32] Ibid, 6: 435–6.

the continuous everyday work of constituting and reconstituting moral life. That requires something closer to universal human bedrock than the modern ideal of the dignity of humans as humans: closer to the moral sentiments and the reciprocal relations of recognition, ethical punishment and reconciliation which they mobilize and direct. It is from these sources that moral judgement acquires its social power and its social authority.

15.7 The elementary forms of the moral life

Moral judgement structures all societies, not just post-aristocratic democracies with a liberal humanist ideal. The moral sentiments of blame, guilt, remorse, and reconciliation are, I believe, elementary structures of human sensibility. They mix and blend in many ways with many other feelings—sentiments of pride and shame mobilized in various honour codes, sentiments of gratitude and resentment, sentiments of disgust and horror. It is not inevitable that they dominate, but it is their nature to do so. Pride and shame, when not corrupted, submit to them. Gratitude and resentment presuppose beliefs about rights and thus are in turn responses to them. Pollution feelings decline when moral sentiments detach from them.

The social practices and philosophical, and religious self-understandings that derive from them vary. But the order of explanation is this way round: from the sentiments to the understandings. It follows that moral judgement, and its distinctive concept of obligation, is not a product of religion.[33] Morality may be conceived in various ways. It may be conceived as the age-old law and custom of our community. Or it may be conceived as the universal law of one sovereign God. In the modern West there is a fundamental shift from these traditional and religious 'command' models to a 'self-governance' model.[34] Moral obligation comes to be conceived as something distinct from both custom and sovereign law, as that which moral agents know through their own conscience. Conscience itself shifts from being the voice of an omnipotent external sovereign to being the voice of one's own true self. Yet through these transformations at the level of content and conception morality itself, the constitution of social relations by the moral sentiments and dispositions, stands firm. Moral judgement persists even as these understandings vary.

A social functionalist could well say that it persists because it plays indispensable roles. The roles of moral judgement are verdictive, disciplinary, and (potentially) emancipatory. They arise because morality judges of reasons for feeling that involve recognition and its withdrawal. For that same reason, moral judgement always starts from a relationship to historically determinate communal judgement—moral common sense.

The verdictive role of moral judgement is to be sensitive to all the sources of practical reasons and *resolve* them in concrete cases, in a way that preserves the categoricity of the moral. Moral judgement serves as an arbiter of practical reasons, though of course in

---

[33] Religion in traditional societies is cosmology. The moral order of society provides an explanatory paradigm for that cosmic order (Skorupski 1976).
[34] See Schneewind 1998 for an account of this shift up to Kant.

many cases it does not get involved at all. But whence comes the knowledge from which these verdicts are delivered?

If anyone has moral knowledge some must have it on the basis of personal moral insight. At one end of the spectrum, moral conviction might be transmitted by trust in the moral judgement of some few wise people who are accepted as having moral insight. There could have been an enormously wise being, or committee of wise beings, that could help us to moral knowledge. (Even then, it could only help: what we freely accepted and trusted would still be the contribution *we* made.) At the other end, moral insight and autonomy might be equally available to all, through consulting their own conscience.

All that moral agency conceptually requires is self-determination, not autonomy (12.4). Even if we are all equally autonomous, however, the epistemic role of community remains. We have already seen one way in which the resolution of practical reasons in concrete cases is accountable to communal moral appraisal—through what I called Hegel's private morality argument in 14.6. As noted there, this is a general point about the dialogical character of all normative knowledge. Personal normative knowledge is possible only through dialogical response to a collective state of judgement—which one can agree with or criticize but which provides an essential framework. Thus moral common sense is essentially involved in moral judgement's verdictive role.

But Hegel's insight into moral life goes further. *Moral* judgement in particular involves a reference to communal judgement that goes beyond the general point that normative knowledge is dialogical. This special relationship to communal judgement arises, as already noted, because of the particular emotions whose reasons it judges, and their connection with withdrawal of recognition—the disciplinary role.

It is instructive to consider again the case of utilitarianism. We have seen the impossibility of getting from pure utilitarianism to morality without a premise that appeals to moral insight (13.8 to 13.10).[35] If pure utilitarianism takes its 'shoulds' (or its warrants) to be moral obligations, i.e. adopts an act-utilitarian moral premise, it is often said to be 'too demanding'. But where does this judgement of excessive demandingness come from? It does not come from a recondite calculation about when, from the standpoint of Good, act-utilitarian behaviour becomes counterproductive. It comes from the judgements of moral common sense about when there is reason to blame, and these involve verdicts about the relative weight of Good-based and other reasons. When does a failure to assist, for example, become blameworthy? It depends on what other reasons were in play. We should judge the question by our own conscience, but it is proper for conscience to take into account what is generally thought—not just because that is the way of normative judgement in general, but because in this case we are making judgements about blame, recognition, and its *communal* withdrawal.

In contrast, a 'post-moral' pure utilitarianism[36] requires no such verdicts because it does not believe in moral obligations. One might say it is not too demanding because it doesn't

---

[35] It is just as impossible to get to morality from the Demand principle alone. The application of this principle presupposes moral judgement.

[36] Discussed in 13.10.

exact anything: any attempt a post-moral utilitarian makes to borrow the force of moral judgement (as against coercion justified on utilitarian grounds) is confused or phoney. There is no more moral force behind its 'shoulds' then there is behind my conclusion that I should take a taxi instead of the car. Not doing what I know I should incurs at most the shame of being irrational (a pain that has less effect on most people than it may have on philosophers). It cannot mobilize the power of the moral sentiments, and thus remains feeble. The verdictive role of common moral judgement disappears because its disciplinary role disappears.

In various ways common sense verdicts of blameworthiness turn on what it is reasonable to expect. There is what you can reasonably be expected to have noticed, considered, etc, what precautions you can reasonably be expected to have taken, what you can be reasonably expected to take on by way of burden. Such judgements of reasonableness are characteristically communal judgements.[37]

This is *not* to say that the accepted morality of the community is always right. Accepted moral judgements can be criticized immanently, from the standpoint of individual conscience. *Pace* Hegel, they can certainly also be criticized from the standpoint of an abstract theory, whether of Good or Right. Galahad (14.4) can legitimately argue that we are not moved enough by the principle of Good. He can dismiss actual blame, and thus actual withdrawal of recognition, on the grounds that it is undeserved. He can argue that the common judgements of blameworthiness fall short of their own immanent standards. But he can also argue that they are simply wrong, that they have got on to a wrong track, by direct appeal to his own conscience or in the light of a general view of the relative importance of Good. Firmness of personal moral judgement may give him the strength to stand out against the community. Nothing I have said implies that he *couldn't* be right. It is only moral judgement itself, not philosophy, that can weigh whether he is dogmatic and stubborn or insightful, responsible, and thus free.

We cannot construct morality either from the purely individual standpoint of conscience or from that of abstract theory. Without moral common sense there is no *point d'appui*. In practice that is recognized by all moral advocates and even by all seekers after moral knowledge, whatever they may think in theory.

Moral common sense can get it wrong; or again, since moral wrongness is relative to warrant, the judgement of a moral community might be right relative to its epistemic warrants, but wrong relative to ours. Furthermore, blameworthiness can diverge from moral wrongness through extenuation. In particular it allows for extenuation through justifiable failure to grasp warrant.

There has, for example, always been a right not to be enslaved. So ancient Greek slavery was morally wrong unless warranted insight into that right was impossible in that

---

[37] There is an affinity here to contractualist approaches to morality of a broadly 'Kantian' kind, such as Scanlon's (1998). But these, including Scanlon's, seem, *prima facie*, to work with a too individualistic notion of reasonable (dis)agreement. To say that their judgements of reasonableness implicitly appeal to a particular tradition of a particular community would be a defence against this objection, not itself an objection. But another difference would remain, at least with respect to Scanlon's theory: our approach does not identify the property of moral wrongness with any property characterizable in terms of reasonable agreement, but with a property characterizable in terms of reason-supported blame. Reasonable agreement belongs to the epistemology, not the constitution, of the moral.

moral community. To argue that it was *impossible* would be too strong. There were voices that questioned slavery;[38] they could have been listened to, and the force of what they were saying recognized. Still, was the average Greek slave-owner blameworthy? There was warrant to believe that slavery was wrong; reasonableness, however, pertains to justification, not warrant. The slave-owner might justifiably, though incorrectly, have thought that slavery as such was not wrong. So might the slaves. They might have been 'legitimately' captured in war. Could a warrior captured in a war reasonably object to his enslavement? Could he justly blame the victor for it? Perhaps only a slave-owner who treated his slaves unjustly by the enlightened understandings of his time would be blameworthy.[39]

15.8 Liberal community: freedom and impartiality

Moral judgement clearly has a disciplinary role; this disciplinary role is also an emancipatory role, a contribution to living in freedom.

Freedom in the fullest positive sense is autonomy: recognizing reasons by personal insight and acting on them. Since knowledge of reasons is dialogical, a judgement based on personal insight into reasons still commits the person who makes the judgement to an assumption about communal judgement. But at this level the implicit community of co-judgers is a highly idealized one. Autonomous moral judgement is possible where *actual* communal moral judgement has little authority or force: in the Gulag, in the war of all against all. It is possible in situations in which the distinctively moral sentiments are baffled or stunned, situations beyond normal moral judgement. Psychically strong individuals may maintain autonomy, inner freedom, even in the Gulag.[40] They can still respond to the practical–normative sources; it becomes a question of determination to act as one can act and sees to be best, of ethical heroism.

But the inner freedom that matters to most people fortunately does not require this level of armour-plated autonomy. What it requires is the freedom of *moral integrity*. This is an ideal of the responsible person, as friend, relative, professional, or citizen. It is an ideal that appeals to a desire to do what can reasonably be expected of one, to play one's part, achieving self-respect and the respect of others while pursuing the concerns of personal life. It assumes not so much full Kantian autonomy as self-determination and an integrity based on the moral emotions and communal moral judgement.

Here the moral sentiments—the sentiment of blame, together with the associated, reciprocating, emotions of remorse, repentance, and reconciliation—can play a significant role. In well-functioning moral life moral judgement forms and reforms both moral personality and the allegiance and trust on which moral community rests. Acceptance of blame grounds a freely accepted discipline that is the freedom of moral integrity.

---

[38] The sophist Antiphon seems to have opposed the doctrine of 'natural slaves'.
[39] According to student notes Hegel thought that Greek slavery was valid but wrong (57, addition). However, he had a different point in mind: the alleged progressiveness, from the world-historical standpoint, of ancient slavery.
[40] Schier 1993.

Through it the wrongdoer recovers standing as an answerable moral agent with whom it is possible to live in free relations resting on trust. Moral integrity, responsibility, 'respectability', is something that only successful heroes or prophets in the wilderness can lightly dismiss.

We are clearly in Hegelian territory: 'The individual…finds his *liberation* in duty.'[41] Freedom as moral integrity requires that the verdicts of moral judgement acquire force, command respect; that requires enough concrete community for a moral common sense to emerge. It may seem odd to use the notion of moral integrity in this way, given its sometimes existentialist connotations. But the basic idea is the undivided self—the self true to itself. It is a modernist fallacy to think that for most people, at most times, integrity is only achievable by a withdrawal from communal judgement that privileges lonely autonomous choice. That may become necessary when well-functioning moral life breaks down, but then it is only possible for a very few. We could call this kind of freedom, freedom as moral integrity, 'Hegelian' autonomy. When Hegel says:

> a man must possess a personal knowledge of the distinction between good and evil in general: ethical and moral principles shall not merely lay their claim on him as external laws and precepts of authority to be obeyed, but have their assent, recognition, or even justification in his heart, sentiment, conscience, intelligence, etc.

he still requires personal normative knowledge but allows for a kind of knowledge that is not full first-personal *insight* ('assent, recognition, or even justification'). Recognition of 'ethical and moral principles' may derive from at oneness with a community, trust in its moral common sense, yet still be knowledge.[42]

Moral common sense can cease to function well either by complete breakdown, as in the war of all against all, or by becoming despotic. In the latter case it undermines freedom instead of enabling it, by giving force without authority to communal judgement. So a balance must be struck. This is the balance Hegel seeks to strike in his account of modern moral life.[43] On the one hand, moral knowledge and the goods of moral life—as against individual ethical heroism—can be empowered only within a determinate moral community. On the other, the claims of individuality and universal impartiality must both find their place. This is true in any community: there are always some accepted agent-neutral moral obligations, obligations of rescue to strangers, for example. And there is always respect for individuality in some shape or form, however minimal. Nevertheless, it seems fair to say that in modern moral life these acquire unprecedented importance.

---

[41] Hegel 1991 (1821): 149.

[42] Hegel 1971 (1817): 503. In more abstractly philosophical terms, 'Kantian' and 'Hegelian' autonomy could be contrasted by reference to warrant relative to an epistemic state versus warrant relative to a person's normative powers (15.8). A Hegelian autonomous act proceeds from person-relative warrant. The normative elements in such a warrant may be testimony-based. In Kantian autonomy the act proceeds not just from warrant but from fully first-personal insight into all the underlying a priori warrants.

[43] It is another question whether his substantive social and political views successfully achieve it. For me, certainly not: I find Mill a much better guide than Hegel, though obviously all guides are highly fallible.

In this modern form of moral life individuality is reflected in the right of conscience and a right of self-governing private life, agent-neutrality in the modern prominence of Good and Right, whose universalism and abstract foundation stands out ever more clearly. These are cosmopolitan principles, requiring concern for the interests and rights of everyone, not just family members, fellow professionals, or fellow citizens.

How thick a community do moral knowledge and allegiance need? Could there be a cosmopolitan 'community'? Would it lose moral judgement?

Moral life within a community starts from the agent-relative and always remains dominated by it, however widely these relations may spread. There is what I am obliged to do because I hold this position in the web of roles, or again, what I am obliged to do because various groups to which I normatively belong have legitimately decided to pursue some goals and I must now play my fair part, or again, what I am obliged to do because of the history of specific understandings that I or my family or lineage have engaged in. Citizenship is agent-relative: we think, for example, that we have obligations to maintain health care for our fellow citizens, which we do not have towards the whole world.

We cannot wholly lose the agent-relative obligations without losing community, for community is a moral entity not a matter of personal preference like a club. The epistemic and psychic importance of allegiance and trust are fundamental to the well-functioning authority and force of moral judgement. They in turn depend in part on the well functioning of the discipline of recognition-withdrawal and thus of some concrete community that plays these roles. These are the essential elements that ground moral confidence.

Thus how thin a community can be depends on how thin it can be while maintaining allegiance and trust. How communal does moral judgement have to be? Or: how much can one rely on Kantian autonomy and explicit agreement alone, as against situated moral personality and community? To emphasize the importance of allegiance and trust need not be a non-liberal standpoint, as one should learn from both Hegel and Mill. Nonetheless, the cosmopolitan strain in contemporary liberalism strongly encourages either post-moralism or an embattled stance of individualist (as against situated) 'moral' integrity. In a stark world of individual and cosmos moral judgement loses its roles.

15.9 Criticism of morality

We have been considering what moral judgement does when it works well. As noted at the beginning, it can also work badly. In this final section the worries about morality we shall consider are not broad philosophical attacks on morality's very coherence: they do not arise from scepticism or nihilism about normative claims in general, say, or from metaphysical doubts about the very possibility of responsibility (as against empirical doubts about how responsible people in fact are). These broad philosophical attacks, if sound, would make it redundant to ask what moral judgement does when it works well. They can only be disarmed at a similarly broad and abstract level, the level we shall reach in Part IV. Granting, however, that moral judgement is not philosophically unsound *ab initio*—allowing that it can have genuine authority and is not in principle misguided—we can consider how it can nevertheless go wrong. In an obvious sense a moral judgement goes wrong when it is false. However, the worry we should consider is a practical worry about morality's potential for *oppression*.

There are cases in which doing one's duty is hard, and cases in which it is hard to know one's duty. Such situations can feel oppressive, but they too are not our concern; these are not cases in which morality is failing to work as it should. The serious worry arises because moral disciplines engage with elementary reactions involving outcasting, remorse, and atonement: reactions which, when corrupted, can be terribly destructive.

Withdrawal of recognition, however temporary and muted, can be a frightening thing. There is thus a healthy human reluctance, especially in well-ordered tolerant societies, or in small-scale societies and groups where expulsion or punishment may be costly,[44] to resort to explicit moral condemnation. If one has to criticize, one prefers to criticize in other terms. So too in the case of a friend one may be reluctant to come even to an unexpressed verdict of blame, because of the chilling, distancing effect it will have on one's attitudes and acts (anger, on the other hand, can be quite therapeutic). Again a child is chilled, thrown back on itself, made to think about what it has done, by being sent to its bedroom. Or so the parents hope (forlornly, perhaps, if it has a computer there). But they may well also worry that their action may have a too disrupting effect, undermining family relations that they want to be close. Explicit moral condemnation is perilous and should properly be felt to be so. Quite apart from anything else, it is right to remember that one may not know all the circumstances, cannot see inside a soul, and so on.

Moral judgement is, indeed, 'judgemental'. This is often an implied criticism: but the whole point of moral judgement is to judge. Moral blame is *meant* to have a psychic and social force that other kinds of disvaluing verdict are not meant to have. A person may be offended by being told his behaviour is crass, or lacking in dignity or pathetic, or ridiculous, or that he is 'letting himself down', but he may instead tough it out and return contempt for contempt. We may think him mistaken in doing so but, we may say, 'that's *his* problem'.

True, such disobliging opinions in practice have great force within particular peer groups, through the desire to belong. But while moral judgement cannot wholly condemn this human tendency it suspects it and seeks to limit it, jealously guarding its own special force. Seriously intended moral condemnation raises the ante; to work on the individual as it should it must retain its power to shock. It purports to speak for the community, the universal, in the way that a criminal indictment comes from 'the people'. It *should* be felt as dangerous, because it legitimizes attitudes of exclusion which must otherwise be kept in check, even if one disapproves in other ways. One cannot just shrug it off as an opinion one doesn't share, or doesn't care about—one must accept it and repent or actively defend oneself by arguing that it is mistaken. A parallel contrast holds between morality and ideals. I can respect the ideals of others, endorse their worth, not just shrug them off, but still not accept them as guides to how I should act. But morality is not

---

[44] See Silberbauer 1991: 22.

something I can just respectfully decide not to live by in that way. I cannot endorse a moral judgement while respectfully deciding that morality is not for me. (Because, for example, the ideal of 'human dignity' strikes me as empty.)

Withdrawal of recognition gives morality, as a positive human institution, its potentially dangerous charge. The honour code of individualist humanism feels less menacing. It can be elevating, especially in contexts where the point is that moral or civil respect are not dependent on class or status. But one should not overestimate the persuasive power of appeals to dignity, to not letting yourself down—not least of appeals to the presumed dignity of being human. The moral feelings are rooted much deeper than a humanistic or religious ideal of equal dignity. Their roots are the most primitive roots of identity and membership. For just that reason, when they are misdirected or irresponsibly inflamed they can turn very ugly—if, for example, they drive a young man to 'become a devoted member of the Hitler Jugend' or a young woman to think it is better to be 'a servile housewife than complete outcast'.[45] What is horrifying in these cases is that emotional forces that should sustain moral integrity are perverted into the very opposite; that routes to recognition provided by remorse and atonement are degraded into their nightmarish caricatures, self-abasement and self-betrayal. Just because the moral emotions are a part of our self-recognition, our sense of 'who we are', their corruption—in civil wars, social panics, identity-undermining interrogations, the hunting out of scapegoats or blameobjects—is very frightening. We are brought up against the pathology and exploitation of attitudes of membership and recognition which normally underlie and are only reluctantly brought to the surface.

In the face of these very real dangers the best we can do is to be alert to and stand up to them, fighting corrupt morality with morality. There is, however, a rather different worry that deserves consideration in this section. It is that morality systemically makes unrealistic assumptions about how responsive to moral considerations people are and can be expected to be, and thereby places blame on those who do not deserve it. To how many people, and to what extent, can we attribute the moral powers: ability to see what moral obligations bear on one's conduct and ability to act in accord with them? It is part of moral common sense that a wrongdoer's inability to act otherwise is extenuating, and there is then the empirical question of how far a wrongdoer could be said to have had the ability in the particular case. But there is also the question of how much insight a person has into reasons and their moral salience.[46]

Thesis (4) in 12.3 asserted the (weak) categoricity of moral obligation: if it is morally wrong for x to α then x has warranted reason not to α. It follows that if a person has no warranted reason to α, they have no moral obligation to α. But what of people who are

---

[45] The examples are Theo von Willigenburg's (Willigenburg 2003: 363), to whom I am grateful for making me think about these issues.

[46] 'Situationist' doubts about the reality of character (e.g. Doris 2002) are also related to this kind of worry, since morality's notion of personal responsibility assumes character, in the sense of steady, self-determined purposes. (Compare Mill: 'it is only when our purposes have become independent from the feelings of pain or pleasure from which they originally took their rise, that we are said to have a confirmed character...the will, once so fashioned, may be steady and constant, when the passive susceptibilities of pleasure and pain are greatly weakened, or materially changed.' Mill (1963–91, vol. VIII: 154.)

insensitive to some morally salient reasons? Do they nonetheless have them? Are they blameworthy if they don't act on them? We encountered a version of this worry in connection with Williams' doctrine of internal reasons (10.6 to 8).

Although we rejected Williams' motivational internalism, we saw the attraction of cognitive internalism. And this has the same implication. Morally salient reasons of gratitude are just not reasons for gratitude-blind Tom (10.8). Borrowing Williams' terms we can say that they are 'external' with respect to Tom, though cognitively rather than motivationally.

We could say that there are reasons for Tom to feel gratitude if he could but know it. But this looks like a *façon de parler*, as when we say that there is reason for a bird to feel gratitude if it could but know it (10.8). We are not really imputing reasons to the bird or to Tom, we are just saying that someone has done them some good. The bird does not fall within the scope of universal generalizations about reasons for gratitude and nor does Tom.

Yet there is a desire to impute these external reasons to Tom, unlike the bird. Williams interestingly asks why this should be:

> what would these external reasons do to these people, or for our relations to them? Unless we are given an answer to this question, I, for one, find it hard to resist Nietzsche's plausible interpretation, that the desire of philosophy to find a way in which morality can be guaranteed to get beyond merely *designating* the vile and recalcitrant, to transfixing them or getting them inside, is only a fantasy of *ressentiment*, a magical project to make a wish and its words into a coercive power.[47]

He evidently assumes that a satisfactory answer cannot be given, and thus moves to the Nietzschean interpretation, which explains our desire to get people who have done vile things 'inside morality' as a resentful, indignant, or vengeful wish to hurt them, a wish that wishes to legitimate itself as the right to inflict due punishment. For due punishment presupposes that the morally relevant reasons can be imputed to the blameworthy.

If we still want to impute these reasons to these people the Nietzschean interpretation may apply: we want more than clear-headed self-defence, we also want to retaliate; the 'fantasy of *ressentiment*' moralizes this desire by saying that these people, really, *can* see the reasons for not doing what they do. It needs to do so because punishment in its ethical sense is an instrument of atonement, reconciliation, and thus envisages that the wrongdoer can be brought to recognize those reasons. Thus the wish to hurt a bad person calls up the belief that they can see the wrongness of what they do: if we gave up the belief we could not justify hurting them as being what they deserve.

If *this* is our thinking it is itself open to criticism from the moral point of view. We should not blame such people for the wrong they do. But surely there is also a more idealistic motive at work: the democratic desire to give everyone equal respect. And there is the feeling, not least among people who most have this desire, that the kind of respect which is most worth having, or even the only kind that is really worth having, is respect for one's capacity personally to recognize and act on the moral law.

---

[47] Williams, B. 1995c: 216.

The consequent desire to insulate moral agency from the actual facts of human psychology creates fictions, such as Kantian transcendental egalitarianism about autonomy (12.4). If we remove the transcendentalism we see that the empirical capacities involved in moral agency are complex and that people may have them in different domains of acting for a reason in different degrees. The fully autonomous human being is an ideal to which few if any approximate.

Consider Tom again. We denied, in virtue of cognitive internalism, that there is reason for him to feel gratitude, and on that basis we denied that he has a moral obligation of gratitude. Several points might be made in response to this.

In the first place some will agree that Tom is not blameworthy for failing to discharge obligations of gratitude, but still hold that those obligations do apply to him. They treat his inability to see the relevant reasons as excusing his non-compliance with the obligation, rather than defeating the claim that he has the obligation. One case for doing so, given the discussion of Chapter 12, would have to be that moral obligation follows ideal, state-relative warrant (5.8, note): it is what an agent who has Kantian moral autonomy, unrestricted normative powers, can recognize as such. This is certainly a possible way to go, but why insist on it? We are not trying to blame Tom. Nor do we have to impute the relevant reasons of gratitude to him by the universalizability of reasons, for we have seen that universalizability is compatible with cognitive internalism (3.9). Furthermore a moral philosophy that strongly ties moral agency to the Insight principle is likely to connect moral obligation to person-relative as against state-relative warrant. However, we do not need to legislate on this: what would be oppressive, on any of these options, would be to blame Tom.

In the second place it could be pointed out that even if cognitive internalism is granted, it does not follow that Tom has no obligation of gratitude. In arguing from cognitive internalism to the conclusion that Tom has no such obligation we implicitly assumed that if there is no reason for him to feel gratitude he can't be warranted in thinking that there is.[48] Yet might he not be warranted in thinking that there is, simply on the basis of what others tell him, even though he can't see it for himself? In that case he has *warranted* reason to be grateful—sufficient reason to believe that there is reason to be grateful—on the basis of testimony, even though there *is* no reason for him (warrant is not factive). In the same way he may know by testimony that this warranted reason is morally salient. And warranted belief that there is morally salient reason is all that moral categoricity requires.

However, this seems a too externalist view of moral agency. Suppose Tom says 'You tell me that there is a reason to say thank you, but I just can't see it? So why should I accept it, and how can you legitimately blame me if I do not?' Can we answer that he should accept our testimony, and is blameworthy for his ingratitude if he does not?

---

[48] Tom may accept that there is reason to say thank you because he knows that people will be hurt if he doesn't, though he doesn't understand why. On that basis, if he can see the moral obligation not to hurt people needlessly, he may see a concrete moral obligation to do some of the things gratitude requires. But this is not seeing the evaluative reason they see: the reason of gratitude.

In general, obviously, I can have a reason to do something simply on the basis that trustworthy people tell me that there is reason for me to do it. They might be sworn to secrecy as to the facts and can't tell me why. But this is lack of direct knowledge of the facts, not lack of personal insight into reason relations. It seems to me that it is appropriate for people to tell me that there is reason for me to do something only if they can legitimately hold that if I knew the facts I would see that there was that reason, or could be brought by free normative discussion to see it. Counter-examples to this general rule rest on appeal to removable disabilities that block the power of normative insight that I do have. So it is not clear that Tom has testimony-based warrant for the belief that he has reason to thank.

The point is that some degree of free, personal acceptance of the relevant moral norm is necessary for moral autonomy. It is hard to say whether this is just a 'modern' requirement. At any rate it seems a good one. To return to the passage from Hegel quoted in the previous section:

> a man must possess a personal knowledge of the distinction between good and evil in general: ethical and moral principles shall not merely lay their claim on him as external laws and precepts of authority to be obeyed, but have their assent, recognition, or even justification in his heart, sentiment, conscience, intelligence, etc.

Personal moral knowledge can derive from such attitudes as trust, faith, reverence, or solidarity. Some people have personal insight ('justification'), others assent, accept, through trust in and reverence for the morals of the community, and even a desire for moral standing in its eyes. Yet they are not blind followers, who are simply acting on what they have been told. They are freely responding, out of spontaneous feeling for the common voice.

Recognizing the complexity and independent variability of moral capacities is important because it helps us to avoid a social and political picture which simplistically divides people into sheep and shepherds: those who just can't attain responsibility and those who have it absolutely. Responsibility—responsiveness to moral reasons—is a short word for a multiform capacity which comes in degrees. It is not a package deal. Developing the various kinds of responsiveness it requires should not mainly be a matter of communing in solitude with one's private conscience (though the degree to which it has to be is a matter of the society in which one lives). It should be dialogical: I come to appreciate reasons which I wouldn't have come to see on my own by listening to what people I respect think. I am willingly recruited into this deliberative community, seeing myself as a genuine member, not a follower. This, surely, is the element of truth in Williams' proleptic theory of blame. A certain ruggedly conscience-driven and egalitarian attitude would emphasize that doing the right thing out of a mere desire for solidarity is doing it for the wrong reason and thus cannot earn respect. The element of truth in this makes it difficult to see what is limiting and ungenerous in it. A more forgiving and worldly wisdom says that motives can't be so finely discriminated, that the desire for respect shades into the desire to do those things that command respect for the very reasons for which they command it, and that the desire for respect, or even honour and glory, is in any case in no way an ignoble desire.[49] These are spontaneous emotional sources on which a well-functioning morality can rightly draw. They are not ways of beating, scaring, indoctrinating, or manipulating people into assent.

But it is time to complete our discussion of normativity by turning, in Part IV, to meta-normative issues.

---

[49] On this Hegel is acute against the purism of Kant and others: see e.g. Hegel 1991 (1821): 124, with its addition.

PART IV

The Normative View

16

THE EPISTEMOLOGY OF REASON RELATIONS

When an appearance is given to us, we are still quite free as to how we should judge the matter.

In order to judge objectively, universally, that is, apodictically, reason must be free of subjectively determining grounds; for if they did determine reason, the judgement would be as it is only contingently, namely, because of subjective causes.[1]

The final part of this book turns to the meta-theory of the normative domain. This domain, as Parts I to III have shown, is the domain of reasons. Our subject therefore is the epistemology and ontology of reasons; our aim is a critique of reasons.

As noted in 1.2, critique, in this Kantian sense, takes a non-revisionary attitude to 'common cognition'—that is, to serious first-order aesthetics, ethics, history, science. Common cognition is ever revisable, but immanently, by its own norms. The Critical question is not *whether*, but *how*, correct claims about reasons in these various fields are possible.

The answer should have a positive and negative aspect. The positive aspect is description: describing our epistemic practice, the conditions which we *actually* think to be required for a normative claim to be warranted, and in which we consider ourselves to have normative knowledge. Showing that we do indeed have warrant when these conditions apply is the negative task. It largely consists in defusing arguments that purport to show normative warrant and knowledge to be impossible, by identifying the faulty philosophical theses from which these conclusions flow. Reasons are not like the Higgs particle or extra-terrestrial life. Claims to know that these exist must stand up against epistemic norms that we apply when we consider whether a hypothesis is justified by the evidence. We know (within a context of scientific theory) what kind of evidence would be evidence that they exist. The question is whether they do. But with reasons it is not a question whether there are reasons. Of course there are. We know there are, but not by inference to a substantive explanation of some data. The question is how we know it: what the epistemology of the normative is.

---

[1] From Kant's *Prolegomena to Any Future Metaphysics*, IV: 290 and *Reflexion* 5413 (XVIII 176)—both passages are cited in Pippin 1997: 35.

It is telling that sceptical, error-theoretic and fictionalist views have most power when directed specifically at morality. Claims about moral obligation are a special class of claims about evaluative reasons, and evaluative reasons are neither more nor less problematic, meta-theoretically, than other reasons. If these worries, considered as specific worries about morality, had their main source at the meta-level one would expect them to ramify. But in fact they borrow their power from substantive criticisms of morality that really have been powerful in our culture, say from Marx, Nietzsche, or Freud onwards. These assert the ideological origin of moral doctrines, or more deeply, the oppressive role and effect of the moral emotions as such. Our present day uncertainties about the very idea of morality are in good part their effect. If people weren't consciously or unconsciously influenced by the idea that morality is a kind of oppression, repression, or enslavement, it would be impossible to explain why they so often think that *moral* judgement raises epistemological or metaphysical doubts that other forms of normative judgement do not raise.[2]

We sought to answer some of this substantive criticism of morality in the previous chapter. In this part of the book, however, we are leaving substantive questions about particular kinds of reasons behind. Our task now is to consider meta-issues about the normative as a whole, on their own merits.

Controversy about the status of the normative has come to have a distinctive shape. On the one side, have been realists, naturalistic, and non-naturalistic, on the other, have been non-cognitivists. Both sides have sought to answer the question of how correct normative claims are possible, in ways we shall consider. However, our main aim will be to show that neither of these opposing stances is required. We shall argue that propositions about reason relations are not about any domain of substantial facts, natural or 'non-natural'. The basic point, embarrassingly obvious and simple, as such basic points tend to be, is that factual and normative propositions are different. Factual propositions state that some fact obtains; purely normative propositions do not. They have no factual content. The difficulty is to see the implications of this simple truth in a perspicuous way.

I have called the resulting stance—cognitivist but irrealist—the Normative view (1.5.8). It applies uniformly to all three kinds of reason: epistemic; evaluative; and practical. They all have the same epistemological and ontological standing. At the meta-level there is a unity of reason, even though at the substantive level there is indefinite diversity.

The Normative view entails rejection of the correspondence or picture 'theory' of propositions, as for brevity one labels it. More accurately speaking, however, it is not so much a matter of 'rejecting' a 'theory' as of showing that there is really no intelligible theory or thesis *there*, as against platitudes acceptable on all sides. The correspondence 'theory' is, of course, a much-discussed subject; our aim in discussing it will not to be to provide new arguments but simply to explain the reasons (in no way novel) for holding it to be a pseudo-thesis. More interesting to us will be the further consequences of this conclusion. We shall see how dissolution

---

[2] Often, it is true, meta-ethical worries about morality fall back on the more general assumption that epistemic reasons have an ontic status that no practical and evaluative reasons have. This, however, does not pick out morality as such, unless the claim is that morality in particular pretends to have that status. In any case the assumption is false, as the discussion of Part IV will, I hope, show. (Bernard Williams' critique of morality interestingly combines all these lines of thought: morality does not have the ontic status of science, nor its unconditionality, and it is oppressive.)

of the putative correspondence theory gives us a much better understanding of normative truth. It is worth emphasizing at the outset, however, that what we are left with is not a *pluralistic* conception of truth, in which a correspondence notion of truth applies in some domains of discourse, while some other conceptions of truth apply in other domains. Such a view is committed to holding that the correspondence view is *intelligible*, and the question then arises of why it does not apply universally. One is forced either to normative realism or to the conclusion that normative 'propositions' are propositions in at best a second-class sense. Contrary to this view we shall hold that the concept of truth is uniform across all domains, and the correspondence conception applies to none of them.

The plan of Part IV is as follows. The epistemology and metaphysics of reasons will be discussed in the first two chapters, epistemology in this one, semantics and ontology in the next. The Normative account that emerges will then be applied to Wittgenstein's famous questions about the normativity of rules, rule-following, and concepts. We shall examine what I call Wittgenstein's open-question argument against normative realism, and show how its outcome can be read as a form of the Normative view. Alternative meta-normative positions will also be discussed there. Chapter 19 discusses some connections between the Normative view of reasons and the metaphysics of freedom and the self. The final chapter sets out the Normative view of certain classical issues raised in the Critical tradition, showing how it amounts to a new form of Critical philosophy.

Our aim in this chapter then is to describe when a person is said to have warrant for a normative belief, or to have normative knowledge: showing the grounds on which we in practice accept or reject such claims. It will emerge that an accurate account of our epistemic practice is inconsistent with taking purely normative propositions to be (substantially) factual. The next chapter will show that the semantics of normative sentences does not require us to take purely normative propositions to be factual either. Semantics is silent on that subject. It is, rather, the correspondence theory of truth that forces on us the unwelcome choice—that of having to take normative claims as either factual or not genuinely propositional at all. On a better account of truth the unwelcome choice turns out to be bogus.

16.1 Facts

First we must look more closely at the notion of *fact*. We distinguished (3.3) between a purely nominal notion of factuality and an ontologically substantial notion. The nominal notion identifies facts with true propositions, or treats them as abstract entities—truths—that stand in one–one relation to true propositions. We understand 'proposition' as the sense or meaning of what is asserted on an occasion (7.3). So the nominal notion of fact is pretty much the Fregean notion: 'a fact is a thought that is true'.[3]

---

[3] Frege 1977 (1919, 1923): 25. Note that in ordinary language facts are possible objects of awareness, not possible objects of belief, whereas propositions are possible objects of belief. If one talks of being aware of a proposition what one means is being aware of it as an object, not of its truth. However, we can be said to be aware of the *truth* of a proposition, or the fact that it is true. So, strictly, nominal facts should be identified with truths as against true propositions: a class of abstract objects that map true propositions.

On this view, if 'Hesperus' and 'Phosphorus' have different senses then 'Hesperus is a planet' and 'Phosphorus is a planet' express different propositions and state different facts. Plainly if 'fact' is taken in this sense, it is trivially true that all propositions are factual. To assert that *p* is to assert the truth of the proposition that *p*, and thus to assert it to be a fact—in the nominal sense—that *p*.

In contrast, a *substantial* notion of fact takes facts to be perfectly distinct from propositions. We can note three distinguishing characteristics of substantial facts:

(1) Substantial facts have substance: a constitution or essence.

It follows that in some cases they may be the subject of a posteriori identity claims of the form 'The fact that *p* is identical to the fact that *q*'. Assertions of distinct factual *propositions* may turn out to assert that one and the same *fact* obtains. Thus the fact that there is water in the glass is the fact that there is H_2O in the glass. (It follows that name–name identities like 'Hesperus is Phosphorus', 'Water is H_2O' are not substantial facts.) The same distinction applies to properties: nominal properties are senses; substantial properties (*attributes* as I called them in 3.3) may be picked out by more than one nominal property[4]:

(2) Substantial facts may, in virtue of their substantiality, cause and/or be caused.

We predicate causal properties of objects, attributes, and facts. An object causes in virtue of having some attribute, an attribute causes in virtue of its instantiation in objects, a fact causes by being the instantiation of some attributes in some objects. For example, it was the fact that poor-quality steel had been used that caused the collapse of the grandstand.[5] Can we say that to be a substantial fact is to have causal standing (to cause and/or be caused)? Or can there be productively insulated substantial facts—substantial facts that are neither caused nor cause, constituted by attributes or objects that are causally inert? We shall argue in 17.3 that substantive factuality *is* causal standing. Irrespective of that stronger thesis, however, facts of which one is objectually aware—those that are apperceived, perceived, or which one remembers apperceiving or perceiving—cause the awareness and are therefore substantial facts. I am aware of a light flashing in the distance, a plane passing by. I am aware of a sinking feeling in my stomach; I am aware of the way you looked just now. This is objectual awareness of facts. My *propositional* awareness that a plane is passing by may result from objectual awareness; but I can have propositional awareness without objectual awareness. I am aware that my favourite pianist is performing tonight; but since I'm unable to get to the concert I do not have objectual awareness that she is performing. I am aware that it is illegal to drive without insurance, but that is not the kind of fact of which I *could* be objectually, as against propositionally, aware. Nor are normative, thus nominal, facts the kind of fact of which I could be objectually as against propositionally aware.

---

[4] There is no nominal sense of 'object'. By 'object' I mean possible referent; the relevant distinction here is between real and irreal objects—see Chapter 18.

[5] Cp. Mellor 1987, 1995.

(3) Substantial facts are ontically cognition-independent: the substantial fact that p and the fact that it is believed or known that p are distinct.

The contrast with nominal facts here is not that nominal facts are cognition-dependent: the point, rather, is that the notion of *ontic* cognition-independence is inapplicable to nominal facts, because it only applies to real objects and, as we shall argue in Chapter 17, nominal facts are not real objects. (Nominal facts are, however, cognition-independent in a purely logical sense: the nominal fact that p neither entails nor is entailed by the nominal fact that it is believed that p.)

The world is the totality of substantial facts. Let us defer the question whether that is an absolute, well-defined, totality (see 20.7 and 20.8). At any rate common sense, scientific and religious thought concern themselves with the world in this sense. When we think in common sense terms of ourselves as thinkers and agents in the world we are thinking of ourselves and our acts as a proper part of this totality. What we do is caused by and causes other facts. The fact that someone stepped out into the road caused me to slam on the brakes, and that caused the car to crash.

Global realism, it will be remembered, is the view that all (non-analytic) propositions are factual, where a factual proposition says that some substantial fact obtains. According to global realism the two assertions 'The world consists of all the facts' and 'The world is everything that is the case' are the same. But on the Normative view they are not the same, because the Normative view is irrealist about purely normative propositions. The world consists of all the substantial facts, but *what is the case* is broader. Take the principle of inference to the best explanation (9.3). It is the case—that is, it is true—that where h is the best explanation of some facts there is reason to believe h; but that is not itself a (substantial) fact—it is a norm.

On the global realist view knowledge of a fact must consist in identity with it or involve production by it or something causally connected with it. The latter relation involves productivity in the object, on the one hand, and receptivity in the knowing subject, on the other. But if we describe the circumstances in which a person is regarded as having a warrant for an a priori belief about reason relations, or a priori knowledge of reason relations, what do we find? We find that the epistemology required by realism does not fit. Knowledge of reasons relations does not require either identity with or causal relation to substantial facts. It involves no receptivity at all. Its epistemic basis consists solely in spontaneity and convergence. To these two notions we now turn.

16.2 Spontaneity

The distinction between spontaneity and receptivity is Kant's. Every judgement involves spontaneity, but Kant thinks that not every judgement involves receptivity: some judgements are based on spontaneity alone. The contrast plays a fundamental epistemological role in his Critical philosophy and it will play the same fundamental role here. However, I believe that the idea of spontaneity should be developed rather differently to the way Kant develops it and given a wider scope than Kant gives it. These differences with regard to the notion of spontaneity will underlie the differences between Kant's overall Critique of Reason and the Normative view of reasons. We shall come back to some of them in Section 16.6.

Spontaneity is a property of responses and dispositions to respond. The basic idea is that a spontaneous response or disposition is one that comes in the right way from, is genuinely that of, the actor. Kant gives this basic idea a causal interpretation: spontaneity, self-origination, is 'original'—uncaused—causation of its activity by the active self. He then takes it that such causation cannot be understood at the empirical level. So spontaneity becomes something whose possibility can be vindicated only by transcendental idealism.[6] We should not follow him in this: spontaneity, as I interpret it, is not as such a causal notion at all, though there can be subversive causal explanations of a person's response which preclude its spontaneity.

A fortiori, spontaneity is not agent-causality. It will be argued in 19.4 that 'agent-causality', understood as a form of causation distinct from natural or efficient causation of states of the person by states of the person, is not required for attribution of freedom. Furthermore all responses—beliefs and feelings as well as actions—can have the property of spontaneity. True, there is a difference between action, on the one hand, and belief and feeling, on the other: you cannot believe or feel at will. Believing and feeling are not things you do or decide to do. However, the notion of agent-causality does not illuminate this difference. *I* do not cause my beliefs or feelings; but then *I* do not cause my actions either. I *do* them. I can cause them in indirect ways of course, such as causing myself to go to the meeting by setting the alarm on my watch. Or deciding to go in 5 minutes may cause me to go in 5 minutes. In these cases something I do causes me to do something else. Similarily, something I do may cause me to believe or feel something. But the idea that spontaneity consists in you *causing* your actions, beliefs, or feelings by a *sui generis* kind of causality is not what I am proposing here. (It also seems that Kant should not identify spontaneity with 'agent-causality' at least as the latter is often understood, for he takes beliefs as well as actions to be products of spontaneity.)

Spontaneity in the sense I am interested in does require that the response or disposition to respond comes in the right way from the actor: that is, from the actor's nature. In this sense beliefs and feelings can be spontaneous, as well as actions. It does not mean 'acting without thinking'. There is a connection, in that what I do 'without thinking' may indeed reveal my true nature. However, a response that issues from profound reflection may also be spontaneous, in the sense of coming in the right way from me. The Critical point is its source. Thus 'spontaneous' contrasts with 'factitious': a factitious as against a truly spontaneous response or disposition is one that is accepted uncritically into one's thinking from others, or one that results merely from a wish to please or to annoy . . . and so on. We can interpret Kant's reflection (cited at the head of the chapter) in this way: 'in order to judge objectively, universally, that is, apodictically, reason must be free of

---

[6] See e.g. Kant's discussion of the third antinomy.

subjectively determining grounds'. 'Subjectively determining grounds', or 'alien causes' to use another of his phrases,[7] are factitious grounds or causes of a response. A spontaneous response is simply one that is free of such grounds or causes.

'Spontaneous' also contrasts with 'conventional'. For example, my disposition to drive on the left in Britain is not spontaneous; it registers my awareness of a convention. Nonetheless following a convention itself always involves the exercise of spontaneity—there is spontaneity in the judgement that a conventional rule applies in such-and-such a way to a particular case, as will be discussed in Chapter 18.

Another pair of terms for the same contrast between 'spontaneous' and 'factitious' is 'natural' versus 'artificial': as in Mill's remark that 'moral associations which are wholly of artificial creation, when intellectual culture goes on, yield by degrees to the dissolving force of analysis'.[8] Wittgenstein uses the word 'natural', for example when he invokes 'natural ways of going on'; here too the notion being deployed is what I am calling spontaneity. 'Natural' captures the idea of something that truly comes from your nature. I prefer 'spontaneous' in part because of some misleading connotations of 'natural'. In the relevant sense, of coming from your nature, it should not be confused with 'innate'—your nature can be developed and formed, responses can cease to be or become spontaneous. (Mill too, immediately before the passage I have just quoted, distinguishes the question whether moral feelings are natural from the question whether they are innate.) However, the main reason for my preference is that it is Kant's epistemological contrast between spontaneity and receptivity that is going to be important to us, even though the notion of a spontaneous response as I am interested in it coincides with Mill's or Wittgenstein's notion of a natural response.

Now in asking myself whether some purely normative judgement I am disposed to make is warranted, I may ask myself whether the disposition is really mine: *is* it what *I* am really disposed to think? I am asking about its spontaneity. So when does a disposition *feel* 'really mine'? Spontaneity in one's cognitive, affective or practical dispositions is typically marked by a certain experienced or felt normative harmony. A disposition to ψ has this feature when it blends with a disposition to take oneself (more or less explicitly) to have reason to ψ. Call this latter disposition, taken on its own (i.e. with or without the actual disposition to ψ) a *normative disposition to* ψ. A normative disposition to ψ is a disposition to judge that there is reason to ψ. We can experience this disposition in a first-person way. It is an *experience, impression or spontaneously persuasive representation of* a given response—belief, feeling, or action—as reason-supported: normatively apt, proper. (This is, I think, what is often meant in current philosophical discussion when someone says they have 'an intuition' that such-and-such: they mean an inclination to believe that feels reason-supported. However, we have reserved the term 'intuition' for the more ambitious sense that it has for intuitionistic realists.[9]) The normative disposition may not be reflectively articu-

---

[7] 'Will is a kind of causality belonging to living beings so far as they are rational. *Freedom* would then be the property this causality has of being able to work independently of *determination* by alien causes...' *Groundwork*, IV: 446.
[8] Mill 1963–91, vol. X: 230.
[9] Recent discussions of 'intuition' in the current broader sense include Bealer 2000; Sosa 2007; Williamson 2007.

lated, nor is it the same as an actual belief that one has reason to ψ. You can believe that you have reason to ψ without having a normative disposition to ψ, in the present sense—for example, you can believe it on the basis of testimony or in some other indirect way that does not involve the first-person experience of seeming to see the reason for oneself. Thus I may warrantedly believe that there is reason to prefer X to Y, because reliable critics have told me so, without knowing what the reason is. Equally, you can have the normative disposition to ψ, without the belief that you have reason to ψ. Your disposition to believe that you have reason to ψ is checked or outweighed in some way. You have the normative disposition to think that every condition determines a set, for example, but you know enough about set theory to be aware of the problems. Yet *still* it feels as though there's reason to believe that: you seem to 'understand' why it must be so.

In normal cases, being disposed to ψ and being normatively disposed to ψ go together. But this unquestioned normative harmony can break down. It may seem to me (in the first-person way) that I have reason to ψ and yet I find I'm not at all disposed to ψ. Or I may have the disposition without the normative disposition. In these cases of normative dissonance I start to question my dispositions. And thus whether I really do have reason to ψ comes into question too.[10]

Suppose, for example, that I experience a normative disposition to admire a particular performance and yet have no inclination to admire it. It seems to me that the performance is admirable; I just don't actually feel any admiration. Given this normative disharmony, I can happily move to a verdict about whether the performance is admirable only if I can credibly 'explain away' one or other of these dispositions. The normative disposition may be explained as resulting from misleading hype or peer-group pressure, for example. Or the failure to admire may be explained away by tiredness, jadedness, or distraction, dislike or envy of the artist, and so on. In the first case, the normative disposition has been subverted; it confers no warrant to believe. In the second case it confers a warrant even though the disposition to admire is absent. In the first case the *spontaneity* of the normative disposition has been cast in doubt, while in the second case the *absence* of a spontaneous disposition to admire has been explained away. Or we could reverse the case: I admire but have no normative disposition to admire. Again normative disharmony may be overcome in a variety of ways. One possibility is that my admiration persists and eventually carries my normative dispositions with it. I come to acknowledge, 'be at home with', new reasons to admire new things.

If there is normative disharmony in my reactions, I'm not warranted in making a pure judgement about reasons just on their basis. I need to sort out the problem, either by achieving harmony or finding a convincing way of explaining the disharmony away. Where there is disharmony I'm not warranted in trusting to the spontaneity of my

---

[10] Persistent and extreme normative disharmony tends to produce a sense of self-alienation. Suppose that I 'can't help' believing everyone is hostile to me. I can see that there's no reason to believe that, but I still can't help thinking it. So now I may experience the disposition as alien or intrusive, not really 'mine'. Alternatively, though I can notionally see the reasons for discounting this disposition, I can't feel 'at home' with them.

responses unless I can do one of these things. Educating one's dispositions is in large part a matter of confronting and resolving such normative disharmonies by free reflection on cases and consequences. That applies as much to set theory as to aesthetics.

We can see the epistemic role of spontaneity by reflecting on how explanations that subvert or explain away the spontaneity of a response (or lack of a spontaneous response) also remove its epistemic value. One could say that they work by showing that the response isn't, so to speak, tuned solely to its object (the object of normative assessment). It is not solely an interaction between the object and the subject's nature that gives rise to the response. There is interference from other factors.

Judging whether one's dispositions are spontaneous can be hard. It may require difficult self-examination. Am I genuinely inclined to see reason to ψ—is that what I *really* think—or have I somehow got gripped by a wrong or partial take on the question? Or do I just want to respond as other people want me to? Or to annoy them? Is there something I don't want to acknowledge here?

Even if my dispositions are in normative harmony, I may have other evidence that my response, though harmonious, isn't spontaneous. A subversive explanation of both sides of the harmony—the disposition and the normative disposition to ψ—may be available. If that can be shown then again my warrant for judging that there's reason to ψ is undermined.

And since the appearance of spontaneity can be subverted by various sorts of debunking explanation of how it came about, self-examination alone may not be sufficient—a third-person view on oneself may be needed. Nevertheless, in many cases of normative harmony one is warranted—as ever defeasibly—in taking one's normative disposition to be spontaneous.

In the light of these remarks about *when* one is warranted in taking oneself to have a spontaneous normative disposition, I propose the following norm of spontaneity for pure judgements about reasons:

> (1) *Norm of spontaneity*: when one is warranted in taking oneself to have a spontaneous disposition to judge that a set of facts π_i would give one reason to ψ then, in the absence of defeaters, that warrants the judgement that the set of facts π_i would give one reason to ψ.[11]

The norm applies to the three types of case in which one can be said to have a reason: sentiment; volition; and cognition. Furthermore—so long as spontaneous normative harmony in my dispositions prevails—if I desire or admire, etc., objects of some type, then I am defeasibly warranted in affirming that there is reason for me to desire, or to admire, etc., objects of that type. Likewise, given the same assumption of normative harmony, if I recognize in myself a will to do a certain type of action (that is, under a certain idea of its character) I am defeasibly justified in affirming that there is reason for me to will to do actions of that type.

---

[11] As the above discussion indicates, I may be warranted in thinking that I *would* have a spontaneous normative disposition to ψ were it not for certain blocking factors, such as distraction, stress, or whatever. That too would produce a defeasible warrant to ψ.

The case of belief is special, since factual beliefs require a basis in receptivity. Thus (1), the norm of spontaneity, applies in the epistemic case only to outright—a priori—reasons for belief, and hence, in turn, only to normative beliefs and their offshoots, if any. Here too, given conditions of normative harmony, if I recognize in myself a disposition to form a normative belief of a given type under certain circumstances, I am default-warranted in affirming that there is reason for me to form a belief of that type under those circumstances. Since factual judgement is always normatively guided, that means that any such judgement is the product of spontaneity as well as receptivity—'receptivity can make knowledge possible only when combined with spontaneity'.[12]

16.3 Normative harmony and reflective equilibrium

It is not always easy to apply the norm of spontaneity, because it is not always easy to recognize one's own disposition, or to judge its spontaneity. Furthermore, beyond the difficulties of self-insight mentioned in the previous section, broader questions of normative stability come into play. Normative harmony broadens into 'reflective equilibrium'.[13] A perceived instability in one's normative dispositions breaks down normative harmony; the search for reflective equilibrium is then the search for a more broadly-based, fully achieved normative harmony. How does this work?

In the first place the *universalizability of reasons* generates a drive to normative consistency. How salient this factor is depends on how particularistic norms are. This issue is substantive: the epistemology of norms is silent about it. Norms must be universalizable, but mere universalizability does not impose general principles in the usual sense, i.e. broad and fairly unqualified formulations. Furthermore general principles, where they exist, may be cast in terms of R rather than S. I argued that this was the case with practical reasons. Neither the principle of Good nor the Bridge principle is stated in terms of sufficient reasons. The Demand principle is, but it leaves open the question of when a demand is morally permissible.

Thus the merely logical demands of universalizability impose no tight constraints. Nor does a normative theory with fewer norms have an inherent epistemic advantage over one that has more. We should not import notions of inference to the best explanation from factual to normative inquiry. Simplicity as an explanatory virtue has no place in the latter, because the relevant notion of *explanation* has no place. The question must always be whether the norms that someone propounds satisfactorily interpret our spontaneous dispositions. How far morality, for example, is constituted by general principles is an immanent question within substantive morality, a question about how generally characterizable the objects of reason-supported blame turn out to be.

---

[12] Kant, *Critique of Pure Reason*, A97.
[13] A very old notion, given new life in Rawls 1971; cp. Daniels, 1979, 2008.

For evaluative reasons in general, reflective equilibrium often turns importantly not so much on universalizability as on *analysis of exactly what one feels*. Thus in aesthetics notions like kitsch, phoniness, sentimentality, speciousness, etc. turn on what the object is inviting or tempting one to feel and what one really does feel, or has serious reason to feel. And in morality it can be important to distinguish a genuine response of blame from a recoil of distaste or disgust, or from contempt for something undignified or low, or from understandable anger at a mean trick. None of these, whether well or ill-based, have the implications of blame.

There are also at least two ways in which norms intertwine with facts, thereby bringing facts into the data for reflective equilibrium—one in the evaluative case, the other in the epistemic case.

In the evaluative case there is the fact that sentiments have factual presuppositions or commitments. If these are undermined, so is the sentiment. Suppose I am afraid of spiders. I know they are not dangerous, but I still fear them, and still have the normative disposition to think that there is good reason for that fear (and hence the disposition to think them dangerous). Here there is normative harmony in the sense of 16.3, but it is undermined by knowledge of the facts. It is undermined because the proper object of fear is the dangerous, and thus the sentiment has a factual commitment. The commitment arises from the norm of fear itself: that there is reason to fear y if and only if y is dangerous. So if I accept that an object is not dangerous, I have to accept that there is no reason to fear it, however strong my dispositions. This is a straightforward case; others are far more elusive. It may be that my disgust or horror at some sexual relations, say incest, is associated with an idea of polluting boundary-transgression. Suppose that certain cross-boundary, classification-defying objects spontaneously dispose people to disgust of a particular kind. Is that an epistemic basis for a norm of disgust?[14] It seems that it can be so only within a certain kind of cosmology, a normative idea of nature, to which we no longer subscribe. Giving this kind of disgust real normative standing requires some such rationale. But we no longer have that notion of transgression of natural boundaries, and thus cannot even conceive the putative fact to which a norm of disgust would refer. Not that seeing things as they are invariably generates loss of feeling. If something really is dangerous, fear really is warranted. If it really is cruel, it really is contemptible. If you really did shrug off what you knew to be your responsibility, blame really is the warranted response.

Facts also intertwine with epistemic norms. In 6.9, for example, we considered the suggestion that the Greeks had warrant to hold the parallels postulate a priori, though we do not. If so, facts can enter into the data for reflective epistemic–normative equilibrium. However, this does not mean that epistemic norms are themselves defeasible. In 20.6, we shall argue against that conclusion: even if warranted a priori reasons are defeasible, it will be claimed that epistemic norms are not. Yet it remains true that the progress of factual inquiry may refine our understanding of our epistemic norms and reorder their hierarchy.

---

[14] The reaction may have had evolutionary functions, to do with reproduction, or with hygiene; but that is irrelevant to the normative question, about whether there is any reason to feel that way.

16.4 Convergence

Our account of the epistemology of reasons has so far left out an essential dimension: that of dialogue, discussion with others. But a purely first-personal reflective equilibrium is not enough for warrant. It needs to be tested against, and can be defeated by, the normative responses of others.

Disagreement can defeat one's warrant for a normative claim. It does so when one finds that one has insufficient reason to believe that any of the disagreeing judgements are faulty. This source of defeat depends on a principle which I call the convergence thesis:

> *Convergence thesis*: if I judge that p, I am rationally committed to holding that *either* inquirers who scrutinized any relevant evidence and argument available to them would agree that p *or* I could fault their pure judgements about reasons or their evidence.

The notion of rational commitment is that discussed in 5.11. That is, I am rationally criticizable if I judge that p while also holding that fault-free inquirers would not judge that p. The thesis applies to all judgements, and thus in particular both to factual judgements and to pure judgements about reasons. Now, as noted in the previous section, factual inquiry might undermine pure claims about reasons—by undermining our grasp of the reason-giving fact we thought we understood, or by refining our understanding of the strength and content of the claim about reasons. Setting aside these possibilities, however, a disagreement concerning a priori claims about reason relations must originate from faulty normative judgement on one or both sides. Thus if other inquirers disagree with me in my spontaneous judgements about reason relations, however well equilibrated, I have to ask myself how credible it is that their judgements, as against mine, are faulty.

How does the convergence thesis arise? Epistemic reasons, like all reasons, are universal: if there is reason for someone in an epistemic field to judge that p then there is reason for anyone in that field to judge that p.[15] To this we can add that it is irrational to judge that:

> p but I have insufficient reason to believe that p.

(This is (13) in 5.11). Now suppose I judge that were it true that Π_i that would give me reason to believe that p. Call this the judgement that q. It would be irrational for me to judge that q if I did not think I had sufficient reason to do so. So by the universality of epistemic reasons I am rationally committed to holding that anyone who shares my epistemic state, but does not agree (on reflection) that q, is faulty in their pure judgement about reason relations, for example, through incompetence, inattention, or insufficient care.

---

[15] See Chapter 3 for elucidations of this with respect to indexicals (3.2 and 3.6) and to cognitive internalism (3.8 and 3.9). Thus, for example, as regards indexicals, if there is reason for me in a given epistemic field to believe that I should leave then there is reason for anyone in 'that' field, i.e. the field containing corresponding indexical facts, to believe that he or she should leave. And given cognitive internalism 'anyone' ranges only over those who are able to grasp the class of reasons in question.

What then if I find that others who relevantly share my epistemic state do disagree with my judgement that q, and I come to the conclusion, in one way or another, that I have no reason to doubt the quality of their judgement? In that case I am forced to doubt the quality of my own. I might start to wonder whether my normative disposition is indeed spontaneous, or whether after all it's in some way factitious, distorted by a special interest, for example. Alternatively, I might conclude that it is genuinely spontaneous but also wrong. In that case I might seek to educate my spontaneity. However, this might fail to work. I might then conclude, in a merely external way, without insight, that my spontaneous responses in this domain are somehow flawed. (My taste in this kind of art, for example, is incorrigibly bad.) Or I might conclude, given enough self-confidence and scepticism, that what the divergence of judgements in this case shows is that there simply are no genuine reasons in this domain—no genuine reason, for example, to admire this rather than that.

Is this argument completely presuppositionless—in that sense 'transcendental'—or is there an underlying assumption that my interlocutors share with me a common basic nature, against which outliers like gratitude-blind Tom (10.8) are judged? On the latter view, reasons would have to be relative to cognitive, affective, or conative communities that share a nature. We shall take up this issue in 20.9. However, it does not affect the present epistemological point, which is that warrant for normative claims requires the twin pillars of spontaneity and discussion with others, and nothing more—no special receptivity to normative facts.

16.5 Receptivity versus self-evidence: intuitionism again

What then is normative knowledge? Applying the discussion of 5.10, we have:

> x knows that p if and only if p, x believes that p from warrant, and that warrant is, in the actual circumstances, a reliable basis for x's belief that p.

It follows that one has knowledge of a norm **N** only if the way in which one comes to believe that **N** obtains is reliable. One such route could be the testimony of authoritative judges. In the end, however, there must be judges whose *first-person* judgement of norms is reliable. Their knowledge of norms is a priori knowledge—which we characterized in 6.10:

> x has (immediate, non-inferential) a priori knowledge that p if and only if

(i) p
(ii) x believes that p on the basis of normative dispositions to believe that p
(iii) which are reliable.

A normative disposition to believe that p is reliable if it tends to produce the belief that p when there is a priori warrant for the belief that p and not when not. As noted in 6.10, the question then arises of the relation between a priori warrant and a priori truth. Is a reliable basis for the belief that it is a priori that p a reliable basis for the belief that p? Our affirmative answer will turn on the irreality of reason relations, to be discussed in Chapter 17. (Note also that, by WK[16], if we believe that *p* from a priori warrant we are warranted in believing that we know that *p*.)

The process leading to a priori warrant is that described in Sections 16.2 to 16.4: spontaneous normative dispositions, the search, where necessary for reflective normative harmony, and discussion with others with a view to checking for convergence. There is no other check on reliability beyond these. My judgement that **N** obtains is not *caused* by **N**. Subversive explanations that undermine my a priori warrant do not work by showing that a required cause *fails* to be in place. In particular they do not work by showing that my belief is not produced by some purportedly substantial normative fact. They work by showing that some 'wrong' or 'alien' causes are in place—the disposition is a factitious product of extraneous factors. The same applies in cases where unreliability consists in the lack of a response. Explaining away this lack will consist in showing that extraneous factors are masking or stunting the disposition that would otherwise be expected. To what then are these interfering factors extraneous, alien? To the *spontaneity* of the response—to the way in which I would respond if interfering factors were absent and my dispositions were working in an active and unimpeded way—in other words, coming from my nature. *Any spontaneous normative disposition has some default epistemic weight.*

The crucial contrast is between spontaneity and receptivity. To postulate a receptive normative faculty is to postulate quasi-perception of some substantial normative fact, involving productive causality on the part of the fact. Nothing at all in a careful account of what goes into the making of normative judgements supports this picture. We do not search for empirical theories of how postulated normative facts supposedly affect the knowing subject—what kind of transmission is involved, or what kind of receptors the subject is equipped with. Anyone who tried doing that would be philosophically confused, not scientifically adventurous. So the choice for intuitionists is to think that some radically inexplicable kind of receptivity is involved or that none is.

Spontaneity is the sole final source of normative knowledge. To be sure, we can say that a person believes a normative proposition to be true because he can see that it is. In saying this, however, we are not saying that the truth of the proposition produces the belief by some natural or non-natural causality. We mean that he has first-person insight into its truth. As noted in 6.1 we can also say that the proposition is self-evident. 'It just seems true as such', 'I don't think it needs any supporting argument or evidence—it's evident or plain in itself'. The proposition itself is evident, or if it's not immediately evident then what it requires is elucidation and clarification to become evident, rather than supporting argument. To think a proposition self-evident is to be spontaneously disposed to judge it true just in virtue of understanding it. It *is* self-evident if that judgement, made on that basis, perhaps through added reflection, is warranted. If you believe it on the basis of that warrant, you are warranted in thinking that you know it. And if it is true and your underlying normative dispositions with respect to that kind of truth are reliable

---

[16] Thesis (14) in 5.10. (See the Synopsis or Appendix.)

you know it. To be a reliable judge of that kind of normative truth just is to have and to respond to reliable normative dispositions. Warrant, however, remains non-factive: from the fact that a purely normative judgement is warranted a priori—self-evident—it does not follow (by logic alone) that it is true.

This notion of self-evidence is not the intuitionistic realist's notion of intuition. On the intuitionist model some propositions are a priori because we can have objectual non-natural awareness of their truth makers. The truth makers are facts consisting in the possession of substantial properties by abstract entities. We argued in 6.2 and 6.3 that this intuitionistic model of a priori knowledge leads to vicious regress. In contrast, our notion of self-evidence postulates no non-empirical receptivity to truth makers for a priori propositions: to say that a proposition is self-evident is simply to say that once clarification and dialogical testing of the proposition has been achieved one is outright warranted in believing it.

Self-evidence is a property only of norms, pure judgements about reason relations.[17] The epistemics of the normative that we have described in this chapter explains what self-evidence is. Normative propositions can be known through self-evidence, because their epistemic basis lies solely in spontaneity and convergence—and because convergence arises solely from the universality of reasons.

There is also a realist model of convergence. It says that reliable knowers will, given the same input to their receptive faculties, produce the same judgement of fact, just as reliable cameras will, given the same input, produce the same photograph. But in the case of pure judgements about reasons we have no need to appeal to this camera model—for in their case the criterion of convergence follows from the universality of reasons alone. In contrast, the epistemics of factual judgements require receptivity as well as spontaneity. To be warranted in believing that it's raining, for example, I must be warranted in believing that I'm receiving relevant information: that I can see that it is, that I'm aware of testimony from someone who sees that it is, and so forth.

This, then, is the crucial lack of parallelism between the epistemology of factual judgements and the epistemology of reasons. The former rests on a conception of thinking beings as receptively linked to states of affairs that are distinct from the receptive faculties to which the links connect. This conception has no role to play in the case of pure judgements about reason relations. If reason relations were properties in the substantial sense, attributes of objects, they would be knowable only by some form of receptive awareness; but in fact our knowledge of reason relations can be accounted for entirely in terms of the spontaneity of belief, will, and feeling. In this case as elsewhere, it remains the case that knowledge is true belief reliably acquired. However, being *reliably responsive* to the way in which reason relations obtain in a given subject-area consists simply in having the developed spontaneous capacity for judging how they obtain in that area. One's reliability can be put in doubt, and one's judgement corrected, by showing that one's responses are not spontaneous or that they conflict with those of judges whose responses are not

---

[17] Given the closure of warrant under itself, they won't all be self-evident.

thereby impugned. Unless convergence radically breaks down, that is enough for us to claim knowledge of reasons. The task that remains, to be taken up in the next chapter, is to back up this account with an irrealist ontology of reason relations.

16.6 Receptivity and spontaneity in Kant

The distinction between receptivity and spontaneity plays a vital Critical role in Kant's philosophy. We have built on it, but we have not followed his interpretation of it. Kant entangles his distinction between spontaneity and receptivity with his doctrine of transcendental idealism, and in particular with the application of that doctrine to the self and freedom. Spontaneity, he rightly thinks, is freedom: it is in this sense of freedom that 'when an appearance is given to us, we are still quite free as to how we should judge the matter'.

But Kant thinks freedom as spontaneity belongs to the noumenal self. Thought and action, considered as products of self-activity, are activities of the self as it is in itself; in contrast feeling belongs to the self's experience and thus to its appearance to itself.

We shall be argue in 19.1 that Kant's application of transcendental idealism to self-knowledge is an error. Even if there were some basis for a kind of transcendental idealism about nature (a question to be considered in 20.8 and 20.9), there would still be no basis for distinguishing between the self as it appears to itself and the self as it really is. Spontaneity is not noumenal.

It is a further error to think that whereas judgement and belief are products of self-active thinking, feeling is not; that it is something that happens to us in the way our sensory experience happens to us. Our feelings can be ours and free in exactly the sense that our beliefs can be: i.e. not in the sense that they can be products of our own will, as our actions are, but in the sense that they can be (unlike the data of receptive sensibility) products of our own thought. Our thought can lead us to see reasons to feel just as it can lead us to see reasons to believe.

Transcendental idealism entrenches this error by disconnecting emotions from spontaneity. I do not say that it necessarily does so. Wherever there is responsiveness to reasons there is spontaneity: Kant could have said this consistently with his transcendental-idealist framework. It seems that what is really at work in Kant's thinking is what in the Introduction I called philosopher's syndrome, a rationalistic blindness to the fact that feelings have their own reasons.[18]

Other philosophical thinkers, who have been more interested in the development and education of character and emotion, have had much to say about spontaneity of feeling. The most obvious contribution of Kant's time was Schiller's *Letters on the Aesthetic Education of Man*. It extends the notion of education from cognition and will to the

---

[18] The closest Kant comes to discussing the epistemology of evaluative reasons is his doctrine of aesthetic judgements in the *Critique of Judgement*. It resembles in some striking respects the epistemology of judgements about reasons that has been set out in the previous sections. *Whenever* I judge warrant I make a judgement that I take to be both spontaneous and universally legislative, in the sense that I enunciate a warrant for anyone in my epistemic state.

feelings, and its notion of education in all these cases is that of a development, or free culture, of spontaneity. Furthermore it develops this account within a framework that is at least sympathetic to Kant. A certain liberal tradition stretches forward from that work (to which the account of thought and feeling in this book is—I hope—a contribution).

It should be grasped as a *fundamental* point that spontaneity plays a uniform role in the epistemology of all three kinds of reasons, evaluative as well as epistemic and practical. In all cases spontaneity is what truly comes from a person's nature. In general, what reasons there are depends on a common nature. Norms are grounded in cognitive communities of beings with the same natural dispositions: we shall come back to this in 20.9.

Despite these divergences from Kant, our account of the contrast between spontaneity and receptivity acknowledges three fundamental Kantian insights. First, pure judgements about reasons involve no receptivity. Second, a judgement about reasons is universal in content. Third, where the epistemology of a judgement involves spontaneity only, and no receptivity, one must take an irrealist view of its objects.

Take the first point, that pure judgements about reasons involve no receptivity. Suppose, for example, that I receive an aural representation as of a higher note followed by a lower note. Such a representation, Kant thinks, has already received significant formation in sensibility; our concern, however, is with the step in which I proceed to *judge*, on the basis of this representation, that I have indeed heard a certain objective sequence of sounds. At this point the understanding applies concepts to the materials provided by sensible intuition. It does so by virtue of its power to recognize epistemic states as reasons to form judgements that deploy concepts—e.g. that x is a higher note than y, that y is later than x. To *have* the concepts is, among other things, to grasp, of various possible sensible intuitions, that they constitute reasons to make judgements deploying those concepts. This capacity of concept application or pure reason-recognition is spontaneous, in that it involves no further form of receptivity. A given epistemic state is the product of various forms of receptivity, such as hearing; but recognizing that it provides reason to make this or that judgement does not involve *another* form of receptivity, to some further domain of substantial facts.[19]

So this Kantian account rejects an intuitionistic epistemology of reasons according to which reason-recognition involves a form of receptivity that is *sui generis* to the understanding. The same applies, in Kant's view, to all pure judgements of theoretical understanding or of practical reason. In no case is any intuitionistic receptivity involved.

Not everyone who uses the word 'intuition' is committed to a realist epistemology of the normative.[20] Yet—through illicit association with that epistemology—talk of intuitions

---

[19] 'Concepts are grounded on the spontaneity of thinking, as sensible intuitions on the receptivity of impressions', and hence '*receptivity* can make cognitions possible only if combined with *spontaneity*' Kant, *Critique of Pure Reason*, A68/B93, A97.

[20] Sidgwick is a notable case. Three of his criteria for ethical axioms (self-evidence, consistency, consensus) coincide fairly closely with the three factors I have mentioned as playing a role in the epistemology of pure propositions about reason (spontaneity; reflective equilibrium; convergence). See Sidgwick 1981 (1907): 338–43. The fourth (which he lists first), 'clarity and precision', raises difficulties which a number of critics have noted—see, for example, Crisp 2002. I read Sidgwick as a cognitive irrealist about practical reason. (See also Shaver 2000.)

tends to relieve one of an important task: finding a sober description of what actually goes on in the epistemology of normative claims. On the one hand, pure reason-recognition is not a matter of receptivity, on the other hand, crucially, that point does not force us to conventionalism or voluntarism about reasons either. Our account of the ontology of normative judgements in the next chapter must help us to see how this can be so, and it must be consistent with the claim that where a judgement is based on pure spontaneity its objects must be irreal.

16.7 Free thought

Like Kant, I believe that pure judgements about reasons involve no receptivity; they are default-warranted by their spontaneity alone. Like Kant, I hold that they are universal in content. Hence in making them we take on a convergence commitment as to what other reasoners should rationally endorse. It follows that there are two important ways in which a pure judgement about reasons can lose its warrant. One can undermine it by showing that its spontaneity was only apparent, and one can defeat it by showing that the convergence to which it commits one does not obtain. The epistemology of the normative thus rests on the twin pillars of spontaneity and unconstrained dialogue. It thereby provides the epistemological groundwork for the ideal of liberty of thought and discussion.

Autonomous activity is activity that arises from one's own insight into warrant. In this respect it differs from play. Free *play* is action that is not constrained in any way, either by external constraints or by reasons other than reasons internal to the play. Hence the positive concept of freedom as autonomy does not apply to it. For free thought is not free play; its ideal aim is insightful knowledge of truth. This makes liberty of thought and discussion a narrower topic than liberty of expression in general. There is a special *epistemological* justification for a principle of free speech—whereas the justification for freedom of expression in the wider sense falls under the general justification of liberty, i.e. the freedom to act as one likes so long as one does not violate the rights of others.[21]

Thought that is genuinely free, that is, autonomous, is spontaneous and open to dialogue. It is ruled by its own norms and nothing else; by reason relations that it discovers through reflection on its own activity. First-person insight into truth requires unconstrained discussion with other seekers for truth, people who are genuinely responding not to dogma but to their own spontaneous normative dispositions. Of course it is possible for one person to be right, and all others wrong, but no one can know that that they are right without engaging in dialogue with others and reflecting on the others' responses. We considered a case in point in 14.6 and 14.7.

---

[21] Obviously the special importance of a political principle of liberty of thought and discussion also turns on important issues that are not epistemological. There are other points to be made about the social value of publicly accessible truth, and there are difficult questions about its proper limits (rights of privacy, confidentiality, etc.). These issues are not our concern here.

Especially in ultimate questions of value, free debate that excludes no one is essential—as a matter of the epistemology of the normative, not just of the ethics of democratic respect. It does not follow that every voice carries equal weight. In free and inclusive debate more and less authoritative voices inevitably emerge. It is *important* that they should—that authoritative voices should not be muffled, or hesitant in taking the lead. It was robustly realistic on John Stuart Mill's part, and not a matter of snobbery or contempt, to take full account of that. Putting it the other way round, one's independence or dignity is not diminished by free recognition of genuine authority in the common pursuit of truth, wherever one finds it. On the contrary, this is a mark of inward freedom.

Mill is the liberal who most penetratingly sees the connection between a liberal principle of free thought and the epistemology of spontaneity and discussion, placing it at the heart of his liberalism.[22] But since one of our main themes in Part IV is the connection between the Normative view and Kant's Critical philosophy, I close this chapter with a quotation from him:

> Reason must subject itself to critique in all its undertakings, and cannot restrict the freedom of critique through any prohibition without damaging itself and drawing upon itself a disadvantageous suspicion. Now there is nothing so important because of its utility, nothing so holy, that it may be exempted from this searching review and inspection, which knows no respect for persons. The very existence of reason depends upon this freedom, which has no dictatorial authority, but whose claim is never anything more than the agreement of free citizens, each of whom must be able to express his reservations, indeed even his *veto*, without holding back.[23]

---

[22] See Skorupski 2010b.   [23] CPureR, A739/B767.

17

THE ONTOLOGY OF REASON RELATIONS

'What is there?' was Quine's famously simple statement of the ontological question.[1] Bullyingly simple, one might say, in that the question means nothing without qualification—and when qualified turns into various questions which are not obviously ontological questions at all: 'What is there to do?', 'What is there left to say?'

So when the fly is let out of Quine's fly bottle does it find that ontological questions are just pseudo-questions? Not so. There are genuine questions to be asked. But they are slippery and elusive, and the answers are hard to state in ways that are not misleading.

This chapter is not a general discussion of ontology. My aim is more limited: to show how reason relations differ from other relations in ways that can be summarized by saying that, unlike those other relations, reason relations are *irreal*. Focusing firmly on these differences will help us to stay on our feet. We shall consider the justification for calling reason relations 'irreal' in Section 17.8.

Nonetheless, some general discussion cannot be avoided. Reason relations are irreal; but then so are fictional objects, so are putatively real objects of thought that do not actually exist. Am I saying that reason relations are fictional? Am I saying that we are committed to an error: thinking reason relations exist, when in fact they do not exist? I am saying neither of these things. How then does the irreality of reason relations differ from that of fictional objects, or of putatively real objects which, contrary to what we think, do not exist? And what about abstract objects—sets, numbers, propositions, and the like? How do they fit in? In sketching the contrasts between different kinds of irreality I shall make claims about irreals other than reason relations which I won't defend at all fully, since that would lead us too far afield.[2] The aim is to clarify what is meant by saying that *reason relations* are irreal, and to show in the following chapters how their irreality is fundamental and unique to the normative domain. My claim will be that reason relations are irreal and objective—not mind-dependent. In contrast, other irreals are mind-dependent.

---

[1] In Quine 1948.
[2] I have found Priest (2005) particularly helpful on the logical issues. See also Priest 2008. And I have learned much from Hilary Putnam's work on the right approach to ontology, e.g. Putnam 2004.

Two general ontological ideas will concern us: the *semantic condition* and the *causal condition*. The semantic condition is that whatever can be thought and talked about is real. The causal condition, which has already been in play in the previous chapter, is that the real is what has causal standing. They can be held to coincide, but I do not believe they do. The causal condition (with 'cause' broadly understood) is indeed basic to our notion of reality. But we should reject the semantic condition.

A first step is to note that this semantic condition is no part of semantics. Semantics assigns semantic values to terms and truth conditions to sentences; to claim that semantic values must be real and that truths must have 'truth makers' is to make metaphysical claims that go beyond semantics.

They might still of course be true. But we shall argue that they have no basis. The claim that whatever we can talk about exists is either non-ontological and trivially true, or ontological and false. Further, it is trivially true that a factual assertion is true if and only if the fact that is asserted to obtain does obtain. We can, if we want, call that fact the 'truth maker'. However, this is not the correspondence theory's distinctive notion of a truth maker: crucially, it does not entail that every truth is factual. Semantics, and the understanding of truth required for semantics, does not force us to treat purely normative propositions as factual—while their epistemology, as we have seen in the previous chapter, is positively inconsistent with doing so.

There are factual and normative propositions: this emerges as a fundamental distinction. Quietism, which denies the distinction by rejecting a substantial notion of fact, is too quiet (17.6); non-cognitivism, insofar as it assumes a correspondence conception of propositions, is deprived of its starting point (17.7).

17.1 Semantics versus metaphysics

Much twentieth-century philosophy endorsed the semantic condition. In that century, there was a powerful source for it: a certain picture of the priority of language, according to which ontology mirrors semantics. In this picture there are sentences and their uses—what is uttered and what could be uttered—and there is what those sentences are about—reality. To be real is to be the semantic value of a (possible) term or variable.[3] However, one can hold the semantic condition without accepting this particular picture. Its most basic source seems to be the surprisingly perennial idea that one cannot think about what does not exist.

Philosophers have always also been attracted by the causal condition. Naturalism accepts this condition and then holds that the only acceptable notion of causation is that which can be studied by the sciences. But non-naturalist ontologies also operate with some notion of causality, in the broadest sense of productive power—they just don't restrict it to the scientific notion.

---

[3] I discuss this notion of priority (associated notably with the Vienna School) in Skorupski 1997a.

If one is attracted by both conditions, one will try to show them equivalent. The aim will be to produce a language which refers to no objects other than those which are real by the causal criterion. Thus either we refer to reason relations, in which case they have causal standing, or we do not *really refer* to any such relations: in which case some non-cognitivist analysis of our claims about reasons must be correct.[4]

I take this equivalence project to be fundamentally mistaken; not because the causal condition is mistaken but because the semantic condition is. The causal condition we shall discuss in Section 17.3. In this and the next section we consider the semantic condition.

We should distinguish from the outset the tasks and requirements of semantics and metaphysics. Semantics provides accounts of the way in which the truth-value of a sentence is determined by the semantic values of its constituent expressions. So it attaches semantic values to singular terms, predicates and operators, and describes how the truth-values of sentences are functions of these. Take Fregean semantics, and consider the sentence 'This fire is hot'.[5] According to Frege, that sentence is true if and only if the concept (in his sense) denoted by the predicate 'ξ is hot' maps the object denoted by 'this fire' into the True. The same goes for a sentence about reasons—say 'The fact that I'm late is a reason to hurry'. Here the truth condition is that the relation denoted by the relational expression 'ξ is a reason for v to χ' maps the sequence <the fact that I'm late, me, the act-type of hurrying> into the True. Call these *Fregean* truth conditions. To understand these sentences is to grasp their Fregean truth conditions in the appropriate way, that is, in accordance with their sense. This involves grasping the senses of their constituents—i.e. their modes of presentation of a semantic value. The sense of the sentence 'This fire is hot' (the proposition it expresses) is a function of the sense of 'this fire' and 'is hot'.

In the context of Davidsonian semantics the term 'truth condition' can also be understood in another way, as referring to the sentence in the metalanguage which gives the meaning (Fregean *sense*) of the sentence. This is the Davidsonian truth condition, and it is the sense in which I shall use the term in this chapter.

Senses, objects, functions (including Fregean concepts and relations) are the *semantic posits* of a particular semantic theory. Their ontological status is another question. Is there such an object as the True? From the standpoint of Fregean semantics the trivial answer is that the True is one of its semantic posits. But does the True *really exist*? Come to that, do substantial facts *fail* to exist, given that they are not among the semantic posits of Fregean semantics? These are questions of metaphysics, not semantics. Fregean semantics does not tell us the answers. It does not tell us that the True really exists, nor does it tell us that substantial facts do not exist.

---

[4] In the case of mathematics, where non-cognitivism is unpopular, this produces the 'Benacerraf problem': Benacerraf 1973.

[5] Different semantic theories will have different abstract objects as their semantic values. I find the Fregean/Davidsonian way of doing semantics most illuminating, and will take it as my framework, but the points I make could be made in other frameworks.

Before going further, however, we must settle on a stable terminology that does not beg questions. Consider this statement:

(1) There are characters in *War and Peace* who do not exist and characters who do.

Here 'exist' is clearly used as a predicate to make an ontological distinction between the fictional characters and the real people who feature in the novel. However, 'exists' can also be used to express the existential quantifier. When 'exists' expresses the quantifier, 'Fs exist' has the same force as 'there are Fs'. Call this use of 'exists' the quantifier use. In this use it is trivially true that whatever domains semantics posits exist. To exist is to be the value of a variable. In *this* sense of 'exists' Fregean semantics says that the true exists.

On this use we could substitute 'There exist' for 'There are' in (1), and would have to substitute some other phrase for 'do not exist'—for example:

(2) There exist characters in *War and Peace* who are not real and characters who are.

Both uses of 'exist' can be found in ordinary language. In this chapter, however, I am not going to use 'exists'? in the quantifier sense, but *only* as an ontological predicate with the sense found in (1). For the purpose of this chapter 'exists', 'really exists' and 'is real' will mean exactly the same thing. Thus when we say that Pierre is one of the characters in *War and Peace* who does not really exist, we are saying:

(3) $(\exists x)(x$ is a character in *War and Peace* and $x =$ Pierre and x does not exist).

I am happy to use the verb 'to be', as in (1), to express the so-called 'existential' quantifier, while denying that it has any ontological force. So I can agree with Quine that to be is to be the value of a variable; but I disagree that this has any ontological significance.[6]

In contrast, according to the semantic condition, if we assert (1), (2), or (3) we must 'admit' all the characters in *War and Peace* into 'our ontology'. If we don't want to admit them we must find some other way to regiment these sentences, in which no variable ranging over purely fictional characters occurs.

This is a metaphysical not a semantic claim. What basis is there for it? As just noted, it is hard to see a basis for it other than the thought that whatever one can think and talk about is real. But why on earth should we think such an extraordinary thing?

The only condition that thought and discourse about any topic must satisfy is that we know and can communicate to each other what we are talking about. We must be able to anchor the topics of our discourse, by means of predicates they instantiate, in such a way as to allow us to refer back to them and quantify over them. This 'anchoring' condition clearly does not entail that the object of our discourse, i.e. its topic, must really exist. You and I can discuss how attractive a character Pierre is: there is something we are both

---

[6] More accurately: 'To be assumed as an entity is, purely and simply, to be reckoned as the value of a variable' (Quine 1961:13). Ordinary language does not have a consistent way of distinguishing the quantifier use and the ontological use, so my usage is to that extent stipulative. Saying that there are still some difficulties to be solved in the planning proposal, for example, is not making any ontological claims: it's the quantifier use. But then nor is saying that these difficulties are real, or that they are not merely apparent but really exist. If, however, we ask 'Did Homer really exist?' we are asking an ontological question.

discussing and we both know what it is. We can discuss Pierre, refer back to the character we were discussing, disambiguate our reference where necessary by using a referential anchor, such as 'the young idealist in Tolstoy's novel who gets involved with Free Masonry'. Pierre instantiates that description, but that does not entail that Pierre exists.

I should emphasize that irreality is not a shadowy form of being, where being itself is understood as an ontological status of which 'being real' or 'existence' is a species. The logical truth, '$(\exists x)(x = x)$'—as in 'Pierre = Pierre, therefore $(\exists x)(x = x)$'—makes no ontological claim at all. Nor is it that Pierre exists 'in thought' but not it 'reality'. Pierre does not exist.

17.2 Existence and actuality

Fictional objects are not the only irreals. There are also objects which some or all people think exist but do not. They are the intentional objects of existence-assuming mental states: I will call them *putative reals*.

Consider the plane that you thought attacked you on your sortie. Some of the planes you thought attacked you on your sortie really existed, some did not. We can wonder whether this particular one, the one you're so sure you saw at 10.30 hours, really existed, just as we can wonder whether Prince Bagration, in *War and Peace*, really existed, or whether Ossian really existed. Similarily, the conspirators can discuss the exits from the building, discuss when to use exit A, B, or C, etc.—even though exit C does not exist. People can have definite thoughts about non-existent objects, and those objects can be referred to *de re*.

From this standpoint intentional identity is not a problem.[7] The conspirators discuss when to use exit C, failing to realize that it does not exist. But we too can refer to it, though we know it does not exist, by anchoring our references to their plans: the exit which they thought existed in the basement. Likewise, fictional characters are not bound to a particular fiction. We can put fictional characters in other fictions. Thus one could write a story about a detective called Smith who lives near Baker Street and knows Sherlock Holmes. The detective in *The Casebook of Smith* who lives in Baker Street and whom Smith knows is the one that Conan Doyle wrote about. If Nicola, having heard of the character Pierre in *War and Peace*, then misremembers and thinks Pierre is a character in Dostoevsky's *Crime and Punishment* she has a false *de re* thought about Pierre, the character in Tolstoy's *War and Peace*.

We can reason about non-existent objects, applying the usual principles of deductive logic. Obviously, however, non-existent objects have no properties that require existence. Both Pierre and Napoleon are written about by Tolstoy. Both of them spend time in Moscow in *War and Peace*. These are properties that do not require existence. Unlike Napoleon, however, Pierre does not spend time in Moscow; he just spends time in

---

[7] Geach, 1967. (The witch that Hob thinks blighted Bob's mare is indeed the one about whom Nob wonders whether she killed Cob's cow. But, as *we* know, she does not exist.)

Moscow in the novel. Spending time in Moscow is a property that requires existence. Similarly, exit C has the property of being thought by the conspirators to have a Yale lock; but it does not *have* a Yale lock, because it does not exist.

Talk of irreals must be anchored by their relations to the real. Hence fictional objects and putative reals, since they have no mind-independent anchor, must have mind-dependent anchors. They purport to be real but no mind-independent anchor is available. Of course if a putative real does exist, as with the plane you thought you saw, or the exit we thought was in the basement, then it can be anchored non-mind-dependently.

The issues can be clarified if we distinguish between existence and actuality. Existence contrasts with non-existence, actuality with (mere) possibility. Pierre is an actual irreal object. He is in *War and Peace*, but (unlike Napoleon) he does not really exist. Tolstoy might not have written *War and Peace*, in which case there would have been no such fictional character as Pierre. So there actually are fictional characters there might not have been. Tolstoy might also have written a novel he did not actually write, with various non-existent characters in it other than those he actually wrote about. There might have been such characters, but there are not. The contrast is between what actually is the case, and what merely might have been.

Fictional objects, and putatively real objects that do not actually exist, are contingently actual but necessarily non-existent. There is no possible world in which Pierre really exists. Furthermore, it is a priori that if Pierre is a fictional character then Pierre necessarily does not exist.[8] It is not, however, an analytic truth that Pierre does not exist. I may not know whether Pierre, the character in *War and Peace* that we are talking about, really existed. (Is Prince Bagration, another character in *War and Peace*, real or fictional?) The same applies to the plane I thought attacked me. If it did not really exist, there is no possible world in which it did—though of course there are possible worlds in which I am attacked by an enemy aeroplane.

To be is to be actual, to be actual is to be the value of a possible variable. We can refer to and quantify over anything actual, whether or not it is real. But can we refer to objects that are non-actual—non-actual possibles? I think not.[9] True, some 'possible objects' are actual. When we refer to the possible ways out of the building, we mean to refer to the *actual* ways out that *could* be taken. We can also talk about various ways things might have been, so ways things might have been, possible scenarios, are actual: they are properties of the way things are. It is actually the case that I might have had a son. But when we consider the scenario in which I have a son, is there some object—my possible son—that we are talking about?[10]

The anchoring condition implies that we can only refer to the actual. When we say that there might have been objects other than there are we are not referring to a subclass of the objects there are. We can indeed *imagine* that I had a son, tell a story about him, refer back to him, etc. So then this son is an actual fictional object. But counterfactual

---

[8] I agree with Kripke that actual objects that do not exist could not have existed. See Kripke 1981 (1972).
[9] Here I believe I disagree with Graham Priest's 'noneist' view (Priest 2005).
[10] This is not the same, of course, as supposing that I actually do have a son.

supposing is not in itself the same as imagining in the sense of 'fictioning'—making up an imaginary object. Fictional characters like Pierre could not exist, whereas the whole point about supposing counterfactually that I had a son is that such a son *could* have existed. This precludes treating a counterfactual supposition about a son I might have had as though it were about an actual irreal: my possible son. Counterfactuals are about actual possibilities, not about non-actual possible objects.

True, 'supposing' blends into 'fictioning'. We can imagine I had a son, called Adam, who joined the army, etc. We now have a shared topic of discourse, Adam. However, there is no non-actual and non-mind-dependent object of which we are thinking. Our Adam is a mind-dependent irreal: it is of course also true that I could have had a son, called 'Adam', etc., but such a son would not have been *Adam*: the imagined son we are talking about. It is an essential property of the Adam we are talking about that he is an object of our imagination. In contrast, when we suppose that I could have had a son, we are supposing that there could have been a person one of whose essential properties would be that he was not a figment of our imagination but my son. Similarly, if we suppose that a detective called 'Sherlock Homes' existed, lived in Baker Street, etc., we are not supposing something about Sherlock Homes. Being invented by Conan Doyle would not be among such a detective's properties, whereas it is an essential property of Conan Doyle's fictional detective.

We can conclude that the semantic condition is a condition on actuality, not existence. Since we can refer both to possibilities and to impossibilities, there are actual possibilities and there are actual impossibilities. The former are propositions which could have been true (or ways things could have been), the latter are propositions that could not have been true (ways things could not have been).

So what of propositions, and in general, of abstract objects? By the semantic condition they are actual and nor merely possible. But do they exist? Nothing said so far either entails that they do or rules it out. At this point, however, we must consider the causal condition.

17.3 The causal condition

It is ancient doctrine (going back at least to Plato[11]) that the real is whatever has the power of acting or being acted upon. True, some philosophies envisage real objects and substantial properties that do not have causal powers as *we* now usually understand 'cause', i.e. as a concept internal to empirical natural science. For example, some theists believe that God exists outside space, time, and causality; Plato holds that universals do; Kant thinks that things in themselves do. Kant also distinguishes something called 'the causality of freedom' from natural causality. However God, universals, and things in themselves are held by these thinkers to produce the world of space, time, and causality, even though they do not cause it in our usual sense. Likewise the causality of freedom is supposed to

---

[11] *The Sophist.*

be a *power* of the self to act. Thus on these views there is productive power even if it is not properly describable as causal power, given what we now usually mean by 'cause'.

In considering the causal condition we should understand 'cause' widely, not restricting it to our modern notion of a cause as something of which an intelligible scientific account can in principle be given. Whether that is the only tenable notion of causation is a separate question. If noumena produce phenomena in a non-natural way that lies beyond the scope of science then the causal condition says that noumena are real. Equally if God creates the world by some non-natural act of will, God is real; if Platonic forms somehow generate or produce or give rise to sensible appearances they are real. Come to that, if some normative realists believe that normative facts cause normative beliefs by a scientifically inexplicable productive relation, their view does not fall to the causal condition. The causal condition as such does not beg the question in favour of naturalism.

Among the objects we can talk about the ones that *exist* are agents or patients of causation. Existents have attributes that they are caused to have, and/or attributes in virtue of which they cause something else. You can find them in the causal net, as caused causes; uncaused causes; or caused non-causes. The causal condition says that a real object has a set of attributes in virtue of which it is affected by and affects other things in its distinctive way.

That causal standing is sufficient for reality should be uncontroversial. It is worth noting, however, the contrapositive: irreal objects have no causal standing. Suppose, for example, that Jim is thinking about Sherlock Holmes. That attribute of Jim can give rise to effects—e.g. Jim may forget what time it is because he is thinking about Sherlock Holmes. Isn't it equally an attribute of Sherlock Holmes? It's true of Sherlock Holmes, the fictional character, that Jim is thinking about him. So doesn't Holmes have causal power, and thus exist?

Once again we have to distinguish between semantics and metaphysics: in this case, between nominal and substantial properties or attributes. The nominal property is a nominal relation: 'x is thinking about y' is, if instantiated, instantiated by both x and y. But the substantial property is not a substantial relation. Thinking about Sherlock Homes is an attribute of Jim; being thought about by Jim is not an *attribute* of Holmes, because Holmes does not exist. Given the causal condition, non-existent objects do not have attributes because, by the causal condition, possession of an attribute is existence-entailing. Suppose, for example, that Jim causes an accident because he is so busy thinking about Sherlock Holmes. It's true to say that Jim causes it but false to say that *Sherlock Holmes* causes it.

So the causal condition is sufficient. Is it also necessary?

In 16.6 we endorsed the Kantian thesis that when the epistemology of a judgement involves spontaneity only, and no receptivity, we must take an irrealist view of its objects. This thesis does not entail that the causal condition is necessary for existence; however, the obvious argument for the Kantian thesis assumes that it is. We assume for the argument that if an object is real it has causal standing. Our other premise is that if it has causal standing we can know it only by its more or less indirect causal effect on us, that is, only by receptivity. Hence if my knowledge of an object involves spontaneity alone, that object is not real.

Conan Doyle does not need receptive faculties to know that Sherlock Holmes lives in Baker Street. Because Holmes is a construct of Conan Doyle's imagination, *Conan Doyle*, as against the rest of us, can know truths about him without recourse to receptive powers. (Of course he may in practice have to resort to memory, consulting his papers, etc. to find out, say, what number in Baker Street it was.) Fictional objects are irreal because they are imaginative constructs, and that same fact means that non-receptive knowledge of them is possible.

But might there not be objects that are real, have no causal standing, and are thus unknowable to us? Why, it might be asked, should there *not* be objects and facts that are real and substantial in just the way that objects and facts with causal standing are—the only difference being that they are causally inert? These objects would have substantial properties but no causal powers supervening on those properties, and thus no power to affect us.

It is true that the statement that $(\exists x)(x$ is causally inert $\& \ x$ exists$)$ is not self-contradictory. Nonetheless, I submit that to exist is to have causal standing. The identity is synthetic. It applies to substantial properties and thereby to objects. To be a substantial property, an attribute, is to have causal standing, where a property has causal standing if an object that has the property can cause or be caused in virtue of having it. To be a real object is to have attributes. This is a 'conceptual' truth in the way that, as will be argued in the next chapter, other synthetic a priori truths are. We cannot make the notion of a causally inert existent genuinely intelligible (as against merely pointing out that it is not inconsistent with pure logic).

17.4 Reason relations and abstraction

So we come to reason relations. By the causal condition reason relations are not substantial properties. *Beliefs* about reason relations have causal standing; but, as we established in Chapter 16, they are not caused by receptivity to causal influence from reason relations themselves. Reason relations are irreal. This is not to deny, as we can now put it, their *actuality*: it is certainly true that there *are* reason relations—there are three, to be exact, and none of them exist.

Two tasks remain: first, to clarify the difference between reason relations, on the one hand, and fictional or putatively real objects, on the other, second to consider the status of abstract objects. I hold that propositions about abstract objects are reducible to propositions about reason relations. But I won't develop the suggestion, since our main concern is the status of reason relations themselves.

Reason relations are not fictions. The difference is the difference between the product or construct of an act of imagination and the object of a cognition. Note, however, that to say (for example) that *Holmes* is a product of Conan Doyle's imagination is not literally true. Products, constructs, are real. It is the Sherlock Holmes stories, not Sherlock Holmes, that are the literal product of Conan Doyle's imagination; it was the Sherlock Homes stories, not Sherlock Holmes, that Conan Doyle caused to exist. Holmes is an imaginative product or construct only in the indirect sense that he is an imagined object within a product or construct, a temporal series of acts of imagination, that really does exist.

So we can say that fictional objects are irreal because they are intentional objects within imaginative constructs. Reason relations, in contrast, are not intentional objects within an imaginative construct. They are irreal because they are objects not of imagination but of *pure cognition*. A priori truths about them are cognition's norms.

There are corresponding differences of epistemology. In respect of Sherlock Holmes, there is an asymmetry between Conan Doyle and everyone else: we can't ask how Conan Doyle knows that Sherlock Holmes lives in Baker Street, but we can ask how others know (by reading Conan Doyle's stories, or hearing about them). In respect of reason relations there is no such asymmetry. We can ask how anyone knows that some pure proposition about reasons holds, and though the answer might be that they know by testimony, it is always possible that it is by personal normative insight, and in some cases it must be. No one person has authority as to what is true of reason relations, in the way that an author has authority over what it is true of his characters.

Thus fictionalism about reason relations is incorrect. Insight is not imagination. Error theory about reason relations is equally incorrect. Reason relations are not *putatively real objects* that turn out not to exist. That view would make sense if we thought of them as putative attributes. There would then be a significant question about whether there actually are any such attributes, or indeed could be. But we do not think this. Nor, finally, are reason relations constructs: truths about them are cognition's laws, *not* our constructs. So constructivism about reason relations is incorrect, as least if it literally claims that reason relations are constructs. (Kant would have agreed, as we shall argue in 20.3.)

All truths about fictional objects and putative reals are truths about minds; but not all truths about reason relations are. In particular, *norms* are truths about reason relations that are not truths about anything else. In this sense we can say that reason relations are neither fictions nor putative reals, but objective (non-mind-dependent), actual irreals.

What then about abstract objects? It might be said that our knowledge of them is indirectly receptive, in that is based on inference to the best explanation of data of which we are receptively aware. And it is certainly true that they feature in explanations of observable data, both in the substantive theory and in its underlying logic and mathematics. If the explanation is good enough, the inference to the truth of the explanatory theory, taken as a whole, is sound. Granting that, however, the further inference to the *existence* of abstract objects, as against the truth of propositions about them that appear in the theory, is a question-begging application of the semantic condition. That a proposition features in the full theoretical statement of an explanation of observable data gives one reason to think the proposition true, in proportion to how much reason there is to believe the explanatory theory. It does not entail that its objects are real—that only follows on the semantic condition. Inference to the best explanation can posit unobservable *causes* of observable events and warrant belief in their reality. However, such explanations do not attribute causal powers to abstract objects, and hence do not show that we have indirect receptive knowledge of these objects.

So are abstract objects another class of objective irreals? If so, do we have a whole new domain of objective irreals: possible worlds, numbers, etc.? I suggest that talk about these objects is reducible to talk about reason relations. This occurs in two steps. Talk of abstracta can be reduced to talk of possibilia.[12] Instead of talking about numbers, for example, we can talk about mathematically possible structures.[13] But in Chapter 8 we argued that *possibility* is itself normative. 'It is possible that *p*' means that there is not sufficient reason in μ to exclude the supposition that *p*. So talk of mathematically possible structures can be further reduced to talk of reasons in μ. Propositions about abstracta are normative propositions. What then about the domain of sense? To talk of the sense of an expression is to talk of its conceptual content. In 18.5 we shall argue that concepts consist in the holding of a priori truths about epistemic reason relations, so that grasping conceptual content consists in knowing epistemic norms.

Our final classification of what we can think and talk about is therefore as follows: the *actual*, which subdivides into *reals* and *irreals*, and then into *non-objective irreals*—fictional and putatively real objects of thought—and *objective irreals*—reason relations and nominal facts (hence also the property of truth).[14]

17.5 Truth and correspondence

We now turn from existence to truth. Here again the difference between semantics and metaphysics is important: the nature of truth is no more a question of semantics than is the nature of existence. But there is also an important difference between truth and existence. Existence, we have claimed, is a substantial property. Truth is not. Truth is a nominal property of irreal objects: propositions.[15]

---

[12] Propositions cannot be reduced to possible utterances and their semantic relations. On the contrary, semantic relations should be reduced to normative propositions about the application of conventions (see 18.2).

[13] This 'structuralist' programme is developed by a number of philosophers of mathematics. See e.g. Putnam 1975, vol. 1, 'Mathematics without foundations', also Putnam 2004: 65–7. Surveys of structuralism are provided in Shapiro 2000 Chapter 10, and in Geoffrey Hellman's chapter on structuralism in Shapiro 2005.

[14] Unfortunately our use of 'actual' and 'real' diverges from Frege's. There is point in his use: 'actual' has a connotation *of acting* that is stronger in the German *wirklich*. But it has seemed to me that to use these terms in Frege's way, given current philosophical usage which contrasts 'actual' and 'possible', would be too misleading. In any case I deny that abstracta *act* on cognition in *any* way. This apart, however, our view of abstracta coincides with his:

> In arithmetic we are not concerned with objects which we come to know as something alien from without through the medium of our senses, but with objects given directly to our reason and, as its nearest kin, utterly transparent to it.
> And yet, or rather for that very reason, these objects are not subjective fantasies. There is nothing more objective than the laws of arithmetic. (Frege 1953 (1884): 115.)

That is exactly what the cognitivist irrealist thinks about senses and reason relations. (Meinong divided objects of thought into those that are and those that are not, and then those that are into those that subsist (abstract objects) and those that exist (spatio-temporal objects). Perhaps the distinction between objects that are not and objects that subsist corresponds to our distinction between mind-dependent and objective irreals. The elusiveness of such questions seems inherent to the elusiveness of 'ontology' itself.)

[15] Crispin Wright's version of 'minimalism' explicitly does *not* claim that 'truth is not a substantial property' (Wright 1992: 24ff). It's unclear to me, however, whether there is genuine disagreement here. If there is, I believe it traces back to Wright's underlying endorsement of the semantic condition.

Still, if we are going to convey the meaning of sentences in an empirical language by writing Davidsonian truth conditions for them, we need to know the meaning of 'true'. What must we know? We must know that 'true' is correctly predicated of a proposition—that is, of what it is said by a declarative sentence in a context—if and only if what is said is true. And we must know that what is said is true if and only if what is said to be so is so. This knowledge is captured by the schemas:

(1) It is true that $p \leftrightarrow p$.

(2) P is true → (P = the proposition that p → it is true that p).

(3) It is true that p → (P = the proposition that p → P is true),

where 'P' is a variable ranging over propositions, while 'p' is a schematic letter.

Any further account of truth has to be consistent with (1), (2), and (3).

(1), we have argued, is analytic (7.4). (2) and (3) can be regarded as implicitly defining the predicate 'true', that is, fixing its reference a priori. If truth is a nominal property, an irreal object of thought, we can do that, since the question whether some unique existent satisfies the definition does not arise. Thus (1), (2), and (3) are a priori, necessary truths.

Because (1) to (3) have this status a Davidsonian truth condition can tell us the meaning of its object sentence. We need no a posteriori knowledge other than that the semantic biconditional which states the truth condition of a sentence (the T sentence) is true solely in virtue of the conventions constituting the object language. If we know this we can get the meaning of the object sentence by understanding the T sentence. We know that 'Snow is white' is true in L if and only if snow is white. And we know that this biconditional is true solely in virtue of the conventions of L. So we know that 'Snow is white' expresses the proposition that snow is white. We know that because we know that the proposition in question is one with respect to which it is *analytic* that it is true if and only if snow is white. So that proposition must be the proposition that snow is white.

Now as just noted, in treating (1) to (3) as an implicit definition of 'true', we commit ourselves to the irreality of truth. The question of existence, which can arise when we fix the reference of a term as discussed in 7.7, does not arise here, since being true is not a substantial property but an irreal object of thought. For the same reason we can regard (1) to (3) as not just a priori but also necessary. This view amounts to the 'minimalist' view of truth—(though it might be better called the 'irrealist' view, since the basic claim is that truth is not an attribute, i.e. a substantial property of propositions).

Contrast the correspondence theory. Put it thus:

(4) P is true if and only if there is a fact to which P corresponds.

Here 'there is a fact to which P corresponds' is not be understood as a merely terminological variant on 'P is true'. (4) is to be thought of as 'explaining' what truth is by expressing a substantial underlying identity: truth *is* correspondence, correspondence being, supposedly, a substantial binary relation between a proposition and a fact. Hence 'fact' in (4) cannot be understood nominally, as *true proposition*. Nor is (4) to be confused with the tautologous factuality thesis: a factual statement says that a fact obtains. In *this* thesis 'fact' occurs in the substantial sense. Common sense adds the substantive claim that there are true factual propositions. In their case, therefore, there is a dyadic relation between the proposition and the fact (if it obtains): namely, what one asserts when one asserts the factual proposition is that that fact obtains. It is true of that fact that it has been asserted to obtain. However, this is not the relation intended by the correspondence theory, for correspondence is meant to be an explanation of what truth *is*, or alternatively, what a *proposition* is. It is thus a claim about all truths, and all propositions. A proposition is a picture of a state of affairs. What makes the proposition true—its truth maker—is that the state of affairs it pictures obtains.

Suppose we hold that truth is the substantial property of correspondence. We will still accept the schema *it is true that p ↔ p*. But we will hold that instances of it are a priori, necessary metaphysical truths, nor merely analytic. The fact that snow is white has an essential, substantial truth-making property: the property of making it true that snow is white. Furthermore, necessarily nothing else has *that* truth-making property. So on this account grasp of semantics requires knowledge of these metaphysical truths about truth making.

Fair enough, it might be replied—it is not as if knowledge of these metaphysical equivalences is like knowledge of a posteriori equivalences, such as that snow is white if and only if grass is green. There would be something wrong with a semantics that required you to know that before it could give you an understanding of its object language, but there is nothing wrong with one that requires you to know these extremely obvious metaphysical truths. To which one might in turn reply that if they really were metaphysical truths it would be inexplicable how they could be *obvious*. Is it just a brute metaphysical fact that the correspondence relation holds between the proposition that snow is white and the fact that snow is white, but does not hold between the proposition that snow is white and Leon Trotsky?

I am not going to pursue this argument or other arguments that have been advanced against the correspondence theory (or other metaphysical theories of truth). They are unlikely to dislodge a well dug-in correspondence theorist. We can point out the counterintuitive consequences of the correspondence theory, notably about normative claims. We can ask what this putative correspondence relation is, and what notion of fact it requires. We can say that it leads into pseudo-questions about what facts there are. But perhaps our best persuasive strategy is to ask why we need it, and to apply Occam's razor if no answer is forthcoming.[16]

One answer is that we need it to explain why 'This fire is hot' is true, when it is true. But what sort of explanation is being looked for here? There is a trivial explanation: 'This

---

[16] Take two famous arguments associated with Frege. The first (Frege 1977: 3–4) effectively points out that if 'S is true' means S*: 'S has a correspondence relation to some fact', we have an infinite regress of substantial facts. (Consider 'S* is true'.) The correspondence theorist will deny that the regress is vicious; to a minimalist at least indicates that the correspondence theory multiplies substantial facts *praeter necessitate*. The other argument (it is not in fact clearly to be found in Frege) is the famous 'slingshot', which reduces all facts to a single fact. This seems less challenging, for it is *too* powerful, in that it is pretheoretically evident that there are many distinct substantial facts. So at least one premise of the slingshot argument must be false. (For critical discussion of the argument, see Read 1996.)

fire is hot' expresses a truth (in English) because this fire is hot and that is what the English sentence 'This fire is hot' means. Here the explanation consists in specifying what proposition is expressed by the sentence and asserting it. Another explanation is that 'This fire is hot' is true because the coal is combusting and giving off high-energy gases. In this case the appeal is to a scientific explanation of what it is that makes the fire hot. A correspondence theorist needs to show that there is some third explanation to be given.

Here is a third kind of explanation: the Fregean *concept* assigned to 'χ is hot' maps this fire into the true because this fire has the *substantial property* of being hot. I agree that that is an explanation, inasmuch as the attribute of heat is identical neither with the Fregean concept which is the semantic value of the predicate, nor with the predicate's sense. The latter items are abstracta posited by the Fregean semanticist, whereas the property of heat, in the sense intended in this explanation, is a concrete attribute of things that has a nature, essence, or constitution which physicists investigate. In doing so, they are not investigating the nature of functions or sets. (The same point could be made within other semantic frameworks.)

But this third kind of explanation can be given precisely because we are dealing with a *factual* proposition. 'Fact' in this context has its substantial sense: a fact consists in or supervenes on the possession of substantial properties and relations by real objects. The third explanation of why 'This fire is hot' expresses a true proposition appeals to this fire's possession of the substantial property of heat: to the substantial fact that this fire is hot. Unsurprisingly, since a factual proposition *says* that a substantial fact obtains, we can explain why it is true by pointing out that the substantial fact it says obtains does obtain. Equally unsurprisingly, however, if there are non-factual propositions the same thing cannot be done for them. Someone who insists that it can be done for every proposition is simply insisting that all propositions are factual propositions. Nothing in semantics entails that. It arises, rather, from the metaphysical picture embodied in the semantic condition for existence: that is, global realism.

A last claim could be made for the correspondence theory of truth. We could see it as a relatively shallow thesis about the meaning of the word 'true': it would simply say that 'It is true that' is properly attached to a sentence only if the sentence expresses a factual proposition. This would no longer be a theory rooted in a correspondence, or picture, notion of the proposition as such.

Cognitive irrealists could accept that, as a proposal about how to use 'true': they could then hold that whereas factual propositions can be said to be true or false, propositions about reasons can only said to be 'correct', or 'valid', but not true or false.[17] Indeed this way of talking has some attraction for a cognitive irrealist who stresses the basic

---

[17] Note the opposite position, which rejects this shallow thesis *without* rejecting the deeper thesis that propositions are essentially depictive. For example, Simon Blackburn calls himself an agnostic about truth as 'an identifiable "robust" property', and inclines to a 'more deflationary' view of truth. On this basis he is willing to attach 'It is true that' to those grammatically declarative sentences which in his view do not express genuine propositions (Blackburn 1998: 318 ff). At the same time, his non-cognitivist argument turns in part on a correspondence or depictive model of propositions. One trouble with this position is that it has to treat truth as a property of sentences, or utterances, whereas minimalism about truth works by treating it as an irreal property of *propositions*; see Section 17.7.

significance of the factual/normative distinction. It makes things perspicuous, but is laborious. Semantics would still need a broad term, such as 'correctness condition', to characterize the condition it attaches to any declarative sentence. On the whole it seems preferable to use 'true' in such a way as to preserve (1) to (3)—in which case the right word for the condition semantics attaches to sentences will be 'truth condition'.

Purely normative propositions have no truth makers, but then nor do any propositions, in the sense of 'make true' intended by the correspondence theorist. In that sense no proposition is made true by a fact. We are not rejecting the correspondence theory for normative propositions, while retaining it for factual propositions. We are rejecting it entirely. But we shouldn't abandon the phrase 'make true' to the correspondence theorist. In more ordinary senses *of course* facts can make a normative proposition true. What makes it true that you are acting wrongly is the fact that you are causing suffering, and doing so because of the pleasure it gives you. In this sense there are, precisely, facts that make normative but *not* factual claims true!

17.6 Quietism is too quiet

We have now placed the contrast between pure propositions about reasons and factual propositions on firm epistemological and ontological foundations. In epistemological terms the basic contrast is between spontaneity and receptivity, in ontological terms, it is between irreal and real objects. The epistemology of the normative is the epistemology of spontaneity—its objects, the reason relations, are irreal. In contrast a factual statement asserts that a substantial fact obtains; it is a statement about substantial properties.

At this point two opposing responses are possible, each of which rejects this fundamental distinction. One reiterates the correspondence conception, the other says that we need no substantial notion of fact at all. On either view cognitivist irrealism about reasons is impossible.

These responses seem to me to have a source in common: a conviction that thought and reality must be isomorphic. The structure of thought and that of reality must either correspond or literally coincide—the relationship must be that of picturing or sheer identity. Hence, whatever we can think about is real. There is a further factor which points towards identity rather than correspondence: rejection of ultimate dualisms. It is a driving force in absolute idealism and in pragmatism. Thus William James: 'anything is real of which we find ourselves obliged to take account in any way'.[18] Now I certainly hold that we 'find ourselves obliged to take account' of reason relations: we do not invent them—they are objective but nonetheless irreal. So my account of reality is not the pragmatic one. More generally, any Critical philosophy must accept a bedrock dualism: in Kantian language it is the dualism of spontaneity and receptivity, for the positivists it was the dualism of fact and decision. We shall come back to these issues in our concluding section, 20.9.

---

[18] James 1911: 101. (James is quoting A. E. Taylor's *Elements of Metaphysics*.)

But for the moment let us consider the Identity view, which identifies facts with truth propositions.[19] It has a negative or quietist aspect; it says that we do not need the notion of substantial fact. From this standpoint our contrast between factual and purely normative propositions has no philosophical significance, and the question of realism about reasons, as we have posed it, does not arise. On this approach one could say that one is as much a realist about reasons as one is a realist about everything else—or, alternatively, one could say that one is an irrealist about *all* propositions and not just propositions about reasons.

However, it is one thing to deny the correspondence theory of truth, and consequently the 'truth makers' it posits, it is another thing to deny the existence of substantial facts altogether. True, substantial facts and properties play no theoretical roles in semantics, and hence are not posited by semantics as such. Fregean semantics, for example, posits objects, functions, sets, and senses; it posits no substantial facts. Obviously, however, that is no argument for denying that there are substantial facts. Tables and fairies, flowers and phlogiston aren't posits required by semantic theory as such—that does not settle whether or not they exist. The question of their existence is settled by branches of inquiry other than semantics, though of course if they do exist we had better have ways of referring to them.

We often talk about facts. Can a quietist argue that all such talk is paraphrasable as talk about the truth of propositions? That looks implausible in causal contexts, where we talk about the causal properties of the facts. And as noted in 16.1, we can be objectually aware of facts, in apperception, perception, and memory. You can be aware of the fact that the room is getting hotter. The complement of awareness in this case is the substantial fact itself.

Denying any substantial notion of fact is an over-reaction to the correspondence theory. It is as though the only way to refute that theory is to knock out one element in the correspondence relation entirely, leaving only propositions. But reality does not consist of propositions. It is not identical with the Concept, the Proposition, or the True Thought.

With the correspondence theory safely out of the way we can accept that a substantial notion of fact quite clearly features in common sense thinking, science, and religious thought. Our basic conception of ourselves places us within a total fabric of facts that constitute reality. Facts enter into causal relations. In particular, our objectual awareness of facts in apperception, perception, and memory involves causal relations between those

---

[19] As John McDowell puts it:

> When one thinks truly, what one thinks *is* what is the case. So since the world is everything that is the case... there is no gap between thought, as such, and the world. Of course thought can be distanced from the world by being false, but there is no distance from the world implicit in the very idea of thought (McDowell 1994: 27).
>
> Given the identity between what one thinks (when one's thought is true) and what is the case, to conceive the world as everything that is the case (as in *Tractatus Logico-Philosophicus*, §1) is to incorporate the world into what figures in Frege as the realm of sense. The realm of sense (*Sinn*) contains thoughts in the sense of what can be thought (thinkables) as opposed to acts or episodes of thinking. The identity displays facts, things that are the case, as thoughts in that sense—the thinkables that are the case. (McDowell 1994: 179)

facts and facts about us. We do not need the Identity theory to acknowledge that we are open to reality in this way. Contrast McDowell:

> What is the point of conceiving truth in a way that turns on the identity of true thinkables with facts?... the point is that it helps me spell out the image of perceptual experience as openness to reality—as how reality itself is enabled to exercise rational control over our thinking.[20]

But rational control is exercised by our sensitivity to objective reason relations, not by the identity of true thinkables with facts. How would the latter help?

The world consists of substantial, not nominal facts. Having said that, there is no reason why our notion of a substantial fact should be neat and tidy. We do not need the ultra-perfectly fitting 'truth makers' that the correspondence theory needs. There is no cut and dried way of individuating facts, any more than with other concrete entities. Nor, as will be argued in 20.8, need it be clear where the boundaries of factuality lie.

17.7 Non-cognitivism is not required

Any Critical stance posits a fundamental epistemological dualism, which following Kant we have called the dualism of receptivity and spontaneity. We have also agreed that this dualism has ontological implications. What is left open is the interpretation of these implications. The Kantian view is that spontaneity-based knowledge cannot be knowledge of empirically real objects.[21] The view of this book is that it is knowledge of mind-independent irreal objects. But in the twentieth century the most characteristic Critical stance is that there *is* no spontaneity-based *knowledge*. There is instead a dualism of cognitive and non-cognitive.

The non-cognitivist version of the dualism makes it a dualism between the contribution of 'the world' via sensory receptivity and the contribution of the actor: the world contributes facts while the actor contributes decisions, rules, or emotional responses. In the twentieth century this broad approach rose from initially crude starting points to high levels of sophistication. Simon Blackburn and Allan Gibbard[22] have developed subtle ways of explaining and to some extent honouring our tendency to treat normative claims as true or false, while still retaining the non-cognitive base that is essential to their Critical stance.

Cognitivists, in response, continue to advance powerful objections, of which the most powerful is the well-known 'Frege–Geach' point. Indeed the basic difficulty that this objection reveals seems to me unanswerable.[23] Furthermore, minimalism about

---

[20] McDowell 2005: 87, in response to Engel 2001.
[21] I restrict it to *empirically* real because of Kant's doctrine of 'pure' or 'original' apperception—according to which the representation 'I think' which accompanies all my other representations is itself an 'act of spontaneity', which as such 'cannot be regarded as belonging to sensibility' (B132). We shall come back to this in 19.1 and 19.6.
[22] Blackburn 1984, 1993b, 1998; Gibbard 1990, 2003.
[23] Geach 1965; Hale, 1986; see also the debate between Blackburn and Hale in Haldane and Wright 1993, Chapters 16–18. The debate continues: as well as Blackburn and Gibbard see e.g. Lenman 2003; van Roojen 1996; Schroeder 2008.

truth cannot help the non-cognitivist, as against the cognitive irrealist. This becomes clear if we accept that minimalism makes truth a nominal property not of sentences but of *propositions*—contents of belief and assertion. It is the view that the proposition that it is true that p is identical to the proposition that p. In contrast, non-cognitivism holds that normative claims do not express beliefs and are not assertions of propositions. It is this initial non-cognitivist contrast between assertion and emotional expression that generates the persistent problem, irrespective of minimalism about truth.[24]

However, a more fundamental point is simply that non-cognitivism is not required. The classic objections that non-cognitivists make to normative realism are indeed sound. But they do not force one to reject the view that normative claims are straightforward assertions like any others: assertions that are true or false in the ordinary sense of those words. In contrast, the positive arguments non-cognitivists advance for their view all require premises we should reject, and in fact already have rejected.

I think there are three serious arguments for non-cognitivism, whose respective premises are (1) desire–belief psychology plus the thesis that to accept a reason is to be motivated thereby; (2) global realism plus open-question arguments; and (3) empiricism plus the thesis that purely normative claims are neither analytic nor a posteriori.[25]

(1) The first argument goes as follows:

> (i) A set of beliefs cannot on its own give rise to any action. To motivate, beliefs must combine with a desire.
> (ii) Practical–normative commitments can motivate.

So

> (iii) Such commitments must consist wholly or partly in having some desire.

So

> (iv) Saying that one has reason to do something is expressing (sincerely or insincerely) a desire to do it.
> (As formulated here the argument leads to emotivism. There can also be a voluntaristic or prescriptivist, as against an emotivist, version of non-cognitivism.)

We have already agreed with (ii) but rejected (i) in Chapter 10. Note also that this argument is restricted to the case of practical reasons. In contrast, we argued in Chapter 10 that there is nothing special about the practical case. Beliefs about reasons, practical, evaluative, and epistemic, can on their own or in combination with factual beliefs cause actions, feelings, and beliefs. Rational explanation has the same form in all these cases.

---

[24] Cp. Divers and Miller 1994; Horwich 1994; Smith, M. 1994a, 1994b. where Michael Smith argues that expressivists who deny that moral claims express beliefs (as against desires) cannot argue that such claims are truth-apt on the basis of minimalism about truth.

[25] They were considered in 10.3, for their bearing on cognitive versus non-cognitive models of rational explanation.

By the same token, non-cognitivism is at its strongest when proposed as an account of *all* reasons, epistemic and evaluative as well as practical. That is what is implied by the other two arguments.

(2) The second argument is short:

(i) All propositions are factual.
(ii) No purely normative claim is factual.

So

(iii) A purely normative claim is not the assertion of a proposition.

On this argument non-cognitivists are non-cognitivists because they are factualists. But, they think, no normative claim could *be* a factual claim. The argument is not restricted to practical–normative claims, and could lead to a variety of non-cognitivist positions, such as conventionalism in the epistemic case.

Here again we have agreed with (ii) but rejected (i). Non-cognitivists are right to think that open-question challenges undermine *all* factualist readings of normative claims—non-naturalistic ones as well as naturalistic ones. This will be discussed in the next chapter. And we have already argued in this chapter that purely normative claims, claims about reason relations, are not about non-natural existents.

(3) The empiricist argument is as follows:

(i) All propositions are either analytic or a posteriori.
(ii) Most purely normative claims are not analytic.
(iii) They are not a posteriori.

So

(iv) They are not assertions of propositions.

This again is a purely general argument which can lead to conventionalism, prescriptivism, etc.

Here we agree with (ii) and (iii) but disagree with (i). The counter-claim, that purely normative propositions are synthetic a priori, takes us to the heart of the issues—as one would expect, given the legacy of Kant. This argument from empiricism seems to me to be by far the strongest argument, for the heart of it is a challenge to the idea that there can be knowledge which is non-apperceptual, non-receptive and non-analytic—and that is indeed the most difficult thing to see. But we have tried to show, in the previous and the present chapter, how it is possible. It is possible, according to the Normative view, because purely normative claims are non-factual propositions. Ontologically speaking they make no claim about the attributes of objects, while their epistemology, as described in the previous chapter, is based purely on spontaneity and dialogue. What is true in empiricism is that all *factual* propositions are either analytic or a posteriori.

Evaluative and moral claims are indeed claims about feelings. That is the truth in emotivism. But they are neither claims about what feelings we actually have, nor are they expressions of such feelings. They are assertions about *reasons* for feelings.

17.8 What turns on 'realism'?

We have said that reason relations are irreal and described this position as cognitive irrealism about reasons. We have now got to a point were it is worth pausing to consider what hangs on these terms. Cognitive irrealism is not be identified with quietism or non-cognitivism, as discussed in the previous sections. But why call it irrealism? Could it not just as well be called realism?

Reason relations are irreal; they have no causal standing. But many things are true of them, for example, that there are three. Is there more than a verbal difference between this position and platonism, i.e. non-naturalistic realism? 'You mean by "actual" (it might be said) what the platonist means by "exists", and you mean by "exists" what the platonist means by "has causal standing"'.[26]

How one chooses to use these words is to some extent a matter of choice—but that does not mean that the distinction one uses them to mark is merely verbal. Is it a verbal question whether the semantic condition, or the causal condition, or both, characterize existence? I don't think so.

Platonism as it is nowadays generally understood is the view that propositions about abstract objects are factual just as propositions about carbon, water, heat, or colour are—the only difference being that, unlike these, abstract objects are causally inert. (Plato was not himself a platonist in this sense, as noted above.)

The only argument advanced for this view is based on the semantic condition. What then of fictional objects and putative reals? A platonist who holds that these also exist has a perfect translation from our terms to his terms (is actual = exists; exists = has causal standing). However, most platonists are likely to go with common sense by denying that such objects exist. The semantic condition then requires that apparent references to such objects must be paraphrased out—with all the difficulties that attend that project. Thus we do not have a perfect translation of the irrealist view—according to which, for example, there actually is a non-existent fictional character known as Sherlock Holmes, about whom we can perfectly straightforwardly talk.

An important difference between fictional objects and putative reals, on the one hand, and abstract objects, on the other, is that the former are mind-dependent whereas the latter are not. There would have been no Sherlock Holmes if Conan Doyle had not existed, whereas it is not true (or just unclear what it means to say) that there would have been no numbers if minds had not existed. But why would this show that $\neg(\exists x)(x = \text{Sherlock Holmes})$? Another asymmetry is that in talking of fictional objects we are talking of objects which in their fictional context are imagined to be concretely real. They are, one might say, *presented* as concretely real, whereas abstract objects are not. But the fact that abstract objects are not presented as concretely real is hardly an argument for holding them to be real.

What of our knowledge of abstract objects? We have noted that truths about them are not known through any kind of receptivity, natural or non-natural. Can a platonist simply

---

[26] Cp. Priest 2005; 152 ff on Lewis 1990; and Burgess and Rosen 1997.

agree? 'You yourself', he might say, 'have shown how knowledge of abstract objects can be epistemically grounded purely on spontaneity and convergence. I entirely agree with your account'. But abstract objects, as the platonist and the irrealist agree, are mind-independent. And mind-independent *reals* cannot be non-receptively known. This doctrine, we have argued, is basic to the Critical stance.[27]

Naturalism says that the natural facts are all the facts. Platonism is incompatible with this view, cognitive irrealism is not. For platonism holds that abstract propositions stand to abstract facts in exactly the same dyadic relation in which concrete propositions stand to concrete facts—but that abstract facts are not reducible to concrete facts. In contrast, irrealism denies that *any* fact stands to an abstract proposition in the way that a concrete fact stands to a factual proposition. That is a difference between the two positions, but is it an argument against platonism? So much the worse for naturalism, a platonist might say. Fair enough. But it is not just a question of being consistent with naturalism, which on some views is no more than a piety of our scientific age. I think we should question whether we have any clear picture of what abstract facts might be, whether we are naturalists, supernaturalists, or idealists. In the next chapter it will be argued that we have no clear idea of what it would be for a fact, *any* fact, to stand in the putative truth-making relation to a purely normative proposition. And I have suggested (Section 17.4) that propositions about abstract objects are reducible to normative propositions.

Realism about reason relations is best understood as the view that they are substantial relations about which there are substantial facts. The idea that there are substantial 'normative facts' can strike one as bizarre, or it can seem to have a bold and forceful air. Either way there's the sense of something provocative and 'queer' going on.[28] That is the characteristic indicator that a philosophical sleight of hand is taking place. Realism about the normative leads to a search for naturalistic truth makers for normative propositions, or to an error-theoretic or a non-cognitivist recoil. But all these responses are uncalled for. They can only seem appropriate if one shares the global realist's faulty account of existence, assertion, and truth.

In conclusion we should note the possibility of a more radically anti-metaphysical view than the one proposed here. Saying that there are Fs and that Fs exist can often, it notes, be just two ways of saying the same thing; in any case both ways of talking have various unproblematic uses in various contexts. There is no *philosophical* question about whether numbers, reason relations, purely fictional characters, or problems to resolve 'really exist'. That phrase too can be used in various ways. When we say that a character in a novel really did exist (and wasn't just invented by the author) we are saying one thing, when we say a problem really exists, and is not just an apparent problem, we are saying another. When we say that there exist two prime numbers between 16 and 22 we are

---

[27] Russ Shafer-Landau accepts that 'moral facts' have no 'independent causal power', but holds that 'we shouldn't deny [their] existence for that reason' (Shafer-Landau 2003: 112). Ralf Wedgwood, in contrast, holds that the causal efficacy of normative facts is implicit in the possibility of responsiveness to normative considerations (Wedgwood 2007). Both forms of realism are inconsistent with the Critical stance. But perhaps Shafer-Landau could accept the weaker stance of irrealist cognitivism; whereas it seems that Wedgwood could not.

[28] J. L. Mackie's word (1977).

saying a third, and when we say that neutrinos really exist and aren't just useful posits we are saying a fourth. The beguiling idea of a single 'world', or 'reality as a unified domain' is a will o'-the-wisp. There is no such thing as a criterion of 'ontological commitment'—that phrase means nothing. Ontology should be swept away as a pseudo-subject. What then remains is a mere tautology: if it is true that there are Fs then there are Fs.

On this view it is misleading to say, as we have said, that reason relations are 'irreal'. But then the term 'realism' as well as the term irrealism' should be discarded, since *both* suggest that some significant 'ontological' question is at stake.

I have considerable sympathy for this view; nonetheless, the position proposed in this chapter seems to me to be more natural. For we do, it seems to me, have a conception of unified 'Existence', or 'Reality'—not just in philosophy but pre-philosophically. If a quantum physicist, or a metaphysical theologian, gives a public lecture entitled 'The Nature of Reality', examining the fundamental structure of matter, or its relation to mind and God, we understand what they are talking about and why they give their lecture its title. Reason relations are not part of the Nature of Reality—not Constituents of Existence—when 'Reality' and 'Existence' are so understood.

Existence in this sense seems to be causal standing, in the wide sense of 'causal' (beginning of this chapter) that we have discussed. If, however, some metaphysician insists that there can be causally inert existents in just this sense of 'existence' then—from the Critical standpoint—a fundamental point remains. It is the distinguishability thesis, discussed in 6.3: no a priori relations hold between distinct existents. Knowers can cognize existents distinct from themselves only through some form of receptivity—be it scientifically describable, metaphysical, or magical. But reason relations are not known in any such way.

Putting aside the question of knowability, however, does the idea that substantial facts are the 'truth makers' for purely normative propositions even make sense? In the next chapter we shall argue that it does not.

18

RULES, NORMS, AND CONCEPTS

Not empiricism and yet realism in philosophy, that is the hardest thing.[1]

One area in which important questions about normativity arise has not yet been considered: language use; and concept possession. What is it to understand a linguistic rule? What is it to grasp a concept? Such questions have been central in philosophy since at least the first third of the last century, and indeed they go to the heart of our Critical theme. We must address them to complete our account of normativity, and to prepare the ground for a final critique of reasons in Chapter 20.

This calls for clarity about the relationships between *rules, norms,* and *concepts*. Norms, it will be remembered, are a priori truths about reason relations. Although the word 'norm' is widely used in a variety of ways, no other sense attaches to it in this book. Rules—conventions—are in contrast not truths about reason relations, or truths of any kind. They are the contents of intentions. What rules hold within a group of people is a fact about those people: their beliefs and their intentions.[2] Concepts, we shall argue in Section 18.5, are constituted by epistemic norms, *not* by linguistic rules.

Yet though a rule is not a norm, grasping a rule requires normative competence. No substantial fact determines what the rule requires in a particular case, hence, what the rule is. This is the elusive moral of Wittgenstein's celebrated discussion of rule-following (Sections 18.2 and 18.4). Examining what is involved in following a rule will lead us to our final discussion of normative realism, both reductive and platonistic.

Wittgenstein's discussion is often thought to go beyond Moore's version of the open-question challenge. Moore, it is thought, aims to establish a point about property identity: no normative property is identical with any property expressible by a non-normative predicate. On this reading it follows that no non-normatively characterizable fact could be the truth maker of a normative proposition; but it remains possible that that there are substantial *sui generis* normative properties, and thus that normative propositions have truth makers. If Moore holds that there are such properties, he is an intuitionistic realist about normativity. Clearly Wittgenstein is not that. Wittgenstein goes further:

---

[1] Wittgenstein 1978 (1956): 325   [2] Lewis 1969.

his point is that judgements about the correct application of a rule are normative, and that no *fact*, natural or otherwise, could be the truth maker of a normative judgement. We have no clear conception of how a *normative* proposition could be *factual*; our attempts to envisage a distinctive kind of 'normative fact' that could play that role are philosophical fantasy.

This reading of Wittgenstein might lead one to the conclusion that his account of following a rule is non-cognitivist. It will be clear by now that he had another option, that of irrealist cognitivism, and we shall spell out how it might be attributed to him. However, we are not mainly concerned with interpreting what the later Wittgenstein actually thought; it is the issue of rule-following, and what it shows about the normativity of cognition itself, that concerns us. Likewise we are not mainly concerned with interpreting Moore, and determining whether it is right to think of him as an intuitionistic realist. As a matter of fact, it seems that he may be best thought of as a cognitive irrealist who holds that normative properties are irreal.[3] If so, he might well have agreed with the argument of the previous chapter. However, we shall proceed by first considering the 'Moorean' open-question argument against normative *naturalism* and then the 'Wittgensteinian' argument against any kind of normative *realism*.

In its time the issue of rule-following attracted so much attention because many philosophers assumed that possessing a concept is grasping a linguistic rule. This had to be a central tenet of the Viennese School, given its scientific naturalism and its basic dualism of fact and rule, or fact and decision. In historical terms, the significance of Wittgenstein's discussion is that it is the profoundest exploration—and undermining—of that standpoint. We must take stock of where that undermining leaves the Critical approach. We shall argue that to have a concept is not to grasp relevant rules but to respond to relevant epistemic norms. Given our irrealism about reason relations that view of concepts supports important tenets of Critical philosophy: its anti-platonism and its commitment to the idea that factual discourse has non-factual preconditions.

The last section of this chapter (Section 18.6) discusses in a general way some questions which have cropped up about all the normative analyses in this book, concerning the order of analysis—what I have called the 'cart and horse' issue.

18.1 Rules and norms

There are some differences of connotation between 'rule' and 'convention'. For example, we are more likely to use 'rule' to refer to what is laid down by some authority, or endorsed by explicit agreement, whereas 'convention' often refers to a rule which just

---

[3] He says that natural properties are those which are fundamental in the sense that 'they are in themselves substantial and give to the object [of which they are properties] all the substance that it has' (Moore 1993 (1903): 93); also that 'the root of the naturalistic fallacy' is that naturalistic philosophers and metaphysicians both think that 'Every truth...must mean somehow that something exists', when in fact 'it still remains a distinct and different question whether what thus exists is good' (Ibid: 176). Moore, in contrast, denies 'that "good" *must* denote some *real* property of things' (ibid: 191). I have been helped here by Tom Baldwin, who pointed out these passages to me. See Baldwin 2010: 288–9.

grows up without any authoritative prescription or explicit agreement. But since such differences won't matter here we shall use 'rule' and 'convention' to mean the same thing. The essential point about a rule or convention is that it is the content of a prescription or explicit or implicit agreement: an individual or collective intention. We can thus ask *what* the content of the prescription, agreement or intention is and how it applies to a particular new case.

Rules can be expressed in apparently normative terms: 'The queen may be moved any distance in any direction', 'The knife should be placed to the right of the plate', 'To obtain medical treatment you must fill in form ABC', 'You are forbidden to park on double yellow lines'. Or in non-normative terms: 'We always meet in the portico of the National Gallery', 'The word that is used to refer to the colour green in English is "green"'. These are factual propositions if they express what rule holds in some context or population; they can be explicitly stated in that way: 'The rule (in chess, in most European countries, in our group, in the English language) is that . . .'

So we have the general form 'It is a rule in C that p', whose instances are true or false factual claims about C. But the rule-content, p, is not itself true or false, even though it is expressed by a declarative sentence. Or rather, it is true or false only insofar as understood to be a statement of what rule obtains.

Rules are not intrinsically normative. The *rule-content* is not in itself normative: it is not true or false at all. Furthermore, whether the fact that a rule obtains in C gives one reason to follow the rule depends on the circumstances. If some body lays down a rule there is the question whether it can permissibly command obedience. If you have reason to play a game of chess by the rules, then you have reason to move the Queen only in certain ways. Equally, if you should avoid that tree then you should brake now. In that sense what counts as playing by the rules of chess is no more a normative matter than the fact that the tree is there.

So in what way can the question of how to apply or follow a rule, of what counts as applying or following it, be a normative question? What is the issue? This has turned out to be a remarkably elusive question.

18.2 The normativity of rule-following

Let's suppose that you introduce a new term into our language: you point to a board in the paint shop painted in a rather unusual colour, and say 'We'll call this colour "brue"'. You have laid down a linguistic rule, which we are happy to go along with. 'Brue' turns out to be a useful new word that gets used quite a lot around the paint shop.

We can express this new linguistic convention by the clause:

(1) 'Brue' in our language denotes brue.

Or equivalently,

Our rule for 'brue' is to call anything brue 'brue'.

To know the meaning of 'brue' is to know the truth of these propositions (which is not the same, of course, as knowing that the sentences that express them are true).

Now let's suppose that on some subsequent occasion I know myself to be remembering your original stipulation correctly, and seeing normally, as I look at a particular shade. I think to myself, perhaps after some hesitation:

> (2) Given the colour of this, it accords with our rule as to what we call 'brue' to call it 'brue'.

Or equivalently.

> Given the colour of this, 'brue' as we use the term denotes it. (2) is true, we might say, because:

> (3) This is brue.

For (2) follows from (1) and (3).

Certainly (2) follows from (1) and (3). Equally, (3) follows from (1) and (2). So can we say that (3) true is because (2) is? No: the right thing to say is that the *sentence* expressing (3) expresses a true proposition because (2) is true.

However, this does not address Wittgenstein's problem. Suppose I'm in doubt about whether it is correct to call this 'brue'. My doubt is not about whether I am seeing the colour correctly, or remembering the concrete details of how you laid down the rule (what you concretely said and did); the doubt is about how to *understand* the rule. In that case I'm also in doubt whether this is brue. The rule is supposed to determine the truth-value of every statement of type (2) (vagueness aside), so if I'm not sure—in these circumstances—about (2) I'm not sure what the rule *is*: not sure exactly what proposition is expressed by (1). I know what is asserted by (1)—what the convention *is*—only if I can correctly judge instances of (2) in the described circumstances, i.e. when I know I'm seeing the colour of this correctly, remember how you laid down the rule, and vagueness is not an issue.

We are now in the territory of the 'rule-following considerations'. It is useful to remember that Wittgenstein was thinking about this problem as a problem for the Viennese fact/decision paradigm.[4] So the question was, does (2) state some fact? If so, what fact? Or does it express a decision?

This is another instance of the by now familiar dichotomy: either we take a factualist option, which gives us dispositionalism or platonism, or we take the non-cognitivist option. Now it seems clear that Wittgenstein was not a platonist about rule-following— this was a position he never took seriously. Contrary to some interpretations, I don't believe he was a dispositionalist either. Some have attributed radical conventionalism to him; but I believe that radical conventionalism was the *impasse* he was trying to avoid, rather than the solution he was proposing.[5] If the Viennese account of language is

---

[4] So I argued in Skorupski 1997b.
[5] See Dummett 1959, 1993; and Stroud 1965. Also Skorupski 1997b.

committed to holding that every rule-application is a new decision, that is a *reductio* of the account.

From the Normative standpoint there is clearly another option. It is to hold that (2) is neither a purely factual proposition, nor the expression of a decision, but that it involves a norm. Whether or not this was Wittgenstein's conclusion (whether or not he *came* to any conclusion), it seems to me to be the conclusion forced by the rule-following considerations. Their true importance is that they refute global realism.

Consider:

> (4) Given the colour of this and given our rule as to what we call 'brue', there's sufficient reason to believe that this satisfies 'brue' (or 'brue' denotes this).

I claim that if you know that (4) is the case you know that (2) is the case. But surely sufficient reason does not in general guarantee knowledge? It does not. Crucially, however in this context it does. It might be true, for example, that there is sufficient reason for me to believe that 'brue' denotes this, even though false that 'brue' denotes this, because I am misperceiving the colour. But in this context we are abstracting from such possibilities. (2) is a judgement solely about what the 'brue' rule requires in this case, *given* the colour of this. This judgement has an ineliminably normative component. The *factual* component is what was said, thought, agreed, about the use of a word, or what the practice with regard to its use has been hitherto. These facts, π_i, are the only substantial facts involved. They suffice to determine a rule only if the *normative* component also holds. The normative component is that π_i are sufficient reason to believe that 'brue' denotes this. 'Denote' is a nominal relation and the fact that 'brue' denotes *this* is a nominal fact. If we, in this special context, have sufficient reason to believe that it does then it does. In saying that I do not mean that (2) and (4) express the same nominal fact: to do so they would have to have the same sense. Nonetheless, π_i suffice to determine a rule about the denotation of 'brue' if and only if propositions like (4) are true.

Given the colour of this, and facts π_i, the judgement that 'brue' denotes this is a judgement of pure spontaneity. It involves no further judgements of substantial fact. The standard epistemology of the normative, the epistemology of spontaneity and convergence, applies. You are disposed to judge that calling this 'brue' accords with the rule: that is the first epistemic basis for your judgement. The only other epistemic basis is the test of convergence; hence Wittgenstein's emphasis on agreement of judgements.[6]

Rules are not norms, but judging how to apply a rule is a normative question. *Given* our rule for 'brue', what makes it true that the rule requires us to call this particular sample, not that one, 'brue'? Nothing other than its colour. But then what determines that this particular colour is the one that it's right to call 'brue'? The original intention, decision, stipulation, lays down no rails.[7] No *further* substantial fact is involved, be it dispositional or platonic. There is only the normative judgement, (4).

---

[6] Wittgenstein 1958a (1953): 242; 1978 (1956) VI 39.
[7] And it would not help if it did: Wittgenstein 1958a (1953): 218–19.

Of course this conclusion assumes that that normative judgement does not itself have a dispositional or a platonic truth maker.[8] So we now turn to consider open-question arguments against these options.

18.3 Moore's open question

The flaw in dispositionalism is that it treats the epistemic basis of a norm as though it was the norm's *content*. Certainly a considered agreement of judgements about the application of a rule has epistemic authority. That is important. But it is also true that it could be wrong, just as any other commonly held normative judgement could be wrong. Whether it is right or wrong always remains an open question. And the point still holds if we idealize the opinion in any non-circular way.

Furthermore (2) is a priori, not a posteriori. It is an empirical question what properties *this* has. But there is no further empirical question about whether it is correct to call this 'brue' in our language, given the properties it has. Yet all discussions of rule-following which assign to (2) a dispositional truth condition—to the effect that a language-community would agree on calling this 'brue' in some non-normatively described ideal conditions—make (2) a posteriori. They reduce a normative claim to an empirical assertion.

However, we should consider reductive normative realism more generally, for Moore's argument is directed against all its forms. A view of this kind holds that normative statements, just like any other statements, state facts; what makes it reductive is that it says that those same facts can also be asserted to obtain by certain *non-normative* sentences. The reducing facts may be physical, psychological, or come to that supernatural. Reductivism may or may not be analytic. If it is synthetic it accepts that normative and non-normative sentences express distinct propositions. But it holds that we can pair normative propositions with non-normative ones in such a way that asserting the distinct propositions in the pair turns out to be, in each case, asserting that some fact—as it turns out the same fact—obtains.

Moore's open-question argument is sometimes thought to fail against the synthetic reductive view, since this view does not hold that normative terms can be *defined* non-normatively. However, as already noted, Moore should be taken to use the open question as a way of establishing not just that you can't define 'good' but also *that the property of goodness is not identical to any property that can be attributed by a non-normative predicate*.

Thus, suppose you believe that a thing is good if and only if it's productive of pleasure. Then still, according to Moore, if you reflect on this you'll see that the property of being good isn't identical to, one and the same property as, being productive of pleasure. Similarly, suppose you believe that one has an obligation to do something if and only if God commands that one should do it. Still, if you reflect on this, you see that the

---

[8] But it does have a Davidsonian truth condition, in the sense of 17.1. The cognitive irrealist reading may differ in this respect from Kripke's (depending on what he would say about truth conditions in this sense—Kripke 1982).

property of being commanded by God is not identical with, one and the same property as, being obligatory.

It is an important point that these questions are open to a priori, purely normative, reflection. Whether a thing is good if and only if it is pleasure-productive is something we determine in that a priori way. Furthermore, even if we decide in this way that the biconditional is correct, we still see a priori that the respective properties are not, could not be, identical. In contrast we quite obviously could not determine whether water is H_2O by a purely a priori reflection.

Hence Moore's open question has purchase in the former case, but not in the latter case, which is exactly as it should be. Consider the 'Euthyphro' question: 'Is it obligatory because it's commanded by God, or is it commanded by God because it's obligatory?' This question would make no sense if there was a property identity here—compare: 'Is it water because it's H_2O, or is it H_2O because it's water?' But it quite obviously does make sense. It's only because we can see a priori that obligatoriness is not *identical* with commandedness by God that we can ask Euthyphro's question.

Likewise it is because we can see a priori that productivity of pleasure is not identical with goodness that we can assert, if we are hedonists, that it is the only thing that makes an action good. The action has the property of goodness in virtue of having the property of pleasure-productiveness. It does not have the property of pleasure-productiveness in virtue of having the property of goodness.

The same points can be made with respect to reason relations themselves. Here the claim would be that R is identical with some relation which can be characterized by a non-normative predicate, 'N':

$$R(\pi_i, t, d, x, \psi) = N(\pi_i, t, d, x, \psi).$$

(A matching account would be given of R_0 and S.)

Given that R ranges over actions, beliefs, and feelings, and that in each of these domains there is an irreducible substantive diversity of reasons, 'N' would have to be an extraordinarily long and diverse disjunctive predicate. It might be replied that R should be regarded as a *different* relation in epistemic, practical, and evaluative contexts. But is there any point in multiplying reason relations in this way? Is there more than one R relation *within* each of these contexts? Does the word 'reason' have different meanings in these different cases? We shall come back to these questions in 20.2 and answer them all in the negative. Still, for the moment let's focus on practical reasons alone.

One popular reductive candidate for practical reasons is instrumentalism:

$$R(t, d, x, \alpha) \Leftrightarrow x\text{'s } \alpha\text{-ing at } t \text{ would advance } x\text{'s objectives to degree } d$$

Here 'N' is 'x's α-ing at t would advance x's objectives to degree d'. This predicate expresses the instrumental relation; the reductive claim is that the reason relation *is* the instrumental relation.

Or suppose we are impartial hedonists:

$$R(t, d, x, \alpha) \Leftrightarrow x\text{'s } \alpha\text{-ing at } t \text{ would advance total pleasure to degree } d$$

Then the reductive claim is that the reason relation *is* the hedonic relation, expressed by the 'N' predicate '*x*'s α-ing at *t* would advance total pleasure to degree *d*'.

Convinced instrumentalists or impartial hedonists need not be reductionists. They can reject these alleged identities.[9] What they hold to be a priori evident, they can say, is that the R relation holds *in virtue of the fact that* the instrumental relation holds, or *in virtue of the fact that* the hedonic relation holds, and hence cannot be *identical* with it. And this is a quite general point that can be made for any candidate N relation.

Now on the Normative account to say that an actor and act satisfy the R relation *in virtue of the fact that* they satisfy some N relation is simply to say that the fact that $N(x, \psi)$ is a reason for x to ψ:

$R(\text{the fact that } N(x, \psi), x, \psi)$.

This gives us a way to pinpoint the fallacy involved in reductionism. The reductive theorist confuses the relation whose instantiation by x and ψ is a *reason* for x to ψ with the *reason relation itself*. When we say that some fact, such as $N(x, \psi)$, is a reason for x to ψ we are not saying that this fact *is* the reason relation. We are saying that it *stands in* the reason relation to x and ψ. And whether it does is always an open question, to be settled by normative insight.

This reductive fallacy is the fallacy Moore in effect identified, though in relation to the notion of good rather than the notion of a reason. The advantage of diagnosing it in terms of the notion of a reason is that it gets us away from the somewhat mysterious notion of supervenience. Reductive theorists may see it as an advantage of their account that it eliminates that mysterious notion. But on our approach it is clear that this is no advantage at all, since we can eliminate it anyway, without reductivism.

A sophisticated version of the reductive approach has been given by Frank Jackson; I would like to examine it briefly in terms of the diagnosis just offered.[10]

Consider the term 'water'. Jackson suggests that its reference is fixed as *whatever it is that has the watery appearances we are familiar with*. We have some beliefs about the appearances of water, and the sentences which express these beliefs are analytic on the term 'water': water is whatever satisfies those sentences. Similarly with the 'moral property terms'. In this case, however, we should take into account that our beliefs about what is morally wrong (say) might be false. So consider instead the beliefs of mature moral common sense—'mature folk morality'—about what is morally wrong. (These are beliefs that we may not yet have arrived at.) Moral wrongness is whatever property satisfies the sentences that express *those* beliefs.

Let's say that from those sentences we can extract a disjunctive predicate '$N(x, \alpha)$' such that:

It is wrong for x to $\alpha \leftrightarrow N(x, \alpha)$.

---

[9] Instrumentalists are perhaps less likely to do so than hedonists, but it seems to me that the explanation for this is more cultural and historical than logical.
[10] Jackson 1998, Chapters 5 and 6.

Can we conclude that wrongness is identical with the property N? The objection is that this commits the reductive fallacy. Wrongness is not *identical* with N; the correct account is that it is wrong for x to α *in virtue* of the fact that $<x, \alpha>$ instantiates the relation N, that is, some disjunct in this disjunctive relation. In 12.2 we analysed wrongness in terms of reason to blame; considered from this point of view the fallacy is particularly clear. Suppose that:

There is sufficient reason to blame x for α-ing ↔ $N(x, \alpha)$.

We have a normative relation on the left-hand side and a non-normative relation on the right-hand side. But the normative relation is not identical with the non-normative relation; what is true is that the fact that $N(x, \alpha)$ obtains, or rather, the fact that one of the disjuncts in this disjunctive fact obtains, constitutes sufficient reason to blame x for α-ing. Suppose the disjunct in question is that x αs in order to cause suffering to others purely for his own pleasure. The relevant identity is this:

the fact that constitutes sufficient reason to blame x for α-ing = the fact that x αs in order to cause pain purely for his own pleasure.

The reason to blame is identical with a fact about the action; but that does not mean that the reason to blame *relation* is identical with a disjunction of properties that constitute sufficient reason to blame.

This diagnosis explains a further objection to Jackson's account: it gets the aprioricity in the wrong place.[11] It is *not* a priori that the basic moral truths are those which mature moral common sense holds to be true—because it's not a priori that mature moral common sense is right. In contrast, the basic moral truths themselves *are* a priori. They express norms about what there is sufficient reason to blame, and their epistemology is the epistemology of spontaneity and dialogue discussed in Chapter 16. (This is a general difficulty for all a posteriori reductive naturalisms about the normative.)

So what moral epistemology fits Jackson's account? Jackson seems committed to holding that it is stipulatively a priori that the beliefs of mature moral folk morality about what is wrong are (mostly?) true, in other words, to taking that as an implicit definition of moral wrongness. Grant, for the sake of argument, that there is some one disjunctive property that will satisfy this definition. It seems that moral knowledge, knowledge of that disjunctive property, requires knowledge of what mature moral common sense would hold. Now we can accept that if you hold that cruelty is wrong you are committed to holding that 'mature' common sense will hold it to be wrong (or rather, that if it does not converge on your judgement then it isn't fault-free—16.4). But it's not *in virtue* of

---

[11] 'The identifications of ethical properties with moral [*sic*: read "descriptive"] properties offered by moral functionalism are one and all a posteriori. What is a priori according to moral functionalism is not that rightness is such-and-such a descriptive property, but rather that A is right if and only if A has whatever property it is that plays the rightness role in mature folk morality, and it is an a posteriori matter what that property is.' Jackson, 1998: 150–1. (There is a possible ambiguity in this passage, about whether rightness is a posteriori identical to some descriptive property, or a priori identical to the property of having some such descriptive property, that plays the 'rightness role'. I am reading it, by analogy with the example of 'water', in the former sense.) Cp. Horgan and Timmons 1992.

knowing what mature common sense will hold that you know cruelty to be wrong—if anything it's the other way round. (And come to that, how does mature moral common sense know what is morally wrong?)

18.4 Wittgenstein's open question

Moore's open-question argument, as we have presented it, is an argument against reductive normative realism. It argues that the property of goodness is not identical to any property that can be attributed by a non-normative predicate. If the open question establishes this, as I think it does, it can do the same for reason relations: it can establish that they are not identical to any relations that can be attributed by a non-normative predicate.

That still leaves open the possibility of non-reductive realism, i.e. the view that reason relations are substantial non-natural relations. Non-reductive normative realism says that normative facts are facts in exactly the same sense that physical (and perhaps psychological, and perhaps supernatural) facts are facts, but are not identical with any of these. Normative facts are *sui generis*. Either they don't have any kind of causal standing, or they affect us by a peculiar causal standing of their own.

On the first alternative we cannot know them (17.5). And even if we assume that they have some kind of causal standing, in virtue of which we are receptive to them, it was argued in 6.3 that an intuitionist account based on this assumption leads to vicious regress—so we couldn't know them even then. It follows that such normative facts could not explain our normative knowledge. But it does not follow that they do not exist. So can we argue more directly that they cannot exist?

Wittgenstein evidently did not take intuitionism about rule-following seriously, and not just because of the epistemological problems it poses. Propositions like (2), he would no doubt have said, don't depict or describe a state of affairs. But why not? Undoubtedly we are pretty close to bedrock here; nonetheless one can find in Wittgenstein 'an argument', or a persuasive consideration, that I at least find impressive. Its basis is that *normativity is not picturable*. Wittgenstein uses it in various places, e.g. here:

> In attacking the formalist conception of arithmetic, Frege says more or less this: these petty explanations of the signs are idle once we *understand* the signs. Understanding would be something like seeing the picture from which all the rules followed, or a picture that makes them all clear. But Frege does not seem to see that such a picture would itself be another sign, or a calculus to explain the written one to us.[12]

His point is that no object of any kind can have *intrinsic* normativity. There cannot be an object whose normative significance we know just by knowing its attributes. No 'picture' of objects and their attributes, whether it be physical, mental, or abstract, can tell us their normative significance.

[12] Wittgenstein 1974: 40.

Suppose we have a table of colours to remind us of their names.[13] Next to each sample of a colour there is inscribed a name. The inscription 'brue' appears on the same line as a sample of brue. This could be a useful aide-mémoire. But could that physical fact *be* the rule for 'brue'? Could it *be* the fact that 'brue' denotes brue? That is, could the property of denoting brue be *identical* with the property of having a token that appears on the same line as a sample of brue? Plainly not. The same would go for a mental table of thoughts about inscriptions and colour images. How then could an abstract, as against a physical or mental, table do any better? What special magic could an *abstract* table have?

Even if we had access to objects and their attributes in a Platonic third world, and had a mapping of terms and sentences onto these abstract objects and facts, that would do nothing for us. These objects and facts, just like physical and mental ones, could not tell us the meaning of the terms and sentences unless they were themselves signs, in which case the question of how they have meaning would arise for them just as it arose for terms and sentences. Abstract objects and attributes could not be intrinsically normative, any more than physical or mental ones could be. The objection does not have to do with the particular world we are talking about. The point is that a normative truth cannot *consist* in a fact about objects and their attributes.

We can apply this to reason relations. Suppose we have a 'table of reasons' in which facts are depicted in the left-hand column and the acts for which they are a reason are depicted on the same row in the right-hand column. It serves us as an aide-mémoire, reminding us of what is a reason for what. Could the reason relation be *identical* with the relation of *being depicted on the same row*? Would it make any difference if the table was abstract rather than physical or mental? Plainly not. A table like that would be useful only if one knew that it depicted, or signified, reasons: i.e. that it gave one reason to believe something about reasons.

If grasp of propositions about reasons is taken to be quasi-perceptual access to a special class of substantial 'reason-facts', these facts have to be picturable in some such way as the abstract table. But no such fact could make a proposition about reasons true. At most it could *signify* what propositions about reasons were true. *Reason relations are not themselves picturable*—physically, mentally, or abstractly. They cannot be identified with *any* substantial relation.

So the fundamental point is not that there may be 'normative facts' but if there are we cannot know them. Rather, the idea of a normative fact is inherently unintelligible. Purely normative propositions are not, and could not be, factual.

18.5 Norms and concepts

Once we have grasped the status of norms, we have the framework for an account of concepts and concept possession. However, the theory of concepts is a subject for books rather than paragraphs. My concern here is only to note some implications of the Normative view.

---

[13] Cp Wittgenstein 1958a (1953): 1; 1958b: 3.

Some concepts may be introduced by defining them in terms of other concepts, but some are grasped in a primitive way, i.e. not by definitions. So what does grasping a concept in the primitive way consist in? It does not consist in mastering some rules of language, even though it may well be true that we acquire conscious mastery of many concepts only by means of mastering a language which allows one to articulate them. Nor does grasping a concept consist in objectual awareness of an entity, though it does involve propositional awareness of reason relations. To grasp a concept, in the sense of having insight into it, or possessing it, is to have spontaneous recognition of a pattern of epistemic norms that involve that concept—to make those epistemic–normative judgements spontaneously. The norms in question are those that warrant introduction and elimination of the concept in thought.

One can say that concepts are epistemic–normative pivots, or switching points. Primitive concepts provide our basic thinking tools: concepts of perception; logic; induction; modality; evaluation—and, of course, the concept of a reason, which runs through it all. To have the concept *brue*, for example, is to have the ability to judge correctly, on the basis of visual experience, when there is warrant to believe that an object is brue, and then to recognize that as a reason to judge that it is coloured, that it is not green or white, but is a particular shade of purple, say. I may acquire the concept by learning the meaning of 'brue'; but possessing the concept is not *identical* with knowing the linguistic conventions governing the use of 'brue'.[14]

To possess a concept is to be sensitive to a pattern of truths about epistemic reason relations in which the concept features.[15] Since these truths may be more or less obvious, and more or less far flung, concepts are not clear-cut items. (If they were, there would be less work for philosophy to do.) There can be vagueness, genuine doubt about what norms they involve. Since more than one concept can appear in a norm, their constitution overlaps. Concept possession is a matter of degree: one often comes to appreciate the implications of a concept slowly, as one thinks through the relevant pattern of epistemic norms.

When we talk about a concept we may be talking about a putative or alleged concept: a concept constituted by a putative epistemic norms which are in fact *false* normative propositions. Take the concept of Good in Chapter 13. An egoist would hold, a priori, that we are never warranted in thinking that anything is Good. There are putative exit norms for the concept of Good, but no entry norm. So this putative concept, from the egoist's point of view, is a defective normative pivot. In one way he understands the 'concept', in another way he denies that there is any such concept.

Or it may be that the sentences we use to express propositions that putatively fix the concept do not even succeed in expressing any. 'Tonk' is a famous example:[16] it identifies

---

[14] In what sense is conceptual role semantics *semantics*? The norms that determine a concept's role in thought aren't linguistic conventions. On the other hand, inasmuch as one has a more 'full-blooded' understanding of a word by grasping more fully the concept it expresses, an account of the concept's epistemic-normative role increases understanding of the word.

[15] I don't mean that you must know these truths, i.e, that you can only have the concept of yellow if you have the *concept* of a sensation of yellow, or the concept of moral wrongness if you have the *concept* of the blame sentiment. But you must have the sensation and the sentiment, and be able to recognize its reason-providing force.

[16] Prior 1960b.

no genuine epistemic–normative pivot—not because the putative norms that supposedly constitute it are actually *false* normative propositions, but because the rules for 'tonk' have not identified any normative propositions at all. The sentences purporting to do so lack sense, because they do not merely mention 'tonk' but use it. (This is not meant to be a clear-cut contrast; the egoist might say that 'Good' is just like 'tonk': the difference is just that we *seem* to grasp the notion of an agent-neutral practical reason, but don't even *seem* to grasp the tonk operation.)

There is also the possibility that a genuine concept turns out not to be instantiated. Colour concepts could be an example. Even though there can be sufficient default reasons to judge that something is red, and sufficient reasons for making further deductions, the default reasons may be defeated and it may turn out that nothing is red. What the concept's extension is depends on the facts. By a perceptual norm, a perceptual impression warrants me in thinking that there is something red there. I can raise the question whether there are unperceived objects that have the attribute of redness (unperceived because too far away, or too small...). I seek an answer to such questions by reference to generalizations connecting redness to other attributes. But it may be that our best theory doesn't refer to the putative attribute of redness at all.

If a theory of concepts is a special theory within the general theory of epistemic norms, that greatly reduces the importance of the notion of *conceptual truth*. Even philosophers who balk at applying the category of analyticity still tend to deploy 'conceptual truth' as an 'explanation' of aprioricity and necessity. And such 'explanations' still seem to assume that conceptual truth is something semantical; that is, the explanatory category *true by virtue of meaning alone* still seems to hover, like a holy ghost, over the proceedings. But on the Normative account a conceptual truth is just an epistemic–normative truth: an epistemic norm that partly constitutes a concept. We can say that the epistemic norms discussed in Chapter 9 are conceptual truths. They are concept constituting and they are true. But their status as conceptual truths in no way *explains* how they can be a priori—it just designates that status. For an explanation, we need the resources of cognitive irrealism. If we have those resources, we have an account of normative knowledge, and need no further or distinct theory of how aprioricity is a matter of conceptual truth. An account of normative knowledge will do what that theory was meant to do.

18.6 Cart and horse: supervenience

At a number of places in this book I have given normative definitions of various concepts: *good; a priori; necessary; probable; morally wrong;* a *right*. In each case a cart before the horse objection can arise. It is time to consider this kind of objection in a general way.

Sometimes these objections deny the proposed equivalence. Hart's objection to the Bentham/Mill definition of rights (which we accepted in 12.6) was of this kind, as was the 'wrong kind of reasons' objection to the buck-passing account of good (which we rejected in 4.4).

In all cases, however, there is a further objection: the true 'cart before the horse'. It arises even though the equivalence is accepted. Euthyphro did not deny that the pious is that which the gods love; he wanted to know whether the gods love it because it is pious, or whether it is pious because the gods love it. Similarly we can ask a hedonist whether an action is good because it is pleasure-productive or pleasure-productive because it is good. He should answer that it is good because it is pleasure-productive: the other answer would indeed get the cart before the horse. Or consider an equivalence of the kind proposed by T. M. Scanlon: A acts morally wrongly if and only if A's action is disallowed by principles that no one could reasonably reject.[17] This is more puzzling. Does the left-hand side hold in virtue of the right-hand side, or is it the other way round? In this case, does the question make sense?

We should distinguish between definitional and explanatory order. In a definition in which the left-hand side of the equivalence is being defined in terms of the right-hand side the order is from right to left. Thus, for example, since 'vixen' is defined as 'female fox' it tends to sound more natural to say that this is a vixen because it is a female fox than the other way round. But if this is a definitional equivalence it does not make sense to ask for an *explanatory* order. Being a vixen is not *caused* by being a female fox, nor does the property of being a vixen *supervene on* the property of being a female fox. By definition it just is that property. Where there is definitional equivalence there is definitional order—but there cannot be explanatory order. In contrast, Euthyphro can sensibly ask which way the explanatory order goes, and, it seems, we can ask which way the explanatory order goes in the Scanlon-type of equivalence.

Thus where we have given definitions of normative terms we cannot admit that there is a significant question of explanatory, as against definitional, order. If there is an explanatory order in either direction our purported definitions cannot be *definitions*. A cart and horse objection can say that there is an explanatory order—that, if correct, is enough to undermine the *definitional* claim. Furthermore, it can say that it goes in the opposite direction to the purported 'definitional' order. Combining these two against the definitions we have offered it would respectively object that:

- There is reason to favour a thing *because* it is good.
- There is reason to blame x *because* x could have recognized the action to be morally wrong and no extenuating circumstances applied.
- It is permissible for x freely to make a demand *because* x has a right.
- There is outright reason to believe that p *because* it is a priori that p.
- The supposition that p is not unconditionally excludable in μ *because* it is possible that p.
- There is reason of degree d to believe that p *because* it is probable to degree d that p.

In each case, where the target predicate is $P(x)$ we have given a definition in terms of a reason-predicate of one kind or another, call it $R*(x)$. So we have:

---

[17] Scanlon 1998, Chapter 4. (This particular version of the equivalence is mine.)

(I) P(x) ↔ R*(x)
(II) P(x) =Df R*(x)

The cart-before-the-horse objection then says that even if (I) is a priori true (II) is false. The P property is not identical with the R* property; the latter *supervenes* on the former.

In all the cases mentioned the intuition lying behind the objection is a 'realist' one, in the sense that it says the reductive definition ignores a property of x which really exists and which explains why x has the R* property. The Normative view will deny that there are two properties involved, and claim that the alleged explanatory property is just a reification that does no explanatory work. Given that the *equivalence* is not in question, how can we try to settle this?

Compare the Fregean definition of direction as an equivalence class of parallel lines. Here again one can object on the basis of a realist intuition that lines are parallel *because* they have the same direction. But realism throws up its own problems. If there were no such existents as directions, would it follow that no lines are parallel? Or again, if there were no such existents as numbers, would it follow that that there aren't as many cows as horses in the field? The realist can answer that directions and numbers necessarily exist; but the point is that realism about directions and numbers gives rise to peculiar questions to which it then gives peculiar answers.

However the intuition in the case of parallelism and direction may be as much an 'absolutist' as a 'realist' intuition, i.e. a tendency to explain relations in underlying absolute or monadic terms. If so, then perhaps in the normative case there is also a drive to explain reason relations in terms of monadic normative properties. The monadic property is somehow thought to be 'out there' in a way the reason relation is not.

It is true of course that if there is reason to ψ we can ask why there is. We are asking for the facts that constitute the reason, or if the facts we are given do not constitute a complete reason, we are asking why they constitute a reason. We can ask in this way why there is reason to favour x, why there is reason to blame x, why it is probable that x. (We cannot ask this about a claim that a proposition is a priori, since that is the claim that there is *outright* reason to believe it.)

But this bring us to the redundant middle man objection. Suppose it is held that there is some proposition that P(x), which supervenes on the facts, and then the proposition that R*(x) in turn supervenes on it. We then have the three-tier structure noted in 12.9, where we considered it for the case of wrongness and blame. Thus we have, for example, the available facts, the probability that supervenes on those facts, and the reason to believe that supervenes on that probability. Why do we need the middle man? Why do we need the notion of supervenience? Why isn't the situation, quite simply, that these facts give us this degree of reason to believe, and that talking about the probability is just another way of saying the same thing? Suppose there is no such distinct property of probability. Does that show that those facts do not, after all, give us any degree of reason to believe? We could also ask this question about the supposed distinct properties of goodness, etc.

On the Normative view we can sweep away all relations of normative supervenience and replace them by reason relations. That applies even to supervenience relations between reasons. Suppose, for example, that there is sufficient reason to ψ, in virtue of the fact that there are such-and-such specific reasons. What that says is that there is sufficient reason to ψ, and the reason why there is sufficient reason to believe that there is, is that there are these specific reasons.

Similarily with the Bridge principle, which we stated as follows:

> Whatever fact gives x reason to feel ϕ gives x reason to do the ϕ-prompted action, in virtue of being a reason to feel ϕ.

'In virtue of' is replaceable by the reason relation:

> Whatever fact gives x reason to feel ϕ gives x reason to do the ϕ-prompted action, and the reason it does so is that it is a reason to feel ϕ.

That is, the reason to do the ϕ-prompted action is that some fact obtains that constitutes a reason to feel ϕ.[18]

How does the reduction of normativity to reasons affect the meta-theoretical debate? Are all the approaches we are familiar with from meta-ethics—realism, non-cognitivism, fictionalism, error theory—possible meta-theories of reasons? As noted in the introduction to Chapter 16, fictionalism and error theory have developed as accounts specifically of morality, and one suspects that they have appeal because of doubts about morality that are not meta-normative. It's hard to see how they could make sense with respect to reason relations in general. Reason relations are the essence of thought, in that thought just is responsiveness to them. To deny that there are truths about reason relations is to deny the objectivity of thought itself.

In principle, however, realism and (sophisticated) non-cognitivism are neither more nor less viable about reason relations than they are about *good* or *ought*. Still, it seems to me that there is somehow less of a psychological block about irrealism with respect to reason relations than there is about irrealism with respect to these other notions. This may have something to do with the reifying or absolutizing tendencies mentioned earlier in this section. In particular, goodness feels as if it is a substantial property, in a way that reason relations do not. But reason relations are just as objective as goodness, and goodness is just as irreal as reason relations.

What there is reason to believe, feel or do is in no way mind-dependent (even if the facts that constitute the reasons are sometimes facts about minds). Reason relations are irreal just because they are the objects of spontaneous thought itself. That is why they are able to play their Critical role. But we shall come back to this in the final chapter.

---

[18] The question arises whether there is an interesting and distinctive relation of supervenience in *any* field—for example, with regard to the mental, or causation. But this is not the place to pursue it.

19

SELF AND SELF-DETERMINATION

Before we arrive at the final chapter of this study, we should take stock of a network of topics that have arisen obliquely in previous parts of the book: apperception; grasp of reasons; the self; will; and freedom. They hang together as ingredients of self-determining agency; they are notions we deploy in understanding ourselves and others as persons. For personhood is, by an ideal if elastic criterion, or a central if not dominant measure, the capacity for self-determination—even if we fall substantially from the actuality of self-determination, or even the capacity.

At the same time it would be well to clarify what can be learned from Kant's powerful treatment of these subjects, and what we must reject. However, we shall reserve one aspect of his view, his meta-theory of reason, for the next chapter (20.3).

It is by no means the aim of this chapter to give a comprehensive discussion of self and self-determination, any more than Chapter 17 aimed to give a comprehensive discussion of ontology. As in Chapter 17, our aim in this chapter is to trace out the implications, in this area, of the Normative view—and their limits. Section 19.1 discusses what apperception is, relates it to one among a number of senses of consciousness, and discusses and rejects Kant's theory of 'inner sense'. 19.2 considers under what conditions we are warranted in attributing self-determination to an entity. 19.3 and 19.4 examine the links between self-determination and, respectively, unity of apperception and freedom. 19.5 to 19.7 turn to ontological issues about reasons, apperceptual facts and persons. Reason relations, we have argued, are actual, objective, and irreal. What then about persons? Are persons real?

19.1 Apperception, consciousness, and 'inner sense'

So far we have characterized apperception in terms of its epistemic role. To recall: x apperceives that p at t if and only if the fact that p is, at t, a monotonic sufficient reason for x to believe that p.

Since the apperceptual fact that p is in x's epistemic state, it constitutes a warrant for x to believe that p. It is *self-warranting*. It can be so because apperception is potential awareness: attention to whether or not an apperceptual fact obtains can be sufficient for awareness that it does obtain. Not that this is a sufficient condition of apperception. Perception too is potential awareness: I perceive a red light only if I can be aware that it is there if I attend to whether or not it is. However, the fact that there is a light there is not itself a sufficient reason for me to believe that there is.

So what is apperception? What is its nature? By the Critical argument, if the apperceptual state and the apperception of it were distinct, apperception would require receptivity (6.3 to 6.4). Apperception would be cognition of a cognition-independent fact. As with perception, therefore, we would have to distinguish between seeming apperception that p and actual apperception. Nor could an apperceptually-based sufficient reason to believe that p be monotonic, since it would fall under the non-monotonic norm of receptivity (9.5).

We must conclude that apperceiving a state is just *being* in that state. With apperceived states *esse* is *appercipi*. To think and to apperceive that I am thinking is one and the same thing. To be in pain and to apperceive that I am in pain is one and the same thing. Several consequences immediately follow.

First, if the apperceptual fact that p *is* the fact that I apperceive that p then it follows that one apperceives only states of oneself. Second, it follows that one's apperceptually-based beliefs are immune to error through misidentification. I could not *apperceptually* know that someone is in pain, is thinking, etc., without knowing that I am.[1]

Second, we must guard against thinking of apperception on the model of perception. The essence of apperceptual states is to be apperceived. Whereas apperceiving that one is in pain is being in pain, perceiving that there is a red light there is not identical with there being a red light there. The content of apperception is itself (which is why I refer to the *apperceptual*, not the *apperceived*, fact that p). That of perception, in contrast, is an ostensible field of independent objects—a field whose objects may or may not exist.

Further, we should distinguish apperception, awareness, and attention. I may be in pain, thus, apperceive that I am in pain, without being aware that I am; and I may be aware that I am without attending to the fact that I am. Similarly I may hear traffic noise without being aware of it, and be aware of it without attending to it. Changes of awareness or attention are not changes at the level of apperception, but attention presupposes awareness which presupposes apperception. When I attend to some element in my perceptual field (an element which I really or apparently perceive), say the computer screen, or the sound of a car alarm outside, I am thinking about, focusing mentally on, that element. However, I can do so only because I am *perceptually* aware of it, and I can be aware of it in that way only because ostensible perception is itself an apperceptual state.[2]

---

[1] On 'immunity to error through misidentification' see Evans 1982, Chapter 7; and Hamilton 1995.
[2] I leave it open whether there are cases which can be described as objectual awareness without perception (e.g., perhaps, blindsight). If there are, one is not *perceptually* aware of the object, cannot *perceptually* attend to it, though one can attend to and answer questions about it.

I can also be aware of, and attend to, my apperceptual states. But apperceptual awareness and attention are no more a species of perception than is apperception itself. Being aware that one is hearing a ringing sound is not perceiving an inner state. Nor is being aware that one is in pain, or of what one is thinking, or of what emotions one is feeling, or of some aspect of one's perceptual experience as experience. To realize, for example, that one is daydreaming—to become aware that one is—is not to suddenly *perceive* that one is. One becomes aware of one's apperceptual states either actively or passively, by attention or as a result of ceasing to attend to something else. Attention may be voluntary, as when one is asked to attend to some aspect of one's visual experience, or it may be involuntary, as when one becomes aware of ringing in one's ears or experiences a sharp pain. Occurrent *thinking* has attention to its intentional object built into it—it is attentive as such. Hence, thinking about what one is thinking, focusing on the thinking as an object, can interfere with it, whereas thinking about one's pain does not 'interfere' with the pain.

I use the term 'apperception' for a number of reasons: partly to emphasize the contrast with perception, partly because apperceptual consciousness is a kind of by-the-way, or going-with, consciousness, and partly because the term consciousness, which could be used instead, is ambiguous.

There is (i) a relational sense. When I hear a bell ringing I can be said to be conscious of a bell ringing. Similarly I can be conscious of a presence behind me, or of my interlocutor's disbelief. In that relational sense of 'conscious', what I am conscious of when I have a headache is my head.

In another sense of conscious (ii) we say that perception, thought and pain are conscious states. They are not states *of* which I am conscious, they *are* states of my consciousness. Consciousness in this sense is feeling, sensing, thinking.

However, there is also a sense (iii) in which I can say 'I wasn't conscious of being in pain' even though I was, or 'I wasn't conscious of daydreaming' even though I was. Consciousness in this sense is awareness. Just as one can be aware or unaware of something in one's perceptual field—a light, a distant traffic noise—one can be aware or unaware of something in one's apperceptual field—of one's pain, of an auditory experience.

Finally there is a sense (iv) in which being in pain, or hearing a bell, are conscious states, but thinking about one's jobs for the day is not. There is 'something that it is like' to be in pain or hear a bell—it is of their essence as *experiences*—whereas there is nothing that it is essentially like to think about one's jobs for the day. (It may be depressing, and cause sinking feelings, but that is not essential.) In this sense of 'conscious', conscious states are those that have an introspectible experiential character, quality or feel: sentient states, one may say.

My term 'apperception' corresponds in part to consciousness in sense (ii).[3] However, a difference may be that consciousness in sense (ii) seems to refer to *occurrent* states. If so,

---

[3] And thus, I believe, to what Ned Block called 'access consciousness' (Block 1995).

apperception is wider. I apperceive what I believe or desire, whether or not I am occurrently thinking or feeling anything. I apperceive what I seem to remember, even if I am not currently engaged in recall. To know what I seem to remember it is sufficient for me to attend adequately to the question. The same applies to belief and desire. True, it may be difficult for me to realize, become fully aware of, what it is that I believe, desire, or seem to remember. I may repress it, in some sense refuse to attend to it. I may need to discuss it with someone else, think about what I have done, how I would feel. Where honesty is painful it may be difficult. However, these are all ways of becoming aware of one's apperceptual states through self-examination. Even though the fact that I believe, or desire, or seem to remember that *p* may be hard for me to realize in the first-person way, I can nonetheless become aware of it in that way. Or at least, only if that is so can I be said to apperceive it.

Apperception is the source of all knowledge of states of oneself acquired in the first-person way: acquiring it 'in the first-person way' just *is* acquiring it through apperceptual awareness. There is no inner perception (other than, in a different and irrelevant sense of 'inner', proprioceptive perception of one's body). There is, it is true, consciousness in sense (iv), sentience: some but not all apperceptual states have an experiential character. But these states are neither objects of inner perception nor perceptions of something inner, i.e. of states of the self or soul.

Kant thought of 'inner sense' as inner perception. Were that a sound way of thinking it would force a distinction between my states as they are presented to me in inner sense, and my states as they really are. This was a conclusion Kant readily accepted—it fitted all too neatly into his transcendental idealism. Indeed it follows from it: any introspectible state exists in time, and time is but a form of sensible appearances, hence any introspectible state can only be a sensible appearance. More: if transcendental idealism is consistently applied, the noumenon of which 'my' introspectible states are appearances is wholly unknowable.

This is the most fateful way in which transcendental idealism distorts Kant's thinking about the self. Apperceptual states are not appearances to me of my noumenal self. We do not need, and should not even accept the coherence of, a distinction between the 'empirical' self—the self as it appears to itself—and the 'noumenal' self—the self as it really is. We should especially reject the way Kant aligns his indispensable distinction between spontaneity and receptivity with the misguided distinction between noumenal and phenomenal self, so that all spontaneity becomes noumenal, and all receptive content phenomenal. He compounds this mistake by aligning belief and will with the noumenal causality of freedom, while aligning inclinations, feelings, emotions with sensations: treating them as appearances of myself to myself in receptivity, and as impediments to my freedom (causes alien to the causality of freedom), rather than as, in some cases at least, products of genuine spontaneity, dispositions of the real me.

The contrast between spontaneity and passivity should be drawn *through* the domain of feelings, beliefs, and actions. There are genuinely spontaneous feelings and there are responses that passively reflect convention, group feeling or whatever. The same goes for what one believes and what one does. Furthermore Kant's transcendental idealism undermines his account of apperception. It forces him to hold that *any* state or episode of which I am introspectively aware in time—not just sensation and feeling, but also thought and decision—must be sensible appearance. Hence the scope for apperception, as Kant handles it, is reduced to zero, or rather, to a contradiction: it becomes a bare consciousness of self-activity, yet not a consciousness of the self, or of the activity, as against its phenomenal product. On Kant's account (if we consistently apply his principle that there is no knowledge of noumena) inner sense takes over and apperception reduces to zero. In contrast the account offered here eliminates the myth of 'inner sense' and identifies *all* self-consciousness (consciousness in sense (ii)) with apperception.

Obviously these points about apperception and spontaneity mark very big divergences from Kant. And yet (as with spontaneity) even on our quite different use of the idea of apperception there are important things to say about it which echo, even if distantly, themes in Kant: about how self-determination requires a certain unity of apperception, a distinction between self and other, and an idea of self as both a subject of apperception and an object placed within a spatio-temporal and causal field of objects. The echoes are, as I say, quite distant. We shall not pursue how distant or close they are to Kant but simply develop them in their own right. But we should begin by reviewing what it is to act for a reason.

19.2 What is it to grasp and act for a reason?

Two rather different kinds of philosophical question are involved. One asks what must be the case, at the physical or functional (sub-personal) level of description of an entity, for that entity to be said to have perceptions, feelings, beliefs, and to act intelligibly from them. We come back to this question in Section 19.5. The other asks, given that the intelligible or interpretative way of describing some entity is warranted, what further specific conditions, if any, are required to impute *reasons* to it? It is the latter question that we are concerned with in this section. Can we, in particular, impute reasons to beings that lack the capacity for self-determination?

We should start from our discussion of the epistemology and ontology of reasons. Knowledge of reason relations is not receptive knowledge of some non-natural domain. The situation is not that a being either has this receptivity, in which case it is a self-determiner, and indeed a potentially autonomous agent, or it does not have it, in which case reasons cannot be imputed to it at all. Acquiring sensitivity to reason relations is not acquiring a new receptive faculty. There is no discontinuous point at which an entity comes into a new relation to a distinct domain of normative fact, and thus becomes a self-determiner. Insight into reasons is epistemically grounded on reflective awareness of spontaneous dispositions alone.

From this perspective, it is easier to see that there need be no sharp answer to our questions. Reason-responsiveness is a matter of degree. There is a continuum in which we begin to think of a being as acting for a reason—then begin to think of it as a self-determiner that makes judgements about reasons—and then as possessing autonomy, authoritative insight into reasons. Since concept possession is reason-sensitivity, it too comes in degrees. Let us trace this development.

A minimum condition on what it is to act for a reason would be this: it is to act from some states that have intelligible content, *in virtue of that content*. That is, it is not just that the state causes the act; specifically, it is because of its content that it causes the act. But since we only ascribe states with intentional content to entities in order to explain their acts *by virtue* of that content this minimal condition is satisfied as soon as we ascribe such states.

A heat-seeking missile registers its environment and alters its direction in virtue of what it registers—its content. If the minimal condition were all that was required we could say that its reason for changing its direction was that it registered a change in the target's flight path. This seems too broad. That was the reason it changed direction, i.e. that was the cause, but can we talk about *its* reason for changing direction? Can we say that it thought the target was changing direction? Talking of what *it* thought, and of *its* reasons for action seems non-literal, a mere *façon de parler*.

With many species of animal, on whatever exact grounds, such ways of putting it seem a lot more apt. Animals of sufficient behavioural complexity can be said to perceive and apperceive, and to be aware of what they perceive and apperceive. An animal can hear a noise, be aware of it, notice it, know that it is a particular kind of noise, react to it. It acts in virtue of the content of what it perceives. That is not just a *façon de parler*. But can the animal be said to have reasons and possess concepts?

A stag jumps away from something that hurts it, swerves to avoid the tree, etc. Why does it do that? Because it feels the pain and sees the tree. It has a perceptual and apperceptual field with propositionally characterizable content. It perceives that there is a tree there (or at least that there is an obstacle in its path), it apperceives that it is in pain. It can be aware that it is in pain, or distracted from it by its need to run fast and accurately through the trees. It knows what is in front of it as it runs. It knows that it is being chased, and is running because it knows that.

Must it have relevant concepts—*pain, what is in front of me, being chased*—to be said to believe these things? When it runs because it thinks it is being chased, is it acting for that reason? Or must it have the concept of a reason to act for a reason? Surely ascription of reasons is a matter of degree. The stag has *some* degree of reason-sensitivity just insofar as it responds selectively to apperceptual awareness of pain, to perception of what is ostensibly in front of it, to the belief that it is being chased. To some degree, likewise, it has the concepts *pain, what is in front of me, being chased*: whatever degree goes with knowing it's in pain, what is in front of it, that it is being chased.

The stag runs away because it thinks it is being chased. The cat waits at the mousehole because it expects a mouse to come out. The dog heads for the back of the shed because it thinks that that's where it's got to be to catch the cat. Are these animals acting for reasons? Our uncertainty about attributing concepts and reasons to them arises partly because we are not sure how 'exactly' to characterize the intentional content of their thoughts. Nonetheless I do not see why we should deny them reasons, unless we also wish to deny them apperception and belief. That would put them back with heat-seeking missiles, which seems wrong. Degrees of apperception and perception go with degrees of reason-responsiveness hence with degrees of concept possession. They form a system which we attribute as a whole, but which we think can develop from primitive levels to highly sophisticated ones.

Obviously there are limits on the range of reasons for which these animals can act. Cognitive internalism (3.9) says that where a being has no potential sensitivity to the reason relation that makes a given fact a reason, that fact cannot, for *it*, be a reason. Clearly there are many reason relations to which these animals are insensitive, even potentially. But why not accept that they are sensitive to *these* particular reason relations: that there's reason to run away, to wait at the mousehole, or at the other end of the shed—even if, inevitably, that is only the best way *we* can put their reason?

This still does not make them self-determiners. A self-determining actor needs to have conceptual resources to make self-auditing judgements: in the first place the concept of a reason, and then concepts of apperception as well as perception, since the self-determiner must be able to ask itself whether it has sufficient reason to believe that it really does perceive. And since this must be based on its spontaneity it must have not just spontaneous dispositions to act, but also spontaneous normative dispositions to beliefs about reason to act.

Even if we think the cat has reasons we don't think it can deliberate about these reasons. It does not deliberate about how strong a reason there is to wait at the mousehole. It does not deliberate about whether there is any reason to expect a mouse, or whether there is more reason to do something else, instead of waiting for a mouse, nor do we think that *it* thinks of itself as acting for a reason. It is extravagant to attribute the *concept* of a reason to the cat. It seems that the cat's degree of reason-responsiveness does not require it. If, however, it is argued that capacities for self-determination are required before we can legitimately impute reasons at all, then it follows that the cat does not act for reasons. And if it does not act for reasons it does not possess concepts. To me this seems to put the bar for reason-sensitivity and concept possession too high. But for our purposes we can leave the issue there. Whatever the best resolution may be, the relevant point for us is that *self-determination* requires the concept of a reason.

19.3 Self-determination and the unity of apperception

Self-determination also requires a unity of apperception on which unities of perception and cognition can build. The main features are as follows.

(i) A self-determiner does not just apperceive this and apperceive that, simultaneously or in succession; it apperceives a synchronically and diachronically unified field.
(ii) Within that apperceptual field it discriminates an ostensibly perceived field of objects, and an ostensibly remembered field of objects.
(iii) It places its perceptual and remembered fields within a single spatio-temporal framework of continuant objects, a framework which both unifies them and extends far beyond them.
(iv) It thinks of—in a sense, experiences—objects in this framework as causally unified in some way.

(v) It locates itself and others within its perceptual and memory field and thus within this spatio-temporal and causally unified framework.
(vi) It identifies itself as *self-determining, apperceptual subject* with itself as *spatio-temporally and causally located object*.
(vii) It places its epistemic field within the framework. The epistemic field extends beyond the perceptual and memory fields but is still only a sub-part of the framework.
(viii) It responds to and sometimes reflects on its apperceptual field in the light of epistemic, evaluative, and practical reason relations which it takes to obtain and by which it determines its activity.

All these powers and activities are presuppositions of the capacity of self-determination. (Of course one can have the capacity without always acting in a self-determining way.) They all come in degrees. At the most basic level, any entity which can be said to act from a capacity to process information about its environment must be credited with an informational field and the ability to update it. The missile registers a moving continuant object which it tracks in a unified field within which it also registers its own motion. But we may think that this way of describing the missile is a *façon de parler*. Further up the scale, an animal that can be said to act for a reason must have a certain unity of apperception proper. It individuates continuant objects within a framework in which it also places itself. It experiences these objects multimodally: for example, as looking a certain way and making a certain sound. Acting for a reason and responding to a unified perceptual field develop together.

An animal that acts for reasons must have (i) to (v) to some developed degree. But it need not be self-determining. Self-determination requires *self-audit*, and this requires (vii) and (viii). Self-auditors must have conceptual self-awareness: they must be able to assess their epistemic states holistically and self-reflectively, applying normative judgements to them. This induces a higher, more thoroughly articulated and developed unity of apperception.

Is awareness of independent objects a conceptual precondition of self-awareness? Yes, if we are talking about the abilities involved in (v) and (vi). To have a unified conception of self as simultaneously apperceptual subject and objective agent one must think in terms of a causally and spatio-temporally unified framework within which one is located as an objective agent *among* other objects. Self-determiners must think of themselves that way, so awareness of independent objects is a condition of self-determination. Might there, nonetheless, exist a *purely* apperceptual, non-self-determining, consciousness of self, without consciousness of continuant objects? Nothing I have said is meant to rule that out, or rule it in.

19.4 Self-determination, freedom, responsibility, and autonomy

As noted in 10.10, Kant conceives autonomous action as acting from warrant without inference from alien causes. To quote again:

> Will is a kind of causality belonging to living beings so far as they are rational. *Freedom* would then be the property this causality has of being able to work independently of *determination* by alien causes... [4]

Freedom conceived positively as autonomy is action from 'reason' alone—in the terms of this book, from full first-person insight into warrant; conceived negatively it is action not influenced by alien causes. Given what Kant means by 'alien causes' the positive and negative conceptions are inseparable. A fully free action is an action for which there is a fully rational explanation in the sense of Chapter 10, an alien cause is a factor that causes one to act otherwise than in accordance with warrant.[5]

Given that beliefs and feelings can have fully rational explanations, the definition of 'will' given in this particular passage, taken strictly, applies to belief and feeling as well as action. In their case too there is 'a kind of causality belonging to living beings so far as they are rational'. It is the determination of belief or feeling by recognition of warrant. In all cases an act so determined falls under the causality of freedom: it is an act that can be rationally explained in the sense of Chapter 10.

In the case of feeling and belief, however, we do not call the causality of freedom *will*. That is because *Willkür*, voluntariness, is absent. Its presence in the case of action involves two points. There is the reality of willpower, noted in 10.10, and of course there is the basic fact that sometimes we can and do *voluntarily* act against warrant.

Should we say that voluntary wrongdoing (action against warrant) is free? There is no straightforward answer to this question; the multiple notions of freedom in our ordinary thinking are too diverse. However, two particular notions of freedom are ethically significant, and important both for Kant and for us in our discussion of reasons: freedom as responsibility, and freedom as autonomy. Each of them goes beyond mere voluntariness.

The significance of freedom as responsibility lies in moral assessment. Its relevance is to the question of blame, for blameworthiness turns among other things on whether the agent had the power to do the morally right thing. Freedom as responsibility is stronger than mere voluntariness: an addict's actions are voluntary, but he may not be a free agent in this sense of freedom. Even if there is a moral obligation to refrain, he may lack the power to do so, in which case he is not relevantly responsive to the moral law. Nonetheless his actions are voluntary and he does them for a reason. Likewise, you stay in bed voluntarily even if you lack the willpower to get up. Like the addict, what you do you do for a reason: it's so comfortable in bed. Suppose you would lack the willpower to get out of bed even if you knew there was an urgent moral obligation to do so. Then you lack freedom in the sense of responsibility. These factors diminish blameworthiness; if the inability really is total, they remove it (though as ever you may still be to blame for having got

---

[4] *Groundwork*, IV: 446.

[5] Negative liberty in the social and political sense involves the related notion of freedom from 'external' coercion. However, this is not the notion we are considering. One may act freely, in the sense being considered here, if one is being threatened, blackmailed, and so on, or even in the Gulag. Giving in to a threat may be warranted; if it is and one acts from that warrant one acts autonomously in the present sense. One's action has a fully rational explanation.

into this state). Voluntariness, in contrast, does not entail even the *capacity* for responsibility, understood as moral self-determination.

Note the asymmetry: freedom as responsibility entails the power to do the right thing—it does not entail the power to do the wrong thing. It is not (as Kant recognized) the view that you are free only if you could have acted otherwise.[6] Suppose you simply cannot tell a lie. On Kant's view that would be no restriction on your freedom as responsibility, your capacity for moral self-determination, for he thinks it is always wrong to tell a lie. If he were right about that, he would be right to think that your inability to tell a lie is no restriction on your freedom as responsibility. If, however, it can sometimes be obligatory to tell a lie, and you are unable to do so even then, that *is* a restriction on your freedom in this sense. But a person who was incapable of ever failing in a genuine moral obligation would not lack freedom as responsibility. So what other kind of freedom would he lack? Or better, why would any such lack matter? This leads us to freedom as autonomy.

We distinguished in 15.8 between 'Hegelian' and 'Kantian' autonomy. The former is more than self-determination but less than the latter. Self-determination involves the capacity to act from reasons which one audits by reference to putative norms that one accepts in some way or other, perhaps just by the command of others. Autonomy requires normative *knowledge*, explicit or implicit. It is action (belief, feeling) from recognition of warrant.

However, recognition of warrant, as we have several times noted, need not be based on fully first-personal insight. One can know by testimony that there exists a purely a priori warrant for an act. Normative *knowledge* of warrant is all that Hegelian autonomy requires; unlike self-determination it *does* require that—not just belief, acceptance. The individualistic Kantian model of autonomy is stronger again, emphatically so in the moral case. In Kantian as against Hegelian autonomy an autonomous act (belief, feeling, action) proceeds not just from warrant but from fully first-personal insight into all the underlying a priori warrants. That applies in particular to moral autonomy. We are expected, as moral agents, to have fully first-personal insight into our moral obligations.

We suggested (12.4) that the capacity for moral self-determination, rather than autonomy, is the only conceptual requirement on moral agency as such. Hegel might well agree; but he makes a powerful case for holding that autonomy in his sense is an indispensable modern ideal of freedom and moral integrity ('subjective freedom'). His case is partly a critique (a constructive criticism) of the individualistic Kantian conception of autonomy, and partly a positive account of the possibility of modern *Sittlichkeit*.

There is the question of what powers or virtues are desirable for members of a modern moral community that harbours a free and flourishing moral common sense. For that inquiry in social and political philosophy, the Hegelian idea of autonomy is the

---

[6] 'One cannot say that the opposite of all actions must be subjectively possible for us to be free...but only of those coming from our sensibility' (*Reflexion* 5619: cp 3868, 6078, 6931; *Academie* vols. 17 and 18). Kant often identifies freedom with autonomy, for example, when he says that morality can be derived from the idea of freedom; however, he also acknowledges that heteronomous action can be free (in the responsibility sense).

appropriate starting point. Yet beyond that, and quite apart from it, Kantian autonomy remains for many of us an ideal of self-developed personal life.

It remains so even if we reject the strong moral significances that Kant attached to it (see 12.4 and 12.5, 15.5 to 15.8). It remains not as a condition of moral agency or absolute final value but as the ideal of a certain personal freedom of mind, will, and feeling, or free and integrated personality. To call it the ideal of self-mastery, or self-governance, would be potentially misleading given the strong association of these phrases with willpower, capacity to make yourself do what you do not want to do, or to act against feeling. A one-sided association of autonomy with these factors loses the ideal's essential connection with fully integrated spontaneity of the whole person. Given Kant's ethically devastating failure to recognize evaluative reasons and their epistemic basis in the spontaneity of feeling, he is certainly open to criticism of this kind—the famous criticism of Schiller.[7] However, the very basis for this criticism is provided by Kant's own abstract account of autonomy: the causality of freedom, which works through spontaneous personal insight into reasons, independently of determination by alien causes. Schiller's ideal, one can say, retains this philosophical basis while correcting Kant's distorted rationalistic view of it.

We do not live in an ideal world, and there are contexts in which autonomy requires action against feeling. Justice, for example, may warrant action against fully-warranted love. Autonomy is not a recipe for peace of mind. Furthermore, it is plausible that cultivating a Schillerian, fully integrated, autonomous personality has costs. It may be psychologically unachievable, in which case the second-best option may be not to sacrifice to its cultivation but to aim for something else. And there are other ideals, such as those of humility or service or unconditional love. Yet the ideal of freedom as Schillerian autonomy is the ideal of classical liberalism, the ideal of John Stuart Mill and other great liberals. Questions about its feasibility and its value in relation to other ideals are therefore questions about the significance and authority of this liberal ideal.

Let us finally ask whether either of these notions of freedom—responsibility and autonomy—involve a causality which is transcendental, as Kant thought; a power that, as far as the empirical or scientific notion of causality goes, is contra-causal?

We do not in general assume that powers or capacities of objects must be analysed contra-causally. So why should we think that the power to do the right thing must be? You can have, right now, the power or ability to do the morally right thing, even though you don't, just as you can have the power or ability to get on your bicycle right now and ride it even though you don't. If an 'alien cause,' such as understandable distraction, prevents you from doing what you could and should do, that may serve as an excuse. But even if determinism is true the mere fact that you failed to do what you could and should do does not *already* give you an excuse. For in the first place, determinism is consistent with power. And second, the cause of your failing to do what you could and should have done—for example, that you couldn't care less—may *not* be an excuse. The question is

---

[7] For an account of how Schiller's ideas of freedom and criticisms of Kant developed, see Beiser 2005.

whether the cause in question removed or diminished your ability to do what you should have done.

Suppose you fail to get out of bed when you have a moral obligation to do so, and suppose you have the relevant power of self-determination: you could have made the effort and got out of bed. In that case you stay in bed freely in the responsibility sense, but not in the autonomy sense. But why *didn't* you exercise willpower? The failure to do so can only be explicable by 'alien causes' and your failure to act will therefore be heteronomous. This is truistic: the causes, whatever they were, were alien causes because they prevented you from acting from the causality of freedom, i.e. from warrant. Even if you didn't get out of bed because there were reasons not to, such as the warmth and comfort of bed, you still acted from alien causes—because these particular reasons weren't good enough, in context, to constitute warrant. However, only if what caused you to stay in bed removed your power to get out of it did you lack freedom as responsibility. How to discover in such cases whether a person's freedom as responsibility was diminished or entirely absent is of course often a great problem, but it is an epistemological problem about the availability of evidence; it points to no underlying incoherence that it requires transcendental idealism to resolve.

Yet plainly, whether we consider the connections between self-determination and apperception, or the connections between self-determination, autonomy, and freedom, we find ourselves echoing indispensable themes in Kant—even as we depart from his transcendentalism.

19.5 Why treat reasons as nominal, not substantial, facts?

In the next three sections we turn to ontological questions about reasons, apperceptual states, and the self.

We have taken reasons to be nominal, not substantial, facts: truths. There are two grounds for doing so.

One of them was mentioned in 3.3. As noted there, some reasons are essentially indexical. Take the fact that JS's name is not on the list of people selected for a suicidal mission. To know that that is a reason for me to be relieved I must know that I am JS—and the fact that I am JS is a nominal, not a substantial fact. Likewise with the fact that JS has been called to reception: I know it is a reason to for me to go there only if I know that I am JS. Nor can I know that these facts are reasons for me to believe that I have been selected, or called, unless I also know that I am JS. It may be replied that these facts are indeed reasons for me—just reasons I do not know. After all we have acknowledged that there can be reason for a person to ψ even though that person does not know there is—this applies whether the reason in question is evaluative, epistemic or practical. So why can't the fact that JS's name is not on the list be a reason for me to believe that I am not selected, and to be relieved about that, even if I do not know it is?

It's true that these facts can be reasons for me even if I do not know that they obtain. However, they cannot be *complete* reasons for me to believe that there is reason for *me* to

ψ. A complete reason for x to ψ is a set of facts with respect to which it is a priori that if they obtain they are a reason for x to ψ. But whether it is a priori that the set of facts in question constitutes a reason for x to ψ will depend on what term is substituted for 'x'. That is because these reasons are actor (agent, person, or thinker) relative, as discussed in Chapter 3. Suppose it is a priori that if JS's name is not on the list and certain further facts about the list obtain that is a reason for JS to be relieved. Then these facts, if they obtain, are a complete reason for JS to be relieved. Since I am JS, they are thereby a reason for me to be relieved. But they become a complete *de se* reason for me to be relieved—a reason that I can know a priori to be a reason for *me* to be relieved—only if the fact that I am JS is added to the set of facts that constitute the complete reason for JS to be relieved. Likewise, there is complete *de se* reason for me to believe that my name is on the list only in an epistemic field which includes the fact that I am JS. In general, where a reason is actor-relative, for me to know that it applies to me it must include indexical facts about me.

There must be complete *de se* reasons if self-determination is possible. The crucial line of thought runs from self-determination through self-audit to the possibility of warrant and thus to the availability, to the self-determiner, of *de se* complete reasons. Since self-audit is first-personal, the relevant complete reasons must be reasons that self-determiners can recognize a priori as applying to themselves, *de se*. Since actor-relative reasons must include indexical, and hence nominal, facts we might as well take it that all reason-constituting facts are nominal facts.

The second ground for taking reasons to be nominal facts is that normative truths can be reasons. In particular evaluative truths can be practical reasons. Thus consider:

(1) The fact that he has frequently treated clients in blameworthy ways is a reason to dismiss him.
(2) The fact that hers was the most admirable performance is a reason to give her the prize.

The reasons cited here—that he has acted in a blameworthy way, that she has performed admirably—are evaluative normative truths, and normative truths are nominal not substantial facts.

True, although the evaluative facts that constitute reasons in (1) and (2) are not themselves substantial facts, they contain an implicit quantifier ranging over substantial facts. To say that he has treated clients in blameworthy ways is to say that there are substantial facts about the way he has treated clients which give sufficient reason to blame him. To say that hers was the most admirable performance is to say that there were substantial facts about it—say its skill and sensitivity—that made it the one there was most reason to admire.

Reasons are ultimately determined by substantial facts and norms. It is in virtue of substantial facts that there is a reason to ψ. The sole exception is a priori epistemic reasons—outright reasons to believe a proposition. Such propositions will be purely normative (or offshoots thereof). Reasons to believe norms do not depend on any substantial fact; their application, however, depends on substantial facts. Thus, in the case of action, when there is *outright* reason for me to α I still have to recognize that a given act is a case of me α-ing to know that I have reason for that act. For example, if there is outright reason to help people in need I still have to recognize that α-ing would help people in need in order to recognize that I have reason to α. It is the substantial fact that α-ing would help people in need that gives me reason to α. Similarly with the case of feeling. There may be outright reason to be annoyed with someone who has cheated you but you have to recognize that they have cheated you.

Could the grounds we have given for treating reasons as nominal facts instead be taken as grounds for treating them as ordered pairs of substantial facts and modes of presentation? Thus:

> The set of substantial facts π_i, presented under the *de se* mode <the fact that my name is not on the list, etc.>, is a reason for me to be relieved.
> The set of substantial facts π_i, presented under the evaluative mode <the facts that made hers the most admirable performance>, is a reason to give her the prize.

This way of putting it does not show that treating reasons as nominal facts is a convenient but dispensable device: on the contrary, it implicitly appeals to nominal facts while concealing what is at stake. Furthermore, normative truths can feature essentially in reasons, but cannot be presented as pairs of substantial fact and mode of presentation. We could, for example, spell out (2) as follows:

> There are some facts about her performance that give one reason to admire it most, and *these facts are a reason to give her the prize in virtue of being sufficient reason to admire it most*.

Or:

> There are some facts about her performance that give one reason to admire it most, and *that these facts are sufficient reason to admire it most* is a reason to give her the prize.

The italicized facts are essential in that the complete reason to give her the prize essentially depends not just on the facts about her performance but on their evaluation. It is not that one and the same set of facts disconnectedly, so to speak, gives reason to admire *and* gives reason to award the prize. But since the italicized facts contain the reason relation they must be understood as nominal.

In 11.1 we made a similar point about the Bridge principle:

> Whatever fact gives x reason to ϕ gives x reason to do the ϕ-prompted action, *in virtue of being a reason to ϕ*.

Here again instead of using the convenient phrase 'in virtue of' we could put the principle explicitly in terms of reasons:

> *The fact that some facts, π_i, give x reason to ϕ* gives x reason to do the ϕ-prompted action.

And once again the italicized phrases express a nominal fact about the reason relation.

When self-auditors think about what they have reason to do they are thinking about what they take to be nominal facts: factual and normative truths that they can grasp as contents of thought. They are not thereby cut off from the world of substantial facts; they must have objectual apperceptual and perceptual awareness of some of these. However, where p is some such substantial fact a self-auditor must still realize *that* p obtains in order to consider whether it is a reason. Substantial facts impinge on the self-auditor's reflection by leading to recognition of factual truths that do or do not constitute reasons; it is these truths that are the *relata* of reason relations.

19.6 The ontology of persons

The self-determiner's data are reason relations and apperceptual states. Reason relations are irreal, reasons are nominal facts—what then about apperceptual states? Is the fact that I apperceive that *p* a substantial fact? And what about the self itself? Is it irreal?

Apperceptual facts have causal standing. They have causes and they cause. The fact that I am in extreme pain causes me to lose control of the vehicle. The fact that I seem to hear a noise causes me to believe there is a noise. Furthermore, we can have irreducibly objectual awareness of apperceptual facts. To be aware of being in pain does not reduce to seeing the truth of a proposition, as being aware of someone's discourtesy reduces to realizing that they are being discourteous, or being aware of the result of an experiment reduces to knowing that it had such-and-such a result. So it seems we should accept that apperceptual facts are substantial facts, in the world.

Nor does the Critical argument (6.3) pose a problem. The question, how is it possible to have non-receptive consciousness of a substantial fact, is unanswerable so long as consciousness is thought of as *distinct* from the fact that is its object. But in the case of apperception (consciousness in sense (ii)) the consciousness *is* the substantial fact. Apperception, unlike the supposed faculty of 'inner sense', involves no distinction between cognition and cognition-independent fact, so the Critical question does not arise. I can know that I am in a particular apperceptual state just by attending to it.

If apperceptual facts are substantial facts are they physical facts? It is hard to see how they could fail to be, given that they have causal standing and given the causal closure of physics. Yet it also seems (to me at least) very hard to answer the classical Cartesian/Kripkean modal objection to physicalism in any convincing way.[8] The essence of apperceptual facts is to be apperceived. On the one hand, that point answers the Critical question, of how knowledge of apperceptual facts is possible, but, on the other, it is also what makes the modal objection seem unanswerable. Being in pain is not identical with being in some state that presents itself by causing pain, in the way that heat is a state that presents itself by causing sensations of heat. Nor, it seems, is it identical with the higher-order, functional, state of being in some first-order state which has such-and-such causes

[8] Kripke 1971, 1981 (1972).

and effects. It is the first-order state itself. It might not have had these causes and effects; some state other than pain might have had the causes and effects pain has. And in any case how could I *apperceive* that I am in a functional state? Self-knowledge of pain would become hypothetical. Each of these lines of analysis offers the prospect of a physicalist reduction but each of them seems to fall to the modal objection or to an objection about the nature of self-knowledge.

What then about the self? Are persons real? They can be referred to (including by the first-person pronoun)—but as explained in Chapter 17, that does not resolve the issue. It is, for example, a substantial fact that Sherlock Holmes is a detective. According to our account in Chapter 17, 'Sherlock Holmes' in the previous sentence refers to Sherlock Holmes, a fictional character. The substantial fact in question is that the author of the detective stories in which Sherlock Holmes appears says he is a detective. Facts about him reduce to facts about what the author of the Holmes stories said. Sherlock Holmes is of course a *fictional* object, whereas persons are not; but the general point is that substantial facts can be expressed by propositions about irreal objects.

So is the self irreal? If an apperceptual state has an independent object in its content, and that object exists, my knowledge of it must be receptively based. But the self does not feature in apperception as an independent object. Nor are these apperceptual states independent of my existence, in the way that they are independent of the existence of their contents. The pain in my knee could not occur without being my experience, but it could occur without my having a knee. My thinking about Homer could not occur without being mine, but it can occur whether or not Homer existed. (According to the account of Chapter 17, again, these states have objects—my knee, Homer—whether or not those objects exist.) My apperceptual states have *being mine* as an essential relation and it is by that essential relation, not by receptivity, that I know myself. Just *because* the self is not an independent object we cannot argue that apperception requires receptivity if the self is real.[9]

However, the invalidity of this argument does not positively show that the self *is* real. As just noted, even if the self is irreal a fact characterized as a relation to it may be a substantial fact. Indeed that is what physicalism must hold. For it must say that apperceptual facts about me are facts about a certain physical body. It may be that some relation other than identity holds between persons and their apperceptual states and physical objects and their physical states: supervenience; constitution; causal interaction; or whatever. But unless the relation is one of identity *strict* physicalism, which says that whatever is real is physical, seems to entail the irreality of persons.

We self-determiners must think in terms of a spatio-temporally and causally unified framework in which we are ourselves located. We do not leave it there however; we inquire ever further into the nature of that framework. What if this further inquiry

---

[9] But if no receptivity is involved in apperceptual judgements should we conclude that such judgements are acts of pure spontaneity? Or should we conclude that apperceptual judgement does not fall under the distinction between spontaneity and receptivity, because this distinction presupposes it? By the principle that knowledge based on pure spontaneity cannot be of real objects, the former option leads to the conclusion that the self is irreal. Kant's claim that the 'I think' that accompanies all my representations is an 'act of spontaneity' that 'cannot be regarded as belonging to sensibility' (*Critique*, B132) seems to be directed to these deeply perplexing questions.

develops a scientific theory of its nature which makes it a causally closed world of purely physical entities? If apperceptual states have causal standing, it seems that we must then find a way to identify them with physical states. And persons must be either physical entities or irreal.

On the one hand, the *subject-dependence* of apperceptual states is essential to their epistemic role in the subject's self-determination. On the other hand, identifying subjects, self-determining selves, with anything physical seems fraught with difficulty. Moreover these difficulties, it seems, would not be solved by simply allowing that persons and their apperceptual states are substantial non-physical objects and attributes—for to conceive them in that way is to conceive them as a further class of *objective* states. But the problem is that apperceptual states seem to be both substantial and subjective, essentially *of* a subject. (The modal difficulties come down to this.) Putting this problem, the problem of subjectivity, in another way, the self seems to be an object of cognition and yet not just another objective existent among existents. Dualism—in the sense of a metaphysics which treats persons as non-physical existents and apperceptual states as substantial non-physical attributes of those existents—simply passes this problem of subjectivity by. Given that other considerations count towards physicalism, there is a strong incentive to persist with the idea that apperceptual states are somehow identifiable with physical states of organisms, or alternatively, and even more perplexingly, that they do not have causal standing after all.

I have no idea of how to progress with either of these alternatives. However, it seems that both would point to the conclusion that persons are irreal—that no metaphysics that makes persons existents in an objective world of substantial facts could do any better. The problem is that persons, selves, are *subjects*.

Compare this with our account of Wittgenstein's treatment of the problem of normativity (18.4). The difficulty there was to see how *any* substantial fact could *be* the fact that a reason relation obtains. In this case it is the difficulty of seeing how any substantial fact, say that a given organism is in a given physical state, could *be* the fact that a self is in a subjective state. In the normative case we were able to conclude that facts about reason relations are not substantial facts, because we could show how it is possible for people to act for reasons, even though reason relations are irreal objects that have no causal standing. That solution is not available in the case of subjectivity, so long as we accept that subjective states do have causal standing. And even if they do not, how could we deny the reality of states that 'there is something like to be in'? What could it mean to hold that the apperceptual given is irreal?

The 'mind–body' problem, or perhaps the problem of reconciling subjective and objective views of the world,[10] is (fortunately) well beyond the scope of this study. The ontological framework developed in Chapter 17 does not solve the central issue, which is that of the nature of subjectivity. At most it helps to clarify what would and would not be implied by saying that persons and their apperceptual states are irreal.

[10] This is how Thomas Nagel formulates it (1986: 27).

19.7 Empirical and intelligible

The distinction made in 10.1 between interpretative and non-interpretative explanations resonates with Kant's distinction between two standpoints, as that features, e.g. in *Groundwork*, 4.452–3. Kant argues that we cannot grasp our freedom from the empirical standpoint in which we see ourselves as part of the sensible world, falling under empirical laws. To think of ourselves as free, we must think of ourselves as also belonging to an intelligible world, falling under laws of reason. The Normative view says that we cannot grasp our freedom from the non-interpretative standpoint. To think of ourselves as free we must think of ourselves as able to act from reasons. Furthermore, on the account of reasons and persons that we have given in this chapter and the previous two, the contrast between interpretative and non-interpretative explanation marks an ontological and not a merely methodological divide. Reason relations are objective and irreal; persons are beings who can respond to these relations. But the similarity ends there: this ontological divide is fundamentally different to Kant's, just because cognitive irrealism is fundamentally different to transcendental idealism.

For Kant the two standpoints on persons are a special case of a completely general contrast between things as they appear and things as they really are. The empirical self belongs in the domain of appearance; it is known by inner sense and falls under the determinism of natural causes. The intelligible domain is that of the self as it is in itself, of reason and the causality of freedom. The application of transcendental idealism to persons forces a lamentable bifurcation of the interpretative standpoint, between the self as it appears to itself and the self as it really is, with the self turning up (against Kant's best Critical principles) on both sides of the transcendental divide.

It must be firmly stated that the contrast between 'intelligible', or interpretative, and 'empirical', or non-interpretative, is not at all a contrast between things as they as they really are and things as they appear. Our inner experience is not an appearance of something noumenal. The intelligible and the empirical standpoints are not, strictly speaking, two standpoints on *us*; that is, they do not both deploy the notion of a person, a self-determiner, in their explanations. An interpretative stance is inherently personal; any non-interpretative stance is non-personal. Intelligible explanations are interpretative in the sense that they deploy the concept of a *reason* in their *explanans*. Non-interpretative explanations do not.

True, there is some nuance here. Purely physicalistic explanations of behaviour plainly do not bring in reasons, persons, or intentional states, at all. But what of biology, psychology, the social sciences? Functional explanations in evolutionary biology may concern themselves with intentional states, states directed to contents, but do not explain them interpretatively, in terms of reasons. It is not clear how rich their conception of these states can be. This may be an empirical question about how fine-grained evolutionary explanations of intentional states can become, how closely they can come to model the taxonomies of the interpretative standpoint, driven as these are by the non-biological concepts of apperception, reasons, and self-determination. Explanations of intentional states in the social sciences, in contrast, need to have an interpretative underpinning (Max Weber's 'adequacy at the level of meaning') to be fully satisfactory. Or at least that is the view of methodologists who think that social science should adopt the categorial framework of persons and reasons.

In any case—wherever in the sciences the line between interpretative and non-interpretative comes—non-interpretative explanations, whether good or bad in their own terms, fall outside the domain of reasons and make no explanatory call on the idea of a person as a self-determiner. In contrast, interpretative explanations refer to reason relations and persons essentially.

But we have argued that reason relations are irreal, and we have left open the possibility that persons are. Could it be that reason relations are the objective and irreal intermediary between the subjective and irreal, and the objective and real?

20

THE CRITIQUE OF REASONS

Were we to yield to the illusion of transcendental realism, neither nature nor freedom would be possible.[1]

In this final chapter we review some main points in our examination of normativity. We then turn to a concluding assessment of the Normative standpoint. By starting from the critique of *reasons*, as against sensibility, or meaning, this standpoint yields a Critical philosophy without transcendental idealism or verificationism. Nonetheless, it shares a fundamental epistemological dualism with any other Critical standpoint: the dualism, in Kantian terms, of spontaneity and receptivity. What makes the Normative view distinctive is its interpretation of this dualism.

We have shown the normative domain to be the domain of reasons. In doing so we took the trichotomy of reasons—epistemic, evaluative, and practical—to be fundamental. In particular, it has been a main theme of this book that evaluative reasons are an irreducible category without which the domain of reasons and the very notion of self-determination cannot be understood.

We have found a diversity of norms—not just, as one would expect, across the categories, but within each category too. The most compact sphere is that of practical norms. Yet here too the Bridge principle only summarizes, rather than genuinely reducing, an indefinite diversity of Bridge principles for particular sentiments. There is no substantial unity, no overarching norm of practical reason, let alone of reason as such.

We review these points in Sections 20.1 and 20.2. In both respects they yield a substantive account of normativity that differs very greatly from the account associated with Kant. Yet, at the meta-normative level, reason relations stand out in a distinctive unity. They are irreal relations whose epistemic bases are spontaneity and dialogue. Because we can think about these irreals truly or falsely, and only because we can, knowledge and self-determination are possible. Reality is the totality of substantial facts; we grasp and act on some of those facts. *Self-determining* thought about the real, and action in it, is possible because the reason relations to which it responds are themselves neither

---

[1] *Critique of Pure Reason*, A543/B571.

constituents of the real nor constructions of our own. They *are*: at once objective and irreal.

I believe that this meta-theory of reasons does not differ significantly from Kant's implicit meta-theory of Reason. In Section 3 I shall argue that it only makes it explicit. However it does so in ways that are unexpected. Perhaps most unexpectedly, as will be argued in 20.4, it reveals Kant's Critical theory to be over-determined. Given cognitive irrealism about 'Reason', or rather, reasons, there is no need for transcendental idealism about the self and nature. From a fully thought-through Critical standpoint, transcendental idealism is quite simply surplus to requirements.

But the rejection of global realism is not. The Kantian motto of this chapter is correct, except that it is the illusion of global realism, as described in Chapter 1, to which we must not yield. To put it another way, dispelling the illusion of global realism does not force us to the transcendental idealism against which, and by reference to which, Kant presents his notion of 'transcendental' realism.

Developing the contrast with transcendental idealism, 20.5 and 20.6 show in more detail how the Normative view underwrites the possibility of knowledge. 20.5 examines how epistemic norms apply to reality. 20.6 considers the force and the intelligibility of scepticism.

20.7 and 20.8 spell out some final implications. The Normative view is perfectly compatible with naturalism—so long as this is not understood metaphysically, as a species of global realism. But, like other versions of Critical philosophy, the Normative view does postulate a fundamental dichotomy of receptivity and spontaneity, and thus cannot completely satisfy the hopes of monistically minded absolute idealists and pragmatists. The knower cannot drop out completely, or melt into the world.

20.1 Reasons and Reason

Talk of 'Reason', and of 'what Reason Requires', can easily mislead. If it is just convenient shorthand for talking about reasons, and in particular sufficient reasons, there need be no problem. Yet the impulse to reify 'Reason' is strong. However obvious it may be, we need to keep remembering that there *is* no entity, Reason, that can literally require or command that we do this or believe that. Nothing other than a legitimately authoritative person, group, church, state, and so forth, can do so. And as an autonomous person I can always review the credentials of such bodies, and criticize what they say. That connection between free thought and Reason gives Reason its powerfully emancipatory role; but in reviewing and criticizing I am not appealing to some other kind of personified entity, Reason, that is set over these persons and bodies as a higher judge. Nor is Reason what *I* truly, noumenally, am.

Thinking of Reason as a power, capacity or competence that persons have—that of recognizing and acting on reasons—is less misleading. This power is what we earlier called rationality (5.11). But it is quite likely still misleading if one thinks of rationality as a single, unified power. Even if it does have some unitary characteristics (a question for empirical inquiry) it is at least very decentralized. We human beings have a whole range of normative competences, and we differ quite a lot in our profile of competence across this range. Although reason relations all have the same meta-status, reasons are indefinitely diverse. There are as many sorts of reason as there are norms, and there are many and diverse norms. Only through collective philosophical discussion do we have a chance of getting a picture, though schematic, of them as a whole.

Kant speculates that there may be some interestingly unitary principle of Reason. See, for example, his remark in the Preface to the *Groundwork*:

> the critique of a pure practical reason, if it is to be carried through completely, [should] be able at the same time to present the unity of practical with speculative reason in a common principle, since it can, in the end, be only one and the same reason, which must be distinguished merely in its application.[2]

He never develops this idea of a 'common principle': unsurprisingly, because it is a hopeless dream.[3] We should never have expected, and we have not found, substantive unity—in the sense of a relatively compact and complete set of norms—either across the three kinds of reasons or within any one kind. Many kinds of facts can be reasons in many different ways. This situation may not please the philosopher with a thirst for unity, but it is our situation.

Some compact and fairly wide-ranging norms can be found. Thus in the epistemic sphere we have found norms of apperception, receptivity, induction, and probability. But norms of induction implicitly rely on background norms that are harder to specify. Consider the elusive norms that implicitly govern what we count as a good explanation. There is simplicity, to be sure, but what normative factors go into judgements of simplicity? How are such judgements weighted by defeasible principles of logic and geometry, not to mention vaguer normative constraints on our picture of the world, such as continuity, contiguity, causal closure, conservation of basic quantities?

In the practical sphere we have found the Bridge principle, the Demand principle and the principle of Good. However, the Bridge principle is actually a schematic summary of an indefinite diversity of Bridge principles for particular sentiments.

In the evaluative domain proper there is no norm that is not specific to a particular emotion. There are as many evaluative norms as there are distinguishable emotions, and distinct kinds of reasons for each of them. In fact emotions are primarily distinguished *by* their norms. These norms sustain an extraordinarily rich and variegated evaluative discourse that is related only in complex ways, and at irregular junctures, to the good and the bad, and the right or the wrong. The point is obscured by undifferentiated talk of 'value'. Is a bizarre or disturbing performance, for example, a good one or a bad one? That depends.

---

[2] *Groundwork*, IV: 391.
[3] Perhaps, however, the common principle Kant has in mind is their common source in spontaneity, rather than their convergence on some substantive common *content*. If so, the Normative view agrees.

Evaluative norms underpin complex hierarchies of value; these in turn play an enormous, and contested, social role. What principles can be extracted from, and can retrospectively warrant, such hierarchies has always been a hard but fascinating topic for moralists and for critics and theorists in aesthetics. It is also a constant topic of everyday discussion. In fact the history of morals and aesthetics is essentially a history of how these hierarchies develop and change, and thus, ultimately, of the way underlying dispositions of feeling are regulated and modified by spontaneity and discussion. We are currently in reaction, at least in theory, against canons or hierarchies of value. To some extent that results from a serious search for more comprehensive valuations, forced on us by a pluralistic world. To some extent it results from bad preconceptions in the meta-theory of value. What, nonetheless, remains striking is the degree of rational consensus there actually is, below the surface, in aesthetics as well as in morals: how large the undisputed territory is. Highly skilled, accurate, and effortless long-distance spitting is pretty admirable in its way. To see nothing in it would be to miss its point. A boy who achieves excellence in this field gets some deserved glory. But who thinks it is as admirable as accurate and effortless tennis? And neither of these achievements is as great as great achievement in art or pure science. It is evasive to say that these are incommensurable: we do not seriously think that. Thinking about such hierarchies of value means thinking hard about how excellences of sheer skill, vision, imagination, rigour, and so on interact, and how qualities like perfect execution, beauty, excitement, insight contribute to the value of their product. Aesthetic theories that attempt to answer these questions rest on aesthetic judgements, which in turn rest on normative reflection about our own feelings.

20.2 In defence of the trichotomy

Our assumption throughout the course of this book has been that the trichotomy of reasons is irreducible. It is time to review the assumption. In principle there are a number of other possibilities (seven); in practice, there are three that we should consider.[4]

First there is what I called (2.9) 'epistemicism about reasons'. Epistemicism says that the only irreducible reasons are epistemic. It asserts the primacy of theoretical reason. A further step is to say that there are no irreducible reasons at all.[5] We can consider this along with epistemicism. Then there is 'pragmatism about reasons'. Pragmatism says that the only irreducible reasons are practical. It asserts the primacy of practical reason. Finally there is the common assumption that there are only epistemic and practical reasons.

They all deny that there are irreducible evaluative reasons. One might think that this is a question separable from strictly meta-normative issues. So it should be; but the preconceptions about reason and feeling that seem to be involved may well have metaphysical

---

[4] The ones that I am not considering are that there are only evaluative reasons, that there are epistemic and evaluative reasons but no practical reasons, that there are evaluative and practical reasons but no epistemic reasons, and that there are no reasons.

[5] This, as I understand it, is John Broome's view in Broome (forthcoming).

bases.[6] Thus one important source of resistance to reducing value to evaluative reasons is a realist impulse to reify value, as discussed in 18.6. But we have argued that this impulse, or realist illusion, should be resisted.

This is a negative point. It still remains possible that there might be more than one way of analysing the circle of normative concepts. So let us consider epistemicism and pragmatism on their own merits.

As noted in 2.9, an epistemicist could postulate a valoric scale of goodness and badness, and/or a deontic 'Ought', taken as primitive. Propositions apparently about evaluative and practical reasons would then analysable in valoric and/or deontic terms. Value and obligation, not evaluative and practical 'reasons', would be basic. What one Ought to do would be determined by what action has the most valuable outcome, or by some set of principles determining what Ought to be done, or some combination of these. A further line of thought would treat epistemic reasons as a priori epistemic probabilities. We would have an irreducible epistemic Ought, which could govern beliefs about these probabilities. On this view reasons would completely disappear as primitives.

Now if we set aside the cart and horse argument as arising from a misplaced tendency to reify value, what is at stake here? Don't epistemicism and the Reasons thesis, which takes reasons as primitive and analyses other normative concepts in their terms, become mere terminological variants? The reifying impulse would hold, for example, that 'epistemic probability that p' and 'reason to believe that p' are not just terminological variants, because how much reason there is to believe that p *depends* on, *supervenes* on, the epistemic probability that p. But once we deny that there is a category of epistemic probabilities, distinct both from both epistemic reasons, on the one hand, and from causal propensities, on the other, we seem to be left with a merely terminological choice.

This is not quite right, however. There are questions of economy, power, and naturalness to consider. The Reasons thesis has these virtues; much of this book has sought to show how and why. We can summarize the main points. First, the Reasons thesis clears up the obscure relation of normative supervenience, which simply reduces to the reason relation. In contrast, epistemicism has to postulate it as basic. Second, by taking evaluative reasons as basic the Reasons thesis links to an independently plausible sentimentalist account of value. It gets behind an undifferentiated notion of 'value'; it illuminates the diversity of valuations and gives a realistic account of their moral psychology. Third, it links with a uniform and natural meta-theory of reasons across all spheres. It shows how different 'oughts' relate to different kinds of sufficient reason, or to sufficient reasons relativized to different epistemic fields. In the value sphere it shows how valuations are epistemically grounded on feelings without reducing them to feelings, or treating them as though they had nothing to do with feeling. It remains for epistemicists to show what compensating virtues their account has.

Let us turn to pragmatism, which says that the only fundamental propositions about reasons are propositions about practical reasons.[7] Now as noted in 2.9, if we restrict ourselves

---

[6] They may of course also have psychological bases. After all we are talking about the preconceptions of philosophers. And might it be relevant that they have mostly been male?

[7] I am grateful to John Broome, Jonas Olson, Andrew Reisner, and Mark Schroeder for helpful discussion of pragmatist lines of thought (although the views about to be discussed are not necessarily theirs).

to a semantic test it is trivially true that there are epistemic and evaluative reasons. That is, there are truth-expressing sentences which contain the corresponding predicates—'reason to β', 'reason to φ', 'reason to α'. So unless pragmatists ignore or deny this point, what they must mean is that epistemic and evaluative reasons, though distinguishable from practical reasons by this semantic test, in fact all fall under the substantive theory of practical reason. What to believe or feel is in reality a practical question. You have reason to believe or feel something just insofar as it will be useful, practically valuable, for you to believe or feel it.

A first response to this claim is to distinguish between reason to believe or feel something, and reason to bring it about that you believe or feel it. In 2.9 we considered two examples. I may be on an extremely dangerous mission which there is no reason to believe I will survive. But if there is something I can do to make myself believe I will survive it, that will greatly aid my peace of mind. So if there is something I can do there is practical reason to do it. I claimed that it is nonetheless true that there *is* no *reason to believe* that I will survive. Again, there may be no reason for me to admire my boss's taste in wine, but it's important for my promotion prospects that I show some admiration. In this case there may be practical reason to bring it about that I actually feel admiration. If so, then there is practical reason for me to bring it about that I admire something which there *is* no reason for me to admire.

Pragmatists might reply by saying that it can be useful to believe or feel something that it is not useful to *make* oneself believe or feel.[8] In other words they determine reason to believe or feel by the usefulness of believing or feeling.

There are two ways to do this—but both of them fundamentally undermine the connection between reasons and self-determination that has been at the heart of our discussion. The first way is to accept the trichotomy as a typology but combine it with a pragmatist view of truth and of value. The second is to deny that the trichotomy is a genuine typology of *reasons*. When we talk about 'reasons to believe'—and perhaps 'reasons to feel'—we are not really talking about the reason concept at all. We are talking not about epistemic and evaluative reasons but about epistemic and aesthetic or ethical *standards*. And whether or not you should adhere to such standards—whether they are normative for you—is a practical question.

Consider the first approach. Reasons to believe that p are, constitutively, reasons to believe that it is true that p—whatever is a reason to believe that p is thereby also, a priori, a reason to believe that it is true that p. To that we can add that a set of facts constitutes a complete reason to believe that p when it is a priori that it does. Hence a complete reason to believe that p must be a priori indicative of the truth of the proposition that p. Now is the usefulness of believing a proposition a priori indicative of the truth of that proposition? The pragmatist about truth will answer that it is; for him therefore the usefulness of believing that p is in general unproblematically both a complete reason to believe that p and a complete reason to believe that it is true that p. If, however, the pragmatic theory of truth is rejected, then the usefulness of a belief is never a priori indicative of its truth. In most cases it is not even a posteriori indicative of its truth. Hence we

---

[8] I owe the point to Wlodek Rabinowicz.

cannot hold that that fact on its own, the fact that believing the proposition is useful, is ever a complete reason to believe the proposition, without breaking the constitutive link between reason to believe that p and reason to believe that it is true that p.[9]

Furthermore this kind of pragmatism about epistemic reasons, even when combined with pragmatism about truth, puts in question the link between reasons and self-determination. It is basic to self-determination that epistemic reasons are relative to epistemic fields, and that warranted epistemic reasons are relative to epistemic states. The fact that it's useful for Carol to believe that p is a practical reason for her to bring it about that she believes that p, whether or not she can know that fact. But her epistemic reasons are knowable facts in her epistemic field. It seems, then, that pragmatists about both truth and epistemic reasons must deny that epistemic reasons are relative to epistemic fields. But in that case, how do they think we can achieve warrant? What warranted, auditable, reasons can I have for thinking that a belief would be useful? How can I come to know that it would be? And are my reasons for believing that it would be useful themselves practical reasons? If so, what warrants them? It seems that this version of pragmatism about reasons is incompatible with the self-determining nature of reasoning.

So we turn to the second approach, which says that when we talk about 'reasons to believe' and 'reasons to feel', we are not really talking about the reason concept. There are standards in science, ethics, and aesthetics, which determine right method and procedure in these subjects. They are external to the actor, in the sense that whether he has reason to adhere to them is an open question—a practical question.[10]

Now first we can ask whether this distinction between reasons and standards is more than terminological. If it is, what is the status of these standards? Are they just conventions? If so are they backed up by something like the Viennese, or conventionalist, account of epistemic warrant? Or is it that we are taking a realist stance, at least for epistemic as against ethical and aesthetic standards, according to which the right standards are those that are in fact, a posteriori, truth-conducive? If so a self-determiner must have reason to believe that they are. Is *that* reason just a practical reason? But then how does the self-determiner know that *it* obtains—i.e. that it is useful to believe in accordance with some particular set of epistemic standards?

Again we have come back to the self-determining nature of reasoning. The fundamental point is that our conception of self-determining actors requires us to picture them working with warranted reasons which they can tell they have by reflection alone. If we try to combine this with an account that eliminates epistemic reasons and replaces them with epistemic standards that there is practical reason to observe, we get a vicious regress. I have warranted practical reason to adhere to some standards only if my epistemic state

---

[9] A similar point will apply to pragmatism about evaluative reasons. If someone holds that the usefulness of admiring something really is a reason for admiring it, and not just a reason for bringing it about that one admires it, then he has an unusual theory of value. What other principled basis can be given for holding that this usefulness is not just a reason to make yourself admire, but actually a reason to admire—on a par with the thing's beauty or brilliance, say? To insist that it is a reason to admire, but not on a par with 'value-based reasons', yet not identifiable with a practical reason to make yourself admire either, is just digging in one's heels in defence of a pointless distinction.

[10] In thinking about this option, I have taken as my model some subtle explorations by Peter Railton of the pragmatist view of epistemic reasons. See Railton 2003; also 2008.

gives me sufficient reason to believe that it would be useful for me to adhere to those standards. How does the version of pragmatism we are considering apply to that sufficient reason? Should we replace this reference, to a sufficient reason for me to believe, by a reference to what the epistemic standards license me to believe relative to my epistemic state? In that case, according to the pragmatist, whether to adhere to those standards is a practical question. I can answer it only by considering whether there is sufficient reason for me to believe that it would be useful for me to adhere to them. But now we have another reference to a sufficient reason for me to believe. To replace it by another reference to epistemic standards just repeats the regress at the next level up.

The concept of warrant rests irreducibly on a notion of what there is reason to believe relative to an epistemic state. In contrast, what there is practical reason for a person to (make himself) believe depends solely on the facts, whether or not known by that person. It thus seems that pragmatism about epistemic reasons cannot make sense of warrant and thus of self-determination. But self-determination is central to the very idea of a reason.

So what is the attraction of pragmatism about epistemic reasons? Perhaps what is tempting is a kind of 'externalism' about reasons which rejects the very idea of warrant. This in turn might be fed by a naturalistic outlook; but it will be argued below that that could only be in virtue of a misconception about how naturalism should be understood, arising from a failure to separate naturalism from global realism. Another possibility is that the attraction stems from a kind of instrumentalism about everything, including one's beliefs and feelings. There is the remarkably influential idea that the instrumentalism about practical reasons has an unproblematic and privileged status that no other account of any other sort of reason has. And that in turn, I suspect, may go back to a combination of naturalism and realism in the meta-theory of the normative. The thought may be that propositions about instrumental reasons have readily available factual truthmakers: natural facts about ways and means. But we have already shown that this line of thought is baseless. We should not accept a realist account of propositions about reasons. And in any case, not merely does instrumentalism have no specially privileged standing as an account of reasons, it is false. The correct account of means and ends is the Transmission principle (4.9).

Finally, we can dismiss the common view that there are just two kinds of reasons: epistemic; and practical. Such dualism falls between two stools. If epistemicism is the right view, value, duty, and Ought are basic and we don't need to postulate practical reasons. (We can stop at the best action, or the one that Ought to be done.) But if the sentimentalist analysis of value and duty is correct, then we need all three kinds of reasons. There is thus no perspective from which the common view is sustainable.

20.3 Constructivism and cognitive irrealism in Kant

Kant is a constructivist, in one sense of that word, about nature. He is often held to be, in another sense, a constructivist about morality. How to understand the notion of *construction* is, in each instance, controversial. Still, transcendental idealism does indeed hold that nature—the spatio-temporal causal field—is a construction by the knowing subject, and Kant says as much.[11] It is a *construction*, not a creation, in that the materials with which we 'construct' things as they empirically are, are supplied by things as they are in themselves.

Can morality—according to Kant's account—be said to be a construction? This is much less clear. Here Kant does not use the constructivist language he applies to nature. And given the basic structure of his metaphysics it is unclear what could be constructed from what.

The *content* of the moral law is in no way contributed, made, or constructed by anyone, including us. Thus:

> No-one, not even God, can be the author of the laws of morality, since they have no origin in will, but instead a practical necessity. [God is] the lawgiver, though not the author of the laws. In the same way, God is in no sense the author of the fact that the triangle has three sides.

This is from the early *Lectures on Ethics*, but the distinction between author and lawgiver remains in the *Metaphysics of Morals*:

> One who commands (*imperans*) through a law is the *lawgiver* (*legislator*). He is the author (*autor*) of the obligation in accordance with the law, but not always the author of the law. In the latter case the law would be a positive (contingent) and chosen law. A law that binds us a priori and unconditionally by our own reason can also be expressed as proceeding from the will of a supreme lawgiver...but this signifies only the idea of a moral being whose will is a law for everyone, without his being thought as the author of the law.[12]

Plainly, whatever may be the sense in which we can be said to give ourselves the moral law, we are certainly not its authors. For that would make it 'a positive (contingent) and chosen law,' whereas the moral law 'binds us a priori and unconditionally by our own reason'. In what sense, then, do we give the moral law to ourselves?

What we give ourselves is not the normative content of the law, or even its 'practical necessity', but its standing as *moral law*. Kant adheres to the Insight principle (12.4): no moral law applies to us whose validity we cannot recognize for ourselves. He also holds that we are autonomous beings; we can know the full content of the moral law in that first-person way. (Indeed, given our absolute, transcendental autonomy, we can presumably know the full content of all norms in that way.) We do not have to rely on others for knowledge of the moral law's content. This is the first respect in which we give the moral law to *ourselves*.

Furthermore, the moral law's standing as moral law does not derive from the decree of any sovereign *other* than ourselves, including God. Still, this is a negative point—in what positive sense are we ourselves the sovereigns? We experience the moral law as *law*,

---

[11] 'the order and regularity in the appearances, which we entitle nature, we ourselves introduce'. *Critique of Pure Reason* A125.
[12] LE 40: 51–2; *Metaphysics of Morals*, 6: 227.

as *obligatory*, in virtue of our own finite sensuous nature (15.5). Our sensuous nature inclines us against it, but it is also *in virtue of that nature*—through our capacity for respect when confronted with its content—that we experience it as binding. Moreover the special point about the practical norms of morality is that we have to impose them actively on ourselves, in the sense that to follow the moral law we may have to override inclination.

Thus 'we stand under a *discipline* of reason' though it is 'our own reason' that gives it.[13] In both respects we differ from the 'Holy Will', which does not experience practical reason as something it must *impose* on itself, but simply acts in accordance with its content. The Holy Will, one might say, deals in warrant but not in moral obligation.

In this sense there is after all a somewhat remote analogy between nature and freedom: we can say that our sensuous nature 'constructs' our experience of the moral law as *law*—as imperatival, binding—in somewhat the way that it constructs our experience of things in themselves as objects in a causally integrated spatio-temporal field. There is an important difference, however: Kant's account of moral experience can be de-transcendentalized much more easily than his account of perceptual experience. When we do that it becomes a phenomenology of what objects spontaneously arouse respect. We have discussed it from this standpoint in 15.5 and 15.6.

There is also another sense in which Kant is often held to be a constructivist about morality. 'Construction' here refers to the Categorical Imperative procedure. The idea is that we 'construct' specific moral principles by application of the Categorical Imperative: by testing whether we can universally will a given maxim. This use of the term 'construction' strikes me as highly misleading, at least if the suggestion is that what *makes* a moral principle true is the possibility of a certain construction. For Kant at least (as against perhaps, some modern Kantians, influenced by John Rawls' account of Kantian ethics[14]) the Categorical Imperative procedure is not constructive in the sense that the content we recognize by following it is a product of the procedure. The procedure is epistemic not constitutive: a way of clarifying to ourselves a content which obtains anyway. (Or at least that is what it would do if it worked.) The same applies to our 'derivations' of the principle of Good and the Demand principle in 13.3 and 14.3. They are not a construction of these principles but a way of recognizing, or better, throwing into relief, their epistemic basis and content.

In sum, if there is constructivism about morality in Kant at all, the construction is not of norms, but of the experience of practical norms as *moral laws*, and of the idea of *moral obligation*.

What then is Kant's view of Reason itself? There is a temptation to think that if Kant is not a realist about Reason he must be a voluntarist. But by now we know that this is a

---

[13] *Practical Philosophy*: 206 (5:82).

[14] Rawls 2000, Chapter 6, especially §5, where Rawls contrast intuitionism and constructivism. But this is not an exhaustive distinction, and neither view need be accepted as an interpretation of Kant. (I should, however, add that it is unclear how far Rawls intends to offer a positive meta-normative view, as against merely disagreeing with intuitionist realism. If the constructive procedure he envisages itself appeals to independent, unconstructed normative truths, an intuitionist could ask how these are known. To distance himself from intuitionism at this point Rawls would have to answer in the cognitive-irrealist way.)

false dichotomy. Certainly, on the one hand, Kant is no realist about Reason. He thinks pure normative judgements are products of spontaneity alone, and not of receptivity to some domain of normative fact. After all what, in Kantian terms, could such a domain be? Would it be phenomenal or noumenal? From a Kantian perspective the question does not even make sense.[15]

On the other hand, however, Kant is no voluntarist either. We are not the authors of the norms that govern our thinking. We recognize them for ourselves as 'practical necessities' in spontaneous reflection. Just as we recognize that a representation falls under a concept through an act of pure spontaneity, of freedom—but cannot be said to *decide* that it does—so we freely recognize, we do *not* decide, what our moral obligations are. We must remember, at this point, the distinction between holding that practical principles have their epistemic basis in dispositions of the will (as argued in Chapter 16) and holding that they simply *are* the content of actual acts of will. The first view is an essential part of the epistemology of practical norms. It is an explanation of what is meant by practical, as against epistemic or evaluative spontaneity. The second view would make us the authors of the moral law and commit Kant to non-cognitivism or subjectivism about the moral law: positions which he by no means holds.

The correct account of Kant's standpoint on Reason (theoretical as well as practical) must thus explain how he can be a cognitivist about moral and in general rational requirements without being a realist about them.[16] That is what the cognitivist irrealism developed in Part IV of this book does. There are indeed a priori mind-independent truths about moral obligations and rational requirements; but these truths are not factual claims, either about the phenomena or about the noumena.

20.4 The Normative view as Critical philosophy

That there is a fundamental connection between the possibility of freedom and the possibility of knowledge is one of Kant's greatest insights. However, once we have cognitive irrealism about reason—about normativity—we do not also need transcendental idealism to vindicate either of these insights. What we can say, by a small but

---

[15] In contrast to Rawls, Irwin (2009: 981–3) argues that Kant is a moral realist. On this reading, Kant's view is that moral claims are claims about the noumenal facts. But just as there is no reason, given the option of cognitive irrealism, to accept Rawls' constructivist interpretation, so there is no reason to accept Irwin's—which flies in the face of Kant's fundamental doctrines: that we can only know the noumena as they appear to us, and that they appear to us only through receptivity.

[16] In an exchange about Kant's notion of self-legislation with Robert Pippin, John McDowell remarks: 'Even in Kant's version of the self-legislation theme, we cannot legislate just anyhow... There are constraints, and that is a moment of receptivity in our legislative power, even in this extreme version in which the constraints are purely formal' (McDowell 2007: 408). Pippin agrees: 'Any model of the self-legislative source of value or obligation must have an "element of receptivity" to it' (Pippin 2007: 427). They seriously misapply Kant's distinction between spontaneity and receptivity, and ignore his distinction between author and legislator. We are not the authors of norms, although we may make them a law to ourselves. We don't decide what they are; we recognize what they are. But this fact, that we are not their authors, does *not* entail that we know them by some special receptive faculty. Reason relations are objective; knowledge of them is nonetheless purely spontaneous, in no way receptive. That is precisely the (apparently elusive) possibility revealed by the Normative view.

philosophically large alteration to the Kantian motto of this chapter, is this: *were we to yield to the illusion of global realism, neither nature nor freedom would be possible.* A reflection on this point will bring together a number of themes from previous chapters.

As we saw in Chapter 5, both knowledge of the world and self-determination by reasons—freedom—presuppose non-empirical cognitive access to reason relations: synthetic a priori knowledge of norms. This non-empirical element in our knowledge of reasons is at odds with all realist views of their ontology. Such views cannot account for the a priori element in our knowledge of epistemic reasons, and the essential role played by that a priori element in rational self-audit. They are forced either to deny the a priori element, which destroys the possibility of warrant, or to defend it by postulating a *sui generis* form of receptivity to a non-natural domain of reason-facts. Yet on closer inspection this intuitionistic realism cannot deliver warrant either (6.4). Either way, in destroying warrant global realism destroys the possibility of self-audit and thus of self-determination. Against realism, the key to understanding how these are possible lies in recognizing the role of normative spontaneity in all three spheres: epistemic; evaluative; and practical.

At first sight non-cognitivism about reasons can do better, in that it purports to show how knowledge of reason relations lies within us. However it seems unlikely, at the very least, that the attempt to develop notions of normative assertion, truth, and knowledge on a non-cognitivist base can succeed. In any case, as argued in 17.7, a correct account of existence and truth makes such an attempt unnecessary. These points are just two sides of the same coin: non-cognitivist reconstructions of our notions of normative truth and knowledge are neither possible nor necessary, because there was no problem with those notions in the first place.

Non-cognitivists are indeed right about one very important thing: that the distinction between factual and purely normative claims is fundamental. But why should that show that there are no normative propositions? On the irrealist view, the distinction *is* a distinction between factual and normative assertions. A factual proposition, the content of a factual assertion, states that a substantial fact obtains, whereas a purely normative proposition, the content of a purely normative assertion, does not. It is for this reason that purely normative propositions can be known a priori: they make no factual assertion. Again rightly, non-cognitivists reject the idea that there is or could be a special kind of receptivity to a *sui generis* domain of normative facts. But this should not lead us to reject purely normative propositions. Their epistemological ground, as we showed in Chapter 16, is sufficiently supplied by the disciplines of spontaneity and discussion.

It seems therefore that the underlying source for normative non-cognitivism must lie in some form of factualism, itself most likely based on either scientism (the Vienna Circle) or a correspondence notion of truth.[17] Both of these we can reject. We should do so anyway, and not just to respond to normative non-cognitivism. Once we free ourselves from the illusion of global realism—the proposition-as-picture illusion—we also free ourselves from the implausible simulations of normative 'proposition' and normative 'truth'

---

[17] See arguments (2) and (3) in 17.7.

to which non-cognitivists resort. Truth, in a perfectly straightforward, unambiguous sense, applies in all domains of judgeable content; but not all judgeable content is factual.

The same point allows us to reject quietism, with its absolute-idealist drift (as argued in 17.6). Rejecting the correspondence theory of truth is not at all the same as accepting the identity theory of truth. It does not lead us to deny that there are substantial facts. Of course there are. When we make a factual assertion we are asserting that some substantial fact obtains. Paradoxical denial of that common sense truth is not needed to defend the possibility of a priori insight into epistemic reasons and thus the possibility of contact with reality.

The insight that not all propositional content is factual content provides the basis for a Critical philosophy that steers between dogmatism and scepticism. But how then do epistemic norms apply to reality? In what sense can they be said to apply to it?

20.5 How do epistemic norms apply to reality?

According to Wittgenstein in the 30s, in logic:

> There is not any question at all...of some correspondence between what is said and reality; rather is logic antecedent to any such correspondence...[18]

In the sentence previous to the one just quoted, he says that the reason why 'logical inferences':

> are not brought into question is not that they 'certainly correspond to the truth'—or something of the sort,—no it is just this that is called 'thinking', 'speaking', 'inferring', 'arguing'.

This raises initial doubts. It looks like an appeal to analyticity, but we have rightly become sceptical about this expansive type of appeal to analyticity as a way out of philosophical questions. In particular, when we consider the development of alternative geometrical and logical calculi, and the force of fallibilism about logic and mathematics itself, it looks implausible—bizarrely dogmatic even—to hold that someone who questions 'logical inferences' can't be said to be thinking, speaking, etc.

Logic and mathematics can, we saw, be couched as a set of universal non-normative propositions. Seen in this universalist way they form part of our total theory of reality. When they are understood in this way, they can certainly be 'brought into question'. It makes good sense to ask whether the best theory would include a non-Euclidean geometry. It makes equally good sense to ask whether a combination of quantum logic and quantum physics would make a better total theory than a combination of classical logic and quantum physics. It makes perfectly good sense to wonder whether para-consistent logic might be the best way to develop our account of reality. And so on.

---

[18] Wittgenstein 1978 (1956), I: 156.

However, Wittgenstein's dictum can be understood as applying to the underlying logical norms of inference. So understood, it is correct—it holds for all norms, including norms of logic. There is no question of some correspondence between norms and reality; in particular, epistemic norms are 'antecedent' inasmuch as there can be factual content only if there are epistemic norms. The norms themselves neither correspond nor fail to correspond to reality. They are not themselves factual, their content is purely normative; but they constitute our concepts (18.5). It is, therefore, indeed analytic that there is no thinking without epistemic norms. Thinking is reason-responsiveness, reason-responsiveness is responsiveness to norms. These are merely definitional truths. So it is analytic that if thinking exists there are norms, even by our narrow account of analyticity. It is this interpenetration of thought and normativity that gives the Normative view its Critical force.

Epistemic norms cannot be said to 'correspond to reality'—but they *can* be 'brought into question'. In what sense is this possible? The answer involves three points which take us back to the notions of monotonicity and defeasibility discussed in 9.4:

(i) Logic and mathematics can be stated as universal offshoots of the underlying norms because those norms are monotonic. Non-monotonic norms, such as those of induction, perception, etc. do not have such offshoots.

(ii) In all cases, nonetheless, the normative formulation is epistemologically and ontologically fundamental.

(iii) Whether epistemic norms are monotonic or not, we can still ask whether they are defeasible.

As noted in 9.4, we can think of epistemic norms as having the structure $R(<\pi_i, e>, x, \beta p)$, where $<\pi_i, e>$ is a pair consisting of the facts that constitute the reason and a field in which it is knowable that π_i. A proposition of this form is a norm if it is a priori that relative to such an e, π_i give x reason to believe that p. Let us for the moment restrict attention to norms that underwrite *sufficient* reasons.

An epistemic norm may or may not be monotonic. If it is, then it is a priori that:

(1) $(e)S(<\pi_i, e>, x, \beta p)$

where e ranges over all epistemic fields in which π_i obtain. To return to the example in 9.4, or-introduction, we have:

(2) $(e)S(<\text{the fact that } p, e>, \beta p \vee q)$.

This norm, in common with all norms, is a priori and necessary. In virtue of its monotonicity it underwrites the universal non-normative proposition:

(3) $p \rightarrow p \vee q$.

For suppose that it is the case that p. Since (2) applies to all e in which it is the case that p, there is no e which warrants rejection of (3). Furthermore, in taking it as a priori that (2) is necessary we take it that the hypothesis $\neg(p \rightarrow p \vee q)$ is unconditionally excludable in μ (the maximal epistemic field, comprising all the facts—8.4).

The principle of natural deduction known as Conditional Proof would be invalid if logical norms were not monotonic. For in general it can be true that $\pi_i \tau_e q$ but false that $\tau_e \pi_i \rightarrow q$. For example, it is true a priori that in any non-defeating field in which x seems to see a red patch there is warrant for x to think x sees a red patch. But this norm does not warrant the conditional: if x seems to see a red patch then x sees a red patch. μ may contain both the fact that x seems to see a red patch and the fact that there is no red patch there: it may be a defeating field. To rule out that supposition we would have to be warranted in taking the conditional, as against the underlying perceptual norm, to be a necessary truth.

The point applies in general to all non-monotonic epistemic norms, which we can formulate as follows:

(4) If x is in a non-defeating e which contains π_i, $S(<\pi_i, e>, x, \beta p)$.

This, if true, is a priori and necessarily true. But we cannot infer that the proposition that $\Pi_i \rightarrow p$ is necessarily true or even true. Hence no universal non-normative proposition is an offshoot of (4).

Point (ii) states that even in the case of monotonic epistemic norms the normative formulation is epistemologically and ontologically fundamental. In no case does the aprioricity and necessity of an epistemic norm derive from any fact. This is the Normative view; it contrasts with the factualist view which holds the opposite: for example, that the norm of or-introduction holds *in virtue* of the universal necessary truth that $p \rightarrow p \vee q$.

Apart from its underlying source in global realism, the latter view picks up some plausibility from the fact that *any* universal necessary truth underwrites a monotonic 'rule of inference'. If all As are Bs, then the fact that this is an A materially implies that it's a B, whatever other facts obtain. If it is necessary that all As are Bs, then suppositions in which something is A but not B are unconditionally excludable. Crucially, however, the universalist direction does not explain how we can ever know *a priori* that such a necessary universal truth holds. At this point we can call on Chapter 6, where we argued that the Normative view gives an account of the a priori, whereas intuitionistic realism cannot do so.

In the case of non-monotonic norms factualism becomes quite implausible. Norms of receptivity do not depend on some universal or statistical fact. Nor do norms of induction. There is no fact in virtue of which enumerative inductive inferences are warranted. They do not depend on any factual truth about universal causation, uniformity of nature, etc. And in virtue of what *fact* could inference to the best explanation be a warranted method of reasoning?

In all these cases, it is true, we can make a rough factual claim. In the case of inductive norms it is, roughly, that the world is such that enumerative inductions, or inferences to the best explanation, will in the long run lead us to true factual beliefs. Call this the factual claim that the world is induction-friendly. (There is likewise the factual claim that the world is friendly to norms of receptivity.) Strawson long ago distinguished these two elements in a discussion of enumerative induction. He contrasted two propositions, '(The universe is such that) induction will continue to be successful' and 'Induction is rational (reasonable)'; holding the second to be analytic, the first to be 'contingent'.[19] The first proposition says that the universe is induction-friendly. The second corresponds to the norm of enumerative induction. According to the Normative view this norm is synthetic a priori, not analytic, but we can still agree with Strawson's main point, which is that its truth does not depend on the truth of the first. And that applies to *all* epistemic norms: their truth does not depend on, 'correspond', to any fact.

We could be frustrated in our would-be inductive conclusions. If they were constantly defeated in improved epistemic states they would be undermined. In that case a meta-induction could warrant the claim that the world is *not* induction-friendly. But this would not be a case in which inductive norms themselves were *defeated*, in the sense in which we are using that word. Indeed we would be applying these norms in coming to the conclusion that the world is not induction-friendly. (We could similarly be led inductively to the conclusion that the world is not friendly to norms of receptivity.)

That leads us to question (iii): are epistemic norms defeasible? The answer, I shall argue, is that no norm is defeasible.

20.6 Are epistemic norms defeasible?

Let **N** be a norm. Then we have the higher-order norm, **N***:

(5) $S(<\emptyset, e>, \beta N)$

N is indefeasible if **N*** is monotonic, that is, if:

(6) It is necessarily the case that $(e)S(<\emptyset, e>, \beta N)$

We can now ask whether the norm yielding this sufficient reason, **N****, is monotonic. If it is not, then the claim that **N*** is monotonic is defeasible: it is possible that there is a strictly improved *e* in which there is not sufficient reason to believe (6). But if the claim that **N*** is monotonic is defeasible, isn't **N** defeasible? Or should we say only that the claim that **N** is indefeasible is defeasible?

Suppose we ask whether we are *warranted* in thinking that **N** is indefeasible. The question can be repeated for higher-order levels (**N***, **N**** ... etc.). I suggest that we are warranted in thinking that an ostensible norm is indefeasible if and only if we are warranted in thinking that there is monotonicity at all these *higher-order* levels. If we have no warrant to think that, we have no warrant to regard the ostensible norm as indefeasible. If **N** is indefeasible it is indefeasible 'all the way up'.

Now even by this test I submit that we are warranted in taking evaluative and practical norms to be indefeasible. Remember that we are not asking whether people who *believe* something to be an evaluative or practical norm are fallible. Of course they are. We all have mistaken normative beliefs. The question is whether a wholly normative evaluative or practical proposition can *be* a priori in *e* but not a priori in *e**. I cannot see how that

---

[19] Strawson 1963: 261.

could be, because evaluative and practical norms are insulated from the facts. They do not intertwine with facts in an epistemic field in the way that epistemic norms (other than the norm of apperception) do. So evaluative and practical norms are indefeasible all the way up.

What then of epistemic norms? Consider first the case of 'logical' norms in the broadest sense, i.e. the whole class of monotonic epistemic norms which have universal a priori necessities as their offshoots. Take the geometrical norms underlying Euclidean geometry.[20] This geometry, understood as a set of universal truths, has been dropped by physics. We no longer accept the parallels postulate. So we must conclude that the norm underlying the parallels postulate, call it PP, is not monotonic when it is stated in terms of S. But it might still be monotonic *if stated in terms of R*. PP then says that the fact that two lines intersect twice is an outright reason to believe that at least one is not straight, thus:

$(e)R(<\emptyset, e>, \beta PP)$

On this approach, we have some outright reason to believe PP, as did the Greeks. We can say one of two further things about the Greeks. One is that they had sufficient reason to believe the parallels postulate to be a necessary truth—but while that sufficient reason included an a priori element, it was not purely a priori. The fit with then available data also contributed, via inference to the best explanation. We too have the same degree of outright reason to believe it, but that outright reason no longer constitutes a *sufficient* reason, because of empirically based theoretical considerations of which we are now aware. Alternatively, we could say that in the Greek context, unlike ours, the outright reason was outright sufficient. On the second view the Greeks' geometrical norm, stated in terms of S, is defeated. But on the first view we can hold that PP is indefeasible, even though the parallels postulate itself, conceived as a non-normative proposition belonging to our theory of reality, is defeated.

This account could be extended to logic in the broad sense as a whole. All its norms are indefeasible so long as they are stated in R. The normative lean towards acceptance is then complemented by the data, producing a *partly* a priori belief in their non-normative offshoots. Perhaps some monotonic epistemic norms, but not others, are indefeasible even when stated in S. For example, consider the following colour norm: the fact that y is green is sufficient reason to believe that y is coloured. By the standards of 7.2 this proposition is not analytic, since there is no way of showing that the conclusion 'y is coloured' is asserted in the premise 'y is green'. But it may still be too closely constitutive of the concept of colour to be defeated. In which case it is a priori that it is monotonic, and hence there is outright sufficient reason to believe the universal proposition that whatever is green is coloured. In contrast, some might argue that the development of intuitionistic logic has shown that excluded middle is not so close to the core of the concept of disjunction as to be indefeasible in S. We have no outright warrant to deny that intuitionistic logic may yet turn out to produce some gain of insight, explanatory or other.

---

[20] We discussed these in a preliminary way in 6.9.

A weakened empiricism about the universal propositions of logic and mathematics would say, in the first place, that our warrant for believing them is always at least partly empirical. Hence, in the second place, they are defeasible. This weakened empiricism is consistent with holding the norms of logic and mathematics to be monotonic when stated in R, and indefeasible when so stated.

We can now complete our argument by showing that all other epistemic norms are indefeasible.

Consider first the norm of apperception:

(7) $(e)S(<\text{the fact that } p, e>, x, \beta p)$

where the fact that p is the fact that x is in some apperceptual state. This norm forms a unique case on its own. On the one hand, it is monotonic, like the logical and mathematical norms, on the other hand, as with the non-monotonic norms we cannot formulate a non-normative offshoot. ('Whenever I am in an apperceptual state I am warranted in thinking that I am in that state' is true but normative.)

Could there be some $e*$ in which (7) is not a priori, perhaps even unwarranted? Suppose the fact that p is the fact that I seem to hear a loud noise. Could there be an e in which that fact is not a sufficient reason for me to believe that I seem to hear a loud noise? It seems not.[21] This norm is indefeasible.

Finally, we have the various non-monotonic epistemic norms considered in Chapter 9. These—including the inductive norms themselves—could all be undermined as our epistemic fields enlarge, as considered in Section 20.5. But undermining is not defeat. Many warrants based on these norms might be defeated, but the norms themselves would not be. Thus non-monotonic norms are underminable but not defeasible. Monotononic norms in contrast—the norms of 'logic' and the apperceptual norm—are neither underminable nor defeasible. So all epistemic norms are indefeasible.

20.7 Scepticism

We cannot fully trace the implications of the Normative view for the analysis of scepticism. That is too large a topic. What follows is more of a strategic summary.

Scepticism follows from global realism; thus the Normative view eliminates that particular source. But there are other possible sources with which it does not deal. Scepticism can develop along a variety of routes. Thus we should not expect the Normative view to provide a definitive answer to all sceptical doubts. That is not its project.

It will be useful to distinguish at the outset a scepticism which questions whether knowledge of reality—the 'external world', the past, other minds—is possible while *not* questioning our knowledge of epistemic norms, and a scepticism which questions

---

[21] 'Loud' is vague, so epistemicists about vagueness would disagree. I am assuming the position argued for in 7.4.

whether we have knowledge of norms. The distinction is between first-order or internal scepticism and higher order or normative scepticism.[22]

A main form of first-order scepticism is based on the principle which I argued in 8.3 is central to eliminative inquiry:

> *The eliminative principle*: in considering whether you have sufficient reason to believe that *p*, you should consider whether you have sufficient reason to rule out suppositions incompatible with its being the case that *p*. If you do not, then you do not have sufficient reason to believe that *p*, though you may have some degree of reason.

Scepticism of this kind applies the principle to our common sense-cum-scientific view taken as a whole (call it the 'the received view'). It asks whether I have sufficient reason to rule out radical suppositions incompatible with the received view—for example, that the world came fully-formed into existence 5 minutes ago, or that I am a brain in a vat, etc.

So long as epistemic norms are not being put in question one can see how the reply to this scepticism must go. This sceptic treats the eliminative principle as the dominant epistemic norm; but that is a mistake. Not all inquiry is eliminative. On the contrary, eliminative inquiry operates *within* a framework of beliefs provided by epistemic norms. Beliefs based on norms of receptivity are not products of eliminative reasoning. Enumerative induction is not eliminative. Nor is inference to the best explanation. You do not, in general, have to *eliminate* all other hypotheses (i.e. show that they *cannot* be true) to have sufficient reason to believe a better one.

Eliminative inquiry presupposes the operation of these other epistemic norms, since it requires us to establish at least a provisional framework of what facts are known, and of what is possible and what is necessary, before we can apply it. The suppositions that it eliminates are those we are warranted in thinking impossible given that we are warranted in accepting this (developing) framework.[23]

To illustrate how this works apply it to the supposition that I am now the subject of an experience–simulation experiment being carried out by medical researchers. Is it possible that I am lying in a hospital bed with electrodes inserted into my brain, or even, perhaps, that I am just a brain in a vat in a laboratory? Is this supposition a genuine contender that has to be eliminated before I can legitimately conclude that I am in my study typing on my computer? No. I know that it is not yet possible to produce such simulations of experience, whether or not it ever will be. Thus this supposition can be eliminated.

Can we imagine a development of the received view in which it could not be eliminated? Certainly. Suppose that plenty of very effective experience-simulation devices come to exist. I know—or seem to know—that there are several in the medical laboratories

---

[22] I have put this in terms of knowledge, but scepticism as I am understanding it questions whether any of our beliefs about the world are warranted as well as questioning whether we have any knowledge of the world.

[23] Mill's *System of Logic*, Book III, is a pioneering discussion of these points. In the 'inductive process' canons of eliminative inquiry come into operation only when generalizations about what is and is not possible have been established on a more primitive basis. The more accurate results enabled by eliminative inquiry spill back and correct the initial rough-cut generalizations.

of my university, and I share a flat with some medical research students who are using them. They go in for practical jokes and have already tricked me a number of times... In this scenario I might have to consider seriously the supposition that I am on an experience–simulation device, and not actually sitting at my desk typing.

Pushing this further, the received view *could* develop in such a way as to produce a sceptical collapse. In one far-fetched scenario, the continuing application of epistemic norms apparently turns out to warrant us in thinking that spontaneous coming into existence of brains in vats is a common occurrence. I would then have to start taking seriously the supposition that I am and always have been a brain in a vat. At the limit I would be forced to fall into doubt about the received view as such—given the undermining facts that, on that view, I seem to know. That is, I have to conclude that if I know such facts I know nothing, and hence, since on the received view I know such facts I do not know the received view to be correct. In this way internal scepticism could go hyperbolic.

Nothing in the Normative view guarantees that this could not happen. Yet this possibility of sceptical collapse remains internal; it can arise only where the received view has, as it turns out, reached a position in which it undermines itself. Hence we can reply to this possibility not by invoking any philosophical thesis but simply by pointing out that what it envisages has not actually happened. Our received view is warranted, not self-undermining. This is a response to scepticism from *within* our epistemic norms.

A sceptic may be dissatisfied with this internal response. He will point out that my reasons for thinking it impossible that I am, say, a brain in a vat are based on a set of beliefs about the world that I am taking for granted. If those beliefs are true, then it is impossible that I am a brain in a vat. But what are my grounds for thinking them true? How do I know that the epistemic state that purports to warrant them is not itself caused by an experience–simulation device? No evidence, he says, can be brought to bear on this question, for whenever I treat something as evidence I am doing so from *within* a received view, a theory, of the relation between myself and the world.

This is now a different route to metaphysical or hyperbolical doubt. In effect the sceptic is now raising the higher-order question: why should we accept the epistemic norms that take us from our epistemic states to an agreed, received view?

The question has power, and global realism is a main source of its power. Indeed if global realism is assumed, there is no answer to it. For on the one hand, as argued in Chapter 6, global realism cannot give an account of a priori knowledge. And, on the other hand, we clearly cannot justify our epistemic norms by appealing to a posteriori knowledge of some facts in virtue of which these epistemic norms hold. Dogmatism becomes the only shelter. Thus Critical philosophy is right to say that global realism forces either scepticism or dogmatism.

In contrast, the epistemology of norms offered by the Normative view avoids that dilemma. Again I do not mean that if we eliminate global realism we have a complete answer to scepticism. A feeling persists that so long as hyperbolic suppositions are *intelligible* scepticism has not been dissolved. At this point we face some elusive questions. Does scepticism *need* to be dissolved to be refuted? Can the Normative view dissolve it by showing these hyperbolic suppositions to be in some way unintelligible?

Perhaps the verificationist responses to scepticism that were influential in the twentieth century, and did purport to show its unintelligibility, have pitched our expectations (as Critical philosophers) too high. And perhaps it is partly in recoil from these expectations that some have come to be resigned to dogmatism. More generally, philosophy currently has a tendency to go for extreme meta-normative solutions: a dogmatic realism, or unyielding non-cognitivism, or error theory. In contrast, the best Normative response is lower profile. Accept the intelligibility of hyperbolic sceptical suppositions, but describe the epistemic norms that warrant the received view, and explain the normative epistemology by which they are themselves warranted. Grant that warrant is not factive; however warranted our norms may be, even if they are indefeasible, it is not *deducible* from that that they are true. Nonetheless, we *are* warranted in thinking they are. Nor could any facts show them to be false, because their truth does not depend on any factual claim. True, internal inductions might undermine the warrant they provide for our factual beliefs, but that has not occurred. The Normative view can legitimately distinguish between fallibilism and scepticism.

This response is strong enough to reject both dogmatism and scepticism; it may well be wise to stop there. Still, there may be a more forceful response, which would not just restrict itself to distinguishing fallibilism from scepticism but would try to show that any higher-order normative scepticism that puts epistemic norms themselves into doubt is unintelligible. I sketch how it would go.

The sceptic raises the following supposition: our epistemic norms are fully warranted by the lights of the epistemology described in 16.2 to 16.4, and in no way internally undermined by the progress of inquiry, but the world is actually quite other than the picture of it that we have built on these norms. In other words, the supposition is that our norms are in no way truth-conducive, and thus not *really* warranted after all.

How do we know, this sceptic asks, that that is not the case? The low-profile response simply says that though the supposition is intelligible it is completely unwarranted. The more forceful response says that it is not clearly intelligible. Only a 'transcendental illusion' (in Kant's phrase: cp. 1.2) induced by global realism, an illusion we cannot fully escape, makes it seem to be.

How might this be argued? We would start from the fact that concepts are not detachable from epistemic norms. To possess a concept *is* to recognize the truth of certain norms that constitute the concept (18.5). We must use concepts in formulating any sceptical hypotheses which supposedly put our very epistemic norms into doubt. Yet if these sceptical hypotheses succeed in doing so, they put in doubt the concepts in terms of which we are trying to formulate the hypotheses, and thus the intelligibility of the hypotheses themselves. The supposition that they are intelligible forces us to conclude that we cannot know they are intelligible.

The sceptic may reply that he has produced no positive hypothesis about how the world actually is (about evil demons, brats in vats, etc.), but only the negative hypothesis that it is radically unlike the way we think it is. Still he is considering the supposition that there *is* some radically alien way that it actually is—*even though* our received view is warranted by our own epistemic practices and in no way undermined by the progress of inquiry. As he thinks of it the received view is, so to speak, internally but not externally warranted. The more ambitious Normative response tries to show (a) that the sceptic must claim that this radically alien way is in principle intelligibly describable; but (b) that it is not, given that our concepts are fixed by our epistemic norms. That is, any attempt to distinguish between 'internal' and 'external' warrant founders on the fact that concepts are epistemic norms. For example, I can intelligibly hypothesize that an evil demon is deceiving me into thinking I have two hands, but *only* on condition that I also concede that in the only sense of warrant there is I am warranted in rejecting that hypothesis; that is, only if I concede that I am warranted in thinking I have two hands, and that no evil demon is making it look as though I have. If I do not concede that, then my hypothesis ceases to be intelligible. I am then trying to apply concepts beyond their bounds. But if I do concede that, then the received view is warranted, in the only sense of 'warrant' there is.

As I say, the less ambitious normative response is good enough. And the more ambitious response, which tries to show the unintelligibility of metaphysical or hyperbolic scepticism, may be thought to appeal still, in some way, to a verificationism that is not justified by a good normative theory of concepts. The question, that is, is whether demonstrating the unintelligibility of scepticism requires only something negative—rejection of global realism—or whether it overambitiously rests on some positive philosophical thesis which is itself unsustainable. But we shall not pursue it further here.

Finally we turn to another form of normative scepticism that is not based on global realism. It arises from scepticism about the possibility of normative consensus. In 16.4 we argued for:

> *The convergence thesis*: when I judge that p, I enter a commitment that inquirers who scrutinized any relevant evidence and argument available to them would agree that p unless I could fault either their pure judgements about reasons or their evidence.

This applies to all judgements, including purely normative ones—in their case the question of evidence drops out. Thus insofar as I encounter purely normative disagreement between my own judgements and others', disagreement about norms, I must either be able honestly to judge that others are at fault in their normative judgement, or conclude that I am at fault—or I must conclude that there is no truth of the matter.

The last option produces scepticism, or rather nihilism, about the putative norm in question. Where we thought there was a norm, there is no norm. Even though this outcome would destroy a part of our assumed normative framework, scepticism based on this possibility is still internal in one sense: it is not connected to global realism. The argument is simply that *within* the dialogical process of inquiry what we initially took to be norms might turn out not to be so. So we can respond in the way we responded to the possibility that our epistemic norms, though sound, undermine themselves in the course of inquiry. It could turn out that they undermine themselves, it could turn out that they fall to fault-free non-convergence—but it has not turned out to be so.

For various obvious non-philosophical reasons, however, this last claim is somewhat difficult to make. We live in a pluralistic democratic culture in which there is plenty of apparently ultimate normative disagreement. This apparently applies even in the case of epistemic norms. Take the question whether we are warranted in believing hypotheses about unobservables, when these are justified purely as inferences to the best explanation, or whether we should regard them purely as useful heuristic devices. Or consider the question whether a religious belief based on faith is warranted. To maintain a view on these issues we must be justified in thinking that the normative judgement with which disagree, however popular, is not fault-free. (Or at least treating that as a real, not merely nominal, option.) Thus if inference to the best explanation is normatively sound but purely faith-based belief is not, then there must be some fault in the judgement of those who disagree.

Given that I accept inference to the best explanation as a norm, I must seek an explanation for why others disagree. I find it by tracing it to the underlying issue of global realism. For anyone who makes an underlying assumption of global realism *should* find it impossible to see how the mere fact that a hypothesis is simple could warrant the belief that it is true. That being so, I can hold that what is indicated, by disagreement about the norm, is not an ultimate disagreement of spontaneous normative judgements that casts doubt on the norm itself, but rather interference from a philosophical dispute. Likewise, if I reject the claim that faith-based beliefs can be normatively sound I am committed to holding that the claim that they are does not arise from the free and untrammelled play of normative spontaneity, but, for example, from people's strong emotional need for religious conviction, or from some other undermining cause.

The appearance of ultimate normative disagreement is even stronger in the evaluative and practical domain. This is why the challenge raised by J. L. Mackie's argument from relativity is so forceful and widely repeated, compared to his more arcane argument from queerness.[24] Mackie's argument from relativity, as against his argument from queerness, has a valid core. *If* there is ultimate, fault-free, normative disagreement about some putative evaluative or practical norm, then that putative norm turns out not to *be* a norm. To defend a norm one must argue that those who disagree with it have misunderstood it, or that their judgement is not genuinely spontaneous, but distorted through carelessness, wishful-thinking, indoctrination, uncriticized 'group think'... or that their spontaneity is in some way faulty, as in the case of gratitude-blind Tom. This can be difficult to do for reasons other than purely epistemological ones. But such difficulties lead us into questions of social and political philosophy which are not our subject here.

20.8 Naturalism

The Normative view is in conflict with global realism; it is not in conflict with naturalism as such. Naturalism says that the natural facts are all the facts there are.[25] Properly

---

[24] Mackie 1977: 36–8.

[25] One might call this ontological naturalism and contrast it with methodological naturalism, the important but vague doctrine that says something like 'Postulate no non-natural facts in your understanding of the world, including your understanding of human beings'. But it seems that this must be based on a heuristic of ontological naturalism. For if there are facts other than natural facts, for example, about human beings, why should we not take them into account in our understanding of the world?

understood, this is where thinking about the world has led: it is the internal product of common sense/science, and should be respected as such by any Critical philosophy, since the critique of our philosophical preconceptions seeks no revisions to common sense.

What then are natural facts? We can take them to be substantial facts wholly constituted by attributes that fall under relations of efficient causality, as this notion has developed within scientific inquiry. A natural fact consists in the possession by some object or objects of some such attribute or attributes. Thus the force of naturalism lies in its notion of causality, which is narrower than the very broad notion of causality, productive power, that we used in characterizing the real in 17.3. Naturalism is a much stronger doctrine than the doctrine that whatever is real can cause or be caused, where 'cause' is used in this very broad way. The latter doctrine, we argued, asserts a necessary identity. But naturalism rules out various substantial facts that some metaphysical doctrines, including metaphysically-based religions, have proposed.

Kant has to reject naturalism. True, he can and does accept the thesis that the natural facts are all the facts there are *at the phenomenal level*. However, facts at the phenomenal level are only facts as they appear. The facts as they really are not natural facts. They have productive power in the broad sense, that is they in some way bring about their appearances. But they are not spatio-temporal and they do not do so by what Kant calls natural causality, for that is a relation that applies only at the phenomenal level. Furthermore, insofar as thought and action is a product of the 'causality of freedom' it is not reducible to any natural fact.

It is not clear whether the Vienna School could accept naturalism. Their individual views varied; there was Schlick's physicalism in his *General Theory of Knowledge* and Carnap's neutralism in the *Aufbau*. However, the question is whether Viennese verificationism as such, considered as a form of Critical philosophy, is consistent with naturalism. This turns on whether it has a sufficiently cognition-independent notion of fact.

Viennese Critical philosophy is naturalistic in the sense that it takes reality to be whatever the categories of a developed natural science would say it is. The natural facts are the true descriptive propositions of such a science. However, the truths of such a science are relative to a system of conventions: to the non-descriptive 'propositions' in the scheme. In contrast it seems to be essential to the naturalist vision, as to common sense, that there are substantial, cognition-independent, facts. The natural facts are thus and so, this way rather than that, 'already there', 'there anyway' irrespective of what we think (1.2). They are substantial, not nominal, facts. Thus in particular they cannot be equated with nominally factual propositions whose truth depends on what conventions we choose to adopt. This being so, Viennese Critical philosophy cannot deliver naturalism any more than the Kantian version of Critical philosophy can. The Kantian critique holds that there are genuinely cognition-independent facts but denies that they are natural facts; the Viennese critique asserts that there are natural facts, and only natural facts, in *its* understanding of 'fact'—but denies that facts are cognition-independent.

These consequences stem from Kant's transcendental idealism and Viennese verificationism, which these Critical philosophies took to be necessary to save the possibility of knowledge. The Normative view denies that they are necessary and rejects them, holding instead that all we need is cognitive irrealism about reasons. So can it make genuine peace with naturalism? Does its critique of epistemic norms respect the cognition-independence of natural facts?

On the Normative view the limits of the world, of the substantial facts, are in a certain sense not clear-cut. The point at issue becomes especially clear if we consider again the status of universal a priori necessities—all those universal propositions that we have characterized as offshoots of monotonic norms (green is a colour; if p then p or q; $7 + 5 = 12\ldots$). These universal propositions are not normative, by our definition of 'normative proposition'. Nor are they factual; nor are they analytic.

As universal propositions they all form part of our theory of the world. Thus if a factual proposition is simply a proposition in this theory, they are factual. However, we have not characterized factual propositions in that way. (That was the Viennese approach.) We have simply said that factual propositions are propositions whose content is that a substantial fact exists. And since the Critical argument (6.3) is that propositions that are factual in this sense cannot be known a priori, we must conclude that these universal offshoots of epistemic norms are not factual.

The weakened empiricism noted in Section 20.5 would say that *no* universal proposition can be known completely a priori, even if in some cases, such as the propositions of logic and mathematics, there is some degree of outright reason to believe them. I think we should accept that there are cases in which our warrant for a belief has an a priori ingredient but is not completely a priori. So in these cases, is the belief for which we have a partly a priori warrant a factual belief? We can only answer that factuality is a matter of degree: complete aprioricity is inversely related to complete factuality. But this, if true, is not inconsistent with naturalism. Naturalism is simply the view that insofar as a proposition is factual, to whatever degree, the fact it claims to obtain is a natural fact.

If factuality is a matter of degree, however, then we cannot think of the world as a well-defined set of absolute facts. This conclusion is reminiscent of the moral Kant draws from the antimonies of pure reason, namely, that we cannot think of 'the sensible world as a whole existing in itself'—we cannot 'think the whole' as an absolute and independent whole.[26] Why not? Not because the sensible world is a dependent, joint product of the interaction between things in themselves and the knowing subject, as transcendental idealism would have it. For the Normative view, 'thing in themselves' don't come into it. It is, rather, because our theory of the world is not an inert picture of nature but a way of thinking about and acting within nature. Our world theory—our theory of what exists and how it works—belongs to our self-determining activity and thus inevitably has normative as well as factual dimensions, which are not in the end neatly separable.

---

[26] Henry E. Allison suggests that the attempt to 'think the whole' arises from a 'theocentric model of knowledge' which, he thinks, is what Kant rejects when he rejects transcendental realism. As I would put it, it arises from global realism, which is what the Normative view rejects Allison 1983: 38, 60.

20.9 Can Critical dualisms be overcome?

All Critical philosophies start from a fundamental epistemological dualism, but they diverge in what other dualisms they then generate. The fundamental dualism is between self-determining thought and its data. It arises from the very nature of self-determination. Viennese Critical philosophy interprets it as the dualism of convention and experience. Like Kant, we have seen it as a dualism of spontaneity and receptivity: the dualism between self-determining thought's own epistemic materials—its spontaneous normative dispositions—and the epistemic materials it receives from something other than itself: the facts as they are. Thus whereas in the Viennese critique the fundamental dualism generates non-cognitivism about Reason, or reasons, it does so neither on Kant's account nor on ours.

One can represent Kant's epistemology as flowing from two basic tenets: (i) knowledge that arises from pure spontaneity is not knowledge of things as they really are, i.e. of real things, existents; and (ii) knowledge that arises from receptivity is not knowledge of things as they really are. (i) leads to cognitive irrealism about Reason, (ii) leads to transcendental idealism. Since spontaneity and receptivity are exhaustive, given (i) and (ii) it follows that there is no knowledge of things as they really are. The Normative view accepts (i) but rejects (ii). Still, it would be glib to leave the matter there. We must take stock of elements in our thinking that genuinely pull towards (ii).

There are a number of these, some of them fuelled by global realism; but the ones I want to consider are those that arise from within the Normative view itself. They concern the possibility of non-convergence.

We inquire into the world within a framework of epistemic norms. Our knowledge of these norms is ineliminably dialogical: it thus presupposes the presence of a cognitive community against which one tests one's spontaneous judgements. Epistemic discipline requires that where these judgements encounter disagreement one must be able to judge (seriously, not wilfully) that others are making a misjudgement, or withdraw one's own.

But could there not be cognitive communities of beings with systematically different normative responses? The concept of a reason is required for the possibility of judgement of any kind; it is in that sense a 'transcendental' concept. But while the concept of a reason can be applied only where there is a determinate framework of norms, there is no particular determinate framework that its very intelligibility presupposes as such. We cannot infer, from the very concept of a reason, that the norms warranted for us are warranted for every community of self-determiners. Could other norms be warranted for other communities?

Take first the case of practical and evaluative norms. Could there not be a community (not necessarily a human community) within which there is no sentiment of gratitude, and thus no insight into reasons of gratitude? Or in which there is no acknowledgement of the Demand principle, and thus of rights based on it? What if this other community acknowledges norms we cannot grasp?

Cognitive internalism (3.9) says that if the other community is blind to some reasons whose force as reasons for us we see, then these are not reasons for them. Hence the norms these reasons instantiate are not norms for them. Symmetrically, if we are blind to some reasons they see, these reasons are not reasons for us. Norms are grounded in cognitive communities of beings with the same natural dispositions. Reasons are judged from within the common sense of such communities, as are faulty judgements on the part of individual reasoners like gratitude-blind Tom. What warrants a particular norm, and the judgement that an individual's judgement is faulty, is spontaneity and convergence within that community.

In effect this introduces a cognitive-community parameter which becomes variable if cognitive communities with radically different natures are introduced. We thus arrive at a fully general theory of reasons, in which common *natures*, cognitive, affective, and conative, are one of the relata of reason relations along with the others we have become familiar with. In particular, this applies to epistemic norms. They will still be universalizable, and because reason relations now include a variable ranging over cognitive communities with varying natures, true. Various cognitive natures have their various cognitive norms, pure universalizable truths about reasons.

The special thing about epistemic norms is that they generate a world theory. If another cognitive community produced a less powerful one than ours we would very likely discount its putative norms. If it converged on ours the significance of the purely normative divergence would fade. But what if the result turned out to be a tie in terms of predictive adequacy? Come to that, what if our own norms produced more than one optimal world view by all our norms of good explanation, taken together?

Can we really understand these supposed possibilities? And if we can, would it be intelligible to ask which world view is really right, even though we couldn't give an answer?

I think we can understand them. We can imagine finding ourselves faced by genuinely conflicting, highly successful cognitive traditions. The longer this conflict went on without resolution the more we would come to be warranted in accepting a strong thesis of underdetermination: the thesis that there is more than one optimal theory of the world, taking into account all epistemic norms.

The conclusion would always remain defeasible. It would always remain possible that new evidence, or new reflection on existing evidence, would undermine one or both theories. And a certain regulative ideal of inquiry, that 'truth is one', would encourage us to expect that and search for it, and discourage us from accepting the conclusion. Nevertheless, to say that a conclusion is defeasible is not to say that it is unwarranted, and it seems to me that in a long run of unsuccessful attempts to resolve or supersede the conflict it would eventually become reasonable to accept that there is indeed more than one optimal theory of the world. There might be no crucial experiment that could decide between the theories—and not just because we could envisage one but lacked the technology to set it up. There would only be balance sheets for both of them, containing different debits and credits but adding up to the same bottom line. This situation might persist for decades or centuries. Every attempt by one theoretical tradition to trump or assimilate the other would be met by an effective reply.

In such circumstances, a meta-induction could eventually warrant the conclusion that no such attempt could be successful. We would have to accept that there was more than one optimal world theory. How would we react to this conclusion?

There would undoubtedly be a disposition to say, on the basis of this history, that it turns out we cannot know how things really are. And there would be an inclination to accept that there *is* some unknowable truth about the world as it really is. This is the disposition that makes something like transcendental idealism attractive. But should we yield to it?

On the one hand, it seems that we can ask, of a whole world theory, whether or not is true. On the other hand, given failure of convergence there is failure of warrant. So we seem forced either to hold that we cannot know which if either of two optimal contenders is true, or alternatively, to fall back to some kind of instrumentalist attitude to our theories, according to which they cannot, taken as a whole, be said to be true or false.

The alternative is to say that the question which world theory is really true is empty. To be sure truth, unlike warrant, is a monadic property of propositions. Epistemic warrant is a relation between fields, natures, and beliefs, truth is not. Nonetheless, even though truth is not explicitly relational in the way warrant is, it is not applicable to whole world theories, but only within them. After all, we are considering *epistemically optimal total* world theories. It makes no sense to apply the notion of truth in this radically trans-theoretical way.

The ideal of 'truth as one' take us no further. This is a regulative ideal, an incentive to pursue inquiry until we have one comprehensive and consistent answer that every fault-free inquirer will converge on; it has no further metaphysical sanction. In the circumstances we are considering we would have to accept that the ideal cannot be achieved—not because we cannot be sufficiently comprehensive and consistent but because there is more than one way to be so.

This is a debate one can have *within* the Normative standpoint—I have formulated it as such, without appeal to any global realism, or appeal to a God's eye point of view. However, it seems to me that within that standpoint the idea that truth is intra-theoretical should prevail. The clear-cut removal of a metaphysical background of realism pulls us that way. Instrumentalism has its well-known difficulties of distinguishing between fact and theoretical fiction; connectedly, it introduces an implausible degree of cognition-dependence. In contrast. the Normative view allows for scientific realism (in somewhat the way that, according to Kant, transcendental idealism allows for empirical realism). It does not quite give us the 'absolute conception of the world' envisaged by seventeeth-century scientific realism. But it gives us as much cognition-independence as common sense requires.

Inquiry into reality could develop in a plural way, with no long-term convergence—even though it has not so far done so. *Any* metaphysical stance has to accept that. But whereas for a global realist this points to scepticism, for Normative Critical philosophy it points to the dictum that 'The world is our world'. The world is our world in the sense that the concept of *the world* is itself an internal concept. It is in terms of norms that hold relative to our nature, and in terms of our cognitive tradition, that we understand it. If it seems anthropocentric to say so, lean on the other foot and remember that we do not in any sense 'construct reality'. Nor do we construct the norms which underlie our world theory. These norms are neither facts about the world nor facts about us. They are objective universal truths about reason relations: irreal, pure objects of cognition that mediate between knowing subject and known world.

Appendix

SYMBOLS, TERMS, AND THESES

Symbols

'R', 'R_o' and 'S' denote specific, overall and sufficient reason relations. '**R**' ranges over any of these (**R** = R, R_o or S).

'W' denotes the relation of warrant.

'p', 'q'—schematic letters standing in for declarative sentences.

'P', 'Q'—variables ranging over propositions.

'x_1', 'x_2', etc. range over *actors*.

'π_i': ranges over sets of nominal facts (truths), including the empty set—or if one prefers, plurally over facts including the null fact. $\pi(y_1, \ldots, y_n)$: a nominal fact about $y_1, \ldots, y_n$.

'Π_i': schematic letters replaceable by declarative sentences. Where 'Π' is replaced by a sentence that expresses a truth, 'π' refers to the corresponding nominal fact.

'ψ': ranges over *responses*, i.e. beliefs (believing that so-and-so), affective states (feeling such-and-such about so-and-so) and actions proper (doing so-and-so).

$\psi(y_1, \ldots, y_n)$: a response directed to a sequence of objects $y_1, \ldots, y_n$. $\psi(y_1, \ldots, y_n, F)$: a response directed to a sequence of objects $<y_1, \ldots, y_n>$ and a property F (as in reason to believe of the sequence that it instantiates the property). $\psi(P)$: a response directed to proposition P.

'β' ranges specifically over beliefs, 'ϕ' over feelings or affective attitudes, and 'α' over actions.

'e' ranges over epistemic fields.

's' ranges over epistemic states.

N: ranges over norms.

'$\emptyset$' denotes the empty set of nominal facts, or the null fact.

'$\ldots \tau_e \ldots$': 'given that$\ldots$in e, it is warrantably assertible in e that$\ldots$'

'μ' denotes the maximal epistemic field—the field consisting of all the nominal facts.

Ep: denotes the act of unconditionally excluding the proposition that p from all suppositions.

Ip: denotes the act of unconditionally including the proposition that p in all suppositions.

Variables, constants, and quantifiers are left implicit whenever convenient. For example:

'R(x, α, t)' = 'There's reason for x to α at t' = '$(\exists \pi_i)$R(π_i, x, α, t)'.

'S(α)' = 'There's sufficient reason for the person in question to α at the given time' = '$(\exists \pi_i)$ S(π_i, x, α, t)'.

'S(p)' = 'There's sufficient reason, in the epistemic field in question at the relevant time, to believe that p' = '$(\exists \pi_i)(x)S(e, \pi_i, t, x, \beta p)$'.

Technical terms (i.e. terms that are used in this book in a specific or distinctive way)

Absolutely complete reason: see **complete reason**.
All-things-considered reason: see *prima facie reason*.
A priori:

(i) A proposition that p *has some degree of a priori support* in e iff there is some degree of **outright** reason to believe it in e.

(ii) A proposition that p is *a priori* in e iff there is **outright** sufficient reason to believe it in e.

(iii) There is *a priori warrant* in s for x to believe that p iff in s x's spontaneous disposition to believe that p is sufficient reason for x to believe that it is a priori that p.

(iv) x has immediate (non-inferential) a priori *knowledge* that p if and only if (i) p; (ii) x believes that p on the basis of normative dispositions to believe that p; (iii) which are reliable.

Apperception: you apperceive the fact that p if and only if that fact is in your **epistemic state**.
Attribute: a substantial **property**.
Autonomy: an autonomous act is an act that proceeds from warrant, thus, a rationally explicable act (see **rational explanation**). 'Hegelian' autonomy: no restriction on the warrant from which the act proceeds. 'Kantian' autonomy: the act proceeds not just from warrant but from fully first-personal insight into all the underlying a priori warrants. See 15.8, footnote 44. On either reading, autonomy is stronger than **self-determination**.
Awareness: objectual awareness (*aware of*): awareness of an existent object or substantial fact by apperception, perception, or memory. Also, awareness of an object of thought or topic of discourse, real or irreal. Propositional awareness: (*aware that*): awareness that it is the case that so-and-so. See 16.1.
Complete reason to ψ: a set of nominal facts of which it is a priori that they constitute a reason to ψ. In the epistemic case, a set of nominal facts is a complete reason in e to ψ iff it is a priori that it constitutes a reason in e to ψ. It is an *absolutely complete* reason to ψ iff it is a priori that it constitutes a reason in all e to ψ.
Defeasible: a (complete) epistemic reason to believe that p in e is defeasible iff (i) the facts that constitute it give reason to believe that p in e but (ii) we 'cannot rule out', i.e. are not warranted in unconditionally excluding, the supposition that there is an $e^\star$ (a strict enlargement on e) in which it is defeated. A proposition is defeasible iff all reasons to believe it are defeasible.
Definitional consequence: derivability by means of the natural deduction rules for conjunction and the universal quantifier alone, plus substitution of explicit definitions. See 4.2.
Epistemic field: x's **epistemic field** at t, $e_{x,t}$, is the set of facts that are accessible to x at t—that x can come to know, discover, at t, whether or not x has come to know them.
Epistemic reason: a reason to believe something. Also, in reasoning, a reason to make a cognitive transition (introduce a supposition, make an inference, exclude a supposition, etc.)
Epistemic self-audit: see **self-audit**.

Epistemic state: x's epistemic state at t, $s_{x,t}$, is the set of facts that p such that the fact that p is an **absolutely complete** sufficient reason for x to believe at t that p.
Evaluative reason: reason to feel.
Fact: A *nominal* fact is a true proposition, or a truth. A *substantial* fact is the instantiation by some objects of some **attributes**.
Final end: see **telic reason**.
Global realism: see **realism**.
Justification: a justified response (belief, feeling, action) is one that raises no criticism of the agent in respect of **rationality**.
Maximal field, μ:—the epistemic field consisting of all the facts.
Monotonic norm: Let 'π_i+' refer to the union of π_i with some other facts. Then:

(i) The evaluative or practical norm $\mathbf{R}(\pi_i, \psi)$ is monotonic iff it entails that $\mathbf{R}(\pi_i+, \psi)$.

(ii) An epistemic norm $\mathbf{R}(<\pi_i, e>, \beta_p)$ is monotonic iff it is necessarily true that for all e that contain π_i, $\mathbf{R}(<\pi_i, e>, \beta_p)$.

See 9.4.
Monotonic reason: a reason that instantiates a monotonic norm.
Neutral reason: see **relative** reason.
Nominal fact: see **fact**.
Norm: a synthetic **purely normative** truth.
Normative proposition: proposition expressible by a **normative sentence**.
Normative sentence: *atomic* normative sentences are sentences of the form:

$R(\pi_i, t, d, x, \psi)$
$R_o(\pi_i, t, d, x, \psi)$ or
$S(\pi_i, t, x, \psi)$.

An *explicitly* normative sentence is one which is either:

(i) an atomic normative sentence

or

(ii) a sentence which is built from sentences which include at least one atomic normative sentence, by means of the connectives of propositional logic, quantifiers, and the truth operator ('it is true that').

A normative sentence is defined as follows.

a. Any explicitly normative sentence is normative.
b. Any sentence which has a normative sentence as a **definitional consequence** is normative.
c. No other sentences are normative.

Normative sentences which are not explicitly normative are *implicitly* normative and sentences which are not normative are *non-normative*.
A *wholly normative* sentence has no non-normative sentence as a **definitional consequence**.
A *wholly normative proposition* is expressible by a wholly normative sentence.
Overall reason to ψ: the degree of overall reason to ψ is determined by the totality of **specific reasons** to ψ (and in the practical case, not to ψ).

Offshoot: a **monotonic** norm warrants outright assertion of a corresponding non-normative universal proposition. This is its *offshoot*.

Outright reason: there is outright evaluative or practical reason for x to ψ iff the null set of facts gives x reason to ψ. In the case of epistemic reasons there is outright epistemic reason in e for x to ψ iff in e the null set of facts gives x reason to ψ.

Overall reason: the degree of reason to ψ when all specific reasons are taken into account.

Property: a *nominal* property is the sense of a predicate. A *substantial* property, or *attribute*, subvenes a causal sensitivity or power, and may be expressed by predicates which differ in sense. See 17.3.

Practical reason: a reason to perform an action.

Prima facie:

(i) A *prima facie* **epistemic reason** is an apparent epistemic reason which may or may not turn out to be a reason when all facts in the relevant epistemic field are considered.

(ii) A *prima facie* **warranted reason** (epistemic, evaluative or practical) is an apparent warranted reason which may or may not turn out to be a reason when all facts in the relevant epistemic state are considered.

(iii) A *prima facie* moral obligation is an apparent obligation which may or may not turn out to be an obligation when all facts in the relevant epistemic state are considered. ('*Prima facie*' contrasts with 'all things considered'—not with '**overall**'.)

Purely normative proposition: a normative proposition from which it cannot be deduced that any fact obtains.

Rationality: the various powers involved in recognizing and responding to reasons. To criticize someone in respect of rationality is to criticize them as inadequate in respect of their possession of these powers or faulty in their exercise.

Reason-supported: x's ψ-ing is reason-supported if and only if there is reason for x to ψ (whether or not x is aware of it or ψs from it).

Relative reason (agent-relative, patient-relative, temporally relative): contrasts with *neutral* reason. See 3.2 and 3.5.

Self-audit: epistemic self-audit is reflective assessment of what one has reason to believe and in particular whether one has reason to inquire further. Self-audit in general is reflective assessment of one's **warranted** reasons.

Self-determination: responding from *what one takes to be* sufficient reasons. Requires that one have the concept of a reason. Self-determining actor, or self-determiner: actor who has the capacity for self-determination. Self-determination is weaker than **autonomy**, in that it does not assume that the ostensible reasons to which one responds are reasons one correctly recognizes as warranted.

Should*: in the epistemic and evaluative case—x should* ψ if and only if there is **sufficient reason** for x to ψ. In the practical case—iff there is *uniquely* **sufficient reason** for x to ψ.

Specific reason to ψ: a distinct fact or set of facts that give reason to ψ, where there may be other sets of facts that also give reason to ψ (or in the practical case, not to ψ.) Sometimes referred to as a *pro tanto* reason.

Substantial fact: see fact.

Sufficient reason to ψ: a set of facts that give one strong enough reason to ψ.

telic reason: if the fact that an action will promote a state of affairs is a complete reason to do it, that state of affairs is a *final end*. The fact that an action would promote a final end is a *telic* reason to do it.

Warrant: there is warrant for x to ψ if and only if x's epistemic state, $s_{x,t}$ gives x sufficient reason to believe that there is sufficient reason for x to ψ. (The notion of warrant can be relativized to the actor's normative powers or to the actor's epistemic state. See 5.8.)

Warranted reason: x has (specific, overall, sufficient) warranted reason to ψ at t if and only if x's epistemic state, $s_{x,t}$ gives x (specific, overall, sufficient) reason to believe that there is (overall, sufficient) reason for x to ψ at t.

Wholly normative sentence/proposition: see **normative sentence**.

Some theses

I
The Normative view

(i) Normative propositions are propositions about reason relations.

(ii) There is a fundamental epistemological and ontological distinction between factual propositions and a priori propositions about reason relations.

(iii) All (synthetic) a priori propositions are in the first place normative.

(iv) Reason relations are irreal objects of true and false thoughts.

II
Some other theses (accepted or rejected)

Bridge principle: whatever facts give x reason to feel ϕ give x reason to do the ϕ-prompted action, in virtue of being a reason to feel ϕ.

Categoricity of morality: it is a priori that if x has a moral obligation to α x has sufficient reason to α (weak categoricity: has reason to α).

Cognitive internalism: π_i is a reason for x to ψ only if x has the ability to recognize, *de se*, that were it to be the case that Π_i that would be a reason for x to ψ.

Cognitivism: about normative claims—the thesis that such claims express propositions, possible objects of belief, which may be true or false.

Critical thesis: no factual proposition is a priori.

Demand principle: if it is morally permissible for x to demand that y αs, the fact that it is is a complete specific reason for y not to fail to α without x's permission.

Empiricist thesis: no synthetic proposition is a priori.

Factualism: all propositions are factual propositions—in a **substantial** sense of 'fact' stronger than the merely nominal sense.

Insight principle: morally autonomous agents can know their concrete moral obligations by means of their own insight into them (Moral version). Rationally autonomous agents can know their warrants by means of their own insight into them (Rational version).

Instrumental principle: if x has objective O, there is reason for x to adopt any means m for bringing about O, the strength of that reason being proportional (a) to the intensity of x's commitment to O; (b) to the cost-effectiveness of m as a means to achieve O.

Internalism: see **cognitive** internalism, **motivational** internalism.

Motivational internalism: there is reason for an actor to α only if α-ing would serve (promote, advance) a motive that the actor has.

Principle of Good: the fact that α promotes Good is a complete specific reason to α, proportionate in strength to the degree to which α promotes agent-neutral goal.

Realism: global realism: (i) all propositions are factual, in the **substantial** sense of fact; and (ii) all facts are cognition-independent. (Local realism: (i) and (ii) for a particular area of discourse.)

Reasons thesis: the sole normative ingredient in any normative concept is the concept of a reason (R, R_o or S). To grasp its distinctively normative conceptual content it is necessary and sufficient that one grasps the concept of a reason.

Transmission principle: if there is reason of degree d for x to pursue O there is reason for x to adopt a means m to achieve O; the strength of that reason being proportional (a) to d, (b) to the cost-effectiveness of m as a means to achieve O.

WK principle: if x is warranted in believing that p then, were x to recognize that warrant and on that basis believe that p, x would be warranted in believing that x knows that p.

REFERENCES

ADAMS, ROBERT MERRIHEW. 1999. *Finite and Infinite Goods: A Framework for Ethics*. New York: Oxford University Press.
ALLISON, HENRY. 1983. *Kant's Transcendental Idealism*. New Haven and London: Yale University Press.
—— 1990. *Kant's Theory of Freedom*. Cambridge: Cambridge University Press.
AUDI, ROBERT. 2001. *The Architecture of Reason*. Oxford: Oxford University Press.
—— 2008. 'Intuition, inference, and rational disagreement in ethics', *Ethical Theory and Moral Practice* 11: 475–92.
AUSTIN, J. L. 1962. *Sense and Sensibilia*. Oxford: Clarendon Press.
BALDWIN, THOMAS. 2010. 'The Open Question Argument'. John Skorupski (ed.) *The Routledge Companion to Ethics*. London: Routledge, pp. 286–96.
BEALER, GEORGE. 2000. 'A theory of the a priori', *Pacific Philosophical Quarterly* 81: 1–30.
BEISER, F. 2005. *Schiller as Philosopher*. Oxford: Clarendon Press.
BENACERRAF, PAUL. 1973. 'Mathematical truth', *Journal of Philosophy* 70: 661–80.
BLACKBURN, SIMON. 1984. *Spreading the Word*. Oxford: Clarendon Press.
—— 1993a. 'Circles, finks, smells and biconditionals', *Philosophical Perspectives* 7: 259–79.
—— 1993b. *Essays in Quasi-Realism*. Oxford: Oxford University Press.
—— 1998. *Ruling Passions*. Oxford: Oxford University Press.
BLOCK, NED. 1995. 'On a confusion about a function of consciousness', *Behavioral and Brain Sciences* 18: 227–47.
BOGHOSSIAN, PAUL AND PEACOCKE CHRISTOPHER (EDS). 2000. *New Essays on the A Priori*. Oxford: Oxford University Press.
BRINK, DAVID O. 1997. 'Kantian Rationalism: Inescapability, Authority, and Supremacy', in Cullity and Gaut, pp. 255–92.
—— 2003. *Perfectionism and the Common Good, Themes in the Philosophy of T. H. Green*, Oxford: Oxford University Press.
BROOME, JOHN. 2000. 'Normative Requirements', in Jonathan Dancy (ed.), *Normativity*, Oxford: Basil Blackwell.
—— 2004. 'Reasons', in R. Jay Wallace, Michael Smith, Samuel Scheffler, and Philip Pettit (eds), *Reason and Value: Themes from the Moral Philosophy of Joseph Raz*. Oxford: Oxford University Press, pp. 28–55.
—— Forthcoming. *How To Be Rational*.
BURGE, TYLER. 2005. *Truth, Thought, Reason: Essays on Frege*. Oxford: Clarendon Press.
BURGESS, J. P. and ROSEN, G. 1997. *A Subject with No Object*. Oxford: Clarendon Press.
BUTLER, JOSEPH. 1970 (1736). *Butler's Fifteen Sermons and A Dissertation of the Nature of Virtue*, London: S.P.C.K.
BYKVIST, K. 2009. 'No good fit: why the fitting attitude analysis of value fails', *Mind* 118: 763–92.
CARLSON, ERIC. 2006. 'Incomparability and measurement of value', in Richard Feldman, Kris McDaniel, Jason R. Raibley, and Michael J. Zimmerman (eds), *The Good, the Right, Life and Death: Essays in Honor of Fred Feldman*, Ashgate.
CARNAP, RUDOLF. 1937 (1934). *The Logical Syntax of Language (Logische Syntax der Sprache)*. London: Kegan Paul, Trench, Trubner.

CARNAP, RUDOLF. 1950. *Logical Foundations of Probability*. Chicago, IL: Chicago University Press.
—— 1956. 'Empiricism, Semantics and Ontology', in Carnap, *Meaning and Necessity*, Chicago, IL: University of Chicago Press.
—— 1963. 'Intellectual Autobiography', in P. Schilpp (ed.), *The Philosophy of Rudolf Carnap*, La Salle, IL: Open Court.
CHISHOLM, R. M. 1963. 'Contrary to duty imperatives and deontic logic', *Analysis* 34: 33–6.
—— 1974. 'Practical Reason and the Logic of Requirement', in S. Körner (ed.). *Practical Reason*, Oxford: Blackwell.
CLARKE, J. A. 2009. 'Fichte and Hegel on recognition', *British Journal for the History of Philosophy* 17: 365–85.
COFFA, ALBERTO. 1991. *The Semantic Tradition From Kant to Carnap: To the Vienna Station*, Cambridge: Cambridge University Press.
CONANT, J. 2002. 'The Method of the *Tractatus*', in E. Reck (ed.), *From Frege to Wittgenstein: Perspectives on Early Analytic Philosophy*, Oxford: Oxford University Press, pp. 374–462.
CRISP, ROGER. 2000. 'Review of *Value...And What Follows*, by Joel Kupperman', *Philosophy* 75: 452–62.
—— 2002. 'Sidgwick and the Boundaries of Intuitionism', in Philip Stratton-Lake (ed.), *Ethical Intuitionism*, Oxford: Oxford University Press, pp. 56–75.
—— 2005. 'Value, reasons, and the structure of justification: how to avoid passing the buck', *Analysis* 65: 80–5.
—— 2006. *Reasons and the Good*. Oxford: Clarendon Press.
—— 2008. 'Goodness and reasons: accentuating the negative', *Mind* 117: 257–65.
CULLITY, GARRETT AND GAUT, BERYS (eds). 1997. *Ethics and Practical Reason*. Oxford: Oxford University Press.
DANCY, JONATHAN. 2000. 'Should We Pass the Buck?', in A. O'Hear (ed.), *The Good, The True and the Beautiful*. Cambridge: Cambridge University Press.
—— 2004. *Ethics Without Principles*. Oxford: Oxford University Press.
DANIELS, NORMAN. 1979. 'Wide reflective equilibrium and theory acceptance in ethics'. *Journal of Philosophy* 76: 256–82.
—— 2008. 'Reflective Equilibrium', in Edward N. Zalta (ed.), *The Stanford Encyclopedia of Philosophy (Fall 2008 Edition)*. http://plato.stanford.edu/archives/fall2008/entries/reflective-equilibrium/
DANIELSSON, S. and OLSON, J. 2007. 'Brentano and the buck-passers', *Mind* 116: 511–22.
D'ARMS, JUSTIN AND JACOBSON, DANIEL. 2000. 'Sentiment and value', *Ethics* 110: 722–48.
DARWALL, STEPHEN. 1977. 'Two kinds of respect', *Ethics* 88: 36–49.
—— 2003. *Welfare and Rational Care*. Princeton and Oxford: Princeton University Press.
—— 2006. *The Second-Person Standpoint: Morality, Respect, and Accountability*. Cambridge, MA: Harvard University Press.
DIAMOND, CORA. 1991. *The Realistic Spirit*. Cambridge: MIT Press.
DIVERS, JOHN AND MILLER, ALEXANDER. 1994. 'Why expressivists about value should not love minimalism about truth', *Analysis* 54: 12–19.
DORIS, J. M. 2002. *Lack of Character: Personality and Moral Behavior*. New York: Cambridge University Press.
DOUGLAS, MARY. 1970. *Purity and Danger: An Analysis of the Concepts of Pollution and Taboo*. Harmonsworth: Pelican.
DUMMETT, MICHAEL. 1959. 'Wittgenstein's philosophy of mathematics', *Philosophical Review* 68: 324–48. Reprinted in Dummett 1978.

—— 1978. *Truth And Other Enigmas*. London: Duckworth.

—— 1993. 'Wittgenstein on Necessity: Some Reflections', in *The Seas of Language*, Oxford: Clarendon Press, pp. 446–61.

ENGEL, P. 2001. 'The false modesty of the identity theory of truth', *International Journal of Philosophical Studies* 9: 441–58.

EVANS, G. 1982. *The Varieties of Reference*. Oxford: Clarendon Press.

EWING, A. C. 1939. 'A suggested non-naturalistic analysis of good', *Mind* 48: 1–22.

—— 1947. *The Definition of Good*. New York: Macmillan.

—— 1959. *Second Thoughts in Moral Philosophy*. London: Routledge and Kegan Paul.

FICHTE, J. G. 2000. (1796–7). *Foundations of Natural Right*. Cambridge: Cambridge University Press.

FIELD, HARTRY. 2000. 'Apriority as an Evaluative Notion', in Boghossian and Peacocke (eds), *New Essays on the A Priori*, pp. 117–49.

FREGE, G. 1953 (1884). *Foundations of Arithmetic* (2nd rev. ed.). Oxford: Basil Blackwell.

—— 1977 (1919, 1923). *Logical Investigations*. Oxford: Oxford University Press.

—— 1979 (1897). *Posthumous Writings*. Oxford: Basil Blackwell.

FRIEDMAN, MICHAEL. 1991. 'The re-evaluation of logical positivism', *Journal of Philosophy* 10: 505–19.

GARVER, NEWTON. 1996. 'Philosophy as Grammar', in Hans Sluga and David G. Stern (eds), *The Cambridge Companion to Wittgenstein*, Cambridge: Cambridge University Press, pp. 139–70.

GEACH, P. T. 1956. 'Good and evil', *Analysis* 17: 33–42.

—— 1965. 'Assertion', *Philosophical Review* 74: 449–65.

—— 1967. 'Intentional identity', *Journal of Philosophy* 64: 627–32.

GIBBARD, ALLAN. 1990. *Wise Choices, Apt Feelings*, Oxford: Clarendon Press.

—— 2003. *Thinking How to Live*. Cambridge, MA: Harvard University Press.

GOLDMAN, ALVIN. 1976. 'Discrimination and perceptual knowledge', *The Journal of Philosophy* 73: 771–91.

GREEN, T. H. 2004 (1883). *Prolegomena to Ethics*. Edited with intr. by David O. Brink, Oxford: Oxford University Press.

GREENSPAN, PATRICIA. 1975. 'Conditional oughts and hypothetical imperatives', *The Journal of Philosophy* 72: 259–76.

GRICE, H. P., and STRAWSON, P. F. 1956. 'In defense of a dogma', *The Philosophical Review* 65: 377–88.

GRIFFIN, JAMES. 1986. *Well-Being*, Oxford: Clarendon Press.

HAIDT, J. and GRAHAM, J. 2007. 'When morality opposes justice: Conservatives have moral intuitions that liberals may not recognize', *Social Justice Research* 20: 98–116.

HALDANE, JOHN AND WRIGHT, CRISPIN (eds). 1993. *Reality, Representation and Projection*. Oxford: Oxford University Press.

HALE, BOB. 1986. 'The compleat projectivist', *Philosophical Quarterly* 36: 65–84.

—— AND WRIGHT, CRISPIN (eds). 1997. *The Blackwell Companion to the Philosophy of Language*, Oxford: Blackwell.

—— —— 2000. 'Implicit Definition and the A Priori'. In Boghossian and Peacocke (eds), *New Essays on the A Priori*. Oxford: Oxford University Press.

HAMILTON, A. 1995. 'A New Look at Personal Identity', *Philosophical Quarterly* 45: 332–49.

HARMAN, GILBERT. 1999. *Reasoning, Meaning and Mind*. Oxford: Oxford Universtity Press.

HART, H. L. A. 1982. 'Natural Rights: Bentham and John Stuart Mill', in *Essays on Bentham*, Oxford: Oxford University Press.

HEGEL, G. W. F. 1942 (1821). *Hegel's Philosophy of Right*, (transl. T. M. Knox). Oxford: Oxford University Press.

——1971 (1817). *Hegel's Philosophy of Mind, Being Part Three of the Encyclopedia of the Philosophical Sciences* (transl. William Wallace). Oxford: Clarendon Press.

——1991 (1821). *Elements of the Philosophy of Right*, (transl. H. B. Nisbet). Cambridge: Cambridge University Press.

HEMPEL, C. G. 1965. *Aspects of Scientific Explanation*, New York: Free Press.

HILBERT, DAVID. 1971 (1899). *Foundations of Geometry (Grundlagen der Geometrie)*. La Salle, IL: Open Court.

HILL, THOMAS. 1985. 'Kant's argument for the rationality of moral conduct', *Pacific Philosophical Quarterly* 66: 3–23.

HOOKER, BRAD. 1987. 'Williams' argument against external reasons', *Analysis* 47: 42–4.

——2000. *Ideal Code, Real World: A Rule-Consequentialist Theory of Morality*. Oxford: Oxford University Press.

HORGAN AND TIMMONS. 1992. 'Troubles for new wave moral semantics: the "Open Question Argument" revived', *Philosophical Papers* 21: 153–75.

——2000. 'Non-descriptive cognitivism: framework for a new meta-ethic', in *Philosophical Papers* 29: 121–53.

——2006. 'Cognitivist Expressivism', in Horgan and Timmons (eds). *Metaethics After Moore*. Oxford: Oxford University Press, pp. 255–98.

HORWICH, PAUL. 1990. *Truth*. Blackwell: Oxford.

——1994. 'The Essence of Expressivism', *Analysis* 54: 19–20.

HUME, DAVID. 1902 (1777). *Enquiries Concerning the Human Understanding and Concerning the Principles of Morals* (ed. L. A. Selby-Bigge). 2nd edn. Oxford: Oxford University Press.

——1968 (1739). *A Treatise of Human Nature* (ed. L. A. Selby-Bigge). Oxford: Oxford University Press.

HURKA, THOMAS. 1993. *Perfectionism*. Oxford: Oxford University Press.

HURLEY, S. L., 1989. *Natural Reasons: Personality and Polity*, Oxford: Oxford University Press.

IRWIN, TERENCE. 2000. *The Development of Ethics, A Historical and Critical Study*. Oxford: Oxford University Press.

——2009. *The Development of Ethics, A Historical and Critical Study, Volume 3, From Kant to Rawls*. Oxford: Oxford University Press.

JACKSON, FRANK. 1998. *From Metaphysics to Ethics*, Oxford: Oxford University Press.

JAMES, WILLIAM. 1911. *Some Problems of Philosophy*, London: Longmans, Green.

KELLY, THOMAS, 2008. 'Evidence', in Edward N. Zalta (ed.), *The Stanford Encyclopedia of Philosophy (Fall 2008 Edition)*. http://plato.stanford.edu/archives/fall2008/entries/evidence/

KOLODNY, NICO. 2005. 'Why be rational?' *Mind* 114: 509–63.

——2008. 'The myth of practical consistency', *European Journal of Philosophy* 16: 366–402.

KORSGAARD, CHRISTINE. 1986. 'Scepticism about practical reason', *Journal of Philosophy* 83: 5–25.

——2008. *The Constitution of Agency: Essays on Practical Reasons and Moral Psychology*. Oxford: Oxford University Press.

——2009. *Self-Constitution: Agency, Identity, and Integrity*. Oxford: Oxford University Press.

KRAUT, RICHARD. 2007. *What is Good and Why: The Ethics of Well-Being*. Cambridge, MA: Harvard University Press.

KRIPKE, SAUL. 1971. 'Identity and necessity', in Milton K. Munitz (ed.), *Identity and Individuation*. New York University Press.

——1981 (1972). *Naming and Necessity*, Oxford: Blackwell.

——1982. *Wittgenstein on Rules and Private Language*. Oxford: Basil Blackwell.

LENMAN, J. 2003. 'Disciplined syntacticism and moral expressivism', *Philosophy and Phenomenological Research*. 66: 32–57.
Lewis, David.1969. *Convention, A Philosophical Study*, Cambridge, MA: Harvard University Press.
—— 1979. 'Attitudes de dicto and de se', *The Philosophical Review* 88: 513–43.
—— 1990. 'Noneism or allism', *Mind* 99: 23–32; reprinted in Lewis 1999.
—— 1999. *Papers in Metaphysics and Epistemology*. Cambridge: Cambridge University Press.
MCDOWELL, JOHN. 1977. 'On the sense and reference of a proper name', *Mind* 86: 159–85, reprinted in McDowell 1998b.
—— 1982. 'Criteria, defeasibility, and knowledge', *Proceedings of the British Academy*, 68: 455–79. Reprinted in McDowell 1998b.
—— 1994. *Mind and World*. Cambridge, MA: Harvard University Press.
—— 1998a. *Mind, Value, and Reality*. Cambridge, MA: Harvard University Press.
—— 1998b. *Meaning, Knowledge and Reality*. Cambridge, MA: Harvard University Press.
—— 2005. 'The true modesty of an identity conception of truth: a note in response to Pascal Engel (2001)', *International Journal of Philosophical Studies* 13: 83–8.
—— 2007. 'On Pippin's postscript', *European Journal of Philosophy* 15: 395–410.
MACKIE, J. L. 1977. *Ethics, Inventing Right and Wrong*. Harmondsworth: Penguin Books.
MELLOR, D. H. 1987. 'The Singularly Affecting Facts of Causation', in *Matters of Metaphysics*, Cambridge: Cambridge University Press, 1991 pp. 201–24.
—— 1995. *The Facts of Causation*. London: Routledge.
MILL, J. S. (1963–91). *Collected Works of John Stuart Mill*. London: Routledge.
MOORE, G. E. 1993 (1903). *Principia Ethica, Revised Edition*. Cambridge: Cambridge University Press.
NAGEL, THOMAS. 1970. *The Possibility of Altruism*. Oxford: Oxford University Press.
—— 1986. *The View From Nowhere*. Oxford: Oxford University Press.
NELSON, MARK T. 1995. 'Is it always fallacious to derive values from facts?', *Argumentation* 9.4 (1995): 553–62.
NEUHOUSER, FREDERICK. 2000. 'Introduction' to Fichte 2000 (1796–7).
NICHOLSON, PETER. 1990. *The Political Philosophy of the British Idealists* Cambridge: Cambridge University Press.
NIETZSCHE, FRIEDRICH. 1982 (1881). *Daybreak: Thoughts on the Prejudices of Morality*. Cambridge: Cambridge University Press.
—— 1998 (1887). *On the Genealogy of Morality*. Indianapolis, IN: Hackett Publishing Company.
NORCROSS, ALASTAIR. 2006. 'The Scalar Approach to Utilitarianism', in Henry West (ed.), *The Blackwell Guide to Mill's Utilitarianism*, Oxford: Blackwell: 217–32.
PARFIT, DEREK. 1984. *Reasons and Persons*. Oxford: Oxford University Press.
—— 2007. *On What Matters*. Oxford: Oxford University Press.
PETTIT, PHILIP AND SMITH, MICHAEL. 2004. 'Backgrounding Desire', in Frank Jackson, Philip Pettit, and Michael Smith, *Mind, Morality, and Explanation, Selected Collaborations*. Oxford: Clarendon Press.
PIPPIN, ROBERT. 1997. *Idealism as Modernism, Hegelian Variations*. Cambridge: Cambridge University Press.
—— 2007. 'McDowell's Germans: response to "On Pippin's Postscript"', *European Journal of Philosophy* 15: 411–44.
PRICHARD, H. A. 2002. *Moral Writings*. Oxford: Oxford University Press.
PRICE, ANTHONY. 2009. 'Review of M. Schroeder, *Slaves of the Passions*', *Philosophy* 84: 291–5.
PRIEST, GRAHAM. 2005. *Towards Non-Being*. Oxford: Oxford University Press.
—— 2008. 'The closing of the mind: how the particular quantifier became existentially loaded behind our backs', *Review of Symbolic Logic* 1: 42–55.

PRIOR, A. N. 1960a. 'The Autonomy of Ethics', *Australasian Journal of Philosophy* 38: 197–206. Reprinted in Prior 1976.
—— 1960b. 'The runabout inference ticket', *Analysis* 21: 38–9. Reprinted in Prior 1976.
—— 1976. *A. N. Prior: Papers in Logic and Ethics*, A. Kenny and P. Geach (eds). London: Duckworth.
PUTNAM, HILARY. 1975. *Philosophical Papers, Volume 1: Mathematics, Matter and Method, Volume 2: Mind, Language and Reality*. Cambridge: Cambridge University Press.
—— 1983. *Philosophical Papers, Volume 3: Realism and Reason*. Cambridge: Cambridge University Press.
—— 2004. *Ethics without Ontology*. Cambridge, MA and London: Harvard University Press.
QUINE, W. V. O. 1948. 'On what there is', *Review of Metaphysics* 48: 21–38. Reprinted in Quine 1961.
—— 1961. *From a Logical Point of View* (2nd edn). New York and Evanston: Harper and Row.
—— 1966. *The Ways of Paradox*. New York: Random House.
—— 1970. *Philosophy of Logic*. Englewood Cliffs, NJ: Prentice-Hall.
RABINOWICZ, WLODEK AND RØNNOW-RASMUSSEN, TONI, 2004. 'The strike of the demon: on fitting pro-attitudes and value', *Ethics* 114: 391–423.
—— 2006. 'Buck-passing and the right kind of reasons', *Philosophical Quarterly* 56: 114–20.
RAILTON, PETER. 2003. *Facts, Values, and Norms, Essays Toward a Morality of Consequence*. Cambridge: Cambridge University Press.
—— 2008. 'Reply to Skorupski', *Utilitas* 20: 230–42.
RAWLS, JOHN. 1971. *A Theory of Justice*. Oxford: Oxford University Press.
—— 2000. *Lectures on the History of Moral Philosophy*. Cambridge, MA: Harvard University Press.
RAZ, JOSEPH. 1979. *The Authority of Law*. Oxford: Clarendon Press.
—— 1990. *Practical Reason and Norms*. Princeton, NJ: Princeton University Press.
—— 2000. 'The Truth in Particularism', in *Engaging Reason*, Oxford: Oxford University Press.
—— 2005. 'The myth of instrumental rationality', *Journal of Ethics and Social Philosophy* 1: 2–28.
READ, STEPHEN. 1996. 'The slingshot argument', in *Logique et Analyse*, pp. 143–4, 195–218.
REICHENBACH, H. 1948 (1935). *The Theory of Probability, An Inquiry into the Logical and Mathematical Foundations of the Calculus of Probability* (2nd edn). Berkeley: University of California Press.
REID, THOMAS. 1817 (1764). *An Inquiry Into the Human Mind on the Principles of Common Sense*. Glasgow: William Falconer.
ROSS, DAVID. 2002 (1930). *The Right and the Good*, ed. Philip Stratton-Lake. Oxford: Oxford University Press.
SCANLON, T. M. 1998. *What We Owe to Each Other*. Cambridge, MA: Harvard University Press.
—— 2008. *Moral Dimensions: Permissibility, Meaning, Blame*. Cambridge, MA: Harvard University Press.
SCHIER, FLINT. 1993. 'The Kantian Gulag', in Dudley Knowles and John Skorupski (eds), *Virtue and Taste*. Oxford: Blackwell.
SCHLICK, MORITZ. 1985 (1925). *General Theory of Knowledge (Allgemeine Erkenntnislehre)* (2nd edn). La Salle, IL: Open Court.
SCHNEEWIND, J. B. 1998. *The Invention of Autonomy*. Cambridge: Cambridge University Press.
SCHROEDER, MARK. 2007. *Slaves of the Passions*. Oxford: Oxford University Press.
—— 2008. *Being For*. Oxford: Oxford University Press.
SCHUELER, G. F. 1995. *Desire: Its Role in Practical Reason and the Explanation of Action*. Cambridge, MA: MIT Press.

SHAFER-LANDAU, RUSS. 2003. *Moral Realism*. Oxford: Oxford University Press.
SHAPIRO, STEWART. 2000. *Thinking about Mathematics*, Oxford: Oxford University Press.
—— (ed.). 2005. *The Oxford Handbook to the Philosophy of Mathematics*, Oxford: Oxford University Press.
SHAVER, R. 2000. 'Sidgwick's minimal meta-ethics', in *Utilitas* 12: 261–77.
SIDGWICK, HENRY. 1981 (1907). *The Methods of Ethics*, 7th edn. Indianapolis, IN: Hackett.
—— 2000. *Essays on Ethics and Method*, (ed.). Marcus G. Singer. Oxford: Oxford University Press.
SILBERBAUER, GEORGE. 1991. 'Ethics in small-scale societies', in Peter Singer (ed.), *A Companion to Ethics* Oxford: Oxford University Press.
SKORUPSKI, JOHN. 1976. *Symbol and Theory, A Philosophical Study of Theories of Religion in Social Anthropology*. Cambridge: Cambridge University Press.
—— 1989. *John Stuart Mill*. London: Routledge.
—— 1993. *English-Language Philosophy 1790–1945*. Oxford: Oxford University Press.
—— 1997a. 'Meaning, Verification, Use', in Hale and Wright (eds), pp. 29–59.
—— 1997b. 'Logical grammar, transcendentalism and normativity', in *Philosophical Topics* 25: 189–211.
—— 1999. *Ethical Explorations*. Oxford: Oxford University Press.
—— 2001. 'Three Methods and a Dualism', in Ross Harrison (ed.), *Henry Sidgwick* (Proceedings of the British Academy, 109): Oxford: Oxford University Press, pp. 61–81.
—— 2005. 'Later Empiricism and Logical Positivism', in Shapiro (ed.), pp. 51–74.
—— 2006a. *Why Read Mill Today?* London: Routledge.
—— 2006b. 'Green and the Idealist Conception of a Person's Good', in M. Dimova-Cookson and W. Mander (eds), *T. H. Green: Ethics, Metaphysics and Political Philosophy*. Oxford: Oxford University Press, pp. 47–75.
—— 2008. 'Sidgwick and the many-sidedness of ethics', in Placido Bucolo, Roger Crisp, and Bart Schultz (eds), *Henry Sidgwick, Happiness and Religion*, Biancavilla-Catania: Dipartimento di Scienze Umane dell'Università degli Studi di Catania, pp. 410–45.
—— 2010a. 'Human Rights', in Samantha Besson and John Tasioulas (eds), *Philosophy of International Law*. Oxford: Oxford University Press.
—— 2010b. 'Liberalism as Free Thought', in Georgios Varouxakis and Paul Kelly (eds), *John Stuart Mill—Thought and Influence: The Saint of Rationalism*. London: Routledge:
SMITH, ADAM. 1984 (1759). *The Theory of the Moral Sentiments*, Indianapolis, IN: Liberty Fund.
SMITH. MICHAEL. 1994a. *The Moral Problem*. Oxford: Blackwell.
—— 1994b. 'Why expressivists about value should love minimalism about truth', *Analysis* 54: 1–11.
—— 1994c, 'Minimalism, truth-aptitude and belief' *Analysis* 54: 21–6.
SORENSEN, R. A. 1988. *Blindspots*. Oxford: Clarendon Press.
SOSA, ERNEST. 2007. *A Virtue Epistemology*, Oxford: Oxford University Press.
STRATTON-LAKE, P. and HOOKER, B. 2006. 'Scanlon versus Moore on Goodness', In Horgan and Timmons (eds), pp. 149–68.
STRAWSON, P. F. 1952. *Introduction to Logical Theory*. London: Methuen.
—— 1963. 'Freedom and resentment', in *Proceedings of the British Academy* 48. Reprinted in Strawson, *Freedom and Resentment and Other Essays*, London: Methuen, 1974.
Stroud, Barry. 1965. 'Wittgenstein and logical necessity', *Philosophical Review* 74: 504–18.
—— 1984. *The Significance of Philosophical Scepticism*, Oxford: Oxford University Press.
SVAVARSDÓTTIR, SIGRÚN. 1999. 'Moral cognitivism and motivation', *The Philosophical Review* 108: 161–219.

THOMSON, JUDITH JARVIS. 1990. *The Realm of Rights*. Cambridge, MA: Harvard University Press.
VAN ROOJEN, M. 1996. 'Expressivism and irrationality', *Philosophical Review* 105: 311–55.
VÄYRYNEN, P. 2006. 'Resisting the Buck-Passing Account of Value', in Russ Shafer-Landau (ed.), *Oxford Studies in Metaethics Vol. 1*. Oxford: Oxford University Press.
VELLEMAN, J. DAVID. 2000. *The Possibility of Practical Reason*. Oxford: Oxford University Press.
WALDRON, JEREMY. 1993. 'When Justice Replaces Affection: The Need for Rights', in Waldron, *Liberal Rights: Collected Papers 1981–1991*, Cambridge: Cambridge University Press.
WALLACE, R. JAY. 1994. *Responsibility and the Moral Sentiments*. Harvard University Press.
WEDGWOOD, RALPH. 2007. *The Nature of Normativity*. Oxford: Oxford University Press.
WILLIAMS, BERNARD. 1981. 'Internal and External Reasons', in *Moral Luck*, Cambridge: Cambridge University Press.
—— 1985. *Ethics and the Limits of Philosophy*. London: Fontana Paperbacks.
—— 1995a. 'Internal Reasons and the Obscurity of Blame', in Bernard Williams, *Making Sense of Humanity*, Cambridge: Cambridge University Press, pp. 35–45.
—— 1995b. 'How Free Does the Will Need to Be?', in Bernard Williams, *Making Sense of Humanity*, Cambridge: Cambridge University Press, pp. 3–21.
—— 1995c. 'Replies', In J. E. J. Altham and Ross Harrison (eds), *World, Mind and Ethics, Essays on the Ethical Philosophy of Bernard Williams*, Cambridge: Cambridge University Press, pp. 185–224.
—— 2001. 'Postscript: Some Further Notes on Internal and External Reasons', in Elijah Millgram (ed.), *Varieties of Practical Reasoning*. Cambridge, MA: MIT Press.
WILLIAMS, ROBERT R. 1992. *Recognition: Fichte and Hegel on the Other*. Albany, NY: SUNY Press.
WILLIAMSON, TIMOTHY. 1994. *Vagueness*. London: Routledge.
—— 2000. *Knowledge and its Limits*. New York: Oxford University Press.
—— 2007. *The Philosophy of Philosophy*, Oxford: Blackwell.
WILLIGENBURG, THEO VON. 2003. 'Shaping the arrow of the will', *Utilitas* 15: 353–68.
WITTGENSTEIN, LUDWIG. 1958a (1953). *Philosophical Investigations*. Oxford: Basil Blackwell.
—— 1958b. *The Blue and Brown Books*. Oxford: Basil Blackwell.
—— 1961 (1921). *Tractatus Logico-Philosophicus*, (transl. D. F. Pears and B. F. McGuinness). London: Routledge and Kegan Paul.
—— 1974. *Philosophical Grammar*. Oxford: Basil Blackwell.
—— 1975. *Philosophical Remarks*. Oxford: Basil Blackwell.
—— 1978 (1956). *Remarks on the Foundations of Mathematics*, 3rd rev. edn. Oxford: Basil Blackwell. (First published 1956).
—— 1979. *Wittgenstein and the Vienna Circle*, conversations recorded by Friedrich Waismann. Oxford: Basil Blackwell.
WRIGHT, CRISPIN. 1986. 'Inventing logical necessity', in J. Butterfield (ed.), *Language, Mind and Logic*. Cambridge: Cambridge University Press, pp. 91–182.
—— 1992. *Truth and Objectivity*. Cambridge, MA: Harvard University Press.

INDEX

Page references in bold refer to the Glossary.

a priori 4, 9–10, 14, 16, 19–20, 22, 23, 75, 119, 137–63, 156–60, 429, **506**
   and reference-fixing 184–5
   no-content view of 137–8, 139–40, 148, 150, 169
   knowledge 20, 22, 137, 160–3, 167, 496, **506**
   propositions 22, 119, 137, 148–50, 152–4, 161, **506**
   support 149–50, 157–8, **506**
   warrants 115–19, 137, 140–1, 150–2, 161, 413–14, **506**
abstract objects *see* objects
actuality 424–6, 430 note 14, 439
Adams, Robert 20 note 21
agent-relative reasons *see* reasons
Allison, Henry 11 note 11, 326, 501 note 26
analyticity 15–16, 18, 80, 164–72, 204, 489–90
   empty-inference approach 167–72
   implicit definition approach 176–8, 185
apperception 3, 21, 119–20, 130 note 27, 142, 144, 150–1, 207–10, 458–62, **506**
   and independent objects 119–21
   apperceptual states, their *esse* is *appercipi* 208, 459, 472–4
   norm of 207, 215, 231, 494
   unities of 464–5
Antiphon 390 note 38
Aristotle 335 note 14
arrogance (as objection to utilitarianism) 360–1, 365
atonement 28, 264, 378–81
attention 108, 113–15, 120, 130 note 27, 459–60
attribute 61, 415, 427–8, 433, **506**
Audi, Robert 138 note 2, 141 note 5
Austin, J. L. 211 note
authority 352, 419
autonomy 5, 21–3, 26, 107, 109, 111, 122 note 19, 133–4, 258–9, 261–2, 301–4, 324–30, 341, 343–4, 362–3, 390–2, 396, 418, 462, **506**
   Hegelian and Kantian 391 note 42, 467, 485, **506**
   egalitarianism about 303–4, 306–7, 395–6, 465–9
   v self-determination 22 note 24, 107, 109, 301–2, 462
awareness 208 note 3, 210, 403 note 3, 459
   propositional and objectual 404, 453, 459–60, 472, **506**

bad 86–7
Baldwin, Thomas 443 note 3
Bayesianism 51, 227–30
Bealer, George 408 note 9
Beiser, Frederick 468 note 7

Bentham, Jeremy 168 note 4, 263–4, 370, 454
Blackburn, Simon 241 note 10, 246 note 18, 433 note 17, 436
blame 28, 131 note 30, 264, 291–300, 304–6, 314, 316, 317–18, 322, 339–40, 343, 350–1, 368, 370–2, 387, 389–90, 456, 466
   and avoidability 376–377
   as withdrawal of recognition 376–82
Block, Ned 460 note 3
Bridge principle, the 3, 24, 27, 28, 29, 263–7, 286, 288, 314, 316, 321, 322–3, 330, 333, 337, 346, 347–53, 356–9, 369, 410, 457, 471, 477, 479, **509**
Brink, David 279 note 17, 299 note 12
Broome, John 50 note 20, 58 note 1, 102 note 35, 132 note 31, 480 note 5, 481 note 7
buck-passing account of good *see* good; of moral obligation 319–20, 350
Burge, Tyler 166 note 3
Burgess, 439 note 26
Butler, Bishop 369
Bykvist, Krister 91 note 23

Carlson, Eric 36 note
Carnap, Rudolf 6, 13, 15–16, 139–40, 168 note 5, 176, 179–80, 220 note 19, 500
Carroll, Lewis 190 note 6
cart before horse objections 89, 91, 156, 200–3, 293, 309, 443, 454–7
categorical imperatives 26, 105–6, 326 *see also* Kant; hypothetical imperatives
categoricity, of morality, of moral judgement 28, 264, 299, 307, 339–40, 344, 387, 394–5, **509**
causal condition, the 30, 421–2, 426–8, 439
causality 30, 235, 262, 414, 421, 426, 468, 500
   agent causality 406
   of freedom *see* freedom
Chisholm, R. M. 101 note 34
Christianity 377 note 15
Clarke, J. A. 374 note 10
Coffa, Alberto 14 note, 16
cognition independence 7–10, 14, 15, 18–20, 137–8, 140, 145–6, 459, 472, 500, 504
   ontic *v* logical 405
cognitive internalism 57, 73–6, 253–6, 266, 306–7, 395–6, 412 note, 413, 502–3, **509**
cognitive, or cognitivist, irrealism 23, 31, 128, 140, 402, 433, 434, 439, 475, 478, 484–7, 501–2

cognitivism 4, 5, 12–13, 119, 242, **509**
common cognition, common sense, common
    conceptions 6, 9, 18–20, 27, 29, 340, 344–6, 348,
    359, 368, 388–90, 391–2, 401, 450–1, 503–4
Conant, J. 140 note 4
concepts 188, 442–3, 452–4, 463, 497–8
conceptual truth 145, 188, 283, 309, 454
conditionals 167–8, 169 *see also* reasons
Conditional Proof 170, 172, 491
conscience 27, 29, 306, 348, 359–64, 367–8, 387–8, 391–2
consciousness 120, 460–2, 472
constructivism 11–12, 429, 484–7, 504
conventionalism 3, 15–17, 139, 179–81, 445–6, 483
convergence 405, 412–13, 415–16, 418, 446, 502–4
convergence thesis 412, 498
Copp, David 297 note 9
cost effectiveness 52, 98–9, 103, 246 note, 315
Crisp, Roger 87 note 18, 91 notes 23 and 24, 345 note 23,
    349 note 3, 417 note 20
Critical argument 140, 144–7, 459, 472, 501
Critical Philosophy, Critical Tradition, Critical Stance 4,
    5–9, 14–15, 17, 18, 19, 20, 29, 165, 290, 400, 403,
    405, 416, 434, 436, 440–1, 443, 477, 487–9, 496,
    500–2
Critical thesis, claim 137–8, 143, 144–6, 152–4, 156, **509**

Dancy, Jonathan 40 note, 118 note
Daniels, Norman 410 note 13
Danielsson, S. 91 note 23
D'Arms, Justin 87 note 18, 264 note 1
Darwall, Stephen 282–5, 295 note 5, 319 note 31, 360 note
    12, 374–5, 383 note 26
defeasibility 43, 123, 150, 156–60, 206, 214–16, 490, 492–4,
    506
definitional consequence 81–2, 154–5, **506**
degrees of belief and feeling 50–2, 227–8
demand 310–14, 323, 352, 354–6,358, 374
Demand principle 3, 26, 27, 29, 92, 263, 322, 347–8, 351–6,
    369, 410, 479, 502, **509**
de re thoughts 120–1
Descartes, René 31, 472
desert 307, 314–16, 381
desire/belief psychology 238, 240–2, 251, 437
desire 24, 268
    and reason to desire 270–4, 277–8
    aim-eliciting sense 239, 250
    categorial *v* particular 274–8
    substantive sense 239
        no distinction between instrumental and final
        239–40, 268
Diamond, Cora 140 note 4
dignity 134, 376, 383, 386–7, 394, 419
dispositionalism 243, 445, 447
distinguishability thesis 145, 441
Divers, John 437 note 24

dogmatism 5–9, 496
Dominance principle 338, 365–6
Doris, J. M. 394 note 46
Double W principle 122–3
Douglas, Mary 377 note 13
Duff, Antony 312 note 27
Dummett, Michael 445 note 5
duties of right 307–8, 312–13, 323

egoism 68–70, 285–7, 318, 324, 326, 328–30, 348–50, 453–4
emotivism 437–8
empathy, norm of 207, 218–19
empirical and intelligible standpoint 475–6
empiricism 14, 19, 149, 164, 166, 169, 187, 203–6, 238,
    242–5, 437–8, 442, 494, 501, **509**
ends 103, 334–6, **507**
entailment 188, 191
epistemic fields 41–5, 156–60, **506**
    in space and time 45–7
epistemic self-audit 2, 21, 58, 109–11, 204, 301, 465, 488,
    508
epistemic states 112–15, 119, 150, **507**
epistemicism about reasons 54, 480–1, 484
error theory 402, 440, 457, 497
esotericism 344, 348, 364–6
Euthyphro 455
    'Euthyphro' question 448
evaluative terms 118
    wholly normative 93–6
    mixed 96–8
Evans, Gareth 459 note 1
evidence 210–14, 271
    indicative 48, 212
    inductive 212, 213–14, 227
Ewing, A. C. 83, 90
exclusion and inclusion (epistemic) 191–5
existence 30, 181, 183, 423, 424–8, 430, 431, 439–41
existentialism, 363
exoteric principle, the 364–5,
expected utility theory 52, 103–4
explanation *see* inference to the best explanation,
    interpretative explanations, rational explanations
expressivism 241 note 10, 246 note 18, 248, 251

facts 16–17, 140, 435, 501, **507**
    factual and non-factual propositions 152–6, 402
    nominal and substantial 7–9, 61–3, 91, 153, 403–5, 430,
        431–3, 435–6, 469–72, 489, **507**
    noumenal and phenomenal 11–13, 156, 427, 475
    reasons as 37, 55–6, 61–3
factualism 7, 10–11, 15, 19, 140, 244, 438, 488, 491, **509**
fairness 307, 314, 316–17, 328
fallibilism 198–200, 489, 497
Fichte, J. G. 373, 374
fictionalism 402, 429, 457

fictional objects *see* objects
Field, Hartry 148 note 12
Fontenelle, B 385
freedom 11, 27, 30, 264, 327, 332, 362, 378, 390–1, 416,
    418, 458, 466–9, 486, 487
  causality of 27, 306, 426, 461, 466, 468, 469,
    475, 500
free thought, dialogue 30, 31, 418–19, 478
Frege, G. 7, 16, 165–6, 173 note 11, 174 note 14, 403
    note 3, 422, 430 note 14, 432 note 16, 435 note 19,
    451, 456
Frege/Geach problem 139 note 3, 436
frequency (and probability) 221–3
Freud, Sigmund 402
Friedman, Michael 14 note 15

Garver, Newton 14 note
Geach, Peter 84 note, 424 note 7, 436 note 21
Gibbard, Allan 2 note, 109 note 2, 292 note 1, 300, 312
    note 27, 436
global realism *see* realism
Goldman, Alvin 128 note 25
good
  'buck-passing' definition of 82–92, 319, 335, 454
  neutral on questions of deontology or teleology 92
  'good for' 84–6, 268–9
  good of a person 26, 84–6, 267–9, 274, 278–82, 285–7
    and rational care 282–5
  functional goodness 84–6, 98–9, 103
  Good, the 336–7, 349, 453
  the principle of Good 3, 26, 27, 29, 263, 322,
    333–4, 337–8, 344, 347–53, 356–9, 369. 389, 410,
    479, **510**
Gödel, Kurt 181 note 26
Gomperz, Theodore 270 note 8
Graham, J. 377 note 13
Green, T. H. 279, 281 note 20, 285
Greenspan, Patricia 101 note 34
Grice, H. P. 168 note 5
Griffin, James 276 note, 357 note
guilt 294, 376, 378, 380, 382

Haidt, J. 377 note 377 note 13
Haldane, John 436 note 21
Hale, Bob 181 note 28, 436 note 21
Hamilton, Andy 459 note 1
Harman, G. 132 note 31
Hart, H. L. A. 309, 312, 454
hedonism 269, 272, 274, 280, 349, 448–9, 455
Hegel, G. W. F. 5, 29, 365, 367, 373, 374, 380, 382, 389, 390
    note 39, 391, 398 note 49, 467
  his 'private morality' argument 363–4, 388, 391, 397,
    398 note 49
  on conscience 361–4
Hellman, Geoffrey 430 note 13

Hempel, Carl 222–3
hermeneutics, hermeneutic principle 267, 291, 299, 381
Hilbert, David 176 note 18
Hill, Thomas 326 note 6
Hillary, Edmund 118
Hobbes, Thomas 318
Hollis, Martin 251 note 34
honour 378, 384–7, 394, 397
Hooker, Brad 252 note 37, 341 note 21
Horgan, Terence 450 note 11
Horwich, Paul 174 note 13, 437 note 24
Hume, David 27, 145, 238, 240, 242–3, 244 note 15,
    263–4, 370
Hurka, Thomas 289 note 30, 361 note 14
Hurley, Susan 38 note
hypothetical imperatives 27, 105–6

ideals 256, 287–9, 384, 386, 468
idealism 279, 434, 440, 489
  German, 264, 373
  transcendental, 10–13, 14, 17, 20, 27, 30–1, 138, 140,
    146, 148, 149, 332, 416, 461–2, 469, 475, 476, 478,
    484–5, 487, 500–2, 504
identity 62, 153–4, 168–9, 473
  intentional, 424
impartiality 25–6, 264, 314, 316, 321–34
implicit definition *see* analyticity
'impossible', definition of 193, 200–1
indifference, norm of *see* probability
induction 213–14, 231
  to necessary truths 214
  enumerative, straight norm of, 151, 213, 215–16,
    223, 495
inference to the best explanation 151, 191 note 7, 218
  norm of, 207, 213–14, 215–16, 405, 495, 499
inner sense *see* Kant
inquiry 45–7
  acts of, 189–91, 199–200
  eliminative, 189–95, 495
  in space and time, 230–1
Insight principle, the 302–4, 307, 341, 344, 362, 396,
    485, **509**
instrumentalism, Instrumental principle, the 104–5, 205,
    238, 245–8, 250, 254, 326, 448, 484, **509**
interpretative explanations 52–3, 70, 236–7, 256–8, 475–6
intuition, intuitionism, intuitionistic realism 12, 18, 20, 22,
    137–9, 141–3, 146–8, 149, 197, 202–3, 206, 291, 328,
    330–1, 348–350, 407, 414–15, 417–18, 442–3, 451–2,
    486 note, 491
  can give no account of warrant 146–8, 487–8
  Brouwerian, 75
irrationality 133
irrealism 4, 5, 12–13, 415–16, 417–18, 420, 424, 427,
    439–41
  irreal objects *see* objects

Irwin, Terence 487 note 15
is/ought distinction 81–2, 97–8

Jackson, Frank 449–51
Jacobson, Daniel 87 note, 264 note
James, William 434
justification 107, 111, 124–7, 132, 237, **507**
justice 25, 26, 307, 309, 313–14, 316

Kant, Immanuel 3, 14, 15, 16, 17, 20, 21 note 23, 64
    note 11, 96, 105–6, 120, 134, 138, 146, 169, 186,
    198, 201, 251, 308, 313, 336 note 16, 373, 398 note
    49, 401, 410 note 12, 426, 438, 469, 473 note 9, 475,
    497, 504
  autonomy and freedom 22 note 24, 26, 107, 122
    note 19, 253–4, 332, 391 note 42, 392
  egalitarianism about, 303, 396, 465–8
  the Categorical Imperative 26, 106 note 43, 323–32,
    362–3, 365, 429, 486
  Critical philosophy, 5–6, 9–13, 487–8, 500–2
  'the fact of reason' 11 note 11, 332
  constructivism and cognitive irrealism in, 11–13, 31,
    484–7, 253, 484–7
  distinction between right and virtue 308, 313
  evaluative reasons, failure to recognise 24, 26–7,
    302–3, 333, 416
  free thought 418–19, 468
  inner sense and apperception 458, 461–2, 472, 475
  spontaneity and receptivity 13, 29, 128, 152, 331, 405–7,
    416–17, 427, 434, 436, 477–8
  synthetic a priori propositions 19, 140, 152 note 15,
    165–7
  respect 26, 134, 334, 378 note 17, 383–7
  will and practical reason 23–6, 235, 262
  Wille and *Willkür* 261–2
  the unity of Reason 22, 479
  see also freedom, causality of; hypothetical imperatives;
    idealism, transcendental
Kantian 18, 20, 21, 25, 26, 74, 118, 142, 148, 156, 201, 323,
    354, 427
Kelly, Thomas 211 note 7
knowledge 14, 19, 23, 30, 290–2
  and warrant 127–30
  and reliability 127–30
  normative 413–14
Kolmogorov calculus *see* probability calculus
Kolodny, Nico 132 note 31
Korsgaard, Christine 238 note 5, 251 note 35
Kraut, Richard 269 note 6
Kripke, Saul 20 note, 182 note 29, 425 note 8, 472

Lenman, J. 436 note 21
Lewis, David 67 note 13, 439 note 26
liar paradoxes 175
liberalism 417–19
logic 164, 169, 186–9, 489–92, 493–4

normative foundation of classical 194
factualist *v* normative conceptions of 203–4

McDowell, John 116 note, 183 note 30, 187 note 4, 218
    note 17, 435 note 19, 436, 488 note
Mackie, J. L. 440 note 28, 499
Marx, Karl 372, 402
mathematical structuralism 430
mathematics 164, 169, 179–80, 489–90, 494
maximal epistemic field 189, 193, 490–1, **507**
Meinong, Alexius 430 note 14
Mellor, Hugh 404 note 5
memory 211
  norm of 207, 218
method of choosing *see* rationality
Mill, John Stuart 213 note 10, 263–4, 281, 289, 311, 325
    note 5, 334, 336 note 17, 391 note 43, 394 note 46,
    407, 419, 454, 468, 495 note 23
  analyticity 167, 169–72
  desired and desirable 210 note 6, 270–1
  logic and mathematics 164, 179–80, 187, 204–6
  moral wrongness and blame 292–3, 370–2
  names 182–4
  parts of happiness 273–6
  rights and justice 308–9, 312, 313
  utilitarianism 338–9
Miller, Alex 437 note 24
modal concepts 186, 202–3
modal logic, normative interpretation of, 195–8
monotonicity 214–16, 459, 490–1, **507**
Moore, G. E. 78, 91 note 23, 442–3, 447–8, 451
Moralität 361–2, 364 note 19, 374
moral integrity 390–2
moral judgement 27, 29, 78, 92, 101, 104 note 40, 348,
    369–70, 387–93
  verdictive, disciplinary, emancipatory 29, 387–92
moral obligation 22 note 24, 28, 44 note 15, 49, 186, 251,
    256, 263–4, 290–1, 298–302, 304, 307–8, 319, 322,
    339–46, 355, 384, 394
morality 26, 27, 28–9, 290–1, 402, 410
  and practical reasons 295–301, 322–3, 348–50, 358, 387
  criticism of 392–8
motivation 239–54
motivational internalism 263, 305–6, 395, **509**
motives 240, 242, 249
Mulligan, Kevin 91 note 23

Nagel, Thomas 63 note 8, note 9; 474 note 10
naturalism 20, 30, 31, 402, 421, 440, 443, 484, 499–501
nature 477, 478, 483, 484–5, 486, 487, 488, 491, 501
'necessary', definition of, 193–5
Nelson, Mark 81
Neuhouser, Frederick 374 note 10
Nicholson, Peter 279 note 17
Nietzsche, Friedrich 294 note 3, 307, 369 note 2, 372, 395, 402
nihilism 81, 392, 498